The History of Art

II: From the French Revolution to the Present

The History of Art

II: From the French Revolution to the Present

Random House   New York

Staff for Random House

Editor
Stuart B. Flexner

Special Editorial Consultant
Jess Stein

Assistant Editors
Leonore C. Hauck
Keith Hollaman

Production Director
Peter Mollman

Staff for Mitchell Beazley

Editor-in-Chief
Jack Tresidder

Senior Designer
Marnie Searchwell

Senior Editor
Paul Holberton

Designers
Paul Bickerstaff
Alan Brown

Editors
Ian Chilvers
Jane Cochrane
Jane Crawley
Katharine Kemp
Jean McNamee
Roslin Mair
Judy Martin
Susan Meehan

Peter Courtley
Gerry Douglas
Jane Owen

Chief Picture Researcher
Flavia Howard

Picture Researchers
Celestine Dars
Tessa Politzer
Sandy Shepherd

Researchers
Julian George
Andrew Heritage
Kate Miller

Production Controller
Suzanne Semmes

Senior Executive Art Editor
Michael McGuinness

THE RANDOM HOUSE LIBRARY OF
PAINTING AND SCULPTURE
© Mitchell Beazley Publishers, 1981

Published in the United States by Random House, Inc.,
New York, and simultaneously in Canada by
Random House of Canada Limited, Toronto.

Library of Congress Cataloguing in Publication Data
Main entry under title:
The Random House library of painting and sculpture.
   Includes index.
   1. Art—History. 2. Art appreciation.
   3. Art—Technique. 4. Artists—Biography.
   I. Piper, David.
   N5300.R24   700   80–28604
ISBN 0–394–50092–X (Four-volume set) AACR1
ISBN 0–394–52130–7 (Volume 3)

Origination by Gilchrist Bros, Leeds and
Scala Istituto Fotografico Editorale, Florence

Printed in the Netherlands
for Random House, Inc., New York
by Koninklijke Smeets Offset b.v., Weert

Contributors and Consultants

Clare Abbott
Francis Ames-Lewis
David A. Anfam
Penny Bateman
Jane Beckett
Sandra Berresford
Peter Bird
Laurel Bradley
Barbara Brend
Ben Burt
Colin Campbell
Shigeo Chiba
A. H. Christie
Alexandrina Le Clézio
Craig Clunas
Susan Compton
Richard Demarco
Peter Draper
K. A. Edwards
Angela Emanuel
Susan Foister
John Glaves-Smith
Jennifer Godsell
Patricia Godsell
Christopher Green
Antony Griffiths
James Hamilton
Martin Hammer
Roberta L. Harris
Anne Harrison
Larissa Haskell
James Hickey
Brian Hickman
Joke Hofkamp
Richard Humphreys
Paul Ioannides
Michael Jacobs
Anne Clark James
Ingrid Jenkner
Marc Jordan
Anne Kirker
Alastair Laing
Nigel Llewellyn
J. P. Losty
Jules Lubbock

B. J. Mack
Melissa McQuillan
Peter Mitchell
Stefan Muthesius
Jill Nicklin
Keith Nicklin
Sarah O'Brien Twohig
Young-sook Pak
Sir Cecil Parrott
Stevan K. Pavlowitch
Richard Pestell
Geraldine Prince
Birgitta Rapp
Michael Ridley
Professor Sixten Ringbom
Malcom Rogers
Irit Rogoff
Sara Selwood
Richard Shone
Evelyn Silber
Sam Smiles
Frances Spalding
Lindsay Stainton
Mary Anne Stevens
Roy Strong
Glenn Sujo Volsky
John Sunderland
Kay Sutton
Margaret Tatton-Brown
Julie Thomas
Rosemary Treble
Philip Troutman
Adriana Turpin
Peter Vergo
Gray Watson
Claudine Webster
Roderick Whitfield
Cecilia Whitford
Frank Whiteford
Gillian Wilson
Rosalind Wood
Christopher Wright
Alison Yarrington
Iain Zaczek

The Random House Library of Painting and Sculpture

STRUCTURE AND ORGANIZATION

This book is one of four independent but interrelated volumes designed to provide a wide range of knowledge about painting and sculpture within a compact but comprehensive library of art. The exceptionally high proportion of illustrations reflects the importance given to visual information. In general, if a work of art is mentioned in the text it is also illustrated—and described in further detail—on the same page.

The organization of the history is, with few exceptions, chronological and geographic, but a particular school or movement is usually followed through to its final development, not treated piecemeal. Though enough context is given to orientate the reader, the aim is not to provide a socio-cultural history but to keep the focus of interest fixed firmly on the paintings and the sculptures themselves.

Particular subjects, or aspects of them, are usually encapsulated within a single two-page "spread". This allows the reader either to begin at the beginning in the conventional way or to enter the book at any point, finding each spread more or less self-contained, though it connects with the others to build up a coherent whole. The spread system allows a double approach; the broad development of art is unfolded in "narrative" spreads, which begin usually with background information and then cover a particular period, movement or region. In the course of the story, some artists arrive of such stature that they have one of these spreads to themselves. An alternative kind of spread, a "focus", is recognizable by a large-scale illustration. Here, the opportunity is taken to pause and contemplate a single work of art. The aim is to convey its essential flavour, sometimes to show why it was specially significant or influential, sometimes to trace out the process of its creation, always to make the reader look at it again, with deeper understanding.

EDITORIAL AND INDEXING METHOD

The locations of works of art shown in this book are not given in the captions but can be found, together with the dimensions and medium, in the list of illustrations that precedes the index. Entries in this list are headed, as are the captions themselves, by the name of the artist or, if this is unknown, by the place of origin or original location of the work. This may be different from the present location; thus "*The Virgin of Vladimir*" appears under the heading CONSTANTINOPLE, where it was made, though it is kept in the Tretyakov Gallery in Moscow.

Titles of works of art are given in italics, but if translation is inappropriate, or the title is a popular one which may not properly describe the image, it is also placed in quotation marks and capitalized—thus "*The Embarkation for Cythera*", "*La Toilette*". The names of monuments or buildings, notably churches, are usually the local names—thus Ste Madeleine, the Residenz. "S." is used for all the Italian variations, San, Santa, Sant', Santo. For Chinese words the pinyin system is used (though the Wade-Giles spelling is cross-referenced to the pinyin in the index). The Latin forms of ancient Greek names have been used except in the historical section on ancient Greek art; thus Hercules in Renaissance art, Herakles in Greek art.

COMPANION VOLUMES IN THE LIBRARY

Though this book is self-contained, with its own index, there are some cross-references to companion volumes in the Library. The introductory *Understanding Art* volume (vol. 1) covers both the formal and the technical sides of painting and sculpture, providing a basic course of art appreciation. *The History of Painting and Sculpture* (vol. 2) begins with Palaeolithic images and traces the development of the Western tradition from Egypt, Greece and Rome through medieval art to the Renaissance and the era of Baroque before the French Revolution ushered in the modern world. In a further *History* (vol. 3), the arts of Islam, Asia and Japan are introduced before the story is told of Western art in the nineteenth and twentieth centuries. Finally the *Dictionary* (vol. 4) provides succinct accounts of the lives and works of more than 3,000 artists, a gallery of portraits and self-portraits, and a comprehensive glossary of art terms and techniques.

Contents: THE HISTORY OF ART

2: Eastern Art by PHILIP RAWSON
Western Art since 1789 by DAVID PIPER

EASTERN ART

Several art traditions of the East have a continuous history far longer than any in Europe, but it was only recently that their greatness came to be recognized in the West. For many centuries, interest in Eastern works of art tended to be specialized – admiration for Muslim textiles, for instance, or Chinese porcelains. In the first part of the nineteenth century a number of French and English painters were captivated by a romantic image of the Islamic world and its decorative arts, among them the French painter Delacroix. Then painters such as Manet and Whistler were strongly affected by the prints of Japan, the Post-Impressionists van Gogh and Gauguin even more so. At the same time the religion, culture and art of the East began to be studied systematically, though scholarship in this area still cannot compare to the breadth and detail of Western art history. During the twentieth century many European and American artists, from Kandinsky and Klee on, have found direct inspiration in the arts of China, India and Japan.

What was it that Western artists found in Oriental art which they could not find in their own traditions? The answer involves not only the arts but also the cultural attitudes and values of the East. Islamic art has cultivated a both geometric and calligraphic idealism, reaching continually into the realm of the abstract – identified in Islamic thought as the archetypal zone of divine creation. Indian art, however, and the South-East Asian art derived from it, tended to express their intuitions through an imagery of cosmic deities endowed with immense, often very sensual charm. The mythic dramas of India are enacted in the language of the dance, but their imagery is set in a time-scale vast beyond human understanding. China was less concerned with the sheer vastnesses of the world. It did, however, see Nature as a constant flow of change, of unbroken appearance and disappearance, and it expressed this sense of unceasing movement in the calligraphic aspect of its painting, which was carried over also into both sculpture and ceramics. Japanese art adapted Chinese insights to its own more intimate view of Nature.

Behind the very diverse expressions of Indian, South-East Asian, Chinese and Japanese arts lie two principal unifying inspirations. First, the external world we perceive is seen not as a phenomenon produced externally by a mechanical Nature but as fragments from a whole, projected through the life experience of each individual. Reality can never be known by collecting its external fragments but must be apprehended by inward focus upon the whole. The second inspiration is the belief that to aim like this for a vision of the whole represents the highest cultural value, and may lead to the individual's release from suffering and anxiety, and perhaps from reincarnation.

These inspirations corresponded quite closely with a tendency appearing in Western art and culture at the end of the nineteenth century – an increasing refusal to try to depict outer reality as if it was somehow independent of the artist, and a search for principles of form rather than for appearances. By turning inward to explore new worlds of form and by making art works as "objects" which do not originate in the natural order of things, modern artists, like those of the East, have tried to extend the spectator's sense of what it means to be material, and their awareness of man's participation in active creation.

ISFAHAN, IRAN (left) View of the court of the Madraseh Chaharbagh, 1706-14

ANGKOR WAT, CAMBODIA (right) View of the temple in the centre, early 12th century

THE WORLD OF ISLAM

SPAIN

Tours

Danube

Tripoli

Istanbul
Bursa
Iznik

TURKEY

Aleppo
Raqqa
Damascus
Jerusalem
JORDAN
SYRIA

EGYPT

Nile

Mecca

Samarra
Baghdad
Tabriz

CASPIAN SEA

Qazvin

Kashan
Isfahan

I R A N

Nishapur

Herat

Shiraz

Mohenjodaro

CASPIAN SEA

TURK

GANDHARA

Kabul

Taxila

Harappa

Indus

Mohenjodaro

Basolhi

Kangra

H I M
A
L
A
Y
A

PUNJAB

Panipat

Delhi
BRINDABAN Katra
Mathura
Taj
Agra Mahal

Yamuna

Osia
Kishangarh

R
A
J
A
S
T
H
A
N

Modhera

Deogarh

MALWA

Khajuraho

Bharhut

Sanchi

Ajanta

Karle Elura

Bombay
Elephanta

D
E
C
C
A
N

Badami

Aivalli

Amaravati

Belur

Kanchipuram

MYSORE

Tanjore

Mamallapuram

Madras

Cochin

SRI LANKA

Sigiriya

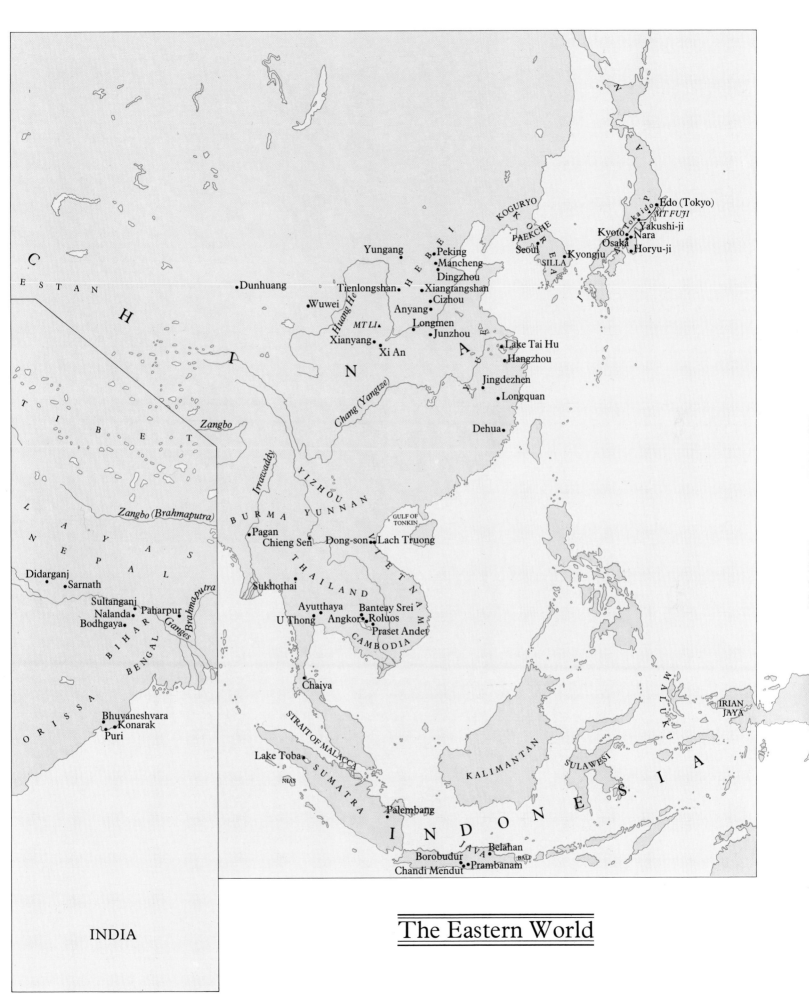

C
ESTAN

Dunhuang

Yungang

HEBEI

KOGURYO

PAEKCHE

Seoul

SILLA

Kyongju

Edo (Tokyo)
MT FUJI

Kyoto
Osaka

Yakushi-ji
Nara
Horyu-ji

Peking
Mancheng
Dingzhou
Tienlongshan
Xiangtangshan
Wuwei
Cizhou
Anyang
Huang He
MT LI
Longmen
Xianyang
Junzhou
Xi An

H
I
N
A

Lake Tai Hu
Hangzhou

Jingdezhen
Longquan

Dehua

Chang (Yangtze)

Zangbo

T I B E T

Zangbo (Brahmaputra)

H
L
I
M
A
L
A
Y
A
S

N
E
P
A
L

Irrawaddy

YIZHOU
YUNNAN

GULF OF
TONKIN

BURMA

Pagan
Chieng Sen

Dong-son
Lach Truong

Didarganj
Sarnath
Sultanganj
Nalanda
Bodhgaya
Paharpur

BIHAR
Ganges
Brahmaputra
BENGAL

THAILAND

V
I
E
T
N
A
M

Sukhothai

Ayutthaya
U Thong
Angkor

Banteay Srei
Roluos
Praset Andet

CAMBODIA

ORISSA

Bhuvaneshvara
Konarak
Puri

Chaiya

STRAIT OF MALACCA

SUMATRA

NIAS

Lake Toba

M
A
L
U
K
U

IRIAN
JAYA

KALIMANTAN

SULAWESI

I N D O N E S I A

Palembang

JAVA
Borobudur
Chandi Mendut
Prambanam

Belahan
BALI

INDIA

The Eastern World

Indian Art 1

India's devastating climate has ensured that we have only the scantiest remains of its early arts; there are huge gaps in Indian art history, even though we know that the Indian peoples have made art in many media since the early third millennium BC: it was then that the first great Indian culture began to flourish in the Indus valley, declining about 1,200 years later. The Indus valley was then well watered and fertile, supporting numerous towns and villages, and at least two great cities, Harappa and Mohenjodaro, with streets on a rectangular plan, granaries and advanced drainage systems. All the works of art surviving, however, are small-scale – hundreds of soapstone seals and clay impressions of seals, pottery, terracotta figures and a handful of tiny bronze or stone sculptures in the round. The seals frequently depict cattle; some represent scenes of bull-wrestling and bull-vaulting before an icon of a head on a pole, both customs that still survive among the aboriginal peoples of India. And one most important religious subject is a male dancer in the company of animals, represented in seal impressions and in one surviving, though damaged, stone sculpture – possibly a remote prototype of the god Shiva.

DIDARGANJ (right)
Yakshi? or *Royal devotee?*
mid-1st century BC?
This paragon of Indian beauty surely continues the technique and scale set by Maurya sculpture now lost: she is well over life-size, the polished surface gleams sensuously, her nude body is plump and luscious, well nourished – in Indian art a sign of wealth and status. The face is individual, and might be a portrait of some royal princess, idealized.

SARNATH (below)
Lion capital, 240 BC
The four lions, once atop a towering Maurya column, were perhaps intended to symbolize the cosmic axis of the world; a frieze below depicts four animals which represent its four corners – indicating the universality of Buddhism. The lions are formalized but lively, and distantly related to lions in Persian art (see vol. 2 p. 29).

After the dispersion of the Indus valley culture about 1800 BC virtually no art is known until stone sculpture appeared during the third century BC, under the patronage of the great Emperor Ashoka of the Maurya dynasty (272-322 BC). An early convert to Buddhism, he set up a series of monolithic pillars at sites associated with the Buddha's career. Most were inscribed with injunctions cut by Ashoka's command, and the pillars, of polished sandstone, have capitals representing imperial animals – lion, bull, horse, elephant – but no base or footing. These are Ashoka's chief memorials, but there was undoubtedly a contemporary and related tradition of wooden architecture and sculpture, all of which has now vanished. It seems indeed that Mauryan sculptors developed techniques of colossal figure carving – the basis of a style of sculpture that continued into the following period.

The Buddha, neither god nor prophet but a human teacher, died about 489 BC. After his death his bodily relics were dispersed, then installed in reliquaries within the solid domes of shrines called *stupas*; the domed shape of the *stupa*, raised on a plinth and crowned with tiers of honorific umbrellas, became itself a symbol

HARAPPA (left)
A buffalo, c.2500-2300 BC
The buffalo often appears on Indus valley seals and was probably essential to the economy. It is fluently drawn, but without such agility as many Minoan seals are (see vol. 2 p. 32). The horns are exaggerated, to suggest its fecund power?

BHARHUT (left)
Yakshi, 2nd century BC
The ancient Indian nature spirits kept their place and meaning within the context of Buddhist art: the *Yakshi* holds a branch of a mango tree (referring to the old belief that the touch of a beautiful woman will make a tree flower), a metaphor of the fruits to be garnered by following the Buddha.

SANCHI (above)
The eastern gate of the Great Stupa, inner side, 1st century BC
The crowded details of the reliefs present fascinating glimpses into Indian life of their time; they depict events from the life of the Buddha (though the teacher himself is not represented) and scenes from his earlier incarnations. A definite

sense of depth is suggested by the overlapping of forms; there are even occasional attempts at foreshortening. The lintels may be based on the painted scrolls used by travelling story-tellers to illustrate their stories – hence the two ends of each appear to be rolled up like a scroll – and the reliefs are to be read in that way, in continuous sequence.

HARAPPA (above)
Ceremonial dancer,
3rd millennium BC
The dancer's body is defined by subtly angled planes, and there is a sense of blithe,

spiralling movement in the figure's twisting torso and cocked leg, without parallel in any other object extant from the early civilization of the fertile Indus valley.

of Nirvana – that Release from reincarnation that is the only end of suffering. The *stupas* became centres of pilgrimage, and were embellished with decorated stone railings, gateways and narrative panels. The earliest sculptural style, in quite shallow relief with rather angular, sharply cut figures, is represented by the remains of the elaborate railings of the *stupa* at Bharhut (second century BC), largely built during the brief Shunga dynasty of northern central India. But the most complete (now restored) early *stupa* is the famous Great Stupa at Sanchi built by the Shatavahana dynasty, rulers of central and southern India from 220 BC to AD 236. The Sanchi *stupa* has four gateways of distinctive shape, carved in more massive relief and with more complex subject matter than at Bharhut. At Bharhut there is no developed sense of space – the relief is more like a translation into stone of an outline drawing – but at Sanchi that characteristically Indian feeling for full, rounded volume is clearly developing. The Shatavahana dynasty, lasting longer in the south than in central India, also built an important series of *stupas* around Amaravati from about 20 BC to AD 300, featuring vividly sensuous

sculptures in white limestone – gracefully carved figures in varied movement. The Shatavahanas sponsored trade with South-East Asia, and the Amaravati style appears in Buddhist settlements on the coasts of South-East Asia and even as far away as Sulawesi.

With the development of Buddhism, monasteries were founded, and in the western Deccan numbers of cave-monasteries were cut in living rock from the second century BC. Their halls, for instance at Karle, were decorated with sculpted images embodying beauty and physical well-being, and with wall-paintings. Unfortunately the earlier (first century BC) paintings on the walls at Ajanta, the most famous of these rock-cut monasteries, have greatly deteriorated, though it is clear that they depicted incidents from the *Jataka* tales (describing the Buddha's previous incarnations) in styles closely related to Shatavahana art.

The first image of the Buddha himself was carved about the end of the first century AD, either in the great cosmopolitan city and religious centre of Mathura, then ruled by a dynasty of central Asian origin, the Kushan, or at Gandhara (see over). Previously it had been improper to represent the Buddha in human

form, but Buddhism was becoming increasingly popular, needing a more personal focus. The humanity of the prince Shakyamuni, who became the Buddha, was acknowledged, though icons suggested his attainment of Nirvana by their transcendent peacefulness.

Buddhism almost from its inception had been split between the stricter form, Hinayana, the so-called "Lesser Vehicle", denying the Buddha divinity but seeking personal Nirvana, and Mahayana, the Greater Vehicle. Mahayana invested the Buddha with divine status, and postulated the existence of divine compassionate Bodhisattvas, beings who would later become Buddhas but had paused on their way in order to assist all mankind to Nirvana. Mahayana Buddhism was to spread eastwards to Tibet, China, Korea and Japan; Hinayana Buddhism had its greatest influence in Sri Lanka and in South-East Asia.

Contemporary with the historic Buddha was another teacher, Mahavira, whose archaic religion is known as Jainism. Jain-inspired sculpture survives alongside Buddhist art, for instance at Mathura, where the remains of what may have been a Jain *stupa* reflect particularly Buddhist sculpture at Karle.

KARLE (below)
The Buddha preaching, flanked by worshippers, 2nd/4th century AD
The magnificent flanking figures are more than life-size and their scanty but elaborate clothing suggests royal status. The figures follow an ideal canon: the males have broad shoulders and chests, firm hips and a virile appearance; their females are in contrast soft and more rounded, with large breasts and hips and tiny waists. Their opulent well-being indicates that the cave is a palace fit and worthy of the Buddha's teaching proclaimed within. Two Bodhisattvas attend the Buddha in the central relief.

AMARAVATI (left)
The presents of King Band-huma, from the *Vessantara Jataka,* late 2nd century AD
Like many such scenes of the *Jatakas* at Amaravati, the relief has convincing depth, filled with figures. The king receives gifts of gold and sandalwood in the presence of his daughters.

KATRA (right)
Seated Buddha, mid-2nd century AD
Making the *abhayamudra* (fear-repelling gesture) the Buddha sits beneath a bodhi tree, attended by royal Bodhisattvas. The linear draperies assist the powerful projection of the massive, heroic figure.

MATHURA (right)
Yakshi, 2nd century AD
The figure conforms to the same voluptuous canon as the donors at Karle (left); even more is made of the soft, undulating shape of the female body. She carries a birdcage and a parrot pecks at her hair, suggesting that *Yakshis* shared the attributes of the courtesans of the day, since one of the accomplishments of these ladies, mentioned in the *Kama-sutra,* was to teach a parrot to talk.

Indian Art 2: From Gupta to Pala

Mahayana Buddhism flourished throughout India and its various kingdoms from the third century BC to the seventh century AD, when the older Hindu religion began to revive and the Buddhist Gupta Empire finally disintegrated. Although a modified Buddhism, Vajrayana Buddhism, continued to be practised under the Pala dynasty in the north-east, the invasion of the Muslims in 1196 destroyed the Pala kingdom and virtually obliterated all traces of Buddhism from India. From about the third century AD, however, it had been carried with their wares by Indian traders and by missionaries all over Asia, and in Tibet and Nepal the styles evolved in Gandhara, Mathura and in the Gupta Empire have developed uninterrupted until the present century.

Gandhara, in the north-western corner of India, was the cross-roads of overland trade routes from both East and West – from China and from the Roman Empire. Numerous Buddhist *stupas* and monasteries, encrusted with stone and stucco sculpture, attest the wealth of its merchants and rulers in the early centuries AD. In contrast to the contemporary art of Mathura (see preceding page), Gandharan sculpture shows the native Indian softness and rounded form overlaid by a strong influence from Graeco-Roman art, visible especially in the mould of the features and in the pattern and comparatively heavy sweep of the draperies. In its turn, Gandharan art had an influence on the sculpture of Mathura and other Indian centres, and was exported by stages as far as China, Korea and Japan.

However, the heartland of Buddhist India was the middle Ganges plain, where the Buddha himself had lived and taught. There the great sacred sites – such as Sarnath, where the Buddha had preached his first sermon; Bodhgaya, where he had attained enlightenment – attracted pilgrims from all over the orient. In this region the Gupta dynasty gained power about AD 320. Early Gupta art developed the types and images established in Mathura, representing the enlightened Buddha and the compassionate Bodhisattvas in "bodies of glory" – supernaturally suave and gentle forms, on which the clinging drapery was represented almost as a transparent veil. These painted sculptures were intended to convey, partly through the very smooth surface of the stone, a condition of radiant peace with which the devotee could identify.

GANDHARA (below)
Standing Bodhisattva,
2nd century AD
Numerous almost identical
Bodhisattvas survive, all
with this fluted drapery and
zigzag hems. Perhaps the
decorative treatment of the
hair and moustache echoes
rather similar features
of Roman sculpture in the
same era (see vol. 2 p. 50).

AJANTA (right)
Flying nymph, late 5th
century AD
The heavenly nymph soars
in flight, as the swing of
her necklace indicates. A
detail of a large fresco of
celestial beings adoring the
Buddha, she has rich ornaments and a splendid turban,
illustrating the luxury and
liveliness of Gupta art.

SARNATH (above)
The first sermon,
5th century AD
The icon depicts the
Buddha preaching the Law
(*Dharma*) in the Deer Park
at Sarnath. The Buddha
compared the rules of right
conduct to the spokes of a
wheel, and his hands are in
the *dharmachakramudra* (the
turning of the Wheel of the
Law), one of many gestures
used to symbolize aspects
of the Buddha's teaching,
here amplified below in a
relief. The elegant, rather
limp hands, softly rounded
face and narrow torso, and
the smoothness, the reticent
carving of the stone, are
typical of the Gupta style.

NALANDA (below)
Seated Bodhisattva,
8th or 9th century AD
The stucco icon, image of
supreme compassion, makes
the gesture of dispensing
gifts (*varadamudra*). Ornate
jewels signify his status as
a royal Bodhisattva – at
Nalanda the chief means
of distinguishing the many
Bodhisattvas from images
of the Buddha. The marked
emphasis on lips, nose and
eyes seems a Pala feature.
Nalanda was an important
centre of pilgrimage and its
style and iconography were
disseminated, chiefly by
means of votive bronzes,
as far afield as Borobudur
in central Java (see p. 30).

PAHARPUR (above)
Shiva and dancing girls,
8th century AD
Pala shrines in Bihar and
Bengal were built in brick,
into which terracotta reliefs
were set in thousands.

The figures have the broad
shoulders and slender waists
of Gupta fashion, but also a
superhuman opulence which
extends even to the details
of jewellery and clothing –
all once brightly painted.

The caves in the gorge of Ajanta are the richest depository of Indian Buddhist painting, although the murals there, and scattered relics elsewhere, can only hint at the state of the art in early medieval India. In Caves 1 and 17 in particular there are substantial remains of huge programmes of wall-paintings belonging to the fifth or sixth century: the drawing reflects the rounded fullness of Gupta sculpture, with smooth, supple contours; the faces are simply but boldly delineated; and the crowded delights of the princely mansions depicted glow with bright colours. At Ajanta there is also a quantity of sculpture of the same period – massively generalized, frontal images carved out of the solid mother-rock (see over). These icons, too, were once painted, and the cells, halls and corridors of the caves were richly and variously decorated from floor to ceiling with a brilliant repertoire of Buddhist legend and belief.

The Gupta Empire was decaying in the sixth century, though it was briefly revived by the cultured conqueror Harsha in the first half of the seventh century. In the eastern part of the Empire – Bihar and Bengal – the Pala dynasty was consolidated about 760. The Vajrayana Buddhism fostered by the Pala kings embraced elements of mystical Hinduism, and in the West it is known after its basic texts, the Tantras, which proclaim all earthly things to be the product of cosmic sexual activity, and therefore essential to the existence of the Great Whole. Orthodox Buddhism asserts that life is without value; Tantrikas claim that life offers positive experiences to be cultivated according to complicated systems of medicine, psychology, metaphysics, ceremonial and magic. The sweet, erotic style of Gupta art was adapted for schemes or tableaux of painted and sculpted figures, both masculine and feminine, which demonstrated the states of mind and body the Tantrika could achieve. The bright colours – blues, greens and reds – of the skin, the proliferation and disposition of arms and legs, these all had a prescribed significance, intended to trigger radiant inner icons in the mind's eye, and so assist meditation.

One great Pala site is Paharpur in Bengal, where the ruin of the mountainous plinth of a Buddhist shrine built in the eighth century still retains more than 2,000 of its terracotta sculptured panels. On each, summary, doll-like figures represent different episodes, anecdotes, truths and admonitions of the great body of Sanskrit literature, both Buddhist and Hindu. There is a greater attention to detail in the stucco icons produced at Nalanda, a large monastic complex and university in Bihar, though the influence of the soft, unbroken contours of Gupta sculpture is still at work. Illustrated Buddhist texts also survive, in a style closely related to the Pala sculpture.

The later Gupta style had penetrated China and South-East Asia, modifying or supplementing the Indian-inspired traditions already established there, but through the Pala dynasty the Gupta tradition was transmitted to Nepal, Tibet and Indonesia. The Buddhism of Tibet is an amalgam of Tantric Buddhism and native necromantic elements, and its pantheon has many deities. Tibetan monasteries were filled with paintings and sculptures on every scale, from miniature to colossal, representing the gods in all their variety of attributes – often calm and of an idealized beauty, reflecting Pala styles, but sometimes gloriously angry and threatening, depicting the fierce aspect of a compassionate Bodhisattva confronted with evil. Nepalese art was yet further modified by an accretion of Hindu elements.

BENGAL (above)
The Ashtasahasrika Prajna-paramita: The Bodhi-sattva Samantabhadra with Tara, the incarnation of Buddhist wisdom, and the dwarf Acharya Vajrapani, c. 1120
The figures preserve the manuscript from harm and attract divine favour.

TIBET (below)
The Heruka in union with his shakti Nairatmya, 17th century?
The attributes held in his 28 hands identify this particular emanation of a Buddha; his union with his female creative energy (*shakti*) symbolizes the unity of the Tantric system.

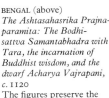

SULTANGANJ (above)
Standing Buddha, early 9th century?
This colossal bronze is a unique survival, an early version of the Gupta style adopted in Nepal. In its frontal view it is close to Nalanda stucco sculpture, but its more delicate, slim, etiolated form is typical of later Nepalese art.

TIBET (above)
Thangka (temple banner): *The goddess Tara, the incarnation of Buddhist wisdom,* late 17th century Thangkas were intended as aids to meditation, and rigid canons governed the disposition, proportions and colours of the images. They had to be framed by two coloured borders – symbolizing the *thangka's* visionary character. Figures and costume are of Indian type; the subsidiary detail of the background depends on Chinese prototypes.

Indian Art 3: Hindu Art

Hinduism had displaced Buddhism as the dynastic religion of central and southern India by about the beginning of the seventh century AD. Soon afterwards, coinciding with a great effervescence of literary activity, as Brahmin scholars put together the *Puranas*, virtually encyclopaedias of Hindu legend, a distinctive Hindu style of art emerged in the south. In the major shrines, under the patronage of a succession of powerful dynasties, halls and galleries of painting and sculpture illustrating the *Puranas* were created, and the chief deities at the heart of the developing Hindu religion – Shiva, Vishnu and the Goddess, Devi – were hymned in colossal, sometimes almost terrifying icons. Though the style of the sculpture was adapted from that of the rock-carving in Buddhist cave-monasteries of the western Deccan (see preceding page), southern Hindu art is characterized throughout its long development by its own elaborate schemes of mythical imagery.

The Chalukya dynasty, which ruled larger or smaller parts of south-west India from the sixth to the thirteenth century, built at Aivalli (Aihole) the first significant group of Hindu temples, with vigorous but relatively crude sculpture representing the deities of the pantheon in a rather limited formal vocabulary. Towards the end of the sixth century, however, at Badami, the Chalukyas undertook the cutting of a series of caves filled with monumental sculpture of more varied expression and of superb quality: its style was influenced by the Deccan tradition of Buddhist carving seen in the caves at Ajanta. There are also a few surviving fragments of painted decorations at Badami (also Deccan in derivation), which echo the stunningly beautiful *Apsaras* painted perhaps 50 years earlier at the rock fortress of Sigiriya in Sri Lanka; the remains at Badami and Sigiriya are all that is left of the enormous cycles of decoration once widespread in the shrines and palaces of early medieval India.

The first powerful patrons of Hinduism on the eastern side of peninsular India were the Pallavas. Their principal cities were Mamallapuram and Kanchipuram, and around Mamallapuram, in numerous rock-caves along the coast, the Pallavas expressed their devotion to the great Hindu deities in a cool and restrained style – the sculpture derived, it seems, from the style of the sculpture of the Amaravati *stupas*, the painting from the styles

ELEPHANTA (above)
Shiva, 8th century
The god is represented as Shiva Maheshvara, that is, in his three aspects – the wrathful Aghora, on the left; Uma Devi, the blissful one, on the right; in the middle the beneficent Tatpurusha. Shiva's awesome image, 3.5m (11ft) high, is one of the main icons of the shrine, carved from the rock in a bold, broad, hieratic style.

BADAMI (right)
Vishnu sitting on Ananta, 578
Smaller reliefs are almost scattered round the huge, sumptuously ornamented icon. Vishnu is usually represented reclining on the Serpent of Eternity (as at Deogarh, see over) but here he sits within its coils in a posture of royal ease, raising his symbols, the conch and the *chakra*. If not so generous in form, he echoes Ajanta work in type, pose and facial details.

AJANTA (below)
Panchika and Hariti, 6th century
From Cave 2, the double icon displays the Buddhist god of wealth, Panchika, and his consort, the goddess of Plenty; like her Western counterpart, Charity, she carries a child. The heavy, rounded appearance of the deities typifies the Ajanta style – due in part to the porous nature of the stone.

SIGIRIYA (right)
Apsaras, detail, late 5th century
In style and technique, the figures closely resemble the 5th-century frescos at Ajanta (see preceding page), though rather freer in execution: the elaborate details of hairstyle and jewellery are drawn directly in colour and the contours later outlined in black. A maid offers flowers and fruit to a lady, who has a body the colour of "ripe corn" – considered a mark of high birth; the maid, on the other hand, has dark skin, over which she wears a transparent red blouse.

MAMALLAPURAM (right)
The descent of the goddess Ganga, mid-7th century
Carved on a huge granite outcropping, the tableau of massive forms is perhaps the most complex medieval Indian sculpture extant. It represents the reward for his austerity of the sage Bhagiratha, the Ganges water; in the rainy season, water runs down a natural cleft in the rock, to become the focus of the action. Each figure is simply and clearly defined, with little ornament, but a fine sense of life; animals – especially the elephants, making their way to drink at the holy river – are represented with sympathetic naturalism.

represented in the caves at Ajanta. The legend of *The descent of the goddess Ganga*, cut into the face of a cliff, is the most famous of the Pallava reliefs; the narrative is episodic, uncompartmented: the different phases of the tale are dispersed over the whole field of the rock and woven together in a single tissue of interacting figures, though these are solid and separate, seldom overlapping. The Pallavas were traders, and their art was exported and took root in Indochina and Indonesia.

North and to the west, inland among the mountains at Elura (Ellora), there is a vast complex of Buddhist, Jain and Hindu caves, all sculpted in related styles between the sixth and ninth centuries – most stupendous among them the Kailashanatha temple, cut by the Rashtrakuta dynasty, successors to the Chalukyas on the west coast. In the icons and narrative reliefs decorating the many shrines at Elura, the sculptors strove to convey a sense of transcendent being, imparting to the figures a tremendous volume and strength; some of them embody such strenuous movement that they seem to be bursting out of their frames.

The sculpted cave at Elephanta, an island off the coast near Bombay, was one of the first of the great Hindu works to arouse the admiration of the West. Elephanta was ruled first by the Chalukyas and then by the Rashtrakutas, and it is unclear which of the two dynasties sponsored its sculpture. The cave is dedicated to Shiva, the awesome god of phallic and destructive power. Only the interior is artistically significant – its great icons, probably once plastered and painted, are flanked by colossal narrative panels (not shown), which, in appropriate scenes, impress the spectator with a sense of erotic sweetness extraordinary on such a massive scale. All the sculpture has a clarity, with smooth and simple volumes, reminiscent of the early Chalukya sculpture at Badami.

After the collapse of the Pallava dynasty, the Cholas, like the Pallavas a seafaring, merchant power maintaining close links with South-East Asia, became dominant in south-east India. The Cholas built plentifully – hundreds of smaller shrines survive, and a few huge pyramidal temples, expressive of imperial ambition. The greatest early Chola temple is the Rajarajeshvaram at Tanjore, in which are preserved not only carvings but also, inside the ambulatory, a unique scheme of painted decoration, including female dancers posing provocatively, performing gymnastically with great fluency. Some of the finest Chola works are bronze icons cast by the *cire-perdue* method, commonly less than half life-size, made to be borne in procession. They are usually of a male or female deity – most often Shiva or Parvati – or sometimes joint images of gods and their consorts; their sensuous elegance and slender proportions are the Hindu paradigms of that ideal canon of beauty first expressed in the sculptures at Amaravati.

In the last phase of purely Hindu sculpture there was a marked tendency towards the decorative. The Hoyshalas, the last dynasty to rule in Mysore (falling to the Muslims in 1386), built temples – with some relation to northern shrines (see over) – displaying simplified figures that are often hardly more than supports for extravagant ornament, deeply cut multiple loops and curlicues. After the decline of the Cholas several dynasties in the south undertook ever vaster schemes of stone and painted stucco sculpture in the decoration of their stupendous shrines; the scale and the need for immense numbers of figures led to a decline in expressive intimacy in favour of superficial magnificence.

ELURA (right)
Shiva's dance in the elephant skin, c. 580–642
Shiva prepares to slay the demon Andhakasura, who has threatened to carry off Parvati. He wears the skin of the elephant-demon, Nila, flayed by Virabhadra, a ferocious form of Vishnu, and strides forward in a highly energetic attack.

TANJORE (below)
Dancing girl, c. 1000
Exaggeratedly contorted, the whirling figure no doubt reflects both the dancing and religious prostitution customary in major Hindu temples of medieval India.

MADRAS (left)
Parvati, 10th century
As the *shakti* (consort) of Shiva, Parvati embodies the strength and potency of the deity. Long-limbed and heavy-breasted, the elegant bronze, 1m (40in) high, recalls the Sigiriya *Apsaras*.

BELUR (right)
Heavenly nymph,
12th/13th century
The age-old image of the Yakshi is reinterpreted in terms of the intricate ornamental detail typical of the Hoyshala period.

COCHIN (above)
Vishnu, late 17th century
As at Badami, Vishnu sits on the Serpent of Eternity, whose five heads form a canopy behind the supreme god; the coincidence of this unusual iconographic motif suggests Chalukya tradition was still strong in the area. The vigorous fantasy of the palace mural is typical of the flowering of wall-painting in the late Hindu period, redeeming a rather lifeless treatment of the figure in a carnival of dense, colourful pattern.

The Kandarya Mahadeva Temple, Khajuraho

After the death of Harsha and the eclipse of the Gupta Empire in the seventh century AD, India was divided into numerous warring kingdoms, ruled mostly by Hindus. These dynasts also vied with one another in building ever more elaborate temples, displaying some of the finest architectural sculpture the world has seen. Indeed in northern India the temple itself was conceived as a sculpture, as a colossal monolith encrusted with an extraordinary wealth of sculptured forms, both figurative and decorative, carved in stone but originally cloaked in plaster and brightly painted.

The Hindu temple symbolized the axis of the cosmos, the mountain Meru, which rises through the different realms of Earth and Heaven, its spire reaching towards the Beyond. Inside the temple tower, the comparatively small sanctuary contained the source of the temple's sanctity, an icon or emblem of one of the major gods or goddesses. Inside and out, the temples were hung with garlands of sculpture, depicting in broad bands most often gods and godlings in their Heaven, entertained eternally by celestial musicians and dancers. Their heavenly delights were imagined to encompass the highest pinnacles of human longing, uncontaminated by the evils and suffering of earthly life.

Wall-paintings also survive in patches in the temples, reflecting the style of the sculpture and conceived not very differently. All the arts of medieval India were informed by one constant idea, derived from the dance-drama, which had flourished in India since at least the second century BC – first to awaken and then to reconcile traces of the powerful emotions felt during that long series of rebirths which every Indian, Buddhist or Hindu, knew he had experienced. Both sculpture and painting reflect the bodily imagery of gesture and posture of the dance-drama, and share in its ultimate aim, to bring the spectator into that supreme emotional condition, *Rasa*, which is a genuine version of Blissful union with the divine ground of being, Brahman. The experience that brings one most intensely to *Rasa* is sexual love in all its variety. Apart from certain images of terrible gods and spirits, Hindu temple art always presents its *dramatis personae* as supremely beautiful, charming to the eye and seductive to the hand.

The early evolution of the Hindu temple is difficult to reconstruct. Shrines of the second century BC have been excavated, bearing some resemblance to Greek temples; but the earliest known example of the developed Hindu shrine, at Sanchi, dates from the fifth century AD. The basic styles and sculptural formulae of the southern Hindu temple (see preceding page) are found from the sixth, seventh and eighth centuries; then in the north superb temples rise, at Deogarh, Osia, Khajuraho; in Orissa, at Bhuvaneshvara, Puri and Konarak; in the north-west, at Modhera. Deogarh, which is early – even possibly of the sixth century – is modest in scale; Khajuraho, built between 950 and 1050, was a huge complex of some 80 temples round a large lake. Of its 25 temples still intact, the shrine of Kandarya Mahadeva is perhaps outstanding; its famous erotic sculptures – the Heavenly Bands – represent Hindu sculpture at its finest.

ORISSA (left)
Shiva and Parvati,
12th century
The icon once stood inside a shrine. Its two deities were carved according to strict canons, described in illustrated manuals: hence the great god Shiva and his consort Parvati have rounded faces "like full moons", noses arched "like parrots' bills", and eyes shaped "like willow leaves".

KONARAK (below)
The Surya temple, detail:
A wheel, emblem of the chariot of the sun-god Surya, 13th century
Surya's temple, known as the Black Pagoda, is famous for its explicitly erotic figure carvings. The wheels support the *mandapa*, the body of the temple, and are carved with the vine and tendril motifs typical of Orissan sculpture. On the temple itself single celestial deities stand at the side of embracing couples.

KHAJURAHO (above)
The Kandarya Mahadeva temple, detail of the Heavenly Bands: *An Apsara, c.* 1000
These pneumatic beauties, swelled with unremitting amorous desire, swarm in Heaven, where their role is to arouse and gratify every possible sexual impulse, and so to reward the heroes and saints for the virtue shown in their earthly existence.

BHUVANESHVARA (left)
The Rajarani temple, detail, *c.* 1000
The celestial girl under a tree echoes the Nature spirit, or *Yakshi*, of early Indian sculpture. Creepers and foliage abound, rising from the supernatural sap felt to be coursing from within the whole temple.

DEOGARH (above)
Vishnu lying on Ananta, 6th century
The supreme god lies on the serpent of Eternity, symbolizing the endless revolutions of time, as described in the *Vishnu Purana*, the cosmic myth relating the activities of the primordial godhead.

KHAJURAHO (above)
The Kandarya Mahadeva temple, detail of the Heavenly Bands, c. 1000
The figures follow standard proportions for fashionable beauty; posture and gesture are always elegant, while the elaborate hairstyles and ornament represent the apex of royal fashion. Clothing is minimal, not interfering at all with our perception of the underlying body, and the sexual attributes are emphasized. Sculptural form is almost totally rounded, evoking memories of erotic sensation and the delights of touch. Above, the rhythmic ornamental forms, the multiplicity of the mouldings, the perpetual pattern of rib rising upon rib, these are intended to excite, in a tempo of visual drumming. The main bulk rises 30m (100ft) high, surrounded by 84 decorated buttresses, and is dedicated to Shiva.

Indian Art 4: Mughal and Rajput

Islam came to India first of all modestly, with Arab traders, to the western seaboard – then as a holocaust. Muslim armies invading from Afghanistan in the late tenth, eleventh, twelfth and thirteenth centuries looted and systematically destroyed every Buddhist or Hindu temple and institution that fell to their arms: not one ancient temple survives in the northwest or the northern Deccan. At first the raids were seasonal – the Turko-Afghan Muslims disliked the pre-monsoon heat – but in 1120 the first of a series of Muslim sultanates was established in Delhi. In the suburbs of the modern city the Q'utb Mosque and Minar still stand, bearing finely cut, purely Islamic sculpture of about 1200.

By this time Persian painters also were employed at the Muslim courts, although nothing survives from before the early sixteenth century. From the same period other manuscripts have come down to us that show an amalgamation of Persian and Hindu styles, so it is reasonable to assume, too, a tradition of purely Hindu narrative illustration. Scattered sixteenth-century manuscripts are sufficient to give an idea of its main characteristics, and Jain manuscripts produced in western India from the fourteenth to the seventeenth century are in a variant mode of the same essential style. In Hindu narratives the figures are types, conventional and repetitive, defined by strong outlines in rather gaudy colours and placed in simplified, almost two-dimensional settings. In the evolved Indo-Muslim style, these elements are transformed by the brilliant colours, highly finished execution and rhythmic draughtsmanship – stemming ultimately from the discipline of calligraphy (see over) – of the more developed Persian painting.

In 1526 the first Mughal Emperor, Babur, won northern India at the Battle of Panipat. The supreme examples of Indo-Muslim painting were produced at the courts of the third, fourth and fifth Mughal Emperors, Akbar (ruled 1556-1605), Jehangir (ruled 1605-27) and Shah Jahan (ruled 1628-58), the builder of the Taj Mahal. Akbar set up his workshop, run by Safavid painters from the court of Shah Tahmasp in Persia (see p. 26), as an instrument of his policy of cultural and religious unification: it produced histories of Akbar's reign to be circulated amongst his Hindu and Muslim feudatories, and each also received the literary classics of the alien culture in trans-

lation. Akbar's atelier evolved a unique style, in which Hindu conceptions and European realism (derived from engravings) were combined in a modified Persian matrix; many compositions were the work of several hands, frequently both Muslim and Hindu – one doing the general outline, another the portrait heads, another the landscape, yet another the colouring. The large miniatures of Akbar's atelier revel in worldly complexity, and aim not only to teach but to fascinate: events are stirring, emotions uninhibited; the whole is a blend of consciously beautiful colour, perfectionist calligraphy and meticulous realism.

Jehangir, who took over Akbar's atelier on his death, had a special interest in botany and zoology: albums of birds, animals and flowers were produced for him, as well as narrative paintings which became somewhat more descriptive and austere, less dynamic. Jehangir's artists recorded the world with dispassionate curiosity – whether it was the largest lion Jehangir had ever shot, or one of his nobles dying of debauch, alcoholism and drugs. Jehangir's son Shah Jahan, however, had a taste for the finely wrought and decorative, to which the fine jades he commissioned also

DELHI (below)
Detail of the sculptured calligraphy on the Q'utb Minar, *c.* 1200

The relief bands embody phrases from the Koran in Persian script. As usually in calligraphy (see over), the rhythms of the vertical and curved, long and short, strokes of the lettering reflect those of the chant.

RAJASTHAN (above)
The marriage of Vasudeva and Devaki, 1525
Within a simple enclosure, schematic figures, typical of early Hindu miniatures, act their parts in the nuptials of Krishna's parents, as told in the *Bhagavata*.

WESTERN INDIA (left)
The Uttaradhyayana-sutra: Mahavira surrounded by dancers and musicians, *c.* 1460
The simple but harmonious colours and naive, sharply outlined figures are common to all Jain manuscripts.

AKBAR'S ATELIER (right)
The Hamsanama (Deeds of Mohammed's uncle, Hamsa): *Gardeners beating a giant trapped in a pit*, *c.* 1570
Closely observed animals and plants, actively posed, delicately modelled figures, are united harmoniously in a brilliant overall pattern.

AKBAR'S ATELIER (below)
The Akbarnama (Deeds of
Akbar): *Akbar's officers
reconcile a rebel, c.* 1590
The anecdotal narrative is
disposed in layers mounting
up the picture; every inch
glistens with a different
colour, but all the parts
are fully legible. Persian
influence is clear in the
colours and composition.

SHAH JAHAN'S ATELIER
(right) Jade cup, 1657
The cup resembles a ripe
gourd, tapered to a handle
shaped into the head of a
wild goat. The wax-soft
appearance is an illusion
(jade is so hard it cannot
be scratched by steel: it
is carved with gems) – an
effect of the lobed shape
and subtle modelling. The
fine jades produced at Shah
Jahan's court were mostly
the work of Persian artists.

testify. But when Shah Jehan was deposed and
imprisoned by his son Aurangzeb, the atelier
was abolished and the artists dispersed, to find
their livings in the bazaars of Delhi and Agra,
or at the lesser courts of Rajasthan.

In these courts, during the tolerant rule of
the great Mughals, artists had been producing
album paintings and illustrations in a purely
Hindu style, although they had learnt from the
example of metropolitan Mughal art to essay
portraiture and historical record, and to work
their figures into a richer landscape. Specifically Hindu, however, is the clear compart-
mentalization of these compositions, reasserted strongly after the demise of the
Mughal atelier. Now recognized as one of the
world's great artistic achievements, Hindu
Rajput miniatures were made from the early
seventeenth to the nineteenth century at the
greater courts in Rajasthan proper and in the
neighbouring Punjab hills. Rajasthan painting
naturally reflected Mughal influences from
Delhi and Agra more directly, but its subject
matter was Hindu and romantic – the legend of
Krishna in particular stimulated an extraordinary output of erotically flavoured paintings. The superb large-format miniatures and

small portraits painted at the court of Kishangarh by an artist of genius, Nihal Chand
(active 1730-50), for his ruler, Savant Singh
(who was also a renowned poet and the passionate lover of the poetess Bani Thani), are
one high point of the Rajasthan school. Nihal
Chand's idealized women have beautifully
rounded and elegant features, and emanate an
erotic aura of delicate, dreamlike poetry.

The Krishna legend was also treated in the
Punjab hills. In a variety of styles, ranging
from the rough and violent in Basohli to the
elegiac and softly atmospheric in Kangra,
painters retailed the progress of Krishna's
allegorical life and love-affairs among the
cowherds and cowgirls of Brindaban. Brindaban is a region on the banks of the Yamuna
river, reinterpreted mystically as the realm
where earth and heaven fuse, just as Krishna
fuses the human and divine. Lines from one of
Savant Singh's poems parallel the seductive,
nostalgic radiance of the Kangra paintings:

"Seeing the idiot world around me, I long
for Brindaban, and the Yamuna's sweet
waters; but life is slipping by. How deeply I
yearn for Brindaban; how afraid I am that life
is slipping by."

JEHANGIR'S ATELIER
(left) *The zebra,* 1621
Inscribed with the legend,
"A zebra, which the Turks
... brought from Abyssinia,
painted by Mansur in the
16th year of the reign of
Jehangir", the painting
records with delicate detail
the liquid eye, the hair of
the forelock, and the soft,
dark muzzle of the animal.
The court painters followed
the Emperor everywhere,
with instructions to note
anything of interest: they
made exact likenesses, but
these lack vigour – unlike
the teeming records of the
reign of Akbar the Great.

SCHOOL OF NIHAL CHAND
(left) *Radha, c.* 1750
Savant Singh idealized
his beloved Bani Thani
in his poetry as Radha,
Krishna's beloved; this
perhaps is a romanticized
portrait of Bani Thani.
The elegant stylization of
facial features – the long
pointed nose and curving
eye – and the refined use
of line are the supreme
distinction of Nihal Chand.

KANGRA (right)
*Krishna and Radha in a
grove, c.* 1780
Sharp details are set in a
range of colours from dark
to a lovely powdery pastel.
The passionate mutual love
of Krishna – an incarnation
of the supreme Vishnu –
and Radha symbolizes the
union of the soul with god.

Islamic Art 1: Calligraphy

The Prophet Mohammed was a combative personality, and the religion he founded, Islam, was dynamic, assertive and zealous to spread his teachings by conquest and force. Within three decades of the death of the Prophet in 632, Muslim Arab armies, surging out across the borders of modern Jordan, had overrun the Byzantine provinces of Syria and Egypt, North Africa as far as present-day Tripoli, and Sassanian Persia as far as present-day Kabul. In the eighth century the Muslims were halted inside the borders of France by Charles Martel at the Battle of Tours (732), and slightly later in Asia Minor by the Byzantine Emperors; by then the heirs of Mohammed, the Caliphs, having transferred their capital to Damascus, ruled all North Africa and Spain, all Persia, all Afghanistan, and large tracts of Turkestan in the present USSR.

Having little developed art and architecture of their own, the Arabs adopted and adapted the traditions of the lands they conquered, employing local craftsmen to rebuild or redecorate previous structures, or to decorate their new buildings with fragments of older ones. Mosaicists of Byzantine training adorned the Dome of the Rock in Jerusalem, the octagonal Islamic shrine established there to challenge the Christian Holy Sepulchre. The Arabs borrowed from Sassanian decorative forms in Persia, from late classical, even Coptic, ornament in Egypt, Syria and North Africa; from this assortment of Graeco-Roman forms they fused selected motifs into a remarkably unified Islamic style, formed and propagated above all in the arts associated with the written word.

The doctrines of Islam, rigidly governing every aspect of religious and secular life, are enshrined chiefly in the Koran, the word of Allah dictated through Mohammed, and also in a large collection of maxims and sermons, the *Traditions*, supposedly spoken by the Prophet. The Arabic text of the Koran was probably established in definitive, edited form by the middle of the ninth century. Its text was always written with a slant-cut reed-pen, in a calligraphy intended not only to convey His message but also, in its beauty, to reflect the glory of God. Calligraphy, the art of writing the sacred book, was regarded as the highest of all the arts, and the calligraphic forms of Arabic letters were soon used as ornament on

IRAQ OR SYRIA (right)
Chapter heading from a Koran, 9th/10th century
Early Kufic script is artless and emphatic; but the gold frame and the leaf-like medallion demonstrate a growing decorative impulse.

BAGHDAD (below)
Frontispiece and text from a Koran, *c.* 1000
Text and ornament are separate here, but in other pages unified. The exquisite Naskh lettering makes this a rare example of its kind.

TURKEY (right)
Hilyah (Description of the Prophet), 1691-92
The Ottoman sultans in Istanbul attracted many artists from Tabriz; early Turkish illumination is often very close to the Persian style. In Turkey, however, a greater degree of naturalism prevailed – apparent in the garlands which adorn the border.

IRAN (left)
Text from a Koran, 11th/12th century
High, exaggerated uprights typical of the Kufic script contrast with a background of graceful, golden scrolls.

NORTH AFRICA OR SPAIN (right) Text from a Koran, 11th century
The Maghribi script, with its bold, rounded but spare serifs, little embellished at first, originated in Spain.

textiles, metalwork, ceramics, furnishings and architecture. As the art of the scribe developed, other forms of decoration, chiefly arabesque and geometric, were introduced to provide elaborate frames for chapter headings and "rubrics" – emphasized phrases.

The earliest scripts used to transcribe the Koran were the Kufic group, developed in the seventh century. They stress the horizontal and vertical strokes, but use loops sparingly. Then the ends of the horizontals and verticals were greatly extended, and even "foliated" with elaborate serifs – a mode probably invented in Egypt in the eighth century. During the tenth century the use of the more curvilinear Naskh script became widespread, and by the fifteenth century six other kinds of script had been developed. To write any of these scripts well demands, according to Islamic tradition, special qualities of personal purity, concentration and even divine inspiration. In its developed form the calligraphy corresponded to the rhythms and cadences of chanted speech, so that the lengths and proportions of the letters were altered, not only to enrich the visual pattern, but also to embody the musical phrasing in which the words were

sung. Though much less individual than Chinese calligraphy, written with the brush, Islamic calligraphy permits the writer some freedom of expression, by allowing him to follow the promptings of his inner ear – within the recognized canons of perfection for each type of script. It was perhaps the scribe's personal urge to express praise and reverence for the sacred book that carried him beyond the forms of the letters themselves into abstract decoration, usually developed out of the calligraphic forms, but also incorporating the geometric and arabesque patterns originating in other arts; once they had been introduced, it was chiefly in manuscripts that these patterns were developed and transmitted.

The arabesque is essentially an S curve, composed of opposing spirals. The relative proportions of the spirals may vary considerably, and the foliage and flowers forming its original basis are usually stylized out of recognition. As in calligraphy, the Islamic aesthetic demands that the hand be schooled to execute the arabesque without any of those tremors or linear faults which indicate a failure of concentration. Beside, or instead of, the arabesque, which was used as a background

linking together the sequences of lines, a repeating geometric pattern – interwoven combinations of circles, squares, pentagons, hexagons, octagons or stars – was used for the frontispieces, especially of Korans of the thirteenth and fourteenth centuries. These are often strikingly reminiscent of masterpieces of Christian Celtic art (see vol. 2 p. 66).

Geometrical shapes have a profoundly important role to play in Islamic art, since they are considered as the archetypes of all form, symbolizing the divinely ordained pattern of the universe. A generalized, "all-over" geometric design was even felt to be superior to the idiosyncratic variations of calligraphy or arabesque, and to represent the closest approach of the human understanding to God's Nature. Though the educated Muslim recognizes that geometrical forms are not in themselves divine, but merely symbols of divinity, nevertheless a kind of geometrical complacency has been the particular disease to which Muslim art has sometimes succumbed. Islam, however, seems to have preserved a continuing consciousness of the sacred function of ornament which other decorative traditions once possessed, but usually have lost.

TURKEY (above)
Basmallah (In the name of God, the compassionate, the merciful), 1834
A religious invocation is spelled out in bird form.

NISHAPUR, IRAN (left)
Earthenware bowl, late 10th century
The intrinsic elegance of Kufic lettering, appearing by itself or in combination, was exploited consummately by artist-potters of the Samanid dynasty (874-999).

IRAN (below)
Tailor at work,
early 17th century
Calligraphic line is elegant, rhythmic, economic, fluid; Riza Abbasi, famous artist of the Isfahan court, translated all these qualities into his masterly drawings.

IRAN (left)
Frontispiece from a Koran, early 16th century
Persian calligraphy had its finest flowering under the Safavid Shahs, and Tabriz became a flourishing centre (see further pp.26-27) for artists and illuminators, and

scribes: there the idea of enclosing, enshrining, the script within elaborately decorated lozenge or star medallions was developed. The lavish use of gold, here exploited in striking contrast with the lapis lazuli, is also typical.

Islamic Art 2: Decorative Arts

The Western distinction between "fine" and decorative art is impossible to sustain when considering Islamic art, and not only because the greater part of Islamic religious art, being non-figurative, would have to be classed as decorative. The basis of all the Islamic arts is painstaking craftsmanship, pursuing an ideal of consummate and laborious flawlessness; in this all the arts are equal. Further, although the highest perfection could be achieved by an Islamic craftsman only with the aid of what a Westerner would call "inspiration", the idea of the artist in the Renaissance sense could never gain ground. The craftsman's achievement was dependent not on inventive genius but on selfless application to his task and on closeness to the source of all skill, God.

The Muslim art that has always been most highly valued in the West is that of textiles. The earliest examples show Islamic adaptation of the traditional motifs of the areas the Arabs had conquered – some fine early silks feature designs based on Byzantine or Sassanian heraldic figures and animals. Soon, however, the weavers, too, were drawing on the developing common repertoire of Islamic art – arabesque and geometric ornament – although

on silks and carpets from Safavid Iran representational images like those in miniature painting (see over) were also included. Weaving, being the product of so many warp and woof threads calculated on the loom almost as on an abacus, could also be a vehicle of mathematical symbolism; so, too, could the sequences of knots forming the patterns of carpets, which were used in the Islamic world not only to cover floors and walls, but also to serve a religious purpose in the mosque. The most laborious and most skilfully woven Islamic textiles are the small rugs on which the worshipper kneels and prostrates himself in prayer. Their design is based usually either on the arched niche, or *mihrab* (with or without its hanging lamp), which in the mosque marks the direction of Mecca, or on the garden of Paradise, complete with symmetrically arranged flowers, shrubs, trees and pools.

The most precious Muslim artefacts are items of metalwork – in gold, silver, steel, bronze or brass – in which the craftsmen of several Islamic dynasties excelled. Vessels, candlesticks, pen-boxes and jewellery all tend to share a common aesthetic, an elegant contour and a lustrous, highly finished surface,

IRAQ (below)
A fragment of silk, 9th/10th century
Islamic appropriation of

Sassanian styles (see vol. 2 p. 25) is clear in the figures, in the tree's stylized foliage; Kufic script runs below.

IRAN (below)
Bronze cauldron, 12th/13th century
Exquisitely incised with animals and interlocking abstract designs, Seljuk

metal artefacts are often further decorated with a unique "animated" script – characters in Kufic and Naskh calligraphy ending in human and animal heads.

IRAN (left)
Carpet, 16th century
A central medallion, the fairly naturalistic forms of animals, and fine scroll and foliate patterns over a rich background – these typify the Safavid carpet.

SYRIA (below)
Brass inlaid basin, 1240
The craft of metal inlay reached a peak in the 13th and 14th centuries under Ayyubid and Mamluk rule, notably in Damascus (hence the term "damascening").

IRAN (right)
Standard, 16th century
Great artistry was applied to the making of weapons under the Safavid rulers. The pattern is a complex

blend of geometric with arabesque; it is symmetrical on the vertical axis, but otherwise not one element recurs. The steel is overlaid with gilt calligraphy.

making it extremely hard to judge by the eye the true thickness or weight of a piece. Weaponry in particular was wrought with a consummate and often minute skill; Islamic craftsmen developed extremely intricate techniques of inlay and overlay (especially of gold and silver on baser metals), in which they have never been surpassed. The decoration was sometimes calligraphic, the calligraphy – a verse from the Koran – being superbly integrated within repeating designs of foliage or rosettes; the approach was essentially linear, reflecting the rhythms of the scribe.

The first major development in Islamic ceramics seems to have taken place in Iraq during the ninth century, at Baghdad and Samarra, capitals of the Abbasid caliphate (750-1258), where a white tin-glaze was produced in imitation of the white Chinese Tang dynasty ware (see p. 38), and soon enhanced with green and blue "Tang" splashes. The refinement in Islamic pottery consists chiefly in the glazes, since the making of porcelain, though it continued to be imported from China, remained an impenetrable secret; the shapes of the vessels display fluent contours comparable to those of metalwork. By degrees the Muslim potters developed their own coloured and lustre overglazes, in which they executed first calligraphy and, later, heraldic designs; by the twelfth century they had applied to pottery most of the arabesque and calligraphic repertoire, and also splendid stylized human and animal forms. A special development of Islamic ceramics was tiling, used for the cladding of mosques or tombs. During the Safavid period in Iran huge decorative schemes were undertaken, and vast areas of wall were scaled with thousands and thousands of decorated tiles – producing an effect comparable in magnificence to the great stained-glass curtaining of European Gothic cathedrals. The tiles were set in plaster in complex geometric and arabesque designs, often on concave and convex surfaces, necessitating the most abstruse mathematical calculations.

The architectural ornament of a mosque consisted not only of ceramic, but also of wooden, stucco and stone sculpture – and the finest Islamic sculpture is architectural. Still recognizable in the design of the furniture of an Islamic mosque are late antique and Byzantine features – the canopy of an early *mihrab*, for instance, hooded in a scallop-shell, or acanthus sprays still adorning capitals. Islam however, developed an inhibition against sculpture in the round or in high relief – sculpture which "casts a shadow" – and Islamic sculpture is characteristically flat, in low relief or sometimes deeply incised, but the integrity of the surface-plane is consistently preserved. Stucco figures do exist, but sculpture consists again usually of arabesque or calligraphy, a dominant inspiration in architectural ornament: carved in relief in stone, the flat characters of the various scripts sometimes underwent surprisingly sensuous variations.

The *minbar* or pulpit of carved wood occupied an honoured place in the mosque, and received the finest wooden (and sometimes ivory) inlay, predominantly geometric in design. Domestic interiors and doors, balconies and screens were also decorated with the most delicate inlay or low relief or fret carving, but the intention seems always to have been essentially religious – to create an atmosphere of peace in which the individual could be mindful of God. That was achieved above all by the demonstration of an overall complex geometric unity, subsuming into one whole the variety among the subordinate elements.

SYRIA (above)
Bowl, 12th/13th century
Before its destruction by the Mongols in 1259, the city of Raqqa was famous for its pottery, close to Iranian designs but with a distinctive greenish glaze.

IRAN (below)
Tiles, late 14th century
The glazed and lustre tiles of Kashan, often featuring, as here, a raised arabesque, adorned the interiors both of private houses and of the finest, richest mosques.

EGYPT (above)
Inscribed marble slab, 9th/10th century
An almost fruit-like quality in these deeply rounded Kufic letters is created in the marble, on which they stand out in bold relief.

TURKEY (above)
Mosque lamp, c. 1557
In the mid-16th century the blue and white glazes of early Ottoman pottery were supplemented with a vivid tomato red – special to the ware made in Iznik.

EGYPT (right)
Pair of doors inlaid with ivory, 13th/14th century
Highly intricate geometry was the delight of Mamluk architects and designers. These precious doors came probably from a *minbar*.

Islamic Art 3: Representational Arts

Although it is often said that Islam forbids representational art, there is evidence in the *Traditions* that the Prophet deliberately did not order the destruction of paintings of the Christian Holy Family. It is, however, true that Islam has no religious tradition of representational art, though there are some manuscripts of later centuries which illustrate the Prophet's life, including certain of his encounters with the divine. Islamic figurative art is generally secular.

There was little early established tradition of painting in north-western Africa and the Arabian peninsula, and Islamic art in these regions remained mainly abstract or calligraphic. Elsewhere, especially in present-day Iraq, Iran, Syria and Turkey, vivid representational styles flourished over the centuries, developing traditions already vigorous in these regions before the Arab invasion. The first Caliphs and the Ummayad rulers (661-750) took over from their predecessors all the traditional trappings of royalty, which included representational art. Artists provided public expression of autocratic power – accounts of battles, the submission of enemies, great animal hunts. We hear, for example, of a tenth-century lord of Aleppo who, after his defeat of a Byzantine army, was installed in a pavilion quickly decorated by his artists with scenes of his triumphs. These princely themes are constantly repeated in the major form of Islamic representational art to have survived, illuminated manuscripts. But it was also the artist's task in early Islamic courts to decorate the private apartments of the nobility, with stucco reliefs and murals representing dancers, wrestlers, buffoons, or, in the baths, images of amorous couples or fighting warriors.

Thousands of illuminated manuscripts were produced under the patronage of Islamic princes and nobles, the majority being works of literature and history. Baghdad was the most important centre in the first flowering of Islamic miniature painting, in the thirteenth century. Though there are a few Byzantine and Sassanian features, the figures, moving with some confidence in three dimensions, are clearly related to a number of ivory carvings surviving from Fatimid Egypt (969-1171), with lively forms active amid scrollwork. The figures also bear a generic resemblance to the highly accomplished, if schematic, figures painted on ceramic dishes (not shown) under

EGYPT (right)
Panel, 11th/12th century
Vital, charming, Fatimid openwork ivory carving has a style quite distinct from that of Byzantine ivories of this date (see vol. 2 p. 61).

SULTAN MUHAMMAD? (above)
Nizami's *Khamseh: The ascension of Mohammed*, early 16th century
Brilliant, flaring colour is the hallmark of Shah Tahmasp's finest painter.

IRAN (above)
Firdausi's *Shahnameh: Bahram Gur slays a dragon*, c. 1340
The mountains and dragon reveal Chinese influence.

HERAT, IRAN (right)
Hafiz's *Divan: Dancing Sufi dervishes*, c. 1490
The fresh, delicate style established by the great Bihzad is quite entrancing.

MIR SAYYID ALI? (left)
Firdausi's *Shahnameh: Bahram Gur slays onagers*, background detail, c. 1525
Disdain for perspectival consistency never excludes the scrupulous observation of flower, stem and leaf.

the Seljuq Turks, ruling in Iran (1037-1194); but the miniatures have greater freedom.

In all Islamic manuscript painting the emphasis is on the outline, which echoes elements of the calligraphic repertoire – a range of straight, slightly bowed, undulant, angled and single- or double-curved strokes. The sculptural solidity of the figures is scarcely felt despite their contoured bulk; unlike even the most stylized figures in Byzantine art, they are described without reference to an underlying bodily structure. They are purely calligraphic entities, enclosing fields of flat colours. These principles remained firm for all Islamic illuminators, even though in Iranian work of the Ilkhanid dynasty (1256-1336) influence from Indian and from central Asian Buddhist painting can be clearly discerned, and later manuscripts also display Chinese elements.

The greatest and most consistent Islamic pictorial art was produced during the late fifteenth and early sixteenth centuries under the Timurid and Safavid dynasties in the cities of Iran, notably Herat, Shiraz, Isfahan, Tabriz and Qazvin. Later, much of high quality was painted in the capitals of the Ottoman Turks, Bursa and Istanbul, but the skill of the Iranian miniature painters has never been surpassed anywhere. The foundations of the tradition were laid probably at Tabriz and Shiraz, but the first great flowering came at Herat. After the death of Tamerlane his son Shah Rukh (ruled eastern Iran 1405-46) gathered round him in Herat a large atelier of painters. Their pictures set what became the standard pattern for later works, with numbers of small figures laid out across an open format, and a high horizon permitting a large area of ground. The colours are high-keyed, and robes and buildings highly decorated; mountains are rendered in ranks of curves, and the earth sprouts with stylized sprays of flowering plants.

The school of Herat produced one of the most famous geniuses of Islamic art in the painter Bihzad (active c. 1470/85-c. 1510/20; not shown). Bihzad's own work is unfortunately at best rare, but he had numerous pupils and followers who faithfully reflect his style. It was Bihzad's essential skill to give to individual figures and groups, within the glowing pattern of their setting, an extraordinary sense of movement and variety. He and his school illustrated notably the legends versified by Nizami in his *Khamseh* and the epic *Shah-nameh* (Book of Kings) of Firdausi, but also the mystic works of Sa'di and Jami and, less frequently, the poetry of the great Hafiz. The Timurid dynasty proved short-lived, but Herat remained an important centre under the Safavid dynasty (1502-1736), though Bihzad himself ended his life in the new capital, Tabriz, in western Iran.

It was in Tabriz in the first half of the sixteenth century that the greatest Safavid painters mostly worked, among them Mir Sayyid Ali, Aqa Mirak, Mirza Ali and Sultan Muhammad, the leading painter in the brilliant court of Shah Tahmasp (ruled 1524-76). The skill of these artists consisted not only in their draughtsmanship but also in their freshly conceived colour sequences, radiating over the surface. (Riza Abbasi in Isfahan was known mainly for his drawing, see p. 23.)

Many manuscripts of Ottoman Turkey were illustrated in a style probably derived from the Safavid schools. More direct was the influence on Indian painting: the techniques of the Tabriz school were transplanted to India by the third Mughal emperor, Akbar the Great, who brought Mir Sayyid Ali himself to India to work for him (see p. 20).

AQA MIRAK? (left)
Firdausi's *Shahnameh: King Khosroes I's war prizes are pledged for*, c. 1530
His emphasis on decorative still life (such as the carpets that superbly follow their own perspectival logic) distinguishes the work of Aqa Mirak. He, too, was a Tabriz painter at the court of Shah Tahmasp, to whom this codex was dedicated.

MIRZA ALI? (right)
Jami's *Haft Aurang: A father's discourse on love*, mid-16th century
Despite the use of vivid, glowing colours applied so precisely that the surface seems almost enamelled, there is nothing stilted or conventional about this vision of a Safavid court at leisure. Their refined pleasures – chess, music, poetry and conversation – are shown with lively and sophisticated immediacy.

TURKEY (left)
Murad III's *Surnama: Sweepers performing before the sultan*, c. 1582
Ottoman art tended to be naive, bold, and generally prosaic beside the poetic delicacy of the Iranians. The subject matter was more limited – scenes of everyday life, ceremonials and entertainments. Here one of the artisan guilds displays its special skill before Sultan Murad III.

South-East Asian Art 1 : Indonesia

Indonesia, the group of islands situated to the south-east of the Asian continent – including Sumatra, Java, Bali, Kalimantan (central, eastern and southern Borneo), Sulawesi (Celebes), Maluku (Moluccas) and Irian Jaya (Western New Guinea) – is inhabited by diverse ethnic groups sharing a complex cultural and artistic inheritance. Human settlement in the region is extremely ancient, but surviving evidence of the distant past is scant and inconclusive: Chinese influence (both of the proto-historic Shang and of the later Zhou – see p. 34) was early felt, and also the influence of the bronzeworking Dong-son civilization, which flourished in Vietnam in the early centuries BC. It is impossible to state with any precision when Indian culture began to exert a significant influence in Indonesia, but the three religions practised there today – Buddhism, Hinduism and Islam – all arrived there from the west.

Apart from Buddhist and Hindu temples (see over), most of the Indonesian art that survives is in perishable materials – carved wood, or textiles – and so must have been made comparatively recently. There are important exceptions, however – a widely dispersed group of megalithic monuments, some of which may be very ancient (though on Sumatra and on the much smaller nearby island of Nias the practice of erecting large worked stones continued into the nineteenth century); and various examples of bronzework after the Dong-son pattern, such as richly decorated sacred battle-axes and large kettle-drums. These drums were cast by a sophisticated *cire-perdue* process and bear shallow reliefs of heads, of figures engaged in ceremonial or of abstract ornament. Some of them may have been associated with rainmaking ceremonies. "*The Moon of Bali*" (not shown), preserved in the temple of Pejeng, is the most famous and sacred of these drums; other large examples are kept by families, while small ones were used for the purchase of brides.

Many of the peoples of Indonesia still live or lived until very recently in tribal societies. Their tribal art has been categorized in two main modes, designated the "monumental" and the "ornamental-fanciful". The megaliths of Nias and Sumatra, and many of the objects created throughout Indonesia in association with rites and sacrifices made to ancestors, exemplify the former; the "ornamental-fanciful" mode, essentially two-dimensional, is reflected in some degree in the bronzes, and finds characteristic expression in the decoration of the houses of the region, in textiles and in painted carvings. The two modes, which, it is assumed, sprang from different sources, are now often found within the same tribal culture, or intermingled in one artefact.

One salient feature common to all Indonesian tribal art (and further afield – it shares some characteristics with tribal art on the mainland, or with Oceanic art, see vol. 2 p. 22) is reverence for ancestors, expressed in many forms. The people of Nias erected their megaliths in honour of dead chieftains, while the Toraja of Sulawesi populate terraces in the cliffs with permanent galleries of standing wooden effigies of the dead, looking out over the rice fields. Numerous wooden carved standing or squatting figures, presumably embodying ancestor spirits, come from Maluku and the north-western tip of Irian. Protective ancestor figures are included in the carved decoration of houses, or in textiles – for instance the ceremonial *ikats* woven by the Dayak of Kalimantan, which sometimes incorporate a lozenge design derived from a

SUMATRA (below)
Ancestor figure?
Colossal and mysterious, the megalith is one of a circle of such stones on the island of Samosir, in the middle of Lake Toba, which perhaps represent ancestors. The conception of the figure seems rather more advanced than that of the famous Easter Island megaliths (see vol. 2 p. 23), surely similar in purpose.

NORTH VIETNAM (right)
The god of wine,
1st century BC
The bronze candelabrum, found in a tomb at Lach Truong, and a product of the seafaring Dong-son people, based in the Gulf of Tonkin, has affinities with works of Zhou China in its incised patterning. The ridges at the mouth are tongues: the god was known as "loosener of tongues".

KALIMANTAN (right)
Ikat textile
Among the Dayaks designs based on the squatting ancestor figure were used to decorate blankets (*pua*) worn at feasts. It was given only to the womenfolk of the chiefs to weave such patterns, since they were conceived to have powers to protect and benefit.

SULAWESI (above)
Ancestor figures
Mortuary festivities are an important aspect of life among the Toraja. Before a host of guests, the dead man or woman, clothed and bejewelled, is placed within a rock-cut chamber; outside, a realistic effigy is put up to signify the continuing existence of the spirit.

frontal view of the squatting ancestor figure. All power is thought to flow from the ghostly realm, and ancestor figures act as intermediaries for the flow of that power.

In some areas, the wooden ancestor figure has instead of a carved head the skull of the dead person attached, and the cult of the skull – essentially an extension of the reverence for ancestors – is widespread. Everywhere heads are collected and treasured, sometimes (among the Batak of Sumatra) in the roofs of family houses, sometimes (among the Dayak of Kalimantan) in village shrines, and some of the most imposing monuments of Sumatra are huge stone troughs made to hold skulls. Headhunting expeditions, launched in order to collect skulls so as to reinforce the "spiritual property" of the group, have or had a central importance in the ceremonial of certain tribes.

The elaborate decoration of wooden houses in Indonesia is famous. The large dwelling-houses of the Batak are often ornamented with engraved and painted abstract designs, and with carvings representing symbolic human breasts, lizards, monster heads and roughly-hewn squatting figures. The houses of the Toraja of Sulawesi, splendid constructions

raised on piles, with enormous flying roofs, are also embellished with carvings and paintings: the façades are decorated with geometric and figural designs, and the post supporting the projecting roof often bears the carved head of a buffalo, chief among their sacrificial animals.

Tribal societies, preserved more or less unchanging in some islands even to the present day, had given way elsewhere often very early to a system of kingship. The arts associated with these kingdoms, recorded from the early medieval period, are both religious (most stupendous is that of Java, see over) and secular. Some of the secular, originally courtly, arts that continue to be practised are the painting, carving and manipulation of puppets called *wayang*, extremely stylized, highly graceful figures (not shown), and the intricate working of small ceremonial swords called *kris*, revered as cult objects chiefly in Java and in Bali. The *batik* textiles of Java are also famous: *batik* is a technique of dying cotton (or, more recently, silk) in elaborate designs by coating the reserved areas, in each dip, with wax, and was developed in the palaces of the petty rulers of Java after the fragmentation of the medieval kingdoms that built its great temples.

IRIAN JAYA (above)
Ancestor figure
Ancestor carvings are seen as the dwelling-places of the spirits of the dead. A skull may replace the usual carved head; and this figure holds scroll-like objects that may refer to the snake – symbol of the power and regenerative force of nature.

SULAWESI (right)
The façade of a house
The abstract patterning of a curvilinear motif based on the horns of a buffalo and a concentric circle is typical of Toraja houses; the richer the decoration on a façade, the higher the occupants' status in the strict clan structure of the village.

BALI (below)
Kris and scabbard
The solemn forging of a *kris* gives the dagger a "soul" and so links the

prospective owner with his ancestors. The blade has characteristically an exaggerated shoulder; the hilt is inset with jewels;

in the earliest examples the hilt was wrought in the shape of a human figure, now elaborately stylized but still discernible.

KALIMANTAN (above)
A hornbill
The Dayaks made images of the hornbill as part of the three-day festivities

in honour of the war-god, Singalang Burong, held on the return of the tribe from a headhunting sortie. The carving is a rather

fanciful representation of the bird, brightly coloured and elaborately modelled, with a characteristic delight in spiral and curl.

JAVA (above)
Batik textile
The cotton is dyed in one of many traditional patterns; in this, made up of inter-

secting circular tendrils, the elliptical spaces are inhabited by tiny creatures of fancy, exhibiting clear affinities with Chinese art.

Indeed it is quite likely that the *batik* technique originated in China, though only in Java did it attain this peak of refinement.

South-East Asian Art 2: Java and Burma

Borobudur in central Java is one of the most extraordinary stone monuments ever made. It is a vast structure, but does not seem to have been a tomb, a palace or even a temple, but instead a profound and intricate expression through architecture and sculpture of Buddhist doctrine – it forms in plan, for instance, a *mandala*. Its construction must have required an army of craftsmen and an architect of genius, but there is no record of who built it or why, although its date is generally assumed to be late eighth or early ninth century AD, and its sponsor a member of the central Javanese Shailendra dynasty (778-864).

Not the least remarkable thing about Borobudur is that it is the culmination of an artistic tradition that seems to have been very short-lived. Western Java had first been settled by Indian traders perhaps in the first century AD, and Buddhist monasteries were certainly established there by the fourth century, but there is no evidence of any significant undertaking in stone – architecture or sculpture – for a further three centuries. The earliest extant Javanese stone sculpture, which is Hindu, dates from the early eighth century, hardly 100 years before Borobudur.

In elevation, Borobudur is a kind of flat, solid pyramid, composed of eight terraces of diminishing size. Around the perimeter of the five lower terraces, which are square in plan, runs a broad, roofless corridor, lined with relief sculpture, and with *Buddhas* sculpted in the round in niches surmounting the walls, facing out over the surrounding country. The three topmost terraces are circular in plan, unwalled, and carry 72 lattice-work *stupas*, bell-shaped, each sheltering a colossal *Buddha*; and the climax of the monument is a single, solid *stupa*, representing Nirvana. Borobudur symbolizes the ascent of a believer, following the precepts of Buddhism, from the baseness of ordinary human existence to the ultimate condition of psychological and philosophical enlightenment – the *stupa* at the apex. The sensation, when emerging from the enclosed walls of the square terraces on to the open levels of the circular terraces, is extraordinary, an intimation of the Buddhist experience of understanding the nature of the cosmos.

The style of the figure sculpture at Borobudur, unique to Java, though clearly derived from India, is characterized by massive, full

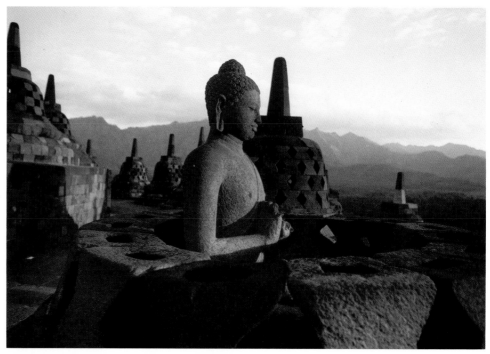

BOROBUDUR (below)
Pippalayana and Bhadra, 8th/9th century
The second terrace of the complex is decorated with reliefs depicting the life of the Buddha and his prior incarnations, the *Jatakas*, which represent, in metaphorical terms, the many virtues of the Buddha. Here his chastity is typified by the legend of Pippalayana and Bhadra, who married but still remained celibate.

BOROBUDUR (right)
One of the 72 *Buddhas*, 8th/9th century
The 72 *Buddhas* in their *stupas* round the topmost terraces denote the phases of enlightenment undergone by a devotee in pursuit of Nirvana. Their huge figures convey great tranquillity – faces smiling peacefully, bodies scarcely inflected, the volumes contained and at rest. No more radiant symbols of Buddhism exist.

PRAMBANAM (below)
Rama and Sita with Lakshmana, early 10th century
The *Ramayana* frieze runs along the terraces beside the shrines of Shiva and of Brahma, and it relates the myth of Rama, a great king and perfect man. He wins the hand of Sita by bending the great bow of Shiva at a tournament held to chose her bridegroom, but is banished from court; he retreats to the forest with Sita and his favourite half-brother Lakshmana. Sita is carried off by the demon-king Ravana, while Rama is pursuing a gold deer sent to mislead him, but Rama rescues her: he has obtained assistance from the King of the Monkeys. So, too, the forms are unrealistic, but highly ornate.

BOROBUDUR (right)
The story of King Sibi, detail: *Visitors arrive in their ship*, 8th/9th century
The ship, with tripod mast and heavy outrigger, seems an accurate representation of the vessels that sailed the Indonesian seas more than 1,000 years ago. The semi-legendary King Sibi was renowned for generosity, and his flourishing, cultured realm was a resort of many visitors from other lands.

CHANDI MENDUT (above)
The Bodhisattva Vajrapani, 8th century
The smooth, round quality of the icon is reminiscent of the Buddhist carvings in the Ajanta caves (see p. 14). The Bodhisattva Vajrapani sits in a posture of royal ease, as befits the supreme lord of divine and powerful beings who are converted to the Buddhist doctrine, and the special companion of the Buddha Shakyamuni.

and rounded forms, with slow rhythms in their movements and compositions. But although the figures are generalized and ideal, the narrative scenes are rich with precise naturalistic detail from contemporary life, illustrating ships, buildings, weapons, furniture, costume. A similar style prevails in the other monuments built by the Shailendra dynasty, among which the shrine of Chandi Mendut is perhaps outstanding. It is much smaller, consisting of a single cell, encrusted on the exterior with decorative and narrative relief panels positioned with a superb sense of design; the interior contains three gigantic stone icons, the Buddha and two Bodhisattvas. Their smooth surface contours are interrupted only by jewellery worn by the Bodhisattvas.

The last of the great central Javanese shrines, Lara Jonggrang at Prambanam, built in the early tenth century, was clearly undertaken as a Hindu rival to Buddhist Borobudur. Originally the enormous complex contained 232 temples, fully provided with icons and covered with relief sculpture. The terraces still display a remarkable series of relief panels summarizing the Hindu classics; Lara Jonggrang also happens to possess some of the

earliest known representations of Indian dance postures (not shown).

In eastern Java, between 927 and the beginning of the sixteenth century, when Islam came, there was a succession of dynasties, which built in stone or brick or cut in the rock a large number of smaller Hindu and Buddhist shrines containing extremely accomplished stone sculpture, both narrative reliefs and large icons. A colossal *Vishnu riding on Garuda* was commissioned in the eleventh century by one King Airlanga, whose portrait it may also be; there is also an enchanting feminine *Supreme Buddhist Wisdom* from Singasari (not shown), carved perhaps to personify a thirteenth-century queen. In style, eastern Javanese art depended on the central tradition, but tended towards more fantastic imagery and a more linear description of form.

Most of the monumental sculpture surviving in Burma is Buddhist. Probably from about the seventh century AD the country was divided between two peoples, the southern Mon and the northern Pyu, both practising Buddhism. After the fall of the Pyu capital in 832 the northern regions were infiltrated by Burmans, who brought with them the cult of

Nats, a mixed collection of beings, including nature spirits, ancestors and ghosts. In time this cult and the Buddhism of their predecessors were merged into a hybrid religion, still a force in Burma today. A tradition of painting and sculpture was established in the time of the Mon and Pyu, and King Anawratha, who in the eleventh century established the capital of the united Burmese territory at Pagan, employed Mon artists in large numbers. Palaces and shrines occupying several scores of acres sprang up, richly ornamented with painting and painted terracotta sculpture, which is still there in Pagan in some quantity today, since in 1286 the city was sacked by the Mongols and virtually abandoned.

Apart from the ruins at Pagan and elsewhere, the heritage of Burmese art consists of a few small medieval bronzes, of high quality, and quantities of carvings and gilt stuccowork of uncertain age: there has been little variation in style. The figures are simplified and generalized, enacting legends mostly of Buddhist derivation in elegant postures reminiscent of the dance; the supreme qualities of Burmese art are its airy spirituality and inspired decorative finesse.

BELAHAN, EASTERN JAVA (left) *Vishnu seated on Garuda*, c. 1042
The sculpture may represent King Airlanga himself in the guise of his patron Vishnu. The sublime peace of the expression of the god contrasts vividly with the wild ferocity of his terrible vehicle, Garuda, who is a kind of bird, and symbolizes cosmic energy.

PAGAN, BURMA (right)
Frescos decorating an arch in the temple of Muy-tha-kut, 11th or 12th century
Inside Burmese temples the painted decoration includes usually fiery jets like those sculpted outside (far right). The two figures are prior Buddhas, part of a scheme depicting scenes from the Buddha's previous lives, which serve as a reminder of the Buddha's teaching.

PAGAN (above)
Terracotta ornament, 12th century
The ornament on Burmese temples is calculated to lend apparent lightness to heavily vaulted structures. The decoration on the arch depicting jets of flame and curling smoke symbolizes (not, however, too literally) the energy generated by contemplating the Buddha.

UPPER BURMA (above)
The Buddha in the bhumi-sparsamudra, 17th century
The Buddha's gesture is to touch the ground, in order to call the earth-goddess to witness his complete fitness to enter Nirvana.

BURMA (left)
Sutra chest, 18th century
In *sutra* chests the sacred texts that every monastery needed were kept; they were sumptuously ornamented, sheathed in gilt gesso, and inset with mirror glass.

South-East Asian Art 3: Cambodia and Thailand

From about the late first century AD, Indian trade settlements began to appear around the coasts of South-East Asia, and became sources for the dissemination of Indian religious practices and ideas. Both Buddhism and Hinduism had taken root in the coastal regions of South-East Asia and in some of the islands, notably Java (see preceding page), by about the fourth century AD.

One of the most important early Indian settlements was at Palembang, near the Strait of Malacca, which acted as a centre for the diffusion of a style based on that of Amaravati (see p. 13): a large bronze icon of the Buddha from Sulawesi is the most splendid (and rare) example of the earliest Buddhist style to permeate the region. But it was in Cambodia that the first distinctly South-East Asian style of high quality emerged, influenced by Indian importation but clearly also dependent on an existing native style of some sophistication, probably worked in perishable materials. This sculpture, both Buddhist and Hindu, evolved in the two monarchies of Fu-nan (second to sixth century) and its successor Chen-la (sixth to seventh century). Stone icons of Hindu and Buddhist deities survive from the latter part of

the sixth century onwards, all single figures sculpted with a strong feeling for volume, even if rigidly defined in frontal view – the mould from which was formed the classic Cambodian style of Angkor Wat in the twelfth century. Associated with the Fu-nan icons are stone lintels from the temples (not shown), which were carved with an opulent ornament – rich foliage, jewellery – which reappears on the early buildings of Angkor.

Towards the end of the eighth century, Chen-la disintegrated, to be re-formed under a new dynasty founded by Jayavarman II (died 850), a son of the old royal family, who had been in exile for some years at the court of the Shailendra in Java. His successor Indravarman (ruled 877-89) had his capital at Roluos in the south-east, but he built the first great reservoir at Angkor, which was to be the largest city in the world before modern times.

Perhaps the most beautiful of all the works of the early Angkor period is at Banteay Srei, a private foundation of the tenth century just outside the capital. The lintels decorating the doorways of the three shrines and subsidiary buildings are effervescent with the most opulent decorative carvings, exuberant foliage and

jewel-strings (symbolizing wealth); exterior panels are carved with standing figures and the pediments with Hindu legends, again amidst profuse ornament. In Angkor itself ever vaster schemes of architectural sculpture were undertaken, reflecting the expanding ambitions of the successive rulers of the growing Khmer Empire. Within the greatest of the mountain temple complexes in the city, Angkor Wat, built in the early twelfth century, more than a mile of stone reliefs recount a panorama of legends from Hindu mythology, in which the heroes are identified with the aggressive and ambitious king who built the Wat, Suryavarman II (ruled 1113-45). The relief, however, is hardly three centimetres (1in) deep; nevertheless the artists were able to mount complex compositions suggesting vigorous movements in deep space.

In 1177 Angkor was sacked by the neighbouring Cham people, marking the end of the era of the great Hindu emperors of Cambodia. About 1200 Jayavarman VII, a grandson of Suryavarman and a Buddhist, began to rebuild the city as Angkor Thom; he erected his own mountain temple complex, the Bayon temple, striving to outdo the Wat in the scale and

SULAWESI (right)
The Buddha, detail, 3rd/5th century
Probably the oldest image of the Buddha in South-East Asia, the icon was perhaps imported from India or Sri Lanka. Undulating loops of drapery – gathered in the bend of the left arm as in the first Amaravati images (see p. 12) – are drawn in grooves across a sleek body.

CAMBODIA (below)
Vishnu, late 7th century
The style of the icon is that of Prasat Andet, one of the major temples of the Khmer kingdom of Chen-la. It combines severity with a certain sensuous charm; its blocky, cubic form is finished smoothly, and the drapery is mainly incised.

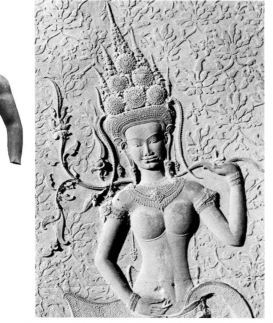

BANTEAY SREI (above)
Pediment, 10th century
The demons Sumbha and Nisumbha fight over the most beautiful of the Apsaras, Tilottama, framed by the elaborate jewel and foliage motifs typical of early Khmer architecture.

ANGKOR WAT (left)
Apsara, detail, 12th century
The heavenly dancing girls of the Wat are dressed in the height of fashion, with elaborate hairstyles and rich jewellery. They stand against rich floral backgrounds, representing the brocade hangings of Heaven.

ANGKOR THOM (right)
Devata, early 13th century
This charming maiden is a divine guardian of a door to the Bayon temple; she is carved with the same precise attention to details of dress as the dancers on the Wat, if less happily proportioned.

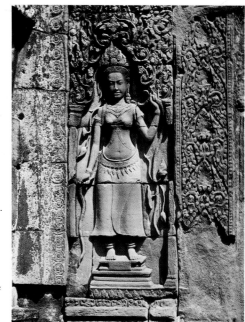

The horse rears in violent
forward movement; men
with rubbery limbs crowd
every available space, in
an exciting scene from the
Hindu epic *Mahabharata*.

quantity of its reliefs. These are rather clumsily executed, however, and their compositions are stiff and hierarchical, although the beautiful *Devatas* who guard its portals are worthy rivals to the divine maidens carved on the Wat. On Jayavarman VII's death, Angkor declined in the face of attacks by the people of central present-day Thailand, and the ideals of absolute kingship which had inspired so much of the art of Cambodia were extinguished.

Neighbouring present-day Thailand had been ruled in the eleventh and thirteenth centuries by the Khmer; before that it had been the domain of the kingdom of Dvaravati, a confederation of the indigenous Mon peoples inhabiting also southern Burma. From the sixth to the eleventh century Buddhist art had flourished there, influenced by regional Indian styles, though the faces usually show features characteristic of the local Mon population, with distinctly marked, out-turned lips and downward-curving eyelids outlined in double channels. After the eleventh century, the northern regions of Dvaravati were infiltrated by the Thai, and when the Khmer disappeared from the scene the Thai moved further south. Shortly afterwards the Burmans moved in

among the Mon peoples in present-day Burma (see preceding page), and the Mon ceased to be an entity.

Like the Burmans, the Thai were animist, reverencing Nature spirits, and remained so even after their conversion to Buddhism. The Buddha was felt, animistically, to embody the supernatural potency of the whole region and nation. There were several rival traditional types of icon: the dominant type was the "Sukhothai", a gracefully rounded, sinuous figure named after the city in central Thailand, but two others deserve mention – the rather squarely modelled "U Thong" type (not shown), popular notably at Ayutthaya in the south, and the more massive, almost crude "*Lion*" or "Chieng Sen" type (not shown) in favour in the northern regions. Colossal brick-and-plaster *Buddhas* were erected inside many shrines: these, now ruined or heavily restored, were modelled according to one of the Thai prototypes, and so were wall-paintings of the Buddha, also lost or repainted; the oldest surviving paintings are on cloth. Buddhism, however, is still a force in Thailand today, and Buddhist art is still being produced which, in conception, owes much to historic styles.

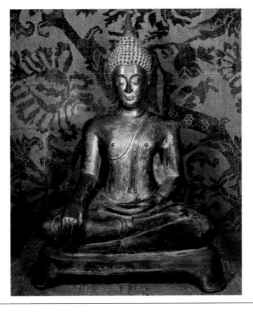

Chinese Art 1: Relics of the Tombs

We should know little of China's Bronze-Age art were it not for the elaborate burial practices of its ruling class. During the early dynasties of the Shang (*c.* 1600-*c.* 1072 BC) and the Zhou (*c.* 1027-475 BC), the important families maintained large subterranean tomb complexes, from which the ancestral dead were conceived to watch over the fortunes of the living. Apart from its already remarkable pottery, some of the first notable Chinese works of art are bronze vessels for use in ceremonies undertaken to appease these spirits: cast by a complex piece-mould process, they bear complicated zoomorphic designs, originally magical and protective glyphs, developed into endless linear proliferations with backgrounds of square scrolling. Many have dedicatory inscriptions inside the bowl, which are among the earliest surviving examples of the archaic Chinese script. The ceremonies grew more extensive and elaborate in the Zhou period: the vessels bear long inscriptions describing the circumstances in which they were cast, but the decoration is often less complex.

Besides the pottery and the bronze vessels, some of the most attractive early works to survive are numerous small bronze or jade

ANYANG (above)
Bronze vessel, *c.* 1200 BC
The vessel represents two owls standing back to back, and displays the Chinese genius for rounded form played against a complex two-dimensional pattern.

NORTHERN CHINA (below)
Incense burner, *c.* 200 BC
The censer reflects the widening spread of Taoist beliefs among the wealthy

classes: it represents a craggy mountain rising from the sea, the dwelling-place of the immortals and fabulous beasts of Taoist mythology.

NORTHERN CHINA
(above) Pictogram, and inscription, from bronze vessels; (below) animal-shaped plaques, *c.* 1200 BC
The first Chinese writing survives on ritual vessels and the so-called "oracle bones" used in ceremonies to decide when and how a sacrifice should take place. The text informs us: "This vessel is dedicated to my father"; it shows symbols combined to express ideas more complex than those of the first "picture-letters".

plaques, which decorated either horse tackle or the pole-tips and hub-caps of chariots. Animals are frequently represented. They are stylized, however, in stereotypes that are recognizably akin to some of the pictograms of the archaic Chinese script on the ceremonial bronze vessels. At the very beginning of Chinese culture an affinity between writing and art was firmly established, never to disappear.

China's history is chequered with periods of destructive political upset. The power of the Zhou dynasty was disintegrating in the eighth century BC, and the succeeding periods – the so-called Spring and Autumn period and the Warring States period – remained unsettled until the establishment of the harshly centralized Qin dynasty in 221 BC. This interim, however, was paradoxically an era of astonishing cultural and technological advance, and during it lived China's two greatest moral philosophers, Confucius and Laozi – the one elaborating a humanistic outlook in a series of famous adages, the latter developing a philosophy ordering man's mystical union with Nature. Artistic production increased in quality and sophistication: luxurious objects of jade, bronze and fine lacquer were wrought in

MANCHENG (above)
Burial suit, *c.* 113 BC
Taoist mythology includes a belief that jade has the power to conserve the body after death. In Han times, even in modest tombs, the

corpse was furnished with costly jade pieces; Prince Liu took the belief to its logical conclusion and had prepared for himself and his wife whole suits, each made of more than 2,000

jade tablets sewn together with gold thread. Each suit, it is reckoned, would have taken ten years to make; the extravagance of early Chinese burial furniture can seem almost oppressive.

34

thousands to satisfy the demands of China's growing class of wealthy landowners. Compared to the glyphic look of Shang decoration, their ornament is playful and refined.

China is a land full of ancient sites awaiting investigation. Since coming to power the government of the People's Republic has conducted a series of model excavations of ancient tombs, dramatically increasing our fragmentary knowledge of its huge past. Some of the most remarkable finds come from the imperial tombs of the Western Han dynasty (206 BC-AD 8), revealing a vigorous and varied artistic tradition. Ornament has an undulating, cursive character, found for instance on inlaid bronze incense-burners – their "cloud" motifs are typical of Han decoration. By then the aristocratic burial customs of the previous era had spread to all levels of society; the funereal pottery found in more modest tombs of Han date is covered with a lead-green glaze, in an obvious attempt to ape the aristocratic bronze, in shapes which also imitate metalwork.

Great care was taken in Han burials to preserve the corpse, not physically by mummification but magically by means of jade emblems placed at all of the body's nine

orifices (including the eyes); the tomb of Liu Sheng, of the imperial family, has revealed entire suits of jade plaques encasing the corpses of the prince and his wife. The dead were customarily surrounded also by representations of the world they knew – figures of attendants, soldiers, musicians, animals – especially favourite horses – models of stoves, granaries, pig-pens, houses. Formerly their servants and animals were slaughtered to accompany lords into the next world, but this practice was abandoned in the fifth century BC under pressure from the Confucians; the substitutes were usually on a small scale, made of wood or clay, although some especially fine bronze figurines are known – among them a "*Flying Horse*" made under the Eastern Han dynasty (AD 8-220). Near Mount Li in western China, the extravagant burial mound of China's self-acclaimed first Emperor, Shihuangdi – the first and only effective ruler of the Qin dynasty (221-206 BC) – more than two thousand life-size terracotta warriors and horses have been excavated, probably a grandiose emblem of the army with which this tyrant enforced his rule. Even early in the Tang dynasty (AD 618-907) royal tombs were

lined with reliefs or paintings of everyday life, and filled with figurines.

The parallel with ancient Egypt is obvious. Art was used as a means of realizing in the spirit world the objects, people and animals the dead would need to use. The material possessions of the dead went with them to the grave, and elaborate precautions were taken against grave robbers. Major tombs of the Qin and Han dynasties were enclosed by huge artificial hills and approached by avenues called "spirit roads", lined with colossal stone guardian figures. Few survived the troubles at the end of the Han period, but near Xianyang, in western China, is a mound believed to be the grave of General He Qubing, who died in 117 BC after a lifetime of harrying the Hunnish tribes to the north of the country. The colossal figures – several horses and a buffalo – which stood before his tomb are the earliest examples of Chinese monumental sculpture to survive, and mark the beginning of a tradition which continued into Ming times. It was probably in the carving of these large-scale sculptures that the skills necessary to the sculpting of the colossal Buddhist icons of post-Han China were developed (see over).

WUWEI, WESTERN CHINA (left) "*Flying Horse*", 2nd century AD
The horse is depicted with one hoof resting on a bird in flight; in the rhythm of its briskly clip-clopping limbs, its bouncing ears and tail, there is a fine sense of its movement. More than 200 similar bronzes were discovered in the same tomb, though this one is unique.

MT LI (right)
A warrior, c.246-210 BC
The figure is a general in full battle regalia, and he holds the highest rank of all the terracotta figures so far excavated from the army of thousands buried near Mt Li. The general is clearly individualized, like the other soldiers; they may even be portraits of the rank and file of the army that Shihuangdi led.

LONGQUAN (above)
One of the Emperor Tai-zong's chargers, c. AD 649
Reliefs representing the Emperor's six chargers in sandstone once lined the anteroom of his splendid mausoleum. The horse is fully caparisoned, moving at a brisk, high-stepping trot; though rather broadly modelled, it is conceived in a naturalistic spirit typical of Tang sculpture.

XIANYANG (above)
Recumbent horse, c. 117 BC
The animal appears to be struggling from the stone out of which it is carved. Disturbingly monumental, it is one of several from the burial mound probably of General He Qubing, and a fitting memorial, as he owed his victory over nomadic tribesmen raiding from the north in 119 BC to horses he stole from them.

Chinese Art 2: Buddhist Art

Buddhism was the chief inspiration of figurative art in China between the collapse of the Eastern Han dynasty in AD 220 and the rise of the Tang at the beginning of the seventh century – and even well after; during the Tang and Song dynasties, however, though the religion never died out in China as it did in India, Buddhism declined, while Confucianism revived and secular art became increasingly important. Entering the fringes of the country from India as early as the first century AD, Buddhism was brought to China chiefly by missionaries from Gandhara (see p.14), and when Buddhism was adopted more widely in the fifth century, after the accession of the Wei dynasty (386-535), the influence of Gandharan art held wide sway.

The iconography of the great works of Chinese Buddhist sculpture and painting is based mainly on two principal Buddhist sacred books, the *Lotus Sutra* and the *Amitayus Sutra*, cosmic texts permeated with an atmosphere of stupendous miracle. Chinese artists were inspired by them to undertake compositions often on a colossal scale in a "transcendent" style; the orthodox Buddhist triad, of the Buddha and two Bodhisattvas, was re-peated again and again (sometimes with other attendants and assisting deities), while the Bodhisattva Maitreya, the Buddha of the future age, was a favourite image of royal, monastic and communal patrons.

The Wei dynasty was only one of six ruling China – some of them concurrently – between the demise of the Han and the reunification of China under the short-lived Sui dynasty (581-618). These dynasts and their nobles were responsible for a series of immense rock-cut monasteries, complete with vast decorative schemes of high-relief sculpture (and painting, though little remains). The chief sites are in the north – Yungang (460-535), Longmen (495 to about 700), Tienlongshan (mainly seventh to eighth century) and the Dunhuang oasis (mainly sixth to ninth century) – and these furnish the most extensive evidence left to us of early Chinese Buddhist art; numerous Buddhist monasteries certainly also flourished in the more southerly cities, but their remains are few. Bronzes also survive, on a smaller scale, matching the enormous major works in imagery and style; large-scale bronze icons in the round also existed, and were probably amongst the outstanding works of Buddhist sculpture, but they were melted down during the later persecutions of the religion.

The stylistic evolution of Chinese Buddhist sculpture begins with the colossal static icons at Yungang, where the smoothly rounded figures are recognizably close to Gandharan work. By the beginning of the sixth century a more linear style predominated, notably among the sculptures of Longmen, where some of the icons are extremely severe figures, with harsh faces. Towards the end of the sixth century, partly due to fresh influence from Gupta India, the sculptures became again more full-bodied, and this trend culminated in the superb *Bodhisattvas*, with well-fleshed torsos in the Indian fashion, of the Tang dynasty (618-907). Many of the great rock-cut icons at the cave sites bear inscriptions testifying to the piety of the individual – maybe a prince – or of the group who commissioned the work. Not only icons were made: numerous reliefs were carved in honour of such a great event as, for instance, the visit of an empress. Numerous devotional stelae were also erected, illustrating in low relief and often in a more dynamic, curvilinear style narrative episodes from the *Sutras*, or sometimes the Pure Land

NORTHERN CHINA (left)
Maitreya, 522
The Buddha of the future is surrounded on his altarpiece by eight tiny Bodhisattvas, while below two donors proffer bowls. The central figure's elaborate draperies with fluted edges, his sharply defined facial features and his bewitching smile – all are features of the many bronzes produced under the northern Wei.

YUNGANG (above)
The Buddha, c.460-70
The tranquil, sensuous aura of Gandharan sculpture has been expanded, inflated, to a colossal scale. The body of the Buddha beneath his robes has become a broad smooth volume, over which sweep undulant draperies, indicated by linear folds.

LONGMEN (right)
An empress visits Longmen, c. 522
Despite the flat carving, the relief conveys a fine sense of forward movement, largely due to the taut arcs of the linear draperies, typical of the sculpture in this cave. Such reliefs may reflect the style of lost wall-painting at the court of the northern Wei rulers.

NORTHERN CHINA (above)
Bodhisattva, 8th century
During the Tang dynasty China re-established trade contacts with India, with immediate consequences in Chinese sculpture: figures sway with easy indolence, displaying plumply elegant forms beneath transparent draperies. The full forms of Indian art are fused with Chinese linearity.

XIANGTANGSHAN (left)
Bodhisattva, c.550-77
The column-like figure is gently, smoothly rounded, in contrast to the sharply delineated jewellery, Indian in inspiration. Yet the air of calm and majestic beauty is closer to the great icon of Yungang than to the Tang figure (above), in which the Gupta influence is stronger. Indian influence is present here, but not yet decisive.

Paradise of Amitabha to which the faithful are transported after death, which is figured in some seventh-century wall-paintings at Dunhuang (not shown).

The aristocratic burial customs of the Han dynasty had subsequently spread to all sections of society, and by the time of the Tang it was usual for every family to furnish their dead in their graves with "spirit figures", ceramic people and animals. Ceramic sculpture had been put to Buddhist use as early as the eighth century, but the earliest surviving examples are tenth-century – figures of Luohans (the original disciples of the Buddha) in which an aspect of Chinese art more familiar to the West emerges – a sharply drawn idiosyncracy of feature and character. The *Luohans* make a strong contrast with the idealization of earlier Buddhist icons, though they, too, are distantly related to Gandharan models – to attendant figures in Gandharan icons of the Buddha. They rapidly became widely reproduced, in sets of 16, in all media; each was individually characterized, some as handsome young monks, others as sages of fantastic character, craggy, bizarre and gnarled figures whose gaunt, bony faces testify to their spiritual

YICHOU (below)
Luohan, late 10th century
It was taught that no one could equal the Buddha; so

his disciples, who reached Nirvana almost as he did, were called merely "worthy ones" that is, *luohans*.

efforts. This new idea of individual personality infected even the *Bodhisattvas* made in wood, clay and stone by the sculptors of the Song (Sung) dynasty (960-1279): these are still ideally plump, and wear rich garments and highly wrought ornaments, but they appear much more as individual human beings than as purely symbolic figures.

Buddhism had never displaced the older modes of thought and custom enshrined in Confucianism and Taoism, and its hold was periodically weakened by politically motivated attacks. The main target of imperial policy, the great monasteries, continued, however, to flourish during the Yuan (1271-1368) and Ming (1364-1644) dynasties, and their halls were filled with painted scrolls, murals and large-scale sculpture – dynamically animated works, vividly coloured, and with a strong illusory presence (the sculptures often had inset glass eyes). Once Buddhism had been extirpated from India, there was no further vitalizing influx from the west; China, however, passed to the east, to Korea and Japan, both traditional Buddhism and that most individual form, founded by the late 5th-century Indian immigrant Bodhidharma, Chan (Zen).

WESTERN CHINA (below)
Devotional stela, 554
The Buddha is central, flanked by his disciples, Bodhisattvas and guardians.

Above, twin Buddhas reveal the *Lotus Sutra* miracle, while the lower tier is given over to the inscription and an incense-burner.

CHINA (below)
Camel with grooms,
Tang dynasty
Such "spirit figures" were provided for the needs of

the dead in the beyond; the lively camel, glazed in a characteristic yellow and green, would act as a beast of burden for the deceased.

NORTHERN CHINA (above)
Guanyin, Song dynasty
The fulsome, elegant figure poses with graceful languor in the *maharaja-lila*, the position of royal ease – a consummate image of disinterested compassion, as benefits Guanyin, who was the special comforter and the protector of mankind.

NORTHERN CHINA (left)
Hanging scroll, detail,
14th century
The colourful figures – a Buddhist manifestation of a Tantric deity, and three Bodhisattvas attending, in a fantastic surround – are typical of Ming Buddhist painting; the skilfully elaborated strands of drapery fly out around, creating a strong, dramatic presence.

Song (Sung) Porcelain

HEBEI (above)
Spitoon, c. 850
The beautifully inflected swelling curves of the pot are typical of the creamy-white porcelain produced in the northern province of Hebei during the Tang era.

HAIDIAN, PEKING (below)
Vase and cover, late 14th century
The copper-red underglaze patterns are more typical of Ming pots, although this is of the Yuan dynasty, a transitional era in ceramics.

JINGDEZHEN (above)
Stem cup, c. 1426-35;
Plate, c. 1723-35
The cup is rather heavily potted and displays the deep blue decoration and glaze of the classic era of

Ming blue-and-white ware. The Qing plate bears an exquisite design of plants flowering amidst rocks, in a translucent silvery glaze – a perfection later marred by over-fussy decoration.

CHINA (below)
Items of Song porcelain:
A Northern celadon bowl, 11th century;
B Jun bowl, probably 12th century;
C Ding bowl, 12th century;
D Cizhou vase, 12th century
Jun ware was valued for its luminous bluish glaze, more opalescent, and softer and subtler, than the heavy olive-green of the celadon bowl, incised with flowers and scrolls. The wares of the Ding factories, in the northern province of Hebei, are some of the most famous of the Song era; the bowl

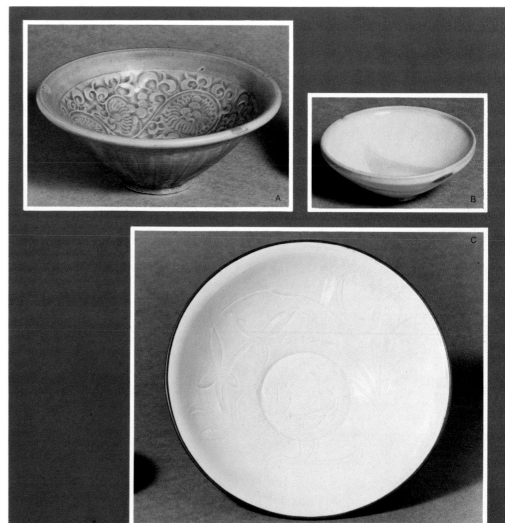

In Western cultures ceramics have seldom attracted major artists, though the Rococo epoch is a significant exception. In China, where porcelain was invented, and where pottery of a quality the West has long envied was produced for hundreds of years, ceramic as a medium had a far-reaching importance, not only because much Chinese sculpture, even on a large scale, is ceramic, but also because the patron classes, from the Emperor downwards, devoted to porcelain as much interest and appreciation as to metalwork or any other art – in some instances, more.

In fact pottery has been produced at very many sites in China since neolithic times (since about 4000 BC) and has been consistently of high quality. But the high-fired, creamy-white wares produced under the Tang dynasty (AD 618-907) are probably the world's first true porcelain, although the invention had been prefigured by a stoneware with an olive-brown feldspathic glaze appearing in southern China in the third century. True porcelain is made of ground feldspathic stone and white kaolin, fired at a very high temperature, when it vitrifies, and is invariably glazed – the glaze

usually also contains some feldspar, and fuses with the body of the pot when it is fired. In the aesthetic of porcelain the form of the pot and the glaze are intimately connected; though the glaze is the chief standard by which the vessel is judged, its effect depends on the way light amplifies the shape that carries it.

Many Tang pots still echo the shapes and decoration of bronze vessels, in a hang-over from the Han dynasty (see preceding page). The crucial development came during the Song (Sung) dynasty (960-1279). The Buddhist Song Emperors paraded a religious poverty, using vessels not of precious metals but of supposedly lowly clay, and therefore took a direct interest in the kilns; the taste for this fine porcelain soon spread throughout the Empire. Typically, Song ware has a subtle, clearly outlined, organic shape, glazed usually in monochrome and often incised with an ornament; but it was produced in many local varieties. Most have blue-green glazes, and are known in the West as celadons; of these some feature a thick, glutinous glaze which produces very refined and suggestive optical effects – including the dull-green Northern celadons, has a freely incised design, a pair of mandarin ducks (symbols of happy marriage) amid reeds and comb-like waves glazed in translucent ivory. The Cizhou vase, of classic *meiping* shape, is of fine stoneware, not of porcelain: the decoration is here more important – bold, purple-black peonies against a buff ground. Its design, though, is applied beneath the glaze; on later porcelain, the colours are enamel, a part of the glaze itself. Song porcelain has a subtlety and simplicity which, compared to later ware, can be called classic.

JINGDEZHEN (above)
Jar, c.1506-21
The design of free-ranging dragons, moving between the vapours of the air and the waves of the depths, is applied in enamels, overlaid by light incised lines.

SOUTHERN CHINA (above)
Bodhidharma, 18th century
The creamy-white Dehua porcelain statuette depicts the Indian philosopher who founded in 520 in China the form of Buddhism known as Chan (as Zen in Japan).

JINGDEZHEN (below)
Meiping vase, c.1662-1722
Bearing the mark of the Kangxi reign, the summit of Qing enamelled wares, the nobly shaped vase was intended to hold a single branch of a prunus tree.

the bluer Longquan ware of the south, the complex Jun celadons with their mulberry flashes, and the crackled grey-blue *guan* ware; others are more thinly glazed, including the greeny-blue *qingbai* ware and also the white, delicately potted Ding ware, in which the incised ornament is important.

In the earlier periods the form of the ceramic was more important; later the glaze and the surface became the chief considerations. The overlap lies in the Song period, and the group of wares called Cizhou seem most obviously to initiate the development away from monochrome to a more elaborate coloured decoration. Cizhou ware has a white or buff ground, on which a fairly simple design is imposed in black or brown. By the beginning of the thirteenth century, potters had learned how to execute their designs in red, green and even yellow enamels – the forerunners of Ming and Qing polychrome wares.

The tendency towards greater surface decoration was consolidated under the Mongol Yuan dynasty (1279-1368). Ornament was applied both in copper red and in cobalt blue – the latter was far more successful and popular, and was continued into Ming times. Under the Ming dynasty (1368-1644) porcelain production was concentrated in the city of Jingdezhen; the bases of a high proportion of Ming pots are inscribed with the monograms of the reigning Emperor (often forged on later wares). Earlier types continued to be made, but taste moved increasingly to favour polychrome glazes: different colour combinations predominated at different times – red, green, blue and yellow; yellow and blue; yellow and green. The Manchu Qing dynasty (1644-1911) pursued the refinement of decoration to its extremes, although Dehua ware – in which religious figurines as well as vessels were made – was valued for its pure white colour and delicate modelling. The various overglaze enamel liveries which became popular in the Qing dynasty – the black, green and rose families – feature an extraordinary variety of design; though the shapes of the pots may have been standardized, their painted decoration was inimitable in another medium because it exploited and harmonized with the curvature of the surface. This is the great beauty of the later Chinese porcelain.

Chinese Art 3: Landscape Painting

The history of Chinese painting extends back well beyond the date of any surviving works: painting emerged as the supreme Chinese art probably during the Han dynasty (206 BC-AD 220). The development of Chinese painting was nevertheless continuous, rooted from the beginning in calligraphy – the art of writing characters expressively with brush and ink – and primarily devoted to landscape – the manifestation of the subtle workings of the Tao, or Nature-as-change.

It was during the Han dynasty that the famous Chinese imperial civil service or "bureaucracy" was created – a class of scholars, poets and men of letters fitted by their education for the administration of the Empire. Painting was part of the gentleman's curriculum, one of the means by which he expressed his personal understanding of the world in a manner worthy of his ancestors. Surviving literature provides plentiful evidence of its theory and practice, which can be supplemented by one scroll, just possibly original, that is attributed to Gu Kaizhi (c.344-406) and illustrates Confucian maxims.

Literature of the Tang dynasty (618-907) records the existence and merits of a number of painters, but few silks or scrolls survive, and those are mostly copies. The great formative period of classic landscape painting was that of the Five Dynasties (907-60) and the Northern Song (960-1127). Its development was stimulated both by the application of Taoist philosophy and by the needs of imperial court ceremonial, it being the crucial role of the Chinese emperor to maintain the harmony between Nature and man; landscapes representing the desired course of Nature's changes were elements in the rituals. But, although many of the outstanding painters of this time were professional members of the court atelier, some of the greatest, such as Li Cheng and Fan Kuan (active c.990-1030), were Taoist recluses. Their landscapes consisted of dense, rocky motifs rising vertiginously through the upright picture. An outstanding professional, active later in the eleventh century, was Guo Xi, whose grandiose spaces are filled with rough terrain and gnarled trees drawn with nervous calligraphic loops.

In the second half of the eleventh century an important group of gentlemen artists – among them the great Mi Fei (1051-1107) – gathered round the statesman, poet and artist Su Shi.

Their outlook was Confucian, and they developed a theory of painting according to which the expressive qualities of the picture were a reflection of the personality of the artist – the work had value as a record of the inspired insight of the artist into the realm of Nature. The demarcation was made which coloured the entire subsequent history of Chinese painting – between the professional, usually the member of an academy, who painted painstakingly and objectively, and the gentleman amateur, who painted when the spirit moved him and in order to cultivate his spirit.

The last Emperor of the Northern Song dynasty, Huizong, an accomplished painter of flowers and birds – an important vein in Chinese painting – lost northern China to the Mongols and died in captivity. One of his sons, the founder of the Southern Song dynasty (1138-1279), set up a new capital in the beautiful city of Hangzhou, and gathered there an almost legendary gallery of major painters. Xia Gui (active c. 1180-1230; not shown) painted huge landscape panoramas with sparse and abrupt "axe-cut" strokes; Ma Yuan (c. 1190-c. 1224; not shown) painted asymmetrical compositions, of which the true subject is the

FAN KUAN (below)
Travelling among the mountains and streams, early 11th century
A massive towering outcrop dominates the scene, above the figures that set its scale. Fan Kuan's painting was felt to be instinct with the energies of Nature.

AFTER GU KAIZHI (right)
Admonitions of the instructress, detail, original c. 375
The silk scroll illustrates Confucian moral precepts: the ladies of the imperial harem are taught conduct – not so much deportment as worldly wisdom. The style has exquisite, wispy grace.

MI FEI (above)
Spring mountains, clouds and pine-trees, c.1050-1100
The misty hills have no outlines but are formed by large blots of ink laid on very absorbent paper. The aim was not to re-create the object in Nature but to express its spirit. "Anyone who talks about painting in terms of likeness deserves to be in a class with the children", wrote Su Shi.

MUQI (right)
A mother gibbon and her baby, c.1250?
Part of a hanging triptych, this image of maternal protectiveness haunts the memory. The mother clasps her child, gazing out at the spectator with a most vivid directness. The two sit on a branch, drawn in rough strokes of fluid ink, with all the careless beauty of Muqi's extraordinarily deft, eloquent and vigorous style.

empty space to one side set off by the strongly brushed rocks to the other. But the artist who created the subtlest suggestions of the infinite void of time and space was the Chan Buddhist monk Muqi (1180–1270?).

During the unhappy years which brought the end of the Song and the establishment of the Mongol Yuan dynasty (1279-1368), several great masters nevertheless emerged. They were highly conscious of the past, and they sought to recapture in their own quite distinct styles the harmony and coherence of early Song painting; then they themselves became paradigms to be imitated by later artists. It was a standard requirement for professional painters of the succeeding Ming dynasty that they could paint in the different style of the six main Yuan painters – Gao Kegong (misty, rain-drenched landscapes), Zhao Mengfu (archaizing, spare calligraphy), Ni Zan (dry but luminous brushwork), Huang Gongwang (superbly fresh landscapes), Wu Zhen (landscapes with a mood of sober melancholy) and Wang Meng (c.1301-85), who became famous for his dynamic rhythms and dense, rich textures, formed by so-called "dragon veins". The great masters of the Ming

dynasty (1368-1644) were yet more numerous, including both amateurs and professionals, deeply imbued with their great heritage, and working largely within the repertoire established by it. They included Dai Jin, Shen Zhou, Wen Zhengming, Jia Ying and Tang Yin (1470-1523); also Dong Qichang, a practising connoisseur who wrote on the history, theory and classification of painting.

The painters of the Qing dynasty (1644-1911) inherited therefore a range of prescribed themes to be treated according to a thoroughly annotated practice. Many good artists continued to work within it, but those who sheered off into individual and sometimes extravagant mannerisms are perhaps more interesting. Two of the greatest of these "Individualists" were Buddhist monks, Zhu Da and Shitao (1630-1717); Shitao invented an original graphic style and also composed the most profound of the many books on the spirit of Chinese painting. The Individualist spirit lived on in the equally bold work of the eighteenth-century painters, but their originality seems originality for originality's sake beside the extraordinarily vibrant effects of Shitao's calligraphy.

GUO XI (above)
Early spring, 1072
For the Chinese, everything shares in a single cosmic principle, the Tao; rocks are living things and man participates in their life. It is this boundless and all-pervasive quality that Guo Xi seeks to capture. The Tao also expresses itself in flux; "the spring mountain wrapped in dreamy haze and mist" contains hints of seasonal change in the flickering lights and shifting compositional lines.

WANG MENG (below)
Forest dwellings at Juqu, c. 1370
Terraces of dense inter-penetrating rock ascend the picture plane, linked by winding lines – "dragon's veins". There is no single compositional focus and the horizon lies beyond the picture space, giving that sense of limitless space which is an expression of the nature of Tao: "Beyond mountains there are more mountains ... Beyond trees there are yet more trees."

TANG YIN (left)
A poet and two courtesans, c. 1500
Tang Yin stands between the scholar-painters and the professional artists; an amateur by temperament and training, but demoted after being involved in an examination scandal, Tang Yin was forced to paint for money. He executed several such elegant, open, lightly coloured pictures of girls from the pleasure quarter of Suzhou, and he became a source of inspiration for 18th-century *ukiyo-e* print-makers in Japan (see p. 49).

SHITAO (above)
The gleaming peak, c. 1700
In his youth, Shitao had travelled all over China, and he often depicted real places, but universalized the experience so that *The gleaming peak* has become all mountains – Shitao is seeking to express "the hidden forces of heaven and earth". The brush-strokes delineating the contours and crevices of the rocks form a complex, spreading network; and Shitao asserted: "A single brush-stroke is the origin of existence and the root of myriad phenomena."

Korean Art

Korean art has always been treated as something of a poor relation amongst the arts of the East, which is a grave injustice to an artistic tradition which has created some of the world's most beautiful objects in a distinctive style. Moreover, Japanese art owes an enormous debt to Korea, for it was via Korea that the Japanese came into contact with Buddhism and Buddhist art, both Korean and Chinese.

Korea's original population was probably related to the Siberian Tunguz; but by the fourth century BC the country had fallen under the influence of its huge neighbour, China. In AD 372 Buddhism was adopted in Koguryo, the nearest to China of the three kingdoms into which Korea was divided – Koguryo, Paekche and Silla – until the seventh century, when all three were united under the Great Silla dynasty, with its capital at Kyongju. Hundreds of tombs from the early Korean dynasties stand ruined on the mountain-sides and the coastal plains; most of them were long ago looted, but from certain large royal tombs some stupendous feats of craftsmanship have survived, such as the crowns from Kyongju – intricate, complex structures assembled from sections of sheet-gold cut into the stereotyped outlines of

sacred trees, with long, swaying "branches" and trailing "fronds" carrying loose, shimmering fillets of gold and jade.

From reliefs and from a few early tomb paintings of the fifth and sixth centuries it is clear that the Koreans followed the Chinese custom of surrounding the dead with images of the world they knew. In the paintings, scenes perhaps derived from Chinese prototypes rather harsher in tone are infused with a gentle and refined expression characteristic of the Korean genius. What remains of the Buddhist temples of the Three Kingdoms is scanty (though literature tells of many magnificent buildings); the more ancient sites obviously provided the prototypes for early Japanese Buddhist shrines. Surviving from the temples are several early Buddhist images, already showing, despite their clear debt to Chinese example, distinctive features of Korean style: quite un-Chinese is their graceful subtlety and the sweetness of their linear modelling – the outlines undulate, floating off into delicate curves of decorative drapery. One of the most famous Korean images is a large seated figure of Maitreya in gilt bronze, now in the National Museum, Seoul. Its almost exact double in

KANG HUI-AN (above)
A sage resting on a rock,
15th century
Against the soft washes of ink in the background, and the calligraphic sweep of the vine, the figure of the sage is sharply drawn; the contrast heightens his cheerful, luminous presence. Zen ideas – the concept of enlightenment won through meditation on the natural world – are surely implicit. Kang Hui-an, an amateur painter in the Chinese sense, was well travelled; his work is related to and holds its own beside both Chinese and Japanese art.

KOREA (below)
Wine pot, late 12th century
During the "Golden Age" of Korean ceramics, in the 11th and 12th centuries, Koreans created some of the finest celadon ware ever known, using a soft, bluish-green glaze on vessels of widely varying shape. Once they had learnt to handle high-fired porcellaneous ware from the factories of Yue, China, they evolved their own unique style.

KYONGJU (left)
Royal crown,
4th/6th century
The tombs of the kings of Silla (in south-eastern Korea) have yielded several elaborate gold crowns, hung with comma-shaped pieces of jade with antler-like branches; these mysterious forms may be connected with shamanistic rituals.

SILLA OR PAEKCHE? (right)
Maitreya, early 7th century
The gilt-bronze Buddha of the future is serenely seated, half cross-legged, in meditation. Compared to other early *Maitreyas* from China or Japan, he displays distinctly Korean features of calm, grace and transcendence; his robes ripple mildly, decorously.

KOGURYO (left)
A nobleman and his wife,
mid-5th/6th century
The ancient tomb-painting still preserves the seated man attended by his wife (who kneels at the right). Strongly outlined and once highly coloured, they bear witness to the refinement of life under the Koguryo in northern Korea. Other tombs have revealed murals of wrestling, hunting and dancing. Chinese artists had infiltrated Korea, and some close parallels have emerged in Chinese tombs.

wood is treasured in the Koryu temple in Kyoto, Japan, and the elongated, graceful "*Kudara Kannon*" in Japan (see over) is traditionally attributed to a Korean artist. Strong Chinese influence, however, is still apparent in eighth-century work, but the colossal, splendid stone Buddha in the Sokkuram in Kyongju (not shown) may be influenced by Indian Mathuran or Gupta sculpture.

The best known achievement of medieval Korean art is in ceramics. After the fall of the Great Silla, under the Koryo dynasty (918-1392), potters evolved a celadon ware related to Chinese celadon both in body and in type of glaze, but inlaid with designs in differently coloured slips in an original Korean technique. The contours of each pot are subtly suggestive of organic shapes, and the painted decorations are brushed freshly and with vitality. From the Koryo period there also survive religious paintings of remarkable courtly beauty (the majority are now preserved in Japan).

Buddhism, the state religion of the Great Silla and the Koryo dynasties, then fell out of favour with the accession of the Yi dynasty (1392-1910). The new rulers fostered a strict Confucianism, which rapidly penetrated the educated and connoisseur classes. Art became predominantly secular. Following the example of the Chinese Song dynasty, official ateliers of artists and craftsmen were established, with carefully defined grades. Professional work was restricted on the whole to formal portraits and to standardized decorative schemes. However, like those in China (see preceding page), Korean amateur or scholar-painters sought to convey their vision of universal change in a highly expressive, calligraphic style – though few works by these early Yi painters have survived. Those of the celebrated Kang Hui-an (1419-65), who had travelled into Ming China, exhibit fairly heavy, dark contours and modelling strokes that are powerful and swift, slightly resembling the style of his contemporary in Japan, Sesshu (see p. 46). An Kyon (1418-94) was greatly honoured for his landscapes. The Yi nobles also appreciated fine ceramics: a white porcelain, sparingly decorated in blue underglaze, was produced for the court, and a coarse pottery (*punch'ong*) was made for daily use. (*Punch'ong* was soon to be particularly admired for its simplicity and directness by the Japanese tea-masters).

In the late sixteenth century Korea became a battlefield, invaded in 1592 by the Japanese under the dictator Hideyoshi, seeking an avenue to attack China. Its treasures were despoiled, and its potters deported to Japan (where they infused new life into the Japanese ceramic tradition). Yet the tradition of amateur painting was maintained by a succession of gifted artists, such as Yi Chong (1578-1607; not shown), the slightly later Yi Jing and the powerful calligrapher Kim Myong-guk. Kang Hui-an's brushwork was revived in the work of Chong Son (1676-1759), but further strengthened and hardened. Although these painters still generally followed Chinese prototypes, their work attained a distinctively Korean character, resembling neither Chinese styles nor the work of Japanese contemporaries. In the eighteenth century the meditative landscape painter Yi In-mun (1745-1821) and the genre painter Kim Hong-do (1745-c. 1818; not shown) achieved an original expression.

The distinctly Korean artistic language emerged above all in the early sculpture, in pottery and in painting, where there is an original sensitivity to the changing course of Nature. The distinctively Korean quality is one of refinement and honeyed delight.

AN KYON (above)
The dream of the peach-blossom garden, 1447
An Kyon's painting of the prince An Pyong's vision is one of Korea's earliest surviving landscapes. The complex, fantastical style reflects Song influence.

CHONG SON (left)
The mountain by the river, 18th century
The first to paint truly Korean landscapes, Chong Son wielded his brush with energy. He freed himself from Chinese restraint.

YI IN-MUN (right)
A young Immortal under a fir tree, 18th/19th century
Yi In-mun, a professional, gave traditional images new, sprightly life. The Taoist Immortal, or sage, is at one with Nature.

Japanese Art 1: Art of the Buddhist Temples

Japan is a treasury of some of the world's greatest sculpture, virtually all of it Buddhist, and at first strongly dependent upon prototypes from Korea and China. Medieval Buddhist art in Japan, however, is often much better preserved than in China or Korea, and, because of the lack of correlative examples, it is often difficult to decide whether a particular piece is imported, or by a native Japanese, or by an immigrant.

Japanese history before Buddhism came is divided into three principal epochs, the Jomon (approximately 7500-200 BC), the Yayoi (200 BC-AD 200) and the Tumulus (AD 200-600). From these periods mostly small-scale ceramic sculpture survives. The neolithic Jomon figurines are of grey and red earthenware, their bodily features defined with ridges and shallow incisions, great round eyes giving the abstracted image life. The Tumulus period takes its name from the great burial-mounds constructed by its rulers, around which quantities of *haniwa* have been found – ceramic cylinders topped by figures of retainers, women, animals and houses. According to an ancient text, *haniwa* were substitutes for the living people and real objects which had in former times accompanied the great into the grave – though archaeology has not corroborated this.

The first wave of Buddhist influence came to Japan from the kingdom of Paekche in Korea; it is reported that the Korean king sent the Emperor of Japan a gilt-bronze image of the Buddha in AD 538. The Emperor declared himself deeply moved by the profound Buddhist doctrine, but because pestilence came in its wake the gift was thrown into a canal. However, more images, and then artists (including one known master, Tachito, from China), followed, and by the end of the sixth century Prince Shotoku, Regent of Japan, was welcoming Buddhism openly. The famous monastery of Horyu in the region of Nara was founded then, among others, and images began to be produced in large numbers. At first Buddhist sculpture was confined to a few subjects only – Shaka (the historical Buddha), Yakushi (the healing Buddha), Miroku (or Maitreya, the Buddha of the future), Kwannon or Kannon (the Bodhisattva of compassion) and the guardian kings of north, east, south and west. Two Buddhist trinities (the Buddha flanked by two Bodhisattvas) in bronze are recorded by the hand of Tori,

JAPAN (right)
"The Kudara Kannon",
7th century
The ethereal camphorwood deity of compassion has the linear grace of Korean art, but was probably carved in Japan (the wood is rare in Korea) – by an immigrant?

JAPAN (left)
A *haniwa*: *A warrior*,
3rd/6th century AD
The burial mound of one emperor of the period had 11,200 such *haniwa*, partly supporting its steep sides.

HORYU-JI, JAPAN (below)
The death of the Buddha,
711
The highly emotive dry-clay group in its artificial cavern is staged on a floor in the five-storey pagoda of the ancient monastery.

JAPAN (above)
Jomon figurine,
1st millennium BC
The earliest art objects found in Japan are clay pots and figurines – small idols decorated with an impressed rope pattern (*jomon*), more vital than any in other neolithic cultures.

YAKUSHI-JI, NARA (right)
The Buddha and two Bodhisattvas, c. 726
The three colossal deities gleam darkly against their great haloes – once gilded, the bronze has blackened with time. Their smoothly rounded limbs show Tang influence – a solidity in contrast to the remote grace of Korean-influenced figures. Though prototypes exist in China, and colossal bronze *Buddhas* are recorded in literature, none survives so huge, or of such quality.

grandson of the immigrant Tachito, who was rewarded for them with a higher social status. The style of this early Japanese sculpture is clearly derived from Chinese examples (compare, for instance, those at Longmen and Yungang, see p.36), often brought to Japan through the medium of Korea – as with "*The Kudara* (Paekche) *Kannon*", traditionally ascribed to a Korean artist. The forms are somewhat stiff and elongated, smoothed into gently gradated surfaces scored with a calligraphy of drooping folds and graceful pleat-ends.

During the seventh and eighth centuries, wood became a favoured medium of Japanese sculptors. It was carved and polished into smoothly undulating volumes, formed by gentle contours, more or less enlivened by linear patterning. One of the finest examples of this period, however, is in bronze, the colossal free-standing Buddhist trinity at the Yakushi temple in Nara, probably of the early eighth century. The drapery lines coil freely about the magnificent and massive *Yakushi*; the Bodhisattvas, too, are plump, epitomizing elegance. Such huge images, probably derived directly from Chinese Tang prototypes now lost, were frequently ordered during the Nara period

(710-84) from each province to celebrate the passing of a plague, an emperor's accession and so on; one which survives at the Todai temple in Nara (not shown) consists of nearly five tons of metal, even though the figures are hollow, cast by the lost-wax method.

Another vein of sculpture, in unfired clay, appears in the freely modelled small figures of mourning disciples in the tableau of *The death of the Buddha* (711) in the Horyu monastery. Each disciple is conceived as a distinct individual. A similar realism charges the magnificent dry-lacquer portrait of the Chinese monk Ganjin, founder of the Toshodai monastery and widely revered as a kind of saint in Japan. From China he seems to have brought with him artists, and a new wave of influence. The huge *Kannon* in the Toshadai temple, 5.5 metres (18ft) high, with its thousand arms (in fact 953) creating around the calm face a fantastic aureole, is also of dry-lacquer. While the *Ganjin* initiates a new and powerful tradition of portrait sculpture, surely related to the trend in China that culminated in the individualistic figures of *Luohans* (see p. 37), the *Kannon* reveals a new ponderous and static style, with drapery of heavy curving folds.

During the Heian period (784-1185) an esoteric sect, the Shingon Buddhists, began to flourish; their prolonged rituals required large numbers of images embodying a ramified pantheon of spiritual powers, each with distinct, often fantastically elaborate attributes. In the eleventh century the sculptors resorted to the technique (*yosegi*) of jointing sections of carved wood in order to produce ever more complex figurations. The elaborate rituals practised during the Kamakura Shogunate (1185-1392) were no longer under state patronage, though much sculpture, both large and of high quality, continued to be made for them, with increasingly dynamic invention and with insistent realism. Two great woodcarvers of the thirteenth century, Unkei and Kaikei, were famous; their statues of guardian deities (not shown) are magnificently menacing.

The Buddhist temples were furnished not only with sculpture but with murals, embroidered banners, figured silks, illustrated manuscripts, drawings and block-printed scrolls. Private individuals owned both miniature versions of the images in the temples and small portable shrines, sometimes carved in precious materials.

TOSHODAI-JI, JAPAN (right)
The priest Ganjin,
before 763
The coloured dry-lacquer statue of the blind Chinese monk (who endured terrible hardship on his journey to Japan) may have been made in his lifetime, perhaps by an artist trained in China.

TOSHODAI-JI, JAPAN (below)
"*The Kannon with 1,000 Arms*", after 759
Dry-lacquer, lacquer over cloth, is both surprisingly light and hard, permitting the artist to treat surfaces in highly elaborate detail, even those of sculptures on a monumental scale.

JAPAN (right)
The Bodhisattva Fugen,
12th century
The plump-faced, gentle divinity, painted on silk, is conceived in terms of fine line and flat colour. Indian and Tang models still exerted considerable influence in this period.

JAPAN (below)
Fudo, 13th century
Fudo's fierce grimace and stalwart stance, conveyed with the forceful realism characteristic of Japanese sculpture of the Kamakura era, clearly evokes his role as the chastiser of evil, immovable and impartial.

Japanese Art 2: Zen Ink-Painting

"Zen" is the Japanese pronunciation of the Chinese "Chan" – the vigorous, fundamentalist Buddhist sect which first flourished in China under the Tang dynasty. It stood for the rejection of the elaborate rites and duties of the traditional Buddhism practised in the great monasteries, with their immense apparatus of ceremonial, their treasures of paintings and sculptures; Zen monks sought enlightenment through personal dedication, through austerity and concentrated meditation, and expected to reach it in the midst of the ordinary course of everyday activity.

During the Kamakura Shogunate (1185-1332) Zen Buddhism was adopted by much of the warrior class. The Shogunates were military dictatorships ruling Japan in the name of a puppet emperor, regarded, together with his courtiers, by the Shogunate as effete, frivolous, fettered by ceremonial. The Shogunates fostered in contrast Zen Buddhism and the caste and code of the Samurai ("Warriors"), whose ethics and prowess were founded on the precepts of Zen. In their martial arts of sword, bow and spear Zen discipline, the training by which enlightenment might be attained, played a significant part. The strokes of the

Samurai had to be spontaneous and immediate, without any extraneous thought interposing between need and act. A similar quality was cultivated in ink-painting.

By the fourteenth century, in the Muromachi period (1333-1573), ink-painting, especially as practised by Zen priest painters, dominated the arts in Japan. It was founded on the ink-painting of Song China (see p.40): pure black Chinese ink (*suiboku*) was the prime medium, and its subjects, too, were drawn from the Chinese repertoire – above all landscapes and the seasons, but also portraits. Its aesthetic demanded directness of vision, the spontaneous reflection of sensitivity to Nature – it was closely based on Chinese canons, but was achieved by the Zen techniques of meditation. A series of painters had gradually established this Chinese style in Japan – among them Shubun (active 14th century; not shown) and Bunsei (active 15th century); the greatest of them was Sesshu (1420-1506), who was perhaps the greatest distinctively Japanese ink-painter, although he, too, was still strongly influenced, like his predecessors, by the great painters of the Southern Song dynasty, including the Zen monk Muqi (see p. 40), but also by

SESSHU (below)
Autumn landscape, late 15th century
Sesshu's achievement was to implant a tradition of landscape painting based on observation. His clear vision superseded earlier ethereal landscape dreams. He varied his use of ink inventively; famous was his *haboku* (broken-ink) style.

BUNSEI (right)
The layman Vimalakirti, 1457
Zen monks sought to avoid ostentation with a simple, personal art. The portrait, beneath a eulogy, captures a direct, sober essence, but in the poverty is richness – the vigour of the sharply angled outlines, set off by quieter, even fuzzy, textures.

EITOKU (right)
Plum-trees by water, 16th century
A series of sliding screens

in the Juko-in monastery are given to Eitoku. Straw brushes (*warafude*) gave his line distinctive spikiness.

MOTONOBU (right)
The small waterfall, early 16th century
The clear, almost pen-like lines of Motonobu's brush recall Sesshu's directness,

but there is a hint, too, of the decorative *yamato-e* which he also practised. Motonobu often added bright colour to the firm lines of his compositions.

the Ming painter Dai Jin. It is reported of Sesshu that while he was studying in China (1467-68) he was regarded as the greatest living ink-painter there. In fact Sesshu's brush-line was harsher and more angular than that of the Song painters, expressing his experience of Nature with greater freedom and a stronger personality, overriding the academic harmony of form and spirit for which the Chinese masters were then striving. Later generations of Japanese artists were to draw continually on his example – not least the painters of the Kano family school.

According to tradition the founder of the Kano school was Kano Masanobu (1434-1530; not shown), who began painting in the soft style of his master Shubun, and then developed a more decorative expression in remarkably clear and balanced compositions, notably in a huge series, mostly lost, of murals and screen-paintings for Zen monasteries. His son Kano Motonobu (1476-1559) consolidated the Kano style in strong and lyrical outlines reflecting his admiration of Sesshu, but also of the styles of the great masters of Song China. Like his father he worked for Zen monasteries, and he did much to gain the Kano school its

official status with the Shogunate.

The great castles on towering stone plinths built by the nobles during the rule of the Momoyama Shoguns (1568-1615) in response to the import of cannon offered huge acreages of wall to be painted – an opportunity to which the Kano artists responded with energy and imagination. The great genius was Kano Eitoku (1543-90), grandson of Motonobu. He injected into the subdued ink-painting style the rich colour and gold-leaf characteristic of the secular decorative traditions of *yamato-e* (see over), and in his screens set huge trees or rocks, drawn in great sweeping lines, against a golden, hazy, immaterial background. Unfortunately little by his hand has survived the destruction of the palaces and castles in which he worked. There are also decorative screens, atmospheric, asymmetrically designed, by his contemporary Hasegawa Tohaku (1539-1610), who is best known, however, for his monochrome painting, and the subtlety of his apparently casual brushwork. The Kano school continued to flourish into the eighteenth century, gradually losing inspiration.

The strict Zen style of painting was given fresh life in the Edo period (1615-1867), when

simplicity and directness was reasserted by Niten (1584-1645), ink-painter and Samurai swordsman, whose brushwork has a corresponding swift, summary quality. Niten's vivid monochrome brushwork was matched by that of his contemporaries Sotatsu (died 1643) and Koetsu (1558-1637), who were not only ink-painters (though not in the Zen style) but also decorative artists, instrumental in the revival of *yamato-e*. The conception of Zen was by this time no longer so austere; the tea ceremony, originally practised by monks as a contemplative ritual, came to be cultivated as more an aesthetic than as a religious activity, and it is from the Momoyama and early Edo periods that the finest, subtly casual, decorated vessels associated with it survive. The renewal of Zen stimulated also the development of the allusive, epigrammatic 17-syllable verse-form of the *haiku* and its pictorial counterpart the *haiga*, perfected by the poet-painter Yosa Buson (1716-83; not shown). A closely similar aesthetic informed the painting practised by Zen monks to test their intuitive insight – an extreme, "minimal" version of the principle that has always guided Japanese ink-painting – to express the most by means of the least.

TOHAKU (above)
Pine-trees, detail of a screen, late 16th century
With almost evanescent strokes of soft brown ink on paper, Tohaku evoked air and mood – a sense of peace in a morning mist.

KENZAN (left)
Ceremonial tea-bowl: *Evening glory*, late 17th or early 18th century
Ogata Kenzan (1663-1743) was himself a tea-master. His enamelled glazes are boldly, playfully dabbed.

KOETSU AND SOTATSU (above) *Deer*, detail of a scroll, 17th century
Sotatsu, who practised in several styles, invented a new technique of modelling by manipulating wet ink. His deer illustrate the calligraphy of Koetsu.

NITEN (left)
Bird and branch, late 16th or early 17th century
Niten is supposed to have attacked paper with ink as if fighting an enemy. His few surviving works, monochrome paintings, typify that vital spontaneity so admired by Zen Buddhists.

BUNCHO (right)
Heron wading among lotus flowers, 18th/19th century. This painting of Buncho (1763-1840) has the typical calligraphic economy and austere composition of the *haiga* style. He was an eclectic artist, studying various Japanese styles and Chinese ink-painting.

Japanese Art 3: Yamato-e

The essentially secular mode of painting the Japanese call *yamato-e*, "Japanese painting", grew originally out of Chinese Tang dynasty styles which penetrated Japan and were assimilated in early medieval times. It was initially a court style, and clearly distinct from the painting (see preceding page), directly inspired by later Chinese example, which dominated the arts during the Kamakura and Muromachi Shogunates (1185-1573). Its more formal, more decorative, more colourful aesthetic was entirely opposite to the spontaneity, intuition and personal expression – usually in monochrome – of the Zen ink-painters, although, as we have already noticed, the two modes interacted to some extent.

Features of *yamato-e* are early apparent in the famous portraits of court dignitaries by Fujiwara Takanobu (1141-1204), reflecting the extremely strict conventions governing the intercourse of the medieval Japanese nobility. The faces now seem highly stylized, with an emphasis on simple, graphic design enlivened with decorative detailing. In their day, however, their realism caused some scandal.

The most important examples of *yamato-e* are painted scrolls. During the Heian period (784-1185) probably Tang Buddhist scrolls imported from China inspired the development of long narrative scrolls, *emakimono*, mirroring the sophisticated and cultured pleasures of the imperial court. A group of the earliest and finest of these illustrates the celebrated eleventh-century novel of courtly life by the lady Murasaki, *The Tale of Genji*, with the scenes alternating with passages of text. The figures, outlined in black ink, are drawn according to a formula; it is their fashionable robes which define their identity and status, rather than the faces reduced to empty ovals, with noses rendered by little hooks, eyes by tiny black ticks. Buildings are mostly roofless and in such projection as to allow a view of interior scenes.

Other narrative scrolls of different type but of a related style were devoted to the lives of Japan's Buddhist saints or to Japan's often ferocious history, retailed sometimes satirically, sometimes highly dramatically. The twelfth-century *Ban Dainagon* scrolls are perhaps the most dramatic. They are remarkable in that successive episodes are integrated into a continuous representation, carried for-

TAKANOBU (below)
The courtier Taira-no-Shigemori,
late 12th century
The courtier's impassive, delicately painted face is offset by the angular, decorative formula of his black ceremonial robe, accented by the sword and *shaku*, a kind of sceptre. Taira-no-Shigemori was apparently a mild, sincere man; here is no vainglory.

KORIN (left)
White plum-trees in spring,
c. 1705-10
The *yamato-e* technique of painting in a kind of dry tempera led to an emphasis on sinuous line, flat colour: diagonal lines animate the surface boldly. Branches running off the frame give a typically Japanese effect of space extending further. (Such patterns inspired Art Nouveau, see p. 121.)

UNKNOWN ARTIST (above)
The Tale of Genji:
An interior with figures,
12th century
With soft, subtle colours and delicate interplay of line, the anonymous artist evoked a mute atmosphere almost of suspense. The tale of amorous intrigue also flattered the Heian nobility by showing their refined pleasure in calligraphy and painting. The novel's 54 chapters were originally illustrated with about 80 or 90 images, of which only 19 survive.

MITSUNAGA? (right)
Ban Danaigon: The flight of the court,
late 12th century
The three extant scrolls of this story are assigned by tradition to Tosa Mitsunaga, active at the imperial court. Ban Danaigon was a villainous politician, who without any grounds or scruple accused a rival of setting fire to a gate of the imperial palace. Here people stare or run or are confused – all sharply characterized – as the smoke rolls forth.

ward in countless vividly drawn, animated figures, barely millimetres high, as the long scroll was unrolled from right to left. All classes of people, from nobles to peasants, are depicted, in a range of hectic gesticulations expressing violent emotions.

The skill in portraying lively genre with dashing line and decorative colour was to be practised and developed vigorously from these early prototypes in a long series of narrative scrolls reaching virtually to modern times. The tradition was dominated by the Tosa family school, established in the conservative and ceremonious environment of the sacred imperial court of Kyoto. The early Tosa artists cultivated refined techniques of surface decoration, with rich colouring and much gold-leaf; during the early Shogunates the school declined, but its decorative splendour re-entered the mainstream of Japanese painting during the sixteenth and seventeenth centuries, having been reanimated by Tosa Mitsunobu (1434-1525; not shown). From the example of the Tosa school the artists Koetsu and Sotatsu (famous also for their experiments in ink-painting, see preceding page) developed in the early seventeenth century in Kyoto a

colourful style, which was taken up by Ogata Korin (1658-1716), an ardent admirer of Sotatsu. Korin's superbly elegant screens and scrolls combined elements from the traditional imagery of Chinese painting (see p. 40) with Japanese folklore, presented in dramatic designs and with an extraordinary feeling for colour and texture. He also painted, in contrast to the formal splendour of his purely decorative works, lively naturalistic studies.

The final and outstanding period of *yamato-e* dates from the removal of the Shogunate from Kyoto to Edo, modern Tokyo, in 1615. Art for the citizens of Edo, an urban class of a new prosperous type, was a matter neither of social ceremonial nor of religious expression, but was purely for pleasure. For their delectation the revived *yamato-e* style was applied to genre paintings such as that of the Matsuura screens, peopled with ladies in gorgeous contemporary dress. Such would be the subject matter of *ukiyo-e* (see over); and the prime medium of the *ukiyo-e* artists, the woodblock print, was developed in seventeenth-century Edo notably by Moronobu (c. 1618-94), who was one of the first to use the process for the mass-production of book illustrations.

Moronobu saw himself as a follower in the *yamato-e* tradition, and signed himself accordingly. Erotic art was practised by all Edo artists; Sigimura Jihei (active late 17th century) made magnificent prints of sexual dalliance, which were very popular.

The range of expression of *yamato-e* extended from its early sophisticated formality to the sentimental, highly opulent and sometimes crude Edo styles; not the least of its many offshoots was the art of lacquer-painting. Several famous painters had experimented with lacquerware, including Koetsu and Korin in the seventeenth century; in China, lacquerware had been made since ancient times and became very popular during the Ming dynasty. During the Edo period the Japanese developed a quite extraordinary skill in painting little lacquer cups and dishes, and in particular the compartmented medicine-boxes known as *inro*. These were attached to the wearer's sash by a cord secured with a *netsuke*, a small carving in wood, ivory or a semi-precious stone. Whether in relief or in the round, within a remarkably small, miniature compass Japanese craftsmen were able to conjure astonishing, fantastic effects.

UNKNOWN ARTIST (left)
A Matsuura screen, early 17th century
A conversation piece of ladies at their leisure, this screen is one of a pair which might once have advertised a textile shop. The patterned kimonos are clearly displayed. A rosary worn by the third figure from the right and a clay pipe in the second screen are Western imports.

UNKNOWN ARTIST (below)
Lacquer box, late 18th century
The range of lacquerware extended from dishes made for aristocrats to utensils for the modestly affluent. Shallow relief was often used, with a great variety of colours, gold- and silver-leaf and metallic dust to give a glamorous sparkle.

MORONOBU (left)
A river-boat party, c. 1682
Moronobu depicted his lovers with unprecedented frankness, reflecting the interests of the public without further pretensions. His prints were considered vulgar by the cultivated and by some artists, but opened the way for the great print designers.

JIHEI (below)
An insistent lover, c. 1685
Jihei adapted his style to the exigencies of his medium; he disposed black and white in a gorgeously ornamental design, with a sweeping line – suitably sensual, for most of his drawings and prints were erotic. His treatment is florid but not unsubtle.

Japanese Art 4: Ukiyo-e

The subject matter of *ukiyo-e*, "pictures of the floating world", first appeared in screens and hanging scrolls (see preceding page), but in the later seventeenth century was taken up by woodblock printers. *Ukiyo-e* prints, published both as illustrations to novels and as independent pictures, were made in the shops of specialist craftsmen to artists' designs, and their typically calligraphic style was already formed in the hand-coloured prints made by Kaigetsudo Ando (active 1700-14) and his associates. In Kaigetsudo Ando's single-figure pictures of famous beauties of the Yoshiwara, the brothel quarter of Edo (now Tokyo), the emphasis was placed on the gorgeous designs of the kimonos, depicted with wiry curves and strong, broad angles in a boldly two-dimensional composition.

Lacquer prints appeared about 1720, in which certain parts of the design, such as the sash of a kimono, were painted with glossy ink, while other parts were covered with glue and dusted with metallic powder – a technique exploited later in the century by Sharaku. The invention of the multi-block colour print by Suzuki Harunobu (1724-70) came in 1765. Harunobu's imagery revolved around a fragile type of woman, almost childish, tripping along the street, or pictured at home lounging or in conversation, or making love: it was Harunobu who established the prevalent mood of *ukiyo-e* during the second half of the eighteenth century, as a vision of everyday reality invested with an elegant glamour.

Amongst a multitude of considerable artists at work during the first maturity of the Edo print were three giants, Koryusai, Kiyonaga and Utamaro. At first the style of Koryusai (active 1765-84) was very close to his master Harunobu's, but after Harunobu's death he began in the 1770s to design to a new, larger format (which soon became standard for other artists) and commenced a long series of courtesan pictures – beauties of the Yoshiwara, standing or promenading either alone or with attendants – whose images he presented in splendid compositions, using sheaves of lines to define cascades of drapery and sweeping folds. He was also pre-eminent in bird and plant compositions, and, like nearly all the other Edo artists, he produced prints showing sexual love in action. Kiyonaga (1752-1815) specialized in extended compositions of figures in an architectural or landscape setting, the landscapes distinguished by a remarkably subtle aerial perspective. His designs were frequently continuous over a number of sheets – two or three or more – bringing extended narratives within the reach of the print.

Utamaro (1735-1806) is often looked on as the greatest of the *ukiyo-e* printmakers. He evolved a new type of female beauty, large-bodied, soft but strong, evoked in broadly looping lines – and also used this type in his illustrations of Japanese legend and folklore. He was fertile in technical devices, introducing effects conveying the transparency of fabrics, and cutting off the figures by the borders of the composition – a trick which was to be admired and imitated by Impressionists (see pp.94ff).

These artists were rivalled at the end of the eighteenth century by a younger generation, including the mysterious Sharaku (active 1794-95). He is thought to have been by profession an actor in the traditional Noh theatre; he turned to prints for ten months in 1794-95, producing at least 136 remarkable portraits of Kabuki actors. His forceful and searching draughtsmanship is relished now, but his harsh characterizations do not seem to have appealed to the public at the time.

KAIGETSUDO (left)
A courtesan, c. 1714
Kaigetsudo Ando (or Anchi) drew the designs, his staff cut the blocks, printed the prints and coloured them in by hand. The lady's kimono is richly decorated with cursive script from a poem: these early prints retained a "raw" quality reflecting accents of the brush in the formation of sweeping arcs, scribbled flutters of line.

HARUNOBU (right)
A lady dressing her hair, 1768
Suzuki Harunobu was the first artist to over-print the drawn black-and-white design with colours, using one block for each colour. His quiet, domestic ladies were inspired, it is said, by a waitress named O Sen.

KORYUSAI (right)
At the gate, c. 1771
The *hashirakake* or hanging-pillar print was intended to decorate wooden pillars in Japanese country homes. Koryusai cleverly adapted perspective to persuade the fashionably dressed ladies to fill the narrow frame.

KIYONAGA (below)
Cherry blossom, c. 1787-88
Kiyonaga's gently coloured scene, the central part of a triptych, catches the mood of a stroll in a park with extraordinary freshness – especially considering its consciously elegant humour and its stylization of tree and robe. No wind rustles the trees, but it is vivid in the lady's touch to her hat, in her fluttering gown.

UTAMARO (above)
Folio from *The poem of the pillow,* 1788

In his erotic prints as in his others Utamaro could combine unusual, effective

angles (emphasizing here the erogenous nape of the neck) with superb design.

Hokusai (1760-1849) had in contrast an immensely long career: in his later years he signed himself *The old man mad about drawing*, and he was indeed an experimental artist, full of humour and appreciation for the oddities of both life and art. Until about 1823 he produced comparatively conventional actor and courtesan prints, and in 1798 one tiny series of *Views of Edo*, his first landscapes. Then between 1823 and 1829 he found fame with his *Thirty-six Views of Mount Fuji* (later made up to 46 prints): no previous *ukiyo-e* artist had taken such a direct interest in the drama of landscape, carried in such a witty and bold design. He was extremely prolific, not only in prints but in bird and flower pictures, illustrated greetings cards and in drawings (his *Manga*) collected from 1814 in 13 volumes.

Hokusai was a major artist, but also a transitional figure, linking the eighteenth century to the nineteenth. Under some pressure from censors, the subject matter of the prints changed: Hiroshige (1797-1858) became the greatest artist of landscape. His *Views*, though certainly influenced by Hokusai's style, abandoned his bravura, and were full of poetic atmosphere, with a sympathetic observation of

the common people about their daily business. Kuniyoshi (1797-1861) developed quite another mode, Japan's rich repertoire of legends, the warfare of the Samurai. In sets of large prints, including triptychs, he illustrated heroes battling against hideous odds and monsters. But the work both of Kuniyoshi and of

Hiroshige is variable; Western influence and declining standards of technical accomplishment were eroding the quality of Japanese prints at just about the same time that Western painters began avidly to collect them, and to incorporate their bold designs and superbly decorative colour into their own work.

HOKUSAI (right)
Folio from *Thirty-six Views of Mount Fuji: Southerly wind and fine weather*, c. 1823-29
Hokusai's landscapes fused observation with pattern: for this quality Japanese prints became famous. The particular quality of the *Thirty-six Views* was their range of mood – here placid and serene, but in *The wave*, (not shown), one famous print of the series, wild, dramatic and spectacular.

HOKUSAI (right)
Folio from *Little Flowers: Peonies and a sparrow*, 1828
Although Hokusai did not introduce bird and flower compositions to the print, he extended its range and elevated its status beyond

that of a proletarian art form. The subjects of such albums as *Little Flowers* were sketched from nature, but in one of the approved Chinese styles. Utamaro also had produced prints of birds, animals, insects, fish.

SHARAKU (above)
The actor Otani Oniji as Edohei, 1794
In the fifth month of the season of 1794, the Kabuki theatre at Edo was playing a tale of intrigue between members of great families, in which a valet, Edohei, conspired with another man wickedly to rob his master. Sharaku's portrait of him is

an intense characterization of his villainy; indeed it was faulted for exaggeration. The bold draughtsmanship is offset by a background sprinkled with mica-dust. Sharaku's are the finest examples of actor prints – one of the main subjects of *ukiyo-e*. The actors were of the Kabuki, not the "highbrow" Noh theatre.

KUNIYOSHI (above)
Folio from *The Heroes of Suikoden: Tameijiro dan Shogo grapples with his enemy under water*, 1828-29
The 108 heroes, engaged in improbable feats, are drawn melodramatically, almost satirically – precursors of the Western comic.

HIROSHIGE (left)
Folio from *Fifty-three Stages of the Tokaido Highway: A shower at Shono*, 1833
Hiroshige, like Hokusai, prepared his prints from sketches. He purveyed rural scenes and country life in a romantic mood, sometimes in rather mannered designs.

THE AGE OF REVOLUTIONS

The French Revolution of 1789 heralded an era of often violent change which, in Western art, was to accelerate throughout the nineteenth century and culminate in the overthrow of the notion that an essential constituent of painting and sculpture was its ability to create an illusion of natural appearances. During this period the patronage of Church and nobility was largely replaced by that of the middle classes and the state, and France completed its eclipse of Italy as the artistic centre of Europe. Yet the wealth of Italy's classical heritage provided a major inspiration to the movement known as Neoclassicism. The art of its most influential exponent, Jacques-Louis David, expressed through the imagery of the distant past a belief in a Utopian future.

Classical principles of reason and clarity were, however, challenged by the new Romantic enthusiasm for the primacy of feeling. A strain of pessimism in much Romantic art reflects a deep insecurity, of which other symptoms were the revolutions flaring through the century. Goya's "Black Paintings" achieved an unparalleled morbid intensity. Another notable characteristic of Romantic art is its reverential awe for Nature; during the nineteenth century landscape became the major single subject of painting.

Towards the middle of the century a Realist movement, socially aware in art no less than literature, directed the sharp focus developed by the Romantics on to very mundane subjects, reproduced sometimes with almost photographic fidelity. The artists who responded most successfully to the development of photography were, however, the Impressionists, who wished to capture the everyday world with as much immediacy as the camera but to surpass it in rendering the sensation of the moment in colour and light.

An opposing movement in the last quarter of the century was Symbolism, which, in its rejection of the realities of the present, has often been seen as a second wave of Romanticism. Links can be found also between the Symbolists and the rather amorphous group known as the Post-Impressionists; many of the artists associated with both styles were appalled by the ugliness of the industrial civilization taking shape and wished to retreat from it, by embracing mysticism, as did some Symbolists, or by turning back to more primitive perceptions, as did Gauguin, or by making a virtual religion of art itself. The struggle of artists such as Gauguin and Cézanne to reshape the physical world in paint according to new, subjective, artistic laws led towards the irrevocable breakthrough of Cubism.

In Scandinavia, Germany and Austria it was the urgency of the movement called Expressionism that made the most significant inroads into the new territory of form opened up by Post-Impressionism. Amidst a maelstrom of cross-fertilizing styles and approaches, the dissolution of naturalism culminating in Cubism led with astonishing rapidity to the institution of purely abstract art, in France, in Germany, in Italy and in Russia. Already before World War I the Futurists were exploiting the new language of art in the creation of a new world, and Constructivism became the artistic language of the early Russian Revolution almost as Neoclassicism had been the artistic language of the French Revolution.

PARIS (left)
View of the grand staircase of the Opéra, 1861-74

BARCELONA (right)
The façade of Casa Batlló, begun 1905

CHICAGO (far right)
The Carson Pirie Scott store, 1899-1904

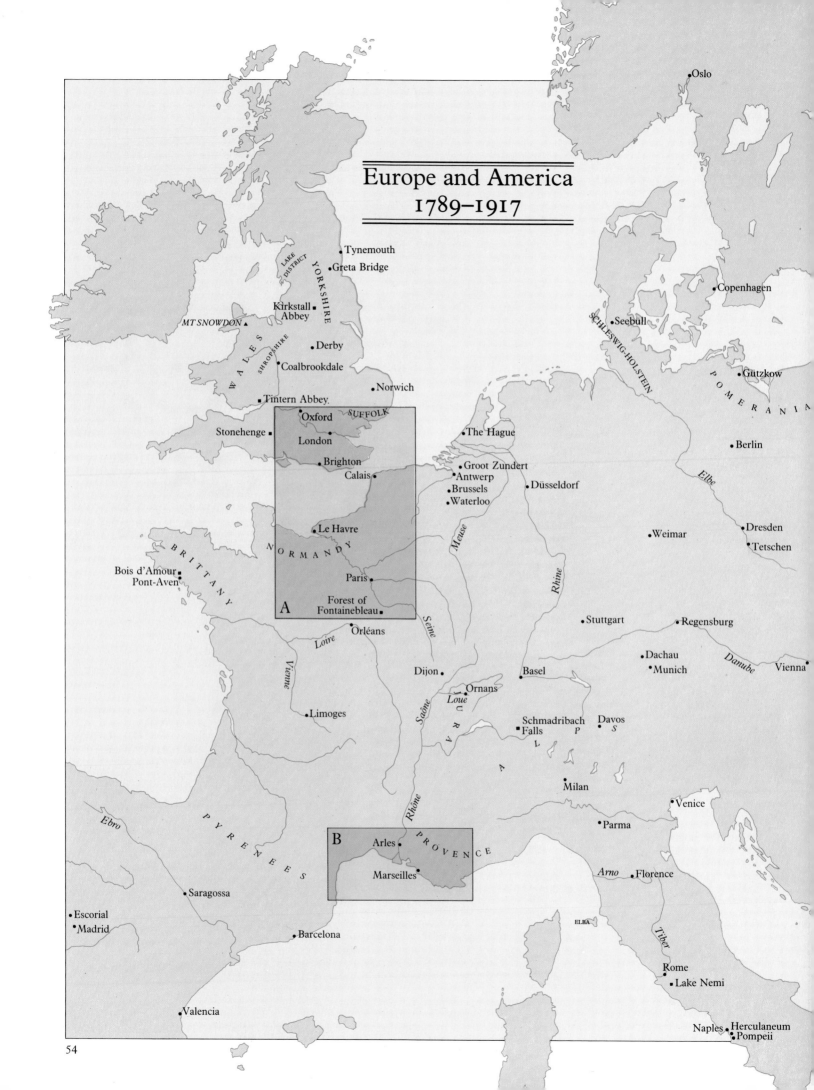

Europe and America
1789–1917

Oslo

Copenhagen

Tynemouth
Greta Bridge

LAKE DISTRICT

YORKSHIRE

Seebüll

SCHLESWIG-HOLSTEIN

POMERANIA

Gützkow

Kirkstall Abbey

MT SNOWDON ▲

WALES

SHROPSHIRE

Derby

Coalbrookdale

Norwich

Berlin

Tintern Abbey

Oxford

SUFFOLK

Elbe

Stonehenge

London

The Hague

Düsseldorf

Weimar

Dresden
Tetschen

Brighton

Calais

Groot Zundert
Antwerp
Brussels
Waterloo

Meuse

Le Havre

NORMANDY

Rhine

A

Paris

Stuttgart

Regensburg

Forest of Fontainebleau

Seine

Orléans

Dachau
Munich

Danube

Vienna

Loire

BRITTANY

Bois d'Amour
Pont-Aven

Vienne

Dijon

Saône

Ornans
Loue
J U R A

Basel

Schmadribach Falls

Davos

Limoges

Milan

Venice

Rhône

Ebro

PYRENEES

B

Arles

PROVENCE

Parma

Marseilles

Arno

Florence

Saragossa

ELBA

Escorial
Madrid

Barcelona

Tiber

Rome
Lake Nemi

Valencia

Naples

Herculaneum
Pompeii

54

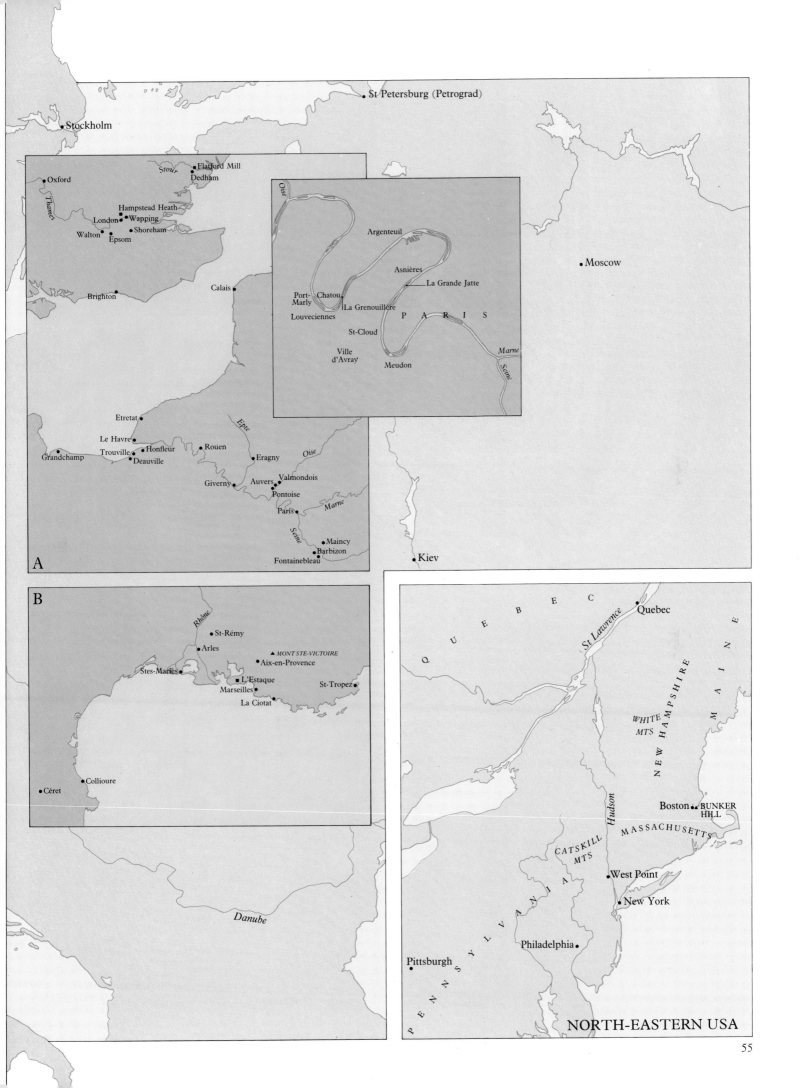

St Petersburg (Petrograd)

Stockholm

Moscow

A

Stour
Flatford Mill
Dedham
Oxford
Thames
Hampstead Heath
London • Wapping
Walton • • Shoreham
Epsom
Brighton
Calais

Oise
Argenteuil
Asnières
Port- Chatou La Grande Jatte
Marly La Grenouillère
Louveciennes P A R I S
St-Cloud
Ville
d'Avray Meudon
Marne
Seine

Etretat
Le Havre *Epte*
Trouville • Honfleur Rouen
Grandchamp Deauville Eragny
Oise
Giverny Auvers Valmondois
Pontoise
Paris *Marne*
Seine Maincy
Barbizon
Fontainebleau

Kiev

B

Rhône
St-Rémy
Arles
▲ *MONT STE-VICTOIRE*
Aix-en-Provence
Stes-Maries
■ L'Estaque St-Tropez
Marseilles
La Ciotat

Collioure
Céret

Danube

Q U E B E C
St Lawrence Quebec

*WHITE
MTS*
N E W H A M P S H I R E
M A I N E

Hudson
Boston ▲ BUNKER
HILL
*CATSKILL
MTS*
M A S S A C H U S E T T S
West Point
New York
P E N N S Y L V A N I A
Philadelphia
Pittsburgh

NORTH-EASTERN USA

David: The Oath of the Horatii

The movement called "Neoclassicism" is discernible from about 1760, and it reached its climax in the paintings of Jacques-Louis David (1748-1825) and the sculptures (see p. 60) of Canova between about 1780 and 1800. Though reference back to the example of classical antiquity was nothing very novel, it had seldom been so wide-ranging and so detailed; Neoclassical artists sought anew the underlying principles of ancient art, and their motivation was often highly moral. Neoclassicism was perhaps the first movement in Western art to put theory before practice.

Knowledge of classical painting and furniture in particular had been greatly extended by the steady growth of excavations in Italy. In 1738 Herculaneum was discovered, Pompeii in 1748; and there was a wave of fashion for things classical, or classical-looking. Although it was later to embody a revulsion against the pretty frivolities of Rococo, early Neoclassicism handled its antique look with distinctly Rococo sentiment – for example in the paintings of David's teacher Joseph Vien (1716-1809). The immensely influential Johann Joachim Winckelmann (1717-68), the first of the great German art historians, was the prophet of the nobler lessons to be learnt from classical art. He found his ideal in Greek art as opposed to Roman, and diagnosed the essence of Greek beauty as "noble simplicity and serene grandeur". His friend and fellow-German in Rome, Anton Raffael Mengs (1728-79), attempted to transpose Winckelmann's theories into practice: his *Parnassus* of 1761, rejecting Baroque illusionism and colour, is laid across the ceiling as if it were a sculptured relief – simple and cold, if not quite noble and grand.

The Scotsman Gavin Hamilton (1723-98), who reached Rome in 1748, though a much lesser artist than Mengs (who was also a superb portraitist), was a seminal figure. He anticipated not only the style but the themes of Neoclassical painting, and in his illustrations of the *Iliad* and in his *Oath of Brutus* hit upon two of the central interests of Neoclassical art, heroic classical epic and moralizing classical history. His *Oath of Brutus* certainly influenced David's *Oath of the Horatii*.

Though it was bred on Italian soil, the impact of Neoclassicism was most concentrated in France, where it came more and more to respond to the moral values expounded by the philosophers of the Enlightenment. Coinciding with the wide-ranging radicalism that culminated in the French Revolution, its mood was stoic, even puritanical; its emphasis was on civic virtue. The Revolution, when it came, endeavoured to base itself politically, ethically and culturally on republican Rome.

In Rome in 1775 David abandoned the influence of Boucher's Rococo for classical art – not only the ancients but also Raphael and Poussin. He painted *The oath of the Horatii*, the archetypal picture of purist Neoclassicism, in Rome in 1784. David said that he owed the subject to the tragedian Corneille, the picture to Poussin, but his classic reduction to essentials was reached only after a long and arduous series of studies (the foot of one Horatius was reworked 20 times). The picture established not only David's reputation but also the relevance of Neoclassicism to current issues.

POUSSIN (left)
Extreme Unction, 1644
Neoclassical painting was as much a return to the rigours of Poussin as to the lessons of ancient art, which Poussin had studied with care (see vol. 2 p. 195). In its language – gestures, composition, use of colour – Neoclassicism differed little, but it was more dramatic, more earnest, less complex.

VIEN (below)
The cupid seller, 1763
The subject is closely related to a wall-painting discovered in Herculaneum, but it was chosen no doubt as an allegory of sexual negotiation – its laxity and prettiness is pure Rococo.

GREUZE (below)
Septimius Severus reproaches Caracalla for seeking his death, 1769
Despite its classical detail, its frieze-like composition, its motifs already unearthed from antique art by Poussin, Greuze's picture failed. Its meaning was unclear.

MENGS (below)
Parnassus, 1760-61
Apollo and the Muses can be traced to antique prototypes, but they are seen through Raphael's eyes. With supreme efficiency Mengs reached a carefully balanced composition and a minute finish, eschewing both passion and rhetoric.

HAMILTON (right)
The oath of Brutus, c. 1763
Because the son of King Tarquin had raped Lucretia, Brutus swore to expel despotism from Rome and create a republic. Earlier artists, following Ovid, had shown the rape; Hamilton, following the historian Livy, stresses moral action.

DAVID (above)
The oath of the Horatii,
1784
To settle the war between
the two states, the three
Horatii brothers of Rome
engaged to fight the three
Curatii of Alba. All died
save one of the Horatii,
who, returning to Rome,
found his sister mourning
one of the Curatii, to whom
she had been betrothed.
Infuriated, he killed her.
David ignores the lurid
and more spectacular pos-
sibilities of the story, and
invents an undocumented
moment – the swearing of an
oath by the three brothers
that they will dedicate their
lives to their country. The
masculine energy of the
brothers and their father is
contrasted with the ladies'
tender compliance with fate;
the brothers' untarnished
devotion to duty is echoed
in the clear, sharp morning
light and in the simplicity,
austerity of the composition.

DAVID (left)
*The lictors bringing Brutus
the bodies of his sons,* 1789
Painted in the very year of
the Revolution, David's
picture was not specifically
political propaganda, but
it strikingly expresses the
moral fervour that fuelled
the Revolution and carried
it to such lengths. Brutus
had ordered the execution
of his own sons because
they had rebelled against
the republic he had founded.
His taut figure, seated with
tightly crossed legs in the
foreground, is a remarkable
image of personal emotion
screwed down by the sense
of moral duty. (The hand
pointing to his head is not
only a reference to a pose
common in classical art,
but also indicates Reason
ruling from the head).
Another such masterpiece,
of 1787, was *The death of
Socrates,* where, too, action
is less the subject than
conscience and consequence.

Neoclassical Painting: The Grand Style

The pure intensity of David's painting in the 1780s was the distilled essence of Neoclassicism, but it did not last long. The outbreak of the French Revolution in 1789 at first provided an ideal climate of opinion; David was prominently active in politics and his art entirely in key with events. *The death of Marat*, 1793, is virtually a canonization of the great revolutionary – a Christian *Pietà* transposed into a secular mode. After the fall of Robespierre, in 1794, David was imprisoned twice, and in the second spell, in 1799, he began *The intervention of the Sabine women*, a subject which could be interpreted as a revulsion against the excesses of the Reign of Terror and the guillotine, and a plea for reconciliation. Formally, its composition was a new development, using Greek models and with a suggestion of sensuality new to his work (some of his own pupils condemned it as being Rococo!)

Napoleon was needed to bring the Revolutionary convulsion under control and harness it to constructive purpose, although this purpose proved very different from the original ideals. David's art, as much as others', became an overt celebration of the Napoleonic Empire. He recorded contemporary events,

sometimes on a vast scale – *The coronation of Napoleon* (1805-07; not shown) includes more than a hundred identifiable portraits. His style became increasingly theatrical and pompous – pageant painting, in the tradition of Veronese, but applied to the heroic events of his own time. In this he had been preceded by American painters working in England, Benjamin West (1738-1820) and John Singleton Copley (1738-1815). West's *Death of Wolfe*, 1771, was a documentary recording General Wolfe's heroic death at Quebec in 1759 – relatively small in scale, yet in the grand style, in modern terms and modern costume.

West's style was modelled most nearly on Poussin, Copley's on Rubens. Both were acknowledged as revolutionary, but neither took the American Revolution as a theme (indeed West became the favourite of George III and succeeded Reynolds as President of the British Royal Academy); that was left to West's pupil, John Trumbull (1756-1843), who had himself fought in the War of Independence. He produced the first cycle of Revolutionary paintings, beginning in 1786, and took them back to America with him in 1816. Like Copley's, Trumbull's style was in a Baroque tradition

DAVID
The death of Marat, 1793
Marat was assassinated in his bath by Charlotte Corday: he suffered from a skin disease, soothed by its medicated waters, and she, inflamed to murder by his radical pamphlets, gained access to him by

means of the letter he holds. David has reconstructed the scene with archaeological accuracy, but has reduced it to its barest essentials, investing it with the most delicate, tender tones; it is still tragic, and with all the emotive force of a Revolutionary slogan.

DAVID (left)
The intervention of the Sabine women, 1799
In David's pictures of the 1780s, women had grieved impotent in the shadows; here they burst to the fore. In the packed but frozen action, like a carved relief, there are innumerable references to earlier artists – Raphael, Poussin, Rubens, Lebrun – and Greek vases; it is a little incongruous.

TRUMBULL (right)
The death of General Warren at the Battle of Bunker Hill, 1786
The splash of colour is the prime means by which the ardour of the fighting is conveyed. Bunker Hill was the first major battle of the American Revolution.

WEST (above)
The death of Wolfe, 1771
Before David's *Death of Marat* West had already used a religious formula, *The Deposition*, to impart an aura of tragedy to an historical event. There are

even 12 colleagues round the dying General, like 12 apostles, but the Cherokee makes 13 (he is in the pose of *Mourners* traditional on grand tombs). Wolfe died in the capture of Quebec, which made Canada British.

STUART (above right)
George Washington, 1795
Stuart complained that as soon as Washington sat for him, "a vacuity spread over his countenance", and it cost him some difficulty to achieve this alertness.

COPLEY (right)
A boy with a squirrel (The artist's half-brother), 1765
Reynolds praised Copley's freshness but faulted his hard lines, cold colours and too particular detail; these the American later avoided.

rather than a Neoclassic one. Copley had staged his *Death of Chatham* (not shown) as a one-man show in London in 1781, outside the Academy – the one-man show was still a novelty, and Copley's example perhaps inspired David's one-man showing of his *Sabine women* in Paris in 1800.

Copley's early work in America, before 1774, had been almost entirely portraiture. He was self-taught, and his knowledge of the European tradition had been acquired largely through engravings, but his extraordinarily vivid portraits show an innate eye for character. In their clarity of contour and often trenchant simplicity, they both anticipate the Neoclassic vision and preserve something of the freshness of the primitive. In England, his style tended to yield to the more atmospheric quality of the English fashion. Another American, Gilbert Stuart (1755-1828), who had started with West in London in 1775, likewise (though openly contemptuous of the Grand Manner) veered more to the fashionable English portrait style, and took it back to America with him in 1793. His subsequent fame rests on his oft-repeated image of *George Washington*.

The greatest of the Neoclassical portrait painters was beyond doubt David. His early portraits are astonishingly realistic, presaging the clear vision of his heroic classical subjects, but more relaxed. Direct portraiture continued all through his career, often of friends or professional men, but the supreme example of his more austere Neoclassic vision is the unfinished *Madame Récamier* of 1800, in which David's sheer painterliness is evident. The best example of his state portraiture is the finely dignified yet equally finely detailed whole-length of *Napoleon in his study*. It is in remarkable contrast to the heady, romantic atmospherics with which Sir Thomas Lawrence (1769-1830; not shown) in England invested the great.

After the fall of Napoleon and the Restoration of the Bourbons in France, David became an exile in Brussels, where he died in 1825. He was a great teacher, and the ramification, modulation and eventual dilution of the Neoclassical style in painting was furthered mainly by his pupils. François-Pascal, Baron Gérard (1770-1837) was one of the most successful, both with portraits and with mythological "history" paintings, but softer, even sentimental in comparison. His portrait of

Madame Récamier is clear evidence of a more fussy and already almost mannered style. Gérard served both republic and Empire, and then switched without difficulty to propaganda for the restored monarchy. Anne-Louis Girodet (1767-1824) was more interesting, though David disapproved of his "poetic" tendencies; these, however, appealed to Napoleon. Although he was regarded in his lifetime as a leader of the classical school, the successor of David, he is also a precursor of Romanticism (with paintings such as *Ossian receiving the generals of the Republic*, 1802, not shown; or *Atala's entombment*, 1808). Napoleon also recognized Pierre-Paul Prud'hon (1758-1823), who was not a pupil of David's, and his painting shows him an heir to Correggio rather than a Neoclassicist (David called him the Boucher of his day). The painter most successful in capturing the glamour of Napoleon in action was David's pupil and close friend Antoine-Jean, Baron Gros (see p. 78), whose high sentiment and drama established a tradition eagerly exploited by the Romantics. The true heir of David's Neoclassical style was Ingres (see p. 84), but the impact of his immensely long career came later.

DAVID (left)
Mme Récamier, 1800
The woman, the stand, the divan are arranged in space like abstract sculptures; and David, having organized and produced funerals and pageants in the Revolution, probably designed both the furniture and her gown.

GERARD (right)
Mme Récamier, 1802
Dissatisfied with David's too severe vision, removing her to the elevation of some dispassionate deity, Mme Récamier commissioned Gérard, who obliged with a portrait of ingratiating softness. It is more human, more affable, perhaps truer to the gentle, winning way of the leading hostess of the Directoire, but much less subtly individualized.

GIRODET (above)
Atala's entombment, 1808
The subject is taken from a novel by Chateaubriand. Atala had taken poison, as she was just about to break her vow of eternal chastity.

DAVID (right)
Napoleon in his study, 1812
The candles are low; the drafts of his legal code are on the table. The time is 4.13 a.m. Napoleon works while his subjects sleep.

PRUD'HON (above)
Justice and Divine Vengeance pursuing Crime, 1808
Prud'hon's allegory uses Neoclassical models from Flaxman and Canova, but these are transformed by dramatic, emotive lighting.

Neoclassical Sculpture

Sculpture could respond more satisfactorily than painting to the ideals of Neoclassicism, in the quest for the quality defined by Winckelmann as "noble simplicity and serene grandeur". Sculpture and drawing offer opportunity for the clear definition of line and contour; the sculptor could achieve a material monumentality, a most solid physical presence, removed, however, from the accidents of ephemeral mortal life by the inexpressive cool pallor of marble. The purest Neoclassical painting, such as David's in the 1780s, strained towards the condition of sculpture.

Although no sculptor emerged of a stature quite comparable to David's, the dismissal of almost all Neoclassic sculpture as cold, academic and lifeless is gravely unjust. An exception was always made for the work of Jean-Antoine Houdon (1741-1828), especially for his brilliantly vivid portrait busts, and certainly his enormous talent and superb technique were untrammelled by dogma or theory. He created a portrait gallery of those men of wit and reason whose influence was felt throughout Europe – Voltaire and Rousseau, Diderot, d'Alembert and many others. He sculpted Jefferson and Benjamin Franklin;

invited to America, he created a stately yet vital statue of George Washington. His flexibility is perhaps best apparent in his variations on the theme of the aged philosopher Voltaire.

Houdon survived the Revolution, and was even privileged to model both Napoleon and Josephine from the life. His enchanting contemporary Clodion (see vol. 2 p. 243) was not so fortunate: his erotic version of the Antique, his delicate, lively little terracottas were too Rococo in feeling for the Puritan austerities of the Revolution, which ruined his career. The sculptor who answered most nearly to Neoclassical taste and theory was the enormously successful Italian, Antonio Canova (1757-1822), born in Venice, but based in Rome from 1780. His early work in Venice had been more or less in key with contemporary French classicizing sculpture, but Rome revolutionized his ideas and his practice. His *Theseus and the Minotaur* of 1781-82 is as uncompromisingly austere as anything he was to carve in his whole career. It shows not the combat but the moment of Theseus' victory, and the idealized figure of Theseus may be an allegory of the sculptor's own triumph over his earlier style – the naturalistically treated, half-

bull, half-human Minotaur. Canova, however, always kept his roots in the world of natural appearances, beginning each day by drawing from the life, but in his finished work he sought another kind of Nature, the realization in art of the philosopher Kant's definition of Nature as "the existence of things in so far as it is determined by general laws". Thus, in perhaps his most famous work, the *Cupid and Psyche*, the idea was evolved from a rhythmic, almost abstract study in clay of the interlocking of two embracing figures, which developed into an image that is at once an idyll of young love in innocence and a distillation of ecstasy. The *Cupid and Psyche* is nevertheless more akin to Roman, or to Roman copies of Hellenistic sculpture than to Greek sculpture of the classic era: that Canova had never seen until his visit to London in 1815, when he was greatly impressed by the fifth-century sculptures from the Parthenon that Lord Elgin had bought from the Turks, where he found "the truth of nature united to the finest forms".

Canova's range and clientèle were wide, his work sought after in Bonaparte's France as in England. In the Augustinerkirche in Vienna, for the Archduchess Maria Christina, he cre-

HOUDON (right)
Denis Diderot, 1771
Houdon conveys even the wit of the observation Diderot seems to making, and has apparently caught him not only in a fleeting moment but in an habitual expression. Houdon's busts surpass even Bernini's in their sheer vivacity.

HOUDON (below)
Voltaire, 1778
The robe could be either a toga or a dressing-gown; it is a timeless foil for the *tour de force* of the head. The hands grip the chair, the body strains forward, the head turns to speak. Houdon made this study – it is in terracotta – just before Voltaire's death.

HOUDON (left)
George Washington, 1788-92
To achieve an utter fidelity, Houdon noted his sitter's features scientifically, and took measurements of his body. Washington's right hand rests on Roman *fasces* and a ploughshare, making him a modern Cincinnatus – the modest Roman farmer who saved his country – but Washington refused to be shown in classical garb.

CANOVA (below)
Cupid and Psyche, 1787-93
The statue intends neither a single nor a multiple viewpoint; in a sense, it has no viewpoint at all. It is an entirely closed image, cold and impenetrable; despite their tense vitality, *Cupid and Psyche* permit no share in the ideal union of their flawless forms. (Try as he surely will, the viewer can never see both faces at once.)

CANOVA (left)
Theseus and the Minotaur, 1781-82
The hard, smooth dullness of the marble reproduces the effect of Roman copies of Greek statuary. The self-imposed absence of expression studiously avoids the "excesses" of Bernini.

It is said that Canova had intended to represent the drama of hero and beast as they grappled – a Baroque subject – but chose instead (advised by his friend the painter Gavin Hamilton) its conclusion, so Theseus could be static, composed, ideally aloof and detached.

ated an impressively original Neoclassic development of the Baroque grandiose funeral monument. Austere in conception, it is none the less dramatic, even theatrical, and rich in a symbolism from which almost all specifically Christian reference has evaporated.

Canova's reclining figure of *Paulina Borghese as Venus Victrix* (1805-07) is the three-dimensional equivalent of David's *Madame Récamier*, but this is far more idealized and, of course, in the smoothest of marble drained of all ephemeral colour. Canova did not achieve, and would not have wished to achieve, the vivid immediacy that Houdon captured from his subjects, and portraiture was not really his *forte*. He developed, however, the convention of the nude heroic portrait – in the female *Paulina Borghese* and in an extraordinary colossal version of Napoleon (not shown). One of the earliest of these nude portraits had been by Jean-Baptiste Pigalle (1714-85) – the seated *Voltaire*, in which the philosopher's aged and shrunken body is shown with astonishing naturalism; the usual heroic portrait statue supplied a more or less realistic head with an entirely ideal torso.

The European market for sculpture was

expanding spectacularly, and continued to do so throughout the nineteenth century. The middle classes began to commission portraits, and, while the demand for grandiose funerary monuments dwindled, it was more than offset by the production of heroic statuary for public places, a celebration of heroes that found its focus in public squares and in national shrines such as St Paul's Cathedral in London or the Walhalla near Regensburg.

The demand was answered by a vigorous breed of sculptors: the heroic mode seemed to have a special attraction for artists from the north, though they found their inspiration in classical Rome, and often settled there for life. The most talented and successful of Canova's heirs was Bertel Thorvaldsen (1770-1844), born in Copenhagen but working in Rome from 1796 to 1838, and patronized by a clientèle as international as Canova's. He took Canova's style towards an even more austere classical simplicity, shedding all last traces of Baroque movement. Gottfried Schadow (1764-1850), a sculptor of very great technical virtuosity, worked in his native Berlin after a spell in Rome, and John Flaxman (see over) had an extended stay in Rome, 1787-94.

THORVALDSEN (above)
Hebe, 1806
Thorvaldsen's goddess of youth emulates classical Greek sculpture, but rejects the columnar folds and the austerity, for instance, of the Erechtheion caryatids (see vol. 2 p. 39): the marble glistens, the contours are luxuriously full and soft.

CANOVA (left)
Paulina Borghese as Venus Victrix, 1805-07
Napoleon's sister poses as the goddess whom Paris judged the fairest, to whom he awarded the apple. It is an allegorical portrait, so Canova had justification for generalizing her features. The virtuoso realism of the Grecian couch on which she lies rivals Bernini's.

SCHADOW (left)
Field-Marshal Blücher, 1815-19
Schadow knew the work of both Canova and Houdon, and preferred Houdon. His statue of the Prussian commander at Waterloo is individual, and imposing, but none too classicizing. Schadow draped a lion-skin over Blücher's otherwise modern costume only at the insistence of Goethe.

PIGALLE (below)
Voltaire, 1770-76
The vigorous head, with its distant gaze fastened on intellectual problems, contrasts with the frailty and rottenness of the body. When exhibited, the statue was found eccentric, and it seems a deliberate mockery of the heroic male nude.

CANOVA (above)
Sketch for *Cupid and Psyche*, 1787
Canova's *bozzetto* reveals him intent from the start on the formal currents that bind his figures together. There is no question of an initial spontaneity the finished work has lost.

CANOVA (right)
Monument to Archduchess Maria Christina, c. 1805
Piety bears the ashes into the open dark door of the tomb, followed by figures moving in the slow flow of an elegiac rhythm. By the lion of Fortitude leans the genius of Mourning.

Neoclassics and Romantics in England

The historians' search for a satisfactory definition of Romanticism in the visual arts still continues unresolved. The confusion arises because, as Baudelaire observed, Romanticism is precisely situated neither in an artist's style nor in his subject matter, but in himself – an inconstant factor. Romanticism continues the high seriousness of Neoclassicism, but tends both to intensify it and to widen its scope, often looking more closely at Nature – whether concentrating on its violent or peaceful aspects – and plunging into politics, feelings and issues of the day; sometimes altogether misfiring under the strain of its ambitions. Style and subject matter are determined by individual taste or principle, for Romanticism was never a coherent movement (coherence is hardly a Romantic concept); nor perhaps was classicism, but the fundamental difference between the Romantic and the classicist is surely that, for the latter, the motive force is rational, while for the Romantic it is emotional.

Goethe, the youthful exponent of Romanticism in Germany, the author of the best-selling early Romantic novel *The Sorrows of Young Werther* (1774), developed into the elder statesman of European culture, for whom classicism was health and Romanticism sickness. In France, Delacroix, in whom Baudelaire discerned the archetypal Romantic painter, himself maintained sturdily (if with Romantic passion) that he was a pure classicist. In England, John Flaxman (1755-1826), the draughtsman and sculptor whose outline drawings were acclaimed throughout Europe as capturing the very essence of classical form, was the friend and the exact contemporary of William Blake (1757-1827), a pivotal figure in any definition of Romantic art.

Flaxman's illustrations to Homer, precise, economic, faultlessly balanced, are in a sense the *ne plus ultra* of Neoclassicism, realizing the ultimate reduction to stark, pure outline. But Flaxman also illustrated Aeschylus and Dante, both poets of vision, and Blake again illustrated Dante, in the same linear terms, though with rather different effect.

The middle ground between classicism and Romanticism was occupied by the Swiss-born Henry Fuseli (or Füssli, 1741-1825). His initial interests were literary, religious and radically political, but he developed an early enthusiasm for the writings of Winckelmann. In 1765, having moved to London, he trans-

lated Winckelmann, but next year, in Paris, met the Romantic philosopher Jean-Jacques Rousseau. Having settled for a career as a painter, he learnt his craft in Rome between 1770 and 1778, and there discarded Mengs' cool interpretation of Winckelmann's Neoclassicism for an exaggerated version of Michelangelo's style. His famous wash-drawing of *The artist moved by the grandeur of ancient ruins* (1778-79) is typical of his emphatic manner – stressing the subjective emotion of the artist rather than any objective antique quality in the colossal fragments. It also illustrates the inherent danger of the emotional interpretation – pushing the sublime to the brink of the ridiculous, and drama into melodrama. Fuseli subsequently drew not only on the Antique, but also on Milton, Teutonic legend and Shakespeare. In works such as his sensational *Nightmare* he exploited subject matter that is intrinsically Romantic, and his strangely perverse erotic visions of sinister women have excited psychoanalytical attention. Yet his compositions remained formally within Neoclassical conventions; although his technique and execution were not adequate to fulfil the originality of his imag-

FLAXMAN (above)
Illustration to the *Iliad: Princes all Hail!*, 1795
Agamemnon sent Ulysses to placate Achilles, having taken his prize. Flaxman emulates the purity of an Athenian black-figure vase.

BLAKE (below)
Newton, 1795
A silhouette of classical beauty and ideal anatomy (derived from a figure on the Sistine Chapel ceiling), Newton the scientist was for Blake an oppressor who attempted to quantify life with a pair of dividers. This is a Romantic view; beside it Flaxman's vision of mental torment (right) lacks emotional power, for all that the stylistic conventions are so similar.

BLAKE (below)
The good and evil angels struggling for the possession of a child, 1795
Orc (Evil), despite his destructive nature, also represents pure energy (indicated by the flames)

vital to man's salvation; Los (Good) is in a fallen state, since he has fettered Orc in a fit of jealousy. Blake parades the schizoid crisis of his Romantic philosophy; his idealized forms are strangely Puritan.

FLAXMAN (above)
Illustration to Aeschylus' *The Furies*, 1795
Orestes, having killed his mother, Clytemnestra, in revenge for his father's death at her hand, was then pursued by the Furies.

FLAXMAN (below)
Monument to Sophia Hoare, 1821
Though Flaxman executed several large-scale works, smaller commissions found him at his best. Christian sentiment emerges despite so much classical detailing.

ination, his distortions and linear attenuations had a considerable effect on the more deeply committed and spiritual art of Blake.

In official eyes, Blake was an eccentric, even thought by some to be mad. He was certainly a loner, a supreme example even among the Romantics of the visionary, the individualist, the radical. He was scornful of the official establishment of art, but he had been a fellow-student with Flaxman at the Academy schools and his earliest work was in the Neoclassic mode, while his enduring belief in an art of shadowless contour was strengthened by training as an engraver. From these beginnings, however, he developed his own style and technique with which to express his vision. Blake is unique in English art in being both a major poet and a major artist: much of his work consists of engraved hand-coloured books in which verse was integrated with illustration, rather as in medieval illuminated manuscripts. In his painting, as in his poetry, he developed a new, personal, exaltedly unearthly and convolutedly obscure mythology, entirely opposed to the cool reasonableness of the age of sensibility. Blake never travelled abroad, but championed revolution, whether in America

or France. He preached enthusiasm and excess. His authority was his own inspiration, his inner eye. But although he abandoned perspective and illusionism, his inner eye could formulate its vision only through the experience of his outer eye, and his style reflects engravings of Michelangelo – perhaps also the influence of the Gothic ogee curve.

Though the personal and intuitive basis of Blake's work was prophetic of the course modern art was to pursue, he was too individual to inspire a great movement. Nevertheless, one rather exceptional aspect of his work founded a tradition that has been fruitful ever since. The elegiac pastoral vision of a series of celebrated minute woodcuts for a translation of Virgil's *Eclogues* (the woodcut reproduced here is more or less actual size) became a source notably for Samuel Palmer (1805-81), during a brief period of spiritual inspiration and dedication in the 1820s. Palmer's early evocations of the landscape about the village of Shoreham in Kent are almost hymns of contemplation and adoration, as if he had rediscovered there the Garden of Eden before the Fall – certainly before the Industrial Revolution.

FUSELI (above)
The artist moved by the grandeur of ancient ruins, 1778-79
Fuseli's adulation of the Antique found expression in a dynamic, exaggerated, muscular figure style based on Michelangelo's work in the Sistine Chapel, though tempered by a measure of Mannerist attenuation.

BLAKE (below)
The circle of the lustful, from Dante's *Inferno,* Canto V, *c.* 1824.
Tales involving infraction of the conventional sexual code – like Dante's of Paolo and Francesca – frequently appealed to the Romantics. Blake depicts the circle of the damned adulterers as a whirl of bliss, with the two young lovers united forever in a halo of bright light.

FUSELI (left)
The nightmare, 1781
Fuseli's picture made his name when exhibited at the Royal Academy in 1782. It is a fantasy of rape, representing oppressively

the terror of the young girl. The horse's head thrusting through the heavy curtains is a typically Romantic symbol of savage power. Fuseli habitually resorted to violent chiaroscuro.

BLAKE (above)
Thenot under a fruit tree, 1821
Palmer called these woodcuts "Visions of little dells, and nooks, and corners of Paradise ... the exquisitest pitch of intense poetry".

PALMER (below)
Early morning, 1825
The scene is recorded with minute attention to natural detail – typical of Palmer's Shoreham period: he saw Nature as an expression of the divinity of its creator.

Francisco de Goya

jaunty angle suggests the
dandy: the image was etched
the year before Goya was
made First Court Painter.

After the splendours of the seventeenth century – the art of Velazquez, Ribera, Zurbarán
and Murillo – the Spanish seemed content to
adopt current international styles without injecting much originality. Close connections
with Italy were maintained through the Spanish dominion of Naples, and major Italian
artists were imported by the Spanish court and
the Church, the principal patrons. Luca Giordano, in Spain 1692-1702, deployed Baroque
rhetoric across the ceilings of the Escorial; the
Venetian Amigoni and the brilliant Neapolitan
painter Giaquinto consolidated late Italian
Baroque in Spain in decorations for the Palace
of the Orient in Madrid after 1734. Both were
appointed court painters, and helped in 1751-
52 to set up the Academy of San Fernando,
which did much to establish artistic standards
and status in Spain. Giambattista Tiepolo
worked in Spain from 1762 to 1770, and the
Neoclassicist Anton Raffael Mengs came with
Charles III from Naples in 1761. The French
Rococo style had been acclimatized in Spain
when the crown had passed in 1700 to the
Bourbon grandson of Louis XIV, Philip V.

Francisco de Goya y Lucientes (1746-1828),
in his beginnings, practised in most of these

varying traditions. Born and trained in Saragossa, then the second city in Spain, he was
soon attracted to Madrid, the political and
cultural capital under the centralizing policy of
Charles III. He did not settle there, however,
until 1773: his initial attempts to win a scholarship at the Academy failed, and in 1770-71 he
was in Italy (notably in Rome and Parma). His
first major commission was for a series of
frescos for the church of Nuestra Señora del
Pilar in Saragossa, which are fully Baroque,
and already show the bold colours and free
handling that were to characterize his later
work. In Rome he had met Mengs, who in
Spain secured him employment designing
cartoons for tapestries to hang in the royal
palaces. Some of these are as lightly frivolous
as diversions by Domenico Tiepolo.

In Madrid from 1773, Goya rapidly became
established as a designer of decorations, as a
virtuoso of religious frescos and as a portraitist. He was prosperous, friendly with a
liberal intellectual set, sympathetic to the ideas
of the Enlightenment, but apparently unmoved by the storms of Revolution raging in
France. He was a familiar in the highest
circles, and became, according to a legend that

might have rivalled Luca
Giordano. He had learnt his
technique in Italy, and the
conception and design echo
Italian example – a double
tier of figures rises in a
vortex against skies no less
luminous than Tiepolo's.

is by no means improbable, the lover of one of the grandest ladies in the land, the Duchess of Alba. The elegance of his several portraits of the Duchess may recall Gainsborough's fluency and lyricism, but their originality is startling even now. The portrait of 1797 shows the Duchess in widow's weeds, wearing rings inscribed *Alba* and *Goya*, pointing with one forefinger to the ground at her feet, where, if you look closely, is written *Goya Solo* (only Goya). The riddle is Goya's own indeed. The lady is imperious, haughty, and commands attention, almost crackling with static electricity. In 1799, after 13 years in the King's service, Goya was created First Court Painter, the highest artistic honour in Spain.

The variety of Goya's art in the years of his prime is inexhaustible. The famous pair of *Majas*, naked and clothed, of about 1802-05, are the most delightful, untroubled celebration of the erotic in all his work. *Maja* is untranslatable: it refers to the dandy cult of Madrid's new proletariat, who dressed with a gypsy flamboyance and an independent pride which it became fashionable on occasions for aristocrats to imitate. Goya drew on this source again for his *Two majas on a balcony*, where the

combination of beauty, coquetry and the sinister is unsurpassed.

Both versions of the *Maja* belonged to, and were possibly painted for, the all-powerful Manuel de Godoy, Prime Minister, Generalissimo of land and sea forces, and lover of the Queen. Goya painted him in 1801 in a design that is both unorthodox and grandly, even pompously, formal. Goya's independence, his disregard of the standard European portrait conventions, is evident again in his extraordinary life-size group, *Charles IV and his family* (1800). The royal family seems curiously gauche in the dazzling plumage of their brilliantly painted costumes – this is the most eccentric state portrait ever painted by an appointed painter to a crown. Although most observers have seen it as mordant satire, the King himself appears to have been pleased.

The problem of Goya's loyalties is a difficult one. During the French occupation, 1808-12, he painted the French dignitaries. When Madrid was liberated in 1812, he had almost finished an equestrian portrait of Joseph Bonaparte, on which he then substituted the head of the liberator, the Duke of Wellington. His superb and appalling vision of the mass-

acre by the French of Madrid citizens on May 3rd, 1808, painted in 1814, seems less a patriotic war memorial than an expression of rage at the horror of man's inhumanity; and towards the close of his long life, in 1824, when Spain was subjected to a repressive regime, he withdrew in self-imposed exile to France, where he died four years later.

The dichotomy in Goya's temperament, the black pessimism that produced the "Black Paintings", had emerged long before, but not in public. The glamorous world of the distinguished and the court seems to have ceased to intrigue him after 1802, when the Duchess of Alba died. Yet the event that is generally thought to have confirmed and released his obsession with the horrific is the severe illness that left him stone deaf in 1793. Devils had appeared in his work even previously, and *Los Caprichos* of 1799, even *The Disasters of War* (though that series was not published in Goya's lifetime) – etchings in which Goya's obsession with the macabre is clearly present – could still be accepted as social satire. The revelation of the "Black Paintings" and allied works such as *The colossus* (see over) of his later years did not come until well after his death.

GOYA (above)
Don Manuel de Godoy, 1801
The 35-year-old supremo leans back in a leisurely pose, gloriously attired, surrounded by the panoply of a military commander, against a dark sky that is seemingly about to erupt with the explosion of war. He seems formidably self-satisfied, gazing beyond the furled standard with an almost cruel delight at some private pleasure.

GOYA (left)
Two majas on a balcony,
c. 1800-14
Like the nude and clothed *Majas*, these girls exude confidence in their gaudy appeal, and flirt with the spectator across the iron balcony. Yet, though they disregard the shrouded men behind them, they are caged.

GOYA (above)
Charles IV and his family,
1800
Replying to Velazquez's "*Las Meninas*" (see vol. 2 p.210), Goya has included himself (dark) on the left; the Queen's uplifted jaw recalls the earlier Infanta's. There is a story that Goya refused to paint one of the princesses full-face as he found her impossibly plain.

GOYA (left)
May 3rd, 1808, 1814
The Spanish insurgents are driven in a seemingly endless stream towards the pool of light and blood in front of the lethal phalanx of firing French soldiers.

Goya: The Colossus

Goya painted *The colossus* (originally called *The giant*) in the years 1808-12, that is in the period when Spain took the full brunt of the Napoleonic Wars for the first time. Character-istically enigmatic and mysterious as the image is, there are grounds for thinking it as much a reflection on war as his famous etchings, *The Disasters of War*, the first of which date from about 1810. Lines from a poem by Juan Arriaza about the wars have been identified as a possible stimulus for Goya's image: "On a height above yonder cavernous amphitheatre a pale colossus rises, caught by the fiery light of the setting sun; the Pyrenees are a humble plinth for his gigantic limbs." *The colossus* may represent the emergent spirit of a defiant Spain against French invasion, but, if so, the people in the picture do not seem confident of success. A related mezzotint (not shown) of a giant seated solitary on a low horizon, brood-ing, dates from about the same period or rather later. Otherwise *The colossus* must speak for itself. The painting is not physically colossal (some 1.5 metres (5ft) high), but its impact certainly is, achieved by the dramatic clash of opposing scales and values. Probably, as in so much of Goya's work, it is more a general, non-partisan statement on the human condition, an allegory of human impotence.

In a famous plate in the series of etchings *Los Caprichos* (or Phantasmagoria, 1796-98), there is a similar clash of reality and surreality. The artist is seen slumped in sleep, and surely nightmare, with a host of bat-winged monsters battering at him. A grave illness in 1793 had left Goya virtually stone deaf; turned inwards by the consequent isolation upon the tumult of his own mind, he became increasingly ob-sessed with the spectres that thronged his imagination. *The Disasters of War*, in which the most appalling miseries and tortures that man can inflict on man are vividly and ruth-lessly rendered, conveys not so much com-passion or anger or patriotic fervour as an appalled fascination and a resigned horror: *This is how it is*, read several captions. But then the plate showing a man impaled on a splin-tered tree-trunk, his arms severed, has the laconic subscription: *This is worse*.

Goya's addiction to the abnormal and vio-lent expressed itself elsewhere, in his scenes of asylums, of religious flagellants, of witchcraft. The accumulating agony and exhaustion of Goya's inner world are mirrored vividly in a late *Self-portrait* showing the artist in the arms of the doctor who nursed him during a second crucial illness in 1819, with omnipresent de-monic figures hovering in the murk of the background. The last manifestation of his morbid obsessions was the famous "Black Paintings" Goya concocted to adorn the in-teriors of his own house on his retirement. To be condemned to live surrounded by these paintings would be a fearsome sentence, but Goya chose as it were to paper his house with them. Painted very broadly, often with the palette knife rather than the brush, in dark and sombre tones, they closely anticipate in their mood and hideous violence the savage pes-simism of twentieth-century Expressionism. Goya's genius was recognized again in the age of Manet and Baudelaire, but his "Black Paintings" appeal specifically to our own.

GOYA
The colossus, 1808-12
The naked colossus is from
one world, the scattering,
running figures in the foreground belong to our puny
planet (only a donkey is unmoved by the panic). Yet the
giant's threat is directed not
overtly against the men and
women below, but against
a force, presumably on his
own scale, out of view on
the left. Superhuman forces
engaged in their own titanic
conflict disrupt and destroy
ordinary people's existence
almost haphazardly. Painted
in a very free technique,
the giant looms upward
phantom-like through cloud,
while the fleeing men and
animals are shaped more
solidly in a swift impasto.

Romantic Landscape in Britain and America

Sir Joshua Reynolds had asserted firmly that landscape was a secondary form of art, inevitably subordinate to the painting of ideal or heroic subjects. Yet within 20 years of his death both Constable (see over) and Turner (see p. 72) were working irresistibly towards the establishment of landscape as the most characteristic achievement of English art.

The changing climate of thought and sentiment reflected the increasing popularity of "back-to-Nature" movements, and the influence of Jean-Jacques Rousseau and of the English Lake poets. The growing fashion for Picturesque tourism, practising a conscious, often rather self-conscious, appreciation of the real countryside, went hand in hand with an increasing demand for paintings and engravings of it. Favourite sites for expeditions and sketchings were the "wilder" regions of Britain – the Lake District and the Welsh mountains – and ruins romantically situated on deserted moors or uninhabited hills.

Subject matter that is explicitly Romantic had been exploited by Wright of Derby – a delight in mysterious moonlight or in volcanic eruptions, even in incandescent visions of the factories of the Industrial Revolution. A French immigrant, the brilliantly professional Philippe Jacques de Loutherbourg (1740-1812) ranged, like Wright, from the Picturesque to the Sublime; in 1781 he exhibited his Eidophusikon, in which he mounted the drama of Nature on the stage – views of natural scenery subjected, by means of artificial lighting and sound effects, to varying effects of sun, storm and lightning. John Martin (1789-1854) developed a strong taste for spectacular melodrama, turning from sensitive landscapes in a traditional manner to apocalyptic visions of lurid plains, canyons and mountains, and gigantic temples of desolation; beneath, minute figures act out episodes from the Bible or from Milton. These explosions of the imagination became widely known in mezzotint.

Meanwhile, however, a relatively realistic tradition, depending directly on Netherlandish example, had persisted; it bore fruit in England at the close of the eighteenth century in the provincial Norwich school, headed by John Crome (1768-1821). His masterpiece, *The Poringland oak*, of about 1818, catches a local, rural subject with all the freshness of a Hobbema: unostentatious, positively ordinary, it seems in hindsight a staging-post to the meditations of the Barbizon school. Crome's younger colleague John Sell Cotman (1782-1842) was of more obvious originality, a master who extracted simplified but bold patterns from the natural landscape.

Cotman's finest work was in watercolour, developing a tradition by then firmly rooted throughout the country, with a wide market in both the aristocratic and middle classes. By the end of the eighteenth century, some skill in draughtsmanship was part of a gentleman's education, and most of the professional watercolourists were also drawing-masters. Much of their work was topographical, but watercolour was also used by painters with aspirations to the Sublime, above all John Robert Cozens (1752-97). His father, Alexander Cozens (c. 1717-86; not shown), had insisted both on working from Nature and on the need for originality in composition. To teach the latter, he published a system based on the idea of elaborating a landscape design from random abstract blots (more or less as Leonardo da Vinci had once suggested). His son evolved, though still in the studio, dreaming visions of Italy or the Alps – Constable was to call him "the greatest genius that ever touched land-

LOUTHERBOURG (above)
Coalbrookdale by night, 1801
The "dark satanic mills" of industry were for a short time the objects of awe and Romantic wonder. Far from provoking dismay at their intrusion into a once lovely valley, these Shropshire furnaces were found "sublime". Loutherbourg later described Coalbrookdale as "worthy of a visit from the admirer of romantic scenery" – an extension of the standard cliff and crag.

CROME (above)
The Poringland oak, c. 1818
Continuing traditions of landscape established by the Dutch, Crome chose a view without obvious drama. Nature herself is found to be a subject of intrinsic worth, honestly painted, not transformed, as by Wilson, into a Picturesque glory, nor infused with Romanticism.

JOHN ROBERT COZENS (above)
Lake Nemi, c. 1778-79
A muted blue-grey tonality characterizes Cozens' Grand Tour watercolours, and a melancholy, thoroughly romantic atmosphere his image of the famous lake near Rome. He made exact topographical notations at the site and then perfected his painting in the studio.

MARTIN (above)
Joshua commanding the sun to stand still, 1816
Martin's paintings are in the tradition of Salvator Rosa, the heroic landscape overwhelming the figures. They offered nothing new in the interpretation of Nature on canvas – they were primarily literary in inspiration – but fascinated a large public in England, France and America.

COTMAN (right)
Greta Bridge, 1805
From relatively simple views Cotman created watercolours of quiet dignity in a unique style, displaying a superb precision of brushwork and facility of design. By his own account, he studied colouring from Nature. He never excelled the masterpieces of his youth, painted on tours in northern Britain between 1803 and 1805.

scape" – "Cozens is all poetry". The brief-lived Thomas Girtin (1775-1802), the friend and fellow-student of Turner, made important technical innovations in watercolour, abandoning the usual practice of establishing the design initially in monochrome. He used a rough off-white paper, on which he spread brilliantly controlled washes, allied with what was at times stippling in pure colours. The result was a solidity and vibrancy that enabled watercolour to rival oil-painting.

The American vision of landscape took some time to shake European blinkers from its

eyes. Washington Allston (1779-1843) spent long periods in Europe, studying with Benjamin West from 1801 to 1808. A friend of the poet Coleridge, he took an essentially Romantic stance – he likened painting to music and sought to express subjective qualities of mood in landscape, and of personality in portraiture. John Martin's emphasis on the confrontation of the human with the divine influenced much of Allston's later landscape, but from his more subtly colouristic style he is often called "the American Titian".

A more specific attachment to the American

genius of the American place was sought by later painters associated with the "Hudson River school". The greatest of them, Thomas Cole (1801-48), observed that "the painter of American scenery has, indeed, privileges superior to any other; all Nature here is new to art". Although preconceived European formulae affected their approach, and some painters tended to introduce strong moral or didactic themes, the Hudson River school at times produced images of an intensity both new and startling – for instance Cole's *Sunny morning on the Hudson River* of about 1821. The most famous work of the leading theorist of the school, Asher B. Durand (1796-1886), *Kindred spirits*, depicts Cole communing with Nature on a ledge over a rocky torrent.

The Hudson River school approach persisted through the nineteenth century, though moving in general away (and happily so) from more grandiose, moralizing, themes towards pure landscape. Several painters developed a delightful variation, genre subjects in landscape, which often reflected the more idyllic side of the ever-advancing western frontier – for instance, *Fur traders descending the Missouri* by George Caleb Bingham (1811-79).

GIRTIN (right)
Kirkstall Abbey, c. 1800
The ruins of the Cistercian Abbey are not recorded in the interests of antiquarian topography, though Girtin has evoked the delicacy of the Gothic tracery and the crumble of old stonework. The Yorkshire countryside and its weather are the real subject of the watercolour. Girtin's expressive, broad handling fully realizes the Romantic potential of the landscape; his work was important in establishing the place of watercolour in British painting. Turner said: "If Tom Girtin had lived, I should have starved."

ALLSTON (left)
Moonlit landscape, 1819
The mood of a Gothic novel (Allston had once attempted to write one) seems to infect his subject. It is invested with haunting tensions, in a fascination for the effects of supernatural forces.

DURAND (right)
Kindred spirits, 1849
Admiring the scenery in a Catskill glen, the two men (Thomas Cole and the poet William Cullen Bryant) create a typically Romantic image, wanderers or solitary figures dwarfed by Nature. Durand's training as an engraver is evident in the unsoftened detail and hard linear technique of the work.

COLE (right)
Sunny morning on the Hudson River, c. 1827
One of the first artists in America to devote himself wholly to landscape, Cole travelled from New York along the Hudson in search of inspiring scenery. The European tradition shows in the use of sunlight to give life to the wooded hills, and in the *repoussoir,* the foreground focus of rock and tree, leading the eye into the distance towards the plain. The Hudson River painters also ranged into the Catskill Mountains of New York and the White Mountains of New Hampshire.

BINGHAM (above)
Fur traders descending the Missouri, 1845
The enchanted stillness of the river belies the wildness of the country, where the

traders bartered with the Indians for furs. There is a Chinese delicacy in the pale tones and the figures of the French trader and his half-breed son in their boat.

Constable: The White Horse

In late 1819 John Constable (1776-1837) was at last elected an Associate of the Royal Academy and was able to sign his latest work, now known as *"The White Horse"*, as A.R.A. The painting remained one of the artist's favourites throughout his life, and in 1829 he bought it back from its first buyer. When exhibited in 1819, it had been greeted with enthusiasm by the critics – "what a grasp of everything beautiful in rural scenery", wrote one, predicting that "this young artist" would soon be at the top of his profession. The "young artist", however, was already 42, and success was coming late. Full membership of the Academy came only in 1829, after the most fruitful decade of his life had come to a close with the death of his wife in 1828, and he himself died nine years later.

Constable had been a slow starter. Son of a Suffolk mill-owner of some substance, he began full training at the Royal Academy schools in London when already 23. Although he always deplored the imitation by artists of earlier painters, he loved and often copied them, Claude as well as Gainsborough, though his affinity to the Dutch masters, to Ruisdael and Hobbema, is perhaps greater.

Constable insisted that the essential source for any original painter must be Nature itself, and that there was no alternative to drawing directly from Nature. His conviction was the foundation of his art, and of his own highly personal style, which became mature only by about 1810, when he was in his 30s. It did not mean that all his work was done in the open air, but he made endless studies, in pencil, in watercolour or in brilliantly free impressions in oil on paper or small wood panels, directly from his subject. Afterwards he used their material in building up his large compositions (what he called his "six-footers"), and for the famous *Haywain*, begun in 1821, he worked through a whole series of compositional variations, from a miniature scale to sketches equal in size to the finished painting. It was an experimental, pragmatic process, and the interrelationship of all these variations is often unclear, but Constable was adamant (though posterity does not always agree) that the finished painting was the climax of the process.

His longing was always to distil the eternal from the ephemeral, and to reveal what he loved to call the chiaroscuro in Nature, the interlocking harmony of the elements. Constable knew Wordsworth, whose poetry answered his painting, and quoted a phrase of his when describing his wish to make monumental "one brief moment caught from fleeting time". Empathy with Nature in all its moods informed them both, though Constable found his inspiration in the domestic, man-made landscapes of his native Suffolk, of Hampstead Heath or in the beaches of Brighton, rather than in the mountains and lakes Wordsworth loved. If there is ever an awesome quality in Constable's work it is in the skies, and in the

CONSTABLE (above)
Oil-sketch for *"The White Horse"*, c. 1819
Constable made a full-scale study in oil before painting his Academy entry – a procedure he later elaborated. This sketch corresponds less closely to the finished work than the several oil-studies for the later *Haywain*, and less closely also to prior studies made from Nature.

CONSTABLE (left)
"The White Horse", 1819
The first of Constable's "six-footers" – huge works devoted to mundane rustic scenes – the picture compelled immediate attention, if only for its size: such a humble subject had never before been presented on such an heroic scale. It was shown under the title *A scene on the river Stour*, "a placid representation of a serene, grey morning, summer". The barge-horse is being ferried across the river between Flatford and Dedham in Suffolk at a point where a tributary interrupted the towpath.

CONSTABLE (left)
Clouds, Sept. 5th, 1822
Constable's series of cloud studies typifies his almost scientific attempt to capture permanently the momentary in Nature.

CONSTABLE (above)
Pencil sketch, 1814
Constable compiled his oils from swift annotations in pencil or watercolour – this became an ingredient of *"The White Horse"*.

CONSTABLE (left)
The haywain, 1821
Constable's view of the house of a close friend, on the Stour near Flatford Mill, was distilled from long acquaintance, from studies made over many years, proving his heartfelt attachment to the scene. His emotional involvement with landscape was intense: he wrote: "The sound of water escaping from milldams, etc., willows, old rotten planks, slimy posts, and brickwork – I love such things. . . . Painting with me is but another word for feeling." The lavish scattering of highlights, "Constable's snow", which give vibrancy to the work, puzzled contemporaries.

mood created by qualities of light – as in the small watercolour of *Stonehenge* with its double rainbow. Constable's love of Nature was both intense and true and faithful: he wrote: "Painting is a science and should be pursued as an enquiry into the laws of Nature". His "experiments" included studies of types of cloud formations, and his results were attempts to establish, in free, swift, open brushwork, the equivalent on canvas of English sunlight running through moist air, the wind rustling foliage and wimpling the water.

Constable's deepest impact, and his warmest reception, was in fact in France. *The haywain* was singled out by Géricault at the Academy in 1821 and in 1824 French critics acclaimed his work at the Paris Salon. Delacroix, entranced by Constable's light aerial key, reworked the background of his *Massacre at Chios* (see p. 81), and Constable's poetry of the ordinary later had effect on the rural meditations of the Barbizon school.

CONSTABLE (right)
Stonehenge, 1836
Ever more vigorous and masterly effects are evident in Constable's later works, especially in this watercolour view of the inherently dramatic "Druidic" megaliths of Stonehenge. A gleaming sky highlights the grey stones, revealing the artist's aim "to give 'to one brief moment caught from fleeting time' a lasting and sober existence, and to render permanent many of these splendid but evanescent exhibitions, which are ever occurring in the changes of external Nature".

Turner: Dawn after the Wreck

The sea, stretching to the horizon and beyond, illimitable as the skies above, is one of the elemental images of Romanticism. It compelled many artists to paint it, yet remained essentially indefinable – seeming, in an evening calm, to suggest a peace beyond understanding, but in storm one of the most formidable agents of inhuman, destructive power in Nature. The career of Joseph Mallord William Turner (1775-1851) was a long one, but through almost all of it he was obsessed by the sea in all its moods, though most of all by its more violent aspects.

Dawn after the wreck is a watercolour painted with the full freedom of Turner's later years, probably about 1840. It belonged originally to a friend, the Rev. Kingsley, but it may well have started as one of what he called his "beginnings", and not necessarily with the idea of being worked up into a "finished" picture for framing and hanging on a wall. Turner kept sketchbooks all his life (all left to the nation, amongst 19,000 or so watercolours, and now in the British Museum). In the later books, hundreds of colour sketches record atmospheric effects, many of which may read to the modern eye as pure abstracts; already in 1799 he told a colleague he had "no settled process", but "drove the colours about till he had expressed the idea in his mind". *Dawn after the wreck* may well have started with

Turner snatching at an effect of turbulence of light and colour and painting very fast, perhaps with the aid of the sharp end of the brush, even fingers. The stability of the composition hangs on the strong yet disturbed horizontal of the horizon, transfixed by the tremulous reflection suspended from the frail sickle of the new moon, which together with the flecks of cloud defines the sky as sky. Then the addition of the title spelled out the Romantic desolation; the sea, the victorious destroyer, subsides, passion all but spent. And possibly after that came the shivering dog with its almost audible howl of mourning.

Turner was very precocious. He started traditionally, as a travelling topographical draughtsman and watercolourist. He exhibited *Tintern Abbey*, a drawing of literal linear accuracy and great accomplishment, in the Royal Academy in 1795, when he was only 20. Unlike Constable, he was able to make himself acceptable to the art establishment and public very early: he was a full Academician by 1802 – a recognition denied Constable, born one year later, until 1829. Gradually, however, as he developed towards an ever greater freedom, his work began to mystify most people. His later pictures were called "fantastic puzzles", but were nonetheless based on the faithful observation of Nature. The first of his famous vortex compositions, *Snowstorm: Hannibal*

TURNER (above): *Dawn after the wreck, c.*1840

TURNER (above)
*Tintern Abbey, c.*1795
Together with Girtin, Turner had copied watercolours by John Robert Cozens – *Tintern Abbey*
reflects the influence of Cozens' wistful tonalities. Such Picturesque views contributed significantly to Turner's income, and first made him known abroad.

TURNER (left)
The slave-ship, 1840
Turner reacted emotionally
to a recent scandal in which
a slave-ship's captain had
thrown overboard those of
his "cargo" dying of fever.

TURNER (below)
*Snowstorm: Hannibal
crossing the Alps*, 1812
Turner attempted to show
the truth of natural fury,
rather than exaggerating
its scale, like John Martin.

TURNER (above)
*The Thames near Walton
Bridge, c.* 1807
Turner seldom sketched
in oil in the open air. This
exception may pre-empt
innovations by Constable.

TURNER (below)
*Sun rising through vapour:
fishermen cleaning and
selling fish*, 1807
The seascapes and harbour
scenes of Cuyp and van de
Velde challenged Turner at
the beginning of his career.
Determined not just to rival
but to excel these masters,
he adopted similar subject
matter, but introduced his
own concern with elusive
effects of natural light.

TURNER (above)
*Venice: S. Giorgio
Maggiore*, 1819
Turner's first visit to Italy
in 1819 was a revelation of
light and colour, a decisive
event in his career. The
freedom of these water-
colours indicates a direct
and revolutionary response
to the haunting, luminous
atmospherics of Venice,
held in pure transparent
tints on a white ground.

crossing the Alps, 1812, was based on a violent
storm he had witnessed two years before in
Yorkshire. In an overarching, overwhelming
paroxysm, Nature rears in all its blind force, in
the biting fury and flurry of snow, cloud and
ice. At the other extreme, his *Burning of the
Houses of Parliament* (1835; not shown) shows
light and fire threatening to consume not only
the centre of Government but the earth and
water as well. Gradually his basic theme
became light itself, in an almost Shiva-like
capacity as creator and destroyer – creator, by
revealing the physical world, destroyer, by
dissolving solid form in luminous veils of
colour. Already in 1816 the writer Hazlitt
complained that Turner's paintings were "representations not properly of the objects of
Nature as of the medium through which they
were seen". It was part of Turner's achievement successfully to transpose into oils the
technique of watercolour, with all its lightness
and fluency, and ability to capture the most
fleeting, evanescent atmospheric effects.

Though the public found such works eccentric ("pictures of nothing, and very like it"),
Turner painted a whole series of pictures,
spread over many years, in which he self-
consciously and provocatively allied himself to
the European tradition, challenging Claude
and Poussin, Cuyp and van de Velde, Wilson,
even Titian, Veronese and Rembrandt. In

paintings such as *The slave-ship*, 1840, he
evoked marine catastrophe in terms surpassing
Géricault's *Raft of the Medusa* (see p. 79) –
here the tormented seas are laced with human
blood. In contrast, his paintings (not shown) of
Norham Castle, made in the early 1840s, are
rich with a radiant serenity, and make a
fascinating comparison with the very similar
viewpoints he had selected at the same site in
the late 1790s: these early watercolours had
been romantic enough, but in the late full-scale
oils the subject is dissolved into insubstantial
mists of glowing, shimmering colour, in which
castle or cattle are mere accents subsumed into
emanations of light.

In his lifetime Turner was recognized as a
genius who might be criticized but not denied,
and in John Ruskin (1819-1900) he found a
sympathetic critic and panegyrist of genius. In
Modern Painters, 1843, Ruskin placed Turner,
as the artist who could most stirringly and
truthfully measure the moods of Nature, at the
culmination of a tradition stemming from
Dürer and the Venetian colourists. Turner and
Constable dominated the subsequent course of
landscape in England, and both were acclaimed in France, though Turner rather later.
The Impressionists took respectful note, if
with reservations; and his work has continued
to have reverberations, not least in the abstract
painting of the later twentieth century.

German and Scandinavian Romanticism

After the magnificent originality of Dürer, Holbein, Grünewald, no outstanding Germanic genius in painting or sculpture had emerged. The great German and Austrian Baroque and Rococo decorators had worked with brilliant virtuosity in an international tradition; the ablest German Neoclassical painter, Mengs, spent most of his working life in Italy and Spain. Nor, to begin with, was there an upsurge in the visual arts comparable to the astonishing Romantic literary activity in Germany. Goethe was established long before his death in 1832 as the presiding genius of European culture, and he was followed by remarkable writers in the Romantic spirit, such as Schiller, von Kleist, the mystic Novalis and Tieck, while the Schlegel brothers' Romantic philosophy was discussed throughout Europe. Napoleon's domination of Europe inspired by reaction a sense of common racial and cultural inheritance amongst German intellectuals, even though the diverse kingdoms and principalities of the German peoples were to remain fragmented for many years yet.

In the 1770s the young Goethe had emerged as the prophet of German Romanticism – in the violence, and colourful appeal to German legend, of *Götz von Berlichingen*, in the introspective melancholy of *The Sorrows of Young Werther*, and in a panegyric of Gothic architecture. At this time Goethe identified art with "Nature", emphasizing the particular rather than the general, and the overriding importance of autonomous "genius", although he came later to feel that the emphasis on feeling over reason was becoming morbidly unbalanced. His involvement with the visual arts continued all his life, and he knew personally the painters Runge and Friedrich.

German Romanticism found its characteristic visual expression in three modes, which often came together in a single work – landscape, overt symbolism, and nationalistic medievalism. In its visionary intensity it was closer to English than to French attitudes, but generally more dour in temper and more concerned with explicitly religious themes. The models from which Romantic landscape developed were provided by the established traditions of pastoral landscape, as is clear in *Northern lights*, about 1790, by Jens Juel (1745-1802), in which a conventional, even tame, formula is opened up on to a limitless ether. Juel taught at the Copenhagen Academy, where both Friedrich and Runge studied. The

FRIEDRICH (right)
Monk by the sea, 1809
Friedrich later removed two boats he had originally included in the landscape, in order to emphasize its starkness and spiritual isolation. On it von Kleist commented: "Because of its monotony and boundlessness, with nothing but the frame as foreground, one feels as if one's eyelids have been cut away" – in terror in the face of infinity.

JUEL (left)
Northern lights, c. 1790
Juel enjoyed a popular reputation for his scenes of the open air, somewhat in the spirit of Gainsborough. Here, however, the picture stimulates curiosity by its very enigma. Who is the man sitting by the gate? Where does the path lead? The gate, notably, is shut on the dissolving distance.

KOCH (left)
Schmadribach waterfall, 1808-11
Earlier such a landscape would have been equated with a desert, but to Koch the elemental forces of Nature conveyed something of the heroic *terribilità* he admired in Michelangelo.

DAHL (above)
Clouds, 1825
The trees and spires rising into the sky are devoid of symbolic meaning. Dahl was interested in Nature only for its intrinsic beauty, and so was close in spirit to Constable; he developed the example notably of Ruisdael.

RUNGE (above)
Morning, 1808-09
Despite the enigmatic and slightly absurd imagery, the painting could stand as an illustration to Wordsworth's poem *Intimations* *of Immortality*, conveying divine unity and rhythm in Nature. In the baby's eyes, every element seems "apparelled in celestial light, the glory and the freshness of a dream".

influential Anton Koch (1768-1839) at first produced classicizing ideal landscapes, echoing Poussin, which, though he retained a firm grasp of structural principles, he later invested with an emotional, Romantic feeling.

The outstanding interpreter of German Romantic landscape was Caspar David Friedrich. Born in Pomerania, he worked from 1798 in Dresden, but his temperament seemed always to retain the cold melancholy of Baltic shores. His landscapes are the purest expression in European Romantic art of the yearning of man for communion with Nature, even if their prevailing tragic sadness speaks of alienation, and ultimate solitude, in the attempt. The essence of Friedrich's message is summed up in his *Monk by the sea* of 1809: the solitary – it must be, doomed – figure is a small dark accent between the voids of land, sea and sky. There was some give and take between Friedrich and his friend, the Norwegian Johan Christian Dahl (1788-1857), but Dahl's interests were more in the naturalistic side of Romantic landscape. He was making detailed studies of cloud formations at the same time as Constable, in the 1820s, quite independently.

Friedrich's work is dense with symbolism (see over), but the symbolism of Philipp Otto Runge (1777-1810) is even more overt. Runge, like Goethe, published a work on colour theory, but was also much influenced by the linear purity of Flaxman's illustrations. He died aged merely 33, leaving only fragmentary witness of his main ambitions. A mystic who might easily have become a Lutheran pastor, he had a virtually religious, all-embracing, dedication to art, and landscape was the only branch of art that could support its intensity, being for him a medium for the comprehensive representation of all the elements of life. He aimed ultimately at a *Gesamtkunstwerk*, incorporating all the arts – poetry, architecture and music. Of his major project, *The Four Phases of Day*, only one vast canvas (subsequently dismembered) was completed, *Morning*. In this the sharpness and delicacy of his vision are brilliantly clear. His portraits are perhaps his most successful surviving works: that of his parents, whose wooden vigour in the relentless light is contrasted with the dewy but also merciless innocence of the grandchildren, is one of the most extraordinary and monumental portraits of the early nineteenth century. In his engravings of *The Phases of the Day*, he condensed his symbolic language into a near-diagrammatic form.

The medievalist and nationalist approach is best exemplified by the Nazarene group. These young artists formed a quasi-religious Brotherhood of St Luke in Vienna in 1809, and in 1810 migrated to Rome, to what would now be called a commune, in an abandoned monastery, where they lived, painted, prayed and sang together. The original leader, Franz Pforr (1788-1812), who had illustrated Goethe's *Götz* in a Dürer-like style, left a striking medieval reconstruction, *The entry of Emperor Rudolf of Hapsburg into Basel*, before his early death. He was succeeded by Friedrich Overbeck (1789-1869). Generally, the Nazarenes wished to fuse the best of early Italian styles (especially Raphael's) with the best of German (Dürer); they also revived early techniques, fresco and tempera, and in this the most talented of them was Peter von Cornelius (1783-1867), who early illustrated Goethe's *Faust*, developing a hard, linear style of great vigour and intensity. However, the example of the Nazarenes, as a breakaway group extolling primitive techniques and ways of life, was perhaps more significant than their work.

RUNGE (right)
Morning, from *The Phases of the Day*, 1803
The series of engravings appeared as *Die Zeiten* in 1805, indebted to the style of Flaxman, and to motifs culled from Bellini and early Renaissance art, but the meaning was new.

In sentiment they perhaps seem close to Blake, but Goethe compared these prints with the music of Beethoven, which "tries to embrace everything and in doing so always loses itself in the elemental, yet still with endless beauty in the particulars".

PFORR (above)
The entry of Emperor Rudolf of Hapsburg into Basel in 1273, 1808-10

This is one of the first large medieval history subjects, depicted in a consciously archaic style.

RUNGE (above)
The artist's parents and his children, 1806
The cool light mercilessly exposes the figures – the suspicious gaze of the old couple, stiffened with age, contrasts with the children's pure absorption with the bright flowers.

CORNELIUS (right)
Faust and Mephisto on the Brocken, c. 1811
The style owes much to Dürer. Romantic artists sought the imaginative and passionate in literature – Goethe's *Faust*, plays by Shakespeare, ancient epic – Homer, Virgil and Ossian.

OVERBECK (above)
Italia and Germania, 1811-28
The physiognomies, dress and colours are based on Raphael. The landscape, too, is Italianate, save for a

Gothic church spire. The wreaths and idealization of the faces emphasize the eternal significance of the encounter. The artist used the composition of a Visitation for the embrace.

Friedrich: Man and Woman Gazing at the Moon

Caspar David Friedrich (1774-1840) has shown the man and woman from behind, beheld by us as they themselves behold the moon. Our own position is uncertain, since we see them from above; no stabilizing foreground links us. They are alone together, as almost all Friedrich's figures are alone, as if alienated, silent, their faces unseen. Beyond them, the moon rides remote in infinity.

The picture is replete with Friedrich's personal symbolic imagery. Thus, for him, the moon represents Christ. The pine trees (Christian faith on earth) are traversed by a stony path (the path of life) winding uphill (towards Christian redemption). The shattered and dying oak tree and the dolmen represent transience and paganism, while the dark abyss falling away to the right shows the way down to temptation and unbelief. However, the impact of the picture is far from being entirely dependent on the spelling out of its symbolism. The success of Friedrich's finest paintings rests on their vivid visual coherence, their credibility as real topographical sites.

The painting is a variation on a design which obsessed Friedrich throughout his career, and which had been established in the haunting solitudes of *Moonrise over the sea* of 1822, in which Friedrich repeats with only slight variations a version of 1819, *Two men contemplating the moon*; here the two men of the *Moonrise* are replaced by the artist himself and his wife. The theme reached its most complex elaboration in *The stages of life* of 1835.

All Friedrich's work is religious, the most astonishing example coming early in his career, *The Cross in the mountains* of 1808, known as the Tetschen altar. It was in fact used as an altarpiece, though it is a landscape, which caused controversy. The sun sets, the old order passes, its last gleams transmuted in the golden figure of Christ on the crucifix, while the rock symbolizes steadfast faith in Christ. The mood has a serene, even optimistic quality unusual in Friedrich's work. The famous *Abbey graveyard under snow*, with the gaunt Gothic choir rising in a snowy graveyard amongst shattered trees, is more typical. Terrifying in its bleak mystery, it is one of the most haunting images of European Romanticism.

Friedrich's predilection for Gothic forms has no doubt some nationalistic significance, and his work included positive references to the German struggle for freedom against Napoleon. But Friedrich's art was essentially non-topical, visionary. "The artist should not only paint what he sees before him, but also what he sees within him. If, however, he sees nothing within him, then he should also omit to paint what he sees before him".

In the 1812 painting of Friedrich by Georg Friedrich Kersting (1785-1847), the artist is seen in an austerely empty studio, summoning up his picture from within himself rather than from outside. Friedrich was nevertheless a close and precise observer of Nature, as a great many drawings make clear. The detailed precision of his drawing reinforces his startling contrast of the mundane with the unearthly. His people may appear in frock-coat or dress and bonnet – dressed, as it were, for office or shopping – but poised on the brink confronting eternity. Usually his figures are unemphatic, often seen from behind. They are simply and exactly described, yet such is their still intensity that the effect is transcendental.

Friedrich's technique could seem somewhat dry; painterly virtuosity, the sensuous delight in the painter's materials, was always strictly subordinated to the image to be produced, in a style descriptive rather than expressive, so that he was for long condemned as a literary painter. Many of his paintings are of twilight or dusk or moonlight, but in fact he was a most subtle colourist. He lived out his life quietly in Dresden, and the considerable attention that his work had at first attracted dwindled, until at his death he was almost neglected – and so he remained until the 1890s, when the Symbolists rediscovered the formidable potency of his imagery. Indeed, echoes of Friedrich are to be found in the greatest of the northern Expressionists, Edvard Munch. Friedrich's art, in fact, was no less revolutionary than the very differently generated landscapes of Constable and Turner. The analogy of his art with Chinese landscape painting, though it cannot be pressed too far, is striking – the vision of man alone in the immensity of a natural world that is the symbol of an infinity beyond.

FRIEDRICH (above)
The Tetschen altar: *The Cross on the mountains*, 1808 Friedrich himself designed the gold frame. On the base, shafts of light around the eye of God echo the rays of the setting sun, while the wheat-ear and grapes refer to the Last Supper. The star above symbolizes both death and resurrection.

FRIEDRICH (below)
A dolmen near Gützkow, c. 1837 These prehistoric burial stones, stranded like wrecks in the sea of time, fascinated Friedrich: they suggested at once human transience and eternity. A dolmen occurs in the left foreground of *Man and woman gazing at the moon*.

FRIEDRICH (above)
Abbey graveyard under snow, 1810 The way in which the once Picturesque attractions of the Gothic past are raised into mystical symbolism is typically Romantic. The skeletal trees and the Gothic ruin endure against time in transcendental melancholy.

A German Romantic poet, Körner, had described a similar, earlier picture as a *Totenlandschaft* (a landscape of the dead). Indeed the monks appear to be carrying a bier into the "bare ruin'd choir" of the church. A mist completes the sense of sepulchral mystery and lost faith.

FRIEDRICH (left)
Moonrise over the sea, 1822 Though ostensibly closely observed and naturalistic, the canvas takes on a near-abstract appearance, with its vertical and horizontal axes and colour contrasts – the reddish browns of the land and the suffused bluish-purple sky. The sea without any horizon, a recurrent motif, suggests infinity and the unknown, against the familiar, homely silhouettes of the gazing townspeople.

FRIEDRICH (below): *Man and woman gazing at the moon*, c.1830-35

FRIEDRICH (left)
*The stages of life, c.*1835
This is perhaps the most
personal of all Friedrich's
images of transience. Sea
and sky shine luminously,
but soon after he painted
them Friedrich had a stroke
from which he never fully
recovered. The painter is
the old man confronting
infinite spaces, while his
children and grandchildren
stand, sit or play close by.

KERSTING (right)
*Caspar David Friedrich
in his studio,* 1812
The painter has shuttered
the lower part of his studio
window, blocking out the
world, the better to visu-
alize his inner world as he
broods over his canvas.
The bars of the window
form a Cross in the sky,
like a delicate blessing.

French Romanticism

The figure who links French Neoclassicism with Romanticism is Antoine-Jean, Baron Gros (1771-1835), considered by David a wayward pupil, yet his favourite. David made over his studio and, he hoped, his principles to Gros when he went into exile after the defeat of Napoleon in 1815. It had been Gros rather than David, in paintings such as *Napoleon on the battlefield at Eylau* (1808, not shown) or *The plague at Jaffa* (1804), who translated the heroic glamour, the legendary quality, of the Napoleonic era into paint. Gros's sense of drama infected his brushwork with a bravura much admired by the Romantics; by 1831, his huge *Napoleon at Eylau* could be identified by a Romantic critic as "the birth of the Romantic school". Although these compositions are in the grandiloquent classic tradition of "history" painting, the formidable and gruesome realism of the corpses in their foregrounds made a profound and lasting impression, especially when the Napoleonic triumph had turned to defeat. Gros's emotional instability, culminating in his suicide, is in key with one aspect of the Romantic temperament.

Not only his work, but the temperament and life-style of Théodore Géricault (1791-1824) –

not least his premature death, aged only 33 – make him an archetypal Romantic artist, in the example of Byron or Chatterton, Chénier or Keats. His first important painting, in the spirit of Gros, the dynamic portrait *An officer of the Chasseurs*, 1812, was offset by *The wounded cuirassier leaving the field*, painted in 1814 when Napoleon was in exile in Elba. Subdued in colour compared with the brilliance of the *Chasseur*, it is an image of defeat, but also of the glamour of death: it was found the more shocking because presented on an heroic scale, life-size. Géricault was obsessed throughout his brief life with images of violence. Horses provided him with one elemental example of power and speed, and in 1816-17, when he was in Rome (where the energy of Michelangelo's style had impressed him), he planned a colossal painting of the traditional race of riderless horses along the Corso; later, in England, he was to paint horses again, and his own death followed a riding accident.

His great masterpiece of 1819, *The raft of the Medusa*, has come to be seen as a manifesto of French Romanticism, much as David's *Oath of the Horatii* had been one of Neoclassicism. Here again, he treated an unheroic subject on

an heroic scale. The subject was topical, sensational, and open to political interpretation. The *Medusa* had been wrecked in 1816, a catastrophe ascribed, if on tenuous grounds, to Government incompetence. The survivors on the raft had endured the horrors of mutiny, exposure, starvation, even cannibalism. The moment chosen by Géricault was the terrible spurious dawn of hope, when a ship was sighted from the raft but passed without noticing. The composition, with its strong diagonal stresses, refers back to Baroque rather than to Neoclassical example, but the moulding of the figures is solidly founded on classical techniques and groupings. Though the theme is so intensely dramatic, even melodramatic, the figures in the finished painting have become idealized, perfect physiques, well-shaven and undisfigured by emaciation or sores; yet Géricault had painted studies for it from actual corpses, even severed limbs, with vivid objectivity. When first exhibited at the Salon, it seems initially to have been uncontroversial, and was even awarded a medal, but it had some *succès de scandale* later in London, and by 1847 the historian Michelet could see in it a comprehensive allegory of the troubles of

GROS (above)
The plague at Jaffa, 1804
Gros invests Napoleon with implicitly royal powers of healing and immunity when faced with plague-stricken troops during his Egyptian campaign. Postures from Italian religious painting, the ghastly realism of victims and the serenity of Napoleon are conjoined to effect his "canonization".

GERICAULT (right)
An officer of the Chasseurs, 1812
David had immortalized *Napoleon crossing the Alps* (not shown) in 1800, with his hero on a rearing horse against a scene of battle. Using a very similar pose, Géricault abandons the cult of personality and glorifies the sheer excitement of battle in the momentary stance of horse and rider, the energy of the paint, the vividness of colour.

GERICAULT (left)
A wounded cuirassier leaving the field, 1814
The vigorous movement of the horse is contrasted with the halting progress of the injured soldier, courageous even in defeat. This was a pendant to the *Officer of the Chasseurs*, and its sombre, apprehensive mood evokes the disillusion which followed Napoleon's fall from power in 1814.

DELACROIX (below)
The barque of Dante, 1822
Virgil is leading Dante into Limbo across the river Acheron, in which bodies of the damned are tossed. The corpses, composition and the Michelangelesque quality of the figures recall *The raft of the Medusa*, although Delacroix's rich colours anticipate the trend of his later painting.

France. Géricault's last works were remarkable studies of mad men and women, painted as scientific case-studies for a psychiatrist friend, but intensely emotive.

When Géricault died in 1824, Delacroix, in his *Barque of Dante* of 1822, had already paid his tribute to *The raft of the Medusa*, and was emerging as the presiding genius of the Romantic movement (see over), though he would never have categorized himself as such. The emotive subject matter used by Delacroix – exotic and oriental themes, violent depictions of animals, historical stories from the Middle Ages as well as from antiquity, and also from the poets of passion, Shakespeare, Tasso and Byron – these were all adopted by many other painters. Landscape, too, was a development especially congenial to the Romantic temperament (see p. 92). Paul Delaroche (1797-1856; not shown) became aligned with Delacroix more because of rows with the Salon and his medievalizing "romantic" subject matter than for his style; his flair for the psychological moment in narrative was weakened by sentimentality, but he was immensely popular.

Géricault produced a few small pieces of sculpture, bronzes of powerful expressive force that anticipate Rodin's quality, but generally sculpture was not a medium that the Romantics found congenial or particularly suitable. François Rude (1784-1855), a loyal supporter of Napoleon, went into exile with David in 1815, until 1827. His ability to fuse Napoleonic classicism with Romantic fervour and drama is strikingly shown in his *Departure of the volunteers ("The Marseillaise"*, 1835-36), for the Arc de Triomphe in Paris. (Napoleonic and Revolutionary themes, forbidden under Charles X, returned to favour after 1830 under Louis-Philippe). Antoine-Louis Barye (1796-1875), who had first trained as a painter under Gros, turned his attention to the popular Romantic theme of wild animals, although his technique, in a prolific output of vivid small bronzes, was naturalistic rather than expressively Romantic. The most remarkable Romantic sculpture of all is Rude's *Awakening of Napoleon*, 1845-47.

By that date, Romanticism in France was established, consolidated by the support of critics and theorists. Middle-of-the-road Salon artists drew copiously if superficially on its achievement. But by then Courbet (see p. 90) was already active in Paris.

GERICAULT (above)
The raft of the Medusa, 1819
The exceptional intensity of Géricault's researches for the *Medusa* resulted in his eventual nervous collapse. The horrible and unheroic ordeal of the victims is elevated by visual reference to Michelangelo and Caravaggio, but no facile moral emerges: Géricault sought veracity, a conscientiously unsparing view of men at the limits of endurance.

GERICAULT (right)
A kleptomaniac, 1822-23
Dr Georget at the Paris asylum commissioned a series of objective studies of the pathological mind, believing that every mental illness was registered in a specific facial expression. Restraint and compassion infuse Géricault's portrait: it captures the sense of the subject's individuality even while the sitter is alienated within his own obsession.

RUDE
The departure of the volunteers, 1833-36
Rude echoes both spirit and structure of Delacroix's *Liberty leading the People* (see over). Recalling the heroism of the people who in 1792 had rallied to the Revolutionary cause, the vitality of the figures shows him realizing fully the dynamic possibilities of gesture and grouping.

RUDE (left)
The awakening of Napoleon, 1847
Rude liked David's blend of classicism and topical reference, though he here transforms it into a mystic archetype of French glory.

BARYE (above)
Jaguar devouring a crocodile, 1850
Many Romantics saw wild animals as metaphors of untrammelled freedom, their savagery expressing a primal urge in Nature.

Delacroix: The Death of Sardanapalus

The first painting Eugène Delacroix (1798-1863) exhibited at the Salon in Paris was his *Barque of Dante* (1822; see preceding page), clearly influenced by Géricault and equally clearly in the Grand Tradition. Though it provoked some criticism it was bought for the royal collection. In 1824 he showed *The massacre at Chios*, which owed something to Gros's *Plague at Jaffa* (see preceding page); but while Gros had celebrated Napoleon serene in the midst of pestilence, Delacroix's *Chios* was a lament, or perhaps a celebration, of defeat. Although it was criticized for its "unfinished" quality, and its bold juxtaposition of colours seemed crude to contemporary taste, it was nevertheless bought by the state.

The death of Sardanapalus was a very different matter. It coincided in the Salon of 1827-28 with Ingres's *Apotheosis of Homer* (see p. 85) – confronting the Neoclassical principles of calm, clarity and nobility with dynamic bravura, colour, violence, exotic subject matter, sensual passion and morbid despair – a manifesto of extreme Romanticism. Delacroix

himself called it "an Asiatic feat of arms against David's Spartiate pastiche".

Sardanapalus is from Byron's drama of the same name. Byron's hero, though certainly of a voluptuous temperament, had in fact committed an heroic, self-sacrificial suicide, but Delacroix described him thus: "Besieged in his palace by insurgents . . . Reclining on a superb bed on top of a huge pyre Sardanapalus orders the eunuchs and palace officers to cut the throats of his women and his pages, and even of his favourite horses and dogs; none of the objects that have contributed to his pleasure must survive him." Hence, a self-indulgent, almost bored figure presiding impassively over a sensual abandon of destruction, in a clash of resonant colour and collapsing shapes.

Sardanapalus represents the climax of Delacroix's developing obsession with death and pessimism, and of his pictures of doomed heroic figures in despair and defeat; and his style was now fully evolved to deal with them – the movement of the paint itself, the chords of colour, being integral to the expression of the

artist's emotion. Delacroix clearly identified himself very closely with Sardanapalus; unlike Géricault's *Raft of the Medusa* (see preceding page) this is a work of personal fantasy, and ultimately remote from reality – no drop of blood obtrudes, for all its violence. Yet it is typical of Delacroix that the artist's involvement is balanced by a disciplined detachment, and the whirl of flesh and pleasure and colour spinning out from Sardanapalus is held within a controlled composition. But public reaction was violently hostile, and Delacroix himself had doubts, referring to the painting as his "retreat from Moscow" and keeping it thereafter unseen in his studio until his death.

In 1830 Revolution displaced the last of the Bourbon monarchs and installed the so-called "citizen-king" Louis-Philippe. Delacroix was a conservative in politics, a cool, impeccable dandy in society, and not one to participate on the barricades, but he painted the spirit of revolution, *Liberty leading the people*. The picture found favour: henceforward he was relatively secure in official patronage.

DELACROIX (left)
The death of Sardanapalus,
1827

DELACROIX (below)
The massacre at Chios, 1824
Byron, whom Delacroix
admired, had passionately
identified with the cause
of enslaved Greece; and yet
Delacroix shows an episode
from the War of Liberation
with a curious ambiguity:
the Turks' indifference is
as striking as the inertia of
their victims. Fatalistic
figures mostly recline in
a fresh, brilliant landscape.

DELACROIX (left)
Still life with a lobster,
1827
The conjunction of still
life and landscape is somewhat bizarre: exhibited in
the Salon in the same year
as *Sardanapalus,* it seems
to intend another kind of
antithesis to Neoclassical
theory and practice. The
tartan plaid among the
disparate objects reflects
Delacroix's current anglo-
philia: he had spent some
months in England in 1825.

DELACROIX (right)
Baron Schwitter, 1826-30
Schwitter was a friend
of Delacroix; the portrait
suggests their intimacy, as
"men of sensibility". Its
nervousness and pensive
elegance, and the freedom
with which the brooding
sky is painted, owe much
to English influences, notably Thomas Lawrence.

His voyage to North Africa in 1832 has been
likened to other artists' voyages to Italy. It
provided him with a source, recorded in many
sketchbooks, of exotic sensuous imagery and
of glowing colour. Its impact is summarized
in his small, famous and influential painting,
Women of Algiers, a memory of a harem
interior into which he had managed to gain
entry, a vision of languor half-asleep in voluptuous, floating colour. Violence however, was
still the theme of much of his later work, and in
an impressive series of small-scale paintings he
depicted horses, lions and tigers, symbols of
power and passion, with a vigour and intensity
rivalling Rubens. However, in his large official
commissions, he moved away from his more
Romantic obsessions. His aloof temperament
had always made him suspicious of the
publicity-conscious postures of militant Romanticism, and it may be that he is equally
significant as the writer of the most elegantly
styled and perspicacious journal in the history
of art, and as the subject of an apologia by
Baudelaire, as for the bulk of his paintings.

DELACROIX (above)
Liberty leading the people,
1830
Although Liberty is more
than a frigid abstraction,
and the People are workers,
not the bourgeoisie who
were in fact triumphant,
this is more a patriotic
than a specifically socialist
work. If it is restrained in
key and composition beside
Sardanapalus, it epitomizes
Romantic rebellion: per-
sonal protest has replaced
David's corporate idealism.

DELACROIX
Women of Algiers, 1834
The surface is patterned in
a close and intricate harmony
of colour, suggesting a new
attention to current theories
on colour complementaries.
The intensity of the almost
abstract design enhances
rather than dominates the
mood of subdued eroticism.
The Impressionists took
note, and so did Matisse.

Painting in Victorian Britain

The nineteenth century in Britain, after victory at Waterloo in 1815, was a period of peace at home and growing prosperity at the centre of a vast Empire. The Industrial Revolution had brought profit; its attendant miseries, in some ranks of the working classes, provoked no political revolution. Queen Victoria's reign (1837-1901) is synonymous with stability. Political life, so turbulent in France in the same period, was comparatively gentlemanly, and so, too, with few exceptions, was British art.

Art was considered as an educative and edifying element in civilized life, to be based on solid principles of Truth, Sentiment and Health. The expounder of these values, John Ruskin apologist for Turner (see p. 73) and then for the Pre-Raphaelites, assumed the stature of a major moral prophet. The maintenance of moral health required wholesome subjects – rural idylls for tired urban eyes, and religious, historical or modern themes with an edifying message. The trend is clear in the work of Sir David Wilkie (1785-1841), known as "the Scottish Teniers". He turned from his lively scenes of Scottish low life to elevated modern themes, such as the highly patriotic *Chelsea pensioners reading the Gazette of the*

Battle of Waterloo. The taste for genre developed in various ways – in fashionable costume scenes from contemporary literature; in picturesque studies of children; in the full-scale detailed documentaries of Victorian life produced by William Powell Frith (1819-1909) in the 1850s.

Crown, aristocrats and commoners generally concurred in taste. Queen Victoria's favourite painter, Sir Edwin Landseer (1802-73), appealed to the national love of animals; indeed his universally popular *Monarch of the glen* was at first intended for the elevated environs of the House of Lords. In the huge project of decorating Pugin's new Gothic Houses of Parliament at Westminster, important elements of national taste were clearly reflected, not only the renewed appreciation of medievalizing styles, but also, in its frescos (not shown), a growing interest in early Italian painting and the art of the German Nazarenes.

The Pre-Raphaelite Brotherhood was the fruition of such trends. The association of seven very young artists was formed in 1848, when their leader, William Holman Hunt (1827-1910), was only 20. Their programme was simple – to express serious, sincere ideas in

HOLMAN HUNT (below)
The awakened conscience, 1852-54
In accordance with Pre-Raphaelite practice, every detail points to the moral

drama – for example, the music on the piano, *Oft in the stilly night,* and the cat under the table playing with a bird. Hunt's concern for realism was tireless.

LANDSEER (below)
The monarch of the glen, 1850
The sentimental appeal of the noble beast, and the

Scottish element, popularized by royal enthusiasm for the Highlands, made this an image familiar in parlours throughout the land.

FRITH (above)
Derby Day, 1856-58
Frith used photographs, and numerous models, for his panoramic picture of racing day. The copyright for engraving was bought before the painting had been begun – the appeal of his ingredients was assured.

WILKIE (above)
Chelsea pensioners reading the Gazette of the Battle of Waterloo, 1822
At this first attempt to touch upon a "serious" subject, Wilkie scored a remarkable hit – it was railed off from delighted crowds at its exhibition.

MILLAIS (right)
Christ in the house of his parents, 1850
Using heavy symbolism to foreshadow the Crucifixion – the wound of the nail in the palm of the Child, the presence of St John and the sorrowing Virgin – Millais created a picture full of

sentiment and meaning. Its awkward poses, reflecting in part the influence of the Nazarenes (see p. 75), and the realistic features (a professional carpenter was the model for Joseph) outraged the dignified piety of the public. This condemnation roused Ruskin to defence.

a truthful way, relying on direct observation of Nature. They found authority in the example of Italian painters before the time of Raphael, whose work they knew mainly through engravings, but in practice what was so startling was their brilliant, luminous colour, helped by the use of a pure white ground. This seemed to many crude and even scandalous: the French critic Taine concluded that there must be "something peculiar in the condition of the English retina". To modern eyes their sharp vividness seems the most exciting phenomenon in Victorian painting; perhaps less so their typically Victorian high moral content. In *The awakened conscience*, 1852-54, by William Holman Hunt, a "loose" woman starts up from her lover's knees as her conscience is called to higher things. Sir John Everett Millais (1829-96) was the most naturally gifted of the group; to his horror, the painstaking, admirably observed and admirably drawn *Christ in the house of his parents*, 1850, caused scandal, and was lamented in a famous paragraph by Charles Dickens, the chronicler of England's social distress, as unacceptable in its naturalism – "to speak plainly, revolting". To modern eyes, nothing could be more whole-

some, and it is a far cry from the provocative Realism of Courbet. Pre-Raphaelitism, as a movement, lasted less than a decade; Holman Hunt continued faithfully in its principles, but Millais, in art-style as in life-style, was slowly absorbed into the Royal Academy, ending as its President.

Dante Gabriel Rossetti (1828-82), a major figure in the group, and a poet, too, nourished in a rather hot-house imagination the most original visions of any of the Brethren. In one of his earliest works, *The Annunciation* of 1850, the integration of symbolism with form and colour created an entirely new image of the Virgin. Something of Rossetti's visionary quality persists in the art of Sir Edward Burne-Jones (1833-98). With Rossetti, the designer William Morris and others, he painted frescos of scenes from Arthurian legend in the Oxford University Union (1857-62; not shown), which constituted one of the last productions of the movement. Burne-Jones' work was admired all over Europe, not least by the Symbolists (see further p. 123).

Outside the Brotherhood, the painter whose practice corresponded to Pre-Raphaelite ideals most closely was Ford Madox Brown

(1821-93). He was well aware of the art of the German Nazarenes, but the Pre-Raphaelites influenced his high key of colour and his dedicated naturalism. His *Work* (1852-65) is a striking "real allegory", like Courbet's *Studio* (see p. 90), though too crowded with minute detail for visual coherence; it is a better attempt to involve the whole range of society. His landscapes make an interesting comparison with the Barbizon school – similar aims pursued very differently. Hunt, too, sought symbolic and moral effects, and moral earnestness steadily inspired the work of George Frederick Watts (1817-1904), whose portraits are still recognized as outstanding. His allegorical subjects became diffuse, overcome by the attempt to portray eternal truths, but in his *Hope* he produced a compelling image.

Watts' didactic earnestness was out of key with the ideal art of the late Victorian Academicians, such as Lord Leighton or Sir Lawrence Alma-Tadema, working in a virtually international academic tradition (see p. 87). But the English art scene from the 1860s was provoked and disturbed by the presence of the American Whistler (see p. 96), who came from Paris with a quite different approach.

MADOX BROWN (right)
Pretty baa lambs, 1851
Painting in the open air, Brown explored ground also covered by the Barbizon school and Impressionism, but in a quite different way, with brilliantly light colour and in minute detail. He pioneered Pre-Raphaelite landscape with Hunt, and Ruskin urged their followers to produce work of even more painstaking naturalism.

BURNE-JONES (left)
King Cophetua and the beggar maid, 1884
Burne-Jones' sombre colour, the softness and grace of his line, are related to the work of Puvis de Chavannes (see p. 122) and to Art Nouveau. The subject, taken from an Elizabethan ballad, is literary and quasi-medieval, but "I mean by a picture", he said, "a beautiful romantic dream of something that never was, never will be".

ROSSETTI (above)
The Annunciation, 1850
The simple primary colours and compressed, elongated space were revolutionary at the time, and unacceptable. The Virgin conforms to a distinctly Pre-Raphaelite aesthetic, with long face, large eyes and wavy hair.

MADOX BROWN (right)
Work, 1852–65
Belief in the moral function of the arts and the necessity for social reform inspired Brown's didactic painting. To the right stand Carlyle and Frederick Maurice, the Christian Socialist; to the left the idle rich and the tramp pass by the workers by.

WATTS
Hope, 1886
Watts' Symbolist image of an emotional state entitled Hope (but equally eloquent of Despair) was reproduced in thousands of delicately

coloured mezzotints. The wan, attenuated figure is strikingly close to those of Puvis de Chavannes (see p. 122). She is blindfold, and holds a harp on which she plucks unheard music.

Ingres: La Grande Odalisque

Jean Auguste Dominique Ingres (1780-1867), a pupil of David's, is said to have assisted in the painting of the famous reclining *Madame Récamier* (see p. 59), for which David seems to have made a nude study, and the pose is echoed in Ingres's own *"La Grande Odalisque"* (The concubine), painted in Rome in 1813-14. It is an essay in the long tradition of recumbent female nudes that stems from Titian's *"Venus of Urbino"* (see vol. 2 p. 145), and one of many variations on Ingres's personal and so successfully realized vision of the nude. Of these the most natural and, in the objective precision of its drawing, the most classical, is the earlier *"Valpinçon Bather"* of 1808, a superbly cool study in pale flesh colours and tones of white, yet also in its secretive way intensely erotic. Ingres's famous command of line is already completely assured.

The domination of contour is in accordance with the Neoclassical principles of David, but the total impression of the *Odalisque* is of a nude seen for its own sake rather than as an illustration of any ideal or heroic theme. It departs from strict Neoclassic canons, both in subject matter and in the way it is handled. Though preceded by many assiduous studies from the life, the anatomy is unnaturalistically modified for the sake of the composition – contemporary critics observed disapprovingly

INGRES (below)
"The Valpinçon Bather", 1808
The effect of suspension of time and gravity is achieved by the diffusion of light, the insistent verticals and the refined contour of the sitter's untroubled repose.

INGRES (above)
"La Grande Odalisque" (The concubine), 1814
The *Odalisque* was commissioned by the Queen of Naples, Napoleon's sister, but never delivered, since the Emperor's fall intervened. Ingres remained in

Rome but sent the picture to the Paris Salon of 1819, where one critic wrote: "Sworn enemy of modern schools, and infatuated with Cimabue, he has taken the dryness, crudity, simplicity and all the Gothic traits with a rare talent."

INGRES (below)
The Turkish bath, 1859-62
A description of a women's bath in Istanbul, and illustrated accounts of oriental travels, inspired Ingres's complex composition, which includes several portraits, though not of Easterners.

INGRES (below)
Oedipus and the Sphinx,
1808, reworked 1825
Ingres enlarged the picture
in the 1820s, filling in the
figure of the Sphinx and
adding the fugitive man,
thereby investing it with
immediacy, and stressing
the element of terror –
the horrible fate of those
who failed to solve the
riddle. Oedipus is posed
apparently in imitation of
the Antique, but Ingres
was not just a stylist: he
wrote: "I copy only from
Nature and never idealize."

INGRES (below)
*Joseph Woodhead, his wife
Harriet and her brother
Henry Comber*, 1816
Each figure is drawn with
admirable precision, each
face carefully portrayed,
traced without shading in
Ingres's unfaltering line.

INGRES (left)
Louis-François Bertin,
1832
Bertin's pose presented a
problem until Ingres saw
him in earnest discussion,
and used this stance. As
the founder of the *Journal
des Débats*, Bertin stood
for the liberal bourgeoisie
and the establishment; this
perhaps aided the portrait's
success in the 1833 Salon.

INGRES (below)
La Comtesse d'Haussonville,
1845
The pensively tilted head
opposes the slope to the
right of the shapes that
constitute the body, thus
restoring equilibrium. The
portrait's visual harmony
is so highly contrived and
abstract that it can be compared, for instance, with the
pure forms of Brancusi or
Hepworth without ridicule.

INGRES (below)
The apotheosis of Homer,
1827
Ingres attached considerable
importance to this work
(for a ceiling in the Louvre
but conceding nothing to its
position), and was hurt by
the lack of due appreciation.

that the back had been elongated by the
equivalent of at least two vertebrae. The effect
is more closely related to the cool, smooth
eroticism of much sixteenth-century Mannerist painting than to Ingres's beloved Raphael.
When finally exhibited in Paris, the *Odalisque*
was found eccentric and bizarre. Only with
"*La Source*" of 1856 (see over) did Ingres
produce an image of the nude that responded
entirely to popular taste.

Ingres's obsession came to a remarkable
climax in the famous *Turkish bath*, completed
when he was 83 (as he noted beside his
signature with a natural pride). This extraordinary welter of nudes, the highly refined
result of a series of searching studies, appears
in the abstract view as a remarkable resolution
of swarming curving forms within a tondo
form. Admired by Prince Napoleon, it was
painted only a year before Manet's notorious
Olympia (see p. 94). Ingres's vision was apparently acceptable partly because it was
clearly placed in an exotic fantasy world.

Ingres's early career was far from an un-
mitigated popular success. Even in lucidly
drawn classical subjects, such as the *Oedipus
and the Sphinx* of 1808, there is something
strange, and the painting was criticized for
being flat and shadowless; he was accused of
being Gothic, of being *un Chinois égaré*, a
Chinaman who had lost his way. Alienated by
French censure, he spent many years in Italy
(1806-24), but in mid-career he became established and returned to Italy (1835-41) as
Director of the French Academy in Rome.
Although artists of opposing views never quite
reached the point of pitched battle, as factions
of writers did at the famous opening of Victor
Hugo's Romantic drama *Hernani*, their anta-
gonisms were ferocious, and Ingres was a man
of high and stubborn temper. At a Salon show,
after Delacroix had left, it is reported that
Ingres demanded that the windows be opened:
"I smell sulphur."

Ingres's influence was extensive and enduring over successive academic generations (but
also on Degas and even on Matisse). The vast
Apotheosis of Homer, 1827, was to remain the
model for many frigid murals. It is a response
to Raphael's *School of Athens*, laboriously and
efficiently executed as if expressly to illustrate
Winckelmann's description of "noble simplicity and calm grandeur"; but its artificiality
discourages the modern spectator.

Arguably, Ingres's most purely successful
work is that in which he was most closely
committed to his own contemporary reality.
The exquisite delicacy of his early pencil
portraits, mostly done in Italy, has rarely been
surpassed, while in minutely detailed and
highly finished parade portraits he was to
mirror the sumptuous material prosperity of
the Parisian bourgeoisie of the mid-century,
and create images of formidable monumentality. Few portrait painters illustrate better
Dostoevsky's note that the portraitist's job was
to catch his sitter at the moment when he
looked most like himself – most individual, yet
representing a whole human social type.
Baudelaire praised the *Monsieur Bertin* of 1832
and the later *Comtesse d'Haussonville* as "ideal
reconstructions of individuals".

Academic Art in Europe

In the first half of the nineteenth century, most of Europe experienced a boom in the production of paintings; a new market opened up as patronage expanded from the top ranks of society to an increasingly large and prosperous urban bourgeois population. The art trade became widely and firmly established: through official exhibitions, through dealers, and especially through mass-produced prints (made possible by technical improvements in engraving processes), pictures reached an enormous clientèle. In sculpture (see p. 106), there was a corresponding demand for small-scale works for domestic settings, and a growing national and civic pride prompted ubiquitous municipal architectural sculpture and statues.

The training of the artists who produced this kind of art was based, almost throughout Europe, in the official academies. This orthodox professional stream of nineteenth-century art was dismissed almost completely by later critics (dazzled by successive progressive avantgardes), and only recently has its long overdue reassessment begun.

The principles of the academic tradition were rooted in the *disegno* of early Renaissance Florence – stressing the importance of drawing, the defining contour of line; the detailed preliminary study; the subordinate role of colour; and the necessity both of classical balance and of "finish". These principles had been upheld in the French Academy by a long line of painters from Lebrun to David. The highest themes were classical or Christian, and the noblest subject was the human form, to which a certain decorum of "nobly" expressive pose and gesture was appropriate. These principles persisted through the nineteenth century, but interiors, sentimental scenes of peasant life, views of exotic lands and customs, portraits, genre scenes in the Dutch mode – these were all also in great demand, painted again in a closely detailed manner.

The dominant figure of the academic, classical tradition was Ingres (see preceding page), whose name became almost synonymous with it, and the polarization between academic classicism and Romanticism was conveniently but too sweepingly summarized in the fierce antagonism (theoretical, practical and personal) of Ingres and Delacroix. In fact even Ingres's classicism could be far from orthodox, and what we now call academic art was not the only kind to receive major official patronage –

INGRES (right)
"La Source" (The spring), 1856
Ingre's generalized nudes gave rise to the type called the *femme de l'Ecole*, which joined sensuality with dewy innocence. His allegorical figure triumphed in the Salon, fetching a ransom.

COUTURE (left)
The Romans of the Decadence, 1847
The moral of Couture's highly-praised historical allegory on contemporary society was: "Crueller than arms, lust descended upon Rome and avenged the conquered world."

FLANDRIN (right)
Theseus recognized by his father, 1838
The studied monumentality and high finish of the work echo Neoclassical example, but it lacks any deep-felt meaning or spirit.

GEROME (above)
The gladiators, c. 1859
With vehement gestures the crowd urge the victor to slay his opponent – a scene presumably calculated to arouse repugnance with a moralistic intention. The artist paid almost pedantic attention to archaeological detail, and his real powers of draughtsmanship earned him the Prix de Rome, the highest accolade the Academy could bestow. His interest in the human figure, evident in these poses recalling the life class, led him eventually to concentrate on sculpture.

MEISSONIER (right)
Napoleon III at the Battle of Solferino, June 24th, 1859, 1863
Scarcely suggesting ultimate victory, the scene of battle is relatively realistic in its spirit. Meissonier used photography to study the movement of the horses.

Delacroix himself was far from unsuccessful – even though the stereotype of the unrecognized genius, the starving Bohemian painter embattled against a philistine public, dates from this period. Considerable fortunes could be made, especially through engravings, and Paris swarmed with artists. Its artistic vitality and the reputation of its training workshops, *ateliers*, run by most of the leading painters, made it the centre of European art, much as Rome had been in the eighteenth century. The highly romanticized reflection of Parisian art student life is to be found in Murger's *Scenes from Bohemian Life* (1849), which was the source of Puccini's famous opera *La Bohème*.

Typical of the middle generation of the academic painters was Thomas Couture (1815-79), though he was more eclectic than some. Couture's vast *Romans of the Decadence* (some 7.5 metres (25ft) wide), exhibited at the Salon in 1847, challenged the great Venetian decorative painters, Veronese or Tiepolo, but it also owes much in construction to Bolognese classicism. The archaeological detail is very accurately researched, and the overall mood, morbid and sensual, was no less in accord with mid-century bourgeois taste, conferring

respectability on a somewhat dubious subject. Not only the nude, but disguised scenes of torture, of female subjugation, were constant themes amongst Salon painters. Couture ran a famous *atelier*, and his students included Puvis de Chavannes, Fantin-Latour and Manet.

Many painters followed more closely in Ingres's path, notably Hippolyte-Jean Flandrin (1809-64), one of his pupils; his *Theseus recognized by his father*, 1838, represents the pure classicizing style, somewhat dry and arid, applied to the pure classical subject. Jean-Léon Gérôme (1824-1904), the most famous of the next generation, likewise exploited classical themes, for instance in his *Gladiators*, but now with realistic violence. Ernest Meissonier (1815-91) was a brilliant master of the small-scale costume or history piece, reducing the Napoleonic campaigns to miniature proportions painted with minute accuracy and great technical virtuosity. The name of Adolphe William Bouguereau (1825-1905; not shown) stands for the extremes of smooth gloss finish; Degas invented the word *bouguereauté* to describe such academic paintings. With Alexandre Cabanel (1823-89), Bouguereau dominated the Salon in the second half of the

century, and was influential in excluding from it all revolutionary work from Manet onwards.

The difficulty of containing artists within the opposing categories of academic or classical and Romantic is exemplified by the work of the extremely talented Théodore Chassériau (1819-56). Cherished pupil of Ingres, he nevertheless developed an expressively Romantic use of colour, stimulated by Algerian trips in 1840 and 1846. The short-lived Henri Regnault (1843-71) was acclaimed in the Salon for his colouristic skill; and elements of Romanticism influenced many of the middle-of-the-road academic artists ("*le juste milieu*"). The conflict between Romantic and classical tends to be overstressed, largely as a result of the violence of contemporary controversy.

In Britain, Frederic, Lord Leighton (1830-96), President of the Royal Academy from 1878, preferred antique themes, but also travelled in the Levant and found inspiration there for his highly polished works, which had much in common with French, as with German, academicism. The ideal conventional art of late Victorian England is exemplified in the reconstructions of domestic Roman life by Sir Lawrence Alma-Tadema (1836-1912).

CHASSERIAU (below)
The toilet of Esther, 1841
The biblical heroine in this exquisitely coloured work is an Ingresque nude, but the moood is exotic, orientalizing. It even seems to anticipate the approach of the Symbolists at the end of the century.

CABANEL (left)
The birth of Venus, 1863
The critic Zola denounced Venus (bought by Napoleon III) as made not of "flesh and blood – that would be indecent – but a kind of pink and white almond paste".

ALMA-TADEMA (below)
The Baths of Caracalla, 1899
Alma-Tadema's precise archaeological environs cloak his languorous ladies in nostalgia. He also evoked daily life in ancient Egypt.

LEIGHTON (left)
The Garden of the Hesperides, 1892
In a sophisticated tondo format, the artist evokes a paradise where daughters of Evening guard golden apples, symbolic of love.

REGNAULT (above)
Automedon with the horses of Achilles, 1868
Painted in Italy, this huge Neoclassic canvas attracted attention for its theatrical effect, bold conception and free, colouristic technique.

French Realism

The movement known as Realism in the arts was formulated with most consistency and authority in France, between about 1840 and 1880. Like the label "Romanticism", the movement from which Realism in part developed and which in part it superseded, "Realism" is applied to concerns far wider than those of an identifiable artistic style. By 1840 some of the consequences of the Industrial Revolution were becoming apparent, among them the concentration of vast populations in the great urban centres, in which proliferating slums new in their scale and density contrasted with the showy display of wealth by the successful classes. Inevitably such violent imbalances within the structure of society began to involve artists, thinkers and writers, who were themselves only part of surges of unrest that found relatively mild outlet in the French revolutions of 1830, but erupted all over Europe and especially in France in 1848 (the year Marx and Engels published their *Communist Manifesto*). Realism relates closely to the philosophical work of writers such as Comte, Fourier and Proudhon; of historians such as Michelet and Taine; of novelists from George Sand to Zola and the Goncourts. As Romantic painting had seemed summarized in the work of Delacroix, so Courbet is the archetypal painter of Realism.

"Painting", claimed Courbet, "is an essentially *concrete* art, and can only consist of the presentation of *real and existing* things." Scenes from the past – classical, medieval, even Revolutionary or Napoleonic – were inadmissible. The emphasis on the present went hand in hand with the new permanence of the fleeting moment made possible by the techniques of photography, initiated by Daguerre about 1827 – photographs were already proving useful to Courbet for his painting by the 1850s. The most remarkable of the French nineteenth-century photographers was Félix Nadar (1820-1910), whose portraits, such as the famous one of Baudelaire, rival any portrait by a Realist painter not only in mere naturalism, but in monumentality and vividness – although in sheer size photography could not (yet) match the epic canvases on which Courbet and others painted scenes from working-class or peasant life, challenging the heroic dimensions of traditional "history" painting (see over).

The most remarkable statement of the ideo-

DAUMIER
Nadar in a balloon, 1862
Nadar was the first man to photograph from a balloon.

The caption reads *Photography is elevated to the height of art*; the craze sweeps the city below.

NADAR (below)
Charles Baudelaire, c. 1863
Celebrities flocked to Nadar's Paris studio, even Baudelaire, though he had declared photography mere naturalism, the enemy of art.

GUYS (left)
Two ladies with muffs,
c. 1875-80
Guys' art was a superior kind of journalism, with an amoral, sardonic delight in life's passing parade. These fashionable ladies represent the comfortable, gentle aspect of the Second Empire, as opposed to the poverty and villainy shown by Millet and Daumier.

DAUMIER (right)
The dream of the inventor of the needle-gun, 1866
Daumier greatly admired Goya's *Disasters of War* (see p. 66), but his image of a gleeful satanic boffin contemplating the efficacy of a new weapon adds a horribly modern dimension, briskly, humorously noted in a datelessly racy line.

DAUMIER (left)
Ratapoil, c. 1850
It is hard to appreciate now what a strong denunciation of the Bonapartist regime this caricature appeared at the time. Daumier had been imprisoned briefly in 1832 for sedition, and so Mme Daumier kept the terracotta original carefully hidden in a lavatory, wrapped up in a straw bottle-cover.

DAUMIER (right)
Rue Transnonain, April 15th 1834, 1834
Daumier's stark lithograph depicted a recent outrage – innocent residents of a Paris tenement block had been killed in a police raid. Its unvarnished realism – it is just like a newspaper photograph – was such that the lithographic stone was confiscated by the state and most of the prints destroyed.

logy behind the Realist movement in painting came from Baudelaire, in a famous essay, *The Painter of Modern Life*. The "modern" (that is, post-Romantic) painter should be a faceless man in the crowd; a dandy, aloof and uncommitted, yet with the clear unprejudiced vision of a child. His subject matter should be drawn from contemporary life and fashion, and his medium should be swift, reflecting immediate impressions, and suitable for wide circulation.

This applied almost wholly to Daumier, and some of it fitted Courbet. Yet the painter Baudelaire chose to typify his thesis was Constantin Guys (1805-92), who was a minor artist by comparison. Honoré Daumier (1808-79) was one of the most original and profound figure painters in oil in the history of art, and a sculptor who foreshadowed Expressionism. His public reputation, however, rested for most of his life on his satirical caricatures, published in journals from 1824, and exploiting to the full the technical possibilities of lithography. His satire extended almost everywhere, but was most often political, directed against the absolute monarchy of Charles X, and then, after 1830, against Louis-Philippe, whom Daumier held to be a turncoat. After

Louis-Philippe had been toppled in 1848, Daumier's wary scepticism was not appeased by the new Republic or by the new Empire of Napoleon III. His crucial strength was his ability to extract from a topical situation a visual image that summarized an essential quality of human life.

Daumier's artistic stature was gradually acknowledged after 1848. Balzac compared him to Michelangelo, the younger generation saluted him and the aging Delacroix even copied his oils – sombre images often very pessimistic in atmosphere. His *Third-class carriage*, about 1862, shows working-class people in an entirely modern situation, unidealized yet monumental in their patient passivity. Contrariwise, he took one of the archetypal symbols of Romantic failure in European literature, Don Quixote, and, in a series of paintings (not shown), invested him with a strangely credible, eerie reality that no other illustrator of Cervantes has begun to approach. His dense yet vigorous paint reflects both Rubens and Rembrandt, and owes something to Delacroix, but its effect, of an image stirring within the paint, is unique.

About the time that Daumier started paint-

ing working-class subjects, in the mid-1840s, Jean-François Millet (1814-75) turned his attention to subjects drawn from the life of the peasantry. In his densely-worked oils, featuring a single peasant, or a small group, at work in a dimly defined, apparently infinite landscape, Millet created a rural, peasant version of heroic painting. As social comment this could be called reactionary or nostalgic, for Millet did not paint the new working class of the cities; to later generations his sentiment, for instance in his most famous picture, *The angelus*, has seemed, in fact, sentimental; the great power of his style, its monumental simplicity, its classical significance, are only now being reassessed.

The opposite of Millet's vision of the heroic countryside appeared in the horrific townscapes of the intense, even neurotic, Charles Meryon (1821-68), a rather isolated figure. Owing to colour blindness he worked in black-and-white: Victor Hugo praised his topographic etchings of Paris, as visions of the city as a staging-post to Hell. Gustave Doré (1832-83; not shown), better known for his illustrations to literary classics, also illustrated the slums in *London: A Pilgrimage*, 1872.

DAUMIER (left)
The third-class carriage, c. 1862
The brushwork is almost grimy, strengthening the impression of dullness and the grinding poverty of the travellers. Without heroism or sentiment, each is firmly and clearly characterized. Painstakingly, Daumier sought perfection in several versions made of this scene.

MERYON (right)
The morgue, 1854
The harsh contrasts of light and shade combine with the scratchy line to conjure up a hauntingly claustrophobic setting for macabre, ant-like figures about their doomed business. Meryon's highly expressive townscapes are just as Romantic as Realist.

MILLET (left)
The sower, 1850
In 1848 the peasantry had rebelled, protesting exploitation and oppression, and Millet's first version of *The sower*, exhibited in that year, was denounced as socialist. In fact his intent was more to evoke the eternal, almost biblical unity of man and land.

MILLET (right)
The angelus, 1855-57
The religious element is now more explicit. The subject had also a personal meaning for Millet, since his beloved grandmother had always stopped, when the angelus was rung, to pray for "those poor dead". Warm colours of evening strengthen the sentiment, without vitiating Millet's firm draughtsmanship. In the 1860s Millet turned to pure landscape (see p. 93).

Courbet: The Artist's Studio

Gustave Courbet (1817-77) painted his huge *Artist's studio* (it is nearly six metres (20ft) wide) in 1854-55. He subtitled it *A real allegory, determining a phase of seven years in my artistic life* when it was first exhibited in his independent "Pavilion of Realism" at the Universal Exhibition in Paris in 1855. The critical reception was very mixed, but the 40 or so works displayed established Realism, or Courbet's personal vision of it, as a powerful movement that could not be ignored.

Courbet himself gave a long, detailed account of this painting, starting: "It is the moral and physical history of my studio." On the right are "all the shareholders, that is my friends the workers, the art collectors. On the left, the other world of trivialities – the common people, misery, poverty, wealth, the exploited, the exploiter; those who thrive on death". It is not clear either from the individual characterizations, or from Courbet's own description (intellectual rigour was never his *forte*), which represent good and which bad

in the left-hand group, but an acquaintance of Courbet's said that the seated huntsman with his dog and the farm labourers behind him stood for healthy country life. Others in the group included workers representing poverty and unemployment in the urban working classes; a destitute old republican of 1793 – all that was left of the heroic legend of Revolution and the Napoleonic Empire – a curé, an undertaker, and a pedlar hawking rubbish. The group on the right includes Courbet's loyal patron, Bruyas, the philosopher Proudhon, the writer Champfleury, and the poet and critic Baudelaire with open book. But the focus of the picture is the artist himself at work, attended by a superbly painted nude (Naked Truth), and a child (Innocence), though it is a landscape of his native Ornans region that is depicted on the easel.

The composition can be construed as a secularized *sacra conversazione* in triptych form; the plaster figure with adjacent skull, behind the canvas, appears to be a crucified

COURBET (above)
Self-portrait with a black dog, 1844
In this, Courbet's first accepted Salon picture, the subject – an informal figure in a rural setting – is in the tradition of van

Dyck and Gainsborough, but the self-assurance of the face, compounded by the low viewpoint, establishes the young man's individuality. This initiates a series of robust, extrovert *Self-Portraits* of some power.

Christ. It also invites comparison with that Neoclassical manifesto, Ingres's *Apotheosis of Homer* (see p.85), but Courbet's central figure of artistic genius (himself) is set in the context of real people from contemporary life ("society at its best, its worst and its average . . . my way of seeing society in its interests and its passions"). The theme has been interpreted in terms of Fourierist socialism – a personal, concrete expression of an association of Capital, Labour and Talent, an ideal harmony of society. Yet the picture also expresses alienation in a way that Baudelaire himself might have approved: there is scarcely any communication between the three groups, or even between some figures in the groups. The artist in the centre is the hope of communication.

As "real allegory" the picture's internal contradictions baffled contemporaries. The people are all real, faithfully and vividly portrayed, but as an event the gathering is impossible, and even its setting, the walls of the studio, is vague and unidentified. The choice

of characters is also far from an adequate representation of contemporary society. However, it made an impression (Delacroix considered it "one of the most outstanding paintings of the times") and it has since continued to fascinate. Not least, it opens a doorway to modern art: here the artist is shown dominant at the centre of the world. In *The studio* not just the artist, but for the first time the "activity of creating art" becomes the subject. In Courbet's self-portraits and in his portraits of his friends, too, the artist as maker assumes heroic stature, even when surrounded by children, as is *Proudhon*.

Courbet had come to Paris from his native Ornans, in the mountainous Jura of France, in 1840. His early *Self-portrait with black dog* suggests his flamboyant and truculent character, though not his lifelong social and political commitment. Even though *The studio* was the last major work in which he tried to programme his political, social and moral ideals, he continued to participate in politics, taking a

prominent part in the Commune of 1871, until, following a brief imprisonment, he was forced into exile in Switzerland, where he died. His artistic and social sympathies are strikingly expressed in the unemotional but monumental *Stone-breakers* (1849; destroyed) – two men shown simply at their dehumanizing task. In the same year he also depicted a small-town funeral, *A burial at Ornans*, on an heroic scale. He always drew on the real, but with great variety and with a brilliantly broad and free style, often laying on with a palette-knife. Courbet's still lifes have a density, a weight of presence comparable with those of Chardin or, for that matter, of Cézanne. His nudes were of a veracity, sometimes unflattering but often also startlingly erotic, that many found offensive. *The bathers*, again a life-size genre subject, allegedly provoked Napoleon III to assault it with his riding whip at the Salon of 1853. Perhaps, however, his landscapes of the Jura (see over) are the best examples of the beauty, the rich, sombre colour, of his paint.

COURBET (left)
The artist's studio,
1854-55
Courbet's great manifesto rejects both academicism, represented by the dusty plaster figure, and Romanticism, symbolized by the plumed hat and the guitar. Champfleury, Baudelaire and Proudhon, however, who are shown in it, expressed dislike of the work, finding Courbet's vanity and the autobiographical tone of the painting distracting. It is in fact the true subject.

COURBET (left)
The stone-breakers, 1849
Courbet wrote to a friend: "I stopped to look at two men breaking stones on the road. It is rare to find an expression of such utter and complete misery; and at once I had an idea for a picture." It was neither expressionist nor sentimental, however.

COURBET
A burial at Ornans,
1849-50
All sorts of people from Courbet's native town posed for this vast canvas, a mirror of provincial life and death. The onlookers' grief, fear and indifference are dispassionately noted; the faces struck Parisian critics as shockingly ugly.

COURBET (left)
The bathers, 1853
The scandal of the 1853 Salon, *The bathers* attracted universal odium. It is an incongruous picture: even if the women are earthily mundane, their extravagant gestures are reminiscent of the nymphs and goddesses of 17th- and 18th-century art, but almost violent.

COURBET (above)
Pierre-Joseph Proudhon and his family, 1865
Proudhon's "thinker" pose and books indicate a larger reality than the man amidst his family (the portrait is set in 1853). Details such as his worn shoes and his daughters' toys enable the viewer to reconstruct the sitter's situation, though.

French Landscape: The Barbizon School

The art of landscape was relatively slow to become established in France; although in England Constable and Turner, in Germany Friedrich and also more modest German and Austrian naturalist painters had considerably broadened its scope, landscape in France at first remained firmly rooted in the tradition of Poussin – the ideal landscape, conceived as a stage for an heroic story. Landscape was officially accepted as a distinct category of art only in 1817, and its acclimatization dates really from about 1824, when the impact of Constable and of Bonington, shown that year in Paris, was sharply felt, though artists were already preconditioned by a growing Romantic concern with the direct study of Nature.

This interest was matched by an increasing attention to the seventeenth-century Dutch painters, and was most fruitful in the remarkable but still underestimated work of Georges Michel (1763-1843). Rather isolated, and neglected by contemporary critics, his landscapes recall those of Rembrandt or Ruisdael, but he was one of the first to work in the open air, and his contention that a landscapist needed a mere four square miles to provide him with subject matter for a lifetime is close to Constable's discovery of the ordinary and everyday.

The brief-lived Richard Parkes Bonington (1802-28) is an important link between the English and French schools; though he was English-born, from the age of 15 he lived mainly in France, and was a friend of Delacroix. If his brilliantly handled genre scenes of medieval and oriental subjects owe much to French example, his landscapes in oil or in watercolour, especially when painted directly from the subject, have an immediacy of effect and brilliance of colour rivalling the native British tradition. He and Delacroix were in turn friends of Paul Huet (1803-69). Political activist on the barricades in the 1830s and, to begin with, dogmatically opposed to academicism, Huet briefly associated with the Barbizon painters, and ended as the so-to-speak official leader of Romantic landscape when Romanticism had become respectable. His output is of variable quality, but, working consistently in the open, he could usually retain spontaneity in his less formal pictures.

Barbizon is a village on the fringe of the Forest of Fontainebleau, where numerous painters worked and often lived, "led" by Théodore Rousseau (1812-67). Rousseau was certainly impressed by Constable, and based

ROUSSEAU (left)
A group of oaks near Barbizon, 1852
A simple rustic view, with the spreading oaks elevated into a splendidly imposing image, a sense of sun and shade, the heavy peace of afternoon – what more could anyone want of landscape? Critics carped at the unconventional composition, the use of broad brushwork and often dense impasto.

BONINGTON (below)
View of Normandy? c. 1824
Bonington made several trips to Normandy between about 1820 and 1828, setting off on the open road, stick in hand and knapsack with painter's gear on his back. The fresh, light spontaneity of this painting is typical of his style; quite probably he painted it north of Paris in the countryside Michel also painted, with different effect.

MICHEL (right)
The storm, c. 1820-30
Michel dramatized the fields and heaths outside Paris with bold strokes of colour within a dark tonality. This is not a finished work but an *ébauche*, an oil-sketch in which the elements of the picture were "blocked out".

HUET (below)
Elms at St-Cloud, 1823
Huet shared the irritation of Academicians faced with "unfinished" works, though he esteemed spontaneity. Like Corot and Rousseau, he kept in the studio his studies, which can now be compared with the exhibited works of the Impressionists.

DAUBIGNY (right)
Snow scene: Valmondois, 1875
Snow scenes were an excuse for the almost abstract play of tones and colours, and were painted by Courbet and the Impressionists. By the 1870s Daubigny was commercially successful and respectable, but also friendly with Monet; as a member of the Salon jury, he gave the Impressionists what support he could.

his work on the close scrutiny and analysis of natural forms on site. He was in fact the ancestor of much academic landscape of the later nineteenth century, and accepted as such from about 1850, but in his early days (consistently rejected by the Salon between 1836 and 1848) he was known as "*le grand refusé*". His work shows him a master of stillness, though his imagination seems sometimes constrained by a rather dour naturalism.

The work of Narcisse Virgile Diaz de la Pena (1807-76) was more immediately acceptable: he painted the Fontainebleau woods with a much freer (sometimes rather flashy) style, and established an enduring popularity. Charles-François Daubigny (1817-78) was, in an historical sense, perhaps more important than either Rousseau or Diaz, for he is the link between their naturalism and the development of Impressionism – he was criticized precisely for producing mere "impressions". He always worked directly from his subject, in which water and sky often played a large part (he used a boat as a floating studio). Early insistence on detail gradually yielded to a more free and open style, with which he achieved remarkable effects of light and atmosphere. In 1865 he was

with Courbet, Monet and Boudin at Trouville, and his influence on Monet was considerable; the spirit if not the technique of his later paintings is closely akin to that of the early Impressionists.

Rousseau and Daubigny had no great political involvement, unlike Courbet and Millet, whose work was far from being confined to pure landscape, and who are generally classified as Realists (see pp. 88 ff). The best of Courbet's landscapes (and the more directly and faithfully dependent on nature, the better they are) combine a material drama with a sense of massive formal structure that has not been surpassed; however, when he introduced emotional elements – animals – he could be almost as sentimental as Landseer. Millet was closely associated with Barbizon from 1849, but only in his latest work did pure landscape play the dominant role in his vision.

The greatest landscape painter of the mid-century presents a curious paradox of Romantic and classic values. Jean-Baptiste-Camille Corot (1796-1875), amiable in person, unambitious, detached from politics, avoiding controversy, went his own admirable, independent way (in 1846, when he was awarded

the Légion d'Honneur, aged 50, he was still being subsidized financially by his father). Crucial to his development was his Italian sojourn, 1824-28, where it was not the awesome aura of the Old Masters that impressed him, but the lucid light of the Italian countryside. There Corot worked directly from the subject, painting generally small-scale pictures, tuned as it were by his perfect tonal pitch, and harmonized by a sense of design as delicate as the finest balance. The crystal clarity of these idylls is partly the result of his technique: he used thinned, translucent paint applied almost in washes but with sharp precision. Back in France, he then developed a poetical type of landscape of an entirely different character, almost a Romantic variation on Rococo dreams of rustic but elegant figures in a silvery-greeny-grey haze of foliage; these, once extremely successful, were subsequently condemned out of hand, and are only now becoming seriously appreciated again for their painterly subtleties. In his later years, in certain figure paintings and portraits (not shown), Corot developed a power of sculptural modelling that surpasses even Courbet's, and is not to be found again till Cézanne.

DIAZ DE LA PENA (left)
Gypsies going to a fair,
1844
For years a familiar figure

in and about Fontainebleau, Diaz painted richly dappled woodland scenes, bubbling with light and bright colour.

COURBET (below)
The Loue valley in stormy weather, c. 1849
In 1849 Courbet spent the summer near Paris with Corot. He used light effects to define space, rather than the conventional structure of planes receding from a sharply defined foreground.

MILLET (above)
Spring, 1868-73
In Millet's late work the forces of Nature assume the epic quality that his labouring peasants once had. His later technique was looser, lighter, more colourful, perhaps under the influence of early Monet.

COROT (above)
The island of San Bartolommeo in Rome, 1825
Such fresh Italian studies, bathed in Mediterranean light, were, for Corot, raw material for more stately, if also very fine landscapes destined for the Salon.

COROT (below)
View of Avray, c. 1835-40
Here Corot animated one of his favourite views with little dabs of paint, in a way that looks forward to the fresh visions of Renoir. These pictures became the foundation of his reputation.

Edouard Manet

Political revolutions rarely lead to the instant stability of the new regime, and the upheavals of 1848 and 1870 in France were no exception. The radical republicanism that toppled Louis-Philippe in 1848 led within three years to the *coup d'état* by Louis-Napoleon, who was established (by plebiscite) as Napoleon III of the Second Empire. His downfall in 1870, after catastrophic defeat by the Germans, was followed by the socialist, even anarchic, Commune in Paris before relative stability was achieved by the Third Republic. The Second Empire was nevertheless a period of brilliant opulence and artistic ferment.

The 1850s and 1860s contained a rich profusion of styles, practised by overlapping generations – Delacroix died only in 1863 and Ingres in 1867, while Courbet, born in 1819, was at the peak of his powers. The rising generation, born mostly in the 1830s, became notorious during the 1860s; pioneering the most fundamental revolution in the visual arts since the Renaissance, they were not yet acceptable to public or academic opinion.

Edouard Manet (1832-83) was early on considered the leader of the avantgarde, although he dissociated himself from formal connection with the painters who became known as the Impressionists. Born of a well-to-do family, he was slightly older than they were, and the image he presented to the public all his life was that of the elegantly conventional man-about-town, just as he appears in the polite effigy by Henri Fantin-Latour (1836-1904). His art, on the other hand (when he emerged from Couture's *atelier*), flouted convention in both style and content.

If Courbet, most clearly in his *Studio* (see p. 90), had demonstrated the artist's sovereignty, showing the artist as hero in the act of re-creating the world, in Manet the germs are visible of that development by which the paint itself becomes the subject. From Realism he learned the importance of taking subjects from contemporary life and treating them on a life-size scale. However, he combined this approach with an audacious adaptation of traditional iconographic themes, sometimes even adopting the style of the Old Masters, especially the Spanish and the Venetians. His *Absinth drinker* of 1859 was rejected by the Salon, although *The guitarist* (not shown) of 1861 was a success; real confrontation came in 1863, when (following noisy controversy over

MANET (left)
The absinth drinker, 1858
Manet's portrait of a local character, well known in the streets round the Louvre, was perhaps suggested by some verses in Baudelaire's *Fleurs du Mal*. It belongs to a genre created by Spanish painters in the 17th century, but its muted tones and lack of spatial definition were disliked by academics, and Manet's teacher, Couture.

MANET (right)
"*Le Déjeuner sur l'Herbe*" (The picnic), 1863
The *Déjeuner* is clearly in direct line of descent from "*Le Concert Champêtre*" in the Louvre (see vol. 2 p. 142) then given to Giorgione. Manet's reinterpretation answers Baudelaire's call to the painter to find the poetry in modern life, and the eternal in the transitory.

MANET (left)
Olympia, 1863
The girl's direct glance and the hostile pose of her black cat implicate the viewer in a scene of *demi-mondaine* life. The jewels, ribbon and slippers, which provocatively enhance her nudity, and the black attendant all suggest that she is a young courtesan receiving one of her clients.

MANET (right)
Oil-sketch for *The execution of Emperor Maximilian*, 1867
The Mexican Emperor had been assisted by the French government, and his death shocked the French public. The soldiers wear uniforms like those of the French Army, but Manet's view is otherwise strictly detached.

the Salon's policy of acceptance and rejection), Napoleon III arranged a Salon des Refusés, an event sometimes still cited as the starting point of modern art. The *refusés* included Manet, Whistler, Pissarro, even Cézanne.

The major scandal was caused by Manet's "*Déjeuner sur l'Herbe*" (The picnic), in which Manet repeated with some exactness figures from a subject by Raphael engraved by Marcantonio. In the engraving (not shown) the three main figures were all nude, but Manet clad the two males in the dark jackets and trousers of 1863, leaving the female figure naked; her direct and unabashed gaze invites the spectator into the picture. The spectators of 1863 mostly rejected the invitation with rage and ridicule. But the manner of the painting was scarcely more acceptable than the subject matter, and upset even Courbet. Manet suppressed the traditional rendering of form in chiaroscuro, with modelling by gradation of tone, in favour of a method that seemed, at first, flat – in fact it caught the effect of unfiltered daylight, simplifying detail, sharpening silhouettes and kindling colour.

In the same year Manet painted his most famous picture, *Olympia*, though he did not submit it to the Salon until 1865. Surprisingly it was accepted, but its reception by the public was extremely hostile. The subject matter, echoing – or perverting – the established tradition of recumbent nudes descending from Titian's "*Venus of Urbino*" (see vol. 2 p. 145) to Goya's *Nude maja* (see p. 64), was found obscene. (The fashionably acceptable version is represented by Cabanel's *Birth of Venus*, see p. 87.) One critic called her "Manet's rancid Olympia". Here Manet even more markedly simplified and emboldened his handling, using no half-tones, but flat colour which he disposed, contrapuntally, in sharp contrasts. The delicate subtlety of the harmonies of blacks, greys, and whites was recognized only years later; what appeared as vulgar banality is now seen as a brilliant metamorphosis of a somewhat over-exploited subject.

From 1866 Manet had the support not only of Baudelaire, but of Zola, a positively pugnacious apologist. Meanwhile, his control of form developed following a visit to Spain, while both his compositions and his aloof, objective approach to his subject matter were influenced by Japanese prints, then just beginning to become popular, and by photo-graphy. Typical is the portrait of *Zola*, which unites still life and vivid portraiture – the casual informality of the writer's working study transposed into a very intricate pictorial structure. In his *Execution of Maximilian* there may be an explicit political comment, but generally Manet's realism was apolitical; as Zola replied to the socialist requirements of Courbet's friend Proudhon, "The artist is at no-one's service and we refuse to enter yours".

In the 1870s Manet's frequent reliance on blacks and greys, on flattened silhouettes, was happily "aerated" by the influence of the Impressionists, though he refused to exhibit with them as a group. His colour key heightened; his handling of paint became lighter, looser and still more deft, and, though he hardly ever (being essentially an urban creature) painted landscape, much of his work became suffused with light, air and movement. His importance as a graphic artist is also considerable; he translated some of his own most important works into prints for wide publication, but also produced some vivid journalism, notably of the Siege of Paris – a black-and-white equivalent of his power of summary description in painting.

MANET (left)
Emile Zola, 1868
The Japanese *Samurai* print and painted screen, and the reproduction of a Velazquez (hidden by one of his own *Olympia*) are a tribute by Manet to the influences on his work.

MANET (right)
Argenteuil, 1874
At Argenteuil by the Seine with Monet in the summer of 1874, Manet became convinced of the value of *plein-air* painting, even though Impressionist interest in the transitory never affected his concern for structure.

MANET (below)
Chez Père Lathuille, 1879
The restaurant proprietor's son posed as an eager lover of the smart young woman. Manet's technique is freer than ever before – note the quick strokes on the hand.

MANET (right)
Civil War, 1871
During the 1870 Commune Manet saw corpses like this on the streets of Paris, and made a rapid drawing, the basis for his lithograph. The body of the soldier in the centre recalls an earlier work by Manet, *The dead toreador* (not shown), but also Daumier's *Rue Trans-nonain* (see p. 88) and a long tradition going back to Mantegna and Grünewald. Here is another example of Manet charging old forms with sharp topical reference.

Whistler: Falling Rocket

James Abbot McNeill Whistler (1834-1903) was a true international – born in Massachusetts, brought up early on in Russia, then at West Point (failed in Chemistry); as a Navy cartographer he learnt the techniques of etching, before his definitive expatriation in 1855, first to Paris, and, in 1859, to London. Wit, dandy and aesthete, he provoked outrage and astonishment in the sedate worlds of High Victorian art and society.

On his arrival in Paris in 1855, as a student, he was struck by Courbet's forceful denunciations of the official art of the Paris Salon after visiting his one-man show, the celebrated "Pavilion of Realism". In 1859, rejected by the Salon, Whistler, with Manet, showed in a later, comparable "counter-exhibition" where Whistler's *At the piano*, modelled by mass and colour rather than line, was approved by Courbet; subsequently, Whistler was profoundly influenced by Courbet, and at times worked alongside him, although his admiration for the tonal subtleties of Velazquez's paintings in the Louvre and for the flattened, schematic patterning of Japanese prints was to prove more enduring inspiration. (Japanese prints began to arrive in numbers in Paris in the 1850s, and in the 1860s Whistler built up a considerable collection of Japanese art.)

From 1859, with his move to London, Whistler fought off the influence of Courbet. His famous *White girl* of 1862, a *succès de scandale* (alongside such landmarks as Manet's "*Déjeuner sur l'Herbe*") at the Salon des Refusés in 1863, reflects something of the wistful characterizations of young women painted by the Pre-Raphaelite Rossetti. It is an exquisite modulation of tones of white, and Whistler later added the definition *Symphony in white no. 1* to the title. This is symptomatic both of his increasing dedication to the subtle gradations of tonal painting and of his belief in the importance of purely formal pictorial values – overriding that of literal representation. His musical titles – *Symphony, Arrangement* and later the famous *Nocturnes* – stress his notion of the harmonics of tone, colour and line – the equivalent of a kind of mood music. Even in portraiture he claimed the supremacy of abstract form over naturalistic representation. His preferred title for *The artist's mother* (1872), one of the most famous of nineteenth-century portraits (and paradoxically, it seems, a most faithful one), was *Arrangement in grey and black no. 1*. In its subdued delicate tonalities it echoes Velazquez, but its flattened space, its exquisitely calculated disposition ("arrangement") across the picture plane – these qualities anticipate the abstract preoccupations of much twentieth-century painting; they also affected younger Impressionists, and indeed Seurat, when the painting was shown in Paris in 1882, and later they were adapted by Intimistes such as Bonnard and Vuillard. As to the subject of the portrait, Whistler provocatively denied the right of the public to be concerned with it; an arrangement in black and white was what it was – "To me", he said, "it is interesting as a picture of my mother, but what can or ought the public to care about the identity of the portrait?" However, in spite of the emphasis here on purely formal values, and elsewhere in his work on instantaneity, Whist-

WHISTLER (above)
Falling rocket: Nocturne in black and gold, c. 1874
In Whistler's words, "The masterpiece should appear as the flower to the painter ... with no reason to explain its presence – a joy to the artist – a delusion to the philanthropist – a puzzle to the botanist." Aestheticism had no room for art expressing the goodness of Nature, as Ruskin saw it.

WHISTLER (left)
At the piano, 1858-59
The counterpoint of black and white already suggests an association of tonality with musical harmonics.

ler was never really at one with Impressionist theory or practice: he was essentially subjective rather than objectively descriptive. His work, however, was equally incomprehensible to his contemporaries.

His confrontation with established British art and the public came to a climax in 1876 with the exhibition in London of *Nocturne in black and gold: Falling rocket*. Painted about 1874, it is a lyrical exclamation of delight at the effect of fireworks, raining coloured fire through the night at a display in a London pleasure garden. The English critic John Ruskin was revolted by it, for reasons that are not entirely clear (for Ruskin had been the champion of the late work of Turner). Then at the height of his prestige as national moral, no less than artistic, prophet, Ruskin in a famous article denounced Whistler for flinging "a pot of paint . . . in the public's face". Whistler sued for libel. The resulting trial was (in retrospect) one of the most entertaining in legal history. Whistler's wit coruscated, even more brilliantly than his painted fireworks. Some of the phrases used have passed into the language. Asked how long he had taken to "knock off" the painting", he answered, "About two days"; asked then if it was for two days' work that he asked 200 guineas, he replied: "No. I ask it for the knowledge of a lifetime". It is a response, provoking applause in the courtroom, that still echoes today. Whistler won, but he was awarded only a token farthing damages, and the costs led to his bankruptcy.

Whistler's harmonics were usually more subdued than those of the *Rocket*, above all perhaps in his twilight meditations on the Thames, transmuting its industrial daytime prose into mysterious dreamy poems – drifts of shadow glinting here and there with reflected lights. Such works as his *Cremorne lights: Nocturne in blue and silver*, 1872, pre-date Monet's mist-hazed accounts of Rouen Cathedral by nearly 20 years.

Delighting in controversy, deliberately provoking antagonism, Whistler was not the ideal propagandist to reconcile British taste with the new values of French art, although towards the end of his life his influence, especially on Sickert, was decisive. His prolific and delightfully sensitive etchings found an appreciative public, however, and his influence on interior decoration was also important; he was a pioneer in simplification, sweeping out Victorian clutter, using clear and plain colours.

WHISTLER (left)
Wapping-on-Thames,
1861-64
The limited colour range may owe a debt to Manet, but the silvery tones and the almost abstract design of masts and rigging behind the obliquely-angled foreground figures are wholly original.

WHISTLER (left)
The white girl: Symphony in white no. 1, 1862
The critic Castagnary thought she was a girl on the morning after her wedding night. Her soulful look, the drooping lily and contrast of pale and vivid colours perhaps suggested his interpretation: the picture seems an elegy for lost innocence.

WHISTLER (above)
The artist's mother: Arrangement in grey and black no. 1, 1862
Whistler's affection for his mother, a devout woman, was deep. Working rapidly, he refined each application of paint to reach a delicate, almost transparent harmony of tones, evoking the gentle resolve of his subject.

WHISTLER (left)
Cremorne lights: Nocturne in blue and silver, 1872
Whistler wrote to Fantin-Latour: "The same colour should appear in the picture continually here and there . . . in this way the whole will form a harmony. Look how well the Japanese understood this". The influence of Japanese prints is not overt, but they were fundamental to this simplified elegance.

WHISTLER (right)
Venetian palaces: Nocturne, 1879-80
The shimmering etched lines make mystery out of nuances of reflected light.

Impressionism 1: The Early Years

Paintings associated with the movement called Impressionism have become perhaps the most widely known, best loved and most easily assimilated pictures in the whole history of art – and delightful to live with, as the rich collectors of Europe and America discovered in the 1890s. The beginnings of Impressionism, however, were not auspicious. The Impressionists advanced in the first place from certain beach-heads established by the Romantics, by the Realists, especially Courbet and the Barbizon landscapists, and by Manet. They were committed to painting the world as they saw it – the world immediately around them, the modern world – that is, to realism, to naturalism, even to illusionism, though this was hardly recognizable as such at first to the public. Their Realist doctrine encouraged painting directly from the subject – if an open-air one, then out-of-doors. Yet concentration on the purely visible revealed an optical world composed of innumerable touches of colour, not necessarily encompassing or describing discrete, three-dimensional forms.

The Impressionist analysis could be undertaken in various ways. Monet and Sisley were more or less non-intellectual, attempting an intuitive apprehension of the effects of light. Others sought a rational analysis of the sensation of vision, as did Pissarro (at certain stages) and especially Seurat, whose pointillism was supposedly scientifically based. A third approach was concerned more with the objects that comprise the visible world, and the separateness and interrelationship of these objects are a major consideration in Degas's figure studies, in Renoir's later work, and above all in Cézanne's.

The movement started to coalesce amongst a little group of fellow-students in Paris between 1859 and 1864 – Pissarro, Monet, Renoir, Sisley and Bazille. They had common interests – Courbet, the Barbizon painters – and from about 1866 found in Edouard Manet a sympathetic elder. They also had in common the enthusiasm of youth, and an enemy, the orthodoxy of the academic Salon painters. However, they were sharply different personalities and were to develop along very different lines. They may initially have had some political affiliation, inevitably left-wing, but only Pissarro remained a committed and active socialist; their subject matter, however, was most often pleasure or pleasurable – people enjoying themselves, landscapes enjoyable to look at, celebrated in lively high-keyed colour. The movement formally emerged only in 1874, when the Impressionists' work had been rejected wholesale by the Salon, and they formed the Limited Company of Painters, Sculptors and Engravers, which staged its own exhibition in the studio of the photographer Nadar. It was then that they were dubbed "Impressionists". Between 1874 and 1886 there were eight exhibitions by the group, though the only important member to exhibit at all of them was Pissarro, and already in the early 1880s there were doctrinal and technical dissensions.

The main immediate precursors of Impressionism were Eugène Boudin (1824-98) and Johan Barthold Jongkind (1819-91; not shown). Boudin's delightfully airy little paintings, especially his seashore scenes, were, like Jongkind's, in the Barbizon tradition, but had an added vivacity and sparkle of colour, Impressionistic in effect. Claude Monet was (with Sisley) probably the most single-minded of the Impressionists (see over); Camille Pissarro (1830-1903), while loyal throughout to their initial premises, was the most aware of the necessity of development, including reaction

BOUDIN (right)
The jetty at Deauville, 1865
Boudin encouraged the boy Monet at Le Havre, and initiated him (overcoming his first reluctance) into the art of painting in the open air. His fresh seascapes abandoned tradition in their informality and lack of structure. Seen always from a distance, and noted rather than studied, these fashionable strollers of the resort are unposed; they are momentarily arrested on the canvas, just like the clouds.

PISSARRO (right)
Red roofs, 1877
The rich colours and thick strokes of paint impart a striking brilliance, without compromising an essential structure. Pissarro was the most perseveringly analytic of the Impressionists, always experimenting in the use of pure colours to render light.

RENOIR (left)
At the inn of Mother Anthony, 1866
Renoir's first monumental group portrait was a tribute to Courbet and to tradition. His approach is Realistic, and academic in its concern for form and structure, but its informality, the careful tonal harmony and experimental brushwork, are new.

RENOIR (right)
Monet working in his garden, 1873
With his "rainbow palette" Renoir infused his often unremarkable subjects with light and warmth and the feeling of summer. Working together at Argenteuil, both he and Monet used tiny dabs of paint, making the picture shimmer, bringing out its surface in blossoming colour.

to new styles and influences. Pissarro's early admiration for Corot yielded to one for Courbet; in a period at Pontoise, 1866-69 (where he was the neighbour of the young Cézanne, and encouraged him), his landscapes reflected Courbet's rather sombre-toned naturalism, which proved unpopular, and he lived in great poverty. In the Franco-Prussian war Frédéric Bazille (1841-70) was killed; Pissarro and Monet took refuge in London, and Monet's example, together with the experience of Constable and Turner, led Pissarro to a lighter palette and a looser technique with which to interpret the creative play of light over the

physical world. Through the 1870s in France, he was almost the anchorman of the movement, with a stubborn, sometimes slow and even occasionally boring scrutiny of nature – "the most naturalist of them all", observed one critic in 1878.

Pierre Auguste Renoir (1841-1919), from a poor family in Limoges, started life as a porcelain painter, which surely fostered his delight in delicate linear brushwork (not really an Impressionist quality) and in the brilliance of high colour translucent over a pure white ground. He first worked beside Monet in 1864, but even his early *At the inn of Mother Anthony*

shows his reliance on the traditional example of the Old Masters – "It is in the museum that one learns to paint", he later said, which is almost heresy to Impressionism. He also, in the mid-1860s, digested Courbet's lessons of monumentality and modelling, especially of the nude. In 1869, with Monet again at La Grenouillère, and in the next few years, he came as close to classic Impressionism as he ever did. Yet he remained obstinately always non-doctrinaire: his paintings are primarily a sensuous response to the pleasure life offers.

Alfred Sisley (1839-99) was in a sense the narrowest of the major figures of Impressionism, from 1870 concentrating solely on landscape in a very light and airy manner, scintillating with pure colour. At times his work is very close to Monet's; he showed great tonal sensitivity, painting floods, snow, mist in subdued colour with delicate subtlety.

Berthe Morisot (1841-95), taught by Corot, married Manet's brother Eugène, and she perhaps influenced Manet towards working in the open air – opening out his style into Impressionistic fragmented colour. She exhibited landscapes and scenes from domestic life at all but one of the Impressionist exhibitions.

MONET (left)
Impression: Sunrise, 1872
This was the painting that earned the Impressionists their name. "What freedom, what ease of workmanship", wrote one sarcastic critic. The title acknowledges that the work is a sketch; Monet exhibited it since it caught as well as any reworking the effect he sought. The lack of "finish", or labour, to which the critics objected, made possible its instantaneity.

SISLEY (right)
Floods at Port-Marly, 1876
Sisley's series recording the heavy floods at Port-Marly on the Seine near Paris are perhaps his most successful works. His style matured slowly, influenced to the last perhaps by Corot; he gradually came to adopt techniques used by Monet and Renoir, applying colour in small areas – almost in a divisionistic way – working intuitively, without theory. There is nothing English in his art; he was born of English parents in Paris.

RENOIR (above)
Mme Charpentier and her children, 1878
Renoir's later career was successful, after he found a market in the late 1870s for his seductive portraits of women and children. He achieves movement, vivid life in bright colour; what matters the bland absence of critical characterization?

BAZILLE (left)
The artist's family, 1867
Bazille was a member of the nuclear Impressionist group, but his development was cut short by his death in war. Just as he had felt impelled to volunteer, so his portrait is formidably respectable; he was conscientiously Realist, and worked hard at it, made sketches in the open air, and also used photographs.

MORISOT (above)
The butterfly chase, 1874
Morisot seems to combine the dashing, varied strokes of Monet or Renoir with the more smoothly graded tones, and favourite silvery

greens, of her teacher Corot. This scene is typical of her informal, intimate glimpses of women and children – though many were interiors. Her subject matter, unlike Manet's, was unoffending.

Claude Monet

Cézanne's famous summary of Claude Monet (1840-1926) contains an essential truth, applicable to Monet's work throughout his long career: "Monet is no more than an eye – but, my God, what an eye." His approach to his art was always pragmatic and intuitive, rather than based on scientific analysis; he was, however, endowed with a formidably stubborn stamina of purpose.

Monet was brought up in Le Havre, and his early awareness of open marine light may well have been a lasting influence, as his exposure to African sunlight during army service in Algiers, 1860-62, certainly was. In Le Havre Boudin (see preceding page) introduced the teenager to the possibilities of open-air painting, to the search for an equivalent in paint to the look and feel of moving light and air; a little later Jongkind, with his sensitivity to changing light and weather, opened his eyes still further.

In Paris, he became a student with the academician Gleyre, and in Gleyre's studio in 1859 his association with the future Impressionists – Renoir, Sisley, Pissarro – began. An early marked influence from Courbet – his use of strong earth colours, his broad, direct technique with the palette knife – yielded to

that of Manet; Monet's own "*Déjeuner sur l'Herbe*" (The picnic; not shown) and his *Ladies in the garden* of 1866 and 1867 are at once a salute and an extension to Manet's *Déjeuner* (see p. 94). They are woodland idylls really, but contemporary, non-mythical, and Realist – a sun-dappled, relaxed bourgeois picnic treated on the heroic scale, life-size, painted from nature – with the interest shifting markedly to the effects of light.

After 1867, and the mass rejection from the Salon of work by himself and his friends, he settled all the more obstinately into his independence, though he often had to live in great poverty. With Renoir at the riverside restaurant and bathing resort of La Grenouillère, painting in the open air, he pursued the interplay of light on restless water, working out for himself by experiment the way that the surface colour of objects and even shadows are modulated into a quite different appearance by reflected light and the neighbouring colours. He tried out techniques of fragmentary brushwork, using pure colours, especially primaries (red, yellow, blue) against their complementaries (green, violet, orange), laid on in short, broad strokes. He became fascinated with

NADAR (above)
Claude Monet, 1899
Monet's patriarchal figure altered little in his last 25 years. At 84, visitors found him still robust – "an impression of rusticity dispelled as soon as he spoke: then one realized how great a spirit he was".

MONET (below)
The cart – snow-covered road at Honfleur, 1865
Jongkind often painted the one scene in different weathers. Jongkind's urge to precise observation and Courbet's vigorous style here combine to influence Monet's early technique.

MONET (left)
La Grenouillère, 1869
Of all the Impressionists, Monet and Renoir were the most interested in scenes of contemporary life, especially the unpretentious and lively gatherings of the Parisian working and middle classes. La Grenouillère, a resort on the Seine near Chatou, was a perfect subject and, painting there, the styles of the two artists came as close as they ever did. Both used fragmented brushstrokes and dots to render the river's shifting surface, but Monet's technique was the broader, with a vibrancy in which the movement both of the landscape and of the people in it is mirrored.

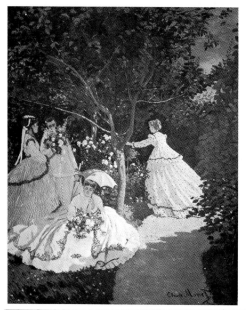

MONET (left)
Ladies in the garden, 1867
Monet's obsessive fidelity to appearances is revealed in the story that he dug a trench in his garden to hold his giant canvas, so he could work directly from nature. He painted it in several sessions from one model in various dresses and poses, but worked only in bright sunlight, in order to retain the unified impression of a brilliant summer's day.

MONET (right)
Gare St Lazare, 1877
Monet explores mainly the vaporous effects of steam and smoke within a light-filled but confined space. Touches of vivid colour, especially red, serve to bring forward more distant forms and to determine the relative positions of the objects in the opaque air.

atmospheric conditions, and painted mists and thaws in which mass and form almost dissolved, until light itself seemed to be the subject – the physical objects hardly more than the means by which light could conjure up its own shape. Traditional linear perspective vanished; the depth of the painting was established by the accuracy of the aerial perspective and the recession of the colours.

In 1870-71, Monet took refuge from the Franco-Prussian War in London, and there, though always critical of their work as a whole, took note of Constable's style and especially of Turner's, whose atmospheric concerns had anticipated his, although Turner had worked with different techniques and from different principles of colour. Back in Paris, Monet, with Pissarro, was the main instigator of the first independent Impressionist exhibition, and it was from one of his studies shown there, of a harbour sunrise (see preceding page), that critics coined the word "Impressionism", which has stuck ever since.

In 1877 Monet began his long series of studies, often repeated from the same spot, of a single motif, shown under different conditions and at different times of day. The *Gare St Lazare* series was the first, continuing the Realist emphasis on themes from contemporary life (the poet and critic Gautier had called railway stations "the new cathedrals of humanity, the centres where all ways converge"). In another sense, however, it was a new departure in naturalism, an attempt at absolute loyalty to the ephemeral effect at a given moment. These series would eventually develop, in his final *Waterlilies*, into the equivalent of musical variations on a theme.

By 1880, Monet's personal relationships with the other Impressionists were beginning to fade, as both they and he increasingly developed their own divergent styles. Monet's work continued very bright in key, but increasingly he abstracted the interplay of colours from the forms on which light kindles them. During the 1880s he travelled extensively, sometimes using a travelling "canvas box": in the box a number of canvases was slotted, and he would move from one canvas to another as the day wore on and the light changed. But he began sometimes (a shift from absolute naturalism) to modify the image before him in the interests of creating a more satisfying colour structure – in this Seurat (see p. 110) may have influenced him. His formal simplifications sometimes resemble Gauguin's or van Gogh's.

Monet's acceptance by the general public came very slowly – in the mid-1880s he was even attacked by the younger generation, including Seurat, and criticized by otherwise enlightened critics. But by 1890 he was at last developing a popular market, especially in the United States, and in some financial security settled in on that long sequence of thematic series – his *Haystacks*, his *Poplars*, his *Rouen Cathedral*; the magical interpretations of London mist over the Thames; and, for all of 20 years from about 1900 till his eyesight failed before his death in 1926, the continuing variations on the lilies in his own water-garden at Giverny. These marvellous and often enormous canvases increasingly became simply harmonious modulations of colour – an effect that was to be noted with admiration by many painters of the second half of the twentieth century. And yet, although Kandinsky hailed the work of his later years – particularly the *Haystack* series – as the inspiration of modern abstract painting, Monet remained to his death a figurative painter, for whom the objects of Nature were the ruling inspiration.

MONET (above)
Two haystacks, 1891
Repeated studies of one motif in varying daylight conditions was the logical result of Monet's life-long concern with instantaneity. He moved from canvas to canvas, registering minute changes in the shimmering "envelope" of coloured light – here that of broad day.

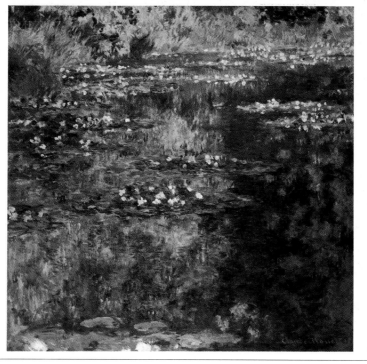

MONET (above)
The cliff at Etretat, 1883
During the 1880s Monet returned to the Normandy and Brittany coast to paint seascapes unprecedented in force and movement. The fury of the waves smacking through the narrow gap of a massive rock formation is captured in brushwork of a new breadth and freedom. But there is no trace of pantheistic Romanticism.

MONET (above)
Two haystacks, 1891
Now approaching sunset dims the palette and blunts the contrasts in an overall red. Kandinsky, on seeing one of the *Haystack* series, suddenly became aware of "the unsuspected power of the palette, which surpassed all my dreams ... At the same time, unconsciously, the object was discredited as an indispensable element of the picture", he wrote.

MONET (left)
The lilypond, after 1900
Though the growing formlessness of Monet's late works is partly explained by his failing vision, more significantly they represent the ultimate development of Impressionism into subjectivity. The recognizable features of the garden – the trees, banks and little Japanese bridge – dissolve in some of the richest, most poetic colour harmonies to be found in painting.

Impressionism 2: The Later Years

By the time of the last Impressionist exhibition in Paris in 1886, such coherence as the original Impressionists had ever had as a group had already largely disintegrated. The shock of novelty was being supplied by younger artists, such as Seurat, whose *La Grande Jatte* (see p. 110) was in the show. Pissarro exhibited some Seurat-influenced divisionist paintings; Monet and Renoir were absent. Degas, who had exhibited at five earlier shows, showed a sequence of pastels of nudes, or rather naked women (see over); yet, although Degas is associated with Impressionism, and he knew all the Impressionists well, it is difficult to call him one of them. He is more adequately described as a Realist (yet all the Impressionists would have claimed to be that). He was closest to Manet, in his insistence upon drawing and his respect for the Old Masters, and, though committed to contemporary subjects, he never worked in the open air or finished his figure studies in front of the model.

In 1886 van Gogh was in Paris; so was Toulouse-Lautrec; the American Mary Cassatt exhibited at the show. Gauguin was in Pont-Aven; both Pissarro and Cézanne had withdrawn from the fray, Pissarro to Eragny

PISSARRO (below)
A view from the artist's window, Eragny, 1888
Using Seurat's divisionist technique – but not his flat, summary forms or shallow space – Pissarro sought to capture the reflections of strong daylight in mingled dots of colour. The result is a spare, rather dull and unevocative painting.

RENOIR (below)
Umbrellas, c. 1881-84
Renoir is surely best loved for his paintings of women

– the sugary, sensual beauty of his standard female face. Here both Impressionist and harder brushwork appear.

and Cézanne to his native Aix-en-Provence, pursuing his lonely course (see p. 112) in modest financial independence following his father's death. 1886 saw the end of Cézanne's friendship with Zola, whom he had known from a boy, with the publication of Zola's novel *L'Oeuvre*, which branded him as an interesting failure. It was interpreted by many as a critical obituary of Impressionism. The original group, whom Pissarro now called the "Romantic Impressionists", were beset by individual problems of style, while their personal relationships had degenerated into what van Gogh saw as "disastrous squabbles".

We have followed the career of the supreme painter of Impressionism, Claude Monet, to his death in 1926 (see preceding page). The later career of Camille Pissarro never compromised his persistent integrity, his faithfulness to his original ideals; but the flexibility of his imagination and his curiosity enabled him to take into account the discoveries of much younger colleagues (he had supported Cézanne, Gauguin and Seurat). Pissarro was sustained by an idealistic belief in the moral and social importance of art ("The most corrupt form of art is sentimental art, orange-blossom

PISSARRO (below)
The Boulevard Montmartre at night, 1897
Despairing of a "scientific" analysis of light, Pissarro reverted to an intuitive

approach, painting with the skill of his hand rather than the calculation of his brain. He caught surface effects, sensations of moving light, more successfully than ever.

PISSARRO (left)
The potato harvest, 1886
In his correspondence with his son Lucien, which is full of intriguing sidelights on the Impressionist movement, Pissarro wrote: "It is only by drawing often, drawing everything, drawing incessantly that one fine day you find to your surprise you have rendered something in its true character." That reveals the artist, not the socialist or idealist. The need to sell work prompted his genre etchings, in which, perhaps, Pissarro's various talent forms a bridge from Millet's approach to that of Gauguin and the Nabis.

RENOIR (left)
The bathers, c. 1884-87
The design derives from a 17th-century lead relief, *Nymphs bathing*, by Girardon, but since these women are presumably bathing at some notional resort, the subject is rendered contemporary. There is a marked conflict between the firm drawing of the foreground nudes and the more Impressionistic treatment of the background; Renoir was seeking, in his own Post-Impressionism, to reconcile them. His nudes are in the grand tradition of Rubens and Courbet, but already show a concern to simplify form and outline.

art which makes pale women swoon"). Technically and theoretically, he saw the point of Seurat's divisionist analysis of light, and tried it out for himself between 1884 and 1888, only to find that it was irreconcilable with other, older principles – spontaneity, instantaneity, all those "effects, so random and so admirable of Nature". Also, his eyesight began to give trouble, and he reverted to a development of his earlier style; his later urban views are quintessentially Impressionistic in style and choice of subject. He achieved some financial security only in the 1890s, but when he died in 1903 he was acknowledged as a great master both by the public and by artists as diverse as Gauguin and Cézanne.

Auguste Renoir also had shown dissatisfaction with Impressionism, and had already declined to exhibit with the Impressionists in 1884. His increasingly solid modelling owes much to a renewed appreciation of the Old Masters, and his later work emphasized, in varying degrees, a formal and monumental quality. His *Umbrellas*, finished in 1884, is a carefully judged, elaborate design, though distinctly contemporary in subject matter. Shortly afterwards, he turned his attention to

the classical and timeless theme of the nude, and his *Bathers* of about 1884-87 was built up in the traditional studio manner, through successive preliminary drawings and studies – the result is quite remote from Impressionist instantaneity. This again was not satisfactory, and, though he continued painting ample and luscious nudes, he reverted to a more colouristic style in the 1890s – perhaps influenced by the brilliance of light he had seen on his trips to North Africa. In his late paintings his colour warmed, becoming even garishly hot.

Towards the end of his life Renoir realized what seems to have been a dream of his youth, and he turned to sculpture. Crippled with arthritis well before his death in 1919, he "dictated" to an assistant some of the most simple, monumental nude sculptures known to art, and they had some influence on the development of twentieth-century sculpture.

After World War I, by the time Renoir and Monet died, Impressionism was almost forgotten amongst working painters, but in the early, exploratory years the Impressionists had notably enlarged the scope of art. They had revealed a world brilliant with light and shot through with colour, and followed through

Realist principles, so that virtually anything in the world was a justifiable subject for art. Monet had identified one of his prime aims as "instantaneity", the translation into paint of a particular subject at a particular time, in a particular condition of light or weather. On the way this was done, photography and Japanese prints had a definite effect. As techniques improved, the camera was beginning to be able to freeze, within the rectangle of the film, the motion of passing life. The snapshot effect was eagerly exploited – by Degas in particular, but by Renoir, too, even in his *Umbrellas* – bodies could be cut off within the frame, and mere fragments could make up a picture. Japanese prints showed how asymmetrical elements in a composition could achieve a similar snapshot effect, and for younger painters, above all Gauguin, how effective strong colours and boldly outlined shapes could be, when distributed across the surface with equal emphasis. Even in the most essentially Impressionist works, such as Monet's series *Rouen Cathedral*, objective sight became difficult to distinguish from subjective vision, and the image represented had to be accommodated to the pattern of the picture surface.

RENOIR (left)
The washerwoman, 1917
The similarity between the heavy form of Renoir's nude and the work of Maillol (see p. 107) is obvious; Maillol had commented (on Renoir's late paintings of equally massive nudes): "That's real sculpture."

RENOIR (above)
Ambroise Vollard, 1908
Vollard, portrayed holding a statuette by Maillol, was a sharp businessman, and a connoisseur of some flair. He opened his gallery in the Rue Laffitte, Paris, in 1894 and became a major dealer in Impressionist paintings. His portrait by Cézanne or by Picasso (see p. 126) is of a quite different kind.

GAUGUIN (right)
Harvest in Brittany, 1888
This is an Impressionist work, but already the design is based on bold, silhouetted shapes (reflecting probably the influence of Japanese prints); colour is applied as frankly as possible. In Brittany Gauguin found an ideal of "primitive" life, and more to paint than only "the real and existing".

MONET (above)
Rouen Cathedral: full sunlight, 1894
After his series of *Haystacks* and *Poplars*, Monet embarked on more than 20 canvases studying the west front of Rouen Cathedral at different times of day from morning to evening.

The intricate forms of the decorative Gothic stonework dissolve in the play of light, and the Cathedral seems to lurk only nebulously behind the clotted brushwork. In this reduction to the purely optical, Realism is fulfilled, and undermined: its limits were made obvious.

Degas: The Little 14-Year-Old Dancer

Hilaire Germain Edgar Degas (1834-1917) was once described by Renoir as the greatest sculptor of the nineteenth century, a claim that may seem exaggerated not only in the light of other sculptors' work – especially Rodin's – but also because *The little 14-year-old dancer* was the only piece of sculpture exhibited publicly in Degas's lifetime. Yet his protégée Mary Cassatt, too, agreed with Renoir.

His reputation as sculptor has in fact only very recently rivalled his long-acknowledged stature as a master craftsman in paint, in pastel and in line. While Monet, Pissarro, Sisley seemed at times to dissolve mass and contour in atmosphere, Degas's artistic ancestry was from the Old Masters, and especially from Ingres. He always retained a profound admiration for Ingres's draughtsmanship. In his Realism, his emphasis on contemporary subject matter, he was entirely in key with Impressionist beliefs, but in his interpretation, in terms of line and silhouette, he was closest to Manet. Like Manet, he was an urban creature: his interest in landscape extended only as far as the race-course. Even there, he always followed traditional studio practice, not working in the open. Like Manet, too, he would cut off his figures at the frame – apparently arbitrarily, but in fact to achieve a calculated balance in the composition. He sought in so doing to enhance the impression of spontaneity and instantaneity, and he delighted in the immediacy of observations made from unusual angles. Yet he said: "No art was ever less spontaneous than mine. What I do is the result of reflection, and study of the great masters; of inspiration, spontaneity, temperament, I know nothing".

His subject matter ranged from the café life of Paris, even its murkier aspects – *The glass of absinth*, 1876 – to its *café-concerts* and of course to the ballet: it is the perennial charm of his young ballet-dancers that has established the enormous popularity of his work. Yet they are not, seen on close inspection, glamorized; indeed Degas's true subject was the animal body objectively observed, whether human or horse. His famous series of nudes bathing, washing, drying, rubbing down etc., were seen, he said, as if through a keyhole. "My

DEGAS (right and far right)
Two views of *The little 14-year-old dancer*, 1880
The critic Huysmans saluted Degas's work as "the only real modern attempt of which I know in sculpture". Comparable *Ballet-dancers* in wax left by Degas as mere sketches usually show more obviously the movement implicit here.

DEGAS (above)
The Bellelli family, 1858-59
The tensions of an unhappy family – Italian relatives of the artist – are shown in the aloof expression of the mother and half-turned back of the father, and also in their spatial relationship. Ingres, Pontormo, Holbein influenced his line, colour and poses and yet Degas's is a wholly contemporary work, already showing his concern for the expressive qualities of the human body.

DEGAS (right)
The glass of absinth, 1876
Degas often used a steep, angled viewpoint to give the effect of a random design, in which human subjects are caught unaware in their characteristic postures. The unbroken zigzag which here leads the eye in and out of the picture confines the dejected figures within a narrow space, reinforcing their mutual alienation.

women are simple, honest people, who have no other thought than their physical activity."

His portraits include some of the most remarkable painted in the whole nineteenth century. Even in a composition as monumental and structured as the early *Bellelli Family*, 1860-62, he achieves vividness, and the informal poses in the tightly organized design produce strong overtones of psychological strain.

From about 1872 he returned again and again to ballet themes, seeking in them the perfect balance between instantaneous, transitory effects of movement and the more general, abstract qualities found in classical artists; he avowed to a patron that he painted ballet scenes "because I find there, Madame, the combined movements of the Greeks". He represented them in all media, especially in drawings, over and over again, moving from oils by about 1880 to pastel applied in many different ways, as his difficulties with failing sight increased. As his control of line became less secure, his interest in colour grew, and so, too, probably his experiments in sculpture.

At his death more than 70 statuettes in wax, amongst many other broken fragments, were left in his studio, and were first cast in bronze in 1921. They were of horses, of nudes, and above all of dancers, modelled with a rough finish but an incomparable grasp of balance and the vital tension of implicit movement. *The little 14-year-old*, on a larger scale, is the only one worked up to a finish. Shown in the Impressionist Exhibition of 1881, it was, in its context, an almost blatant manifesto of Realism – a wax figure, with real hair, a satin ribbon, a muslin tutu. In the original wax model Degas had also supplied satin shoes and a linen bodice (though covered with wax). In the bronze casts, though, hair, ribbon, and tutu are "real", the remainder is metal, and the rather pert, plain face is not coloured – it is almost time-worn for a 14-year-old. The public seems to have found the extreme naturalism of the statuette disconcerting, and yet, for all its naturalism, *The little dancer* is in formal terms superbly sculptural, entirely in the round, only to be understood and grasped by the spectator's movement around it. Within, it is taut with intimations of movement.

DEGAS (below)
A dancer on stage with a bouquet, 1878
Japanese prints lie behind the bisection of the figures on the far left by the edge of the canvas, and the lack of linear perspective. Even in the dancer's triumph, in the ungainly stance of the chorus, the sheer physical effort of it all is stressed.

DEGAS (left)
Woman drying her feet, c. 1885
The detachment with which Degas studied the female nude (almost always, before, treated with a conscious delight) is due not to his "misogyny" but rather to an utterly unromantic approach to the visual world. His interest lay in the private language of the body, and in the relations of form to space. Yet in the velvety textures he created in his experiments with pastels, in the light held almost under the skin, in the tense contours of his models, the sensuality is undeniable. Degas's transformation of conventional media was of pioneering significance.

Sculpture in the Later 19th Century

In terms of quantity, sculpture reached new heights during the second half of the nineteenth century – the city centres, parks, public buildings, churches and cemeteries of the Western world are still populated by its products. There was also an increasing demand for sculpture on a smaller scale, as an element of bourgeois interior decoration, met by the development of patent pointing machines. Reduced facsimiles of famous works became available to all, in unlimited editions and in all sizes. The statuary of a living sculptor could also be published in this way, and reproductions became an important element in his income – like engravings for painters.

Within the wide variety of eclectic styles flourishing in Europe and America, a persistent Neoclassic strain was perhaps dominant. Classicizing sculpture adorns the neo-Gothic Albert Memorial in London (1864-76; see vol. I p.203). One of the most popular images of the century was the Canova-derived *Greek slave* by the American Hiram Powers (1805-73), shown at the Great Exhibition of 1851. The Englishman John Gibson (1790-1866) produced a *Tinted Venus* – reverting, historically quite correctly, to the Classical Greek practice of colouring marble – which caused a stir when exhibited in London in 1862. In Germany, rather later, the sculptor Adolf von Hildebrand (1847-1921) seems sometimes to have drawn inspiration from Archaic Greek *Kouroi*; he restated Neoclassical principles with resounding influence, though more by his writing – above all *Das Problem der Form*, 1893 – than by his carvings. The gifted Alfred Stevens (1817-75) was a sculptor of a rather different order, reinterpreting with rare sensitivity the Renaissance vision of Raphael and Michelangelo – most ambitiously in his unfinished monument to the Duke of Wellington in St Paul's Cathedral, London.

The major contribution to sculpture came from France. Jean-Baptiste Carpeaux (1827-75) developed from Rude's Romantic sense of drama and movement a "painterly" sculpture of great verve and virtuosity. His masterpiece, the delightful group, *The dance*, 1869, made for the façade of the Paris Opéra, is positively Rococo in its animation and gaiety. But one genius presided over the last quarter of the century, and came to establish his supremacy over all European sculptors – Auguste Rodin (1840-1917). No sculptor had made such an impact since Bernini; Rodin virtually regenerated sculpture as a major art form.

Rejected as a student by the Ecole des Beaux-Arts, Rodin was beset by difficulties in his early years, but by 1875 he had saved enough to finance a visit to Italy, during which the influence of Michelangelo's work became decisive. In 1877, aged 37, he exhibited *The Age of Bronze* at the Paris Salon. This aroused great interest, and criticism; accusations that it was a direct cast of a living model now seem absurd, but indicate how revolutionary its treatment of the nude then seemed. It was certainly far more naturalistic than anything else in the Salon, being endowed with life and movement not only in the configuration but also in the texture and play of light on the body, and not least in the expression of internal emotion through physical form. In this, in bestowing permanence on the transient moment, Rodin's sculpture was comparable to contemporary Impressionist painting, but its symbolic content was alien to Impressionist theory, and the vitality of its modelling depends on an accurate understanding of anatomy and the study of Renaissance and classical example. With *The Age of Bronze* and the

GIBSON (above)
The tinted Venus, 1851-52
Long used to monochrome Neoclassical statues, the public was not won over by Gibson's innovation. Now it seems not so startling: the colours are cosmetic, adding little realism. The Venus is too respectable, in type, pose and polish.

POWERS (right)
The Greek slave, 1843
The ingredients for the stunning success of the slave girl were probably her nubility and shame; her chains excited both compassion and lust. The treatment and theme have many parallels in contemporary academic painting.

STEVENS (right)
Monument to the Duke of Wellington, detail: *Valour and Cowardice*, 1858-1912
Stevens died long before his greatest work had been completed. His design had won the competition held in 1858; in 1867 the model was ready. Its architectural frame, surmounted by the Duke's equestrian statue, is traditional, but the figures, here Valour and Cowardice, on the other side Truth and Falsehood, have a welcome vigour and simplicity, in contrast to the ornate and fanciful confections created in profusion in his time.

HILDEBRAND (left)
The Hubertus fountain, detail: *The archer*, 1907
Hildebrand's hard and pure bronze typifies his severe Neoclassicism. He insisted that the image be conceived in the material of which it was made – unlike Rodin, who transferred images into bronze or stone as it suited.

CARPEAUX (above)
The dance, 1866-69
Carpeaux's work broke all sorts of academic rules: it was exuberantly sensual, anatomically incorrect and vivaciously unmonumental. One offended critic found that its Bacchanalian figures reeked of wine and vice, but they are innocuous really.

figures that followed it, Rodin staked his claim as a sculptor in the heroic mould of Donatello and Michelangelo. From 1880, when the French government commissioned an entrance portal for the new Museum of Decorative Arts – The Gates of Hell (see over) – that claim was acknowledged.

From 1880 to his death in 1917 Rodin was offered a series of public commissions, almost all of which, however, were delayed or rejected, because of financial problems (The burghers of Calais) or public opinion (Balzac). His colossal Balzac, finished in 1898, caused a storm of protest – it was cast and set up in Paris only in 1939 – yet it is certainly the most original and artistically satisfying work of public monumental statuary made during the nineteenth century. Throughout his career Rodin also worked in portraiture, at his best conveying vivid impressions of the head as the index of the mind and spirit, and made thousands of drawings. In his small statuettes, modelled with remarkable freedom, he created images anticipating the Expressionist vision. His impact was overwhelming on subsequent generations, who could not, however, advance from it but only react against it.

In France, the finest reaction to Rodin came from Aristide Maillol (1861-1944). An admirable painter, he turned to sculpture only when he was 40. His noblest work is all on the theme of the female nude, which he saw in terms of classical repose and restraint; the storm of Rodin's emotionalism evaporates in serene calm. In its simplicity of form and volume, Maillol's work is also comparable to the sculptures carried out by Renoir's assistant to his dictation in his old age (see p. 103); arguably, however, Degas (see preceding page) was the greatest sculptor of this generation, though more limited in scope than Rodin.

The highly original Italian Medardo Rosso (1858-1928) became celebrated as an "Impressionist" sculptor, perhaps with more justice than Rodin. His extraordinary group Conversation in a garden, 1893, seems full of the verbal echoes and silences of a Chekhov play, solidified for a moment into physical substance. His bust "Ecce Puer" seems to come as close as sculpture can to an Impressionist dissolution of form. The future, however, lay with Hildebrand's search for form that was "true to its material" (see p. 146).

RODIN (left)
The Age of Bronze, 1875-76
The life-size figure was first exhibited under the title The vanquished; it was later also called Man awakening to Nature. It is a symbolic representation of an emotional state not strictly defined – in this it is "Post-Impressionist". The generalized, smooth form of the academic nude has been broken up into a more realistic unevenness, giving light and movement.

RODIN (right)
Honoré de Balzac, 1892-98
Rodin considered Balzac his most daring work, and modern critics have agreed, recognizing the novelty of both concept and artistic means. He eschewed both the realism of conventional portraiture and idealism, gradually evolving an image symbolic of the novelist's creative genius and power. The full-length bronze, the outcome of intensive study, has a megalithic quality. No ornament or allegorical device mars the sweeping line of the robe; essential to the image is its rough finish, conveying strength.

RODIN (left)
The burghers of Calais, 1884-86
Rodin wanted his sculpture to be felt as well as seen, to be set where these men had walked, on the cobblestones of Calais. Each of the hostages (to Edward III of England, who freed them in the end) has a new mood – obstinacy, hope, despair.

MAILLOL (below)
Young girl with drapery, 1910
Maillol's sturdy progeny of static female nudes contrasts with Rodin's fluid, expressive and naturalistic art. He alters nature for the sake of structure and stresses geometric form.

ROSSO (right)
"Ecce Puer", 1910
The features emerge as if through a veil, a mystical premonition of something unformed. Having visited Paris in the 1880s, Rosso knew Rodin's work, and his theme of flux (see over).

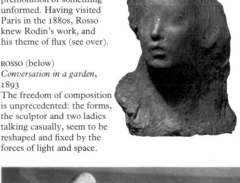

ROSSO (below)
Conversation in a garden, 1893
The freedom of composition is unprecedented: the forms, the sculptor and two ladies talking casually, seem to be reshaped and fixed by the forces of light and space.

Rodin: The Gates of Hell

The commission for the great portal that came to be known as "The Gates of Hell" was offered to Rodin by Antonin Proust, Minister for Fine Arts, in 1880. But the museum for which the Gates were intended was never built, and the Gates themselves were still unfinished when Rodin died, in 1917.

The prototype was provided by the most famous doors in Western art, those made by Ghiberti for the Baptistery in Florence in the fifteenth century (see vol. 2 p. 100). Rodin's initial drawings show a similar division into panels, but this framework gradually dissolved in the creative flow of Rodin's imagination, until each leaf of the doors, in its upward and downward surge, became more reminiscent of the movement of Michelangelo's *Last Judgment* (see vol. 2 p. 133). Originally, the iconographic stimulus had been religious, provided by Dante's *Inferno*, and *The thinker*, central above the two leaves of the Gates, was at once an imaginary portrait of Dante and a symbol of man's creative mind. *The thinker* was to be Rodin's most famous image, repeated on a monumental scale in marble and bronze, and widely reproduced on a small scale.

The Gates became, amongst other things, the storehouse in which Rodin accumulated a repertory of images (more than 200) on which he was able to draw for the rest of his life. His inability to finish the Gates seems not to have worried him greatly: they responded to the continual flux of his creative imagination; Rodin compared the project with Gothic cathedrals – "Were they ever finished?" That, however, illustrates a clear limitation of his genius: creation was for him a continuous process, and a final resolution of a complex composition, especially of groups of figures, escaped him. *The burghers of Calais* (see preceding page) remains a gathering of single figures, linked by their psychological tensions rather than by any formal compulsion. The Gates of Hell is made one unit by the architectural framework of the gateway, but Rodin's figures spill all over it, thrust forward and dissolve into it. This flux of becoming, of waxing and waning, corresponds to the movement of the pliable clay in the artist's fingers. Rodin was not a theorist, but he believed profoundly that the artist should create form by the working of his imagination through his fingers into the clay – the antithesis of the procedure of his revered Michelangelo, who cut away the block to reveal the figure as he met it in the marble. Rodin was quite happy that his clay be translated into marble as well as bronze, but the carving was done almost invariably by assistants. In those remarkable sculptures in which a highly finished figure, or fragment of a figure, emerges to pristine perfection in the midst of rough-hewn marble, he used the effect of Michelangelo's unfinished statues, but for different ends. Michelangelo's figures are not finished; Rodin's express his fascination with the contrast of formed and inchoate, finite and infinite, with flux and with the mystery of birth.

The iconographic content of the Gates was altered and developed no less than the sculptural form, but the overall mood remains coherent. Dante's *Inferno* is transformed into a Baudelairean symbol of Hell in the mind.

RODIN (left)
Detail of the Gates of Hell: *Ugolino*, 1882
Rodin's first version of *Ugolino* predated the idea of the Gates. An ogre who ate his children, in Rodin's Hell he is one of the most tellingly "damned". His muscles strain, his mouth hangs open, his eyes stare madly and cravingly. The clutching figures reflect the frenzy of the whole.

RODIN (below)
The thinker, 1880
Rodin's starting point was Michelangelo's *Lorenzo* (not shown), who embodies the Contemplative Principle in the Medici Chapel in S. Lorenzo in Florence. Deeply tinged with the intellectual pessimism of the 1880s, the image suggests creativity without resolved outcome. Rodin at his own wish was buried beneath a cast of it.

RODIN (below)
Crouching woman, 1882
Rodin's most concentrated work on the Gates, in the earlier stages, coincided with a passionate affair: some of the gloomy figures inspired by the *Inferno* are also driven by the most violent, pressing eroticism.

RODIN (above)
The Danaid, 1885
Rodin found the poses that evoked a mood or emotion by letting his nude models move around the studio as he sketched. The finish of his marble work contrasts with the roughness of his bronzes – his aim was a blurred luminous quality rather than a high polish.

RODIN (right)
Nero, c.1900–05
Rodin made thousands of pencil-and-wash drawings, in which he could exploit the same tensions between volume and movement on the surface that vitalize his sculpture. In these free drafts the subject is often ambiguous – this is like a Renoir nude struck mad.

RODIN
The Gates of Hell,
1880-1917
Anatole France commented
thus: "You will not find
monsters in the Hell of
Rodin ... the evil demons
through whom these men
and women suffer are their
own passions, their loves and
hatreds; they are their own
flesh, their own thought."

Seurat: La Grande Jatte

La Grande Jatte, named after a weekend resort on the banks of the Seine popular among Parisians, was begun in 1884 and finished in 1886, and exhibited in that year in the last Impressionist exhibition. Seurat's admission to the show, due largely, it seems, to Pissarro's championship, caused dissension among the original Impressionists. Indeed this picture is obviously at variance in very important points from the practice of Impressionism – so much so that subsequent historians distinguish the style evolved by Seurat with the label "Neo-Impressionism". The interest in light, in colour created by light, and in a very high key of colour, is still dominant, but the technique is both more fragmented and more precisely (even at times mechanically) worked out. In its contemporary subject matter *La Grande Jatte* is still Realist, but the effect in sum and detail is as if the Impressionist vision had frozen: the sense of implicit movement, the feeling for ephemeral effects, are rejected in favour of a timeless, highly formalized, monumental quality. Realist in some aspects the image may be; it is in no sense naturalistic.

Georges Seurat (1859-1891) was a seemingly orthodox, docile student at the Ecole des Beaux-Arts in Paris, 1877-78, working a great deal in the Louvre, studying there intensely the masterpieces of traditional art from Greek classical sculpture to the Italian and northern Renaissance. However, he extracted his own conclusions from them, and was probably already interested in theoretical writings on colour, such as those published by Michel-Eugène Chevreul and others, leading to the demonstration that juxtaposed colours mix in the human eye, and that the colour so mixed is purer than any pigments mixed on the palette. By 1881 Seurat had developed a highly original drawing technique in black crayon, extracting simplified and very solid figures by the subtle and exact control of tone. His early painting in colour always tended towards a similar simplification: even his small oil-studies, painted in the open, direct from the subject, moving gradually towards the lighter palette of the Impressionists, demonstrated his primary interest in an exactly articulated composition, plotted with equal emphasis across the picture plane, using simplified silhouetted shapes, and increasingly shallow space.

By 1883, he was developing the technique known as pointillism, a system of applying paint in isolated dots of pure colour. His first major work in this technique, on the grand scale of ambitious Salon pictures, "*Une Baignade, Asnières*" (A bathing scene at Asnières), was finished in 1884. The subject, urban recreation at the riverside, was an Impressionist one, and the innumerable preliminary studies likewise reflect Impressionist practice; but their integration into the whole was a studio process, and an austere call to order of the chaotic, multitudinous impressions with which nature assails the eye.

The exhibition of *Asnières* in 1884 and of *La Grande Jatte* in 1886 established Seurat as the spearhead of the new avantgarde. The exponents of Neo-Impressionism, Pointillism or Colour Divisionism were supported by critics such as Fénéon and the Belgian poet Verhaeren, but older Impressionists (with the exception of Pissarro) read *La Grande Jatte* as a counter-Impressionist manifesto.

For Seurat, "the purity of the element of the spectrum is the keystone of technique", and he continued to work with tireless industry towards the perfection and simplification of his system until his premature death from an unidentified illness in 1891. He had continued to produce *grandes machines*, major exhibition pictures, extending his subject matter to further aspects of modern urban life, even adapting motifs from the abstracted imagery of posters and fashion plates, but always resolving his pictures into immobile patterns, even when his subject was the sea or his theme motion, as in his last big canvas, *The circus*. "I want", he said, "to make modern people move about as if they were on the Parthenon frieze, in their most essential characteristics."

Apart from his impact on Pissarro's style in the 1880s, Seurat's work inspired only one disciple of significance, the prolific Paul Signac (1863-1935), who remained to the end faithful to the divisionist principle and technique, although his vision was less subtle and more coarsely handled.

SEURAT (left)
La Grande Jatte, 1884–86
Seurat's biographer, the
critic Fénéon, described the
picture: "It is four o'clock
on Sunday afternoon in the
dog-days. On the river the
swift barks dart to and fro
... A Sunday population has
come together at random,
and from a delight in the
fresh air ... Seurat has
treated his figures in a
summary or hieratic style,
like a Puvis de Chavannes
(see p. 120) gone modern."

SEURAT (right)
The yoked cart, 1883
The rich colour and the
seemingly casual design –
cutting off the cart at the
edge of the canvas – re-
call "pure" Impressionism.
Seurat, however, achieves
a still image purged of all
superfluous detail, evoking
a mood of calm expectancy.

SEURAT (below)
*Seated boy with a straw
hat*, 1883-84
Seurat liked to sketch in
black crayon on thick white
paper; its textured surface
enabled him to achieve the
fine tonal gradations which

characterize his atmospheric
drawings. Sometimes, like
this one, they were studies
for larger pictures (this is
the youth on the left in the
Asnières canvas); yet they
possess all the qualities
of finished works of art.

SEURAT (above)
"Une Baignade, Asnières"
(A bathing scene at
Asnières), 1883-84
Seurat's method was based
on contemporary scientific
theory, even if the separate
dots of colour are not small
enough to blend in the eye,
as presumably he intended.
(This was pointed out only
some 40 years later.) But
Seurat's "scientific" basis
helped to justify his artistic
aim, to capture on canvas
the essence of appearances.

SEURAT (right)
*The "Bec du Hoc" at
Grandchamp*, 1885
The dynamic mass of cliff
against calm sea and sky
rears imposingly; Seurat's
dots and strokes vibrate
before the eye, enlivening
the surface – much as the
less regimented brushes of
Monet or Renoir also did.

SIGNAC (above)
*View of the marina at
Marseilles*, 1905
Seurat's divisionism and
deliberated arrangement
of forms is here enlivened
by vibrant "Fauve" colour

(Matisse was a friend).
Signac had earlier painted
working-class or industrial
scenes, perhaps with implicit
social comment; he was a
professed anarchist. Seurat's
politics were less definite.

SEURAT (above)
Study for *The circus*, 1890
Seurat was later influenced
by the philosopher Henry,
who proposed that certain
analysable factors in a com-

position determined what
emotional message it had:
upward curves and leaping
forms here signal gaiety.
He sought "to do Poussin
again", but from science.

Post-Impressionism 1

The term "Post-Impressionism" was coined by the critic Roger Fry for the title of his exhibition in London in 1910-11, *Manet and the Post-Impressionists*. Cézanne, Gauguin, and van Gogh were strongly represented, also Seurat and Signac, but more thinly; in Fry's second "Post-Impressionist" show, 1912, the range extended even to Picasso and Braque. Though the term can be applied so loosely as to be almost meaningless except as a rough chronological indication, it has persisted. In fact, the major artists to whom it is generally applied shared only a stubborn, often belligerent, refusal to be like anyone else; each, in varying degree, was a loner, misfit or outcast, voluntary or involuntary, not only from the artistic orthodoxy of the time – the Paris Salon – but even from ordinary society. Yet all of them passed through Impressionism, and their mature paintings are developments from Impressionist beginnings.

The beginnings of Post-Impressionism date from the years when Impressionism, as a movement of artists with common theories, practice and sympathies, was disintegrating – that is, the mid-1880s. Within a few years, after seeing the 1891 Salon des Indépendants in Paris, the Belgian poet Verhaeren was writing: "There is no longer any single school, there are scarcely any groups, and these few are constantly splitting. All their tendencies make me think of moving and kaleidoscopic geometric patterns, clashing at one moment only to unite at another, which now fuse and then separate and fly apart a little, but which all nevertheless revolve within the same circle, that of the new art." Within the new art, the sympathy of one master for another was not always obvious: Gauguin always reverenced Cézanne, but Cézanne thought Gauguin was no painter at all, and told van Gogh that he (van Gogh) was mad. Degas was intrigued by Gauguin's works and bought several, but Monet never took Gauguin seriously. Only Pissarro seemed genuinely and selflessly open to objective appreciation of honest explorations in all styles: in 1886 the first and greatest of the "primitives", Henri Rousseau le Douanier (see p. 140) had first exhibited and provoked huge hilarity – only Pissarro recognized the quality that the apparent naivety of drawing and the imagery concealed.

Subsequent historians have tended to distinguish two fundamental trends in Post-Impressionism. The pursuit of formal values is seen as the basic concern of Seurat (see preceding page) and of Cézanne. They are claimed as the spiritual ancestors of several of the major explorations of the twentieth century, notably Cubism and much modern abstract art. By contrast, the revolutionary ways in which other artists realized form have been interpreted as means rather than ends, the ends being the most vivid expression possible of the artist's emotion: so such artists as Gauguin and van Gogh can be categorized as precursors not only of the Fauves, but of the whole Expressionist movement. One trend has been seen as moving towards the objective and the classical; the other towards the subjective – an intensification of Romanticism. Such interpretations must be viewed with caution – the Romantic qualities evident in Cézanne's early work, for example, are not expunged in his very last paintings: they are still there, though differently expressed, for they were an integral part of his temperament.

The "Post-Impressionists", as the epithet implies, were mostly of a younger generation than the founding fathers of Impressionism, and they revolted against their elders while

PISSARRO (right)
Paul Cézanne, 1874
Pissarro encouraged the young Cézanne, persuaded him to exhibit at the first Impressionist show (1874) and never lost confidence in him. He followed Manet's *Zola* (see p. 95) in posing his sitter with pictures relating to him, chiefly a caricature, top right, of Cézanne's early mentor, the great Courbet.

GAUGUIN (below)
Vincent van Gogh, 1888
Gauguin distorts colour to reflect Vincent's obsession with sunflowers, unbalancing the painter in relation to his canvas; he simplifies line, abandons modelling, makes an abstract pattern. His new art had evolved in early 1888 in Brittany, a few months before his visit to van Gogh in Provence.

VAN GOGH (left)
Self-portrait, 1888
Van Gogh had such a rage for Japanese art that he gave his strongly modelled self-image slanted eyes. Inspired by a custom of Japanese painters, he began exchanging portraits with colleagues. This picture, finished before he left for Arles, was dedicated "to my friend Paul Gauguin".

CEZANNE (below)
The rape, 1867
Cézanne's concern to use the brushwork itself as an element of the composition is apparent in his earliest paintings. At this time he used to send Zola poems which, like Zola's Realist novels, and like this picture, have melodramatic, violent themes – an urgent quest to penetrate the heart of life.

taking many of their discoveries for granted. The great exception was Paul Cézanne (1839-1906). Unlike his contemporaries, notably Monet, Renoir and Pissarro, he always had before him the prospect of financial stability, although his prosperous father kept him on a meagre allowance until his death in 1886, when Cézanne was already well advanced in middle age. His early style, deeply imprinted by both Delacroix and Courbet, was sometimes flagrantly Romantic, with sensational subject matter, for instance that of *The rape* of 1867, painted in a thick, often seemingly clumsy style. Associating in Paris with his old school-friend, Zola (admiring the Realism – almost brutalism – of Zola's novels), he suffered repeated rejection from the Salon in consort with the Impressionists. His portrait of the dwarf *Achille Empéraire* (1868-70), a grotesque subject treated with heroic emphasis, the paint applied thick and coarse, was not simply rejected but excited positive revulsion. This was what Cézanne later referred to as his *couillarde* (approximately, "gutsy") style, broadly painted with trenchant use of the palette-knife; it lightened under the influence of Pissarro especially. Cézanne worked with

him for periods at Pontoise and Auvers, and the impact of Impressionist practice is first visible in works such as *"La Maison du Pendu"* (The suicide's house) of 1872; but already here a very solid, almost diagrammatic sense of underlying structure, foretelling his later development, is perceptible. He returned to his native Provence for short periods in 1876 and 1878, and was there more permanently from 1883; following the death of his father, he was able to devote himself undistractedly to his endless battle with the intractable landscape that confronted him (see p. 118)

The 1880s were a watershed; it was then that

Western art was released from the representational concerns with which it had been preoccupied since the Renaissance. Of the pioneers of this modern art, van Gogh (see over) died in 1890, Seurat in 1891, the same year that Gauguin (see p. 116) left for Tahiti. Cézanne continued unsung until the new century. Each asserted in his own way the absolutism of his own personality. Twenty years later, in the first decade of the twentieth century, the great revolutionaries of modern art were to act on that independence to the point of taking the visible world to bits and reassembling it according to their own vision.

CEZANNE (left)
The little bridge at Maincy, 1882-85
Cézanne's reconstruction – no longer an imitation – of what he saw was always based on a careful analysis of colour, light and shade. Unlike Gauguin, or van Gogh sometimes, he never abandoned the modelling of volume by tonal gradation, though his brushwork had also a purely surface value.

VAN GOGH (below)
Montmartre with windmills, 1887
Van Gogh's interpretation of Impressionism, which he had adopted just the year before, was entirely individual. In Paris he had admired Monet's brilliant brushwork, and Pissarro had led him to heighten his key. But only Vincent could give a placid view such urgency.

CEZANNE (left)
Achille Empéraire, 1868-70
Cézanne elected to present to the jury of the Salon of 1870 this huge portrait of a dwarf, just because it would certainly displease them; it was duly rejected. He was, it seems, in revolt against everything. The portrait has an alarming force in its contrasting colours, thick brushwork, and very subject.

CEZANNE (left)
"La Maison du Pendu" (The suicide's house), 1873
Under Pissarro's tutelage at Auvers, Cézanne briefly became a true Impressionist, conveying a vibrating light with much brighter colours.

VAN GOGH (right)
The bridge at La Grande Jatte, 1887
The thick strokes of the brush are undisguised and, with colour, give this work its underlying structure.

Vincent van Gogh

In his short life Vincent van Gogh (1853-90) produced over 800 paintings and a comparable number of drawings; before his death he had sold in total two pictures. Yet he has become perhaps the most widely loved and reproduced painter in the history of Western art. In his posthumous fame the drama of his personal life plays an integral part – documented not only in his extraordinary autobiography in paint, his self-portraits, but in the running commentary contained in more than 700 vividly articulate letters, mostly to his devoted brother and supporter, Theo van Gogh.

He was born, in 1853, with dual affiliations, to religion and to art. His father was a parish priest at Groot Zundert in Holland; three of his uncles were art dealers. His first acquaintanceship with art was from the dealer's side, at The Hague and then for a spell in London. Dissatisfied, he started to train for the Church in 1876, only to realize that his radical view of Christianity was incompatible with orthodoxy. Living in great poverty, he began to draw seriously when he was 27, and so gradually realized his true, final and fatal vocation, to which he surrendered with the fervour of a convert; he had only ten years left to live.

The first five years (1880-85) of his new career were spent in Holland in painful self-training, in physical privation and constant emotional strain. From the beginning his subject matter was the earth and those who worked it; his social concern was crucial. In life, he acted on similar compassionate principles, even setting up house with a prostitute and her child. But while the message of his gospel in art and life was love, his temperament, ferociously independent and egocentric, made it impossible for him to sustain a close relationship with anyone, except Theo.

Vincent's work in Holland culminated in his masterpiece of 1885, *The potato eaters*, which is still traditional, though painted expressively dark in sombre greens, browns and blacks. In late 1885, he moved to Antwerp, and there discovered Rubens; his palette lightened, his touch became freer; and he also became fascinated by Japanese prints. Independently, he was beginning to discover that colour could have its own laws and meaning irrespective of the true colours of the subject matter. His letters reveal his longing to perfect his art, to establish new contacts and see the most modern painting. In February 1886 he arrived in

VAN GOGH (above)
Self-portrait, 1890
The intensity of expression, reinforced by the icy background of swirling strokes, is characteristic. This was painted only a few months before the artist's suicide.

VAN GOGH (left)
The potato eaters, 1885
Van Gogh consciously used the colour of dirty potatoes and heavy, simplified forms so as to convey poverty. As a trainee missionary he had shared the peasants' misery. In seeking to express it as lucidly as he was able, he began to cross the bounds of conventional naturalism.

VAN GOGH (right)
Sunflowers, 1888
On his arrival in Provence in 1888 Vincent reacted to southern warmth and the sunny colours around him in joy. His dashing strokes of paint recall Impressionist techniques, but the twisted lines and the concentrated colours of the series are full of an original power.

VAN GOGH (right)
The night café, 1888
This is the little café in Arles where van Gogh and Gauguin drank together. It is a nightmare – the harsh lighting, giddy perspective and hunched, lonely looking patrons create the effect. The colour symbolism is attested in Vincent's own description of the work. "I have tried to express the idea that the café is a place where one can ruin oneself, go mad or commit a crime", he wrote. "I have tried to express as it were the powers of darkness in a low public house, by the use of soft Louis XV green and malachite contrasting with yellow-green and harsh blue-greens – and all this in an atmosphere like a devil's furnace of pale sulphur".

VAN GOGH (above)
Sailing boats coming ashore, 1888
The simple, bold lines of the boats at Stes-Maries, near Arles, rendered them very suitable subjects for paintings and sketches that emulate Japanese prints. His careful arrangements of lines, shapes and patches of colour reflect Vincent's study of such prints – and he and Gauguin learnt from them not simply design, but bold, non-naturalistic hues.

Paris, and there the impact of the work of the Impressionists revolutionized his painting.

In February 1888, he went south, to Arles. He was still passionately concerned with the social responsibilities of art and the necessity of the modern artist's involvement in life and the whole of life. He envisaged at Arles the establishment of a sort of artists' commune, interlocking with the local community. Yet his own painting was becoming ever more personal and subjective, and even mystical. His famous *Sunflower* series was conceived as a symphony in yellow and blue: the colours sing (the musical analogy recurs in his letters). But he also conceived these pictures as Gothic rose windows, to be decorations of his new home, the intended sanctuary and cradle of a new way of art and artistic life. His co-founder of the commune he hoped was to be Gauguin, but Gauguin's brief stay ended in a violent quarrel, in Vincent's frustrated assault on Gauguin, followed by his mutilation of his own ear and the macabre gift of the bleeding fragment to a prostitute in a brothel. On recovery, van Gogh realized that he was on the brink of insanity – more than that, he had been over it at least once. In May, 1889, he with-

drew voluntarily to an asylum at St-Rémy, but there continued frantic production (some 150 paintings) for the next year. In May 1890, he moved again, living as the patient and guest of a remarkable physician and connoisseur, Paul Gachet, until, overwhelmed by a final crisis of despair, he shot himself on 29 July 1890.

In the south, van Gogh had soon abandoned objective, "scientific" analysis of colour according to Impressionist doctrine. He continued to use, in the Impressionist manner, touches of different colours alongside each other, but generally his brushwork became stronger and more rhythmic, and colour took on its own symbolic function. Thus in his *Night café*, he wrote, he used "colours not locally true from the point of view of the stereoscopic realist, but colour to suggest any emotion of an ardent temperament". The quality of paint, laid on thick and rough and violent, is no less telling than the use of colour. Yet he remained rooted in his subject matter, and one reason for his differences with Gauguin was his distrust of the latter's "abstraction". In *"La Berceuse"*, his portrait of the postman's wife, Madame Roulin, the flat patterning is clearly influenced by Gauguin, and

later he had doubts about it for that very reason. As he painted it Vincent had come to think of it almost as a religious image, a *Madonna*, and as the focus of a polyptych surrounded by his sunflowers like candelabra. His idea was that "sailors, who are at once children and martyrs, seeing it in the cabin of their Icelandic fishing boat, would feel the old sense of being rocked come over them and remember their lullabies".

In the last year of his life, the whole Provençal landscape and its sun, moon and stars were caught up in the impassioned desperate swirl of his paint, and became molten. The image became a symbol of emotion ranging from despair to intoxicated exaltation.

Though he was virtually unknown when he died, the extent of van Gogh's achievement was revealed in a series of exhibitions in Europe and America during the next 25 years. The Fauves, the German Expressionists, all acknowledged him. Following the publication of his letters, he became a romantic hero of book and film, a stereotype – like Rimbaud – of the doomed artistic genius. Endless reproduction still seems unable to drain his drawings and paintings of their demonic vitality.

VAN GOGH (right)
"La Berceuse" (Mme Roulin rocking a cradle), 1889
After his breakdown van Gogh returned to his series of portraits of Mme Roulin, the postman's wife. She holds the ropes of a cradle in her hands, soothing the unseen baby and the viewer. The lack of modelling and the strong pattern reveal a concern for abstract as well as expressionist effects.

VAN GOGH (below)
Field with a stormy sky, 1890
Vincent's late paintings of landscapes around Auvers are essentially subjective: the vast open fields and the troubled skies express his melancholy and loneliness. The painting is structured solely by the brush-strokes and the choice of colour.

VAN GOGH (left)
Dr Paul Gachet, 1890
In letters to Gauguin and his brother Theo Vincent described his portrait in passionate terms. He was trying to create a new kind of portraiture, based not on the imitation of appearances but on the intensification of character. He gave his friend "the heartbroken expression of our time", projecting on to Gachet his own feelings.

VAN GOGH (below)
Country road by night, 1890
The paintings Vincent made in the asylum at St-Rémy unequivocally reveal madness – the rushing path, the hallucinatory sky, the greens lurid in the bursts of spiky corn. The retaining elements of the design – the figures, the horse and trap – are swept away by the violent flow of brush-strokes.

Paul Gauguin

Gauguin's fierce independence, his rejection of centuries-old principles of Western art, surely owed something to his lack of any early training in art at all. Paul Gauguin (1848-1903) was born of mixed blood – French and Peruvian Creole – in a family in which bizarre traditions of violence, rape, sudden death and intellectual radicalism were strangely mixed. His youth in Peru and France was followed by six years in the merchant marine, and then (1871-82) by a successful career as stockbroker; he became a collector of Impressionist paintings, and experimented as an artist himself to such good effect that by 1879 a small statuette of his had been accepted for the fourth Impressionist exhibition, followed by seven paintings in the show the year after. By 1883, when he gave up his career to devote himself entirely to art, he was already questioning Impressionist principles. Between 1886 and 1891 he became the focus of a group of artists at Pont-Aven in Brittany, making a first brief visit to exotic lands (Martinique, in 1887) and spending two fraught months (which have become famous) with van Gogh in Arles in 1888.

These were years in which Gauguin ceaselessly questioned himself and his art, amid increasing difficulties: from affluence he sank to acute poverty, and to his great sadness he was separated from his wife and children. After he had rejected Impressionism, which he came to regard as "shackled by the needs of probability", the first fully realized statement of his aims came in *The vision after the sermon* of 1888, a vision of Breton peasant women rapt in silence and prayer, as if in church, as they behold in a blazing red field the winged angel, gold and brilliant blue, wrestling with Jacob – the women, too, seem winged with the weird shapes of their *coiffe* head-dresses. One critic categorized this art a little later as "idea-ist, symbolist, synthetic and subjective". While the construction acknowledges the basics of traditional perspective (and the looming foreground figures set against the action beyond recall Degas), the impact of Japanese prints is clear, and far-reaching – the schematic composition, the flat fields of unbroken, shadowless colour, the exploitation of silhouettes; even the stance of the wrestlers and of the bull are borrowed from the Japanese. The use, however, of heavy outline filled with pure colour, as in medieval enamelwork, and hence known as "*cloisonnisme*", owed much to Emile

GAUGUIN (above)
Bonjour, M. Gauguin, 1889
In contrast to its buoyant model, Courbet's *Bonjour,*

M. Courbet (not shown), in his sombre picture Gauguin stands in peasant's sabots grimly, outside the gate.

GAUGUIN (above)
Self-portrait, 1888
Gauguin was proud of his "Peruvian savage" features and when he sent van Gogh this portrait explained that he identified with the hero of Victor Hugo's Romantic novel *Les Misérables*, the outlaw Jean Valjean. In the background is a *Self-portrait* by Bernard, apparently with eyes closed – inner eye open.

GAUGUIN (right)
Be in love and you will be happy, 1889-90
Gauguin claimed: "Good health, independence in one's work, and regular love-making – that's the secret". In "primitive" art and its raw forms he found forceful sincerity and directness, by-passing civilized veneer; but he also found monumentality.

GAUGUIN (below)
The vision after the sermon, 1888
Gauguin's starting point was probably a painting by Bernard, a simple design in which he had shown Breton women in their traditional costumes. This, though, had no symbolic content. In the Gauguin the field is red as the aura of the vision; the cow recalls a Breton rite, the blessing of the horned beasts while the lesson of Jacob and the angel was read in church. The picture is based on a real event, but literal naturalism has been expunged; the colour seems arbitrary, but is fused with line and shape to present an idea in "synthetic" terms – a new symbolism of form.

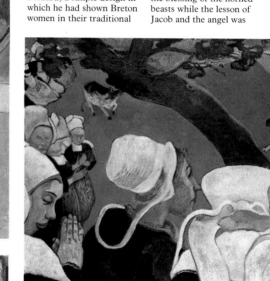

GAUGUIN (left)
The spirit of the dead watching, 1892
During his first visit to Tahiti, 1891-93, Gauguin moved away from the clear-coloured, boldly-lined art of his earlier Breton stay: conventional composition and modelling re-emerge, but in a rich, exotic context. Gauguin was fascinated by Polynesian mythology and ancestor-figures, although he imposed his own notions on the imagery he borrowed, injecting his own "indescribably sacred horror".

Bernard, one of the group in Pont-Aven. Above all, colour takes on a symbolic and emotional significance – a spiritual dimension.

Gauguin's art had become an art of imaginative concept rather than analytical observation. "Art is an abstraction", he wrote, and described his brilliant *Self-portrait* painted for van Gogh at Arles as "absolutely incomprehensible, of course, being so abstract. At first it looks like the head of a bandit ... personifying also a discredited Impressionist painter. The drawing is quite special (complete abstraction), the eyes, the mouth, the nose are like flowers in Persian carpets, thus personifying the symbolic side. The colour is pretty far from nature ... All the reds and violets streaked by flames (are) like a furnace radiating from the eyes, seat of the struggles of the painter's thought."

Gauguin knew the leading intellectuals of the day, notably the Symbolist poet Mallarmé, but eventually reacted decisively against the sophisticated theorizing, the material corruption and complication of Western civilization, and left for Tahiti in 1891, in search of primitive values and simplicity. Harassed by poverty and illness, he was forced to return to

Paris in 1893; leaving Europe again in 1895, he remained in Tahiti till 1901, in constant conflict with the authorities on behalf of the natives. Then he moved to the Marquesas Islands, where he lived until his death in 1903.

His genius was remarkably versatile. From about 1889, he revived his early interest in sculpture; the relief *Be in love and you will be happy* of 1889-90, which at the time he considered his "best and strangest work", is very much non-naturalistic, yet the roughly carved forms, enigmatic in meaning, have immense physical density and gravity. His mind and hands were for ever restless; he would carve a walking-stick, or experiment with pottery (inspired originally by oriental pots in the Musée Guimet in Paris). His woodcuts and zincographs have an uninhibited vigour; his distortion was combined with a feeling for the possibilities of the material, which had a decisive effect on the revival of the woodcut. In painting, his Tahitian works have become the most popular, due no doubt to their mysteriously dreamy subject matter, their offer of escape to a golden primitive land – even if their serenity is profoundly melancholy; but while the Pacific gave him new themes, it did not

enlarge the formal language with which he expounded them. The famous, and vast, picture that he painted "feverishly day and night" before an abortive suicide in late 1897, *Where do we come from? What are we? Where are we going?* was intended as his spiritual last testament. It was indeed his most ambitious synthesis, reassembling in its mysterious panorama mostly symbolic figures he had already used in earlier compositions – not least the enigmatic idol, in Gauguin's description "joining substance, in my dream in front of my house, with the whole of Nature reigning in our *primitive soul*". The symbolism is hardly ever explicit or explicable verbally, as opposed to the Symbolism of Puvis de Chavannes or Odilon Redon: Gauguin said of Puvis (see p.122) that he "explained" his idea but he did not "paint" it.

Nevertheless, because of its purely decorative qualities and its "literary" echoes, his work tended to be depreciated in an age too conscious of purely formal values, though his primitivism was seen to be significant. Gauguin, however, is one of the major founding figures of modern art. "I have tried to vindicate the right to dare anything", he wrote.

GAUGUIN (left)
Noa Noa, c. 1893
Gauguin would scratch and score the surface of his woodcuts to create a varied effect. He adopted this one for the cover of his autobiography, *Noa Noa*, 1901.

GAUGUIN (right)
Nevermore, 1897
The naked girl exudes a rich tropical warmth and a mood of superstitious dread; Gauguin used eerie, dusky colours deliberately.

GAUGUIN (below)
Where do we come from? What are we? Where are we going? 1897
The monumental frieze emanates holy sanctity like an icon, but it is a dream without specific meaning.

Cézanne: Mont Ste-Victoire

The year 1886 was crucial for Cézanne, then aged 47. His father died, leaving him a comfortable fortune, and he was at last able to seal with marriage his 17-year-old liaison with Hortense Fiquet. In the same year his friendship with Zola, dating from their school-days, came to an abrupt end, and in the 20 years remaining to him he left home in Provence increasingly rarely. He became more and more touchy and suspicious, almost a recluse, even after long-delayed recognition came rapidly, indeed spectacularly, after the dealer Vollard's exhibition of about 150 of his paintings in Paris in 1895. His life was concentrated on the stubborn battle with his art – the battle to achieve a reconciliation of the three-dimensional world confronting him with the two-dimensional limitations of his canvas. In 1903 he wrote: "I am beginning to see the Promised Land"; in 1906 he wrote: "I am old and ill and have sworn to myself to die painting". In October 1906 he collapsed after being caught in a storm while painting outdoors, and died a few days later.

These later years were occupied with still lifes, figure painting – ranging from portraits to more general, monumental themes – and landscapes. Still lifes enabled him to structure his compositions before painting; even so in the finished work traditional perspective and true shapes were distorted in answer to the needs of harmony and the stability of the whole. The portraits were painted, like the still lifes, in a long process of profound analysis: giving up his portrait of Vollard (see p.126) after 115 sittings Cézanne was "not altogether displeased with the shirt". Yet in some portraits, built up laboriously touch upon touch like all the late work, the response to individual character can still be almost lyrical.

Cézanne was also preoccupied especially with the theme of nude, female figures in a landscape, or *Bathers*. The subject is still surely Impressionist, stemming from Manet's *"Déjeuner sur l'Herbe"* (see p. 94), but the picture goes much further, not just in its distortions, but in Cézanne's attempt to create something durable, "like the art of museums".

Most of all in his last years Cézanne painted landscapes, which allowed him the greatest breadth for the development of his style and necessitated working from and with nature. He had several chosen local views to which he returned, but the favourite – and one that has become almost as much a cult image as Mount Fuji in Japanese art – was Mont Ste-Victoire. His technique, building up a pictorial structure by the schematic overlay of colours applied mostly very thinly in short, square strokes of the brush, had been developing during the 1870s, at its peak in watercolours. In the London *Mont Ste-Victoire with a great pine*, 1885-87, the composition, though framed by the arabesque of a foreground tree, is determined by the logical recession of the planes or blocks of colour. Even the outline contours usually reveal themselves on close inspection to be built up of crisply defined patches of colour, of astonishingly subtle and varied shades. In the silence, the frontal monumentality of the scene, Cézanne surely achieves his avowed wish, to do Poussin again

CEZANNE (below)
Mont Ste-Victoire with a great pine, 1885-87
In the early days of the long struggle with Mont Ste-Victoire, details of the landscape survive the artist's attempt to translate his sensations into paint and so achieve a "harmony parallel to nature". In a related watercolour, these details are clearer still, and the diagonals sharper, the frontality less firm.

CEZANNE (above)
Mont Ste-Victoire, watercolour, 1906
In the late paintings, oil or watercolour, detail is unimportant; it is unclear precisely what – a house or a tree – is represented by any given patch of colour. The patches, overlapping and interlocking, build up their own coherent form. It was Cézanne's belief that "in the contrast and connection of colours – there you have the secret of drawing and modelling". There is a great variety in the brushwork and the tones of colour, sometimes gentle, sometimes savage.

CEZANNE (left)
The Philadelphia *Mont Ste-Victoire*, 1904-06
Rich colour applied in a mosaic-like pattern builds up and integrates the land and sky, held on the canvas with hallucinatory power. Cézanne's conversation in these years revealed that he felt that in his later views of Mont Ste-Victoire he was coming close to his goal.

CEZANNE (right)
Still life with onions, c. 1895-1900
Form and colour echo each other across the canvas; greens complement pink onions, the rim of a glass is tilted up, a plate bent, in the interests of overall harmony. Cézanne took so long painting that fruit and vegetables shrivelled; he used wax substitutes.

from nature: this is classical form. In his final contemplations of Mont Ste-Victoire, he used the same method still more austerely to extract – or abstract – his picture from the mass and profile of the landscape. The version in Philadelphia of 1904 may or may not be unfinished – Cézanne tended to advance work over the whole canvas simultaneously, so that, whenever he stopped, that stage cohered as a whole; this is faceted by those square brush-strokes, those sharp, even harsh, edges or planes of colour, into unconsoling yet majestic solidity – even in the sky. Yet there is, too, a sense of urgency: the silhouette of the mountain has become a beak or prow – aggressive or defiant. Cézanne's analytic-synthetic method was also a transposition of his own temperamental reaction to the sensation ("*ma petite sensation*") the landscape aroused in him.

Indefatigable as he was in his search for objectivity, Cézanne's example in paint nevertheless went far to establish the supremacy of the modern artist's subjectivity: the world is his, to translate into his own terms as he will.

CEZANNE (above)
Self-portrait with a goatee, c. 1906
In his last *Self-portrait* Cézanne treats himself as dispassionately as a still life – in contrast to van Gogh's or Gauguin's self-expressive images. In the reduction of his head to a compendium of hollows and planes of colour, the basic grammar both of Cubism and of Fauvism is implicit.

CEZANNE (left)
"The Great Bathers", 1898-1905
Whereas the early *Bathers* are often relatively static, rhythmic forces permeate the huge canvases of later years. These nudes seem to be primeval, fashioned of stone or wood, part of the cathedral-like structure of the forest. The picture is constructed with colour – pale shades of blue, ochre and green dappled by light.

Post-Impressionism 2, and Art Nouveau

The wild landscapes and the Atlantic coast of Brittany had attracted artists from the early nineteenth century; the little village of Pont-Aven, in particular, had been "discovered" by French painters in the 1860s, and was already an international artists' colony by the time Gauguin arrived there. Gauguin (see p. 116) stayed in Pont-Aven on various occasions between 1886 and his final migration to the Pacific in 1895. He worked out there the principles and practice of his mature style, and became the natural leader of a group of young artists, notably Emile Bernard (1868-1941; not shown), Maurice Denis (1870-1943; not shown) and Paul Sérusier (1863-1927).

Though able painters, Bernard (who had disputed with Gauguin the claim of having first used highly simplified forms and flat colour) and Denis are more important as theorists and propagandists: Denis, aged only 20, was responsible for a dictum in 1890 that has since been quoted in contexts he would not have dreamed of, and has served as a key tenet of several developments in modern art: "A picture – before being a war horse or a nude woman or some little genre scene – is essentially a flat surface covered with colours ar-

ranged in a certain order." It was Sérusier, however, whom Gauguin instructed one day in a celebrated painting lesson in a Breton wood: the result, a cigar-box lid roughly brushed with – at first glance – an abstract colour pattern, was later shown by Sérusier to his fellow-students at the Académie Julian in Paris. It became known as *"The Talisman"* and had a catalytic effect on these young painters, soon to coalesce as a group called the Nabis (a Hebrew word for "prophet").

Common to most artists of this group was a Christian religious fervour and a harking back, like the Pre-Raphaelites, to early Italian art. But its two most distinguished members ignored pious themes and treated contemporary, often everyday, subjects in the new style – an approach described as "Intimisme". Edouard Vuillard (1868-1940) transformed his banal, homely interiors into beautifully balanced compositions, most successfully on a small scale. In his portrait of his *Mother and sister*, the two figures are simplified into strongly patterned, almost flat, forms, and the surface of the picture, compartmented into a bold decorative design, is held in tension by the room's sharply exaggerated recessions. Yet the

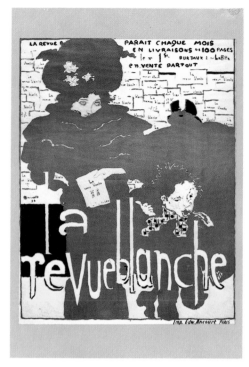

BONNARD (above)
La Revue Blanche, 1894
"The most Japanese Nabi", as Bonnard was hailed by an admiring critic, showed in his graphic art a unique assimilation of the spirit and principles of *ukiyo-e* colour prints. The formal qualities of his poster are openly oriental, even if the wit is peculiarly French.

BONNARD (left)
Nude in the bath, 1937
Vibrant with the light and colour of southern France, Bonnard's mature work is also suffused with a gentle nostalgia for time past. Until the death of his wife in her 60s he continued to portray her tenderly as a slim nubile girl, the model and mistress of his youth.

SERUSIER (above)
"The Talisman": landscape in the Bois d'Amour in Brittany, 1888
Gauguin virtually dictated the picture to his young disciple: "How do you see these trees?" he asked. "They are yellow? Well then, put down yellow. And that shade is rather blue. So render it with pure ultramarine. These red leaves . . .? Use vermilion."

VUILLARD (right)
Mother and sister of the artist, c. 1893
Vuillard may have gained his first fascination with contrasts of texture and pattern from his mother, a seamstress and designer of fabrics. She often appears, sewing or in repose, in his rather claustrophobic, but always affectionate, views of quiet, cosy domesticity. Vuillard later became a successful portrait painter.

VUILLARD (above)
The laden table, c. 1908
Vuillard's experiments with mixed media might have been encouraged by Degas's

earlier innovatory effects. Here he has applied pastel and gouache to a ground of distemper, achieving near-Impressionist spontaneity.

figures are still lively likenesses of specific individuals. Pierre Bonnard (1867-1947) was sharing a studio with Denis and Vuillard in 1890, and he, too, showed a masterly sensitivity and control of two-dimensional design in his everyday incidents. His most remarkable work, however, came very late in his career, in a great series of nudes painted in the 1920s and 1930s, in which he developed the luminous and sumptuous colour of late Monet.

In their early work both Vuillard and Bonnard reflect the asymmetrical balancing, the idiosyncratic perspective, the overall patterning so characteristic of the great masters of the Japanese print, and both were closely involved with the brilliant flowering of lithography in the 1890s – with the development not only of the *livre d'artiste* (see over) but also of the poster. Bonnard seems to have preceded Toulouse-Lautrec, who established the poster definitively as a major art-form.

Henri Marie Raymond de Toulouse-Lautrec (1860-1901), like Gauguin and van Gogh, was a misfit in society; in his case, the basic cause was physical abnormality. A grotesque dwarf, an alcoholic, he nevertheless created, in his brief life no less than in his work,

an heroic legend that has fascinated posterity. Degas's draughtmanship was always a prime inspiration for Lautrec, and he shared with Degas a fascination for metropolitan low life, the theatre and the circus; his eye was just as sardonic and unsentimental, but he also infused his characters with sharp individuality, and his vivid distortions can serve expressive as well as formal purposes. Brilliant as some of his paintings are, he found graphics his most congenial medium: he became perhaps the greatest poster designer ever. He, too, echoes the example of Japanese prints, in a witty economy of sinewy line, clear colour and strong silhouette, and in an exquisite balance between the rectangular format, the image and the lettering. Lautrec's looping forms, his exaggerations, link his graphic work with the international phenomenon of Art Nouveau.

Art Nouveau was primarily concerned with architecture and design, the applied arts. It fused its many sources of inspiration into an entirely original mode of expression, imparting to any object or design a sense of organic growth, often with erotic overtones and often fantastic in conception. It inspired, too, a handful of painters and draughtsmen of major

consequence. In England Aubrey Beardsley (1872-98) drew erotic and sinister images in blackest black on white in an extraordinary fusion of elements from Japanese prints, Greek vases, Celtic interlace, Pre-Raphaelite dream and Rococo, that seemed the epitome of 'nineties decadence. Beardsley became famous through his illustrations for the periodical *The Yellow Book* and for Oscar Wilde's *Salomé*, and achieved international celebrity before his death by tuberculosis aged 26. He was known all over Europe, for instance in Vienna, where Gustav Klimt (1863-1918), the most original painter associated with Art Nouveau, led the Austrian Sezession (formed by analogy with the German Sezessions, see p.130). Klimt's work became progressively less naturalistic: though the heads of his figures are modelled in the round, bodies, draperies and background dissolve into a flat mosaic of colour, swirling line and spirals. His determined defence of the artist's freedom of expression in the face of a reactionary society was crucial for the growth of Austrian Expressionism (see p.195); and, formally, many of the Expressionists throughout Europe took important elements from Art Nouveau, not least Munch (see p.128).

TOULOUSE-LAUTREC (left)
Self-portrait, c. 1890
A hard strain of realism belies the decorativeness of Lautrec's café art; his caricature displays fine linear control and sad wit.

TOULOUSE-LAUTREC (right)
The English girl at "Le Star", Le Havre, 1899
The nicely judged pastel colours set her off; a swift line seems to capture the girl in full brazen giggle.

BEARDSLEY (below left)
Salomé: "J'ai baisé ta bouche, Iokanaan", 1894
The Baptist's head rises like a flower on a stem of blood – a gruesome subject chilled by the calligraphy.

TOULOUSE-LAUTREC (left)
Jane Avril at the Jardin de Paris, 1893
Lautrec's inspiration was Montmartre's *demi-monde* – whores, and dancers, who appear in lithographs and posters in angled poses full of flounce and movement.

KLIMT (above)
Judith, 1909
Obsessive Symbolist *motifs* – female treachery and the severed head of Holofernes (probably a self-portrait) – set in a vivid, even jarring, patterned ground, charge the air with neurotic energy.

Symbolism

In late nineteenth-century France, in a mood both of political disillusion, after the Franco-Prussian War and the Commune of 1870, and of reaction against materialism and scientific rationalism, Courbet's insistence on a concrete art of "real and existing" things had lost much of its force. The Romantic emphasis on the imagination was sustained and revived. The artists who had briefly come together round Gauguin at Pont-Aven in Brittany had sought to express internal feeling, and those who then cohered in a group called the Nabis had spoken of themselves as Symbolists. But perhaps the most remarkable Symbolist, Odilon Redon, stood somewhat apart from that group, and work with an obviously symbolic content was already being produced by older artists, notably Moreau and Puvis de Chavannes.

For these painters literary sources were almost more significant than visual ones – the Symbolist movement crystallized around the doctrines and poetry of Baudelaire, Gautier, Mallarmé and Verlaine. Baudelaire was the arch-prophet of Symbolism. In his seminal *Fleurs du Mal*, published as long ago as 1857, he had written (in the sonnet *Correspondances*) of scents, colours and sounds communicating

not merely sensations, but states of mind. He implied that art, too, could give rise to states of mind and ideas independent of material reality – whether verbally, visually or musically. A typically Symbolist development was the *livre d'artiste*, a book in which text (usually poems) and images (usually lithographs) co-exist as aspects of one meaning, though the text does not "explain" the images nor the images "illustrate" the text. (An early and significant work of this kind had been Mallarmé's translation of Edgar Allan Poe's *The Raven*, with lithographs by Manet.) Baudelaire's aesthetics were developed by Verlaine and the major Symbolist poet Mallarmé, and Huysmans's novel *Against Nature* was virtually a Symbolist manifesto, with its archetypal "decadent" hero, des Esseintes, connoisseur of art, especially the art of Moreau and Redon.

Gustave Moreau (1826-98) was long disregarded, as being compromised by outmoded academic conventions in his figuration and by his "literary" content, which an admittedly modern sensibility could not redeem; he is now recognized as a crucial transitional figure (a role of which he himself was conscious). He painted on two scales – large, very heavily

worked oil-paintings and small, often weirdly incandescent watercolours. In both the subjects were the same – portentous and lurid landscapes or interiors with haunting mythological figures. The Surrealists naturally considered him an important precursor, but also his watercolours were reassessed in the light of Abstract Expressionism and Tachisme, while in his old age a remarkable group of future celebrities found in him a sympathetic teacher; they included Matisse and Rouault.

Puvis de Chavannes (1824-98) seems to present much more obviously a similar discrepancy between an apparently conventional, almost chilly, academic technique and a mysterious content. In fact Puvis's strange stillnesses, his wan, attenuated figures in lonely landscapes, are rendered evocative not only by the power of his imagination, but by his calculated and systematic use of distortion, and by their reduction to an almost two-dimensional pattern. His impact on Gauguin's schematic surface patterning is clear, while his cool, chalky colour and his enigmatic silences are echoed in Picasso's early work in Paris.

Odilon Redon (1840-1916) found a more satisfactory technique with which to realize

MOREAU (above)
The unicorns, c.1885
Certain details of costume suggest that Moreau made use of a set of six Gothic tapestries, *The Lady and the Unicorn*, in the Musée Cluny, Paris. Painted in oils and in watercolour, the surface is encrusted as if with gems, an effect achieved not only by rich impasto, but by rubbing and scratching the canvas; Moreau often incorporated into his composition the accidental images so made.

REDON (right)
Meadow flowers in a vase, after 1895
Redon's mastery of black and white was equalled by his achievements in the pastel medium. He was fascinated in youth by the botanical and zoological studies of Charles Darwin, and insisted on scientific reality, later, as the basis of his art. It is as if close scrutiny has heightened his perception of the object until it appears to glow with hallucinatory clarity.

imaginative concepts, by placing, as he put it, "the logic of the visible at the service of the invisible". His disconnected imagery, his repertoire of disparate and fragmentary symbols and of concocted elements of the imagination, anticipate the Surrealists' attempts to represent the inner worlds of dreams and of the Unconscious closely. Until the 1890s he worked almost entirely in black and white, but then moved to pastels, achieving a brilliant vibration of colour in which the simplest of themes, a vase of flowers, takes on a positively unearthly intensity.

Symbolism came closest in France to being a coherent movement in the fine arts with a clear-cut programme, but symbolic imagery flourished elsewhere in Europe, although formally it was usually much more traditional. Indeed a Symbolist kind of other-worldliness pervaded even orthodox academic painting. In England Sir Edward Burne-Jones was the first of the Pre-Raphaelites (see p. 82) to establish a European reputation, when his dreamy unexplained visions of pale women, so close in mood to those of Puvis de Chavannes, were exhibited and admired in Paris. The work of Dante Gabriel Rossetti, with its recurrent

REDON
Orpheus, after 1913
Orpheus was torn apart by frenzied maenads who cast his head, still singing, into

a river. Afloat in iridescent colour, he typifies *le poète maudit* (the accursed poet), destroyed by the beloved Symbolist *femme fatale*.

theme of the *femme fatale*, was even more mysterious and visionary. Even George Frederick Watts made an original contribution – his *Hope* of 1886 (see p. 83) is a fascinating contrast to Puvis de Chavannes's earlier painting of the same title.

In Belgium, the weird Neo-Rosicrucian group was a focus of Symbolism, though its members still painted in academic or conventional styles. The most striking of them was Fernand Khnopff (1858-1921). His most famous painting, *The caress* (1896; not shown), a male figure embraced by a leopard with a human head, is perhaps more bizarre than convincing, but the dreamlike, irrational intensity of *Memories* (1889) – superficially a banal representation of a tennis party – has all the inexplicable compulsion of Puvis de Chavannes or Burne-Jones at their best. In Germany, the Swiss-born Arnold Böcklin (1827-1901) exercised a transitional and seminal role rather akin to that of Moreau in France. His paintings, essentially traditional and academic in technique, are rooted in Romanticism, and have a remarkable power to evoke the supernatural – never more memorably than in his enduringly famous *Island of the dead*.

ROSSETTI (right)
Astarte Syriaca, 1877
By the mid-1860s Rossetti had developed beyond the strong medievalizing bent of his early painting, and was interested in Venetian art. Astarte's rich glazed greens surely owe much to Veronese. Her dark beauty – and that of many similar lavish and sinister exotic Venuses – was modelled on William Morris' wife, Jane. Their sexuality was often comparatively explicit – in one the bitten pomegranate held by a Proserpina is a cryptic image of a vagina.

BURNE-JONES (below)
The mill, c. 1870-82
The presence of the Three Graces, which derive from Botticelli, might suggest a classical idyll; in fact the other age or world so wistfully evoked is neither antique nor medieval, even though it echoes both. The technique hardly offends academic canons, but the main figures are disposed across the foreground in a long, flattened frieze.

KHNOPFF (above)
Memories, 1889
The two foreground figures were both modelled, one from life and one from a photograph, on the artist's sister. As in a dream, one senses obscure significance in the calm expectancy and clear, unfocused gaze of these women, who seem to float rather than walk.

BOCKLIN (below)
The island of the dead, 1880
The gaping doors of what seem to be tombs hollowed out of rock and the black spires of cypress trees – traditionally associated with death – have probably suggested the painting's title; Böcklin was content to call it simply "a dream

picture". Böcklin perhaps influenced Chirico, whose Surrealist "dummies" are anticipated in the blunt, faceless heads of the two tiny foreground figures. They are there to impart a sense of epic vastness (which recalls the settings for Wagner's operas – *The Ring* was produced for the first time at Bayreuth in 1876).

American Art in the Later 19th Century

A sense of national and cultural unity and identity began to consolidate in the United States only after the end of the Civil War in 1865: Emerson, in some ways the keeper of the new American conscience, proclaimed: "Our long apprenticeship to the learning of other lands draws to the close." The variations made by American artists within the European traditions took on an increasingly distinctive American character. Some talented artists had of course already explored the possibilities of American landscape and American genre (see p. 69), and in the early nineteenth century numbers of local, "primitive" artists had flourished, including some who in a European context might have been tamed into an average professionalism, but, in America, retained a forthright, uncompromising vision. This innocent directness is also to be found in the work of the early American photographers.

The outstanding professional painters of the late nineteenth century fall into two groups – those who remained based primarily in America and those who were more cosmopolitan or were indeed expatriates. The former developed, much along the lines of European Realist painting, an emphasis either on physical detail or on a more psychological realism, and Eastman Johnson (1824-1906), the major forerunner, developed from the one towards the other. From Maine, he studied for six years at Düsseldorf, The Hague and Paris, acquiring from these diverse sources a fine technique in naturalistic detail and a taste for genre subjects, and from Couture in Paris he gained a respect for well-structured composition. Back in America his lively *plein-air* paintings of rural subjects (perhaps already nostalgic for a vanishing way of life) and also strong portraits became very popular.

Winslow Homer (1836-1910) is more often claimed as the archetypal American painter of the later nineteenth century. Conscientiously naturalistic ("When I have selected the thing carefully, I paint it exactly as it appears"), he was influenced by photographic reportage – recording rather than dramatizing. Visiting France in 1867 he received the message of Japanese prints, of Manet's flat tonal surfaces, but Impressionist colourism affected him little. His characteristic subjects of the 1870s, youths at play on the Massachusetts coast, are lightly drawn, fresh and vigorous. Later, preferring watercolour, he began to turn to more dramatic themes, the heroism of man's

HOMER (right)
"*Breezing up*", 1876
This picture was greeted as Homer's "greatest hit" with that conservative body, the National Academy of Design in New York, in 1876. The sea spray and scudding clouds are fresh and lively. The theme of children enjoying themselves was more popular than ever in the year that Mark Twain published his novel *Huckleberry Finn*.

JOHNSON (above)
The old stagecoach, 1871
For the American nation and its artists, Johnson, Homer and Thomas Eakins especially, the 1870s were formative years. Here the outmoded coach symbolizes the end of an era, a game for these post-war children. Johnson was an enthusiast for outdoor painting, but his approach was academic.

HOMER (below)
Inside the bar, Tynemouth, 1883
Homer's watercolour shore scene, with its monumental fisherwoman who almost defeats the elements, was completed after he had left England for America in 1883. The strong two-dimensional design seems a response to the new French developments in painting.

EAKINS (right)
The Gross Clinic, 1875
Eakins wanted his large picture to be exhibited at the 1876 fair to celebrate American Independence. To his chagrin it was hung in the First Aid tent. An art critic found it "powerful, horrible ... fascinating". It is a remarkable statement of American positivism, enterprise, hope and will.

struggle against Nature, the pioneering spirit, and finally to Nature itself – the violence of the elements, particularly the sea.

The realism of Thomas Eakins (1844-1916) was applied more to figure painting and to portraiture. In Europe (1866-70) he learnt much from the Spanish masters and from Courbet's forceful Realism; the honesty of his own work often shocked contemporaries, and he was dismissed from the Pennsylvania Academy for posing a male model nude before female students. His masterpiece is the monumental *Gross Clinic* of 1875, showing a surgeon at work in his operating theatre amongst his students. If there are obvious echoes of Rembrandt's *Anatomy lesson of Dr Tulp* (see vol. 2 p. 216), Eakins proves himself a worthy successor, presenting the scene dramatically and yet with reverence and with compassion: science becomes intensely human. Eakins also produced wax models of horses in motion which owed much to the revolutionary photographs (see over) of Eadweard Muybridge (1830-1904), who showed for the first time how a horse really galloped.

There was a sturdy strain of realistic painters active at this time, often most successfully

in still life. The finest of these was William Michael Harnett (1848-92), a craftsman of exquisite, vivid accuracy: the underlying formal quality of his compositions, their almost abstract intensity, have very recently revived interest in him. Albert Pinkham Ryder (1847-1917) was the most original among the more subjective and idealistic painters; his lyrical and poetic response to sensory experience is in the Romantic and Symbolist tradition, but his generalized forms and broad rhythms were something of an anomaly in his time.

Whistler, greatest of the expatriate painters, has to be seen in the European context (see p. 96). Mary Cassatt (1845-1926), from Pittsburgh but of French stock, moved to Paris in 1866, and after her work had attracted the attention of Degas at the Salon of 1872 she became associated with the Impressionists. Her stills of civilized everyday intercourse are like vignettes from a Henry James novel; her favourite motif, mother and child, repeated perhaps too often, made her very popular.

John Singer Sargent (1856-1925), born of rich American parents in Italy, lived all his life in Europe, though he made forays to the United States. His great technical gifts were

developed in the studio of the highly skilful, fashionable painter Carolus-Duran in Paris, and probably Duran inculcated in Sargent his lifelong reverence for Velazquez and Hals, but much of his early work is Impressionist. His youthful success in Paris was blasted by a violent row over his portrait of *Madame Gautreau*, and Sargent then settled in London; there, though some still found his work eccentric, he became the outstanding portraitist of the Edwardian era. He is the last major exponent of the British portrait tradition, stemming from van Dyck through Gainsborough, Reynolds and Lawrence. He had all their glamour – the command of lavish and opulent movement, the ability to "orchestrate" his sitters' individuality in fluent line and brilliant colour, but he also had a sardonic eye, and at his best he refused to flatter his patron's features into fashionable beauty. Perhaps his masterpieces are his few large-scale shadowy groups, showing a rare skill in the disposition of figures in space – conversation pieces brimful of silence. He was, too, a brilliant watercolourist; the large murals he undertook in Boston in the United States at the end of his life are less successful.

HARNETT (left)
My gems, 1888
Harnett collected *objets* for his still lifes while on tour in Europe. Later he painted them, artfully disposed, with minute care.

CASSATT (right)
The bath, 1892
Though domestic, intimate scenes were far from rare in this period, few were so tender as Cassatt's solemn pictures in pastel colours. The clarity of the design, the viewpoint and the juxtaposition of plain colours owe much to the example of Japanese prints. Cassatt had an important role in infiltrating into American art Impressionist ideas, and in forming Impressionist collections.

RYDER (above)
Moonlit cove, c.1890-1900
Ryder's small simplified seascapes have a mystical, symbolic dimension. He wrote: "The artist should

fear to become the slave of detail. He should express his thought and not the surface of it." In a sense he is in the tradition of Allston, though not really pantheist.

SARGENT (above)
Mme Gautreau, 1884
The American society lady's *décolletage* and pronounced superiority outraged Salon visitors in Paris in 1884. Sargent – more gregarious than revolutionary – moved to London in the hope of a more sympathetic reception.

SARGENT (left)
The daughters of Edward D. Boit, 1882
An opulent, shadowy interior provides a perfect foil for the youthfulness and artlessness of the sisters, daughters of an American expatriate in Paris. The composition derives directly from Sargent's studies of Velazquez.

Art in the 20th Century: A New Constitution

The year 1900 marks with reasonable accuracy a great divide in the history of Western art, a revolution potentially more fundamental in its consequences than any change of direction since the collapse of Hellenic values in the fourth century AD. The first, ferocious challenge to the established order had been the French Revolution, the intellectual, moral and spiritual impetus for which had sprung in large part from the writings of the early Romantics. Romantic ideas as far as the arts were concerned gathered strength during the nineteenth century – if each individual and his conscience were to be free, so inevitably was the artist, and his function came increasingly to consist primarily in the truthful expression of his own self. Therein lay authenticity, originality and integrity. The artist began to look within himself just as much as he looked at the external world, and Picasso would insist: "I paint forms as I think them, not as I see them."

The rejection of the Renaissance tradition of naturalistic representation – what has been called "the retreat from likeness" – had already begun in the work of the Impressionists, for all their emphasis on scientific observation. Of all the Impressionists Monet was probably

the most dedicated to truth to Nature, but he himself compared his huge late paintings of the floating surface of his pond at Giverny to music, and worked and reworked this most ephemeral image in a protracted effort to express not just the subject but its effect, its meaning for him. In the laborious marriage of the world of appearances with the needs of purely pictorial structure that Cézanne battled to achieve, representation was losing out in the artist's fanatical urgency to remain true to his inner self – Cézanne's "*petite sensation*", his little sensation. His principle of conscientious

disintegration of the visible world and its reconstruction in the artist's own terms had an immediate heir in Cubism. On the other flank of the revolution Gauguin and van Gogh, prophets of Symbolism and of Expressionism, were struggling to reduce to order sensations of a more cataclysmic kind, and the subject matter of their art was even more obviously the artist himself, the private person of the artist rendered public.

It followed inevitably that the function of art became increasingly uncertain. Its religious purpose, consistently there probably since its

CEZANNE (left)
Ambroise Vollard, 1899
Cézanne's late portraits were treated almost like his still lifes – highly structured and patterned, the product of numerous sittings. Cézanne studied Vollard's shirt hardly less intensely than his face.

PICASSO (below)
Ambroise Vollard, 1910
The step from Cézanne's portrait seems logical: Picasso appears to have executed with confidence what Cézanne struggled to achieve in his unfinished portrait. Vollard the man becomes an abstraction.

MONET
(below) *Waterlilies*, and (above) detail, 1900-09
Their scale, and Monet's wish to encircle a room with his wall-size shaped

canvases, anticipate the procedure, even some aims of Abstract Expressionists. They incite the viewer to a reflective mood, to the contemplation of colour.

UNKNOWN RUSSIAN
(left) *A yellow cat*, early 20th century
Lubki, or folk woodcuts, were an inspiration on the one hand to Larionov and Goncharova in their progress to Rayonnism (see p. 156) and on the other to Chagall (see p. 185), who borrowed freely from folk imagery to set aglow his own fantasy.

UNKNOWN AFRICAN
(right) Ancestor figure, late 19th century
The formal and expressive range of African tribal sculpture (see vol. 2 p. 16) was so wide that artists could choose from it what suited them, once they had begun to look. A wooden figure of the Congo Luba reveals that even for the massive, simplified forms of 1920s "Neoclassicism" tribal art was relevant.

first known appearance in Palaeolithic cave-paintings, almost disappeared, and its traditional secular themes – such as the celebration of civic or national virtue – seemed no longer relevant. Even private patronage, and the role of the domestic user in supporting and promoting art, became suspect: the validity of the easel-painting itself came into question – what was it for? One major agent in the liberation of painting and sculpture from the slavery of imitating the natural world had been photography, invented in the 1830s and subsequently refined until it acquired the ability to record the world in motion. The recording of the visual appearance of the world had been the monopoly of art for centuries; with that removed, its practical justification was undermined; art became so much more a luxury.

Uncertainty about the nature and purpose of art is apparent not least in the noise of the debate, the dogma and anathema, the manifesto and counter-manifesto, the "isms" that constitute the development of art during the first half of the twentieth century. After 1900 the process accelerated by which an avantgarde emerged in an exhibition challenging the established art of the moment, and then itself solidified into an established art to be challenged by a new avantgarde group mounting its own exhibition, and so on: the necessity for originality, the hunger for novelty, became paramount. Artists deliberately seeking alternative means of expression began to seek inspiration in alien traditions – above all in "primitive" art, partly because it was at furthest possible remove from academic conventions. Picasso and Matisse and others, including the Fauve painter Vlaminck and the Cubist sculptor Lipchitz, eagerly collected tribal art, and the influence of African masks on Picasso's revolutionary proto-Cubist "Demoiselles d'Avignon" is unmistakable (see p. 148). The British sculptor Epstein had one of the most important collections of tribal art ever in private hands; Moore was obsessed in his early career by Pre-Columbian sculpture. Many of the Blaue Reiter group in Germany, notably Klee, studied also the "primitive" or folk art of their own country, and in Russia this interest was reinforced in some by socialism.

The development of twentieth-century art has also reflected the changed conditions and perceptions, the catastrophes and the continuing uncertainties that have affected the world.

A whole way of life perished in the 1914-18 War; centuries-old preconceptions of stability, of continuity, were being proved unsound. Einstein formulated the Theory of Relativity in 1905 – the year Picasso began studies for "Les Demoiselles d'Avignon". Kandinsky reported himself aghast at the news that Rutherford had split the atom. Solid matter was solid no more, and, following the investigations of Freud into the Unconscious, human consciousness and human identity were revealed as fronts and pretences. Some significant movements, however – Futurism, De Stijl – responded with missionary optimism to the new scope of the new world.

Almost all these avantgarde groups were at first greeted with indifference or hostility by the general public. Partly as a result of the Romantic notion that the bourgeoisie must be shocked, startled into life out of deadening habits and ossified imagination, a gulf opened between the artist and his audience. From the first fully abstract paintings of Kandinsky onwards the traditionally brought-up Western observer has had no familiar subject matter to engage and retain his attention; he has been left suspended in a void.

TOLTEC ARTIST (below)
Chacmool, 12th century
Chac, god of rain, holding a basin at Chichen Itza in Yucatan, inspired the heavy reclining figures of Moore. "Primitive" stone monuments set an example in the reaction to Rodin's light and texture.

MUYBRIDGE (below)
Two men wrestling, 1887
Muybridge's "stills" of men and animals not only instructed artists, they even opened up a new approach to depicting motion; both Duchamp's *Nude descending a staircase* (see p. 168) and Futurism presuppose him.

(above) *Paul Cézanne and Camille Pissarro*, 1872
The two men unmistakably are artists: Cézanne is wearing a smock, a work uniform. But their status is dependent on an ability to paint good pictures.

ARNATT (below)
I'm a real artist, 1972
Keith Arnatt (born 1930) is also clearly an artist, but he himself does not know why, or in what: it is his art to offer this question for discussion.

DEGAS (right)
Princess Metternich, 1861
The photograph adorning the Metternichs' visiting card by Eugène Disderi was patently "borrowed" by Degas for his (unfinished) portrait. He has copied not only the pose but the tonal values; photography is surely a factor behind the "cool", flattened tones recurrent in painting from Manet to Pop art. It has profoundly affected both the what and the how of figurative art – both used as an aid and emulated.

DISDERI (left)
Prince and Princess Metternich, c. 1860

Edvard Munch

"No longer should you paint interiors with
men reading and women knitting. These must
be human beings who breathe and feel and love
and suffer. I would paint such pictures in a
cycle. People would understand the sacredness
of them and take their hats off as if in church."
This self-directive, an entry written in his
notebook by Edvard Munch (1863-1944)
when he was in France in 1890, formulates an
aim that he was to pursue until the end of his
life. He disclaims the cosy anecdotal genre of
the Realist tradition popular in his native
Norway (and most of Europe), and implicitly
commits himself to a humanist vocation in
which he would act as a prophet or priest.

Such an idea was the antithesis of the
claimed objectivity of the Impressionists –
though their influence was even then, in 1890,
lightening Munch's palette – but more in key
with Gauguin's objectives and virtually at one
with van Gogh's belief in the power of art to
communicate truths of existence to ordinary
people. It was not, however, a message either
of consolation or of joy. Munch's youth was
profoundly disturbed by the deaths of his
mother and sister from tuberculosis, and by
the aggressiveness of his father, a doctor, who

seems to have come close to religious de-
mentia. Later, as a student, he was involved
with a radical group of writers in Oslo, the
"Christiana Bohemians", influenced by Zola's
harsh dissections of society and by Ibsen's
questioning plays of the 1880s. In this climate
Munch settled compulsively on his perennial
themes – the intense expression of inner states
of mind (usually suffering rather than pleasure); the union of man and woman in love,
and the failure of union: no painter has surpassed him in the depiction of loneliness, and
few have equalled him in conveying an awareness of the doom that haunts the passion of
love, even though it is a theme implanted in the
European imagination from Dante's Paolo and
Francesca onwards. Woman has never been
more vividly realized as both destroyer and
creator than in Munch's *Vampire* or *Madonna*.

Abroad during much of 1889-92, Munch
was influenced in France not only by the philosophy latent in Gauguin's and van Gogh's
work, but also by their formal innovations.
Gauguin's flowing contours, his simplification
and occasional distortion of natural form, his
juxtaposition of broad areas of bright, contrasting colour, these were of seminal import-

inferno of his tormented
imagination – a simple and
telling, if theatrical, image,
and clearly Expressionist.

MUNCH (left)
The kiss, 1892
The two bodies, so merged
in an embrace as to become
one form, might be viewed
as symbolic of union and
fulfilment. But Strindberg,
in his critical commen-
tary on *The Frieze of Life*,
conceived it as "the fusion
of two beings, the smaller
of which, shaped like a

carp, seems on the point of
devouring the larger, as
is the habit of vermin,
microbes, vampires and
women". In a later, variant
woodcut Munch simplified
the forms even further, and
incorporated in the design
the grain of the wood itself
– an innovative practice –
in a violent statement of
great power and economy.

MUNCH (above)
Madonna, 1895
The Madonna, remote in
her ecstasy, emanates the
force of life, terrible in its
impersonality; her red lips,
nipples, navel and halo
recall "Our Lady of Pain"
of Swinburne's poetry. In
a later lithograph Munch
added an embryo, cower-
ing as if in fear of the life
into which he must be born.

MUNCH (right)
Vampire, 1895
Strindberg found expressed
here his view of woman as
the seductress and destroyer
of man: "A rain of blood
flows in torrents over the
accursed head of him who
seeks the misery, the divine misery, of being loved
– or rather, of loving".

MUNCH (above)
Puberty, 1895
Women at varying stages
in their maturity occupy
a central role in Munch's
art: for him, the progress
of female development was
a gripping symbol of the
primary experiences of the
journey through life – birth,
sexual awareness and death.

These, for Munch, were all
fraught with fear; and the
anxiety which dominated
his view of heterosexual
love is explicit in this
girl's pitiful nubility –
she stares out, crossing
large hands, overshadowed
by her growing femininity,
which seems to hover like
ectoplasm in her shadow.

ance to Munch's art. For Munch, however, it was always the inner needs of the subject matter that shaped its outward form, and in a highly expressive and definite manner; with Gauguin it was more often the mood that compelled the subject matter into form, and the significance could be imprecise – Gauguin's "*inquiétude de mystère*" (mysterious disquiet). In contrast, it is Munch's desolations, his desires and his fears, that overwhelm.

Between 1892 and 1908 – the finest period of Munch's art – it was Berlin, not Paris, that provided him with audience, stimulation and patronage – and controversy. The forced closing of his first show in Berlin in 1892 led directly to the founding of the German breakaway group, the Berlin Sezession (see over). By 1908 he was famous, not only in Norway and in Germany, but internationally. In 1908, too, following a wretched love-affair apparently both passionate and absurd, and after various squalid brawls, he withdrew, an alcoholic and in what he called a "complete nervous collapse", to Dr Jacobsen's sanatorium at Copenhagen. The parallel with the crisis in van Gogh's career is striking, but with Munch sanity ultimately prevailed. For the rest of his

life he lived almost entirely in his native Norway, largely withdrawn from society. His fame, however, spread, and in 1933 he received the ultimate accolade as a leader of modern art, when 82 of his works were branded as "degenerate" by the Nazis. Having rejected all contact with the Quisling regime established in 1940, he bequeathed to Oslo on his death in 1944 all the works left in his possession; it is still to Oslo that those interested must go to experience the full range of his achievement, especially his later mural decorations.

The "cycle" that he had hoped for in 1890 was in part carried through, but only within his overall production. He linked a sequence of paintings under the general title *The Frieze of Life*, of which 22 were exhibited together at the Berlin Sezession in 1902. These, in their power, both formal and emotive, to convey *fin-de-siècle* disillusion and a sense of man as a victim, are perhaps his masterpieces. He was by this time, however, translating his themes into other media, and establishing himself as one of the greatest of printmakers (he learnt much technically from the printer Auguste Clot in Paris, who also worked for Vuillard and Bonnard). In his lithographs, and sometimes

in his paintings, he tried deliberately to relax conscious control of the hand, anticipating later experiments. His most remarkable and original graphic work was in woodcut, where his technical virtuosity was matched by an ability to distil his subject into its stark and startling essentials; his woodcuts were to have a profound impact on Expressionist idiom.

In his later years Munch moved towards a freer, lighter style, especially in his murals, designed to be "at one and the same time peculiarly Norwegian and universal". Like almost all twentieth-century large-scale institutional decorations, they verge on the banal, and his smaller work remained more satisfactory, although it became repetitive. However, his long series of self-portraits maintained their early quality, and the very late *Self-portrait between clock and bed* is an image of man in his loneliness as haunting as anything that Munch had realized before. His influence had permeated the ideas of the German Expressionists well before he died, but it is perhaps only since 1945, when Paris ceased to dazzle to the exclusion of other schools, that his towering stature in twentieth-century art has become universally recognized.

MUNCH
(near right) *The scream*, oils, 1893
"One evening I was walking along a path, the city on one side, the fiord below. I felt tired and ill . . . The sun was setting and the clouds turning blood-red. I sensed a scream passing through Nature; it seemed to me that I heard the scream. I painted this picture, painted the clouds as actual blood. The colour shrieked."

(far right) *The scream*, lithograph, 1895
When translated from oil-paint into a graphic medium, Munch's images became still more sharply defined and more potently charged: instinctual panic is expressed in swirling rhythms in the sky, the lake and in the figure, drawn up in a tortured echo of the natural forms.

MUNCH (below)
Self-portrait between clock and bed, 1940-42
Standing in the narrow space between the time that remains to him and the bed on which he is shortly to die, the artist faces mortality against a backdrop of his paintings. But although the theme is sombre, the brilliant, sunny colours stress a positive, perhaps even a triumphant, pride: his art will survive his personal extinction.

MUNCH
History, 1910-11
The decoration of the new assembly hall of Oslo University (1910-15) gave

Munch the opportunity to paint a set of murals on the themes of learning, beauty and the continuity of life. *History* is one of

three main panels and shows Age passing tradition on to Youth against a background of fiords – Norway – and below an oak tree – the

Tree of Life perhaps. The simple design, cool tones and monumental forms led the committee in charge to call it "Greek in spirit".

Impressionists and Expressionists outside France

A ferment of change was transforming the arts everywhere in Europe at the turn of the nineteenth century, although Paris was its most spectacular and most clearly defined focus. The restless movement of artists, and their eagerness to experiment, led to complex cross-fertilizations, and sometimes to disconcerting changes of direction within a single artist's style. In the 1890s in Holland, for example, where painting, though leavened by Impressionist colour, was still generally very traditional, the highly talented Jan Toorop (1858-1928) could blend the linear rhythms of Art Nouveau with both the emotional and literary subject matter of Symbolism and an exoticism owing something to memories of his native Java – and yet during the same period he was also painting pure divisionist pictures.

Toorop was a member of Les Vingt (The Twenty), a group founded in Brussels in 1883 which, before it was disbanded in 1893, had greatly assisted the dissemination of Post-Impressionist art by organizing enterprising exhibitions – showing Rodin, Monet, Redon, Seurat, Gauguin, van Gogh and Cézanne. Another member of Les Vingt was James Ensor (1860-1949). Some of Ensor's earlier

paintings were remarkably precocious – interiors foreshadowing Vuillard – and the work for which he is best known was produced in less than two decades before 1900; after 1900 his inspiration seems to have failed. His imagery – macabre, jagged, grotesque, reverting obsessively to the theme of the mask – was to be echoed immediately by the German Expressionists, and so was the style with which it was conveyed: a master of traditional composition if he so wished, Ensor chose to disrupt convention into chaos, and to distort and to make deliberately ugly in order to express a profoundly pessimistic view of mankind. His most famous picture, the huge *Entry of Christ into Brussels* of 1888, seems in places almost splattered with his vitriol, and was too much for Les Vingt. Etching was perhaps his most effective medium, but even broadcast in prints his vision was individual to the point of obscurity; in his isolation, his inability to come to terms with life, he followed the pattern set by van Gogh and Munch and to be followed again by several German Expressionists.

Germany proved to be the natural home of Expressionism. Without an acknowledged national capital until 1871, the culturally dis-

united states of the German-speaking peoples had nevertheless produced a number of flourishing artistic schools in their leading cities – in Munich and Berlin, but also in Düsseldorf, Dresden, Vienna and Weimar. The predominant style had been naturalistic, academic, high-gloss, often applied with great virtuosity to genre subjects or portraiture; in the 1890s the official or semi-official bodies were challenged by breakaway groups, generally called *Sezessionen*. The symbolic signal for revolt seems to have been the forcible closure of an exhibition of Munch in 1892, when the Munich Sezession was formed; the Berlin Sezession followed in 1898-99, led by Max Liebermann (1847-1935), an able and sensitive interpreter of Impressionism, to which he had turned not long before; but Liebermann could not go along with the Expressionist Neue (New) Sezession (see p. 134) which challenged his group in 1910. Liebermann remained, however, the grand old man of German art.

The other chief exponents of the Impressionist style in Germany, tending always, though in individual ways, to modulate it according to the German tradition of lyric

TOOROP (left)
The three brides, 1893
Three ghostly women stand enmeshed in an intricate web of Art Nouveau line – a nun, the bride of Christ, an earthly bride and the bride of Hell (another manifestation of the Symbolist *femme fatale*; her necklace of skulls recalls Kali, the Hindu goddess of death).

ENSOR (right)
The murder, 1888
Ensor's blend of sadism and fantasy makes him a modern Flemish successor to Bosch. The delicacy of his line, and whimsical distortions, make his theme yet more macabre – a fairy tale turned to nightmare.

LIEBERMANN (left)
The parrot man, 1902
Influenced at first by Hals, *plein-air* painting and the

Barbizon school, Liebermann felt Manet's impact in the 1890s, then became increasingly Impressionist.

ENSOR (above)
The entry of Christ into Brussels, 1888
The fantastic mask-faces

of the people reveal a host of worldly concerns; Jesus' foredoomed entry is retold in terms of the modern city.

naturalism, were Fritz von Uhde (1848-1911), Lovis Corinth (1858-1925) and Max Slevogt (1868-1932; not shown). Their progress, however, was not easy; a vivid illustration of their difficulties is the fact that as late as 1908 Kaiser Wilhelm sacked the Director of the Berlin National Gallery, Hugo von Tschudi, because of his purchase of modern French paintings.

In sculpture, the influence of Rodin was paramount, but the major sculptors in Germany all developed styles in which profoundly personal emotions were expressed in severely simplified forms of great intensity. In his suffering figures Ernst Barlach (1870-1938) resolved the artistic problems of social realism more nobly than any artist encouraged by a totalitarian state (whatever its persuasion) has since succeeded in doing. Wilhelm Lehmbruck (1881-1919) evolved a fusion of classical reminiscence, German Gothic and the sensuous monumentality of Maillol. His strangely elegant, almost narcissistic figures – modelled rather than carved – in their simplified planes, their lean attenuation, are redolent of haunted melancholy. Käthe Kollwitz (1867-1945) was driven by sympathies with the poor and oppressed akin to Barlach's, but her art was more

personal: in her many self-portrait drawings she created an archetypal image of bereaved and suffering womanhood (her only son was killed in World War I, her grandson in World War II). Barlach, Lehmbruck and Kollwitz all found printmaking a satisfying medium, and, though she was a compelling sculptor, Kollwitz's best work was graphic; her lithographs, with those of Ensor and the woodcuts of Munch, prelude the Expressionists' resuscitation of the print.

Another woman pioneer of modern art was Paula Modersohn-Becker (1876-1907). She was encouraged by the dealer Vollard, and met Cézanne; her own work was more in key with the Nabis than with the forceful expressiveness to be developed by her younger compatriots. They responded to the message of the work of Gauguin, van Gogh or Munch but were increasingly aware of the contribution that their own Nordic genius must add to it; and much that they so startlingly developed had been foreshadowed in Germany, for instance by the critic Fiedler, who had declared that "the visual aspect of an object breaks free from the object and appears as a free, independent creation".

KOLLWITZ (above)
Woman welcoming death, 1934-35
Kollwitz's *Cycle of Death* uses taut line and menacing shadow to convey both a fear and desire for release. An intensely personal grief is stripped of egotism, pared down to barest essentials.

UHDE (left)
At the summer resort, 1892
Uhde was a member of the Munich Sezession of 1892. His fresh and uncloying version of Impressionism, influenced by Liebermann, was still close to *plein-air* Realism, being much less brightly and freely painted than the French original. There is even a faint echo of Runge's Romanticism in the aureoled child, who recalls the children in *The artist's parents* (see p. 75).

LEHMBRUCK (above)
Kneeling woman, 1911
The expressive elongation may derive from Rodin; the richly modelled surface is directly Rodinesque. Also Maillol could be cited. But the bowed head and docile pose, like that of some lost Virgin Annunciate, impart a distinctive spirituality – alien to France, but widely found in German sculpture.

MODERSOHN-BECKER (below)
Mother and child, 1906
The mother's heavy, almost animal body encloses the vulnerable form of the baby within a protective curve. Gauguin's impact is clear, but this is a powerful and tender image that has now an added poignancy, as it was painted the year before the artist died in giving birth to her first child.

CORINTH (below)
Morning sunlight, 1910
Corinth's Impressionism was encouraged by study in Paris and then in Berlin under Liebermann. Beside Uhde, his handling is much freer, but sentimentality is perhaps too evident; the sensuous, warm flesh tones of the model, his wife, show his admiration of Rubens.

BARLACH (above)
The solitary one, 1911
Barlach was a friend of Kollwitz, who shared his sympathy with the miseries of the poor and lonely; he aspired, he said, to celebrate "the human condition in its nakedness between heaven and earth", in poetry and prints as well as sculpture. He felt an affinity with the great Gothic woodcarvers, though in most figures the influence of Rodin seems paramount. This is almost bursting with some massive sorrow, too great to bear.

Nolde: The Last Supper

"With light strokes I traced 13 figures on to the canvas, the Redeemer and the 12 Apostles seated at a table in the warm spring night, the night before the Passion. This was the occasion when Christ revealed His great idea of redemption to His beloved disciples. I obeyed an irresistible impulse to express deep spirituality and ardent religious feeling, but I did so without much deliberation, knowledge or reflection ... While working on *The Last Supper* and *Pentecost* I had to be artistically free ... These paintings marked the transition in my development from reliance on external optical stimulus to that of experienced inner value."

When Emil Nolde (1867-1956) painted his *Last Supper*, the genesis of which he was later to describe, as above, in his memoirs, he was already 43. He had been a slow developer. Brought up on a farm in Schleswig-Holstein, in the remoteness of north-east Germany, he always remained a somewhat solitary figure in the German Expressionist movement, with an almost hermetic, mystical dedication to his artistic vocation. He became a full-time painter only in 1894, but he had nevertheless by 1900 acquired considerable experience, in Munich, in Italy and in Paris, and had worked at Dachau in the school of Adolf Hölzel (1853-1934; not shown), whose use of symbolism and of expressive colour was probably very important for Nolde. Nolde's style evolved through Impressionism, but his real mentors were to be Munch and Ensor.

Nolde discovered or consolidated the themes that would preoccupy him for the rest of his life between 1900 and 1910 – religion, Nature (especially the wilderness of northern plains or the elemental forces of the sea), figure painting and, not least, flowers. These, however, he painted according to his inner vision: "All the free fantastic paintings of this period came into being without any prototype or model, without any well-defined idea ... a vague shape of glow and colour was enough. The paintings took shape as I worked." From such conceptions there evolved his idea of "passive artistic creation", defined in 1942 as "the moment when a spark glows in the darkness and grows, if the circumstances are right, into a leaping flame."

The handling of Nolde's *Last Supper* is indeed a far cry from the traditional formulae evolving from the famous prototype by Leonardo da Vinci (see vol. 2 p. 128), though the force behind it owes something surely to the tortured anguish of Grünewald's religious painting. In its harsh, summary drawing, in its echoes of tribal African or Oceanic sculpture, in the strident reds and yellow greens and the compression of figures within the picture space, the painting is unequivocally in the mainstream of German Expressionism. But the religious impact is Nolde's own, and his only peer as a religious artist in the twentieth

century is Rouault (see p. 143), also a great master of glowing colour. Nolde, however, lacked Rouault's sexual disgust, and also his formal restraint, for Nolde could unleash his brush in a wild gaiety of swirling paint in which the figures dissolve.

As a prolific printmaker, exploiting the technical potential of both woodcut and lithograph, Nolde had an importance in the development of Expressionist graphics. Yet perhaps his most remarkable achievements were in watercolour: in this medium, in the incandescent intensity with which he could kindle colour into blaze on paper, he has no peer in the twentieth century.

After he had briefly, in 1906-07, been a

member of Die Brücke, Nolde withdrew to a farm in the northern German fastnesses at Seebüll (where a foundation now houses much of his work); and became more and more a recluse. The Nazis (of whom Nolde at first approved) declared him a "degenerate" artist, but, though he was officially forbidden to paint, he produced innumerable compositions in miniature (his secret "unpainted pictures") during World War II, and subsequently, in an astonishing burst of energy before his death, painted full-scale versions of a great many of them. Well aware of the example of van Gogh, Gauguin and Munch, he rivalled them in the intensity of his vision, in which he formulated an original, elemental imagery of great power.

NOLDE (left)
The Last Supper, 1909
Early in 1909 Nolde had been dangerously ill; on his recovery he began painting a series of religious works – *The Last Supper, Pentecost, The mocking of Christ* and *The Crucifixion*. He said: "I stood almost terrified before my drawing, without any model in nature – I was about to paint the most profoundly significant episode in the Christian religion! ... Had I felt bound to keep to the letter of the Bible or dogma, I do not think I could have painted these deeply experienced pictures so powerfully."

ENSOR (left)
Intrigue, 1890
Ensor was one of the first European artists to break traditional constraints on expression – turning to use the ugly and disturbing. In what seems to be a carnival there is here no festivity; the masks reveal an inner evil; the smiles are leers. Nolde, trying to give form to a personal vision, took up Ensor's example, conveying his emotion through garish colour and coarse features.

NOLDE (above)
A Friesland farm under red clouds, c. 1930
The wild and desolate landscape of Seebüll with its vast expanses of sky suited Nolde's fervent, solitary nature. A visit to China in 1913 perhaps stimulated the vivid hues and liking for pattern typical of his later watercolour style.

NOLDE (right)
The prophet, 1912
This is one of a series of woodcuts that Nolde made in 1912. He had earlier been associated with Die Brücke and he, too, was attracted by the German origin of the technique, and the powerful crudity of the kind of image it produces.

NOLDE (above)
Early morning flight, 1950
Nolde's late oil-paintings are all enlarged versions of watercolour improvisations, with glowing colours, free brushwork and a dreamy or

mystical quality. Perhaps these are spirits heralding the coming of morning; the subject matter is usually fanciful or fey, expressing a joyous vivacity that had seldom appeared earlier.

Expressionism 1: Die Brücke

In 1905-06 a little band of young students at an architectural school in Dresden formed a group they styled *"Die Brücke"* (The Artists' Group of the Bridge). Their aim was to create a modern artistic community, like the Pre-Raphaelites, the Nazarenes, or Gauguin and van Gogh before them, but they were fired with a more aggressive missionary zeal. Very young themselves (the eldest, Kirchner, was only 25), they addressed themselves to the young: "One of the aims of Die Brücke is to attract all the revolutionary and surging elements – that is what the name signifies." Their ideals were to be achieved by their communal activity, and were to be propagated by travelling exhibitions of their work.

Die Brücke were concerned with the social role of art, and in this they differed from the Fauves (see p. 142) in France, although they shared with them a delight in the resonance of contrasting, non-representational colours. Both groups, formulating their revolutionary styles in about 1905 – simultaneously and, to begin with, quite independently – naturally took advantage of the formal explorations of the Post-Impressionists and of Art Nouveau, and also shared an excitement in the expressive

distortions and simplifications of so-called "primitive" art – for Die Brücke, the Oceanic and African collections in the Zwinger Museum at Dresden. In the Germans' work, however, which is angular, often harsh and crowded with detail, there is an emphasis on the Nordic tradition, stemming from Gothic art, from Grünewald and the great print-makers of the fifteenth and sixteenth centuries. The painters of Die Brücke created psychological tensions in their work recalling those of Munch; they were reluctant, however, to admit Munch as kindred spirit, and Munch himself, at his first sight of the work of one of the group (Schmidt-Rottluff), exclaimed: "May God protect us; evil times are coming."

The three outstanding founder members were Ernst Ludwig Kirchner, Karl Schmidt-Rottluff and Erich Heckel. They were followed by Max Pechstein and Otto Mueller, and Emil Nolde (see preceding page) was briefly a member in 1906-07. The manifesto of the group was cut on wood by Kirchner – in the broadsheet tradition – and published in 1906, when its first exhibition was held, in Dresden. By about 1910, the leading members of the group were working in Berlin, where, rejected by the

KIRCHNER (above)
The artists' group of the bridge, 1906
In choosing the emblem of a bridge the group wished to represent themselves as a link between the arts of past and future. They may have found the metaphor in Nietzsche's *Thus Spake Zarathustra*, a work they admired: "Man is great because he is a bridge and not a goal; he is only fit to be loved when he is a transition and a failure."

KIRCHNER (left)
Artists of Die Brücke, c. 1926
A compressed and flattened space is occupied by the angular, almost contorted figures of Mueller, seated, and Kirchner himself, with Heckel and a bespectacled Schmidt-Rottluff standing to his right. The group is portrayed as it was in the years before its dissolution.

KIRCHNER (right)
Street scene, 1913-14
Kirchner was fascinated by the people he observed in the streets of Berlin, by the movement of passers-by, dawdling or purposeful, by the anonymity of crowds, out of which a face might take form with startling immediacy. He registered the people he saw almost as caricatures – here they are shimmering repetitions of the fashionably dressed woman in the foreground, sporting the exaggeratedly tall and slender silhouette favoured just before 1914.

SCHMIDT-ROTTLUFF (above)
The sun in a pine wood, 1913
Against the warm ochres of the trees and the earth, the intensity of the sunlight is suggested in its whiteness. All form has been reduced to bold, violent simplicity, though both subject and mood have their roots in the landscape tradition of German Romanticism.

KIRCHNER (left)
The couple, 1923
The woman's features reflect Kirchner's interest in African tribal masks, while the theme, rendered in brilliant acid colours, is typically Expressionist – the tensions of sex – but not harshly or bluntly treated.

Berlin Sezession, they formed a rival association, the Neue Sezession, with Pechstein as president. In 1910 Herwarth Walden, a dynamic and eloquent champion of Expressionist art in all media, started his influential periodical *Der Sturm* (The storm), and in 1912 established a gallery of the same name in which the work of Die Brücke was shown along with that of the leading artists of the various revolutionary movements in Europe. By then, however, the coherence of Die Brücke was disintegrating: they had resigned from the Neue Sezession, losing Pechstein, who continued to exhibit with it, and Kirchner's *Chronicle of Die Brücke* of 1913 proved an obituary: the group dissolved that year.

Ernst Ludwig Kirchner (1880-1938), most articulate and most gifted of the group, was also the only one of its members to have had any formal training in painting, although he shared with the others a taste for awkwardness in composition. He delighted in subjects full of movement, cabaret or circus scenes; he was a prolific printmaker, and a sculptor, but is seen at his most striking in his painted nudes and haunting street scenes: these, while they reflect in some degree the successive impacts of

Munch, of Fauvism and of Cubism, convey Kirchner's characteristic sense of urban and erotic desolation. His sensitivity was unable to stand the horrors of war, and in 1916 he suffered a breakdown; following his recovery his art became more decorative, lacking his earlier intensity. Condemned as "degenerate" by the Nazis, he committed suicide in 1938.

Karl Schmidt-Rottluff (1884-1976) developed a powerful command of simplified shapes and summarily modulated planes of strong colour, angular and interlocking. His landscapes painted in this idiom, from about 1911, have a magical and mystical intensity. After World War I, his work tended to be softer, more decorative, but in one famous print of 1918 he crystallized the horror of the trenches in an image of Christ, chopped and hacked on to the woodblock. His strength comes through most purely in his prints, and it was especially in the relatively coarse medium of the woodcut, whether black and white or coloured, that he and others of the group found their most striking and original expression. Erich Heckel (1883-1970), likewise a great printmaker, was a gentler talent; in his early work, angular like all Die Brücke images, his

figures are possessed by anxieties, emaciated by them. He was profoundly moved by the great Russian novelists; his most famous painting, the claustrophobic *Two men at a table*, 1912, was dedicated to Dostoevsky.

Max Pechstein (1881-1955), who joined Die Brücke in 1906, offended less against conventional taste than the others, and so became more swiftly successful. The decorative quality of his work was closer to that of the French (he was strongly influenced by Matisse), while his reliance on the forms of tribal art was intensified by a South Seas tour in 1914. Older than the others, Otto Mueller (1874-1930), who joined the group in 1910, retained a softer, more delicate lyricism in contrast to their forceful expressiveness, and preferred pastoral to urban subject matter.

Mueller, dying in 1930, was spared the persecution that the Nazi artistic pogrom of the 1930s brought upon the others, all condemned as "degenerate" artists, their works confiscated, sold or even burnt. Indeed the achievement of early German Expressionism, its forceful relevance to the tragic condition of twentieth-century man, began to impress a larger audience only after 1945.

HECKEL (right)
Two men at a table, 1912
The atmosphere, pervaded by anxiety and suspicion, is a characteristic both of Dostoevsky's novels and of many of Heckel's paintings at this period. These men face each other, seemingly tortured by mutual distrust, before an image suggesting a dead Christ of a Gothic *Deposition*; psychological anguish is vivid in their rigid, angular forms and in the relationship of their hands to the knife lying between them on the table. We seem to be witness to the moment of suffocating tension that precedes an act of fearsome violence.

MUELLER (above)
Nudes on a beach, 1920
Gypsies, and nudes in landscape settings, these were Mueller's favourite themes. Their elongated bodies and graceful air of slightly fraught melancholy recall Lehmbrück's sculpture.

Mueller never adopted the strident colour favoured by his colleagues in Die Brücke: his pale, chalky palette enhances a wistful mood. But the figures have an angularity typical of Die Brücke. His prints are more Expressionistic.

SCHMIDT-ROTTLUFF (left)
The head of Christ, 1918
The woodcut reached its apogee in the art of Dürer and Holbein in the early 16th century, after the first printed images in Europe had appeared in Germany. Its national and medieval origins commended it to Die Brücke, and also its intrinsically "primitive" or stubborn handling, here exploited to forceful effect.

PECHSTEIN (right)
The harbour, 1922
Pechstein appears among the artists of Die Brücke as the chief practitioner of French ideas and methods. Fauve works such as this, though frankly derivative, have, however, a tension (here, perhaps, in the loud reds) lacking in French art.

Expressionism 2: Der Blaue Reiter

Der Blaue Reiter (The Blue Rider), the second of the two major early groups of Expressionist painters in Germany, was, unlike Die Brücke in Dresden and Berlin, quite a loose association that did not nurture a single specific style and did not envisage communal activity. It was formed in Munich in 1911-12 as a splinter group of the New Artists' Association which the Russian artist Wassily Kandinsky and others had founded in 1909; it, too, was headed by Kandinsky, with Gabriele Münter, Alfred Kubin and Franz Marc. Der Blaue Reiter (the name was taken from a picture by Kandinsky) was really a board or committee, which succeeded, before its dissolution at the outbreak of World War I, in realizing only one issue of an art publication, *The Blue Rider Almanac*, and in organizing two exhibitions. Other major artists associated with the group were August Macke, Alexei van Jawlensky and Paul Klee.

Der Blaue Reiter took its final form several years after Die Brücke, founded in 1905, but many of its members had been active in Munich since the late 1890s. Munich had by then become a fertile art centre, almost rivalling Paris, and attracting artists from both west and east. From 1896 two influential art magazines had been published from Munich, *Jugend* (Youth; sponsoring Art Nouveau) and *Simplizissimus*, notable especially for its graphic art. Der Blaue Reiter, compared to Die Brücke, was much more cosmopolitan in outlook, and the aim of its exhibitions was "simply to juxtapose the most varied manifestations of the new painting on an international basis ... and to show, by the variety of forms represented, the manifold ways in which the artist manifests his inner desire". Included, besides paintings by the Munich members, were works by Picasso, Braque and Delaunay (the last perhaps was the most influential on the group), by Malevich and Arp, by the recently deceased Douanier Rousseau and also paintings by the composer Schönberg. In its *Almanac*, Der Blaue Reiter published a remarkable variety of Naive, exotic and "primitive" material – African and Oceanic, Mexican and Brazilian objects; Russian and German folk art; Japanese prints; Bavarian glass-painting; children's art (especially important for Klee's development). The common factor in all these was their freedom from the constraints and conventions of European "fine" art; suggesting possibilities of expressing the artist's "inner necessity" more directly. The philosophy was that of Nietzsche: "Who wishes to be creative ... must first blast and destroy accepted values."

Wassily Kandinsky (1866-1940), born in Moscow, was the oldest of the group. Having studied law, he turned artist and migrated to Munich only at the age of 30, in 1896. His early work in Germany shows him modulating the styles of the time – Post-Impressionism, Art Nouveau, Fauvism – into a personal, distinctly Russian, fairy-tale vision expressed in rich and glowing colour. Having exhibited not only with the Munich and Berlin Sezessions but also in Paris, he was already moving in theory towards abstract art by about 1905; he later observed that even as a student he had found subject matter more of a hindrance than a help in painting. Only in 1912, however, when he was already working on his apologia, *Concerning the Spiritual in Art*, did he reach abstract art in practice (see over).

Together with Kandinsky, the Munich-born Franz Marc (1880-1916) gave Der Blaue Reiter an intellectual calibre Die Brücke never had. He had started as a student of philosophy and theology; fascinated by the physical grace

KANDINSKY (left)
Composition no. 4 (Battle), 1911
In what is at first sight an abstract work, figurative features may yet be found – in the rainbow spanning a gorge and the parachuting "matchstick" figure above. However, no other members of Der Blaue Reiter attained this degree of independence from the physical world in expressing "inner necessity".

MARC (right)
Deer in a forest II, 1913-14
Marc's search for a visual system in which to express his conviction of an "inner mystical structure of the world" was aided by a visit in 1912 to Delaunay. His debt to Orphism (see p. 151) is here strongly marked.

MARC (above)
The fate of the animals, 1913
Marc aspired to give form not to the visible world but to a subjective impression of it: "How wretched, how soulless", he wrote, "is our habit of placing animals in a landscape which mirrors our own vision, instead of sinking ourselves in the soul of the animal so as to imagine its perceptions."

MACKE (right)
Kairouan I, 1914
The crucial African journey made by Macke and Klee in 1914 (see p. 192) is evoked in exquisite tints applied in an almost abstract order.

and essential innocence of animals, he painted them at first naturalistically; then he evolved a counterpoint of form and colour, in which the sinuous rhythms of animal life invigorated broad planes of brilliant, joyous colour bearing no relation to the subject's "natural" hues – Marc's famous blue and red horses. In these an awareness both of Cubism and of Orphism is evident, and by 1913 Marc was moving to almost pure abstraction. His mature paintings are some of the most striking images of twentieth-century art, and his death in action at Verdun one of its greatest losses. Yet almost comparable was the death of August Macke (1887-1914). In sensitivity the most gifted of the group, in his last few years he produced enchantingly lyrical and elegiac visions of urban life – elegant women, children in the park – a poetry of the city very different from Kirchner's sinister evocations. He visited Paris often, but his art, far from being diluted by Fauve, Cubist, or Orphic example, was strong enough to absorb their influences into his own intensely personal view, expressed through shifting planes of colour.

Kandinsky's compatriot Alexei van Jawlensky (1864-1941) was never formally a mem-ber of Der Blaue Reiter, but was closely sympathetic to its aims. Much influenced by the Fauves (he had met Matisse in Paris), he used strong colour in flat planes and often in heavy linear contours, and his work was increasingly invested with an almost mystical feeling. His most memorable imagery was provided by the theme of a very simplified mask-face on which he played endless variations. Also important were Gabriele Münter (1897-1962), one of the few women artists in the group, who lived with Kandinsky until his return to Russia; Heinrich Campendonk (1880-1957; not shown), painting very stiff, primitive-looking images reminiscent of the glass-painting of Bavarian folk art; and Alfred Kubin (1877-1959), primarily a graphic illustrator with a fantastic demonic quality. Paul Klee was also working entirely in black and white when Kandinsky first came into contact with him in Munich, but then began to explore the delicate, infinitely subtle watercolour techniques that he was to deploy and develop for the rest of his life (see p. 192). But Wassily Kandinsky, self-proclaimed founder of abstract art, was undoubtedly the major force.

MÜNTER (right)
A man at a table (Wassily Kandinsky), 1911
Münter concentrated on landscape, but her portrait of her lover also shows her Fauve-influenced style – areas of bold, unmodelled colour enclosed in heavy black contours. Objects are simplified in "primitive" fashion but the execution is vigorous and assured.

MACKE (left)
People at the blue lake, 1913
More than Marc, Macke dissolved modelled form in flat, floating colours almost alone constituting figures and setting. This tendency to generalize had its root in the aim, common to Der Blaue Reiter artists, to convey a universal truth behind surface appearances.

KLEE (below)
An animal suckling its offspring, 1906
The Bavarian folk craft of painting on glass aroused the interest of several Der Blaue Reiter artists, but Klee was the most active in the medium; he worked mainly in black and white and delighted in the sometimes unforeseen effects of the technique, retaining them in the final image.

JAWLENSKY (left)
Woman meditating, 1912
Jawlensky's colour tends to be hotter than that of the French Fauves, and there is a rather more charged quality to his work. Though he often gave his subjects rather heavy features, his brush-strokes could almost be called painstaking; they are more minute than bold.

KUBIN (below)
The egg, c. 1900
A tragic childhood and an obsession with the macabre – it is said that he liked to watch the recovery of corpses from the river – dominated Kubin's graphic work, which was essentially Symbolist in direction.

Kandinsky: Study for Composition no. 7

Composition no. 7 is one of the largest and most elaborate of the series of *Improvisations* and *Compositions* in which Kandinsky moved gradually, between 1910 and 1914, towards the elimination of all figurative or representational elements in his work. This study, of 1913, at first sight seethes, a hurly-burly of colour in conflict – colour that in places melts tenderly, even amorphously, and in others is hot, sharp and strident; here and there are sharp scratchy scorings or criss-crosses of lines. On longer inspection, the implications of the title, a *Composition*, may seem more valid. There is a main focus of attention in an emphatic clench of forms, of thunderous blue and of heavy black left of centre, while the rectangle of the painting is divided by a diagonal from lower left to upper right. Below this is relative calm, above it all is turbulence. The onlooker's first impression may be of uncontrolled explosion; longer acquaintance reveals that the explosion is profoundly excogitated.

Wassily Kandinsky had already completed his fundamental treatise *Uber das Geistige in der Kunst* (Concerning the Spiritual in Art) in 1910, though it was not published until 1912. In this, and his other theoretical writing, the argument is often obscure, but he was grappling with the huge difficulty of explaining the inexplicable, the unanalysable – the abstract values of colour and form completely detached from all representation of nature or objects. Very conscious of the danger of non-figurative art becoming mere vapid decoration, Kandinsky nevertheless believed that in pure colour and pure form the artist could find direct and valid expression of his mind or spirit. "The harmony of colour and form must be based solely upon the principle of proper contact with the human soul." Towards this end he worked out definitions of the qualities of colours and forms, but these, when not patently obvious, are generally highly subjective. One ready parallel with the art to which he aspired was, however, music: his own comments, and titles – *Improvisation, Composition* – indicate this clearly. For all his legal background, Kandinsky was always attracted by mysticism (particularly the theosophy of Madame Blavatsky), while his faith in materialism, in the value of the object, had been undermined by scientific revolution – the splitting of the atom.

Kandinsky's distrust of subject matter goes back to his student days in Moscow, when he saw one of Monet's *Haystacks* (see p. 101), in which the subject was dissolved into shimmering light and colour. Then in Munich, probably in 1910, he saw in one of his own paintings lying the wrong way up, in a subdued evening light, an apparition, a harmony of colour, line and form "of extraordinary beauty, glowing with an inner radiance"; and this precipitated the final conversion to non-figurative art: "Now I know for certain that subject matter was detrimental to my paintings." Kandinsky claimed to have been the first to paint purely abstract pictures – or rather non-figurative ones. The Cubists and others likewise "abstracted" their compositions from their subject matter, but never became completely detached from the object. Kandinsky's claim can be and has been contested, but it is clear that he was indeed the first to establish abstract art as a consolidated and valid mode of expression.

Following the revelation of his upside-down painting, Kandinsky did not proceed immediately to absolute non-figuration, nor did he altogether abandon landscape or other subjects even when he had. Figurative motifs, while becoming increasingly schematic or ves-

KANDINSKY (left)
Study for *Composition no. 7*, 1913
Kandinsky found "vistas of purely pictorial possibility" in the "shock of contrasting colours, the checking of fluid spots by contours of design, by the mingling and the sharp separation of surfaces".

KANDINSKY (right)
Composition no. 7, fragment no. 1, 1913
Apocalyptic struggles have been seen in these studies; but also the first visual equivalent of "consciousness on a psychic level".

KANDINSKY (below)
The first abstract watercolour, 1912
Is Kandinsky's title true? There are rival claimants. The difficulty is that all the short-listed works were long in the artists' hands and might well have been repainted later. This is the favourite, as it seems fully balanced, not an experiment.

KANDINSKY
(left) *Improvisation no. 30 – Cannons*, 1913; (right) *Black lines*, 1913
Both works are abstract, though Kandinsky agreed that his own title *Cannons* and their clear intrusion might reflect the constant war-talk of the time; and *Black lines* seems eerily prophetic of aircraft being strafed in bursts of fire.

KANDINSKY (below)
Two poplars, 1913
Kandinsky did not become an abstract painter overnight; the landscapes he continued to produce until 1914 reveal no impassable gulf between painting the soul and painting trees.

tigial, persist in some of his paintings as late as 1920. Before 1914, however, he had already singled out the Unconscious as the mainspring of his work. Thus of *Improvisation no. 30 – Cannons* he wrote that it was "painted rather subconsciously in a state of strong inner tension. So intensively did I feel the necessity of some of the forms that I remember having given loud directions to myself, for instance, 'But the corners must be heavy'." This may suggest a closer parallel with the Abstract Expressionism of American artists in the 1950s than is really justifiable. Kandinsky's workings, his intuition, were always controlled by an inner discipline, and there are more than 12 preliminary studies for *Composition no. 7*; the final painting took three days.

World War I disrupted Kandinsky's career. Returning to Russia, he painted relatively little, and after the Revolution was busily employed as an artistic administrator, although his work found no favour with the young Constructivists. During this time, however, he was refining his practice towards the geometric, "hard-edge" style that he was to develop fully on his establishment, in 1921, in the Bauhaus (see p. 190).

Le Douanier Rousseau: The Merry Jesters

ROUSSEAU: *The merry jesters, c.* 1906

In the forest, a self-conscious, jokey little clutch of three brown furry animals of uncertain species gazes unblinkingly upon the spectator, as if posed for his camera. A fourth just protrudes at the bottom right corner; a fifth, somewhat melancholy, is erect in the middle distance, and on a branch a leaden bird sits leering. The jungle is a tapestry-like texture of subtly contrasting greens, in patterns of spear-like or heart-shaped sprays of leaves, grasses and magnified fronds; a large, exotic, white, pagoda-like flower rises primly vertical on the left; there is a glimpse of sky above. No shadows are cast. Suspended (by what?) in front of the central group is an inverted milk-bottle and a back-scratcher. *The merry jesters* is an impossible fiction: both the logistics and the significance of the action are inexplicable. But the gaze of the animals confronts the spectator with bland assurance. Mystery reigns, a dream is being dreamed, and yet the conviction of reality recorded is stunning. The prominent curvaceous signature of *Henri Julien Rousseau* at bottom left is an integral part of the design.

Henri Julien Rousseau (1844-1910) spent his adult career, until 1885, when he retired, as an official in a Parisian toll-house: hence he is always known as "Le Douanier". Though he is often categorized as "primitive", "Naive", "Sunday painter" or "amateur", he justly considered himself a professional. Personally Rousseau was indeed naive, innocent, distressingly gullible, pompous and absurd, and at times in trouble with the police (in a film he would have been played ideally by Charlie Chaplin), but he was unshakably convinced of his own destiny and of the grandeur of the contribution he had to make to the Glory of France. He claimed to have "no master but Nature and some advice from Gérôme and Clément" (two leading academic painters); he saw himself as "one of our first Realist painters", and observed to Picasso that they were the only two great modern painters, "I in the modern manner and you in the Egyptian". He had exhibited in Paris from 1885 on, but generally provoked only derision from the public. From about 1905, however, he was patronized by a few leading critics and dealers, especially Wilhelm Uhde (the first critical champion of the so-called "Naive" painters) and Vollard; and was celebrated as a sort of mascot by some of the leaders of the avant-garde, including Picasso, Apollinaire, Léger – but also as their peer, at a famous banquet in Picasso's studio in 1908. After his death, his work was hailed especially by Der Blaue Reiter; Kandinsky considered that Rousseau was arriving at the same goal as he and his colleagues, though by a completely different route. His work has continued to find a delighted response – from Dadaists, Surrealists and Pop artists, and from the public.

Rousseau's subject matter was of great variety, including not only the Parisian suburbs, of which he was the visual poet, but portraits of formidable four-square directness, allegorical compositions in the Grand Manner, flower-pieces, and above all the series of large-scale exotic fantasies inspired by his wanderings in the parks, botanical gardens and zoo of Paris. Naive though he was, untrained, working painstakingly across the canvas, diligently "filling in", he had a superb intuitive sense of design and composition, and this, and the range and intensity of his imagination, establish him well above the Naive painters who have since emerged. Uhde discovered one of them in his own household, in the shape of a housemaid, Séraphine Louis (1864-1934). The Naive painters were established as a serious – if awkward – component of twentieth-century art by Uhde's exhibition "The Painters of the Sacred Heart" in 1928, which also featured the postman Louis Vivin (1861-1936), the gardener André Bauchant (1873-1958) and the one-time circus wrestler Camille Bombois.

ROUSSEAU
The toll station, c. 1890-91
Here worked Le Douanier (not in fact as a customs officer, but as a collector of taxes levied on goods coming into Paris). Seurat's influence is apparent in the studied composition, in its contrived formality.

ROUSSEAU (above)
The ball players, 1908
The movement is conveyed almost solely by the interaction of the stripes on the player's shirts: Rousseau had the most sensitive and subtle command of colour. He was the first painter to make modern phenomena – football, flying machines – star in his compositions.

SERAPHINE (left)
The paradise tree, 1929
Séraphine painted vivid visionary trees and flowers peopled with lips and eyes. They are decorative, and yet there is an element of magic in them. Séraphine used to paint in a trance – informed, so she said, by a guardian angel – and would permit no one to see her at work. Sadly, once she was "discovered", she lost this happy source of inspiration.

VIVIN (above)
Notre Dame, Paris, 1933
Front and side views are combined – a reversion to Egyptian principles. Uhde boldly baptized Vivin "the Canaletto of modern Paris".

BAUCHANT (right)
Cleopatra's barge, 1939
Bauchant was still unknown when Diaghilev decided to employ him to decorate the sets for one of his ballets.

Fauvism

At the Salon d'Automne of 1905 in Paris, a critic found a classicizing torso in pale marble as if trapped amidst a pack of canvases of ferociously exuberant colours. His exclamation, "*Donatello au milieu des fauves!*" (Donatello amidst the wild beasts), baptized one of the most important movements of the early twentieth century – though it was barely cohesive enough to be called a movement, and very brief-lived.

The central figure amongst the Fauves was always Henri Matisse (see over), and that particular brilliance of colour and freshness characteristic of Fauvism in its prime recurs in his painting again and again until his very last work, in cut paper, in the 1950s. Matisse, Albert Marquet and Georges Rouault had all worked in Gustave Moreau's studio at various times between 1895 and 1899, and Moreau's expressive command of glowing colour surely affected all of them. Some 15 years, however, before Fauvism startled the public, Gauguin had defined a quality essential to it: "Instead of trying to render what I see before me, I use colour in a completely arbitrary way to express myself powerfully." In 1901, the work of another forerunner, van Gogh, had been dis-

MATISSE (below)
The gypsy, 1906
At the height of his Fauve period Matisse's exuberant handling of paint and rich

colour had a forcefulness moderated in his later art. Yet the form is defined in the abandon of colour: Matisse studied Cézanne.

played in Paris in a retrospective exhibition at which Matisse first met Maurice de Vlaminck. In 1903, dissatisfied with existing annual exhibitions, a group including Renoir, the Symbolist novelist and critic Huysmans and Rouault founded the Salon d'Automne (Autumn Salon) and gave that year a memorial exhibition of Gauguin; this was followed in 1904 by a large retrospective of Cézanne and in 1905 by the burst of colour that precipitated the Fauve painters' sobriquet.

Artists allied to those already mentioned in elements of style, though they never associated as an organized group, included André Derain, Raoul Dufy and Georges Braque. The adherence of some to Fauvist principles was brief indeed. André Derain (1880-1954), in the south of France in 1905 with Matisse, distilled brilliant, dazzling canvases from the light of the Midi sun, and soon afterwards in London, rather surprisingly, painted equally luminous, if cooler, versions of the river Thames. But within a year or two he had abandoned his brilliant palette, and an essential conservatism tamed his later ventures into Cubism. Georges Braque's Fauve period was even briefer, though to it are due a handful of the most

DERAIN (above)
The harbour at Collioure, 1905
Derain's sense of colour was transformed by strong sun: sunlight seems to burn in the unmodulated dashes applied on a white ground.

BRAQUE (below)
The little bay of La Ciotat, 1907
The seascape is only barely outlined, the arrangement of strokes almost abstract. There is a marked delicacy, and care for composition.

DERAIN (left)
Effects of sunlight on water, 1905
Derain once compared a tube of paint with a stick of dynamite, but he never, like Vlaminck, advocated arson. In the dazzling explosion of colour there still lurks structure – a firm horizon, for instance. His canvas is like a pointillist work energized and saturated.

DUFY (below)
Riders in the wood, 1931
Influenced by Marquet and Matisse's Fauve paintings, Dufy adopted the wild and free use of colour which distinguished the group, but, unlike most others, he was moved by a concern for an everyday realism and by a love of decorative effects, throughout a long career.

subtle and sensitive pictures in the style, and by late 1907 he was moving, with Picasso, into Cubist rigours (see p. 148).

For Raoul Dufy (1877-1953), who had started as an Impressionist, the Fauve vision proved too intense and exclamatory; soon he developed that characteristic lightness of touch, that elegant and witty calligraphy with which he was to describe the pleasures of leisure – beaches, yachts and racecourses – in later decades. Albert Marquet (1875-1947) was always more traditional, though he had a sure skill in extracting the essence of the scene before him, and after a brief explosion of colour as early as 1900 reverted to a more subdued tonal painting, exquisitely controlled.

Georges Rouault (1871-1958) perhaps never belonged emotionally to the Fauve movement: the closest of the Fauves to Moreau (and curator of the Musée Gustave Moreau in Paris), he was driven – by moral indignation, by a fascination with the scatological and, ultimately, by profound religious conviction – far away from the spontaneous hedonism and delight in decorativeness of the others. In this he was the direct heir to the Symbolists, while technically, in his *cloisonné* patterning of col-our strongly reminiscent of the compartmentation of stained-glass windows, he followed the example of the painters of Pont-Aven. His prostitutes and clowns glow sombrely as if in the fires of Hell. Rouault is a direct link between Symbolism, including Gauguin, and the more ferocious output of German Expressionism, and he also ventured into graphic art, in his series of black and white prints "*Miserere et Guerre*" (War and pity; not shown) produced between 1914 and 1918. He stands apart, as perhaps the major religious artist of the twentieth century.

Maurice de Vlaminck (1876-1958) was the most committed of the Fauves, apart from Matisse, from whom in character he was very different: he was self-taught, anti-intellectual, fiercely scornful of the art of academies or museums. He was also for a short time a professional cyclist and peripatetic fiddler; he used to wear wooden ties varnished in bright colours, and indulged in hearty eating contests with Derain and the poet and critic Apollinaire. "I have never 'thought about art' . . . I wanted to burn the Ecole des Beaux-Arts with my cobalts and vermilions and I wanted to interpret my feelings with my brushes without thinking what had gone before me." Profoundly stirred by the van Gogh exhibition in 1901, he unleashed his harsh primaries of red, white and blue against Vincent's favourite yellows, oranges and greens with forceful and sometimes discordant clangour. The vigour of his attack on the canvas can produce the feeling in the onlooker that he is passing though these streets and landscapes at speed, as if on Vlaminck's racing cycle, but in his later work impatience weakened his compositions.

Vlaminck's urge to convey the fleeting impression with the greatest possible immediacy was characteristic of the initial Fauve approach: the aim was to achieve the maximum force of expression in colour and in the movement of the brush – the more violent the contrast between the colours the better. The real world served only as a point of departure in the creation of an image that had conceptual or existential rather than representational value. Once the initial excitement – an essentially youthful excitement – had passed, the style could only degenerate into mannerism, as often in Vlaminck's later work. It was above all Matisse who had the stamina and discipline to control and adapt it to a developing art.

MARQUET (right)
Hoardings at Trouville, 1906
Under Matisse's influence Marquet used the Fauves' strong, unmodified colours for a time, but he was never as wild as the nickname. He would paint in bright tones one day, browns and greys the next, composing finely balanced pictures with a minimum of detail.

VLAMINCK (below)
Landscape with red trees, 1906-07
Vlaminck's best landscapes were composed in primary colours in which freshness becomes almost tangible. He would often squeeze the paint directly from the tube on to the canvas, with scarcely precedented freedom from constraint.

ROUAULT (above)
The prostitute, 1906
Although he exhibited at the Fauve Salon of 1905, Rouault stood apart from the Fauves in important aspects of style (he did not use pure colour) and choice of subject matter. His harsh brushwork and bold use of line evoke the prostitute with expressive power, creating a symbol of the degradation of man.

ROUAULT (left)
The face of Christ, 1933
Rouault remained true to his artistic convictions: the bold contours and deep colours which marked his work in his Fauve period, featuring clowns and social outcasts, later served his mainly religious themes. And yet his vigour was not dependent on colour, and is unsoftened in his graphics.

Matisse: Le Luxe II

"With '*Le Luxe II*' ", George Heard Hamilton has observed, "Matisse completed and closed the Fauve revolution." By the time the painting was finished, in 1908, Henri Matisse (1869-1954) was no longer young, but in the previous years he had refined, consolidated and then unleashed his feeling for the expressive possibilities of luminous colour, first fostered in Moreau's studio ten years earlier.

Unlike his fellow-Fauve Vlaminck, Matisse was a conscientious student of the art both of the past and of his contemporaries: "I have never shunned outside influences. I should consider that an act of cowardice, and bad faith towards myself. I believe that the struggles that an artist undergoes help him assert his personality." In the late 1890s he was painting landscapes very much in Impressionist terms, with, however, at one stage (sometimes called "proto-Fauve") greater audacity of colour contrast than the Impressionists had ever shown; in 1900, though he was then quite the reverse of rich, he bought Cézanne's *Three bathers* (not shown), and certain compositions on the same lines show Matisse thereafter grappling with problems of form as well as colour. A crucial lightening and kindling of colour seems then to have been sparked by a summer spent at St-Tropez with Signac.

Matisse painted "*Luxe, Calme et Volupté*" in 1904-05, applying the divisionist technique in almost doctrinaire fashion, producing a mosaic of short stabs of colour. The result is somewhat stilted and inert, but it is nevertheless the point of departure for "*Le Luxe II*" (a shortened version of the first title, which was a phrase from Baudelaire) and for much of Matisse's future career. It states above all the theme of the female nude, but also the artist's mature quest for "an art of balance, of purity and of serenity devoid of troubling or disturbing subject matter ... like a comforting influence, a mental balm – something like a good armchair in which one rests from physical fatigue". Nothing, perhaps, could seem further from that ideal than the Fauve explosion of colour that came in 1905 (see preceding page), but in the great canvas "*La Joie de Vivre*", nearly two and a half metres (8ft) wide, which he finished in the following year, that aim is almost completely achieved. The divisionist technique has yielded to clear contour, curvaceous line – though there is little depth; the scenery seems composed of stage flats. Perspective is abandoned, and the figures and their scale are arbitrary, attenuated or distorted as the rhythms of the design may require. Technically, the picture owes much to Gauguin, and much also surely to the sinuous linearism of Art Nouveau. Its theme is Arcadian – such a vision as has haunted European fantasy since Titian's *Bacchanals* (see vol. 2 p. 145), a terrestrial paradise that not only Signac and Derain but also Renoir, Gauguin and Cézanne had glimpsed.

Then "*Le Luxe*" I and II come as the climax of this development – the process of reduction and elimination of inessentials in the design, the distillation of Matisse's art to its characteristic flat colour and line. The theme is still *Bathers*: indeed the two major figures are adapted from two on the left edge of "*La Joie de Vivre*". In the study, "*Le Luxe I*", the brushwork is relatively loose, the colours broken, the contours tentative, and auras, or penumbras, around the figures, though diminished, are present here and there. In the final version, "*Le Luxe II*", the clarity of contour is final, the penumbras eliminated; the ragged edge of the cloud is now smooth. The line is comprehensive, incisive, incomparably economic. The colour is lucent.

Matisse did not share Vlaminck's urge to translate impression into instant expression. "I want to achieve that state of condensation of sensations which makes a picture ... a representation of my mind." The sentiment may suggest a close relationship between Matisse and the early Cubists, but the *Luxe* series and *The dance* of 1910 could be read almost as anti-Cubist manifestos. Although Matisse's painting subsequently went through a phase sometimes described as "constructivist" – a sharp disciplining of the lyrical curve of his line – his pure singing colour and his characteristic fluent arabesque line were to be reasserted in the 1920s and 1930s (see p. 184) and not least in the remarkable colour cut-papers he made in his 70s and 80s (see p. 228).

MATISSE (below)
"*Luxe, Calme et Volupté*", 1904-05
The title is a phrase from Baudelaire's *Invitation to the Voyage*: "There, all is order, beauty, luxuriance, calm and voluptuousness." Cézanne's *Bathers* theme is treated in Signac's style.

MATISSE (above)
"*La Joie de Vivre*", 1905-06
Here Matisse reached an expression unmistakably his own (greatly disappointing his mentor Signac). His soft, flat tints and strong curves exhale a serene bliss; some of the nudes retain from "*Luxe, Calme et Volupté*" their penumbras, on which they recline pneumatically.

MATISSE (right)
The dance, 1910
Matisse detached the group of dancers from "*La Joie de Vivre*", transforming the distant, relatively loose-knit circle into a tighter design, a fully independent picture. The fast tempo of a *farandole* performed at the famous Moulin de la Galette inspired him. The rhythmic lines of the figures are even bolder than those of "*Le Luxe II*", a lithe pattern in themselves – the rapid development of Matisse's flat colour and flowing line reaches culmination.

MATISSE (above)
"*Le Luxe I*", 1907
Viewing the full-scale oil-sketch for "*Luxe II*" the critic Barr felt that, after study, "the earlier picture ("*Luxe I*") grows on one despite its faults or perhaps because of them. The sense of experiment and struggle sets up a tension that holds the interest by comparison with the decorative grace of the second version."
The light is unnatural, but the colour more realistic than in Fauve paintings, the forms more modelled.

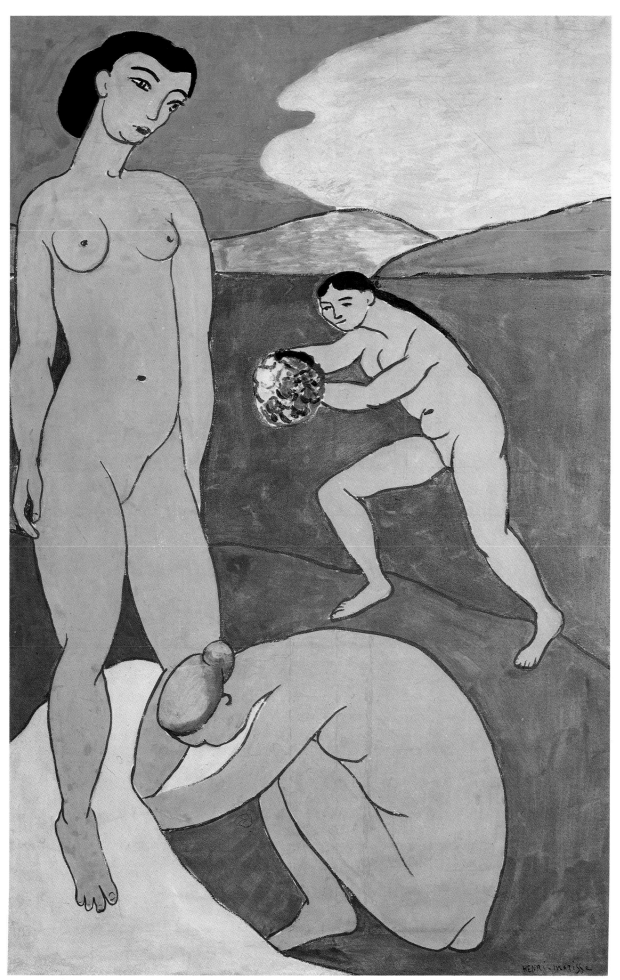

MATISSE (left)
"*Le Luxe II*", 1907-08
Matisse's teacher Moreau
is said to have remarked:
"Henri, you were born
to simplify painting."

Brancusi: The Kiss, 1910

BRANCUSI (left)
Sleeping Muse, 1910
The sculptor explored his
ovoid theme throughout
his life, even in portraits;
no previous sculptor had
dared such concentration,
stripped of superfluity.

Born of prosperous peasant stock, Constantin Brancusi (1876-1957) trained in his native Romania first as a craftsman in wood and then in an academic school of fine art. In 1904 he made his way to Paris. Briefly (1906-07) he worked in Rodin's studio, but then, with the independence that was characteristic of his whole career, cut loose with a comment that has become proverbial: "No other trees can grow in the shadow of an oak-tree."

His early work was in fact strongly reminiscent of Rodin or of Medardo Rosso, but from 1907 to 1910 he evolved a revolutionary mode of sculpture. Its basis was "truth to materials", ideas advocated notably by the German sculptor Hildebrand, and stated by Brancusi in these terms: "We must try not to make materials speak our language. We must go with them to a point where others will understand their language." His guiding principle was the fusion of content with form and with the medium. He early abandoned modelling (except for preliminary studies) in favour of direct carving (most of Rodin's carving had been done by assistants), and his fastidiousness and feeling for his material never lessened throughout his career, though he experimented continually with the presentation of the same idea in different materials, usually polished marble or brass.

The years 1907-10 were the exact period of the Cubist breakthrough (see over). Brancusi, however, was only superficially affected by Cubist art; though *The kiss*, on which he was then working, is literally cubist in shape, it does not attempt the disintegration beloved of Cubist painters, but is a straightforward sim-

BRANCUSI (left)
Sleeping Muse, 1906
The head emerges from, or
sinks back into, roughened
marble, in Rodin's manner.
It was one of Brancusi's
first direct carvings, the
portrait of a close friend.

BRANCUSI (below)
The table of silence, 1937
Like his *Endless column* (see
vol. 1 p. 204), also at Tirgu
Jiu, Brancusi's stools and
table repeat unvaryingly
one simple unit or module.
The forms unite the geometric and organic in a
sublimation of them both.

BRANCUSI (above)
Bird in space, 1919
Brancusi was fascinated
by the infinite: "All
my life I have sought
the essence of flight.
Don't look for mysteries.
I give you pure joy."

plification. In its chunkiness it is characteristic of one persistent aspect of Brancusi's work – a delight in the strong, rough-hewn forms that he knew from Romanian folk art, and also found again in African tribal sculpture, which clearly had a lasting influence on his vision. Such hard angular forms he often used for the bases of his sculptures, in rugged contrast to the sculptures themselves (bases and sculptures were in fact integral).

The contrary, and best-known, element of Brancusi's style is the smooth, exquisite finish, and the reduction of superficial detail until his model virtually vanishes in the primal form of the whole. "Simplicity is not an end in art", he once said, "but one arrives at simplicity in spite of oneself, in approaching the real sense of things. Simplicity is complexity itself, and one has to be nourished by its essence in order to understand its value." This creed is vividly illustrated by his progressive treatment of one form, evolving from naturalistic studies of a sleeping head: an early stage is represented by the *Sleeping Muse* in Bucharest of 1906; by 1909, it is purified into the polished and immaculate egg-form on which the human features are little more than adumbrated. Later, it could become pure egg. This primal ovoid form is at once very concrete and very ideal; encapsulating generation and birth, it is the blank on which human features will take shape. "What is real", wrote Brancusi, "is not the external form but the essence of things." He succeeded in fact in reconciling the tangible external with the ideal essential as no sculptor had done before him.

By 1910, the grammar and syntax of Brancusi's art was established, and so, too, the recurrent motifs on which he was to produce ever more refined variations during his long life. Generally withdrawn from the turmoil of artists' cliques and of public life, he worked aloof in Paris in a high white studio (which he bequeathed to the state, and which is preserved in Paris at the Centre Pompidou). Early accepted by fellow-artists, Brancusi took some time to be more generally accepted. In 1926, a famous turning-point in the popular history of modern art was provided by the legal victory won over the American customs, who claimed his bronze *Bird in space* was liable for duty as raw metal. But his fame was international before he died – it was already claimed that he was the greatest sculptor of the twentieth century, an assessment which Brancusi himself did not challenge.

In 1934 Brancusi was commissioned by his native country to work on a monumental scale: at the small town of Tirgu Jiu was set up the longest version (more than 29 metres (96ft) high) of his *Endless column*, a pole repeating the same motif over and over again, and theoretically extensible to infinity; also a great gateway incorporating once again the theme of *The kiss*, and a vast circular stone table, ringed with stone seats each composed of two hemispheres, awaiting some conference of giants who will never come – *The table of silence*.

It was Brancusi's achievement to abstract into three-dimensional stone or metal the essence of physical life, as if one could postulate from his birds or his fish all the fishes and birds that have ever been.

BRANCUSI
The kiss, 1910
Through the many versions of *The kiss* (perhaps most famous was the first, on the grave of a young suicide in Montparnasse cemetery, Paris, 1910), Brancusi stayed with his original image and material, rough stone. His form expresses both the block and what a kiss is in essence. His influence was crucial to 20th-century sculpture, from Modigliani to Moore.

Cubism 1: Picasso and Braque

The achievement of Pablo Picasso (1881-1973) reveals an astonishing stamina and inventiveness continuous through almost three quarters of the twentieth century. His fame has echoed beyond the confines of art and art history, placing him in a select category of genius – one of the names known throughout Western civilization, with Shakespeare, Michelangelo, Rembrandt, Napoleon.

Son of a Spanish art teacher, Picasso trained in Barcelona, and established a precocious reputation in Paris between 1900 and 1906. In his prolific "Blue" and "Rose" periods (1901-04; 1904-06) he drew on the example of Toulouse-Lautrec, Art Nouveau and Symbolism to create strange, haunting, melancholic images of lonely figures from the ranks of the deprived or outcast. In 1906-07, however, he performed the first, and most radically violent, of those changes of course that characterize his career, in "Les Demoiselles d'Avignon". Executed in 1907, it was not yet a fully resolved Cubist composition. Like Fauve painting (though Picasso never had a Fauve period), it rejects naturalistic colour, Renaissance perspective, consistent lighting – but it also rejects the sensuous pleasure of the

Fauves, and their flat, bright colours. There is certainly depth, the forms jut out from the picture; here and there it seems to incorporate views of the subject seen from different angles. The heads are treated in three different ways: the two central ones are closely related to two primitive Iberian sculptures that Picasso owned, while the head on the left (reworked) reflects the style of Ivory Coast tribal masks, and the two on the right, violently rehandled in the last phase of painting, relate to sculptures from the Congo. The realization of the power of African and Oceanic art had struck both Derain and Matisse in 1905-06; it was not, however, the expressive, emotional potential of "primitive" styles that was decisive for Picasso, so much as their freedom from illusionism, their lack of inhibition in amalgamating different views and aspects into one image.

Georges Braque (1882-1963) had been introduced to Picasso by the controversial champion of the avantgarde, the flamboyant poet and critic Guillaume Apollinaire. Like everyone else, Braque was initially bewildered by the *Demoiselles*, but he felt compelled to come to terms with it. In his "*Grand Nu*" (Great Nude) of the following year, 1908, the

BRAQUE (above)
Houses at L'Estaque, 1908
In 1908 Braque discovered both Cézanne and Picasso. The volumes and the space of a hilly countryside are evoked in firmly modelled, sombre, elemental blocks in a jigsaw of jutting forms composing an architecture.

PICASSO (left)
Life, 1903
The group is suffused with a vague timeless sadness, typical of Picasso in his Blue period. In this he was essentially Symbolist, like Puvis de Chavannes (see p. 122). The forms are classical: *Demoiselles* was a kind of auto-iconoclasm.

BRAQUE (below)
"*Grand Nu*" (Great nude), 1907-08
Braque's monumental nude is a variant on one of the *Demoiselles* figures, no less bold in distortion, more severely sculptural. Later Braque said that African masks had opened horizons for him, helped him towards fresh, instinctive creation.

PICASSO (above)
"*Les Demoiselles d'Avignon*", 1907
Avignon is a reference not to the French town but to a famous street in the red-light district of Barcelona. The painting is more a record of work in progress, of an artist in the process of changing his mind, than a resolved composition: the forms are dislocated, inconsistent in style, in fact unfinished. It is still a disturbing picture, and in 1907 more so – overthrowing perspective, single viewpoint, integral form, local colour, decorative colour; it was also a travesty of the great theme of nude *Bathers*, running from Cézanne to Matisse.

"primitive" distortion is very strong; both object and space are arbitrarily modelled. But more evident in the Braque is the Cubists' debt to Cézanne: especially momentous was his technique of modelling in terms of interlocking and overlapping planes, his subjects being sometimes not only arbitrarily lit, but seen from slightly different angles: his patchwork of blocks of translucent colour, deployed across the whole surface, produced an effect of depth and volume without destroying the flatness, the integrity of the painting.

Between 1908 and 1910, often working closely together, Braque and Picasso perfected a joint style. Their harmony at this time was such that the question of primacy, who discovered what first, is controversial, and perhaps otiose. It was Braque's *Landscapes* of L'Estaque that in 1908 provoked a critic to speak of "cubes"; the movement was subsequently called "Cubism".

Their early Cubist work, up to 1912, fell into two phases, subsequently known as "analytical" and "synthetic". In the analytic phase, 1909-10, the more solid massing of forms of their first Cubist paintings gave way to a technique in which the contours of form were dissolved, so that one form opened and fused with another, and with the void of space surrounding it. The elements of form were taken apart and reorganized, not to sum up the essence of the subject comprehensively but rather to re-create it as a picture. The notion of a painting as a *peinture-objet*, an object in its own right independent of its subject matter, was abroad by 1910. Yet Cubism was claimed as a realist art, and its connection with its subject matter was never wholly lost, though it became tenuous. Picasso's "portrait" of Vollard of 1909-10 (see p. 126) is informed by a strong personal presence, and was greeted, it is said, with warm recognition by Vollard's dog; in that of Kahnweiler, however, late 1910, the sitter's individuality is scarcely hinted at. In Braque's and Picasso's still lifes of 1910-11 and early 1912 (known as their "hermetic" or esoteric period, when they reached their furthest point of abstraction) the subject matter appears to be incidental to the perfectly articulated structure of fragmented planes.

"Synthetic" Cubism was in part a reaction against the abstract tendency of the analytical phase. In 1911 both artists had included in their compositions stencilled capital letters, fragments of words (often puns, sometimes obscene – Picasso's humour could never remain repressed for long). When early in 1912 Picasso created his *Still life with chair-caning*, using extraneous objects stuck to the picture surface – the first collage-painting – he introduced reality literally and physically, reaffirming in the midst of abstraction ties with everyday ephemera. Picasso's collages were a development of Braque's experiments in the same year with *papiers collés*, pasted cut-papers which acted both as formal elements of the composition and representationally, yet at the same remained obdurately just objects. Once the synthetic principle – building up, putting together, rather than breaking down, rearranging – had been formulated, the conceptual nature of both artists' work became ever more marked.

In autumn 1912 Picasso moved to Montparnasse, where he was no longer a neighbour of Braque. Braque's subsequent career, interrupted by active service in World War I, was more one of refinement than of innovation (see pp. 178, 228), while Picasso, a neutral Spaniard, continued throughout the War and after to widen his scope (see pp. 178, 202, 228).

PICASSO (below)
Daniel Henry Kahnweiler, 1910
Kahnweiler was Braque's and Picasso's dealer, one of the Cubists' first patrons. He sat for his portrait more than 20 times, but it remains ghostly, veiled by the fragmented planes of the pictorial structure.

Expression of personality is not the artist's goal, it is rather that complex reconstruction of forms symptomatic of analytical Cubism in its last stage. Yet Picasso implanted in it recognizable details, the hands, button and watch-chain of the waistcoat, as if to help out the spectator.

BRAQUE (above)
Still life with fish, c.1909-10
Even in the most austere phase of analytical Cubism Braque never quite lost his elegance and lustrous colour. In his *Kahnweiler* (left) Picasso tantalized the eye with the play of plane and counter-plane in what must be a solid face; Braque's slightly earlier picture vibrates in scintillating blocks across the surface. It is more spacious, and the process of abstraction is less opaque, less riddling.

PICASSO (right)
Still life with chair-caning, 1911-12
A scrap of mechanically printed oilcloth with a pattern of caning is stuck to the picture, mocking the reign of illusionism over centuries of Western art. Collage almost embodies the principle of synthetic Cubism – the construction of a picture with materials that are, once arranged, the subject of the painting. It was in 1911 that Braque had first used lettering in his pictures to this end, and Picasso soon joined in. The rope that replaces the conventional gold frame is a further touch, asserting literally self-containment – it is, it does not represent.

BRAQUE (above)
The man with a pipe, 1912
Braque and Picasso had developed Cubist painting together, almost neck and neck, using each other's inventions to extend the scope of their art with astounding rapidity. The Cubist use of *papier collé* is attributed to Braque, and *The man with a pipe* is a very early example. The extension of the idea to an art all of collage was an invention of Picasso. Braque was a craftsman's son, quick to fasten on to new devices which Picasso used more imaginatively: so, Braque taught Picasso to use a comb on wet brown paint to produce the effect of wood-graining; Picasso promptly exploited it to represent a woman's hair.

Cubism 2, and Orphism

Picasso and Braque (see preceding page) stood aloof from the usual means of making their work known – the various annual exhibitions in Paris – but their ideas and practice were on display at the gallery of their exclusive dealer, Kahnweiler, and soon attracted attention. Cubist works by enthusiastic followers began to appear just as Picasso and Braque were moving from analytical to synthetic Cubism – first at the Salon d'Automne in 1910, then in the Cubists' own room at the Salon des Indépendants in 1911, whence they were invited to Brussels in the same year. Events were known in Germany and Italy almost as soon as they unfolded in Paris. Picasso and Braque were included by Roger Fry in his second Post-Impressionist exhibition in London in 1912, inducing rage and fury; the epoch-making Armory Show exhibited Cubism to a startled New York in 1913. In 1912 the painters Gleizes and Metzinger published *Cubism*, which ran through 15 editions before the end of the year; Apollinaire in 1913 produced *The Cubist Painters*; A. J. Eddy's *Cubism and Post-Impressionism* appeared in America in 1914. Picasso had made Cubist sculpture as early as 1909, and others soon followed (see p. 178).

GRIS (below)
Homage to Picasso, 1911-12
When he applied analytical Cubism to its perpetrator,

Gris achieved a sober, cool architecture distinct from Picasso's (whose neighbour he had been since 1907).

Juan Gris (1887-1927) had observed his fellow-Spaniard Picasso's early Cubist ventures very closely, and had also made his own independent study of Cézanne. Having begun to paint seriously only in 1911, he made a sensational début at the Salon des Indépendants of 1912 with *Homage to Picasso* – a methodical rearrangement of Picasso's person executed with great assurance. Developing with remarkable speed, by the end of the year he had established a distinctive style: while Braque and Picasso had seemed to move around their subject, to take views from different angles, and then as it were to reshuffle them into pictorial coherence, Gris set each facet of his model – each seen from a single, relatively consistent viewpoint – in a compartmented framework, rather like the leading of a stained-glass window. He eagerly adopted the new techniques of synthetic Cubism, collage and *papier collé*, but unlike Picasso and Braque did not tone down his colour. He soon increasingly abstracted form to fit his compositional needs, a method he described succinctly: "I begin by organizing my picture: then I define the object." "It is not picture X which manages to correspond with my subject

LEGER (right)
Nudes in the forest, 1909-10
This is an ambitious canvas on a monumental scale, and the choice of subject – three woodcutters at work like machines – introduced a Courbet-like Realism to the Cubist repertoire, reflecting Léger's belief in "the people". Further, in astonishing contrast to the static compositions of Picasso and Braque, the figures, the hills and the trees seem to thrum with a vigorous sense of action. Muted greys and greens reflect a dappled forest.

GRIS (above)
The wash-stand, 1912
Gris' synthetic Cubist still lifes were constructed with draughtsman-like skill and intellectual precision; he disposed his forms in mathematical relationships set up by a dissecting grid. Under the curtain, a mirror represents the mirror: it is a mirror, and reflects as one – rather a witty collage.

GRIS (right)
Landscape at Ceret, 1913
Gris often worked beside Picasso, Braque and Derain in southern France. The landscapes of Braque were solidly modelled, subdued in colour; Gris responded with rich, high-keyed colour harmonies, accentuating the flatness as if the picture were made of loose parts from a broken kaleidoscope.

LEGER (above)
Contrasting forms, 1913
Roughly painted highlights on Léger's characteristic cylinders flatten the plane, disrupted by split solids interpenetrating; angular shapes counterpoint round ones. The pyramidal organization assists the sense of monumentality; the movement may reflect the impact of the Futurists.

but subject X which manages to correspond to my picture." Deeply interested in the geometry of proportions and the mathematics of formal relationships, he was a leading contributor to the first exhibition of the Section d'Or (Golden Section) in 1912.

The Section d'Or artists were committed to Cubism but aware of its limitations: they wanted to reinstate colour and movement, and to expand its range of subject matter. They arrived at a resolved pictorial structure not by a reduction of the objects represented but by the application of the laws of musical harmony, of ratio and proportion. Amongst their members were the future exponents of Dada, Francis Picabia and Marcel Duchamp, and Fernand Léger. Fernand Léger (1881-1955) remained a Cubist throughout his career, but from the outset his aims went beyond those of Picasso and Braque: he wanted his work to reflect, to appeal to and to enhance the lives of ordinary people, so his subject matter was more important to him, and more emotive. His training as an architectural draughtsman gave his designs a clarity and precision of outline which emerged as an essential characteristic of his style, consolidated during and after World War I (see p.178). His earliest exhibited work in the Cubist idiom was *Nudes in the forest* of 1909-10: the forms are chunky, contained by their outlines and not opening into one another, and there is more than a hint of traditional perspective; in marked contrast to Braque and Picasso, there is a strong sense of movement, almost of clash and tumult. Already the form that obsessed Léger all his life, the cylinder (which earned him the title "tubist"), is dominant. He was then influenced, in the Section d'Or, to experiment with pure or nearly pure abstraction, notably in his series *Contrasting Forms*, 1913-14.

Robert Delaunay (1885-1941) moved quickly towards a completely abstract art, and one primarily concerned with colour. His *Eiffel Tower* series of 1910 demonstrates his grasp of Cubist fragmentation but also his feeling for the rhythms and contrasts of colour – his prime concern during the most important part of his career, the few years before World War I. His initiative was christened "Orphism" by Apollinaire, who found in it "pure" painting, a close analogy to music. By 1912 Delaunay was experimenting with colour wheels on circular canvases, as in his series of *Circular Forms* – the first completely non-figurative paintings by a French artist. Colours were to act on each other reciprocally "in simultaneous contrasts", creating form and movement in space: "Colour is form and subject; it is the sole theme that develops, transforms itself apart from all analysis, psychological or otherwise. Colour is a function of itself." Delaunay's wife Sonia Terk and Frank Kupka (1871-1957) also turned very early to abstraction, Kupka applying colour theory and musical harmonies to his own "mystical" Orphism.

Although by 1914 Delaunay's painting had almost nothing in common with Cubism, Cubism proved a liberation for him, and for numbers of major artists who rapidly worked through their own understanding of it and advanced beyond it. Having observed Cubism in Paris, by 1914 Mondrian (see p. 188), back in Holland, was developing his own austere abstraction, and Orphism strongly attracted notably some artists of Der Blaue Reiter (see p.136). The Futurists soon discovered (see over) that Cubism could serve their purposes. Though for some years to come Cubism remained controversial with the general public, it was already a fact of life.

DELAUNAY (right)
The Eiffel Tower, 1910
Delaunay sought a novel expression – of sensation, of the movement of light and the rhythm of structure, not as fixed at one moment or seen from one aspect, but as sensed "universally". The dynamism of the Tower is conveyed in crumbling, buckling, lurching forms.

DELAUNAY (below)
A window, 1912
The starting-point was an open window in sunlight through which reflections of the city (Delaunay was fascinated by the city) are seen. Thence he developed a series of virtually non-figurative paintings, with almost transparent planes of light in prismatic colours making crystalline patterns.

KUPKA (left)
The disks of Newton: study for a fugue in two colours, 1911-12
The interaction of colours was the theme of several series by Kupka. Here he sought to demonstrate that rotating wheels of colour, static disks energized by contrasting colours, create an effect of radiant white light. His experiments were intended to create "something between sight and hearing". Like Delaunay's, Kupka's interest in energy is a parallel to Futurism.

DELAUNAY (right)
Circular forms: sun and moon, 1912-13
Delaunay had created his first pure non-figurative painting by 1912, having arrived by a path utterly different from Kandinsky's (see p. 138). The Russian had insisted that abstract art must be founded on a "proper contact with the human soul"; Delaunay was more intellectual than intuitive, and demanded a self-sufficient abstraction: "So long as art does not free itself from the object, it remains descriptive . . . degrading itself by using defective means." There was nothing mystical in Delaunay's art, which was an "absolute" investigation of the movement of colour in harmony and dissonance.

Futurism

The emergence of Futurism, the most aggressive, the most politically conscious and (Dada apart) the noisiest of the important early movements of twentieth-century art, was signalled by the publication in February 1909 of Marinetti's call to action, *The Founding and Manifesto of Futurism*. Filippo Tommaso Marinetti (1876-1944), poet and playwright, was aligned politically with Gabriele d'Annunzio and later (until 1919) with Mussolini in the attempt to consolidate the recently federated component states of Italy into a modern, glamorous, vigorously nationalistic unity. He was the instigator, the theoretician and the voice of the "art of the future", rejecting all art of the past (*"le Passéisme"*) for a new art that would celebrate technology and scientific advance, psychoanalysis and all things modern. A more or less simultaneous supporting manifesto was signed by five artists, Umberto Boccioni (1882-1916), Carlo Carrà (1881-1966), Luigi Russolo (1885-1947), Giacomo Balla (1871-1958) and Gino Severini (1883-1966). Their underlying philosophy was greatly influenced by Henri Bergson's *Creative Evolution*, in which the importance of continual forward-looking development,

conditioned by universal dynamism and flux, was stressed. Successive manifestos claimed that dynamism and flux, in colour and in form, should power the new art.

Italian painting at the turn of the century had been generally conservative; there was no avantgarde, and little awareness of avantgarde developments in Paris. Two painters, Giovanni Boldini and Antonio Mancini, both had international reputations – Boldini as an almost fatuously skilful master of society portraiture, in what Sickert called his "wriggle-and-chiffon" style; Mancini for a blurred, atmospheric version of Impressionism – but the only truly major talent to emerge in Italy had been the sculptor Medardo Rosso (see p. 107). Rosso's mirroring of the fleeting moment of time and of form coming into being had some relevance for the Futurists. It was, however, an integral part of the Futurists' purpose to remedy what they felt to be a national shortcoming, and to create an art worthy of Italy – of the new Italy, not that of its artistic past; their movement was unusual in that its artistic practice was preceded by theoretical exposition – those manifestos, verbose, declamatory, arrogant and provocative,

which set the pattern for so many later variants in twentieth-century art. Marinetti's first famous broadside, however, had real panache: "We shall sing the love of danger, the habit of energy, boldness . . . a new beauty – the beauty of speed . . . a roaring automobile, which seems to run like a machine gun, is more beautiful than '*The Victory of Samothrace*'."

The problem of matching the programme with works of art worthy of it was not so easy. Futurist works were first exhibited in Milan in 1911, but it was recognized that Paris, the international focal point, must be attacked, if the movement were to be established. The first Futurist exhibition was staged in Paris in February 1912. Accompanied by a vigorous public relations campaign, it attracted great attention, but also considerable derision, although Apollinaire reviewed the exhibition with respect. The show then circulated in London, Berlin, Brussels, Amsterdam, Munich and elsewhere: everywhere it aroused interest spiced with alarm, but Futurism certainly became known, its works were sold, and its influence was felt wherever it was seen.

Futurist techniques owed much initially to Neo-Impressionist practice – breaking down

BALLA (right)
The street lamp, 1909
Balla's chief interests remained limited to the representation of light and movement, provoking rebuke from colleagues who felt that Futurism should champion radical, universal issues in a changing world.

BOCCIONI (below)
The city rises, 1910-11
The tempestuously surging waves, 3m (10ft) across, had sensational impact when launched in exhibition. The implicit radical politics were also likely to shock. Boccioni, like Balla, took up Divisionism at the turn of the century, informed by French example, pursuing the characteristic Divisionist effects of luminosity and scintillation. But these paintings were static, and Boccioni's Futurist ideals demanded movement. The Divisionist dots now became blurred with high speed.

BOCCIONI (below)
Farewells, 1911
The emotions of parting are Boccioni's theme: this is the centre of his triptych

States of mind, in which he hoped to force "colours and form to express themselves", that is, the energy latent within them. Cubist

devices appear amid "force lines", in an abstraction of a steam locomotive leaving. Delaunay (see preceding page) was a main influence.

BALLA (right)
Dynamism of a dog on a leash, 1912
The comic quality of the little dog survives the seriousness of the intent, the quasi-scientific study of motion, captured with Balla's usual delicacy. His superimposition of successive movements owed much to chrono-photography – studies by Muybridge (see p. 127) and others of the running horse or the moving human body, in "stills" taken in quick succession. Duchamp was later to apply the same principle in his *Nude descending a staircase* (see p. 168), though he claimed to have arrived at that image before he knew Futurism.

the colours into small fragmentary patches. Divisionism seemed the best means of reproducing the effect of light kindling and moving in colour, of form dissolving into flux, into speed. The treatment was applied to urban and political subject matter: one of the earliest fully Futurist paintings was Balla's dazzling *Street lamp*, 1909; here, however, movement and direction are indicated and defined by lines, "lines of force". The first Futurist attempts to convey the impression of velocity were sometimes somewhat naive – the indication, for example, of movement in a limb by showing it in different positions. The best-known example is Balla's delightful *Dynamism of a dog on a leash*, 1912; the same device was put to more serious, sharply dramatic use in Carrà's *Funeral of the anarchist Galli*, 1910-11.

Most satisfying, in terms of formal resolution, was the Futurist work produced by Boccioni. His huge *The city rises* of 1910-11 is impressive, but the violence of the divisionistic foreground, in tumult, does not marry happily with the naturalistic surge of the new city behind it; Boccioni in fact found his best form only when, in Paris in 1912, he carefully studied Cubist techniques. That these were

known to some of the group earlier is clear from such paintings as Carrà's *Funeral*, and Severini had been living in Paris since 1906, returning to Milan in 1911. It was Boccioni, however, who grasped how aptly the Cubist technique of interpenetrating planes, of one form opening into and fusing into another, could be applied to the very different aims of Futurist movement, so as to create an effect of simultaneity. Yet surely the most original of Boccioni's subsequent achievements came in the form of sculpture, in which he claimed to have realized "not pure form, but *pure plastic rhythm*: not the construction of the body, but the construction of the *action* of the body". He was indeed so successful in his aim that his striding *Unique forms in continuity* was compared favourably by later critics with the Hellenistic "*Victory of Samothrace*" (see vol. 2 p. 42) explicitly derided by Marinetti.

Boccioni died as a result of an accident in 1916. The vital spark of Futurism did not survive World War I, although adherents kept its name alive until about 1930, working in stylized, diluted and mannered versions of its original form. Its impact, however, had been considerable, not least on Dada.

BOCCIONI (above)
Unique forms of continuity in space, 1913
The complex forms of the bronze figure arose from Boccioni's investigation into the phenomenology of moving muscles. Hence his image of strength and speed, a "force form, the equivalent of the expansive power of the body".

BOCCIONI (left)
Development of a bottle in space, 1912-13
Boccioni was the first to translate successfully into three dimensions the Futurist faith in dynamic form, analysing the object in the Cubist manner. The bottle's roundness seems to expand around it while the neck screws upwards.

CARRA (above)
The funeral of the anarchist Galli, 1910-11

The desired effect, shock, was achieved by depicting the subject, the riot which

broke out at the funeral, in violent, glaring colours and savage, stabbing forms.

SEVERINI (left)
Pam-Pam at the Monico, 1910-12
Severini's *Pam-Pam* was a hit at the 1912 Futurist exhibition in Paris – the gaiety of a dancing crowd caught by Futurist means.

RUSSOLO (above)
The revolt, 1911-12
Russolo himself saw this work as the "collision of two forces, the force of the revolutionary element made up of enthusiasm and Red lyricism against the force

of inertia and reactionary resistance". Russolo was a keen political activist, the most literal exponent of Futurist thought, fond of grandiose, often absurd gestures expressed in bold colour and brave new form.

British Art: The Vortex

The standing of the British Royal Academy had been seriously undermined in the last two decades of the nineteenth century. The imagination of its members had ossified, their views were reactionary; worse, the standards of instruction in its school had sunk abysmally. More and more young students had found that Paris offered the only worthwhile training, but then found little recognition of their work in England. Although alternative schools and splinter groups of artists increased, generally English taste proved stubbornly slow to appreciate the discoveries even of the Impressionists, first shown in London in the 1880s.

The most important figures associated with the New English Art Club, founded in 1886 "with a view to protesting against the narrowness of the Royal Academy", were Walter Richard Sickert (1860-1942) and Philip Wilson Steer (1860-1942). Steer had studied in Paris in 1882-84; by 1889, his work was reflecting the high key of colour, raised horizon and broken handling of the Impressionists, and it even suggested at times knowledge of Seurat. For a brief spell, Steer snatched down on to a canvas vivid and original lyrics of sparkling light and vitality, though later he

reverted to competence. Sickert was more consistent in quality, and seriously exploratory, throughout his long career. His friendships first with Whistler, then with Degas, established his standards; he kept to a low key of colour, a muted tonal subtlety, and in particular his reliance on drawing and delight in unorthodox "snapshot" compositions reflected his lifelong admiration for Degas. Sickert spent much time abroad, and even showed in Paris with modest success. His theatrical subjects recall again Degas, but also the Intimistes, especially Vuillard; though he never attempted flat Nabi patterning, and veered to the sensational or anecdotal, he was at his best Vuillard's peer. His "Intimiste" masterpiece is *Ennui*, of which he painted several versions from about 1913. He remained always the most professional and committed English painter of his generation, uneven in quality but inventive until the end. Even he, however, was initially unable to stomach the shock of the two Post-Impressionist exhibitions staged by the critic Roger Fry (1866-1934) in 1910 and 1912.

The Camden Town Group, formed round Sickert in 1911, included able painters of contrasting tendencies – those close in style to

Sickert, such as Spencer Gore (1878-1914; not shown) and Harold Gilman (1876-1919); but also Robert Bevan (1865-1925, not shown), who had worked in Pont-Aven and applied flat colour and strong outline to scenes of horse fairs and urban streets; and many seeds of dissension, not least the irascible Wyndham Lewis. By 1911 Augustus John (1878-1961), destined to be a brilliant, erratic portrait painter, had already done his most original work – a kind of insular Fauve revolution, a series of broadly and boldly brushed little paintings, of an intensity he never recaptured. His sister Gwen John (1876-1939), refusing all group or doctrinal affiliations, isolated, finally a recluse, was the greater painter. Her work was muted, almost conventional in technique, but her variations on her chosen theme, the solitary girl, reveal an individual talent.

The Vorticists made their impact partly in paint and stone, partly in noise, argument and theorizing. The group centred round the turbulent figure of Wyndham Lewis (1884-1956), painter, novelist, myth-maker, aggressive controversialist. He set up the Rebel Art Centre in 1913, with its periodical *Blast* (a self-styled *Review of the Great British Vortex*, whence the

STEER (left)
Children paddling, Walberswick, 1894
Steer's Impressionism became especially lyrical when his introverted sensibility was touched by the fragile play of children.

GILMAN (right)
Mrs Mounter, 1917
Cézanne and van Gogh have influenced, respectively, the broad modelling of facial planes and Gilman's bright, expressive, molten colour.

AUGUSTUS JOHN (below)
David and Dorelia in Normandy, c. 1907
A springtime freshness, a handling perhaps recalling Goya, lend a gypsy air to an English family portrait.

SICKERT (left)
Ennui, c. 1913
Sickert has mastered his early problem in grasping solid form, arriving at a controlled composition in a tightly organized picture. Virginia Woolf admired the melancholy aura of this portrait of a marriage grown irremediably stale.

GWEN JOHN (right)
Girl with bare shoulders, c. 1910
Gwen John's understated style had its origin in her study of Whistler's tonal values. From 1903 she lived permanently in France; the female portraits she painted then reveal subtle and acute strength and sympathy.

poet Ezra Pound gave the movement its name). Lewis' own painting at this point was "Cubo-Futurist": he had been much influenced by the Italian Futurist Marinetti, who visited London in 1914. Although no one in England yet grasped the principles of Cubism, this misunderstanding does not disallow the individual and valid character of the Vorticist style, in its response to an urban and mechanistic environment. From the "vortex" of twentieth-century life Lewis aimed to precipitate what was in effect a classical structure, precise, cool and metallic, yet charged with emotional force. His most impressive colleagues were William Roberts (1895-1980), who has always challenged Lewis' primacy in Vorticism, and who in the late 1970s was still producing paintings of formidable logic in the same style though figurative; David Bomberg (1890-1957); and Christopher Richard Wynne Nevinson (1889-1946; not shown), applying a mechanistic, sometimes Légeresque vision to the experience of war. Lewis himself after World War I became increasingly figurative, and completed some remarkable portraits.

Two sculptors were amongst the most original talents of Vorticism, both foreign-born. Jacob Epstein (1880-1959), born in America, had met Picasso, Brancusi and Modigliani in Paris; he was a discerning collector of African and Polynesian sculpture, and also knew the Mexican and Buddhist traditions. His early work is a remarkably eclectic fusion of elements from such sources, electrified by a passionate Expressionist urge that must owe much to his central European and Jewish ancestry. His public commissions in London and in Paris (the tomb of Oscar Wilde) provoked violent controversy. His most comprehensively ambitious work, however, was *The rock-drill*, a haunting vision of mechanistic man. Realistic expressive modelling was nevertheless Epstein's essential talent, and he became an outstanding portraitist (see p. 198).

Henri Gaudier-Brzeska (1891-1915) made brilliant, reductive line-drawings as economical as those of Matisse, and his best sculpture shows a fierce vitality galvanizing simplicity of form and a feeling for his materials. He fell at the front, fighting in the French Army; the horrors of the first global war would mute the vitality of the avantgarde in British art for about a decade after the peace of 1919.

LEWIS (left)
Ezra Pound, 1939
Though Lewis was loudest in crying Vorticism, those few Vorticist paintings by him that have survived are less striking than those by Roberts. His portraits of the literary avantgarde, painted much later, are his best work as an artist: he has revealingly evoked the intellectual restlessness of Pound; his portrait of T. S. Eliot is equally good.

BOMBERG (below)
In the hold, 1913-14
The huge geometric canvas reveals a desire for order, though the order contains strong movement. Bomberg, the most programmatic of the Vorticists, rejected "everything in painting that is not pure form".

ROBERTS (below)
The diners, 1919
The Cubists' influence on Roberts' early work persisted in the continuing figurative bias of his art. It retains a sense of order and harmony, but seems barely capable of confining the energy of his subjects.

GAUDIER-BRZESKA (left)
Red stone dancer, 1913
This is an early example of a distinctively 20th-century sculpture: forms clearly inspired by tribal African art are combined in a classical harmony. But their contortions have also mesmeric dynamism.

EPSTEIN (above)
The rock-drill, 1913-14
Epstein later removed the support, a quarry drill, to leave only the cast bronze bust (the photograph dates from 1914). The impact is considerable: the machine has become a modern metaphor for sex, terror, power.

Russian Art 1: Symbolism to Suprematism

Though the frontiers of her vast territories border on both East and West, Russia had for some centuries turned to Europe for cultural inspiration. Her greatest national achievement in art had been the icon (rooted in Byzantine tradition, see vol. 2 p. 62), but even the finest examples remained begrimed with the smoke of candles and incense until the superb clarity of their line and colour was revealed when many were cleaned for the Romanov exhibition in Moscow in 1913. During the nineteenth century, however, distinctly Russian variations on Western styles had been evolving in the main cultural centres – the influence came mainly from France, from Realism, then from Symbolism and Art Nouveau.

One of the most important of the several groups of artists that formed in pre-Revolutionary Russia was The World of Art group in St Petersburg (Leningrad), which drew also on the strong indigenous tradition of peasant folk art: it included Alexandre Benois (1870-1960), Leon Bakst (1866-1924) and Mikhail Vrubel (1856-1910); Vrubel developed a personal, very Russian, anxiety-ridden Symbolism. The group also included Sergei Diaghilev (1872-1929), the great impresario

of ballet, and an innovator of genius in exhibition techniques: he first brought Russian art to western Europe, to Paris at the Salon d'Automne in 1906. This success encouraged further ventures, reaching a climax in the famous revelation of the Ballets Russes to Paris in 1909. Until 1914 successive seasons dazzled Paris with Russian culture – the music of Rimsky-Korsakov and Stravinsky, the dancing of Pavlova and Nijinsky, the choreography of Fokine, the décor of Benois and Bakst.

The explorations of the leading French Post-Impressionists were revealed in Moscow rather than in St Petersburg by the collections of three extraordinarily enterprising Moscow merchants, Riabuchinsky, Morozov and Shchukin. Shchukin owned 40 Picassos – including major Cubist works – and 37 Matisses; all bought direct in Paris, and even commissioned works. Riabuchinsky specialized in Rouault, but further founded a magazine and promoted exhibitions in Moscow; his exhibition of 1908 included works not only by the great Post-Impressionists but also by the Nabis and the Fauves. Two of the major pioneers in the revolutionary Russian abstract movements were particularly interested in the

BAKST (above)
"L'Après-midi d'un faune (Vaslav Nijinsky)", 1912
Sinuous rhythms of Art Nouveau evoke the grace and energy of the Ballets Russes' brightest star. The title, a phrase by Mallarmé, inspired Debussy's music, danced by Nijinsky.

GONCHAROVA (right)
Monk with a cat, 1910
The attempt of the Russian avantgarde to combine their native traditions with the current trends in Western painting is quite clear: the monk, recalling a saint in an icon, is rendered in broad and bold Fauve brushwork.

VRUBEL (left)
Six-winged seraph, 1904
The fragmented areas of rich but sombre colour and the hieratic pose owe much to glowing medieval mosaic (Vrubel had once worked in Kiev as a restorer).

BENOIS (left)
Backdrop for Stravinsky's Petrouchka: The fair, 1911
Benois's great contribution to stage design lay in his view of the production as a picture, the stage a canvas where the single elements all combined to create a visually dazzling scene.

LARIONOV (right)
Summer, 1912
Naive peasant art was the inspiration and model for four pictures by Larionov depicting the seasons of the year. The figures have a slightly comic appeal, but the uncompromising crudity reflects the profound dissatisfaction with academic modes of representation which led finally to total rejection of the object.

Nabi and Fauve use of broad and expressive flat patterning in vivid and emphatic line, but applied it to their own existing interest in the techniques and vision of Russian folk art: these were Mikhail Larionov (1881-1964) and his partner Natalia Goncharova (1881-1962).

Both Larionov and Goncharova drew deliberately on the crude, broad imagery of *lubki* (popular woodcuts, see p. 126), and later on the still cruder but vividly expressive graffiti of soldiers' barracks. The direct coarseness of the expression they achieved was unparalleled in Europe, even by the German Expressionist movements. Larionov initiated his own exhibitions, and at the first ("The Donkey's Tail" in Moscow in 1912) he included early, still figurative, works by Tatlin and Malevich. In 1913 he launched Rayonnism.

Rayonnism – not really a movement, the total production being a few paintings all by Larionov or Goncharova – was part of the headlong development in Russia in the years 1911-17 from the figurative to the non-objective, which made Moscow a prime centre of European avantgarde art. Malevich described his works of 1912-13 as "Cubo-Futurist", and this term indicates the basic

principles of the movement in its first stages, if it is not too strictly analysed. There was a seething ferment of often contradictory ideas; several very different styles might be represented in one exhibition. Rayonnism, however, was the expression of Larionov's belief that Cubism had not produced the final answer; it offered an alternative, entirely modern imagery, powered by principles close to those of Italian Futurism: it was an investigation of the interaction of rays of light sprung from the surfaces of (unseen) objects. This was virtually a purely abstract art. Both Larionov and Goncharova, however, soon withdrew from the Russian scene, following Diaghilev to Paris in 1914 and 1915 as ballet designers. The pursuit of abstraction was continued in Moscow by Kasimir Malevich (1878-1935) and Vladimir Tatlin (see over).

Malevich was born in Kiev of humble Polish-Russian stock. Coming to Moscow, he worked his own way through Impressionist and Cézannesque manners, but by about 1908 he was treating themes of peasant life (like Goncharova) in broad, "tubular" fashion. The tendency to the geometric very quickly increased, but differed from contemporary

French Cubism (though surely influenced by it) not least in Malevich's use of a bright peasant palette. Already by 1913 (he claimed) he had created his earliest "Suprematist" works in designs for an opera: one set was completely abstract, a white square and a black square. His first exhibited Suprematist work (1915) consisted of a simple combination of geometric elements. Though they were non-objective, Malevich gave them emotive and associative titles (*In a state of tranquillity; Painterly realism of the footballer*). His geometric forms increased in complexity, but for Malevich always had their roots in an extra-terrestrial mysticism – his "semaphore in space". From complexity he proceeded to the ultimate simplicity and purity, to the quintessential reduction of the famous *White on White* series of 1917-18. His progress to complete non-objectivity, unlike Mondrian's, was not by abstraction from natural forms, but from a more conceptual basis. Suprematism was the "supremacy of feeling in creative art". The more materialist and functionalist Tatlin and Rodchenko, having first joined Malevich in Suprematism, proceeded to reject it for the still more austere concepts of Constructivism.

GONCHAROVA (above)
Cats, 1911
Rayonnism, according to Larionov, denotes "spatial forms which arise from the intersection of reflected rays of various objects, forms chosen by the will of the artist". "In this way painting parallels music while remaining itself. Here begins a way of painting which may be pursued only by following the specific laws of colour and its application to canvas." But while Larionov's own work approached complete abstraction, the motif was often still recognizable in the vivid, angular shapes of Goncharova's canvases.

MALEVICH (right)
Suprematist composition: white on white, c. 1918
Suprematism could go no further; a variation in the texture of the brush-strokes is the only means distinguishing the smaller square from its background.

MALEVICH (left)
Woman with buckets, 1912
Although it bears an extra-ordinary resemblance to Léger's tubular forms, Malevich's Cubo-Futurism seems to have developed independently and ahead of

the French approach to a truly non-objective art. Malevich admitted a social concern – the woman with water buckets is a peasant – which is another striking parallel with Léger (see his *Nudes in the forest*, p. 150).

MALEVICH (above)
Black trapezium and red square, after 1915
Experiments with collage led Malevich to concentrate on the formal relationships between geometrical shapes, which appear on the white ground like *papiers collés*.

Here the large trapezium exerts a subtle influence over the smaller shapes – distorting the squares and rectangles and the oblique lines into so many echoes of its fundamental form. These works quickly had an impact, not only in Russia.

Russian Art 2: Constructivism

The history of avantgarde art in Russia from about 1915 through the 1920s to its final obliteration in the 1930s by the promulgation of social realism under Stalin is complex and confused. Much of its documentation has vanished, including many of the works of art themselves, and the very existence of the movement has been expunged from the record. There are, however, four currents, now merging, now conflicting, that can be discerned – the pure abstract art with mystic overtones (Suprematism) of Malevich (see preceding page); the equally pure, materialist Constructivism of the brothers Pevsner and Gabo; the equally materialist counter-Constructivism of Tatlin and Rodchenko with its political and social commitment, developing into post-Revolutionary "Productivism"; finally, the high-art principles of Kandinsky.

The springboard for Constructivism, as for so many other developments in twentieth-century art, seems to have been Cubism in Paris, and specifically Picasso. In 1913, Vladimir Tatlin (1885-1953), associated in Russia with Larionov, and already aware not only of Cézanne but of both Fauve and Cubist explorations, visited Picasso in Paris, and saw there Picasso's experiments with collage, applied in three-dimensional constructions – in paper and string, and then in sheet metal, wood, wire. A basic concern of Russian Constructivist sculpture was to be the treatment of space rather than of mass. The void was as important as the solid. (Gabo was later to say: "I can use the same space in different positions in the same image.") Back in Russia, between 1913 and 1917, Tatlin produced painted reliefs, followed by relief constructions which included "corner reliefs", suspended on a wire across the corner of a room, in which he discarded the age-old convention of the frame or a base. Above all, these works abolished figuration, abolished even abstraction that referred back to identifiable objects.

Alexander Rodchenko (1891-1956) was associated with Tatlin from 1915, and moved early into purely abstract geometric designs – "compass-and-ruler drawings". Influenced by Malevich's command of dynamic non-figurative design, he expanded the application of these principles to different materials, from chunky constructions in wood that are as spare as Minimal art – or the paintings of Mondrian – to hanging constructions that introduced

RODCHENKO (below)
Composition, 1918
Rodchenko was dedicated to "the absoluteness of industrial art and to Constructivism, its sole form of expression". He had turned early more to design than to art, and his training in a rigorous draughtsmanship appears in abstract compositions with the linear precision of technical drawings. In 1922 he gave up fine art to apply his principles to photography, typography and the design of furniture.

TATLIN (right)
Relief construction, c.1915
Tatlin's constructions of 1913-17 are known only from photographs. Tatlin's motto was "real materials in real space"; in these "counter-constructions", the absence of any frame, which would physically and symbolically distinguish the work from its context, is a sign of the integral relevance of art to life. Not only are these works non-figurative, they were also made out of flimsy and perishable materials rather than from bronze or stone.

MAYAKOVSKY (below)
Revolutionary poster, 1920
The crude, forceful images, recalling those of peasant woodcuts, spell out with uncompromising brutality the propaganda syllogisms of the Reds, written below: "(1) If we don't wipe out the White Guard utterly (2) White Guardism will rise again. (3) If we kill off the landowner and just stand back (4) then Vrangel (a general in the White Guard) will stretch out his hand for the worker. (5) Until the Red Flag flourishes (6) we cannot throw down the rifle."

MAYAKOVSKY (above)
Set design for *Misteria Bouffe*, 1919
Mayakovsky, a playwright and poet (ranked by some the equal of Bertolt Brecht) was a fervent advocate of Bolshevism, and predicted its triumph in his verse drama *Misteria Bouffe*. Its strident, declamatory quality is echoed in this angular design, influenced much by "Cubo-Futurism".

UNKNOWN ARTISTS
(above) "Agit" train, c.1919
The exuberantly painted railway carriage recalls, in all but the subject matter, a gipsy caravan. The decorative forms of Russian folk art found favour with the artists of the Revolution partly as authentic expressions of the working peasantry; these rather naive images, injected with a Futurist dynamism, are combined in exhortation to Communist victory – the red banner reads: "Long live the Third International!"

physical movement – purely abstract kinetic sculpture. Movement soon became a dominant feature in Constructivist art.

The success of the Revolution in 1917 united the most remarkable Russian artists in a common endeavour for a brief but hectic, heroic four years, 1917 to 1921. The brothers Naum Gabo (Naum Pevsner, 1890-1977), the sculptor, and Antoine Pevsner, at that point a painter, returned from Munich and Paris respectively. Kandinsky came back from his long sojourn in Munich (see p. 136) to become an administrative figure in the ambitious re-organization of the Russian galleries. In conditions of great difficulty and deprivation, art was harnessed nevertheless vigorously to Revolutionary ideals. Propaganda shows, produced by artists and actors, were toured in trains and boats; vast celebratory pageants were staged. The décor of these events was violently modern, closely related to early Constructivist sculpture. In 1917 Tatlin was a principal collaborator in the decoration of the Café Pittoresque in Moscow, an early attempt to combine Constructivist decoration with a Futurist life-style in a centre where the avant-garde met, involving art inextricably with life.

After 1919, Lenin encouraged the nascent film industry – hence the early masterpieces of pioneering geniuses such as Sergei Eisenstein. Vladimir Mayakovsky (1893-1930) was one ardent promoter of revolutionary values in poetry, plays, posters and stage designs.

As Gabo later remembered the ferment in Moscow in the early Revolutionary period, each artist brought "something to the clarification of another's work; our activities went on incessantly in both theoretical and concrete experiments at the workshops of the schools and in the artists' studios." Rifts and schism soon began to appear, however, not only from ideological differences but also from clashes of personality – Tatlin, a neurotically jealous character, had already come to blows with Malevich late in 1915. In 1920 Malevich, having mounted a triumphant last exhibition of Suprematism in 1919, announced that "fine" art was over, and turned to "laboratory" art. By 1923, in Petrograd, he was concentrating primarily on the application of abstract design to architecture. Kandinsky had reacted with a programme concerned with aesthetic investigation of the basic property of line and colour, and in his subsequent work

(see p. 190) was clearly much influenced by Malevich. Pevsner and Gabo were also concerned essentially with a modern version of Art for Art's sake (see p. 180). Tatlin's group, however, demanded the abolition of art – as an obsolete aestheticism spawned by a now-extinct capitalist society. Tatlin had envisaged the noblest project for the heroic celebration of the ideals of the Revolution, in his famous Tower of 1919-20 (see over), but after 1920 his Constructivism merged into Productivism, the construction of a socialist design for living, art applied to life for materialist, functional ends.

Pevsner and Gabo and Kandinsky (and also Chagall) withdrew to pursue their own ideals in freedom. The political and social bias grew until exploratory art was swamped in the 1930s in dogmatic social realism. Malevich fell foul of Stalin's reactionary repression, as did Mayakovsky, who committed suicide.

An important figure in the 1920s, coming and going between the West and Russia, a fertilizing agent in the development of crisp typography and of the poster, was the elegantly versatile El Lissitzky (1890-1941), who produced also playful, supremely decorative geometric paintings that he baptized *Prouns*.

RODCHENKO (right)
Hanging construction,
c. 1920
The artist, standing in the background, is seen through the spokes of his sculpture. Virtually all his work is lost, and known only from contemporary photographs, which cannot convey their crucial kinetic qualities.

AFTER RODCHENKO (below)
Hanging construction,
original *c.* 1920
Rodchenko made laths into fragile elliptical spirals, geometrically developed forms suspended from the ceiling with wire, slowly revolving as the air blew. They were an advance on Tatlin's "corner reliefs", free in space but fixed static between two walls.

GABO (above)
Head of a woman, 1917-20
Gabo converted mass into empty space by making up his *Heads* from inclined planar surfaces, of either metal or cardboard. The abstract impulse already underlying Gabo's works incurred only disapproval in the Russia of the 1920s, when socialism demanded the sacrifice of creative freedom for the support of industry and state policy.

LISSITZKY (left)
Proun 99, 1924-25
Lissitzky's background was even more technical than Rodchenko's: he trained as an engineer before applying his skill in design to such cool, Suprematist-derived compositions. Cubism and the mechanistic images of Duchamp also made major contributions to his style.

Tatlin: Monument to the Third International

Vladimir Tatlin (with pipe) *beside the maquette for his Monument to the Third International*

Vladimir Tatlin's *Monument to the Third International* reads at first sight as an austere three-dimensional exercise in non-objective form, an open spiral with its axis slanted against firm verticals. But it has become also a romantic, nostalgic monument to the artistic side of the ideals of the Communist Revolution in its first euphoria – ideals which, like the monument itself, never materialized. Commissioned by the Revolutionary Department of Fine Arts from Tatlin in 1919, the full-scale monument was to be erected in the centre of Moscow; the height proposed was some 400 metres (1,300ft). It was intended, however, not as a symbol, but as a "union of purely artistic forms (painting, sculpture and architecture) for a utilitarian purpose". The functional "body" of the construction would have consisted of a glass cylinder, a glass cone and a glass cube, contained within the open steel framework (painted red). The three elements were to house different functions, from conference and executive accommodation to a topmost information centre including a projector to illuminate the sky above with slogans. These elements were to revolve slowly, and independently and at different speeds, while the whole was to teem with human movement.

Much later buildings were to realize some elements of this programme (the Postal Towers of Stuttgart or London, the transparent colossus laced with escalators of glass at the Centre Pompidou in Paris – but Frank Lloyd Wright's Mile-High Skyscraper has likewise yet to be built). Tatlin's scheme never went further than scale models, one of which was shown at the Exhibition of the VIIIth Congress of the Soviets in December 1920. It seems in fact not to have advanced beyond the form of an almost purely sculptural design, though this indicated clearly how the proposed mechanical and human movement of the completed project would be matched by the formal movement of the basic spiral. This quality of movement was by then a dominant stylistic motif of Constructivist principles (see preceding page). Tatlin's model foreshadows many developments in later sculpture, setting an aspiration of unequalled scale and grandeur.

The formal element of his design was, however, strictly subordinate to its function. In his *Programme of the Productivist Group*, 1920, clearly written as counter to Gabo's *Realist Manifesto* of slightly earlier (see p. 180), Tatlin had redefined Constructivism in terms of two compound words, "*tektonika*" and "*faktura*". The first relates to social and industrial processes, the second to the progression through these techniques towards a logically achieved goal. "*Tektonika* is derived from the structure of communism and the effective exploitation of industrial matter. Construction is organization. It accepts the contents of the matter itself, already formulated. Construction is formulating activity taken to the extreme, allowing, however, for further tektonical work. The matter deliberately chosen and effectively used, without, however, hindering the progress of construction or limiting the *tektonika*, is called *faktura* by the group." Tatlin's ideas committed art entirely to industrialization, to a degree that only communism could make possible.

In theory, all ties with the past were broken. In practice, the only cloud-caps into which Tatlin's Tower would ever soar were those of insubstantial dream. Even the theme of such a monument has obvious roots in stubborn continuing traditions from the past, such as the designs of the Neoclassical architects Boullée or Ledoux or Rodin's *Monument to Labour* – even the Eiffel Tower. The practicability of Tatlin's design is also more than doubtful, and it would in construction no doubt have run into problems as severe as those of an earlier forerunner – the Tower of Babel.

Tatlin, like Rodchenko, but unlike so many of the other most gifted artists of those four "heroic" years of the new artistic dawn after the Revolution of 1917, remained committed to his motherland and to the ideological aspect of art for the rest of his life. He was director of the department of the "culture of materials" in the Research Institute for Artistic Culture (INKHUK); he became primarily a theatrical designer, but still in line with the aspirations of the *Monument* were his designs for a glider or air-bicycle, based on the study of insect flight, and baptized as *Letatlin* – a compound of his own name and the Russian verb for "to fly".

TATLIN (right)
Drawing for *Monument to the Third International*, c. 1920
An austere formal structure was to be transformed by the presence of people into living sculpture: "Least of all must you stand still or sit in this building, you must be mechanically transported up, down, carried along involuntarily ... creation, only creation."

TATLIN (below)
Letatlin, 1932
Tatlin's fascination with the dream of flying was also shared by Rodchenko and Malevich. The urge to transcend gravitational laws was perhaps one and the same with that of the Russian space programmes making a breakthrough only some 30 years later.

RODIN (above)
Monument to labour, 1893-99
Rodin's project was, like Tatlin's, never realized.

TATLIN (above)
Bent-tube chair, 1923
Traditional materials, wood and leather, are used in this innovatory design.

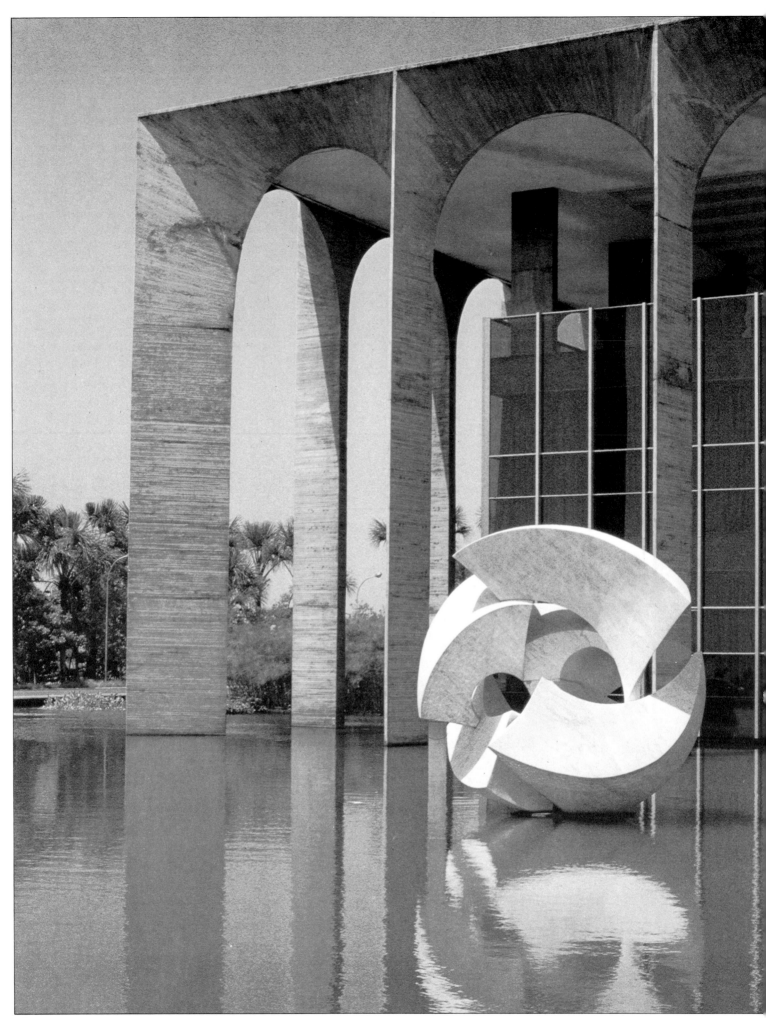

THE TWENTIETH CENTURY

The years since 1915 have witnessed more rapid changes than in any earlier period, in art no less than in science. The Cubist break with traditional methods of representation opened up an extraordinary range of artistic possibilities, and Cubism was to influence nearly all the most adventurous art of the years between the Wars. But the post-1914 avantgarde was distinguished above all by an urge to go beyond stylistic innovation, to work for a change in life and society as a whole. In so doing they called into question the very nature of art, and the interrogation has continued to this day, with little sign of ceasing.

The changing priorities of advanced artists were manifested most dramatically in the international Dada movement, for which the catastrophe of 1914-18 was evidence of cultural corruption. The survivors and successors of Dada who formed the Surrealist movement were as uncompromising in their rejection of established society, though their art was more positive, emphasizing the liberating role of the imagination and the Unconscious.

On the more formal side, the pioneering abstraction of Kandinsky and Malevich was carried forward by a group in Holland which also had social aims – De Stijl, whose austere geometric approach was intended to create a less individualistic form of culture. Such far-reaching ambitions did not survive the further shock of World War II, and the concerns of the most influential post-War artists have tended to be more personal. The persecution which accompanied Nazism drove many of Europe's best artists to America. Their interaction with a generation of talented and energetic American artists, and with a society not only wealthy but receptive to novelty, brought about, for the first time in history, artistic leadership in the New World rather than the Old.

The receptivity of the art market and of art critics to new ideas, and the establishment of great institutions dedicated to fostering contemporary art, are in striking contrast with the hostility against which advanced art struggled through the second half of the nineteenth century. Furthered by the mobility of ideas, images and people, abstraction became in the 1950s almost the dominant orthodoxy of art in the West.

Such ready acceptance has perhaps blunted the edge of satirical art, which might otherwise have proliferated in a contemporary culture addicted to satire; Pop, the post-War movement most akin to Dada, had none of its anarchic intent. In spite of noisy debate, perhaps the most conspicuous feature of contemporary painting and sculpture is the great variety of activity recognized as art, ranging as it does from theatrical flamboyance to Conceptual art, stressing idea rather than product and employing forms that are often as visually unremarkable as can be imagined. In the final section of this history these various movements are given equal consideration, though the likelihood is that the passage of time will, as always, reveal a different order of significance.

BRASILIA, BRAZIL (left)
The Foreign Office, begun 1957

BERLIN, GERMANY (right)
The AEG Turbine Factory, 1909

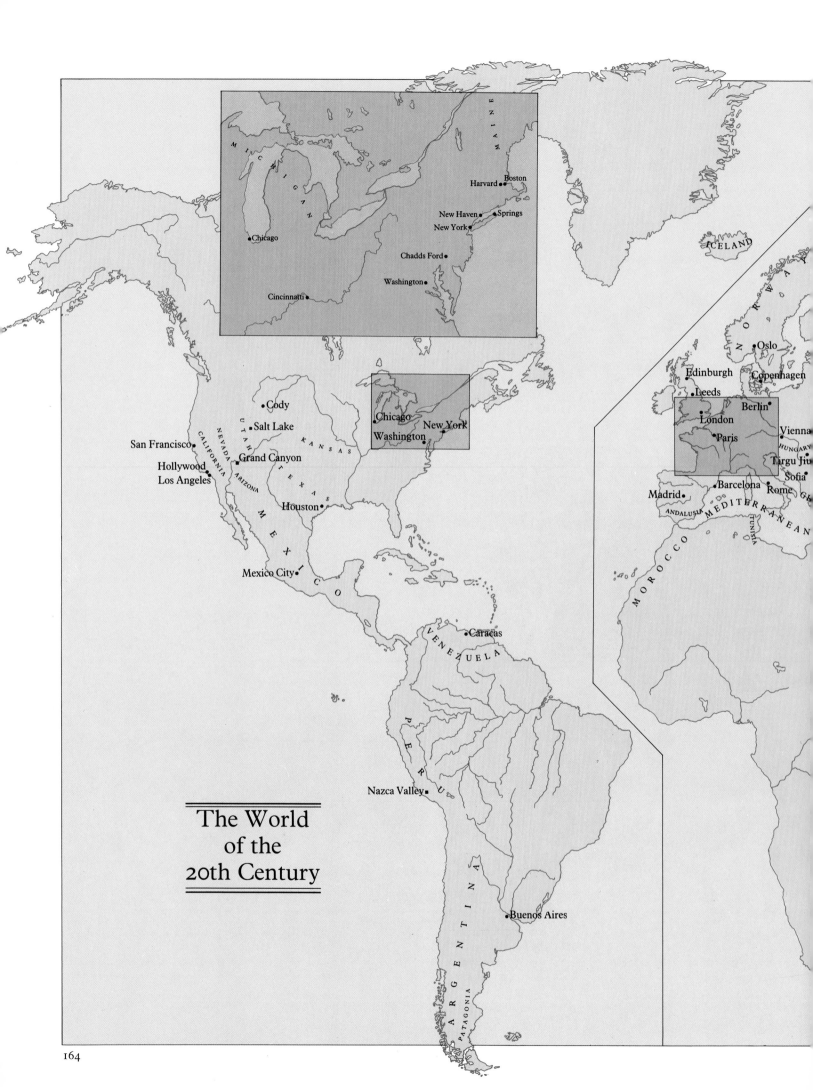

The World
of the
20th Century

Moscow•

•Bucharest

ARMENIA

GREECE

SEA

•Jerusalem

•Cairo

EGYPT

WALES

•Manchester
•Nottingham

•Northampton

Cookham•
•London
Shoreham•

Amsterdam•
Rotterdam• •Amersfoort
         Utrecht

•Düsseldorf

Cologne•
    •Bonn

•Paris

Mannheim•

Zurich•
Berne•

•Guernica

Antibes• •Vence

•Belsen

Berlin•
•Hanover •Dessau

Weimar• •Buchenwald
         Dresden

•Dachau
Munich•

•Salzburg

Venice•

•Bologna

CAMBODIA

•Hiroshima •Tokyo

AUSTRALIA

Sydney• •Little Bay

Melbourne•

165

Dada

The orgy of destruction that convulsed the Western world between 1914 and 1918 checked the progressive spirit that had animated the arts in the years just before. Activity was not stifled (two global wars proved unable to quell Picasso's genius), but the most significant movement took the form of a revolt against the culture and the corrupt, complacent values (many felt) that had encouraged the suicidal massacre of trench warfare. "Modern civilization" was itself to be destroyed, and the instrument to be used was not art but "anti-art" or "non-art"; there was no thought of development or replacement, even if "non-art" proved in fact to hold the seeds of just that, a new art, a new development.

The intense frustration engendered by the War erupted simultaneously in widely separated centres. Its protagonists were mostly very young, in their early twenties, and most had "opted out", avoiding conscription in the shelter of neutral cities such as New York, Zurich and Barcelona. By 1918, however, even before the Armistice, the movement was igniting in blockaded, hungry Berlin, and by the following year the groups were linked by an exchange of visits between the leading figures

and a spectacular barrage of publications – periodicals, revues, manifestos – rather than by exhibitions. The title by which the movement came to be known was "Dada".

Some of the iconoclastic activities of Marcel Duchamp (see over) in New York in 1914-15, and not least his "ready-mades", were precociously Dadaist in spirit, but the movement first started into life as such in Zurich, when Hugo Ball (1886-1927) founded the Cabaret Voltaire there in 1916. With him were associated some who would become famous names in art between the Wars – notably Jean or Hans Arp (1887-1966). The most demonic activist, however, was the Romanian poet Tristan Tzara (1896-1963). All forms of expression were conscripted to serve in the protest – cabaret performances; meetings designed to provoke controversy and even (sometimes successfully) riot; events that had much in common with those to be dubbed in the 1960s "Happenings". The name itself is a nonsense word; accounts of its origin are contradictory, but it is a word common in many languages, and universal in baby-talk the world over. According to Breton, "Dada is a state of mind". According to Arp, "Dada is, like

Nature, without meaning. Dada is for Nature and against Art . . . Dada stands for unlimited meaning and limited means. *For Dadaists life is the meaning of art.*" Dada's first manifesto, by Tzara, 1918, offered no programme, no apologia, no explanation. As a revolt the movement involved a complex irony, being dedicated to the destruction of a society of which it was nevertheless a part, and, almost by definition, there was also dissension in the attitudes of the Dadaists. Henchman to Tzara in Zurich was the volatile Francis Picabia (1879-1953) – Picabia, having participated in Cubism, had already been inciting artistic revolution with Duchamp and Man Ray (1890-1977) in New York and in 1916 in Barcelona. Together in Zurich Tzara and Picabia preached an increasingly subversive view of art and a nihilistic vision of life itself. Ball left for Berne; the German Richard Huelsenbeck (1892-1974), a founding member, had left for Berlin in 1917; when Tzara followed Picabia to Paris in 1920 the Zurich phase of Dada was over.

In Germany, the prime centres were Berlin, Cologne and Hanover. The Berlin version, triggered by Huelsenbeck, was satirical and actively political, its targets more narrowly

ARP (below)
Collages of squares arranged according to the laws of chance, 1916-17
Arp declared that the law of chance could be experienced only by means of a "complete devotion to the Unconscious"; further, that "anyone who followed this law was creating pure

life". His acknowledgment both of an innate creative drive and of a standard of aesthetic beauty sets Arp slightly apart from those Dadaists who were chiefly concerned with chance as an anarchic means of subverting established art; but it led directly into the realms of Surrealism.

MAN RAY (left)
The rope-dancer accompanies herself with her shadows, 1916
Though it is painted in oils, the picture owes a patent debt to collage. Solid blocks of shadow contrast with the delicate star of the dancer and the sinuous line of her rope.

PICABIA (below)
"*M'Amenez-y*" ('Take me there), 1919-20
Nonsensical references in capital letters to pots of castor-oil and crocodile's dentures make up Picabia's provocative, iconoclastic composition; it presages his ultimate outrage, a blot of ink of 1920 that he chose to title *The Blessed Virgin*.

PICABIA (right)
I see again in memory my dear Udnie, 1914
By 1910, soon after he had met Duchamp, Picabia applied his gift for colour to delicate experiments with abstract forms, with a decidedly Cubist bias. In New York in 1913, he developed, in response to

its technological marvels, his "machinist" style; here, mechanical and suggestive biomorphic forms combine in a dynamic composition. Gabrielle Buffet-Picabia once said: "His activity was utterly gratuitous and spontaneous . . . it never had any programme, method or articles of faith."

and precisely defined than elsewhere. Its armament was a number of magazines – *Club Dada, Der Dada* – produced between 1918 and 1920 by Huelsenbeck, in company with one Johannes Baader; Raoul Hausmann (1886-1971) became the editor of *Der Dada*. These periodicals deployed a raucous use of exploded and explosive typography and photomontage. The Cologne version, 1919-20, was by contrast biased towards aesthetics even if only in the sense of being anti-aesthetics. It included two major artists – Arp (see further p.181) and Max Ernst (see p.172). Ernst, with John Heartfield (see p.194), exploited satirical collage techniques using popular printed material, in free play with the grotesque and the weirdly erotic, often foreshadowing Paris Surrealism; the Paris connection was confirmed when Ernst moved there in 1922.

In Hanover, Kurt Schwitters (1887-1948) invented *Merz*. Rejected by Berlin Dada as being too bourgeois, he was nevertheless, of all of them, perhaps the most enduringly committed to Dada principles, stubbornly individualistic, anarchistic and fantastic. *Merz* (a nonsense name from a torn scrap of print with the word *kommerziell*, meaning "commer-

HAUSMANN (above)
The art critic, 1920
Hausmann's photomontage

is typical of Dada weaponry – satiric invention, boast, scorn, ridicule, abuse.

cial") was the title of a magazine (1923-32), and was applied to his art, which he practised in Germany, in Norway, where he took refuge from the Nazi regime in 1937, and from 1940 in England. He never adopted the extreme "anti-art" stance, but he used the detritus of urban life – bus tickets, torn newspaper, cartons, broken bits of wood or metal – in collages or relief montages, transforming his base materials into exquisitely balanced and unified compositions. He was obsessed by the ideal of a *Gesamtkunstwerk*, an art that included all forms of art. His first *Merzbau* (including a chamber named "The Cathedral of Erotic Misery") was an endless construction of bits and pieces that wandered horizontally through the rooms of his house, vertically up through its floors and even out of the windows. This *Merzbau* in Hanover was destroyed by bombs in 1943; another in Norway was burnt in 1951; something of an English version was salvaged by the University of Newcastle.

Paris, though not until 1920, witnessed the climax of Dada, which began with a performance supporting an exhibition and ended in riot. But soon its impetus was sapped, and by 1924 it was ripe for take-over by Surrealism.

MAN RAY (right)
Crossroads, 1934
The leading lights of Dada and Surrealism are featured: from upper left to bottom right are Breton, Ernst, Dali, Arp, Tanguy (who looks oddly "punk"), Char, Creval, Eluard, Chirico, Giacometti, Tzara, Picasso, Magritte, Brauner, Peret,

Rosey, Miró, Mesens, Hugnet and Man Ray. Self-projection was a trait common to most of these artists; they made wide use of their own and each other's *personae* – often bizarrely clothed and posed. In this the forerunner had been Alfred Jarry (died 1907), author of *Ubu Roi*.

BAADER (below)
Collage A 92-22, c. 1920
Baader (Dada name, Ober-Dada) took eccentricity to

its limit; he caused uproar in Berlin Cathedral by shouting at worshippers "Christ is a sausage!"

SCHWITTERS (above)
"Arbeiterbild" (Worker-picture), 1919
The word *Arbeiter*, printed in red on a scrap of paper, gives the collage a name but not a message or purpose – rather, its socialist references are ignored. Stripped of associations, it becomes merely part of a harmony of colours and textures.

SCHWITTERS (right)
Ambleside, 1945-48
Dada tended to underline the original functions of *objets trouvés* in order to make their appearance in other contexts all the more absurd. Schwitters' deeper concern with abstraction led him to use materials in a way that freed them from their mundane identities.

Marcel Duchamp

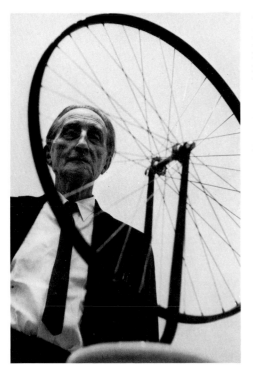

Marcel Duchamp (1887-1968) was the dandiacal cat who walked by himself through the highways and byways of modern art from his first important exhibition in 1912 till his death more than half a century later. Wherever he walked, controversy sprung up in his wake, and since his death his historical importance has become increasingly clear. Two of his brothers also made significant contributions: Raymond Duchamp-Villon was one of the most important sculptors associated with the Cubist movement (see p. 178), his career cut short by premature death, while Jacques Villon (1875-1963; not shown) had a long, very professional career, especially as a printmaker.

Marcel Duchamp became a member of the Cubist Section d'Or group in Paris (see p. 150) in 1912. His early experiments reached their climax in his *Nude descending a staircase*, 1911-12, one of the most famous of all twentieth-century works of art. In it he was clearly aware of Cubist techniques of dismantling an object into its constituent planes, then reshuffling them, and perhaps also of Futurist dynamism (though he denied that); he was certainly also aware of novel photographic techniques which showed the body in progressive stages of a movement, and his *Nude* does just that, but the stages are consolidated into an image of arresting originality. Sensing trouble, Duchamp withdrew it from the Salon des Indépendants exhibition; the following year, in the Armory Show in New York, it aroused clamorous controversy. By then, he was already preparing for his masterpiece, *The bride stripped bare by her bachelors, even*, known as "*The Large Glass*" (still incomplete in 1923, though he then signed it). Work on it began in 1915, in New York, where much of his subsequent activity took place – an activity not so much as an artist but as an iconoclast, an anti-artist and a conceptualist. "I wanted to get away from the physical aspect of painting. I was much more interested in re-creating ideas in painting. For me the title was very important ... I wanted to put painting once again at the service of the mind." His early work had been influenced by Cézanne, by the Fauves; then into the Cubist world he reintroduced the human figure as prime subject, still disintegrating it, but in "*The Large Glass*" presenting it in terms of a pseudo-scientific diagram, in which nonsense mechanisms are activated by human desires.

Marcel Duchamp
Duchamp's art was always intellectual, not emotional, as if it were a chess game of ideas. It was continuous: he reworked, reinterpreted or developed his early, famous works later in life (in 1965, for instance, he exhibited a reproduction of the *Mona Lisa* with the title *Shaved*). It led nowhere, if only in the sense that every gambit implied a counter-gambit; one consistent trend in his later response was that the nature of the art is dependent on its spectator.

DUCHAMP (right)
Nude descending a staircase no. 2, 1912
Duchamp's approach to the abstraction of form was not so analytical or committed as that of the members of Section d'Or, which may explain their disapproval of the painting. But it was no more favourably greeted in the USA. Duchamp's prime inspiration was the mechanics of movement, as the three sets of dotted lines indicate, showing the rotation of the hips as the body moves through space.

AFTER DUCHAMP (right)
Fountain, original 1917
In submitting a urinal for exhibition Duchamp was in effect undermining the assumption, held even by the avantgarde, that a work of art requires an artist. Although the Society of Independent Artists might pride itself on its freedom from bourgeois taste or convention, this *Fountain*, authorless and blatantly vulgar, forced it into just such bourgeois attitudes of outrage as it would condemn in others.

DUCHAMP (left)
A cemetery of uniforms and liveries – the bachelors, 1914
A study for part of the lower half of "*The Large Glass*" shows male sexuality in terms of implements like pistons or syringes. Duchamp called the group "the matrix of Eros".

AFTER DUCHAMP (left)
The bride stripped bare by her bachelors, even ("*The Large Glass*"), original 1915-23
Duchamp's non-picture (it is not an easel-painting, anyway, being on glass) needs an elaborate verbal commentary; even then it defies critical assessment. It is perhaps the first example of Conceptual art, being as much a scheme or a plan as an art object. Essentially it represents the two forces that will also figure in the later "*Etant Donnés*" – male (in the lower panel), female (in the upper). Desire for sexual union is translated into an automatic process, divested of all sentiment but seemingly still prone to chance. This reconstruction was made in 1965-66 by the Pop artist Richard Hamilton.

His first published statement (1915) was entitled *A Complete Reversal of Art Opinions, by Marcel Duchamp, Iconoclast*, and he never ceased to question conventional responses and expectations regarding art. The invention of the "ready-made" principle was also of 1914-15: he claimed the right for anyone to choose virtually any object whatsoever, and by choosing it, and in some cases signing it, to establish it as a work of art. Early specimens were a bottle-rack, a snow shovel and a ventilator; the most notorious the urinal signed *R. Mutt*. The latter, offered for the exhibition of the Society of Independent Artists as *Fountain* in 1917, was rejected. Duchamp resigned. At this period, he was closely associated in New York with Picabia and Man Ray, and promoted two Dadaist revues, *The Blind Man* and *Rong Wrong*. He was indeed the *guru* of the New York Dada movement, and probably the only Dada artist to sustain its anarchic values and contradictions with uninhibited zest during a long career right to the end.

In 1918, he virtually gave up painting, and devoted himself to chess. He created another of the most mesmerizing images of twentieth-century art, simply by endowing a repro-duction of the *Mona Lisa* with a moustache and goatee and subscribing it with an obscene French pun, *L.H.O.O.Q.* (She's hot in the tail). This was another shot against received attitudes to art; it violated the most famous of all masterpieces, contradicted the idea of the sanctity of art and of the value of the unique art object; it swore against good taste – or any taste. "I have forced myself to contradict myself in order to avoid conforming to my own taste." But he also might deny that he was "anti-art": "Whether you are 'anti' or 'for' it's two sides of the same thing."

His work, or his not-work, his life-style, foreshadowed many aspects of mid- and late twentieth-century art. An arch-Dadaist, he became a prophet for the neo-Dadaist elements especially of Pop art. He was a star for the Surrealists. His experiments with "mobiles" – first with a bicycle wheel revolving on a stool – anticipated kinetic art (see p. 180). His exploitation of chance was shared by others but he anticipated the Abstract Expressionists, when "*The Large Glass*" was broken accidentally in 1937, by rejoicing, and incorporating the breaks with loving care in the reassembled work. Perhaps above all he prefigured the Conceptual trend of the 1960s and 1970s. He expected audience participation, believing "it is the SPECTATORS who make the pictures". He lived on paradox; he was cultivated, intensely sensitive and gifted, devoting much time to chess and to calculating the risks of roulette. He refused to live from his art, though towards the end of his life he agreed to allow limited editions of facsimiles of his *Fountain*, doubtless thereby debunking the prestige as a unique art object that the original had acquired since he signed it 50 years before.

Not the least of his baffling and endlessly fascinating innovations was the injection of relentless irony into serious art, the questioning of all accepted values; he took advantage of any fortuitous offering that took his fancy, descending or soaring into coarse buffoonery. Yet in 1961 he stated: "I'm nothing else but an artist . . . I couldn't be very much more iconoclastic any more." After his death, it was revealed that his masterly inactivity of the previous quarter-century had in fact been diverted on and off with the creation of a final masterpiece, a large tableau, "*Etant Donnés*" (Given that . . .), featuring a life-size peepshow of a nude through a door.

DUCHAMP (above)
"*The Large Glass*" (broken state), 1937
In Duchamp's meticulous reassembly of his broken original there was perhaps an urge to rule chance. Systematically paradoxical, paradoxically systematic, he had tried in the 1920s to find a way of always winning at roulette; here he played chance at art.

DUCHAMP (right)
L.H.O.O.Q., 1918
Duchamp's annotated post-card of Leonardo's *Mona Lisa* was first of all one more "ready-made", even if it has also been seen as the quintessential Dada work of art, being at the same time quite puerile and profoundly anarchic. The joke still runs – variations on it keep appearing.

AFTER DUCHAMP (right)
"Ready-made",
original 1913
The wooden stool with a bicycle wheel was the first of the "ready-mades", mass-produced, mundane objects taken out of context and presented to the viewer as art. The adjustment in the viewer's mind was of more significance than the form, to which Duchamp attached no importance, although these works usually reveal his interest in mechanical movement and were fairly new technological devices.

DUCHAMP (below)
"*Etant Donnés*" (Given that . . .), 1946-66
Reinstating in his name the unique art object, Duchamp's widow refuses permission to reproduce what the spectator can see through the cracks in the door – an allegorical peep-show of the human condition? Behind, there is a waterfall, in front of which reclines a nude (sprawling suggestively) with a gas burner – this "illuminating gas" and the cascade are the "given".

Art in Italy: Metaphysical Painting

The most prominent avantgarde group in Italy in the early twentieth century, the Futurists (see p. 152), continued after World War I, but their impetus was spent. With three important exceptions, Italy produced no innovators in art of international renown until rather later – for example, the sculptors Marini and Manzù (see p. 230). The exceptions were Chirico, Morandi and Modigliani; Modigliani really belongs to the "school of Paris" (see p. 182).

Giorgio de Chirico (1888-1978) trained as an engineer before turning to painting, first in Athens and Munich, then settling in Paris in the years of ferment (1911-15). There he moved in avantgarde circles, and was celebrated by the poet and prophet Apollinaire (of whom he painted a famous portrait), and yet he remained essentially unmoved by the French discoveries, from Impressionism to Cubism, though the art of his early period could not have been conceived without the freedom these movements had established. Chirico's concern was primarily with content; form and technique were only the means by which the content could be expressed. He was far closer to the Douanier Rousseau than to such other pioneers as Cubist Picasso, Matisse or Kandinsky. His imagery was essentially figurative and illusionistic, though the illusion was not of the everyday world but of an alternative reality that was later to be called "surreal". In its formulation he owed something to the dreamlike visions of Symbolist painters – his tall and still figures, enveloped in their own isolation, are prefigured in some of the works of Böcklin or Kubin. His strange poetry was certainly influenced by the writings of the philosopher Nietzsche, while his combinations of symbols often seem ready for Freudian analysis.

Chirico's stillness is that between dreaming and waking, and ominous. The setting is urban, the ground is paved, the vistas are of arcaded buildings or monuments under an implacable sultry sky, but civilization has been deserted. The images are described with intense conviction and according to traditional conventions, but the conventions are garbled: obsessed with the poetry of perspective, Chirico played tricks with it, exaggerating it, using different systems in one picture, exploiting it as an emotional device as well as a structural one; the hard light casts shadows, but the lighting is often inconsistent, and the shadows fall like a threat. Chronological in-

CHIRICO (below)
The dream of the poet (Guillaume Apollinaire), 1914
Chirico's picture offers no suggestion of physical likeness. The unidentified, Napoleonic-looking bust in sunglasses, while echoing the blank eyes of classical statues, is also a metaphor for the introspection of the blind seer. Fish-mould and tailor's dummy are images from Apollinaire's poetry.

CHIRICO (below right)
The nostalgia of the infinite, 1913-14
Chirico said that we experience "the most unforgettable moments when certain aspects of the world ... suddenly confront us with the revelation of mysteries lying all the time within our reach, which we cannot see ... Their dead voices speak to us from nearby, but they sound like voices from another planet."

CHIRICO (above)
The mathematicians, 1917
"The phenomenal world", as Nietzsche had once observed, "is the adopted world which we believe to be real." Chirico's pencil-drawing introduces uneasy oddity and confusion into the "most certain" of the sciences – the geometers have become a jumble of their own instruments in a dazzling Cubist parody.

CHIRICO (above)
The enigma of the hour, 1912
The architecture is oddly dislocated so that everyday locations seem mysterious; we are invited to relate them to inner experience by Chirico's emotionally resonant titles. Thus deftly he evokes melancholy, loneliness, departure and the disquieting impassivity of the inanimate world.

CHIRICO (right)
The child's brain, 1914
Underlying Chirico's art was a childlike naivety, a yearning for that state of grace or innocence in which time seems hardly to pass, and in which the incomprehensible is accepted unquestioningly. This sinister looming figure has led some critics towards a Freudian interpretation.

congruities abound – a locomotive may intrude on the timeless townscape, and time itself is sometimes shown stopped. *The enigma of the hour* was painted in 1912, its two tall main figures frozen to statues, the only movement the febrile flicker of the fountain, the clock stopped for ever at six minutes to three.

From about 1915, Chirico's desolate piazzas or stages became increasingly "peopled" with the abandoned equipment of life. Set squares, blackboards and easels, surgeons' gloves etc. congregate around mannequins like tailors' dummies, with egg-shaped heads sometimes bland, sometimes with an ancient symbol for infinity instead of eyes. Chirico returned to Italy in 1915, and in 1917 encountered the Futurist painter Carlo Carrà (see also p. 152); for about a year, Carrà produced imagery obviously inspired by Chirico's vision, but in a more delicate, lyrical mood. This was the brief flowering of the "Metaphysical" school (the adjective occurs earlier in some of Chirico's titles), and its rationale, or rather irrationale, was set out by Carrà in a book, *Metaphysical Painting*, in 1918. There he claimed a continuing validity for Renaissance techniques applied to twentieth-century imagery – of the

irrational, the Unconscious. Chirico's impetus, however, wavered, though he began to be recognized as an artist of major importance. Back in Paris from 1924, he inevitably became associated with the Surrealists, whose vision he had so vividly anticipated, but his own work lost intensity. In the 1920s he worked in the classical idiom widely used at the time, and finally turned back, almost disclaiming his earlier work, to an archaic, purely traditional academic style and subject matter. It is his early work that has lasted, still potent and inexplicably compulsive while the fantasies of many Surrealists already seem period pieces.

Giorgio Morandi (1890-1964) was briefly associated with the Metaphysical school about 1918-19. His still lifes then were confrontations of objects, sharply defined but not behaving according to everyday expectations – casting shadows that do not belong, or presenting an illogical structure. They were painted in much the same grey-green and ochreous palette as Chirico's, and each object, as in Chirico, had its own human presence, isolated in a concentrated stillness. These qualities were to persist, though Morandi's gaze shifted in about 1920, and settled on the three subjects

that were to monopolize the rest of his life – still lifes of everyday utensils (bottles, jugs); vases of flowers; and deliberately unpicturesque, sometimes positively banal landscapes. He worked quietly in Bologna, teaching and painting: his studio was one room in a modest flat. He travelled abroad only once, briefly. His paintings were usually small. It was only towards the end of his life that he was becoming recognized as perhaps the most important painter Italy had produced since 1900 – a twentieth-century Chardin. He was also a master of tonal etching, and his hazy etched landscapes are more compelling than most of his painted ones. He moved away from the harshly delineated techniques of Chirico, and behind his mature vision one can always sense the presence of his first love, Cézanne. His bottles and pots are posed as it were self-consciously: each has its own concentrated individuality, yet the interrelationship of each to each is indissoluble. Morandi's endless variations on his chosen theme are never monotonous, partly because a sense of strangeness persists all through his career – essentially that "Metaphysical" otherness which Chirico, Carrà and he had divined earlier.

CARRA (below)
The engineer's mistress, 1921

Carrà wished, in painting, to "express the mysterious life of ordinary things".

MORANDI (below)
Still life with a pipe, 1918

Even in this early Metaphysical work the objects have a unique intensity.

MORANDI (above)
Still life, 1937
Basic to Metaphysical art was a sense of alienation from everyday reality; but from this attitude Morandi soon departed. His simple arrangements of domestic

objects came to reveal the search for a principle of universal order, recalling again Cézanne in some ways; each is an apprehension of formal relationships hard won from an intense concentration of observation.

MORANDI (right)
Still life, 1938
Morandi's work, unlike that of his fellow Metaphysical painters, shows an interest in the sensuous properties of brushwork. Avoiding the distractions of perspective or a widely ranging palette, he used the delicate shapes of his chosen objects as a means of confining tonally modulated areas of paint. These shimmering objects induce a quiet meditation.

MORANDI (above)
Landscape with the River Savena, 1929
The Emilian landscape is

rendered in broad planes delicately cross-hatched, in varying textures quietly united in a flat pattern.

Max Ernst

In 1961, Max Ernst (1891-1976) revised for publication a selection from his own utterances, autobiographical notes in the third person. The text begins: "First contact with the sensible world: on April 2nd at 9.45 a.m. Max Ernst hatched from the egg which his mother had laid in an eagle's nest and over which the bird had brooded for seven years. It happened in Brühl, six miles south of Cologne. There Max grew up, and became a beautiful child. . . ." Clearly then, the habit of poetic fantasy, the superb egocentricity, the ability to dislocate the structure of the visible world and to reassemble it in the compulsive imagery of an alternative reality, these were all with him in the egg. They were to persist and flourish.

In the first decade of the twentieth century the theories of Freud, the concept of the Unconscious, were becoming widely known, and certainly were relevant to the development of Ernst's imagination. He enrolled in the University of Bonn for a degree in psychiatry, but found academic disciplines distasteful: "The young man, eager for knowledge, avoided any studies which might degenerate into breadwinning." His prime concern was painting. He seems to have been virtually self-taught, but in 1910-11 he saw the work of the most advanced artists: he was also, when visiting asylums, astounded by the art of the insane. August Macke introduced him to the Blaue Reiter group and in 1913 he exhibited with Macke, Kandinsky and others in Berlin. He met Robert Delaunay, and was dazzled by Apollinaire's verbal acrobatics; he made a first short visit to Paris. Early in 1914 he met Jean Arp, a lasting friend and influence.

"On August 1st 1914 Max Ernst died. He was resurrected on November 11th 1918 as a young man who aspired to find the myths of his time." He was in fact a gunner on active service; appalled by the experience of war ("Howl? Blaspheme? Vomit? . . ."), he was ripe for Dada. He found Arp again; he also came across scientific drawings of micro-organisms, and harnessed their strange shapes into a biomorphic imagery that the Surrealists later found irresistible, as did Arp. He discovered Chirico, which sparked off his first collages. "*Aquis Submersus*" (Plunged in the waters) of 1919, perhaps his first major painting, shows a clear debt to Chirico; it was shown at the first Cologne Dada exhibition. At the second exhibition, which was entered through the men's

Max Ernst
Ernst was an exponent of Dada in Cologne; in Paris from 1922, he was one who led it into Surrealism.

ERNST (right)
"*Aquis submersus*" (Plunged in the waters), 1919
The debt to Metaphysical painting is clear – blank, empty space, still statues – but the mood is both weird and almost merry. It rejoices in simple visual puns – the blank reflection in water of the clock-faced moon, an impossible diver inverting the shape of the dummy that grins in the foreground.

ERNST (below)
Katerina ondulata, 1920
The chevron design on the angular construction is in fact a piece of wallpaper, which Ernst has overlaid with gouache in a kind of *papier collé* in reverse.

ERNST (right)
Men shall known nothing of this, 1923
Dedicated to André Breton, the work incorporates many of the Surrealists' *leit-motifs*. A vast sky, an empty desert, are the setting for an erotic theme spelled out by a poem on the back of the canvas, which explains the image as an ideal of cosmic and sexual harmony.

ERNST (below)
The elephant Celebes, 1921
Grotesque mechanical forms that nevertheless suggest humans or animals recur in Ernst's work. This vivid, monstrous mix of vacuum-cleaner and elephant shows a developing Surrealist illusionism; by including some intelligible images within a still irrational composition, the artist can disturb more profoundly than with just the bizarre.

ERNST (above)
Hundred-headed Woman: Germinal, my sister, 1929

Engravings from popular Victorian fiction are set upon by sadism, corruption.

lavatory and which included works offered up for destruction, a collage of his was condemned as pornographic, but the pornographic element in it proved to be Dürer's print *Adam and Eve* (see vol. 2 p. 152). Some of Ernst's work of this time (probably influenced by Picabia) also presents nightmares of mechanical or scientific apparatus animated by human desires, somewhat like Duchamp's.

Ernst was interested neither in the political nor in the caricatural possibilities of Dada. Always attracted to Paris, he gravitated there in 1922. His reputation had preceded him. André Breton, soon to be the major prophet of Surrealism, had organized an exhibition of Ernst's collages in 1920; the greatest Surrealist poet, Paul Eluard, illustrated a volume with Ernst's images. By the time of Ernst's arrival in Paris, the brief Dada explosion there was almost spent, and the movement was ripe for consolidation into an orthodoxy by Breton.

The realistic element in Ernst's work was by now established. For him it was necessary to touch off "the strangest poetic sparks by bringing together two seemingly unrelated elements on a plane unrelated to both" – an effect vividly achieved, for example, by the juxtaposition or conjunction of two widely disparate but realistically rendered objects (such as a female torso and a bird's head) by the collage method. In Paris Ernst, in company with others such as Picabia, Arp, Man Ray, experimented with new techniques for precipitating images hidden in the unconscious mind. By 1923 he was working on paintings in a fully Surrealist vein, and in 1924 Breton announced the official birth of Surrealism as a coherent movement, soon to become a weird orthodoxy, and ultimately a dogma. In 1925, Ernst discovered a technique which was to prove most rewarding for him, *frottage* – a texturing achieved in simple form by rubbing pencil, chalk or even paint on paper laid over strongly grained wood or another textured material; subsequently elaborated by divers methods. This technique served him admirably in those characteristic paintings, at first glance naturalistic visions of moonlit forests, that turn on closer study into fearful dreams.

Ernst was never one to fit easily into an orthodoxy, and committed various heresies against Breton's gospel. His activities were vigorously diverse. His great collage novel, *La Femme Cent Têtes* (Hundred-headed woman), was published in 1929; he collaborated in films with Buñuel and Dali, designed sets and costumes for Diaghilev and the Ballets Russes. In 1938, he quit the Surrealists. In 1941, after being interned in France as an enemy alien, he moved to New York and there was briefly married to his second wife, the collector and art impresario Peggy Guggenheim. The fertility of his imagination, his technical inventiveness and improvisation, flourished unabated: in 1942, in *Man intrigued by the flight of a non-Euclidean fly*, he used a drip technique, preceding Pollock. In 1949, he returned to France, to become ultimately a French citizen. The mood of Ernst's paintings is often reminiscent of the haunted desolations of his great German Romantic predecessor, Friedrich, even if his pictures of the 1930s frequently seem omens of the nightmare about to take substance; his vision of *Europe after the rain*, painted 1940-42, could be a prophecy of the earth's surface in radioactive mutation after the atomic bomb. In his later years, Ernst's mood mellowed; at all times his wit and humour could break free, while his technical virtuosity, his range of glowing colour, are as brilliant as any painter's of modern times.

ERNST (left)
The great forest, 1927
Enchantment and terror, Ernst's feelings when he first entered a forest as a child, are recaptured in the almost fungal effects of his *frottage*, evoking "a new, incomparably vaster domain of experience".

ERNST (right)
Man intrigued by the flight of a non-Euclidian fly, 1942
A puzzled "geometric" man gazes in comic confusion at a fly, its dizzying motion conveyed in drips of paint (from a can circling above).

ERNST (below)
Europe after the rain, 1940-42
Even if inspired only by doodles or random images, such visions are convincing as descriptions of other, wholly credible realities.

Surrealism 1: Figurative

"Surrealism: noun, masculine. Pure psychic automation by which one intends to express verbally, in writing or by other method, the real functioning of the mind. Dictation by thought in the absence of any control exercised by reason, and beyond any aesthetic or moral preoccupation. (Encycl., Philos.) Surrealism is based on the belief ... in the omnipotence of dreams, in the undirected play of thought."

The definition comes from the *Manifesto of Surrealism* published by Breton in 1924. André Breton (1896-1966), the so-called "Pope" of Surrealism, deplored the nihilistic and destructive character of Dada; nevertheless he built on many Dada ideas to create a movement with a comparatively coherent philosophy, although, like Dada, it was as much a total way of life as an artistic credo. Fairly rapidly it developed into an orthodoxy, prone to disruption, heresy and schism, though it was armed (at least in the "Pope's" view) with powers of excommunication.

Surrealism was essentially a revolt against the intellectual concerns of Cubism, against formalist art, Art for Art's sake, against abstraction. Breton himself was a dedicated student of the work of Freud. Initially Surrealism

was primarily literary, claiming as ancestors writers such as Rimbaud, Lautréamont, Jarry or Apollinaire (who had first used the term "surrealist"). "Pure psychic automatism" – the untrammelled expression of the Unconscious – is easier to achieve in writing than in the more complex, more constraining materials of the visual arts, which – especially sculpture – inhibit the desired spontaneity of free association. On the other hand, painting could trap a dream into physical substance, and in the works of Chirico (see p. 170) the Surrealists found a language of dream imagery

that for some seemed almost definitive. Tribal art had again particular significance, and the congruence of incongruous objects, most vividly achieved in Ernst's collages, remained a staple of Surrealist imagery. The ideal text for a Surrealist painting had been provided by Lautréamont's famous phrase, "as beautiful as the chance meeting on a dissecting table of a sewing machine and an umbrella".

The movement early included artists enlisted from the ranks of Dada, some of them major, such as Ernst (see preceding page) and Arp (see pp. 166 and 181). It fostered its own

DALI (above)
*The temptation of
St Anthony*, 1947
Dali has admitted a frank respect for the themes of the European tradition; St Anthony's persecution by the devil is reinterpreted as a confrontation with unconscious forces.

MAGRITTE (right)
Time transfixed, 1939
Some kind of logic in the relationship of seemingly unconnected objects may give Magritte's best work its power to disturb. The fireplace recalls a tunnel, the engine's smoke evokes the function of the hearth.

MAGRITTE (above)
The human condition, 1934
The perfect continuity of the landscape across the easel and window imparts an uneasy sense that the removal of the easel would reveal a frightening void. The idea might have come from the artist's early experiments with collage.

DALI (right)
The persistence of memory, 1931
Dali rejoices in fetishes and obsessions. His famous soft watches were allegedly inspired by the experience of eating Camembert cheese. He loves to set images of decay in a golden glare at once heavenly and sinister. He paints dream-pictures; Magritte made illusions.

major artists, such as Miró, Dali and Magritte, but other major artists, not formally linked with the movement, also began to exploit imagery properly classifiable as Surrealist. Indeed, in the 1920s and 1930s, Surrealism was the dominant avantgarde art in Europe.

Two main trends co-existed. One was dependent on figuration, on the precise reproduction of natural forms – generally juxtaposed, transposed, displaced or mutated far from real situations. The other moved towards abstraction, to an imagery without specific reference to forms found in nature, to forms generated within the Unconscious (see over).

The most remarkable of the figurative painters was the Belgian René Magritte (1898-1967), who perfected an academic, naturalistic, illusionistic technique of accurate, flatly prosy description. Apart from a brief stay near Paris in 1927-30, when he met Breton and exhibited with the Surrealists, Magritte spent a discreet and industrious life in Brussels, painting the impossible with calm and confident conviction. Magritte was the most accomplished disappointer of conventional expectations, exploiting astonishing discrepancies of scale (an apple fills a room; a loco-motive bursts through a giant fireplace); denying the laws of gravity; endowing the sky with a material substance that can be cut out and put on to an easel. His strangeness is heightened by his use of everyday objects: the hero of many of his later pictures is the man in urban uniform – coat, bowler hat, sometimes a brief-case – as expressionless in the even light as a tailor's dummy. The ambiguity of the relationship between the object and its painted image is stressed constantly – a faithful likeness of a pipe, inscribed *This is not a pipe*.

The quietness of Magritte's method had the result that his achievement was for some time undervalued; public attention to the Surrealists concentrated rather on the frenetic activities of the Spaniard Salvador Dali (born 1904), *provocateur-en-chef* of the bourgeoisie from his first association with Parisian Surrealism in 1927 onwards. Like Magritte, however, his technique was that of nineteenth-century academic naturalism, applied to unreal (or a mixture of real and unreal) subjects as if they were real. He worked in many media, in writing, painting, jewellery, film – including, with Luis Buñuel, the famous Surrealist film *Un Chien Andalou* (An Andalusian dog) – but perhaps above all in his own fantastically moustachioed person, in a spectacular public career often virtually like show business – a giant egocentricity powered by an energetic paranoia. His relations with official Surrealism, at first euphoric, later became strained.

A more constricted talent, but one that introduced an individual and enduringly mysterious note into the range of Surrealist imagery, was that of another Belgian, Paul Delvaux (born 1897). In paintings of the 1930s and since he has realized a world of lonely alienation, suburbs of desolation haunted by trains and trams, peopled by silent waiting women who prove on closer inspection to be all identical – perhaps the most intense realization of dream or nightmare achieved by any Surrealist. However, he was not formally associated with the Surrealists; nor was Maurits Escher (1898-1972), a Dutchman. Escher was not strictly a Surrealist at all, though he is most easily considered in that context. His best-known works are his brilliantly calculated games with perspective, presenting with great precision quite different images interpenetrating with such ambiguity that the eye cannot establish where one begins and the other ends.

MAGRITTE (left)
Man in a bowler hat, 1964
The epitome of bourgeois respectability, a bowler-hatted man figures in many of Magritte's meticulous scenes of visual absurdity.

DALI (right)
The Venus de Milo of the drawers, 1936
The image suggests today Melanie Klein's theories that the infant desires to excavate the maternal breast, not only to suck.

DELVAUX (below)
The village of the sirens, 1942
Idealized forms set in a space recalling Chirico evoke an erotic dream.

DALI AND BUNUEL (above)
Still from *Un Chien Andalou*, 1929
A hand swarming with ants is one of the film's milder images; its gruesome early sequence provoked a riot. Breasts, buttocks abounded.

ESCHER (above)
Still life and street, 1937
Tricks of perspective and scale in Escher's work can induce a sense of hallucination in the viewer. His prints became popular in the 1960s "drug culture".

Surrealism 2: Abstract

The representational side of Surrealist art appears at its most successful in the work of Magritte, Dali (at his best) and Delvaux (see preceding page), and in the work of certain other artists who in their variety and achievement escape categorization in any one mode. Picasso (see p. 202) was one, Ernst (see p. 172) was another, and Arp (see p. 181) yet another, and in the 1930s Giacometti, a late-comer. Nor can Henry Moore (see p. 200) be considered without reference to Surrealism, or Surrealism be considered without reference to the continued carryings-on of Marcel Duchamp (see p. 168), Picabia and Man Ray (see p. 166).

The non-representational wing of Surrealism was no less vigorous. The work especially of Arp was more often non-figurative than not, but the major artists most consistently independent of natural phenomena were the Spaniard Joan Miró (born 1893) and the Frenchman André Masson (born 1896), who had studios side by side in Paris and who both joined Breton's Surrealist group at its launch in 1924. For a time both experimented freely with "automatic" drawings, the visual counterpart of the crucial technique or non-technique of Surrealist irrationalism, "auto-matic" writing: its intention was to allow free association so as to find, if possible, an absolutely spontaneous expression. Both found the development of Cubism, whether into the rigid doctrinaire theories of Gleizes, or towards the austere geometric reductions of Mondrian, sterile and inadequate to their needs. Masson's outlook was conditioned permanently by appalling experiences in World War I; he was obsessed by the domination of the rule of tooth and claw in all life, animal or human, and his work is a release of the violence of base instincts. He was himself a violent man, who bellowed emotive phrases while he worked, and often physically attacked unsatisfactory canvases. By 1926 he was exploiting chance and accident as part of his technique: he would scatter sand over canvases previously spread in haphazard areas with glue, and then, at great speed, orchestrate their random configurations and textures into loose rhythms of brushwork and colour. The images that appeared were brutal; they gradually became more specific, and horrific creatures emerged. In 1929, Masson withdrew from the official Surrealist cadre, and some find his work of the 1930s less intense and less successful. How-

TANGUY (below)
The palace of windows at the rocks, 1942
In order to purge himself of all conscious intention, Tanguy is reputed to have painted his randomly titled compositions upside down.

MASSON (above)
Furious suns, 1925
The expressive potential of "automatic" writing and drawing was promoted by Breton, in whose theories Masson found the means to "seize at last the knife immobilized upon the Cubist table". This transformation of Cubism made him, later, a crucial link in the chain from Picasso to Pollock, from Cubism to Abstract Expressionism.

TANGUY (right)
The more we are, 1929
Tanguy taught himself to paint after seeing a work by Chirico in a Parisian shop-window. He had been a sailor, and the memories of his marine experiences are even more obvious in his early works than later, when he enlarged his forms: biomorphic, yet painted in metallic colours, they cast harsh shadows over a landscape of apparent infinity.

MASSON (above)
The battle of the fishes, 1927
Masson's spontaneous line learnt to make shapes, so to speak, in a Cubist school. But Cubist splintering has been energized to express movement, rage, instinct.

MIRO (below)
Dog barking at the moon, 1926
We recognize a few simple figurative images while at the same time allowing that they are visionary elements belonging to another, wholly fantastic, personal reality.

ever, in America during World War II, moved once again by the horror of man's inhumanity to man, he reverted to more "automatic" procedures, and his work of these years influenced the subsequent emergence of the Abstract Expressionist school after the War.

Yves Tanguy (1900-1955), largely self-taught, was taken into the Surrealist squad by Breton, and from 1926 discovered and developed his own vivid and original imagery, a realization of the hallucinatory state of mind in a convincing alternative to the dreams formulated by Chirico. Tanguy's imagery often seems submarine, suggesting an endless sea-bed littered with debris, some of it resembling ominous amoeba-like organisms previously unknown to science. Increasingly he developed the contrasts and variety of his textures, so that his pictures might be classed as a kind of Metaphysical Dutch still-life painting. Forms grew beneath Tanguy's brush under their own mysterious prompting, so he maintained, rather than by any intervention on his part.

The most prolifically various, most genial and also generally the most optimistic of the practitioners of abstract Surrealism was Joan Miró, though Miró himself has always dis-missed suggestions that his work is abstract; for him, his armoury of fantastic forms always signifies real objects. He was, like Picasso and Dali, one of that brilliant breed of new Spanish artists who arrived in Paris in the early twentieth century but, unlike Picasso, he returned constantly from Parisian turmoil to his native country. Immediately after World War I Miró was working in a style of meticulous realism, from which the development of his mature style emerged almost abruptly, like a butterfly from its chrysalis, about 1924-25, certainly encouraged by his contacts with the new Surrealist group. Some commentators on Miró have been obsessed with the sinister overtones in his work, with omens and signals of catastrophe, and in his darker works (especially during and after the Spanish Civil War, 1936-39) such signs are certainly there, but again and again a positive gaiety sparkles from his canvases – ferocious, often, but with the ferocity that one finds in children's art.

Miró's imagery was fully established in a famous canvas of 1926, *Dog barking at the moon*, which one might well suspect to be the original fount from which the comic strip *Peanuts* developed. His strange images tend to be biomorphic, similar to those of Arp, and his fantasy is often close to that of Klee: unknown but convincingly possible organisms take shape, defined in clear outline and sharp lucent colours – primary reds, blacks and whites predominate. Words and phrases sometimes float on the canvas: Miró admitted no differentiation between poetry and painting, and claimed that his work always grew from "a state of hallucination, provoked by some shock or other, objective or subjective, for which I am entirely irresponsible". Irresponsible or not, the initial conception is then marshalled by an unerring sense of design, of space and interval, into a strange formal harmony. During World War II, in Spain, he turned his attention to printmaking, and later to sculpture and especially ceramics. He began afterwards to work on a very large scale, in giant murals such as those for the Terrace Hilton Hotel in Cincinnati (1947; not shown) or the ceramic walls of the UNESCO building in Paris (1958). In his restless inventiveness he was prepared to investigate the possibilities of any medium, often in collaboration with specialist craftsmen, and the fertility of his vision has never slackened in his long career.

MIRO (right)
Painting, 1933
By the 1930s Miró had achieved his full artistic maturity, making dramatic use of colour; against the ground of limited primary colours bizarre, expressive organisms are suspended, absurd, idiotic, profound.

MIRO (above)
Aerial acrobatics, 1934
Miró's inherently graphic imagination tends to revert to linear creatures: these dance, float and wriggle in and about his pictures, apparently engaged in gentle, endearing games, in defiance of the laws of gravity.

MIRO (below)
The wall of the moon, 1958
His growing interest in the interaction of broadly handled abstract lines and colours attracted Miró to large-scale projects – these tiles adorn a wall of the UNESCO Building in Paris.

Cubist Developments

Cubism had been transposed into three-dimensional form, into sculpture, before World War I. Picasso once said that it would be enough simply to cut up an early Cubist painting, then assemble the pieces "according to the indications given by the colour", to be confronted by a sculpture. He had turned to sculpture even before 1910, and was to indicate many of the directions in which twentieth-century sculpture would develop in his *Glass of absinth* of 1914. But his later excursions into welded iron are best considered in relation to the mainstream of his work (see p. 202).

The work of other Cubist sculptors revealed rather different preoccupations, though most "opened up" form as the painters had done, introducing voids where one would expect solids, making out of voids distinct shapes. The two most original experimenters were Raymond Duchamp-Villon (1876-1918), the elder brother of Marcel Duchamp, and the Russian Alexander Archipenko (1887-1964). Archipenko created in his *Walking woman* of 1912 the first pierced-form figure sculpture of the modern era, conveying a dancing rhythm in its abstract arrangement of convex and concave curves. He also experimented with

"primitive" forms, inspired by African and Egyptian art, and with figure constructions cut from glass, wood or sheet metal. His initial vigour, however, later subsided, during a long career, into an increasingly mannered elegance. Duchamp-Villon applied Cubist theory to sculptural form with perhaps the greatest success: his *Horse* of 1914 achieves a fusion of the mechanical and organic in a concentrated expression of elemental energy, of strength and thrust, that seems also to answer Futurist needs – even more than Boccioni's work. But Duchamp-Villon's career was interrupted by war, and he died from fever in 1918.

Other sculptors venturing into the Cubist idiom included Henri Laurens (1885-1954; not shown), Jacques Lipchitz (1891-1973) and Ossip Zadkine (1890-1967). Lipchitz – who heartily disliked the new ideas propagated by Brancusi (see p. 146) – remarked: "Cubism was essentially a search for a new syntax. Once this was arrived at, there was no reason for not employing it in the expression of a full message." His early sculpture, in its marvellous and strong simplicity, remains the most impressive, for instance the justly famous *Bather* of 1915. Subsequently he elaborated style and

ARCHIPENKO (left)
Walking woman, 1912
Here space is expressed for the first time as a volume – holes represent forms, the woman's head and torso. The solid elements echo the painted forms of Picasso, his guitar curves.

DUCHAMP-VILLON (below)
The horse, 1914
There is little left of the naturalistic form, save a suggestion of the horse's head, a leg and a hoof. The subject is animal energy, resolved into spring-like spirals. There are links with Futurism: Duchamp-Villon had met Boccioni in 1913.

PICASSO (above)
The glass of absinth, 1914
Picasso's sculpture was the logical extension of his painting: the spoon is real, like elements in his "synthetic" collages; the bronze vessel is opened out, "analysed", and the whole structure brightly coloured.

ZADKINE (below)
The destroyed city, 1953
A tormented Atlas, both resisting and imploring, Zadkine's pierced bronze is violently contorted and torn. Emulating Rodin's ability to express a state of mind, he achieved a rare concentration of expression.

LIPCHITZ (above)
The bather, 1915
The geometrical precision of Lipchitz's figure evokes architectural rather than natural, human, structure. The sources of inspiration were tribal and archaic objects, which he collected.

content – approaching very close to Juan Gris' later style of synthetic Cubism – during a long and successful career, from 1941 in America. Laurens, a friend of Braque, produced at one point Cubist polychrome reliefs and constructions in wood, plaster and sheet metal, but later on developed a very different style – monumental organic forms, in which a feeling for swelling volume was predominant. Zadkine was never so purely Cubist; he exploited a jagged style, sometimes like a jazzed-up version of Cubism, but his finest achievement came in a few later works, such as *The destroyed city*, 1953, revealing an Expressionist intensity in his memorial to blitzed Rotterdam.

Painting could never be quite the same after the early Cubist developments (see pp. 148-151). Picasso and Braque went their separate ways; indeed, there was a rift between them. Braque, while retaining and exercising to the full that autocratic power over the anatomy of his subject matter which Cubist practice had revealed to him, relaxed from Cubist severity to become one of the most seductive decorative painters of all time, with a profoundly sensuous feeling for texture, for "*la matière*" and for colour. Juan Gris (not shown here) con-

tinued single-mindedly developing a rigorous, cool Cubism during the War and after, until illness sapped his strength before his early death in 1927. But Cubism continued also to provoke counter-movement, dependent but reactive development: "Purism" was the brainchild of Amédée Ozenfant (1886-1966) and Charles Edouard Jeanneret (1887-1965). Its tenets were set out in *After Cubism*, published in 1918: Cubism was held to have lapsed into mere decoration; Purism was a call to order, in which subjective fantasy would be eliminated and a crystalline architectonic structure established. A few paintings of serene clarity emerged, but Ozenfant became more important as a teacher and propagandist, while Jeanneret, under the name of Le Corbusier, went on to become perhaps the most famous of twentieth-century architects.

Fernand Léger (for his earlier work see p. 150) also associated with the Purists; their fascination with simplified machine forms was highly congenial to him. He, however, enriched the rather narrow and ultimately arid Purist doctrine with ingredients rejected by the Purists as impure, amongst them a profound sense of solidarity with working people,

brought home by his experience with "miners, navvies, workers in wood" in the Engineering Corps during World War I. He had also been dazzled by the beauty of machinery, such as "the breech of a 75 mm gun, which was standing uncovered in the sunlight; the magic of light on white metal ... Once I had got my teeth into that kind of reality, I never let go of objects again." He came to see painting as a reflection of – even a confrontation with – twentieth-century technology: "The work of art must bear comparison with the manufactured object." In fact a painting such as "*Le Grand Déjeuner*" (The feast) of 1921 amounts to a statement of serene classicism, almost a contemporary reformulation of Poussin, though despite its "Grand Manner" it retains an intimate charm. In the mid-1920s Léger was still painting in an essentially Purist manner – highly formalized still lifes. Later, this austerity was relaxed (see p.229) in favour of freer contours and looser spatial arrangements. But his integrity and his certainty of touch held fast throughout his career, while he was able to respond imaginatively to all kinds of contemporary work: "Léger", as Ozenfant said, "can make good Léger out of anything."

BRAQUE (above)
Kanephoros, 1922-23
Braque's series of Greek basket-carriers is sombre, but his fluid brushwork has a lush, decorative ease.

OZENFANT (left)
The jug, 1926
The Purists felt Cubism had become too whimsical, too like "embroidery and lace-making", when it had a mission to accomplish. Like the artists forming De Stijl at the same time, about 1917, the Purists shared a common style, governed by a geometric precision and by economy of means; but the Purist pictures were figurative. Theirs was an art for the contemporary world, but it had a timeless quality and a universal validity that recalled Neoclassicism. Ozenfant painted vases and vessels of everyday life in a sharp-edged style, in flat, rather deep colour.

LEGER (left)
"*Le Grand Déjeuner*"
(The feast), 1921
A time-honoured theme is matched by a monumental style; here, in contrast to the engine-like dynamism of early Léger, the figures are static. Yet they have a mechanical impersonality: their rounded limbs have a metallic form and texture.

LEGER (below)
Still life with arm, 1927
Léger's early fascination with mechanical forms and everyday life foreshadowed his "New Realism", an art in which objects robbed of their normal values become symbols of a new world. An arm is isolated, no longer human, and bowl and fruit are fragmented in what still is a Purist kind of Cubism.

Sculpture between the Wars

The once relatively firm divisions between the branches of the arts began to dissolve in the twentieth century. Major and minor artists tended to experiment in all sorts of media; in particular, painters frequently turned to sculpture – not only Picasso (see p. 202) and Matisse but also Ernst, Dali (see p. 175), Magritte, Miró. Already by 1913 Marcel Duchamp was including non-sculpture in his non-art campaign: when he mounted a freely revolving bicycle wheel on a kitchen stool (see p. 169), he announced not only the "ready-made" – and the right of the artist to make anything a work of art or part of one simply by selecting it – but also the beginning of one of the major innovations of twentieth-century art, moving sculpture. By 1920 he had even begun to experiment with optical effects in his *Rotative plaques*, which foreshadow kinetic and Op art in the third quarter of the century.

Brancusi and the Cubist sculptors had opened up the main avenues to be explored in standing sculpture. In eliminating superficialities to reveal the essential core and shape of mass, Brancusi (see p. 146) brought the sculptor back into harmony with his material, sponsoring "direct carving". The Cubists (see

preceding page) were primarily modellers or constructors, opening up the solid mass, giving value to voids, and exploiting new materials, such as welded iron. The scope or subject matter of sculpture ranged from the surreal to Constructivist abstraction.

The Russian Constructivist Naum Gabo, actively involved with Revolutionary art in Russia after 1917 (see p. 159), by 1922 realized that abstract art for the foreseeable future had no home in the communist state. He moved to Berlin in 1922, and his elder brother Antoine Pevsner (1886-1962) followed him in 1923. These two transplanted Constructivist principles and practices into the West. They defined their art in their *Realist Manifesto* of 1920 as "the realization of our perceptions of the world in the form of space and time . . . We construct our work as the universe constructs its own, as an engineer constructs his bridges, as a mathematician his formula of the orbits." The Constructivist sculpture existed simply as an object in its own right, governed by its own laws, but crucial importance was attached to the concept of movement: "A new element, kinetic rhythm, is the basic form of our perception of real time." Gabo's first kinetic

PEVSNER (below)
Marcel Duchamp, 1926
Pevsner had met Duchamp in Berlin in 1923. His little "homage" portrait consists of copper (originally zinc) and celluloid plates set on a wooden ground: he had in Gabo's celluloid heads of this period some precedent, but the faceted construction most recalls early Cubist portraits. A strong spirit inhabits its robotic form.

DUCHAMP (left)
Rotative plaques, 1920
Duchamp's experiments in kinetic art and in an art of optical illusions were spiced with a fine sense of the futility of it all – gadgets without purpose.

GABO (below)
Kinetic sculpture (Standing wave), 1920
Gabo made his first motorized construction in 1920. The vibrating rod creates in time a defined space, neither a mass nor a void.

PEVSNER (above)
Torso, 1924-26
Pevsner first produced sculpture in the 1920s. His thin copper sheets enclose spaces which form the volume of the torso, "utilizing emptiness and liberating us from solid mass" (*Manifesto*, 1920).

GABO (right)
Sculpture at Bijenkorf's, Rotterdam, 1954-57
Searching for a huge, free-standing image, Gabo came upon the idea of a tree of steel, its members twisting like branches. He said his sculpture was "the image of order – not of chaos".

construction (1920) was an erect moving rod, electrically oscillated. Later, he abandoned physical movement in favour of movement indicated or implied. He experimented continually with new materials, especially flexible and transparent plastics. The commission for the Bijenkorf Store in Rotterdam enabled him at last (1954-57) to realize his concepts on a monumental scale, in a steel and bronze wire construction nearly 26 metres (80ft) high. Gabo's brother Pevsner turned, under his influence, from painting to sculpture, and subsequently often achieved an exquisite marriage of high precision and poetry, echoing machine forms; Pevsner was always essentially concerned with movement.

Constructivist austerity did not evoke a wide popular response. The American Alexander Calder (1898-1976) moved towards a more sensuous poetry: initially an engineer, his fantastic experiments with animated toys excited Surrealist attention. Contact with Miró but also, more unexpectedly, with Mondrian influenced his first "stabiles", free-standing metal structures with moving elements; these in turn flowered into his famous "mobiles" (the term was coined by Duchamp). These

were inspired by the idea of "detached bodies floating in space, of different sizes and densities ... some at rest while others move in peculiar manners. Symmetry and order do not make a composition. It is the apparent accident to regularity that makes or mars a work." His career continued long after 1945 (see p. 231).

A still closer connection with living matter was developed by Jean (Hans) Arp, a poet as well as a sculptor. Early linked with Max Ernst and with Dada (see p. 166), he was associated with the Surrealists from the time he first exhibited with them in Paris in 1925. By 1914 he had experimented with coloured reliefs of cut-out plywood, abstract, but expressed in biomorphic shapes. With Sophie Taeuber (1889-1933; not shown), whom he married, he worked in paper, tapestry, collage, creating "pictures that were their own reality, without meaning or cerebral intentions". Arp intended his material to take on its own shape; it was the role of the artist to create the conditions in which the work of art could create itself. His commitment to nature, however, was unshakable: "Art is a fruit on a plant, like a child in its mother's womb." This principle was developed more fully in the 1930s, when he turned

to modelling and then carving in the round: his organic forms are highly successful, best in marble, pure white and smoothly rounded, complete and superb alternatives to nature's own organic forms. In these he often came close to Brancusi, still active if aloof like a sage in his white studio (see p. 146).

The early work of Alberto Giacometti was perhaps more essentially Surrealist than was Arp's or Calder's – especially the series of enigmatic, magical constructions he made before his break with official Surrealism in 1935. Subsequently his work was to be much more Expressionist (see p. 232). Julio González (1876-1942), compatriot and friend of Picasso in Paris, was a prime innovator in the application of techniques of forging and welding iron to sculpture. Though very close to Picasso, in the 1930s he developed an independent, tough vein of imagery; starting always from the human figure, he achieved a formidable austerity and strength.

Many of the major sculptors of the 1930s (such as Henry Moore – see p. 200) consolidated their careers after World War II, but almost all the post-War developments are to be found in embryo in the work of the 1920s.

CALDER (above)
Romulus and Remus, 1928
Like Klee, Calder "took a line for a walk", but a walk in space, with a line of wire. The twins suckled by a wolf are figurative; later Calder became more abstract, but not completely so; simpler, but always light, fanciful.

ARP (below)
Human concentration, 1934
Arp regarded his sculpture as "concrete", not abstract – his forms are organic, not artificial, conditioned by his chosen material, and derived from nature. The artist's Unconscious and chance played their part.

GIACOMETTI (left)
The cage, 1932
Associating with Arp and Miró in Paris, Giacometti created subtly suggestive sculptures, rediscovering strangely altered in them when completed "images, impressions, facts which have deeply moved me".

GONZALEZ (right)
Maternity, 1934
González evolved his daring reduction in welded iron in the 1930s, uniting "real with imaginary forms ... suggested by established points or perforations." New forms evolved through truth to these new materials.

Modigliani: Chaim Soutine

In 1917 in Paris Amedeo Modigliani (1884-1920) painted Chaim Soutine. Modigliani and Soutine were colleagues and drinking companions. Modigliani set his friend within the rather narrow compass of a tall canvas, which he had by then established as his chosen format for single portraits. Cézanne had used a similar scheme, and Modigliani had been impressed no doubt by Cézanne's example, his unflinching confrontation with his sitters; but the format also accentuates Modigliani's characteristically elongated, attenuated vision. His subject is reduced to an almost schematic formula of a long oval (the body, with the hands looped to clasp somewhat primly) linked to a second, smaller oval (the head) by an elongated neck (when his sitter was female, it grew sometimes swan-like). In Soutine's portrait there is a minor elaboration in the formula, provided by the compartmentation of the picture space by the corner of the room and by the rudimentary table with the glass, perhaps witness to their shared interest. However, the variations that Modigliani achieved within this simple, almost monotonous scheme were remarkable: Chaim Soutine is subtly but strongly characterized, an individual human being. Details are subordinate to the painter's need for a certain balance and rhythm in the composition, but the likeness is there, even though the neck is long and the eyes somewhat eccentrically aligned. There is surely a reflection of Soutine's character in the handling, and especially in the choice of colour. In his early paintings, Modigliani relied on a very limited, rather sombre palette of ochres, greys, browns and beautiful muted reds (with a pale fluid blue glint for the eyes); the strong colours used here may acknowledge the violence of colour of Soutine's own painting (see over).

Modigliani's colours may well have been influenced by the similar palette of Cubist painting, or even by that of Cézanne, but otherwise, apart from occasional angular distortions (which as much reflected the idioms of African art), Modigliani's style was not fundamentally affected by the Cubist revolution. His work vividly illustrates just how cogent traditional figurative painting can be in the hands of a great talent, taking what seemed profitable from avantgarde explorations and proceeding along its own course. Modigliani, from an Italian Jewish family, academically trained in Italy, came to Paris in 1905 or 1906. He rapidly established the Douanier Rousseau and Picasso as his idols, but his dependence on Italian tradition was ineradicable, and his linear fluency, his elegance, seem to echo Florentine Mannerist art, or Botticelli.

One might not perhaps guess from this portrait that both Modigliani and Soutine belonged to that group of artists sometimes known as *les peintres maudits* – doomed or accursed painters, the archetypal Bohemian artists of popular legend. Modigliani, however, was fatally infected by tuberculosis even before he came to Paris, and there his excesses of drink and drugs, combined with extreme poverty, hastened his death at the age of 36; the macabre coda to which was the suicidal fall of his mistress Jeanne Hébuterne with their baby daughter from a fifth-floor window the following day.

His legend, and the strict, even mannered limitations within which he worked, have in part obscured the remarkable strength and subtlety of Modigliani's work. Besides portraits, he also painted nudes, again in the same sinuous elongations, but with a freshness both pristine and evocatively sensuous. His modelling is achieved by the subtlest gradation of tone and hue; the dominant quality is always linear, and some of his prolific drawings are masterpieces of comprehensive economy. His ambitions as sculptor were furthered by Brancusi's example; he created in a series of tall enigmatic stone heads, in which an African mystery is combined with that of Archaic Greece or Egypt, some of the most haunting "archetypal" images of modern art.

MODIGLIANI (below)
Reclining nude, c. 1919
So harmonious and graceful is the line that one does not at first notice a dislocation of hip and torso as radical as any to be found in Matisse. Though the older man exercised a profound influence over Modigliani, studies such as this seem also to refer back to the great European tradition of reclining nudes, to Giorgione and Ingres – more sensuous than Manet.

MODIGLIANI (below)
Head of a young woman, 1907
The cool, subdued tones are typical of what the artist later liked to dismiss as his "Whistler period". His work became brighter and more sculptural after the major Cézanne exhibition of 1907.

MODIGLIANI (left)
Study for a stone *Head,* 1909-15
The severely simplified shapes give the impression of being exercises in pure geometric drawing which, almost fortuitously, come together to suggest a human face. Within this reduction of form to essentials there is also a cool spirituality that is even more apparent in the carved stone *Heads.*

MODIGLIANI (right)
Head, 1911-12
Tuberculosis forced the artist to abandon sculpture in 1915; however, in a few years he had created from a knowledge of West African figures and Greek *Kouroi* some immensely powerful images. These heads have a refined monumental grandeur, confuting any notion of Modigliani's art as slight.

MODIGLIANI
Chaim Soutine, 1917

The School of Paris

The label "school of Paris" indicates a climate of opinion, an arena of artistic activity, rather than a coherent style prevailing in Paris in the 1920s and 1930s. The city's standing as the major centre of European art had been clearly established during the nineteenth century, and then in the brief years of the Cubist revolution before 1914. Once World War I was over Paris resumed its ascendancy as the leading art market of the world, sustained not only by artists but also by dealers, patrons and an interested public frequenting exhibitions that often provoked invigorating controversy and scandal. Paris was also the global centre for *haute couture* and *haute cuisine*, and much Parisian art answered comparable appetites for the sensuous and delectable. But the best of it was also informed by traditional French virtues – Chagall later said that on his arrival in Paris in 1910 he went directly "to the heart of French painting, where everything showed a definite feeling for order, clarity, an accurate sense of form".

An astonishing profusion of artists resident in Paris were foreign-born. Spain provided not only the major luminary, Picasso, but also Gris, González and Miró, and Dali arrived in

the late 1920s. There came Modigliani from Italy, Mondrian from Holland, Brancusi from Romania. From Russia came Chagall, Soutine, Zadkine, Pevsner, Larionov and others, and finally Kandinsky. The ferment of ideas, the scope for spectacular individuality, the atmosphere of political, religious and social tolerance, these were no less potent magnets for artists than the prospects of a livelihood, which sometimes anyway did not materialize.

The impact of Cubism was registered by all artists of any stature working in Paris, but in varying and very different degree; those who developed more or less within its original principles are considered on page 178, and Picasso himself on page 202. The painters generally grouped as "school of Paris" turned to the figurative rather than the abstract – they included Picasso and Utrillo, for example, rather than Brancusi or Mondrian. The figuration often had a romantic tinge – Pascin's Bohemian prostitutes, Balthus' erotically wistful adolescents, the sinuous languor of Modigliani's men and women (see preceding page). Especially Matisse's continuing work, though he was living as much on the Riviera as in Paris, accorded with this dominant mood.

UTRILLO (above)
Sacré Coeur, Paris, 1937
Utrillo evoked a Sunday afternoon Paris, a sleepy monotony of Montmartre streets and squares that the bustle of tourists has now disturbed. His charm derives largely from the directness of the design, its easy understatement, its lightly touched colour.

PASCIN (below)
Nude with a green hat, 1925
Pascin was a member of a circle including artists as diverse as Modigliani and Chagall and Soutine. His dreamy female nudes recall both Impressionism (Renoir) and Symbolism (Redon and others), but reveal a study, too, of Cubist structure.

MATISSE (right)
Odalisque in red trousers, 1922
That superb patterning of line and colour evolved in Matisse's early work (see p. 144) was developed and enriched still further in

the lush harem settings of his *Odalisque* series. The flat decorative elements are offset by the rounded form and radiant flesh of the nude; Matisse reworks Delacroix and Renoir in his own unheady, unheated idiom.

SOUTINE (above)
Oscar Miestschaninoff, 1923
In 1923, the year in which his reputation was firmly founded in Paris due to the patronage of the American collector Dr A. C. Barnes, Soutine painted his friend and fellow-Russian, the sculptor Miestschaninoff (1886-1969). Through bold distortions of form and of colour, Soutine expressed nevertheless alienation and distrust: Miestschaninoff becomes a pained Pierrot.

SOUTINE (right)
The carcase of an ox, 1925
Soutine is reported to have said: "In the body of a woman Courbet was able to express the atmosphere of Paris – I want to show Paris in the carcase of an ox." In the 1920s Soutine's painting came increasingly close to the northern genre tradition – to Chardin and to Rembrandt, whose *Flayed ox* (see vol. 2 p. 246) was in the Louvre. Soutine visited abattoirs, and even brought a carcase home to paint.

Maurice Utrillo (1883-1955) was born into the purple of romantic artistic legend, the illegitimate son of Suzanne Valadon, dishwasher, acrobat, model, friend and mistress to great Impressionist painters and, not least, an artist of considerable talent. Utrillo himself became an alcoholic before he was 20. He established, largely self-taught, a highly personal vision of streetscape, often empty and shuttered, melancholic, expressed most typically in a subdued palette of greens, greys and pale blues over a predominant white: though repetitive, he was a master of the poetry of the Parisian banal. Chaim Soutine (1894-1943), Russian-born, arrived in Paris in 1913 and became a close ally of Modigliani. His violent and impassioned style surely owed much to van Gogh (even if he denied it); though he was a profound admirer of Cézanne, his vision had an explosive quality. His subject matter was often macabre – for example carcases, overtly inspired by Rembrandt. His landscapes could swirl as if molten, but perhaps his greatest strength was in figure studies and portraits, in which his distortions and savage brushwork and colour contrasts were tempered by a delicate perception of character. Jules Pascin

(1885-1930), born in Bulgaria of Spanish-Jewish and Italian stock, worked in Paris from 1905, and again from 1922 until his death by suicide. Between 1914 and 1920 he was in the United States, and took American citizenship; his reputation was higher in America and Germany than in Paris, but in the exotic gaiety, the sophistication of his drawing and his delicate colour, he has seemed to others very French – and he could reveal both the frivolity and the ugliness of the Parisian *demi-monde* with an incisiveness worthy of Lautrec.

The Russian Marc Chagall (born 1887) is also generally described as "school of Paris", but escapes categorization with the same effortless levitation as the figures that hover in mid-air and swoop and swirl in his pictures. His "Naive" style and his imagery deriving from Jewish folklore absorbed what they needed, and no more, from successive Cubist revelations; Breton in due course was to salute him as a Surrealist – with Chagall, he said, "The metaphor made its triumphant entry into modern painting." In the threatened, anti-Semitic climate of the 1930s Chagall's imagery seems to have become clouded, but after the War the infectious joyfulness of his

visual poetry rekindled, and in a great variety of media. He had become a master of print-making before World War I (working especially for Vollard), and afterwards he branched out into ceramics and stained glass, and theatre design. But his style remained remarkably coherent, governed by his delightful, if often inexplicable, fantasy world.

Other exiles included the Russians Eugène Berman, an inventive stage-designer above all, and Pavel Tchelitchew, who was also a theatrical designer, and a Surrealist (both of these are associated more with New York than with Paris) and Balthus (Balthasar Klossowski de Rola, born 1908). Of Polish origin but born in Paris, Balthus worked alone and secluded for many years and became widely known only late in life; his peculiar ability was to produce strange atmospheric tensions in delineating the psychological unease of adolescence with minutely detailed realism.

Many artists of the school of Paris were scattered by World War II, and after it most lived elsewhere, while the art scene became decentralized and international, though it focused dramatically for a time after 1945 on the school of New York.

CHAGALL (left)
The cock, 1928
The Unconscious was for Chagall a bottomless well of imagery, but he could not accept the Surrealist attempt to exploit it at the expense of the artist's control. Here, the cock and its circus-like rider are fused in consummately balanced harmony of line and stippled colour, in an exquisitely luminous space.

BALTHUS (below)
The living room, 1941-43
The conventional realism of the bourgeois living room is strangely, paranormally, disturbed by the strained poses taken by the young girls; Balthus evokes the quiet dawn of their sexual desire. The space is still, laden with unearthly calm; an abstract rhythm unites shapes across the surface.

CHAGALL
The Asher window, Haddassah University Medical Centre, Jerusalem, 1960
The cycle of 12 stained-glass windows symbolizes the 12 tribes of Israel with zodiac signs, animals and

a host of other images, but not the human form, in compliance to Mosaic law. Chagall's religious ideals and his sense of the past have increasingly animated the fantasy world of his painting, and in Jerusalem found fitting expression.

Art in Holland: De Stijl

During the 1914-18 War Holland successfully maintained her neutrality. In relative stability a small group of Dutch artists was able to consolidate a movement in art that would have perhaps a more pervasive influence in the Western world than any other in the twentieth century, though most lastingly in the fields of architecture and applied design. The leading spirits were Piet Mondrian (1872-1944) and Theo van Doesburg (Christian Emil Maries Küpper, 1883-1931); the movement took its name from its journal *De Stijl* (The Style), first published in 1917 and last in 1932, with a memorial number for van Doesburg. By then the movement had fragmented. Bart van der Leck (1876-1958) was initially an important representative in painting, and the major sculptor was the Belgian Georges Vantongerloo (1886-1965), moving towards geometrical constructions based on mathematical calculations, which were to influence architects perhaps more than fellow-sculptors. Among the architects and designers the most important was Gerrit Rietveld (1888-1964). Mondrian, the most important representative in all Europe of the Constructivist trend, is considered separately (see over), although he was,

with van Doesburg, the most articulate apologist for the underlying philosophy and theory of De Stijl (which he preferred to call Nieuwe Beelding, or Neo-Plasticism).

This Dutch group, with members representing various disciplines, had initially a greater coherence and wider ambitions than most avantgarde Parisian groups – it was almost like an academy. In the first issue of *De Stijl*, van Doesburg expressed its aim – "to state the logical principles of a style now ripening, based on a pure equivalence between the age and its means of expression . . . We wish to pave the way for a deeper artistic culture,

based on a collective realization of the new awareness." The rampant individualism and subjectivity that had become the norm from Romanticism onwards was to give way to an essentially classical, anonymous, collaborative art with a universally comprehensible frame of reference. The group hoped to create for all aspects of life total environments unified in a coherent style. In practice, like most avantgarde novelties, De Stijl was initially treated mostly as outrageous and meaningless.

The commitment was to an abstraction of a ruthlessly austere order – a reduction of form according to a strict grammar of flat surfaces,

VAN DOESBURG (right)
Contra-composition V, 1924
Van Doesburg issued the manifesto of Elementalism, his splinter movement, in 1926, but between him and Mondrian there had been trouble before that. Van Doesburg remained true to the right angle, but with his diagonals deliberately destabilized his pictures. He was influenced by the dynamic abstracts of the Suprematist Malevich.

VAN DOESBURG (above)
The cow, 1916-17
Two intermediary stages explained how the final abstract arrangement was developed from the model.

VAN DOESBURG (below)
The card-players, 1916-17
The subject and the basic scheme is taken, in homage, from the series by Cézanne, but not the rigid flatness.

VAN DOESBURG (right)
The card-players, 1917
Even in this strictly De Stijl painting there is a volatility of movement foreign to Mondrian.

straight lines and right angles. Colour was cut back to three primaries, red, yellow, blue, and the neutrals, white, black and grey. But in the minds at least of the artists concerned these stark essentials were radiant with symbolic life, and reflected an underlying ideal unity and harmony of the universe – a concept derived in part from oriental mysticism and Western theosophy. Specifically, visual equivalents for the basic facts of nature were found in the vertical (the active principle) and the horizontal (the passive); the three primary colours could embrace all emotions, and black and white were clear as night and day. A longing for a universal style had emerged before; De Stijl stripped off all the frills.

Van Doesburg's works, though highly competent, often seem to illustrate a theory rather than to live as paintings in their own right; he was above all a restless, roving, tireless propagandist for abstract art. In his early work, as in Mondrian's, the initial process of abstraction can be traced as if through demonstration models. His *Card-players* of 1916-17 reflects the impact of Cubism and of Cézanne, but the figurative theme is reduced to a patterning of flat shapes and colours, with straight lines

predominant. Shortly afterwards, van Doesburg distilled the composition down to a schematic design expressed purely in terms of straight lines, and it would be impossible for the onlooker who was not aware of the first version to divine its origins. His famous *Cow* was exhibited beside a photograph of a standing cow in profile, with a demonstration of the principles and stages in the creation of a geometrical abstraction from a natural theme.

Having arrived about 1918 at variations on the theme of rectangular shapes distributed according to a proportional system – less spare, but perhaps more mathematically logical than Mondrian's – van Doesburg evidently found his pictures a little tame. In the early 1920s he introduced strong diagonals, which seem positively violent in contrast to Mondrian's purities of that decade. Van Doesburg's *Contra-compositions* were more dynamic and better attuned to the 1920s tempo; Mondrian found them heretical, and there was a rift between the two artists. Van Doesburg, the champion of abstraction, was always prepared to modify his art in the light of other developments – he associated with Dadaists, with the Bauhaus and (as also was Mondrian) with the

Parisian Abstraction-Création group, who were profoundly influenced by De Stijl.

Van der Leck, having entered into simplifications much like van Doesburg's perhaps as early as 1910, had reached by 1918 a most elegant and precise symmetry – in his *Composition* of that year, for instance, the elements are balanced with an unarguable finality; it proved perhaps a dead end, and in the 1920s he began to move back into a more figurative idiom. De Stijl principles were given three-dimensional form by Vantongerloo; his structures were built in straight-edged, cubical blocks until well into the 1930s, when he introduced curves; "I might have known", Mondrian somewhat resignedly commented on this latest deviation. But set in motion amongst the applied arts De Stijl principles proved astonishingly fertile and enduring: Rietveld's classic armchair of 1922 – looking as if it were built to a blueprint by Mondrian – would not seem out of place in a shop today. De Stijl ideals of clarity, certainty and order have been abroad in the world of art ever since, although perhaps only Piet Mondrian, the major prophet and practitioner of the movement, kept faith until death with its principles.

MONDRIAN (right)
Composition, 1917
Mondrian's progress in abstract painting until 1917 had been gradual and independent; with the birth of De Stijl he was affected by joint developments, and his work came very close to that of van Doesburg and van der Leck. This was desirable; it was consistent with a belief in universal values, with the pursuit not of a style but of the style.

VAN DER LECK (below)
Composition, 1918
Van der Leck was in part motivated by his social concerns to join De Stijl, with its Utopian ideals. He did not have Mondrian's single-minded commitment to abstract painting, and in his abstracts chose not to reject diagonals. Here nevertheless the urge to reduction is strong; only one detail obstructs total symmetry of the shapes.

RIETVELD (left)
Armchair, 1917
The spare, uncompromising rigour of the chair demonstrates De Stijl tenets just as fully as the paintings.

VANTONGERLOO (above)
Construction of volume relations, 1921
The straight line, the right angle, the flat surface reign supreme, as in the paintings.

Mondrian: Composition in Yellow and Blue

Towards the end of his life Piet Mondrian wrote: "It is important to discern two sorts of equilibrium in art – (1) Static balance (2) Dynamic equilibrium ... The great struggle for artists is the annihilation of static equilibrium in their paintings through continuous oppositions (contrasts) ... Many appreciate in my former work just the quality which I did not want to express, but which was produced by an incapacity to express what I intended to express – dynamic movement in equilibrium." At first glance *Composition in yellow and blue*, a classic specimen of Mondrian's most successful period, the 1920s and 1930s, may indeed impress the spectator as a precisely static balance; only on longer contemplation does the

tension between the component forms become more positive and vital. The forms – seven rectangles, one yellow, one blue, the rest pure white, compartmented by black lines of varying thickness – are a consequence of Mondrian's early discovery "that the right angle is the only constant relationship, and, through the proportions of dimension, its constant expression can be given movement, that is, made living". Mondrian's ability to avoid inertness in the most austere designs becomes clear when successive variations on a compositional theme are considered together: though the basic formula in each case is the same, the number of satisfactory resolutions appears infinite.

Piet Mondrian, born in Amersfoort, near Utrecht, was trained in Amsterdam in the prevalent Dutch naturalist tradition, but was soon affected by modern trends – Symbolism, Neo-Impressionism. Almost from the start a pronounced feeling for linear structure and a strong contrast between horizontal and vertical shaped his compositions; constant throughout his career was the ascetic austerity of his spiritual quest for essential truth. (It owed much no doubt to his strict Calvinist background; he was a committed theosophist, and deeply influenced by the philosophical writings of Schoemaekers.)

In 1911-14 Mondrian was in Paris, and was attracted by Cubist theory and practice, but "gradually I became aware that Cubism did not accept the logical consequences of its own discoveries, it was not developing abstraction towards its ultimate goal, the expression of pure reality". Mondrian's urge to extract the essence is illustrated in variations on several themes early in his career, of which those on the tree are the most famous – moving from relatively naturalistic drawing, through vividly unnaturalistic and expressive colour, to linear and faceted simplification, resolved in nearly complete abstraction.

In Amsterdam, during World War I, Mondrian found sympathetic support for his views especially from Theo van Doesburg; De Stijl was established (see preceding page). In 1919

Mondrian moved back to Paris, where he remained until another war drove him first to London, then to New York. His living quarters in Paris were eloquent of his commitment to De Stijl theories – floor, walls and furniture were all integrated into a unity of design, a total environment. It was in Paris that Mondrian pared away his compositions to their utmost simplicity, reducing the number of elements, using a square rather than a rectangular canvas, banishing grey from his palette as too indecisive. He made diamond-shaped canvases from 1919 onwards, their diagonals acting as taut stays against the vertical and horizontal thrusts of the black lines: many paintings are in black and white

alone. *Fox-trot A*, 1930, is one of the most austere but also vital examples of his "dynamic movement in equilibrium". The title reflects another aspect of Mondrian's character; he was addicted to dancing and to jazz, and the theme recurs in the latest development of his style, in the four years in New York (which he loved) before his death in 1944.

Mondrian sought a completely objective quintessence in his art, and yet his paintings are not analysable or translatable in terms of scientific or mathematical formulae. They remain in the end a subjective statement, their success dependent on the exquisite sensibility with which the dynamic equilibrium is poised – his "equivalence of opposites".

MONDRIAN (left)
The red tree, 1908
The desire for order is implicit (as in Cézanne, as in Seurat) not only in the stark, elementary subject but also in the controlled strokes, neatly juxtaposed, of the brush. Fauvism has liberated the colour.

MONDRIAN (right)
The flowering apple-tree, 1912
Cubism has intervened. It has hastened Mondrian to break down the forms into elements reconstituted on the canvas. But there is little depth; and soon he was to discard volume altogether.

MONDRIAN (left)
Composition in yellow and blue, 1929
Mondrian's work was underpinned both by a rigorous sense of truth and by a profound belief in order. Human society was moving into a new age, in which, if there were order, there would be greater happiness. Of this art was an aspect.

MONDRIAN (above)
Fox-trot A, 1930
Mondrian observed that no loss of equilibrium was entailed in a square picture hung diagonally, although diagonals inside the picture destroyed its containment, introducing an alien commotion. He deplored other De Stijl artists' use of curves.

MONDRIAN (above)
Broadway Boogie-Woogie, 1942-43
Passionate about dancing, Mondrian was inspired by the jazzy pace of Boogie-Woogie in his last works. This painting, a delighted salute both to jazz and also to the dizzy street-grid of Manhattan, is a highly controlled explosion of colour

in a complex composition from which black has been entirely eliminated, though the other colours, red, blue and yellow, are Mondrian's usual primaries – the change does not betray principle. In 1944, only weeks before his death, he explained: "True Boogie-Woogie I conceive as homogeneous in intention with mine in

painting – destruction of melody, which is the equivalent of destruction of natural appearance; and construction through the continuous opposition of pure means ..." to achieve dynamic rhythm. *Victory Boogie-Woogie* (not shown), his unfinished last painting, hung diagonally, has the same clean clear rhythm.

Art in Germany: The Bauhaus

The Bauhaus was founded by the architect Walter Gropius (1883-1969) in Weimar in 1919; it moved to Dessau in 1925-26 and to Berlin in 1932, and was closed by the Nazi regime in 1933. The name and concept, however ("Bauhaus" is not precisely translatable into any other language; it means "building house" approximately), have certainly survived the repression of the institution itself.

The founding *Manifesto* of 1919 opened with the sentence: "*Das Endziel aller bildnerischen Tätigkeit ist der Bau!* (The final goal of all activity in the visual arts is the complete building)." It continued: "It was once the most distinguished task of the visual arts to adorn it; they were inseparable components of the great building. Today they exist in self-sufficient isolation, from which they can be rescued only by the conscious co-operation of all working people. Architects, painters and sculptors must recognize anew the complex, composite nature of a building, in all the parts of its entity. Only then will that work be imbued with the architectonic spirit that it has lost as 'Salon art' . . . Art is not a profession. There is no essential difference between the artist and the craftsman."

The inspiration for this gospel of creativity came from Henry van der Velde, active from before World War I in Weimar as a prophet of synthesis in art and of "pure form"; from the tenets of William Morris and the Arts and Crafts movement; not least from the example of the medieval guilds. Yet though Lyonel Feininger's woodcut frontispiece for the *Manifesto* showed the new unity of the arts in terms of a medieval cathedral, the Bauhaus, unlike its progenitors, welcomed the new technology of the Machine Age with enthusiasm, working to take full advantage of it structurally, theoretically and aesthetically.

Bauhaus teaching in each subject began with a six-month foundation course: each course was under the guidance of a *Formmeister* (concerned with fundamental principles of form and creativity) and a modern craftsman. Students were very much apprentices, and theory and practice were tightly allied; some of the Bauhaus textbooks became classic documents for the arts world-wide – Klee's *Pedagogical Sketchbook* (1925) and Kandinsky's *Point and Line to Plane* (1926). However, the curriculum was in continual evolution, as a matter of principle. In the early years of trial

FEININGER (below)
Frontispiece for the Bauhaus *Manifesto*, 1919
The socialist cathedral (still Expressionist, but also dynamic with light) was to "rise one day . . . from the hands of a million workers like the crystal symbol of a new faith".

MOHOLY-NAGY (below)
Light-space modulator, 1922-30
Moholy-Nagy was a true mechanic-artist, applying art to industrial design and technology to art. He was fascinated especially by the media of light: the *Modulator* activates space by reflections and shadows of its revolving forms.

KANDINSKY (above)
On high, 1920
Kandinsky's encounter in Russia with Suprematism (see p. 159) led him into a disciplined style with a more geometrical basis: this cool austerity was further influenced by the Bauhaus spirit. The free personal expression of his Munich abstracts has been sacrificed in the creation of a more concrete order.

KANDINSKY (right)
Rows of signs, 1931
Kandinsky's hieroglyphs are like Miró's Surrealist forms subject to a regimen. They are a synthesis of pure, constructed forms and intuitive, suggestive ones.

KLEE (above)
Italian town, 1928
Klee made many references in his notebooks to the common structural ground of buildings and paintings: this was directly reflected in canvases that combine abstract arrangements of colour with lines defining planes, blocks and space of an architectural character. With the move to Dessau in 1925-26 the Bauhaus became more concerned with architecture and design, and Klee participated in this new spirit whole-heartedly. He left only in 1931 when functionalism – an interest in the "truth" primarily of technological materials – began to predominate.

and experiment, the emphasis on the theory of form and the nature of materials, on the sciences and on manual and technical skills, was balanced by the spiritual, even mystical intensity which notably Kandinsky and Klee brought to teaching – there was a positive awareness of the irrational side of creativity. But from 1923 the architectural side became more dominant, as the uniting factor of all the artistic disciplines, closely knit under the influence of László Moholy-Nagy (1895-1946), Josef Albers and Marcel Breuer (born 1902). Then it was primarily in the fields of architecture and industrial and interior design – furniture, ceramics, textiles – that the Bauhaus made its greatest impact – the establishment of a basic grammar of spare, functional design, taking advantage of new techniques and materials, of mass-production no less than plastics. The aims of De Stijl were taken up and developed; the emphasis was increasingly Constructivist rather than Expressionist.

It was a crucial element in Gropius' genius that he could attract and recruit a cosmopolitan staff of the very highest calibre. His early appointments included the Swiss Johannes Itten (1888-1967) and Lyonel Feininger

(1871-1956), American-born but of German extraction. Feininger had earlier been decisively influenced by Art Nouveau and by Delaunay's Orphism, but from this he developed his personal lyrical dreams, abstracting architectural forms into delicate crystalline structures. The Russian Wassily Kandinsky was closely associated with the Bauhaus between 1922 and 1933, and there defined further the stricter, more geometrical development of his non-figurative work. Paul Klee, who had earlier associated with Kandinsky in Munich (see p. 137), was on the Bauhaus staff from 1920 to 1931, returning to his native Switzerland in 1933 (see over). A crucial and dynamic personality at the Bauhaus between 1923 and 1928 was the Hungarian Moholy-Nagy, on whom the revolutionary work of the Russians Malevich and especially El Lissitzky had had a decisive impact. Moholy-Nagy's interests, irrepressibly various and inventive, extended beyond painting and sculpture to experimental work in photography, film, even light itself as a medium for art; into theatre, ballet and typography. Despite the quality of its staff, however, the Bauhaus bred no outstanding painters and sculptors among its

students, and opportunities for free painting and sculpture diminished, until one of the most gifted painters there, Oskar Schlemmer (1888-1943), commented: "Painters are no more than a necessary evil there." Gropius (and Moholy-Nagy) left the Bauhaus in 1928, and under new direction the school entered a more functionalist phase; the political slant leant increasingly actively towards the Left and as an inevitable consequence it was closed by the Nazis in 1933.

The Bauhaus principles of design and of the relationship of art and industry, its theory of form and its teaching methods were not extinguished, but on the contrary broadcast through the Western world as former members of the Bauhaus became refugees from Nazi oppression. The strongest Bauhaus impact came in the United States, where Moholy-Nagy established in Chicago (1937-38) the Institute of Design, and Albers became a leading figure at Black Mountain College (see p.220); Feininger, Gropius, the typographer Herbert Bayer, the master designer Marcel Breuer and the last Director of the Bauhaus, the architect Mies van der Rohe (1886-1969), all moved to America.

GROPIUS (above)
The Director's office at the Weimar Bauhaus, 1923
Shape and colour are ruled by clean lines, clear light.

MOHOLY-NAGY (below)
Yellow cross, c. 1923-28
Balance and space, static and kinetic movement were Moholy-Nagy's concerns.

BREUER (above)
Steel chair, 1925
Inspired by the handlebars of a bicycle, Breuer made the first tubular steel chair – strong, light and compact.

SCHLEMMER (right)
Concentric group, 1925
As master of the theatre workshop, Schlemmer had studied actors' positions and spatial relationships.

ITTEN (left)
Benign light, 1920-21
Itten's dedication to the properties of colour, both physiological and psychological, gave his abstracts a firm, systematic basis. This multi-colour diagram of subtle tonal gradations was issued as a study aid; it was followed by a series of expressive and lucid grid paintings, which amount to more than merely didactic expositions of his theory, though Itten's reputation as a teacher has tended to overshadow that of his art.

Paul Klee

Perhaps more than for any other great modern artist, the essential biography of Paul Klee (1879-1940) is his art, but his art remains triumphantly inexplicable. It does not respond very well even to commentary. For instance, historians tend to contradict each other flatly at a basic level – what is the prime motive of his work, the formal construction or the inspiration of the imagination? But in the most famous of his apothegms, Klee spoke of drawing (or at least of his drawing, or at any rate of some of his drawing) as "taking a line for a walk". In a variation of that, the image of a man taking a dog for a walk may come to mind, the reasonable man and the instinctive dog linked by the line of the leash, moving together in unpredictable rhythms, indissolubly.

Paul Klee was born in Switzerland into a family, part German, part French in origin, of professional musicians. Klee himself was a violinist of high calibre, and the movement of his compositions often seems closer to music than to the visual art of the other major artists of his time. And yet Klee was responsive to almost any visual stimulus, including that of the most advanced art being produced around him. By 1914 he had seen in Munich the work

of Der Blaue Reiter artists, and had been himself loosely associated with that group; he had travelled in Italy, spent almost a year in Paris in 1912, and travelled in 1914 with Macke in Tunisia. He was aware not only of Renaissance art but also of Byzantine and Coptic; he made reference to the colourism of the Fauves, to Cézanne's use of colour, to the Cubist colourism of Delaunay – but also to the colour patterning of Islamic carpets. He came to know the work of Douanier Rousseau, as also the "primitive" art of Africa and Oceania, and the drawing of children and of the insane. He was widely read in German and French poetry. Yet it is absurd to talk of influences in the case of Klee: he came, he saw, he digested. He was nourished.

He was based in Munich between 1906 and 1920 (with a break for army service, 1916-18), and the contact with Der Blaue Reiter, and especially with Kandinsky and Marc, decisively confirmed his belief in the spiritual well-springs of artistic creativity. Until 1914 his work was almost entirely in black and white (see p. 137) and generally in a Symbolist, Expressionist tradition deriving from artists such as Böcklin and Ensor, but with a very

Paul Klee
"He was a man who knew of day and night, of sky, sea and air. But ... our language does not suffice to express such things, and he had to find sign, colour or form", commented a devoted friend of Klee's.

KLEE (right)
Motif of Hammamet, 1914
The cube-like architecture set in shining sands under an intensely blue sky is fabricated into a patchwork of the local colours; the texture of the paper, visible through the paint, gives a shimmering effect.

KLEE (below)
The country child, 1923
Klee's first application for a teaching post was turned down because the board of governors found his work "frivolous"; now the value and significance of fairy tales are better understood and respected.

KLEE (above)
The vocal fabric of the singer Rosa Silber, 1922
The title, as so often with Klee's paintings, is a play on words: Rosa Silber is a name but also means "rose silver", the main colours. The canvas is just a piece of rough material on which patches of colour, letters (evoking a musical notation) and patterns are delicately disposed so as to suggest the structure of a sound.

KLEE (left)
Mask with small flag, 1925
Klee's fertile imagination and prolific output – 8,926 works in all – are the more astounding in that there is so little repetition within his work, though it is instantly recognizable. Instantly, too, he dazzles and entrances. It is, however, possible to see underlying preoccupations, such as the human face. But compare Kandinsky's *On high* (see preceding page).

original blend of fantasy and wit. He first made his name with etchings, influenced in style by Dürer. His progress towards colour is charted in his early journals and letters, and in 1914, in Tunisia with Macke, the bright desert sunlight transformed his vision as it had Delacroix's and Renoir's before him: "Colour has taken hold of me; I no longer have to chase after it . . . I and colour are one. I am a painter." He was then already 35 years old. The contribution he was to make in colour was a revelation of inexhaustible variations and permutations, of melody and harmony, probably unequalled in its variety. His subsequent production was remarkably prolific, amounting to rather more than 8,000 paintings and drawings.

Klee's appointment to the Bauhaus teaching staff in 1920 was of great importance to his art, even though the Bauhaus ethic, towards the end of his time there, had hardened into an active inhospitality towards painting. He taught there (see preceding page) not only painting but also textiles and stained-glass design, and an intimacy with his materials is an outstanding feature of his work. The Bauhaus gave Klee first a financial independence he had never had before and secondly encouragement

to proceed with an intellectual analysis of his own work. His *Pedagogical Sketchbook* of 1925 was the second of the 14 Bauhaus manuals edited by Gropius and Moholy-Nagy; a primer for his students, it illustrates vividly the tenets that underlie Klee's unique marriage of scientific and mathematical precision with the organic processes of the imagination. In 1923, in the course of a lecture *On Modern Art* (published only in 1945), he formulated a famous metaphor which still seems the most illuminating comment on the nature of his art – the metaphor or simile of the tree.

"The artist has studied this world of variety and has, we may suppose, unobtrusively found his way in it. His sense of direction has brought order into the passing stream of image and experience. This sense of direction in nature and life, this branching and spreading array, I shall compare with the root of the tree. From the root the sap flows to the artist, flows through him, flows to his eye. Thus he stands as the trunk of the tree. Battered and stirred by the strength of the flow, he moulds his vision into his work. As, in full view of the world, the crown of the tree unfolds and spreads in time and space, so with his work. Nobody would

affirm that the tree grows its crown in the image of its root ... Different functions expanding in different elements must produce vivid divergences ... (The artist), standing at his appointed place, the trunk of the tree, does nothing other than gather and pass on what comes to him from the depths. He neither serves nor rules – he transmits."

In 1931, Klee left the Bauhaus to take up a professorship at Düsseldorf, whence the Nazis expelled him in 1933. He settled in Berne, near his birthplace; his last years were clouded by illness, but his work continued. His later painting tended to be rather larger in scale (though all his work has a comparatively small format) and was sometimes sombre with an imagery and colour that seem to reflect his awareness not only of approaching death but also of the imminent tragedy of war. Yet the variety of Klee's imagery confounds categorization; it ranges from the menacing to the most delicately witty or nonsensical.

Historians have sometimes been reluctant to accept Klee's great stature, but that perhaps was before the propagation of the maxim "Small is beautiful"; there was some confusion about the importance of scale.

KLEE (right)
"*Ad Parnassum*", 1932
A mountainous landscape is portrayed in what Klee called his "divisionist" style, after Seurat. Tiny scales vibrate over a surface of modulated colour.

KLEE (below)
Fire in the evening, 1929
This belongs to the series of "magic squares" which occupied Klee from 1922 to the end of his life – these exquisite harmonies in major and minor keys disclose his musical talents.

KLEE (above)
Death and fire, 1940
Painted in the year of his death, *Death and fire* is a product of Klee's aim to "create much, spiritually, out of little". Klee could discover the world or more in the page of a notebook as surely as the poet Blake could in a grain of sand.

KLEE (left)
Under the angel's wing on a steep path, 1931
Not only was he a gorgeous colourist; Klee was also a magician with the pen or the pencil. Images of angels frequent his later work.

Expressionist Developments, and Neue Sachlichkeit

The term "Expressionism", used to categorize a certain kind of art and to distinguish it from other kinds, first became current about 1910. It is applied to an art in which the artist dominates his subject matter to the point of distorting its appearance, so as to express in the most forceful fashion possible his own view of the world, and to make a comment – generally but not necessarily critical – on its nature. "Expressionism" seems to describe aptly the work of several German artists active in the early years of the century – those of Die Brücke and Der Blaue Reiter, even those of Dada – but also to apply to many working in Germany after 1918 and to several outside Germany – Kokoschka in Austria, Permeke in Belgium, Rouault (see p.143) in France.

Two of the most brilliant second-generation German Expressionists emerged directly from the politically orientated Dada group launched by Huelsenbeck in Berlin in 1917 – Grosz and Heartfield. George Grosz (1893-1959) began as a satirical caricaturist, and his best work was defined by an acid-sharp and relentlessly hard line throughout. His running commentary on German social and political life in the aftermath of war was one of the most savage and

GROSZ (below)
Dusk, 1922
Grosz's watercolour and pen drawings of urban scenes

are peopled with hard-faced burghers, war-victims and leering women, personifying inhumanity and suffering.

scathing made on any society ever, exposing the oppression and exploitation of the poor of Berlin by the military and capitalist classes in brutally explicit scenes of murder, prostitution and urban degradation. His characters – notably his bull-necked, squash-faced, cigar-smoking men with shaven heads – are profoundly disturbing and convincingly evil. Technically, he early on became aware of the dynamic Futurist style, then exploited brilliantly the fragmenting methods of Dada, including montage; his urban settings often echo those of Metaphysical painting. Grosz's overt, ferocious, utterly uninhibited satire was driven by an irrepressible and courageous anger against injustice (he was prosecuted on several occasions) but was countered by an ambivalent romanticism. Though he had been a member of the German Communist Party since its foundation, when with the coming to power of the Nazis he could no longer work in Germany he moved not to Russia but to America (becoming an American citizen in 1938). There, though his original satiric bent found expression occasionally, the impetus of his art was sapped, and his painting tended to become soft-edged (very close to Pascin's). His

GROSZ (right)
Eclipse of the sun, 1926
The images in *Eclipse*, one of Grosz's own favourite paintings, are savage – the men of money, without their heads, conspire with the fat decorated general, epitome of bloodthirsty cruelty. The expression of political comment in such allegorical form was novel in painting.

DIX (below)
The match-seller, 1920
Dix's work is exclusively devoted to human beings, to their greed, brutality and to their suffering. He began his pictures of war-victims in 1919, with views of the crippled ex-soldiers seen on the streets of Dresden. His vision is beyond pity or sentiment: the dachshund pisses on the match-seller.

HEARTFIELD (above)
War and corpses, 1932
Heartfield's photomontage was used in Spain in 1934 as a communist poster, the decoration round the neck of the hyena being replaced by a swastika. Photography was for Heartfield a new international and populist language, which he exploited, and expressionistically manipulated, to reveal the inner truths of human society.

HOFER (left)
Three masqueraders, 1922
Hofer strove to probe the visible world as the Neue Sachlichkeit artists did, sharing their aesthetic of disillusionment. However, he refused to accept the "Expressionist" label – his roots lay in a classical idealism transformed by the influence of Cézanne and disturbed by the shock of service in the trenches.

friend John Heartfield (Helmut Herzfelde, 1891-1968), an active revolutionary, used photomontage as a weapon of social satire with an unsurpassed visual wit and efficacy.

Otto Dix (1891-1969) also made his mark in the early 1920s as a cutting and cynical satirist of contemporary society; horrific experience in war and disillusionment afterwards were bitterly expressed in his pitiless linear precision, his clear, often brilliant colour and modelling, and his formulation of repulsive human types. In the mid-1920s, he was the dominant personality of the trend known as "*Neue Sachlichkeit*" (New Objectivity), also called Magic Realism. The label "*Neue Sachlichkeit*" was coined for a projected exhibition in Mannheim in 1923 of "artists who have retained or regained their fidelity to positive, tangible reality". In that sense it was a reaction against abstraction and against the earlier Expressionist destruction of form, but in other senses it sustained some central characteristics of Expressionism – the directness of the artist's confrontation with reality, his use of distortion to emphasize his view of the world. The artist's emotion was, however, to be held in tight control, in a concentration that often invested his work with a neurotic, eerie tension.

There was no co-ordinated movement of Neue Sachlichkeit, and artists practising variations within it were working at several centres in Germany during the Weimar Republic; they included Carl Hofer (1878-1955), Franz Radziwill and Georg Schrimpf (1889-1938). Their work was not tolerated by the Nazis and, though few of them left Germany, most of them radically altered their styles after 1933.

Meanwhile there had been an extraordinary ferment of intellectual and artistic life in Vienna early in the century, nurturing Freud, Schönberg and the Vienna Sezession. Following on the work of Klimt, a fierce strain of Expressionism flared in the haunting psychological intensity of the portraits of Richard Gerstl (1883-1908; not shown), who committed suicide, in the works of Oskar Kokoschka (1886-1980) and in the starved, aching eroticism of Egon Schiele (1890-1918). Kokoschka was initially the *enfant terrible* of the Viennese art scene, a picturesque, flamboyant personality and a strenuous exhibitionist; he began there a long series of portraits (see p.229), including a continuing sequence of *Self-portraits*, that constitute a great part of his

achievement. In these, and in his figure paintings, the delicate exploratory line combines with broken and shifting depths of colour to produce an extraordinary strength of mood. After World War I he travelled extensively, and in Paris began a series of large landscape panoramas, Impressionistic in their brilliance of fragmented colour, Expressionistic in their tumultuous atmospheric vigour.

The Expressionist urge seems to have been a northern characteristic, and after the first inspirations of the Dutchman van Gogh and the Norwegian Munch it nowhere produced a richer harvest than in the Germanic countries, although it appeared in Italy, in the work of Scipione, and in the dour paintings of the earth and the peasantry by Constant Permeke (1886-1952) in Belgium. In Germany itself, Expressionist freedom was anathema to Nazi doctrine. Systematic suppression of free art culminated in the exhibition of "Degenerate Art" in 1937; Germany destroyed or dispersed the most remarkable achievements of her visual arts since the time of Dürer and Grünewald. And yet Max Beckmann (see over), living in obscurity in Amsterdam, continued his formidably apocalyptic painting undeflected.

SCHRIMPF (left)
Boy with a rabbit, 1924
The emergence of a rather stiff realism in Germany during the 1920s owed something to Rousseau's Naive reconstruction of reality. Schrimpf's gently romantic, unpretentious paintings are typical of the style – simple, monumental forms smoothly painted, carefully modelled.

KOKOSCHKA (right)
Lovers with a cat, 1917
Kokoschka's free brushwork distances his *Lovers* from their 16th-century source, a painting by Cranach, and creates a lyricism highly charged with emotion, as if the brush-strokes themselves were spiritual emanations. In this way he could, too, create violent, Promethean visions of human suffering.

SCHIELE (left)
The embrace, 1917
Schiele's own restlessness, in his personal life, seems to suffuse *The embrace*, this contorted clutching amidst crumpled sheets. The male figure is a self-portrait. His eroticism (which had occasioned his arrest in 1911) is anguished, but the complex, angular lines riot with a decorative rhythm.

PERMEKE (right)
The sower, 1933
Permeke's subject is clearly social realist, but a moral is not explicit; his massive figures have a chthonic, or elemental, timeless being. In their dignity and pathos they recall 19th-century heroic pastoral paintings, and late work by Millet.

Beckmann: Departure

The figures are almost clamped in heavy black
outlines, and the space they occupy bears in on
them and compresses them still further – the
claustrophobic effect is overwhelming. The
subject matter is unconscionably brutal, and
worked with an appropriately coarse violence.
Yet man in the lifetime of Max Beckmann
(1884-1950) proved to be only too capable of
the imprisonment, mutilation and mental torture that ravage his first triptych, *Departure*.
The colour is generally sombre, kindling with
the glow and flush of a stained-glass window,
and the three panels read as a sort of post-
Christian altarpiece recording the events of a
modern Revelations. Triptychs soon became a
favourite form of Beckmann's, and their violent, complex themes, evoking the circus, the
stage and classical myth in a very Germanic
interpretation, have, though always personal,
a resonant twentieth-century relevance.

Max Beckmann began his career as a painter
in a relatively orthodox style. His independent
spirit, however, amounted already to high
arrogance: his reaction on his first visit to

BECKMANN (left)
Quappi in pink, 1932-34
Whatever Beckmann made
of his own image in his
revealing *Self-portraits*,
he always painted his wife
Quappi as a lady, indeed
almost as a fashion-plate.
Both line and colour here
recall Die Brücke styles.

BECKMANN (above)
*Self-portrait with
Quappi Beckmann*, 1941
Fear and grim resignation
are expressed in these two
faces. With deep shadows
Beckmann dramatizes their
plight as refugees; he has
been spurned as an artist
but he remains formidable.

Paris, aged 19, was: "What's there, I know already." This confidence was matched by a striking ability. He had established a reputation by the time of his first one-man exhibition (in Frankfurt) in 1911, and by then he was demonstrating two qualities that would persist throughout his career – his ability to control large and complex compositions, and an obsession with horrific subject matter.

Before World War I, Beckmann had encountered in *Der Blaue Reiter* the belief of Franz Marc in an art "seeking and painting the inner spiritual side of nature", together with a demand for utter artistic objectivity towards the thing represented. In 1914, Beckmann worked as medical orderly on the front, but was released in 1915, apparently after a nervous breakdown. The experience of the horror of war proved the turning-point for his view of nature and of man. Stylistically and emotionally, his examples became Bruegel, Signorelli and the brutal assault on the emotions of Grünewald, while his stark and heavily outlined figures, massive within the frame,

directly recall the fierceness of Die Brücke artists, of Kirchner and also of Rouault. In his stubborn insistence on veristic representation he is close to some painters of the Neue Sachlichkeit, but Beckmann's intellectual stature, his ego, the thrust and concentration of his vocation, set him apart from all his German contemporaries; indeed the power of his achievement has caused some critics to compare him with Picasso (characteristically, Beckmann himself suggested that Picasso's *Guernica* (see p.203) was a distorted Beckmann). Undoubtedly he was a myth-maker of the order of Picasso, capable of creating a world of events rationally and even symbolically inexplicable, yet which are compelling as illustrations of hidden but eternal truths.

Beckmann seems to have absorbed what he needed from the compositional methods of the Cubists, but the structural – as it were materialist – concerns obsessing modern movements did not involve him. "Self-realization is the urge of all objective spirits. It is this Ego for which I am searching in my life and in my art

... My way of expressing my Ego is by painting ... Nothing could be more ridiculous or irrelevant than a 'philosophical conception' painted purely intellectually without the fury of the senses grasping each visible form of beauty and ugliness."

Naturally one subject to which he reverted constantly in his search for his ego was his own person – a range of *Self-portraits* in which he appears in various disguises or with strange attributes – horns, saxophones – or as a character in one of his mythologies, or, most tellingly, foursquare as a modern urban man, often in suit and bowler hat, an implacable, unplaceable presence. Leaving Germany on the eve of the Nazi exhibition of "Degenerate Art" in 1937, he established himself in obscure isolation in Paris, and then in Amsterdam. "Nothing shall disturb my composure" is a note that recurs in his diary for the catastrophic year of 1940. In America from 1947 till his death three years later, he re-emerged into critical acceptance, and his stature has since continued to grow.

BECKMANN (left)
Departure, 1932-35
The triptych form evokes a long tradition in north European painting, from Gothic altarpieces to Hans von Marées' Symbolist art in the 19th century, and Nolde's religious triptychs in the 20th. Beckmann began to exploit the full symbolic and monumental potential of the form in 1932 with his *Departure*, the first of nine finished triptychs. The shadow of Christian imagery hangs over its mythical subject: in the left-hand panel the figure bound to a column echoes the flagellation of Christ. Beckmann's friend Perry Rathbone explained *Departure* in these words: "The side panels symbolize, on the left, man's brutality to man in the form of a callous executioner and his victims; on the right, the unbearable tragedy that Nature itself inflicts on human life as symbolized by the mad hallucinations of a woman encumbered by the lifeless form of a man. Out of this earthly night of torment and anguish, the figures of the central panel emerge into the clear light of redemption and release, embarked for eternity." Beckmann said that the centrepiece was the end of the tragedy, but could not be understood except as one part of the whole.

Art in Britain between the Wars

In Britain between the Wars there was almost a national resistance to Expressionist and non-figurative art. Portraiture flourished, mainly conventional, but sometimes given new twists by such artists as Augustus John and Wyndham Lewis (see p.155); and Jacob Epstein, though continuing to be controversial (provoking the public to tar and feather his mildly Cubist carving *Rima* (not shown) in 1925), came to find his *forte* more and more in modelled portrait busts, which recall Rodin rather than his own Vorticist beginnings. With Augustus John, Walter Sickert was the grand old *enfant terrible* of British art, a leavening force on the fringe of English conservatism; in his last work Sickert developed a broad, almost Expressionist grasp of form that foreshadowed Francis Bacon.

The implications of Post-Impressionism, of Fauve colour, of Cubist structure, were not at first developed very far. A pioneering modernist group was the Seven and Five Society, formed in 1919. Its most important member was Paul Nash, who went on to organize in the early 1930s Unit One, which brought together some outstanding though diverse artists in the promotion of abstract art. Unit One included

Barbara Hepworth, Henry Moore and Ben Nicholson, all highly professional and austerely critical of the general sloppiness of the English response to post-Cubist developments. Succeeding Roger Fry, the leading propagandists of modern art were the poet, novelist and critic Herbert Read (1893-1968) and Clive Bell (1881-1964), who first in 1914 justified abstract art with his notion of "significant form"; the meaning of a work of art consisted not in its subject or message but in the experience of its formal qualities. Then during the 1930s the arrival in Britain of artists in flight from the Nazi threat on the Continent

had a profound effect. They included Gabo, Gropius and Mondrian – all closely associated with the architect Leslie Martin and with Ben Nicholson, who with Gabo edited *Circle*, a mainly Constructivist periodical. In 1936 the International Surrealist Exhibition in London was the most comprehensive showing yet; presiding at its opening were the high priests of the movement from France, including Breton.

The most original, and successful, of the British Surrealists (if one excludes Moore) was Paul Nash (1889-1946), but it is typical of the British temperament that when Nash exploited "found objects" they were nothing like

NASH (right)
Landscape from a dream, 1936-38
The British Surrealists responded rather uneasily to the dogmas of militant Continental Surrealism; it never became a way of life. Beginning with realistic landscape, Nash was then influenced by Chirico: here he places figures from his own complex mythology in the recognizable landscape of the Sussex coast.

EPSTEIN (left)
Jacob Kramer, 1921
Retaining the spontaneity of a free sketch, Epstein brought expressive vigour, craggy conviction, to the traditional portrait bust.

NICHOLSON (below)
White relief, 1935
Nicholson was concerned with what Read had called

"the art of determined relations" – the relation of plane to plane, colour to colour, texture to texture.

NASH (left)
"*Totes Meer*" (Dead sea), 1940-41
What appears at first to be a stark lunar landscape was in reality a dump for enemy aircraft shot down in the Battle of Britain. These fragments piled into the pit of a disused quarry became for Nash "a great inundating sea ... It is hundreds and hundreds of flying creatures which invaded these shores ... By moonlight, this waning moon, one could swear they began to twist and turn as they did in the air. A sort of *rigor mortis*? No, they are quite dead and still." In World War I Nash had also painted remarkable evocations of desolation.

SUTHERLAND (right)
Entrance to a lane, 1939
Unlike Nash, Sutherland kept the creatures of his imagination and landscape separate, though in these highly charged evocations of the Welsh countryside he regenerated much of the intensity and lyricism of Samuel Palmer (see p. 63). "Organic abstractions" of poetry and mystery, they are underpinned by a close scrutiny of nature. Sutherland was a leading practitioner at this time of a "neo-Romantic" movement in British painting.

Duchamp's bicycle wheels or urinals. Nash relished the imagery provided by driftwood and flints and pebbles. War brought out his expressive powers: in 1940-41 he created one of his most vivid images, "*Totes Meer*" (Dead sea), a frozen sea of which the dead waves are the shattered wings of German aircraft. He found his most personal vision in a late series of intense, brooding landscapes with a strong Surrealist element; these almost rival the visionary dreams of Samuel Palmer (see p.63).

Henry Moore, too, owed much to Surrealist example but is considered separately (see over). Leading the more austerely abstract front of British art was Ben Nicholson (born 1894). His affiliations with Continental developments, early on notably with Picasso's linear style and with Cézanne's colour modulations, and later with Mondrian, are obvious, but at all stages of his long career his independence, the distinct and original nature of his contribution to modern art, have been striking. He always moved in and out of figurative art and abstraction with complete confidence (see p.227); his concern with pure form had its finest expression in his best-known works, the *White reliefs* of 1934-39, shallowly cut and

carved with geometric precision, as definitive as any Mondrian.

Barbara Hepworth (1903-75), married to Nicholson until 1951, was the most distinguished sculptor of her generation in Britain after Moore, moving from biomorphic to geometric forms, exploiting the play of void against solid, and piercing mass even before Moore did. Though her allusions to nature and to landscape are far less overt than Moore's, she once described her carving as a "biological necessity". Her forms are refined to very simple shapes with an extremely subtle finish.

Graham Sutherland (1903-80) was a late starter, finding his form first in landscapes of Wales in the mid-1930s. After World War II he developed a convincingly eerie skeletal imagery which won him an international audience. His most enduring work, however, may prove to be the best of his portraits, on which he embarked in 1949 with a celebrated, vivid and almost grotesque likeness of the writer Somerset Maugham. (His *Sir Winston Churchill* (1954) was found too unflattering by its subject, whose wife had it destroyed.)

Sir Stanley Spencer (1891-1959) was an anomaly in the twentieth-century art world, with

his profoundly religious sensibility coupled to a raging and tormented sexuality. He saw eternity in the bricks and mortar and the village gardens of Cookham by the Thames; in his greatest work, his large-scale decorations for Burghclere Chapel, Berkshire, in the 1920s, his obsessive care for detail was married into a mystic, beatific vision of moving pathos and yet great serenity. Spencer scarcely changed his style at all, unimpressed by the formal revolutions in art going on around him. Victor Pasmore (born 1908) did, and his career, and the reactions to it, illustrate very well the English difficulty in coming to terms with modern art. His earlier painting was developed in the so-called Euston Road school – a somewhat austere reaction by avantgarde figurative painters to the growing vogue for abstraction. He then underwent conversion in the late 1940s to a vigorous non-figurative style, to Constructivist designs in wood, metal and plastic, and that led on, as it had with Tatlin and Malevich, to involvement with architectural projects. But many British connoisseurs, unmoved by the elegance of his constructions, mourn the loss of the most sensitive English painter of landscape in the twentieth century.

HEPWORTH (right)
Three forms, 1935
Hepworth progressed to a pure abstraction rapidly and with assurance: this, her first completely non-representational sculpture, appeals both to senses and to intellect. Between the exquisitely smooth marble forms, so dauntingly white, the spatial relationship is both rigorous and sensual. Hepworth was firmly in the school of "direct carving".

SUTHERLAND (left)
Somerset Maugham, 1949
Sutherland's principle was to define his sitters by their habitual gestures and expressions – which led to a caricaturist's cruelty. Maugham's shrewdness – or sourness – is conveyed in the narrowed eyes, hawkish pose and arrogant tilt of the head; he almost looks like one of Sutherland's insect-like biomorphisms.

PASMORE (below)
The quiet river: the Thames at Chiswick, 1943-44
Painted in oil, the scene has all the ethereal mist and limpid quality of the finest watercolours. These silvery tones conjure up a nebulous Whistler-like twilight, yet the firm spare elements within it have an abstract force; there are some Seurats with the same meditative stillness.

SPENCER (right)
The resurrection of the soldiers, 1928-29
Stanley Spencer, too, has to be compared with Blake, but Blake the eccentric visionary and myth-maker, not Blake the illustrator of Thornton's Virgil (see p.63). Here the victims of World War I rise up from death; enemies join hands; a man in the foreground sees Christ on the altar.

PASMORE (above)
Snowstorm (Spiral motif in black and white), 1950-51
Pasmore moved through landscape to abstraction, until pure form supplanted

every external reference. This title was suggested by the finished work; no storm suggested the abstraction. His abstract reliefs may also be utterly impersonal.

Henry Moore

Henry Moore (born 1898) was the son of a miner in the northern English county of Yorkshire. The ancestry suggests a closeness to the earth, to soil and to rock, to the mute evidence of past geological upheaval in the fabric of the physical world. It may not be coincidence that Brancusi, that other elemental sculptor of the twentieth century, came also from a stock close to the earth, in Romania, at the other, eastern, extremity of Europe. To both was given the power to retain even in their most abstract and revolutionary work a contact, at times almost electric, with the vital roots. Their imagery was very different – Brancusi reducing to formal essence, Moore much more prodigal; Moore more prone, like nature, to imperfection, but subject in his profusion to marvellous felicities.

After early experience as a soldier in World War I, Henry Moore studied at a provincial school of art, at Leeds, but came in contact there with an unusually enlightened collector of art, Sir Michael Sadler, who introduced him to the critical writings of Roger Fry and Clive Bell. Fry expounded the importance of "direct carving", and Moore's sensitivity to the inherent nature of his materials, his reliance on

their "feel" to guide him to their final shape, remained constant since that time. Through Bell in particular Moore was led to an appreciation of "primitive" carving, especially Pre-Columbian; later, from 1921, in London, he was to explore the cluttered ethnographic collections of the British Museum, although he also came to realize, as a student and then as a teacher at the Royal College of Art, the importance of drawing from the life: drawing was for him "a deep, strong, fundamental struggle to understand oneself as much as to understand what one's doing".

His carving in the 1920s, much of it on the theme of *Mother and child*, was strongly shaped by Pre-Columbian example; he began then his first experiments with the image he was to make peculiarly his own, the reclining figure, and on a visit to Paris in 1926 came across a cast of the reclining Toltec *Chacmool* from Chichen Itza (see p.127) with a shock of recognition. The Leeds *Reclining figure* of 1929 shows the Pre-Columbian influence fully assimilated and transformed, the body's rhythm emphasized, as Moore began to develop the potential of a freer, rounder form, loosed from the rectangularity of Pre-Columbian sculp-

Henry Moore
Moore was widely known by the 1930s; his international reputation was secured when he won the sculpture prize in 1948 at the Venice Biennale.

MOORE (left)
Mother and child, 1924
The mood and rhythms of the figures are inspired by archaic Mexican sculpture: Moore said he admired its "tremendous power without loss of sensitivity".

MOORE (right)
Reclining figure, 1929
With one exception, the *Reclining figures* which constitute more than half Moore's work after 1924 are female – earth-mothers reduced to elemental mass, close to the earth in their posture and their essence.

MOORE (above)
Composition, 1932
Moore produced during the 1930s a superb series of biomorphic abstractions by "direct carving", in which

form evolved in response to material – hence their purity and simplicity; those superfluities which before Brancusi concealed essence are rigorously eliminated.

MOORE (above)
Bird basket, 1939
The form is hollowed, both void and solid constitute the form; the wires enhance the tension between them.

MOORE (right)
The Tilbury shelter, 1941
The air-raid shelters of World War II seemed to Moore "catacombs filled with exhausted bodies".

ture. In 1929, too, he pierced his first hole through solid mass. In the early 1930s, with Hepworth, Nicholson, Nash and others he formed Unit One, a group united by its common interest in design "considered as a structural pursuit". His experiments continued with both *Mother and child* and *Reclining figure* themes, and in them reflections from contemporary masters are clear – Picasso's late-1920s giants on a seashore (see over); the nearly abstract biomorphic forms of Brancusi, and especially of Arp. Moore endorsed Surrealist principles – he had always acknowledged the tutelary guidance of the Unconscious – and was encouraged to make use of the accidental in his art, of found objects, pebbles and driftwood, more or less altered by the artist. He wrought his surfaces into organic, rhythmic patterns, and pierced and hollowed out his work, sometimes tying geometric striations of strings taut across the opened forms. In 1936 he exhibited at the International Surrealist Exhibition in London.

When war came in 1939, Moore began his famous drawings as an official war artist: in the prostrate swathed figures of Londoners sleeping in underground stations, sheltering from the Blitz, he found a subject to which the son of a miner could respond whole-heartedly. His series of shelter drawings, entirely unsentimental in their humanity, topical yet also timeless, touched a chord in a far wider public than he had reached before.

By the end of the War Moore was acknowledged internationally, as the greatest British sculptor since the Neoclassic Flaxman. A prodigious worker, and complete master of his art and craft, he could come to terms with the Renaissance tradition, carving (within his own *Mother and child* theme) a more naturalistic *Madonna* for St Matthew's, Northampton. Simultaneously he began exploring a *Helmet* theme – a metaphor of the womb, form enclosed within form, void and solid in complex interaction. He introduced totemic standing figures, draped seated females, bone-like and egg-like forms; besides massy biomorphs and monumental, immobile or sometimes struggling figures, he also made more geometric or mechanistic, straight-edged and slab-like constructions. He turned to bronze, with a series of family groups, and to marble (he spent long summers at the quarries in Carrara where Michelangelo had been before him); one of his *Helmets* was in lead. Bronze, golden or roughly scored and dull, and wood, swelling with a patterned grain, were the media of his major works of the 1960s; in bronze he produced notably huge abstracts, two or three pieces gaunt or interlocking in compelling inter-relationship. His prolific output included both private work (numbers of finely attenuated miniature bronzes) and public commissions on a colossal scale for sites all over the world.

After he abandoned teaching in London in 1939 Henry Moore lived in the country, first in Kent, later in Hertfordshire. The undulating rhythms of the English landscape, its profiles, its swells and surges in vales and hollows, were answered in his mature work by the interplay of solid and void, and the finest of his *Reclining figures* are hauntingly evocative metaphors for the English landscape, spirit and substance. During the 1970s, working on an ever larger scale, he set much of his work in the landscape, standing close to the earth beneath the sky. His eightieth birthday in 1978 was celebrated with an exhibition of his cavernous voids and mysterious masses in Hyde Park, London, and over them swarmed thousands of children with an instinctive delight.

MOORE (left)
Reclining figure, 1945-46
In his large elmwood figure for the Cranbrook Academy of Art, Michigan, Moore worked sculptural rhythms through the body, locking inside it an infant's form.

MOORE (right)
Madonna, 1943-46
Concerned that the image should be appropriate to its Northampton church, Moore created a classical icon of placid dignity.

MOORE (below)
Two forms, 1966
Moore's later biomorphic abstractions, massive and complex, are often sculpted for landscape settings, and he himself supervises their placement. Like megaliths, the forms suggest the vital strength of natural forces.

MOORE (above)
Helmet head no.1, 1950
The idea of an inner form both trapped and protected by its shell gave Moore another fruitful theme with which to continue exploring external and internal form.

Picasso between the Wars

Having invented between 1907 and 1914 with Braque (see p.148) a mode of pictorial expression, Cubism, so fundamentally revolutionary that it seemed to overturn the entire Renaissance tradition of illusionism, Pablo Picasso proceeded to demonstrate in the years between the Wars that this was not necessarily so. The importance of Cubism was in no way diminished, but the most astonishing aspect of Picasso's subsequent work is its variety, the uninhibited freedom with which he was able to work in entirely different styles simultaneously, sometimes even in the same painting. These styles ranged from virtually naturalistic to near-abstract representation. The variety of media that he employed – not only painting, drawing, etching, sculpture, but also poetry and, in 1941, a play – and the sheer output of his work are scarcely less extraordinary. For Picasso, no style that could be retuned to answer his needs was obsolete.

In 1917, Picasso went with the poet and writer Jean Cocteau to Rome, and the impact of Roman monumental statuary and of the High Renaissance is obvious in a sequence of monumental "antique" figure compositions that he painted sporadically over the next decade; in these the overwhelming sense of massiveness is usually offset by the two-dimensional effect of the setting of the figures. At the same time (from as early as 1916) he was producing shaded pencil-drawings, realistic likenesses of his sitters incised with the most delicate strength, that are clear homage (and challenge) to the pencil-portraits that Ingres had perfected a century before in his years at Rome. In love, Picasso recorded faithfully and tenderly the literal appearance of his new wife (the ballerina Olga Koklova) and their child, and even extended this treatment to domestic still life. One such still life dates from 1919, the year in which he was painting brilliant variations on the same theme in a pure (if very free and painterly) late Cubist style.

In 1921 Picasso applied the austere techniques of synthetic Cubism to a major composition, *The three musicians* (not shown). The subjects consist of a Pierrot, a Harlequin and a monk – characters of his Blue period, here reconstituted in terms of a jigsaw mosaic of brilliant, flat colour. Their mood is ambiguous; some construe them to convey gaiety, others find them sinister. Three years later, in *The three dancers*, 1925, a similar composition

Pablo Picasso (1881-1973)
Picasso's work between the Wars no longer falls neatly into "periods"; rather, he demonstrated virtuosity at all he tried, without limit.

PICASSO (right)
Ambroise Vollard, 1915
From 1915, in a series of pencil-drawings, Picasso captured a generation of famous faces. A touch of caricature is offset by an almost sentimental quiet; even in this naturalistic image, as in the earlier Cubist portrait of Vollard (see p. 126), Picasso asserts independence from nature, through subtle distortions.

PICASSO (right)
Guitar, 1920
The diverse styles which Picasso used and reused in the 1920s included the continued development of synthetic Cubism; Gris and Mondrian influenced his more severe designs with flat, geometrical forms.

PICASSO (below)
The three dancers, 1925
The scene seems to embody a dictate of the Surrealist Breton, that "beauty must be convulsive or cease to be". The sharp colours, the jagged edges and the wild gesticulations of arms and legs electrify the canvas.

PICASSO (above)
Three women at the fountain, 1921
Picasso's "sculpturesque" matrons seem to intensify the dignified solemnity of their classical prototypes; also the serene, smoothly painted forms of Raphael and Ingres are echoed and transformed – for Picasso, great art was never dead.

PICASSO (above)
Seated bathers, 1930
Summers spent in southern France probably inspired the series of monstrously distorted *Bathers*, who lie nonchalantly beside clear Mediterranean sea. Their inside-out forms are like painted Cubist sculptures.

has been galvanized into a frenzy of movement, suggesting the staccato of early jazz or the Charleston, though again interpretations of the picture – as ominous or merry – vary considerably. About 1930, he opened up his earlier "antique" monumental figures into hollowed but massive constructions with pin heads and one Cyclopean blank eye whence all mind has withdrawn, disposed on the shore of what could be the sea of eternity. These creatures look suggestively Surrealistic, and Breton indeed claimed Picasso as a Surrealist; Picasso had sympathy for the movement (and exhibited in the great Surrealist exhibition of 1925), though he never condoned procedures such as "automatic" writing. About 1929-30 there was a fresh burst of sculptural activity, including open iron constructions.

The hedonistic facet of Picasso's Latin temperament is undeniable, and was sumptuously and abundantly illustrated in some colourful, curvaceous nudes of about 1930. And yet by about 1930 a violent and pessimistic strain was becoming more insistent. It reflected no doubt the increasing tensions of the looming Depression, of the threat of war, and also of the break-up of Picasso's marriage. The use of

distortion becomes even more acute; the inventiveness does not flag (dating from about 1929 is the brilliant invention of the combined profile and full-face view in the drawing of a head), but in many works the mood and technique are far harsher. Certain themes are developed in obsessive variations – the 100 etchings of *The Vollard Suite* (not shown), partly inspired by Balzac's novel *The Unknown Masterpiece*, and exploring the relationship and interaction of model and sitter (a theme that haunted Picasso until his death, see p.228); the meditations on bullfighting and on the enigmatic figure of the Minotaur, a half-sinister, half-pathetic symbol of irrationalism – culminating in one of his most complex etchings, *Minotauromachy* (1935; not shown).

The pessimistic strain took on full force in the enormous canvas *Guernica*, painted in 1937 in revulsion at the news of the bombing of an undefended town of that name in Spain. The power of this painting to convey the tragedy, horror and ruthlessness of modern warfare probably converted a far wider section of the public to accept the relevance of modern art to the ordinary person than any other single work. It is an allegory, expressed in terms of

the bullfight (the Minotaur again), but there are also motifs reflecting the real effects of indiscriminate bombing of civilians, though Cubist techniques, presenting objects seen simultaneously from different viewpoints, disintegrate their naturalistic appearance. In *Guernica* Picasso synthesized the themes, moods and techniques of his whole career, his imagination convulsed and concentrated by the anguish of the event. In 1945, however, came the less well-known but hardly less moving *Charnel-house*, surely precipitated by the horrific revelation of the Nazi centres of genocide, Buchenwald, Belsen, Dachau, and their multitudinous wasted corpses. The symbolism of *Guernica* is abandoned, and silence drained of colour replaces the almost audible scream of the earlier vision. Picasso found himself unable to bring the picture to completion, but its impact is nonetheless awesome. "Painting", he said, "is not done to decorate apartments; it is an instrument of war against brutality and darkness." Though Picasso's art was to continue in self-regenerating variety for nearly 30 years more (see p.228), *Guernica* and *The charnel-house* seem to close an era not only in his own career but in our civilization.

PICASSO (left)
Nude in an armchair, 1932
The direct sexuality of
the woman, satisfied and
warmly relaxed, is simply
conveyed in a harmony of
smooth, curving line and
in clear, sunny colour.

PICASSO (below)
Guernica, 1937
Violent condemnation of
indiscriminate massacre
gave Picasso's art a new
dimension; the allegory,
with its timeless images
of horror, roused an era.

PICASSO (left)
Woman's head, 1931
As Breton noted, Picasso
had "no prejudices about
materials": in his metal
assemblages, the pieces –
a colander for example –
retain their identity while
becoming part of something
new. The Spanish sculptor
González taught him how to
weld iron, but the forms
Picasso created are pure
Picasso, uniquely Picasso.

PICASSO (right)
The charnel-house, 1945-48
Picasso defined the artist
(and himself) as a socially
conscious "political being,
constantly alive to heart-
rending, fiery or joyful
events" to which he reacts
accordingly – here in a
deeply meditated requiem.

Early Modernist Art in America

By the end of the nineteenth century, somewhat belatedly, America was beginning to generate its own artistic independence. The main teaching centres were the Pennsylvania Academy and Chase's Art School in New York, still propagating the nineteenth-century tradition of European realism, though it was applied to American subject matter; these bodies, like others elsewhere, tended with the years to become more academic, more conservative. In 1908, they were challenged by a vigorous group known as "The Eight". The Eight had formed in direct reaction to the restrictive exhibition policy of the National Academy, and their first show, in 1908, had something of the aura of a Salon des Refusés; it was, however, very successful.

The Eight included artists of fairly diverse styles, ranging from a realism relying ultimately on Courbet and early Manet to a mood and technique very much aware of French Impressionism. Several members, however, propounded a naturalistic interpretation of some of the harsher aspects of American life, urban or agricultural – often emphasized by a sombre palette – which led to the description "Ashcan school", the name by which they are now unfairly remembered. The leader of the group was Robert Henri (1865-1929); trained at the Pennsylvania Academy and then at the Académie Julian in Paris, he had a swift and expressive style (form should be "rendered according to its nature, but it is not to be copied"), but was perhaps above all an inspired teacher. George Luks (1867-1933) and John Sloan (1871-1951) held on to the vision of Eakins and seventeenth-century Dutch realism; both had started as newspaper illustrators, and a feeling for immediacy, with a quick instinct for telling detail, stayed with them. Sloan, strongly influenced by Henri, was fascinated by the life that teemed on and off urban streets, in the slums (it was his work that precipitated the epithet "Ashcan"); although his style changed key after 1914, lightening in colour and moving towards a more generalized, abstracted treatment of form, he had a great impact on the most remarkable of the American urban realists, Edward Hopper (see over). George Bellows (1882-1925), a pupil of Henri's, though not one of the Eight, was another gifted realist, with a psychological insight into the drama of street life and of popular sport.

The assertion of independence by The Eight in 1908 stimulated others in the following years, culminating in February 1913 in the now legendary Armory Show. Alfred Stieglitz (1864-1946), one of the most brilliant early twentieth-century photographers, had run since 1905 various avantgarde galleries in New York, in which advanced American and European work was shown, but the Armory Show was the first large-scale display of the revolutionary movements in European art that a wider American public had the chance to see – even though more traditional painting, both American and French, outweighed in numbers the more innovatory kind, and the balance of representation was very uneven. Public protest was loud and sharp, although all four paintings by Marcel Duchamp found buyers. The show was crowded, however, and in a reduced form travelled to Chicago and Boston.

The Armory Show is established in history as the starting point of modern American Art. From then on the works of modernists from Europe (mainly Paris) were shown frequently, and the American avantgarde (most of whom had worked for a time in Europe before 1914) began to find a public. Georgia O'Keeffe, wife

HENRI (left)
The masquerade dress, 1911
Henri's life-size portrait of his wife Marjorie, a newspaper cartoonist, has impact, but is a superficial picture. The auburn-haired beauty has a majestic, posed elongation that owes much to Sargent, but falls short of his panache and brilliance.

SLOAN (below)
McSorley's Bar, 1912
This was one of two works exhibited by Sloan in the Armory Show. More than 1,600 pieces of sculpture, paintings, drawings, prints were shown, provoking cries ranging from "Anarchists, bomb-throwers, lunatics and depravers!" (the magazine *Art and Progress*) on. Sloan's painting might well be described as European Realism (Manet, Degas) with an American subject, but its evocative instantaneity is in its own right superb.

LUKS (above)
Hester Street, 1905
Luks was stimulated by the vivacity and colour of the New York slums and their way of life (he was himself a flamboyant character). He recalls French artists who freed their brushwork under Impressionist influence but did not adopt it entirely.

BELLOWS (left)
Stag at Sharkey's, 1909
The excitement and thrill of an illegal boxing match are typical of Bellows' subject matter: he carries the violence of the action over into swift paintwork. His interest in movement recalls Eakins and Homer; this is distinctly American in both subject and style.

of Stieglitz, pursued a long career far into the second half of the twentieth century, with a highly personal, lyrical style (see p. 210). One of the most original of the avantgarde was Marsden Hartley (1877-1943), affected more by German than by Parisian explorations (he knew the work of Der Blaue Reiter); though his usual theme was the rugged mountains and coast of New England, he also concocted bold and brightly coloured variations – almost with the effect of mosaic – on the unlikely theme of German militarism, and his fascination with flags announced a continuing inspiration for avantgarde Americans, from Stuart Davis to Jasper Johns. John Marin (1870-1953) also evolved a Cubist variation very much his own, nearest perhaps in spirit to the work of Robert Delaunay, but combining vigour with delicacy to remarkably decorative effect in watercolour, his subjects often Manhattan or the seas and islands of Maine in summer.

The achievement of the early pioneers of international styles in America is still undervalued elsewhere; at its best, its positiveness and individuality are no less striking than its variety. Arthur Dove (1880-1946; not shown) combined an advanced degree of abstraction

DEMUTH (below)
I saw the figure 5 in gold, 1928
The poem that provides the theme, *The Great Figure* by William Carlos Williams, has a description of a fire-engine, emblazoned with the figure 5, flashing noisily through the wet, dark city.

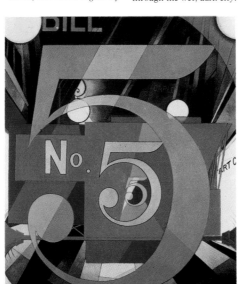

with mystic but potent evocations of natural forms, which could be in effect Symbolist. The splendidly talented Joseph Stella (1877-1946), in a dynamic sequence of kaleidoscopic variations on *Brooklyn Bridge*, naturalized a virtuoso, romantic form of Italian Futurism in New York. Abstractions with a strong geometric structure were developed from Cubist inspiration in the 1920s by Charles Demuth (1883-1935) and other "Precisionists", though Demuth's most celebrated painting is stated with the startling forthrightness of a poster – *I saw the figure 5 in gold*. It is a direct ancestor of developments to come in Stuart Davis (see p. 210) and then Pop art.

In the Depression of the 1930s various federal programmes of sponsorship for art were established, which aided all sorts of artists, but especially assisted a revival of traditional figurative painting in genre and landscape – known as Regionalism. Something of the same spirit animated social realist painters such as the idealistic Ben Shahn (1898-1969) and Edward Hopper; his evocative vision of urban atmospherics seemed at first uniquely American, but has since come to apply to almost any great city in the world.

MARIN (right)
Maine Islands, 1922
Marin, as Homer not long before him, felt a strong affinity with the rocky seascape and the shifting light of the Maine coast. The loose composition of washes is trapped on the paper by a brutal abstract frame.

HARTLEY (left)
A German officer, 1914
Hartley was an unsettled soul, who spent much of his life travelling in Europe and in America. His work ranges from such patterned, textured abstractions as this to raw landscapes and also figurative paintings.

SHAHN (below)
The prisoners Sacco and Vanzetti, 1931-32
Bartolommeo Vanzetti and Nicola Sacco were tried for robbery and murder, and on circumstantial evidence were found guilty and executed: there was uproar, an American Dreyfus case. Shahn presents the pawns in jerky worried sympathy, without giving the answers. This is one of a series of 23 paintings Shahn made recording their progress. With it he made his mark.

STELLA (left)
Brooklyn Bridge, 1917
Brooklyn Bridge was for Stella a vital symbol of America. He described it as "a weird metallic apparition ... supported by massive dark towers dominating the surrounding tumult of the surging skyscrapers with their Gothic majesty sealed in the purity of their arches ... It impressed me as the shrine containing all the efforts of the new civilization of America".

Hopper: Nighthawks

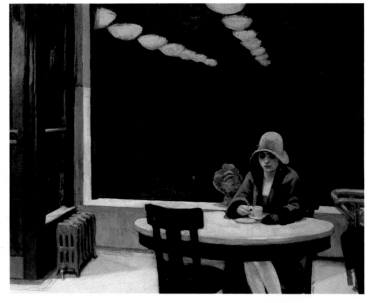

HOPPER (right)
Nighthawks, 1942
Hopper loved a long, low
light, defining structure
with firm clarity: in one
sense his compositions and
his handling are ruthless.
Inside a grid of vertical
and horizontal, human life
is held in a spotlight or
bubble; outside is desert.

HOPPER (above)
The automat, 1927
Hopper's admiration of
Degas is specially clear in
this work, so close in mood
to *The glass of absinth*
(see p. 104). In both, girls
sit in listless isolation –
Hopper's even more alone.

HOPPER (right)
Night shadows, 1921
The series of etchings he
made between 1915 and
1923 established Hopper's
career and subject matter.
The severity of the design
is enhanced by the stark
contrast of black and white.

HOPPER (above)
Approaching a city, 1946
Hopper said he was trying
to express the emotions he
felt when he approached an
unknown city by train.
"You realize the quality of a
place most fully on coming
to it, or on leaving it."

BURCHFIELD (right)
The old farmhouse, 1932
Hopper's observations on
the younger Burchfield's
painting can very often be
applied equally to his own,
for example: "By sympathy
with the particular he has
made it epic and universal."

BENTON (left)
City activities, 1930-31
Benton is remembered as
Pollock's teacher, but was
a painter in his own right,
a fine observer of town and
country life and the leader
of the Regionalist school.
This is one of his murals in
the New School of Social
Research in New York.

Edward Hopper (1882-1967) is the great visual
poet of big-city ennui, of the lonely desolation
of emptied streets and blankly windowed
houses, of skies and pavements scoured by
light and wind. *Nighthawks*, one of the most
haunting images in which he captured this sensation, is unusual in the quantity of human
participants; for Hopper, master of depicting
two people contiguous but without communication, four was a crowd, and here the group of
three might be involved in a desultory exchange of talk – this amounts almost to pande-
monium. But in fact the figure on which the
picture pivots is the fourth one, the man with
his back towards you, solitary, closed in on his
own silence, plumb central. Further, the
human "action" of the picture is distanced
from you by the sheet glass that encloses the
snack bar, which underlines the onlooker's role
as an outsider, almost as a voyeur. The snack
bar is the main source of light, spilling on to the
pavement, revealing the streets to be empty; a
footfall would be startlingly loud, and a threat.
It seems the dead hour of the night, with these
four people washed up haphazard in the fragile
shelter of the light and the glass.

Hopper, a dour and austere man, was not
one to indulge in sensual felicities of colour and

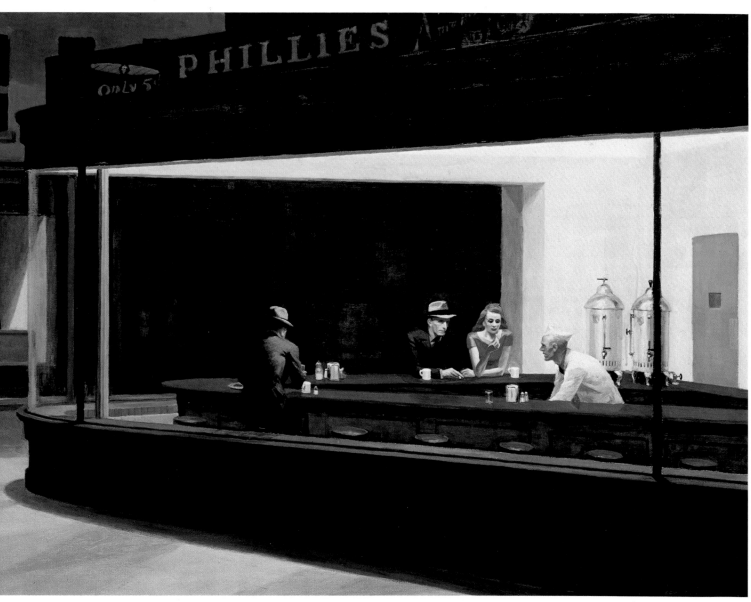

texture and line, of the feel of paint, but the raw harsh colour of the lit interior is offset very effectively by the sombre yet positive colour of the exterior setting. The mood is closely comparable to that expressed by Chirico in proto-Surrealist terms, but Hopper's realistic vision may be more convincing as a statement of the condition of twentieth-century urban man. Hopper's characters are real, unlike Chirico's puppets or statues, but they are far from home, in transit, and one of his most telling subjects is the hotel room, sometimes allied with a view of the railway tracks. Hopper's images of contemporary life touch on a nerve also exposed by the best of the realist novelists – Theodore Dreiser or Sinclair Lewis – a nerve touched again and again in certain films of mid-century – the streets and bars where Humphrey Bogart walked, the "blues" singers, the lyrics of jazz ("Every time we say goodbye, I die a little …").

The career of Edward Hopper, moving from poorly acknowledged beginnings to a position admired and accepted in all quarters, is a healthy reminder of the strength of the realist figurative tradition in the face of the once increasing fashion, especially in sophisticated New York, for abstraction and non-figurative

work. Hopper himself did not condone the move to abstraction: to him it seemed arbitrary and, in the end, frivolous and self-indulgent – not that he was in any way a slavish imitator of superficial phenomena. "My aim in painting is always, using nature as the medium, to try to project upon canvas my most intimate reaction to the subject as it appears when I like it most."

Hopper had been a pupil of Henri's, and retained a lasting admiration for him as an inspiring teacher, though it took some time to shed Henri's brisk, swift approach to painting. Trips to France before 1910 (after which he never went abroad again) seem not to have impressed him profoundly ("The only real influence I've ever had was myself"), though the mood of much of his work has something in common with that of Meryon's etchings, and he admired in Degas a quality which he also found in his compatriot Sloan – "the surprise and unbalance of nature". Vacancy and expectation co-exist. His people lack both characterization and movement, as if they are puppets of fate, and he did not share the social, humanistic concerns of some of the Ashcan school – he preferred "to paint sunlight on the side of the house". Some of his most potent images are of emptiness – a lonely room, or a

mansarded house looming against the sky.

The story of Hopper's career is that of his work – withdrawn from public life, ignoring artistic polemic. Nevertheless many of the painters collectively christened Regionalists shared his preoccupations – the painters of small-time America, the city and the country. The emptiness that Hopper found in the city Charles E. Burchfield (1893-1967) found in the farms of the Mid-West, though he tended towards a more nostalgic melancholy. The realism of Thomas Hart Benton (1889-1975) was more exuberant, sometimes taking a form recalling rather the allegories of British painters such as Ford Madox Brown than the instantaneity of Degas or the Ashcan school; and the contrast with Stuart Davis (see p. 210), juggling more formalistically with contemporary images, is even greater. Yet landscapes, urban scenes, interiors, the passive, the unspectacular, the commonplace could sometimes be structured by other realist painters than Hopper into pictorial drama, and this peculiarly American strain has continued all through the twentieth century, not quite forgotten amid the rage and fury of Abstract Expressionism and vindicated anew in the work of Andrew Wyeth (see p.226).

The Mexican Muralists

The great indigenous traditions of art in Central and Southern America were smothered when European supremacy was established. The cultural effect of the Catholic colonialists was to re-create in America the setting and way of life of Spanish or Portuguese cities. In architecture, some variations of strikingly exuberant fantasy were built, but painting and sculpture were derivative and generally not of high quality. The emphatic and dramatic style of Zurbarán was a lasting influence. In some areas, however, local folk art extracted out of European religious iconography a colourful imagery of its own, and a few painters of more sophisticated talent emerged, such as Melchor Holguín in Bolivia.

In the twentieth century, important artists from Latin America have made significant contributions, but they have been active on the international scene, and generally based in Paris. In Mexico, however, from the Revolution of 1910 onwards, an indigenous national school became very active, and attracted an admiring or horrified attention both in the United States and in Europe. Working often in a medium and on a scale that had almost lapsed in Europe – monumental mural

decoration – its art was harnessed (under official patronage) to Revolutionary political and social programmes as nowhere else in the world, except in Russia, but the Mexican solution was artistically far more imaginative than the platitudes that by the mid-1920s were swamping the brilliant exploratory Russian art of the early Revolution.

In the late nineteenth century there had developed in Mexico a strong strain of popular imagery in the graphic media, published in the so-called "corridos", vehicles for both journalism and popular history. José Guadalupe Posada (1852-1913) had evolved a personal idiom in woodcut and lithograph, Expressionist, formally speaking, in that he used distortion to emphasize his message. In his fantasy world of weird skull-topped characters both the Mexican obsession with death and the Mexican talent for savage caricature were prominent. His popular art, commenting often controversially on current affairs, was a significant precedent for the subsequent development of Revolutionary mural-painting.

The tradition of mural-painting had never died out in Mexico, surviving from the decorations of Pre-Columbian cultures (see vol. 2

p. 18) through the colonial versions of European Baroque styles in the churches. The revival of its techniques and its widespread application were sponsored consciously by the necessity, in a Revolutionary situation, to instil in a largely illiterate populace a sense of national and socialist identity; the programme was educational and inspirational, and in that its aims were similar to those of medieval church decoration. The major agents in the realization of this programme were the famous triumvirate of Rivera, Orozco and Siqueiros.

Diego Rivera (1886-1957) turned against the academic training offered in Mexico City, and between 1907 and 1921 was based almost entirely in Europe, settling in Paris, where he was associated with the Cubist painters, although by 1915 he was establishing a personal, poetic naturalism, expressed in a delicate linear style. On his return to Mexico in 1921, he became involved in a Revolutionary artists' commune, and worked towards the evolution of a straightforward, heroic, naturalist style that should both exploit the formal discoveries of modern art and be immediately comprehensible to the people; he studied the traditions of Mexican folk art, and experimented

RIVERA (right)
Mexico today, Mexico tomorrow, 1936
Part of a huge mural cycle in the National Palace of Mexico City, *The history of Mexico* (begun in 1929), this compartmented crowd of somewhat static figures constitutes a critique of Mexican society. Rivera, with Siqueiros, was one of the leading members of the Mexican Communist Party, but here he denounces the corruption of communist Revolutionaries as well as oppression by the fascists.

POSADA (above)
The alcoholic, c. 1912
Posada always remained close to the people whom he entertained or horrified. His workshop was a focus for the younger artists.

RIVERA (left)
A hymn to the earth, 1926-27
Rivera's fresco scheme exudes the crude power of the new mural movement. The message, justifying the collectivization of Mexican land after the Revolution and exalting the peasant worker, is made through symbols. On the altar wall a huge nude represents Mother Earth in harmony with nature and modern technology.

OROZCO (right)
The people and their false leaders, detail, 1937
Orozco's subjects reflect a wider view of humanity than that of Rivera or of Siqueiros: he was idealistic, but he was not politically active, though he was passionately concerned with the suffering of the common people. He conveys his bleak view of reality in an almost satirical style, with monochromatic tones and expressive brushwork.

with the techniques of early Italian fresco-painting. His themes were deployed in terms of labour, of mining, farming and industry; he celebrated the triumph of creative labour and the destruction of the evils of capitalism, poverty and the established Church. His imagery, and the spelling out of his message, can be distastefully crude, but his control of huge, complex compositions, his sheer energy, can be overwhelming.

José Clemente Orozco (1883-1949) was a second major force, contributing savage caricatures to the Revolutionary cause from 1910. But he developed a wider view of the Revolutionary struggle than did Rivera, and in his greatest series of murals in Mexico, at Guadalajara, which he executed after a stay in the United States, 1927-34, some have felt the titanic force of an artist of universal relevance. The third of the triumvirate, David Siqueiros (1896-1974), was the most politically active, abandoning painting altogether in 1925-30 for politics, imprisoned, exiled, fighting in the Spanish Civil War. The most spectacular Mexican artist of his time, he exploited both folklore and Surrealist and symbolic effects in his social realist synthesis; he used photo-

graphs and new techniques such as air-brushing. Like Orozco's and Rivera's, the rhetoric and bombast of his subject matter can carry enormous impact.

The pattern of official patronage in Mexico was far from consistent: the three main muralists all spent time abroad, and some of their major commissions were carried out in the United States, where their work had a profound effect on American realist painters of the 1930s and later, especially on those associated with the political left. Orozco undertook murals in California and on the East Coast; Rivera worked at the Rockefeller Center. Their most important work, however, was in the public buildings of Mexico itself, constituting a programme of social realist art unmatched in quality or scale anywhere else. The continuing Mexican tradition of mural-painting in bold colours on a colossal scale is unique in the world, though too often it tends to pastiche (usually of Pre-Columbian art).

Often ranked beside Rivera, Orozco and Siqueiros is Rufino Tamayo (born 1899), whose best works are his easel-paintings, in which he successfully synthesized modern European styles with Mexican folklore.

OROZCO
Man of fire, detail (above) of the cupola (below) at Guadalajara, 1938-39
Orozco's human torch is one of many dramatic and disturbing images in the great series of frescos,

begun 1936, at Guadalajara. The cupola, vaults (see far below) and the smaller areas of fresco in the Hospicio Cabanas amount to more than 12,000 square metres, painted by Orozco virtually without assistance.

SIQUEIROS (left)
The portrait of the bour-geoisie, detail, 1939
From 1939 Siqueiros had immense impact on mural-painting in Mexico. In the 1920s he had founded the Communist Syndicate of Artists in an effort to organize artists into an idealistic, unified force, but he had not found his place in the development of mural art. Here, in this detail from a huge scene, which was at first entitled *The image of fascism*, the high gloss of his mature style, enhanced by the use of spray-guns and of thick enamel, has a modernity which contrasts with both Rivera and Orozco.

OROZCO (above)
Machine horse of the conquest, 1938-39
The symbol of warfare and conquest, trailing chains

of slavery behind it, has an almost medieval-looking linear strength and rough-ness. The rider brandishes above the flag of Seville.

SIQUEIROS (left)
For the full safety and social security at work of all Mexicans, 1952-54
The miner, leading doctors and intellectuals towards a better life, represents the power of the working man: the style is typically dynamic. Siqueiros also designed the chamber, with parabolic curves.

TAMAYO (above)
Sleeping musicians, 1950
Tamayo has been labelled "decorative" in contrast to the monumental, apocalyptic mainstream of Mexican painting. Certainly he has none of the cosmic torment of Orozco, and he remains unaffected by the miseries of his subjects. Matisse was of rather greater interest.

The Sources of Abstract Expressionism

During the 1930s there had been an increasing influx of major European artists to the United States, refugees first from Hitler's repression in Germany and then from total war. Picasso and Matisse and Miró did not come, but Grosz, Léger, Albers and Mondrian did, and also – seminal for the triumphant emergence of American painting in the 1950s – practitioners of Surrealism, Tanguy, Masson, Ernst, and its "Pope", André Breton. There was also, in Marcel Duchamp, the enigmatic presence, disruptive yet fertilizing, of ongoing Dada.

The significance of these artists for the new American movement was generously acknowledged by Jackson Pollock, destined to be its most famous star, as early as 1944: "The fact that good European moderns are now here is very important, for they bring with them an understanding of the problems of modern painting. I am particularly impressed with their concept of art being the Unconscious." Yet the very presence of these exiles in the USA indicated the exhaustion of their native European climate; where indeed could art flourish and find a new relevance for a world in violent flux, except in America? The United States emerged in 1945 as the most powerful nation in the world; during the War, unoccupied, unbombed, it seemed, in spite of its colossal military commitments to East and West, to have inexhaustible reserves of energy on which even the arts could draw.

The American public, though mainly in New York and only gradually and reluctantly, had become acclimatized to the shocks of modern art since 1913 and the Armory Show. A network, both cultural and commercial, was building up to sustain and increase its interest. The foundation of the Museum of Modern Art in New York in 1929 was a milestone: it was to develop not only as a museum in the old sense, but also as an active patron and trend-setter. Some of the most famous American private patrons and collectors (notably Gertrude Stein in Paris) were expatriate and orientated to Europe, but others – most famous among them Peggy Guggenheim (1898–1979) – were active and creative agents in America itself. Official acknowledgment of responsibility for the arts, including the avantgarde, had been demonstrated by the Federal Art Project of 1935.

Among indigenous painters, the key transitional figure linking pre-War with post-War American art was Stuart Davis (1894–1964), who brought a concentrated integrity to his pursuit of pictorial structure. (In a curious parallel to George Stubbs' months-long investigation of equine anatomy in confrontation with horses' carcasses, Davis more or less shut himself up during 1927–28 in contemplation of an egg-beater.) Davis' contribution can be seen as an American extension of Cubism: he was at times close to Léger, but he used colour very differently, bright and clear, solid and flat: "People used to think of colour and form as two things. I think of them as the same thing." This, together with his conspicuous modernity, his celebration of the banal vocabulary of everyday urban life, was a decisive influence on artists of the 1940s and 1950s, and then on Pop art. Also significant were the Precisionists, a loosely unified group who portrayed contemporary America in a hardedged, boldly coloured version of Cubism; with them for a time was Georgia O'Keeffe (born 1887), who in a long career developed an increasingly abstract imagery, based on magnified organic forms and on the rolling, windswept plains of Texas.

American artists looked to the East as well as to the West; they also looked to native art,

DAVIS (left)
Lucky Strike, 1921
An illusionistic collage from cigarette packets was Davis' answer to Cubist *papiers collés*; he showed a dazzling virtuosity in the tight restructuring of his fragmented urban imagery.

DAVIS (right)
Ultra-Marine, 1943
The forms seem to stomp through Davis' pictures in jazz-like rhythms, in a magnetic dance: "Colour in a painting occupies different positions in space" was his comment.

NAVAJO ARTIST (below)
"Sand painting", 1966
The painting is performed by a medicine-man, as part of his healing ceremony.

O'KEEFFE (above)
Light coming on the plains II, 1917
The lyrical and evocative shapes of O'Keeffe's work hover on a delicate border between representation and abstraction pure and free.

MATTA
Stop the age of Hemorr, c.1942
Matta's imagery combines study of ancient cultures with an extensive reading of science fiction and of South American novels.

American Indian and Pre-Columbian. Pollock was fascinated by Mayan glyphs, and was intrigued by Navajo "sand painting", not so much its form as its ritual and the manner of its painting, in large gestures and on the ground. It was the supposed motivation of such "primitive" art, its vital and direct contact with the Unconscious, that chiefly interested the Abstract Expressionists. The Chilean Surrealist Roberto Matta Echaurren (born 1912), who lived in the United States from 1939 to 1948, was instrumental in bringing to their notice the American Indian cultures that suggested his personal mythology.

The two main forerunners of Abstract Expressionism were Arshile Gorky (1905–48), Armenian-born, settled in the United States since 1920, and Hans Hofmann (1880–1966), German-born, who migrated to America in 1930. Gorky by 1942 had arrived at a very free calligraphic brushwork, very bright in colour, often entirely without figurative reference. "I never finish a painting – I just stop working on it for a while. I like painting because it's something I never come to an end of." Such statements, no less than his paintings, indicate his importance as a transitional figure for

HOFMANN
Untitled, 1943
Much of Hofmann's work is founded on his theory of "tensions" – he believed conflicting forces should be contained in a painting, in a tenuous equilibrium.

Abstract Expressionism, but his painterliness always reflected his European origins. Hofmann established a profoundly influential school in New York in 1934. He not only was able to provide a forcefully articulated theoretical support for non-figurative art, but remained very open to the stimulus of the new. In particular he reflected Symbolist ideas, of the independence of the world of art from the world of appearances; he used colour to express mood as Kandinsky had, yet retained a feeling for form that stems from Cézanne and Cubism. Anticipating Pollock, he had even experimented with "drip" techniques in 1940, but his own most magical colouristic inventions, coming at the end of his life, express a radiant serenity very far from Pollock's.

Mark Tobey (1890–1978) was never part of the Abstract Expressionist movement; rather, his work ran in parallel with it. He was crucially influenced by oriental example – by Japanese Zen philosophy and painting (see p. 46) with its own kind of "automatism".

After World War II New York was established with remarkable speed as the world centre of avantgarde art, displacing Paris, and so remained for the next 15 years.

GORKY (right)
Water of the flowery mill, 1944
Gorky, born in Armenia as Vosdanig Adoian, emigrated first to Russia and then to America, where he worked through the styles of the fathers of modern art, Picasso and Cézanne, of the Surrealists Miró, Matta, and of Kandinsky. He developed a personal Surrealism that verges on Abstract Expressionism; mercurial forms coagulate and merge, as fluid as the rich paint creating them. A devastating fire in his studio, an operation for cancer, a car accident that prevented him painting, his wife's adultery and his own impotence precipitated the artist's suicide at 44.

GORKY (above)
The limit, 1947
Greys and blacks pervade the works painted during the depression of Gorky's last years. Despite their appearance of spontaneity, even of automatism, they evolved from sketches, sometimes squared up and transferred to the canvas.

TOBEY (below)
Forms follow man, 1941
These frenzied meshes of agitated lines and forms Tobey once called "white writing"; they were directly inspired by his study of oriental scripts. Though his work seems sometimes to anticipate Pollock's, it is not so free, and on a small scale.

HOFMANN (left)
Radiant space, 1955
Hofmann brought with him to America long experience of teaching, in Paris and in Munich. This he imparted to the fledgling Abstract Expressionists attending his school in New York. In later work he managed to amalgamate his European and American careers in paintings of an expressive abstraction often somewhat like de Staël's (see p. 224).

Jackson Pollock

Jackson Pollock (1912-56) was born in Cody, Wyoming. His father was an unsuccessful farmer, and later a government land surveyor: Pollock, in his teens, experienced the vast, elemental landscape of Arizona and the Grand Canyon and also, on surveying trips with his father, came into contact with Indian culture. Moving to New York in 1929, he was taught by Thomas Hart Benton (see p. 206), a leading figure in the American Realist tradition, portraying the rural and small-town Midwest. His subject matter only briefly influenced Pollock, but possibly Benton's rhythmic control of paint and his truculent, independent character made an impression that was to last. Pollock's restlessness was expressed in long, lonely hitch-hiking journeys about America; an addiction to alcohol began very early. In 1938 he started work for the Federal Arts Project and managed to stay with it, somewhat unsatisfactorily, until it ceased in 1943. By then he was in analysis. In the same year, 1943, he signed a one-year contract with Peggy Guggenheim, the most prestigious collector and dealer in wartime New York, and in a group exhibition at her gallery was singled out by the critic Clement Greenberg, who was in no small part responsible for establishing Pollock's controversial fame. In 1945, Pollock married the painter Lee Krasner and moved to Springs, Long Island. There he remained based, while his work became celebrated not only in New York but throughout the world. In 1956, he was killed in a car crash.

By the time of his death, Pollock was already a legendary figure, having fulfilled the public's expectations of a Bohemian artist by outrageous behaviour to match his outrageous pictures. Physically large and impressive, he was also gentle and somewhat inarticulate, almost shy, when sober; when drunk, he would become violently aggressive, hell-bent on shattering the conventions of ordinary society. The existence of his psychological difficulties is well attested, though the interpretation of them differs; it is clear, however, that he had a core of violence – seeking, and sometimes finding, release in his work – which could be irritated beyond control when he was threatened by success, by acceptance by the society whose conventions he scorned but on whom he depended for his livelihood. To his Jungian analyst, his condition when painting suggested "a parallel with similar states of mind ritually

NAMUTH (above)
Jackson Pollock, 1952
Namuth's photographs contributed to Pollock's fame, especially after his death. Magazine articles proliferated, discussing Pollock's private life in as much detail as his art. He was the first American artist to become a star.

POLLOCK (below)
Self-portrait, 1933
Pollock was often to be found in the Benton home in his early days in New York. Benton commented: "He was mostly a silent, inwardly turned boy, and even in gay company had something of an aura of unhappiness about him."

POLLOCK (left)
Going west, 1934-35
The influence of Benton is present not only in the subject matter but also in the undulating contours, in the thick, turbulent paint. Some of this, however, may reflect Pollock's youthful admiration for El Greco. He studied with Benton for two years; he thought his time with Benton was "important as something against which to react very strongly, later on".

POLLOCK (right)
Pasiphaë, 1943
The wife of King Minos of Crete, Pasiphaë, was impregnated by a bull and so produced the Minotaur. The original title was *Moby Dick*; both legends featured huge, primordial animals. Between the Wars Jung had begun to inter-

pret myths as metaphors of the working of psychic energies; Pollock, in the early 1940s, painted a set of works inspired by myths in which elemental forces seem to figure. *Pasiphaë* bears a strong resemblance to Picasso's *Guernica* (see p. 203); Pollock had copied some preliminary drawings.

induced among tribal societies or in shaman-istic trance states''. He was anti-intellectual, though highly intelligent, and drew deli-berately in his mature work on the irrational depths of the Unconscious.

Pollock's early work was influenced by the Mexican Revolutionary painters: they taught him, it has been said, by their expressive, often violent use of paint, ''that art could be ugly''. The large scale of Mexican work, especially the murals, impressed him, and Siqueiros introduced him to new materials and tech-niques, of crucial importance in Pollock's development, since his style was not only conditioned but even generated by his media and the way they could be handled. Picasso and Surrealist influences (especially from Miró) had their effect on Pollock's tumultuous figurative symbolism of the late 1930s. In the early 1940s, Pollock's ''totemic'' period, his work was full of mysterious forms associated with those primordial strata of the imagination from which ''primitive'' art was thought to emerge. The preoccupation with symbols van-ished about 1946, and the non-figurative, ''all-over'' work for which he is famous began. His method is well known from Hans Namuth's

photographs and films of him ''in the act'', and from his own description.

''My painting does not come from the easel. I hardly ever stretch my canvas before paint-ing. I prefer to tack the unstretched canvas to the hard wall or the floor. I need the resistance of a hard surface. On the floor, I am more at ease. I feel nearer, more a part of the painting, since this way I can walk around it, work from the four sides, and literally be *in* the painting. This is akin to the method of the Indian sand painters of the west. I continue to get further away from the usual painter's tools, such as easel, palette, brushes etc. I prefer sticks, trowels, knives and dripping fluid paint or a heavy impasto with sand, broken glass and other foreign matter added. When I am *in* my painting, I'm not aware of what I'm doing. It's only after a sort of 'get acquainted' period that I see what I have been about ... the painting has a life of its own. I try to let it come through ...''

With paint trailed, dribbled, dropped, splashed, smacked across expanses of canvas – often huge – the resulting object is an im-mensely complex network of linear colour. It denies traditional perspective, emphasizes the

flatness of the picture plane yet also creates a mysterious depth in its interstices. The method recalls Surrealist ''automatism'', though Pollock also claimed: ''I *can* control the flow of the paint, there is no accident, just as there is no beginning and no end.'' To a bewildered public the result was at first insult-ingly incomprehensible, meaningless, devoid of form, yet as Pollock's work settles in history its original quality, then felt to be expressive of anger, revolt, even mindless violence, takes on enduring conviction; while losing none of its vitality, it seems now a classic statement.

There was a desperate, doomed aura about several artists associated with Abstract Expressionism, and Pollock's death, whether self-inflicted or drunken or purely accidental, seemed the necessary fulfilment of a death-wish. Intensely subjective, Abstract Expres-sionism demanded of its practitioners a total, almost religious, commitment but, with no established structure of tradition to support them, they were way out on their own, and for some the loneliness, the strain of freedom, proved too much. They were, in fact, true pioneers. The originality of the Abstract Ex-pressionists was their American own.

POLLOCK (left)
No. 32, 1950
Pollock produced a number of works between 1950 and 1952 using black paint only. Their rhythmic quality has since been likened to jazz improvisations with their off-beat tempi and sudden stresses. His habit of numbering his canvases has been explained by his wife, Lee: ''Numbers are neutral, they make people look at the picture for what it is – pure painting.''

NAMUTH (above)
Pollock painting, 1950
Namuth also photographed Pollock at work, and made two films of the progress of a painting from start to finish. ''It was a great drama'', Namuth said, ''– the flame of explosion when the paint hit the canvas; the dance-like movement; the eyes tormented before know-ing where to strike ... my hands were trembling.''

POLLOCK (left)
Convergence, 1952
This is one of Pollock's last paintings using the ''drip'' technique; in his few late works he reverted to a more formal method. It was originally one of the black paintings, and the scrawling network of black lines and splashes can be seen beneath the trails of floating white and primary colours – fixed in a state of flux, seething and dynamic.

Abstract Expressionism: The New York School

The term "Abstract Expressionism" seems to have first been used in Berlin in 1919; rediscovered in America about 1929, as relevant to aspects of Kandinsky's early abstract work, it came into general currency about 1946 to describe the work of a group of American painters centred in New York – though they only very loosely formed a group, and denied that they were abstract. An alternative label, "Action Painting", was coined in 1952 by Harold Rosenberg (born 1906); he and Clement Greenberg (born 1909) were the most influential critics, apologists and expounders of the new movement, which became known also as "The New York school". By 1955, it had become almost a new orthodoxy, matched by parallel or dependent movements in Western Europe under various titles – "Tachisme", "Art Informel", "Abstraction Lyrique"; in whatever guise, it was the expression of fervent individualism, and the communist cultures of Eastern Europe rejected it entirely.

Some of the European, native American and oriental antecedents of Abstract Expressionism have been suggested on page 210. The American upsurge differed from most European abstraction precisely in that it did not depend on an initial abstraction from perceived nature. The paintings had no context in the European tradition of representation or illusionism. The whole painting – the support, canvas or board, and the paint on it – became both subject and object, its primary reality; it was not an abstraction but a physical presence. This presence was emphasized by the very large scale on which most of the Abstract Expressionists worked.

Action painting was carried out at arm's length, with wide and rhythmic sweeps of a large and loaded brush, if brush were used; or, in Pollock's style, the artist almost climbed into the canvas, laid flat on the floor, and swung and dripped paint from the can. From such techniques the "all-over" character of the paintings emerged naturally. The limits of the canvas edges might impose a shape, although Pollock often cut his work for stretching and framing only after he had finished painting. As traditional concepts of composition, space, volume and depth were jettisoned, so the flatness of the picture plane came to be respected, and the varying insistences of colours, in ambiguous relationship with it, came to be

STILL (below)
1957-D no. 1, 1957
Still's enormous canvases dominate the spectator. Their effect is enhanced by the flames of paint which seem to move in and out of the canvas, suggesting that what is there is only a part of something even larger.

KLINE (above)
Orange and black wall, 1959
The major part of Kline's work is in black and white – so stressing the stroke – but throughout he also used colour; his pictures became increasingly larger – this is literally of mural size.

KLINE (left)
Mahoning, 1956
Mahoning is a county in Pennsylvania, Kline's native state. He habitually painted what seem to be memories of the local landscape, an industrial area dissected by numerous railway lines.

GUSTON (left)
Dial, 1956
Guston used to paint very close to his canvas for hours without stopping, so that he became completely immersed in his painting. Using different tones he built up throbbing areas of colour – hence the title "Abstract Impressionism".

GUSTON (right)
Untitled, 1958
Blacks and dark greys start to appear in Guston's work in the late 1950s, and these paintings are more sombre in mood. The brushwork is freer; he lets the viewer trace in the movements of the brush all the hesitations and doubts that are integral to the action of painting.

cherished. The physical action – or exertion – of painting became almost as much an end as a means, and the resulting imagery was the most direct expression, visceral rather than intellectual, of the artist's unconscious being.

Painting was a process of self-discovery by the artist. Artists' selves, however, obviously differ, and so the work of the leading figures in the movement differs likewise, not only in the expressive imagery that they used (or that used them) but in their techniques and attitudes. They can be categorized, if only for convenience, within two poles, the active, and the passive or contemplative. The passive element was common in some degree to all of them, in that they were the instruments of the Unconscious; and they all acted in "psychic improvisation". In some, however, the activity is violent and aggressive in gesture: as time passes, Pollock (see preceding page) and De Kooning (see over) emerge even more clearly as the outstanding figures at this end of the spectrum. The contemplative procedures of Mark Rothko and Barnett Newman mark the passive end, and they are considered beside the later, more colouristic painters (see p. 218). The work of Philip Guston, Clyfford Still,

Franz Kline, Robert Motherwell, Adolph Gottlieb and the ever experimental and articulate Hans Hofmann seems to lie between these two poles; except Hofmann (see p. 210), who was of an older generation, these are the painters illustrated here.

Clyfford Still (1904-80), always a detached figure, worked on a very large scale, his characteristic image being a heavily impasted, jagged form silhouetted in dramatic contrast against a broad, even plane of colour. Philip Guston (1913-80) had his own, highly personal variation, sometimes called "Abstract Impressionism"; from this he moved to a more expressive style in the late 1950s. The vigorous gestural work of Franz Kline (1910-62) has sometimes been compared to gigantically enlarged fragments of Chinese calligraphy; his best-known work was fiercely black and white, but he early began using colour, too. Robert Motherwell (born 1915), originally a scholar rather than a painter, was one of the theorists of the movement – articulate, involved with Existentialist philosophy, seeing painting as an essentially ethical activity. His work is bold and simple, often with symbolic, sometimes figurative and even political connotations.

Still's close contemporary Adolph Gottlieb (1903-74) exploited Surrealist imagery in the 1930s, but was also deeply interested in Indian art, and from this he developed in the 1940s his so-called "pictographs", characterized by very Freudian imagery. In the 1950s, his theme became abstract *Imaginary Landscapes*; these he distilled still further, and at the same time expanded to heroic scale, in his *Burst* series, variations on the theme of an overriding solar orb, luminous above an explosion of colours on Earth – paintings with an apocalyptic presence. The mystic vision developed by the younger painter Sam Francis (born 1923) was lighter, more optimistic – a series of large canvases of the 1950s in which colour runs, coalesces and spills over the canvas. Once described as a "portrait of the surface of the unconscious mind", the result, formless, evanescent as clouds moving in the upper air, invokes meditation. Francis is arguably not of the New York school, since he worked both in Japan and in Paris: his canvases sometimes have the effect almost of a late Monet *Waterlily* painting, while they look forward also to the so-called "colour-field" painting of the 1960s (see p. 218).

GOTTLIEB (below)
Black and black, 1959
Gottlieb's *Burst* series explores the relationship between two shapes, circle and rough rectangle, which have symbolic resonances – of harmony and violence, of freedom and control.

MOTHERWELL (above)
The voyage, 1949
The title is a tribute to a poem by Baudelaire, *Le Voyage*, which described modern art as travelling into unknown territory, much as Motherwell felt he and others were doing.

MOTHERWELL (right)
Elegy to the Spanish Republic no. 34, 1953-54
Motherwell denied that his *Elegies* – there are more than 100 – were political; he called them "general metaphors of the contrast between life and death".

FRANCIS (left)
Summer no. 2, 1958
Francis was Still's pupil in San Francisco and was influenced by Pollock's "drip" technique. He took as his basic theme tensions created between splashes and dribbles of vibrant colour against brilliantly white grounds. Unlike many Abstract Expressionists of the older generation his work lacks symbolic content; he was concerned solely with the emotive values latent in colour, especially white, to him "ringing silence ... an endless, ultimate point at the end of your life".

De Kooning: Woman I

DE KOONING: *Woman I*, 1950–52

DE KOONING (above)
Woman sitting, 1943–44
The thin washes of paint, the muted, delicate tones and graceful drawing recall some works (see p. 210) by Gorky, a fellow-European sharing with De Kooning a studio and an admiration for Picasso and Cubism. Gorky, however, painted very few figurative works.

DE KOONING (right)
Excavation, 1950
Although De Kooning was at his closest to complete abstraction in *Excavation*, its shapes tend to suggest wild ghostly dancers. The painting was very heavily worked, reworked, scraped, rubbed and slashed, until its surface accumulated a solid, densely charged, intricately meshed relief.

DE KOONING (below right)
Study for *Woman*, 1949–52
Greenberg had described De Kooning's aims, before the *Women* alienated him, with sympathy – to recover "a distinct image of the human figure, yet without sacrificing anything of abstract painting's decorative and physical force".

DE KOONING (right)
Woman, 1943
No more than a fraction of De Kooning's 1940s work is extant. His reluctance to finish a painting was ingrained; if possibilities of further work on a canvas seemed unpromising, then often he would destroy it.

DE KOONING (below)
Woman on the dune, 1967
Splayed legs and a toothy grin are the only parts of the woman that are clearly decipherable; the rest of her is inextricably united with the riotous landscape.

The stature of Willem De Kooning (born 1904) is today clear: he was, with Pollock, the strongest and most original force amongst the painters associated with Abstract Expressionism. The intensity of dispute about the relative success or failure of his various shifts of style and subject is perhaps more telling as a witness to his importance than as criticism. While he was always committed to the physical, gestural side of Abstract Expressionism – a true, relentless Action Painter – De Kooning's work represents a figurative element in the movement: figuration seems to lurk in the tormented surface of his paint almost throughout his career: it emerges irresistibly, thrashing demonically through it.

De Kooning migrated from his native Holland to New York when aged 23. By 1939 he was a member of the group soon to be known as the New York school, and especially close to Arshile Gorky. In the 1930s he had painted, in rather delicate greyish, pinkish, greenish tones, alternately pure abstracts and what was virtually traditional figuration. By 1948, when he had his first one-man show, De Kooning's work was generally similar in effect to Pollock's – vigorous, gestural, and often in black and white, for he could not always afford to buy colour, although he was already celebrated in New York avantgarde circles. In

Excavation, an important work of 1950, he did use colour; as soon as this abstract had left the studio he was at work on *Woman I*. He continued to work on it for two years (it has been called "a noble battlefield rather than a completed painting"). Finished, or at least desisted from, in 1952, it was exhibited, with five other *Women*, *nos II–VI*, at his third one-man show in 1953; bought by the Museum of Modern Art, it became one of the most widely reproduced paintings of the 1950s and at the same time a focus for pugnacious controversy amongst not only public but critics: the two most influential critics of the New York avantgarde disagreed violently, Clement Greenberg attacking with the rage of one betrayed, Harold Rosenberg remaining De Kooning's most loyal and articulate supporter. The believers in a rigorously abstract art were dismayed; the general public was shocked by the gross grinning ugliness of De Kooning's presentation of a classical subject, "the idol, the Venus, the nude", as he said.

On first impact, the image is indeed sinister, threatening. It has been construed as a satire on women, an ejaculation of fascinated horror at sexuality, an attempt at exorcism of the threatening Black Goddess or Earth Mother. De Kooning has insisted that it is also funny (specifically, "hilarious"), and that its banality

is deliberate ("I seem always to be wrapped in the melodrama of vulgarity") – this banality was later to be exploited, in very different techniques, by Pop artists. The ferocious leer is a sharpening of the toothpaste smile of magazine pin-ups: De Kooning liked to cut the smiles from the magazines, and in a *Woman* study of about 1950–51 the cut-out smile is pasted directly on to the oil-paint. ("I felt everything ought to have a mouth.") Portions of the anatomy of the *Women* were interchangeable: De Kooning often did drawings of details and tried them for size, pinning them here or there on the canvas.

Violence, energy and ambiguity are staple characteristics of De Kooning's work, but they are not used destructively; instead they are activated as part of the process of establishing an aesthetic order. In his later work, there is an element of landscape involved in the paint, and the female figures in the landscapes all tend to merge back into the vigorous brushwork: many of his later paintings seem closer to pure abstraction, and some find in them a falling off in power, compared to his earlier work. De Kooning is probably not worried. He once said: "Painting the *Woman* was a mistake. It could not be done . . . In the end I failed. But it didn't bother me . . . I felt it was really an accomplishment."

Abstract Developments 1: Colour-Field

Several important artists in America in the late 1940s and the 1950s were experimenting with the use of flat areas or fields of colour to induce contemplation in the beholder – even to a pitch of mystic intensity. Most of them are generally described as of the New York school and as Abstract Expressionists, but if they were Abstract Expressionists they were very much on the passive wing of that movement, in contrast to the agitation of Pollock or De Kooning, though it is hard to draw a dividing line – Clyfford Still's work, for example (see p. 214), can be thunderous in mood, but is positively severe in contrast with Pollock's action. The work of these artists was on a very large scale, in which it differed sharply from the related investigations of Albers and others, the scale being necessary to the creation of the effect.

The senior and most distinguished of these "colour-field" painters was Mark Rothko (1903-70), Russian-born, but brought up in the United States; he has been described, with Still, as the chief exponent of the "American Sublime". He had first exhibited in 1929, and by about 1940 was working in an expressively Surrealistic vein, busy with biomorphic imagery not unlike Gorky's (see p. 211). By 1947,

however, he was evolving the formula to which he was to remain faithful for the rest of his life. This formula, though generally interpreted on a monumental scale, is almost as simple as that of Albers' square (see over). Rothko's rectangular canvases proffer, on an even-coloured ground or field, two or three rectangles of different colours, varying in width or in height but seldom in both, disposed precisely horizontal or vertical. There, however, precision ends, for the colour is washed or stained with shifting tones, shifting luminous intensities, while the edges of the rectangles blur out of definition until the colour seems to float – and, so powerful and intense is the impression of mysterious radiance flooding from these great canvases, the spectator in contemplating them may seem almost to float, too.

"I am for the simple expression of complex thoughts", said Rothko, and indeed his best work invites and seduces to always unconcluded meditation. It is at its most potent when several canvases surround the onlooker, as in the series, on an heroic scale, at Harvard and in a chapel at Houston, Texas, which reproduces for a twentieth-century sensibility the effect of Bernini's Cornaro chapel (see vol. 2 p. 190) –

ROTHKO (above)
Central green, 1949
Rothko declared that he set out to use colour in such a way that it would stimulate in the spectator an emotional reaction, such as ecstasy or melancholy.

ROTHKO (above)
The Rothko room, Tate Gallery, London, 1958-59
Rothko required progress "towards clarity, towards the elimination of all obstacles between the painter and the idea, and between the idea and the observer. As examples of such obstacles I give ... memory, history, geometry."

NEWMAN (right)
The third, 1962
A writer and dialectician as well as a painter and also a sculptor, Newman has had battles of words with many; one of his best witticisms is "Aesthetics is for the artist as ornithology is for the birds."

NEWMAN (above)
Concord, 1949
By rejecting utterly all the traditional ingredients of painting, such as depth, figuration, shape or form, Newman believed that he was making an assertion of freedom. He once said in an interview that if the world could read his work correctly it would abolish all state or totalitarian control of the individual.

totally involving the onlooker, who becomes a participant. Rothko's first such commission was for a set of convases to decorate the Four Seasons restaurant in the Seagram building in New York: he produced in fact three sets, each more sombre in colour, and finally withdrew from the commission altogether. He later selected eight of the final set to be hung in the Tate Gallery, London, where he knew his paintings would be hanging under the same roof as Turner's.

Barnett Newman (1905-70) was associated with Rothko and Motherwell in the founding of an art school on Eighth Avenue, New York, in 1947 and with the Abstract Expressionist group in general: he worked for a time on the magazine *The Tiger's Eye*, which voiced the opinions of many of the group. In his mature work he arrived at even more simplified solutions than Rothko, and was never influenced by the gestural painting of Pollock. His formula already by 1950 was closer to the investigations of Mondrian or of Constructivism than to those of either Rothko or Pollock, although, like Pollock, he sought inspiration in the elemental art of the North American Indians, finding there a "terror before the

unknowable". In his formula, however, the mystical aim is distilled down to the sparsest symbolic geometry: the composition is that of the rectangular canvas, essentially a field of colour divided by one or more vertical stripes. Newman seems to have seen this reduction also as an assertion of the sublime; though his paint is still laid on, applied not stained, and the brush-marks remain, Newman's work is unimpassioned in character, and essentially "cool" in the sense that the young abstract painters of the 1960s would be cool. Close in mood both to Newman and to Rothko was William Baziotes (1912-63), though he developed a style that verged on the figurative as theirs never did; his paintings contain often relatively complex shapes suggestive of animate or inanimate forms.

One figure crucial to the development of colour-field painting was Helen Frankenthaler (born 1928). After working in a Cubist tradition, she moved into an Abstract Expressionist key in the early 1950s, making a significant development of Pollock's "drip" technique. In a painting of 1952, *Mountains and sea*, the paint, rather than being dripped and trailed on the prostrate but primed canvas, is instead

stained or soaked, diluted very thin into raw, unprimed cloth, and becomes integral with it rather than applied. The method allows the spontaneity and immediacy of Pollock's work, but mutes his "bravura rhetoric". Through Frankenthaler's work generally there emerges a sensation of landscape, of lyricism, of lightness and airiness.

When in 1952 Morris Louis (1912-62) visited New York from Washington, he was as much impressed by *Mountains and sea* as by Pollock's work, and in 1954 he developed a refinement of its technique, using thinned acrylic paint, very liquid, on unprimed cotton duck. In his series called *Veils*, the translucent colours, the weave and texture of the cloth, drift down in inextricable unity: the illusion of depth, reduced in Pollock's work but still present there, is eliminated. In his last works, influenced partly by his younger friend, Noland (see p. 222), he produced his *Unfurled* and *Pillar* series, in which he set off rivulets or stripes of opaque and brilliant colour against a vast white blankness of the canvas. His work became increasingly impersonal, closer to the hard-edge colour investigations of Albers (see over) and others.

BAZIOTES (left)
White bird, 1957
Baziotes differs from most Abstract Expressionists in his attention to subject matter, though he was no more willing to be tied down by it than the rest. His images are free forms.

FRANKENTHALER (right)
Mountains and sea, 1952
The seminal importance of this painting's technique has tended to overshadow its fine formal qualities. Frankenthaler abandoned in later work its whipping, wiry lines of charcoal.

LOUIS (below)
Floral, 1959
The achievement of Louis' mature work was built on a foundation provided by Frankenthaler. Louis said of her: "She was a bridge between Pollock and what was possible".

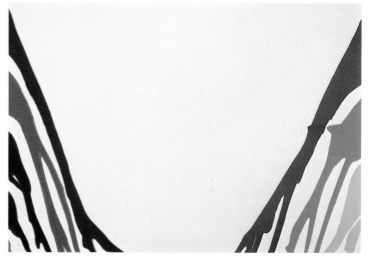

LOUIS (above)
Gamma zeta, 1960
The expanse of "unfurling", nearly 4m (12ft) across, bound only by the banks of rivulets, suggests an abyss into which the spectator is drawn. The scale of the canvas makes it possible to take it in as a whole only from a great distance, and as the viewer approaches there is a growing feeling of magnetic attraction and of unavoidable engulfment.

Albers: Homage to the Square

The post-War movement in painting that shocked and dazzled the eyes of the Western world in the 1950s was the Abstract Expressionism of the New York school. The scale of their paintings, the unorthodox behaviour of the painters – the noise of it all – diverted the attention of the media and the general public from other, parallel trends in art. These did not, however, wither away. Problems of harmony and proportion in abstract painting were being explored by Josef Albers (1888-1976), who had been teaching at Black Mountain College in North Carolina since 1933, when he migrated there from the Bauhaus (see p. 191), closed in that year by the Nazis.

Albers was a quintessential product of the Bauhaus. He was there first as a student and then as a teacher, and was concerned as much with the applied as with the fine arts, working on the Constructivist side of Bauhaus theory, in the glass and furniture workshops. The clarity and irreducible economy of his future painting was already present in his stained or sand-blasted glass, and in his furniture designs – he was responsible for one of the first laminated wood chairs. In North Carolina, where he had a reputation primarily as a teacher, he explored the relations between geometry and colour in a series of paintings, *Variations on a Theme*, but only after he had moved to Yale, in 1950, did he begin in earnest the sequence called *Homage to the Square*.

Homage to the Square consists of hundreds of paintings and prints all within a square format; though they vary in size, they all feature three or four squares, superimposed – a nest of squares positioned with vertical but not horizontal symmetry. Some are distinguished, within the series, by lyrical subtitles (*Distended, Softly spoken, Curious* etc.); some are only numbered. Albers used the formula to demonstrate his abiding belief in an essential dichotomy of art, "the discrepancy between physical fact and psychic effect". Thus the linear structure of his square pictures is of the most simple, unarguable clarity. The colour structure is created likewise in evenly applied paint, straight from the tube; the colour of each of the three or four squares usually has no variation of intensity, and so should be completely inexpressive of any quality other than its particular blueness, redness – its local colour. In fact, in the eyes of the onlooker, the flat picture plane becomes three-dimensional as one colour seems to advance, another to recede, according to its nature; furthermore, the pure evenness of colour within each square is affected optically by reaction to its neighbours – and all the colours shift character as the light in which they are seen changes. The colour is a mystery floating on the canvas, independent of the lines which contain it.

ALBERS (right)
Fugue, 1925
This is a good example of Albers' Bauhaus work, on opaque glass. The colour is removed through stencils to reveal the glass beneath.

ALBERS (below)
Variation in red, 1948
Each of the *Variations on a Theme* has the same basic geometry in varied colours.

ALBERS (below)
Transformation of a scheme no. 24, 1952
The disturbing optical effect prefigures Op Art. This, too, is from a series.

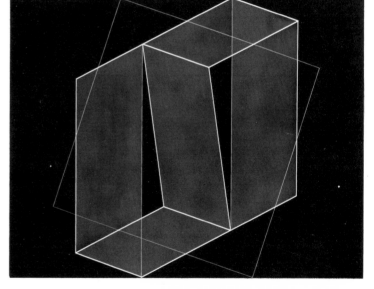

ALBERS
Studies for *Homage to the Square*:
(left) *Rain forest*, 1965;
(right) *R-NW IV*, 1966
In all the variations the largest square measures 10 units; the other squares set within it measure a varying number of units or half units. These two show a progression from base to top of $\frac{1}{2}$:1:4:3:1$\frac{1}{2}$; across the ratios are 1:2:4:2:1. *Confirming* (far right) has four squares, not three; the ratios are from base to top $\frac{1}{2}$:$\frac{1}{2}$:$\frac{1}{2}$:4:1$\frac{1}{2}$:1$\frac{1}{2}$:1$\frac{1}{2}$; across the ratios are 1:1:1:4:1:1:1.

ALBERS: Study for *Homage to the Square - Confirming*, 1971

Albers thought long and deeply on colour phenomena; his treatise *Interaction of Color* was published in 1963. He also played with another form of optical illusion in a series of linear drawings, black on white or vice versa, called *Structural Constellation* – the abstract equivalent of Escher's famous figurative nonsense drawings (see p. 175). He was not, however, the slave to a need to produce a closed logical system, and in *Homage to the Square* he presents the problem in an endless series of solutions, or variations, of the unreconciled yet reconciled co-existence of colour and geometrical linear structure on his canvases. He was

also a poet, and some of his poems state the paradox with equal wit and clarity.

Initial confrontation with a single Albers painting may be disappointing: they need really to be seen in a sequence, when the variation in scale, in the internal relationships of the nesting squares, but above all the play of colour over and through the invariable physical fact of the square, make their full impact.

Homage to the Square was the climax of Albers' remarkable career as a transitional figure between the European traditions and the new American. His work evolved from the European, non-objective art of the Construc-

tivists – of the early Russians, of Mondrian and De Stijl – through the aesthetic, and the moral and social commitment, of the Bauhaus. It is European in scale, best when small and intense (his large-scale murals were done by assistants from his blueprints); some have likened his *Homage* to Monet's famous series. His heirs, however, were the Americans of the late 1950s and the 1960s, who, while respecting the Abstract Expressionist achievement, found in his work a pattern and an intense colour sensation on which they could build (see over). Later again, his interest in perception became relevant for Op and even Conceptual art.

Abstract Developments 2: Hard-Edge and Minimal

Ad Reinhardt (1913-67) emerged as a major figure in the 1950s, pursuing with rigour an impersonal abstraction dominated by purely formal problems. Reinhardt had been working in a fairly geometric, rectangular style since the late 1930s, unaffected by the expressive, gestural work of Pollock and De Kooning; by the 1950s he had reduced his elements even further than Newman and Rothko (see p. 218): he painted series, each in terms of a field of one colour – red, blue and, finally, black. At first glance these may seem just rectangular canvases painted in one colour; the component rectangles or squares lurking in the colour only gradually emerge. His aim was "art-as-art", to be achieved only by reduction to the ultimate abstraction – "no other art or painting is detached or empty or immaterial enough" – and his severity was highly influential.

The impersonal effect of Reinhardt's and also of Newman's and Albers' canvases provoked a strong response from the younger artists who would form the "hard-edge" wing of colour-field painting. Kenneth Noland (born 1924) looked at Pollock but "could gain no lead from him". As it had been for his friend Morris Louis (see p. 218), Frankenthaler's

technique of colour-staining was seminal for Noland, and he, too, integrated his acrylic colour into the substance of the cloth, not applying it to the surface as Newman did, in oil; colour materializes in the shape of his picture. Like Louis, too, he would become obsessed by one image, working through variations on it until its possibilites were exhausted. Unlike Louis', however, Noland's colours, in a lucid high key, are usually defined with geometrical precision by a knife-sharp contour, the "hard edge". His first series, concentric rings of colour within the white field of the unprimed canvas, dates from the late 1950s and early 1960s. About the same time, Jasper Johns (see p. 236) was investigating the same image, as a *Target*, but with very different aims, moving towards Pop art; Noland's interests, however, have more to do with the workings of colour vision, afterimages, induced colours and the like – Op art. Later on, in variations on a chevron theme, Noland shifted the image to an asymmetrical position on the canvas, and then allowed the image to form its own white field and to dictate the shape of the picture: in works such as the elongated-diamond-shaped canvases of about

NOLAND (above)
Ember, 1960
Though moving towards a hard-edged style, Noland sometimes in this series would leave the outer ring unfinished, suggesting that the whole is pulsating and expelling unwanted energy.

NOLAND (below)
Apart, 1965
For two years Noland was at Black Mountain College with Albers; the fruits of their contact are evident in Noland's hard edges, his concentration on one image, the kind of image he chose.

REINHARDT (below)
Untitled, 1948
Reinhardt's earliest work shows the assimilation of various abstract styles: prime and prior was the

influence of Mondrian (not least the late work, see p. 189) and of Stuart Davis. His paintings of the 1930s are hard-edged and bright in colour, but during a period

of close contact with the Abstract Expressionists in the 1940s he softened both the angularity and the colour of his painting. Reinhardt's intention, to

produce an art devoid of any external associations, was shared by Rothko and Newman, but his work is purer, if only because its emotional effect is less.

OLITSKI (below)
Green goes around, 1967
Olitski's works have been described as "the first fully abstract version of Impressionism". They are built up from layers of

sprayed paint which shift in hazes across the canvas with a result reminiscent of the atmospheric effects of Monet's *Waterlilies* (see p. 126); Olitski spent a year studying in Paris.

REINHARDT (left)
Black painting, 1960-66
Reinhardt has described his progression towards the black squares as a search for an image like that of the Buddha, which he once called "breathless, timeless, styleless, lifeless, deathless, endless". His ultimate aim was, he said, "to paint and repaint the same things over and over again, to repeat and refine the one uniform form again and again" – which is a Minimal art.

1966, the unity of image, colour, surface and object is absolute. Some of his vast horizontal-stripe paintings are only centimetres tall, but several metres long (Barnett Newman had preceded him in this kind of narrow painting, but vertical, in the early 1950s).

The Russian-born Jules Olitski (born 1922) had moved by the early 1960s into pure fields of colour, saturating (using a fine spray) un-primed canvas with paint, obliterating linear design, depth of space and all composition other than the shape provided by the (usually vast) rectangle of the cloth. Ideally, he once said, he would like "nothing but some colours sprayed into the air and staying there". The colour is indeed lusciously rich, sometimes too sweetly rich for some palates. In one phase – whether in a nod in the direction of Abstract Expressionism or in an ironic snook against it – there is gesture sprawled at just one edge.

The development of hard-edge painting in the 1950s and early 1960s can be read as stages in the progress towards the "ultimate abstraction" that Reinhardt sought, into the utterly impersonal realm of Minimal art (see further p. 246); and yet that progress was undertaken by distinctively different personalities. Ells-worth Kelly (born 1923) and Al Held (born 1928) both reflected in their work European sensibilities, each having spent some time in Paris in their twenties, setting on a flat-coloured ground large, clear-cut, flat-coloured shapes that seem to echo Matisse's cut-paper pictures (see p. 228) or the flat reliefs of Arp rather than any American example. Kelly in particular was influenced by the European Constructivists and produced paintings and prints composed of bold, striking colours set one next to the other; though he was not so obviously con-cerned with optical effects as Albers, Kelly's work has a similar impact. Forms abstracted from natural ones seemed to linger behind Kelly's images in the early and mid-1950s, but then, perhaps finding it difficult to resolve satisfactorily the relationship of image to col-our field, he moved into true Minimal art with featureless sculpture – at its simplest, two sheets of metal, coloured. Al Held first attemp-ted to reconcile Pollock and Mondrian, then moved into the Abstract Expressionist orbit with very heavily pigmented work. By the late 1950s, however, his constructions, while still heavily painted, were greatly simplified, but on a very large scale: one remarkable series was structured on capital letters of the alphabet. In 1964-66 came the colossal, 17-metre (56ft) long *Greek garden*, and then his work, no longer classifiable as Minimal, moved towards the three-dimensional.

The archetypal hard-edge Minimal painter in those years was perhaps Frank Stella (born 1936). By 1958-59 he was implicitly criticizing the energetic gesturing of Abstract Expres-sionism in an austere group of black canvases, patterned with concentric, geometric, very thin lines: his aim was "to force illusionistic space out of the painting at a constant rate by using a regulated pattern. The remaining problem was simply to find a method of paint application which followed and complemented the design solution. This was done by using the house-painter's techniques and tools." He advanced to aluminium and copper stripes, and to very strongly shaped irregular canvases, which, hung on a wall, do not so much deco-rate it as take charge of it. He has experimented with shapes of many kinds, using vivid, often harshly discordant colour, sometimes fluor-escent, applied utterly impersonally: with Stella the individualism crucial to Abstract Expressionism was finally eliminated.

KELLY (below)
Four panels, 1964
The term "hard-edge" was coined by the Los Angeles art critic Jules Langser in 1958; it was then taken up by the British-born critic Lawrence Alloway and applied to a tendency in American painting of the early 1960s. The clean, clear colour and forms of hard-edge work constitute a homogeneous surface – without figure or ground.

HELD (above)
Greek garden, detail, 1964-66
A decisive factor in the development of hard-edged painting was the European sojourn of its practitioners – Held, Olitsky, Kelly and Noland, who were all studying in Paris in the late 1940s and the 1950s, and so were not closely involved in the onset of Abstract Expressionism. Reacting to the style of Pollock and others, Held wanted, he said, to "give the gesture structure".

STELLA (below)
Port aux Basques, 1969
Stella insists that his work is totally objective. In an interview in 1966 he declared: "My painting is based on the fact that only what can be seen there is there. It really is an object. All I want anyone to get out of my paintings, and all I ever get out of them, is the fact that you can see the whole idea without any confusion. What you see is what you see". This non-associative colour and weaver's pattern corroborate his words, but his recent art is exuberant.

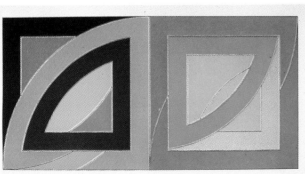

STELLA (above)
Black adder, 1965
Although shaped supports have often been used in the past in altarpieces or in canvases for specific locations, in this century few artists before Stella had experimented with the painting's shape. Arp had, Chirico had, but for them shape was not the prime subject. Mondrian's *Fox-trot* series offered some precedent. But for Stella shape is inseparable from what shape contains, the one determining the other.

Informal Abstraction in Europe

When World War II ended, some European refugees remained in America, to be integrated into the American scene; others returned to Europe. Those who returned tended to go back to Paris: there was Picasso like a living monument. But for many Picasso was now an Old Master; the interests of the so-called "middle generation" lay in other directions, some of them strikingly parallel to those of the rising New York school of Abstract Expressionism, but initially quite independent of it. In France, these tendencies had various labels, corresponding to the niceties of underlying theory, if not so obviously to definable differences in practice – "Art Informel", "Tachisme", "Abstraction Lyrique", "Art Autre" – now generally called "Informal" art. They were essentially a reaction of the irrational and spontaneous against Constructivist abstraction, for instance in Mondrian.

Jean Fautrier (1898-1964) had painted during World War II a series called *Hostages*, inspired by victims of Nazi brutality – images built up in thick, clotted layers of paint. Their modelling was rudimentary in any naturalistic sense, but they revealed great feeling for refined colour and for the sensuous quality of the raw material of paint. Wols (Wolfgang Schülze, 1913-51), German-born, was early associated with the Surrealists (Miró, Tristan Tzara, Ernst) in Paris, but took to drawing and painting as his primary activity only during the War – his work was intensely subjective, an expression of his psychic reactions to experiences endured in these years. Like Fautrier, he used densely worked paint textures. Wols' later paintings, however, are a record of the activity of manipulating paint rather than an attempt to evoke associations; the parallel with Pollock is striking – the doomed charisma, the alcoholism, the social and artistic nonconformity – and both died young. But Wols was an Existentialist, a friend of Sartre, and his paintings do not express exuberance as Pollock's so often do, but often seem the very image of alienation. Hans Hartung (born 1904), another German-French artist, was painting abstracts by 1922, and even before the War had formulated his own characteristic, linear style – clusters, bundles or sheaves, usually sharp and brittle, often on a field of translucent colours. This is a sort of calligraphy responding directly to unconscious energies – "drawing flowing from the fingers", as Wols once described his own work. Pierre Soulages (born 1919; not shown) achieved similar contrasts with broad, elemental bands of black, resonant against white.

By 1947 Georges Mathieu (born 1921), self-styled founder of Abstraction Lyrique, propagandist and publicist of verve and panache – "the fastest painter in the world" – was painting in spontaneous splashes, with paint squeezed from the tube, worked with the fingers, in a rapid but elegant calligraphy of colour whipped across a plain background. The affinities with Pollock's Action Painting (though Mathieu worked quite independently) are clear; Mathieu, too, worked on a very large scale. His avowed purposes were different, however: Mathieu aimed to create in his abstract painting the equivalent of traditional epic "history" painting, and above all – this applies to all the painters of the Paris school, except Dubuffet, when compared to the leading American Abstract Expressionists – Mathieu's work is somehow stamped with European qualities of tastefulness and succulence, and lacks the elemental force of the Americans.

European delicacy and suggestion are most exquisite in the work of the Russian-born

WOLS (left)
The blue phantom, 1951
The mysterious forms that inhabit Wols' paintings resemble huge monocellular organisms. He disliked, he said, "too much ambitious purpose and gymnastics".

DE STAEL (right)
Figure by the sea, 1952
De Staël's brilliant and sensitive colour harmonies were stimulated by trips to Morocco and the South of France: this was painted at Antibes shortly before his suicide. A friend of Braque's, he painted not "psychic improvisations" but constructed evocations.

FAUTRIER (above)
Head of a hostage, 1945
Fautrier's source, though he has abstracted from it, was decayed human heads. The agony of his theme is conveyed not by realistic rendering of the wounded features, but by a hacked impasto, pink-tinged, which merely suggests some brutal mutilation. Fautrier's later works are like reliefs, the paint is laid on so thickly.

HARTUNG (right)
T 1955-23, 1955
Hartung's work is typical of Art Informel: his lines are a record of a release of the artist's energy. If his painting is compared to Kline's (see p. 214), then the problem in assessing the European equivalent to American Action Painting is clear: Hartung's work has been judged "eloquent" or "monotonous"; Kline's work has a brash vigour that is neither of these.

MATHIEU (below)
Painting, 1952
Speed, for Mathieu, was essential, to prevent ideas and memories hampering the brush's dancing rhythm.

Nicolas de Staël (1914-55). His chords of colour and his infectious delight in the sheer sensuous qualities of his paint ("*la matière*") were unrivalled in his generation. His art was a development of Cubism, and he found himself unable to resolve, at least to his own satisfaction, the equation he sought – the union of an abstract picture surface with the natural image of reality. Expressed in rather different terms, a comparable concern with surface textures and the integrity of materials appeared elsewhere in Europe, in Spain in the work of Antonio Tàpies (born 1923) with its rough,

decaying, scrawled and scratched surfaces, and in Italy in the rags, sacking and bandages of Alberto Burri (born 1915).

Nearest to the American Action Painters in uninhibited, even brash vigour were the artists of the brief-lived CoBrA group (the original members came from Copenhagen, Brussels and Amsterdam), which held together from about 1948 to 1951. The Dutchman Karel Appel (born 1921) was the major talent here, assaulting the canvas with stridently savage slashes of colour, sometimes abstract, sometimes swirling into crude imagery. The most

original spirit of this European generation was, however, the Frenchman Jean Dubuffet (born 1901), who settled into full-time painting only in the 1940s; his first exhibition was in 1944. Initially taking Klee's ideas perhaps still further, he found models of a fiercely direct expression of the Unconscious in the paintings of the insane and of children – "Art Brut".

The variety and quantity of Dubuffet's output has been formidable. In the late 1940s and the 1950s his characteristic media were sand, earth, glue, clinkers etc., with pigment mixed in, bashed and scratched into vitality to reveal weird primordial creatures, foetuses, fertility figures and the like. But Dubuffet's variations on different combinations of materials to produce new relationships are almost unclassifiable. In the early 1960s, he experimented extensively with a brilliantly coloured all-over imagery he called *L'Hourloupe*, or *The Twenty-Third Period of My Works*. In these sometimes enormous canvases – one is 8.2 metres (27ft) long – a coagulating writhe of interlocking squiggles resolves itself on closer inspection into an endless jig of small totemic frenzied creatures. Through much of his work there runs a sort of manic gaiety; it vividly expresses many of the main preoccupations of the post-War period, including the paradox of highly cultured, self-conscious and sophisticated urban man deliberately seeking out the primitive, the Unconscious, the ugly.

APPEL (right)
A bird with a fish, 1956
The members of CoBrA shared a common interest in "primitive" and Naive art and in automatism. In most of his work Appel's dynamic, violent textures are used to express natural forces, animal vitality.

TAPIES (below)
Pale blue composition, 1956
Tàpies combines sand, glue and matt, cracked paint in severe compositions, "when dull, inert matter begins to speak with incomparable expressive force". His attitude to materials was almost moral; formulated in the mid-1950s, it was highly significant for the 1960s.

BURRI (right)
Sacking with red, 1954
Burri began to paint when he was a prisoner of war in Texas: there he had to paint on pieces of sacking instead of canvas, and his post-War work contains similar wasted materials – sacks and rags roughly sewn and torn, often singed, splashed with paint. His *Sacchi* (Sacks), resembling stained bandages, express Burri's war experiences, but are also a metaphor for decay and destruction, for the mortality of mankind.

DUBUFFET (left)
The very rich earth, 1956
All the myriad variety of the cells making up a speck of earth is suggested in the variegated mosaic of the painting. It contains, however, a figure – goblins like this inhabit most of Dubuffet's clotted abstracts.

DUBUFFET (right)
Uncertain situations, 1977
This recent work seems to be directly inspired by Dubuffet's collection of Art Brut: crude cartoon figures like those found in children's drawings are in abundance. All save one are enclosed in capsules, from which some strain to be free – a comment perhaps on contemporary existence.

Wyeth: Christina's World

More sorts and kinds of people have responded directly to the paintings of Andrew Wyeth (born 1917) than to any other post-War American painter, yet his work remains controversial. In many accounts of post-War painting, for which the great American breakthrough of Abstract Expressionism is the springboard, he is simply omitted as an anachronistic irrelevance, yet not only is *Christina's world* (in the Museum of Modern Art, New York, since 1949) one of the best known and loved images of American art, but in 1976 Wyeth was given a major one-man retrospective exhibition in the Metropolitan Museum.

Andrew Wyeth is the son of N.C. (Newell Convers) Wyeth, a distinguished illustrator and painter. Brought up as it were breathing art, he proved a precocious virtuoso, and had his first one-man show in New York when he was only 20. In 1939 he came to know a brother and sister called Olson, on a remote farm in Maine; he spent the summers there, painting the farm, the region and a series of remarkable portraits of Christina Olson until her death in 1967. The first impact of *Christina's world* (finished in 1948) is eerie and troubling: the figure of the girl, seen from behind, twisted

WYETH (left)
Christina Olson, 1947
Christina is sitting on the doorstep of her house. Late afternoon sun falls on the lined and wrinkled face and frail body, and it casts a strange shadow on the door behind her, which is as weathered as she is. She is looking out across the fields towards the sea: Wyeth said she reminded him of "a wounded seagull".

WYETH (above)
Christina's world, 1948
Wyeth was devoted to his sitter; he said: "*Christina's world* is more than just her portrait. It really was her whole life and that is what she liked in it. She loved the feeling of being out in the field, where she couldn't go, finally, at the end of her life ... a lot of it came out of what she told me." The composition was prompted by a sight of her from a window in the house, when she had been out getting vegetables, "pulling herself slowly back towards the house".

WYETH (left)
Grape wine (Willard Snowden), 1966
In his portrait of a farm labourer Wyeth draws on sentiment, but cannot be convicted of any sentimentality to weaken and dilute his formal mastery. But adverse critics dislike his nostalgia, and the way in which he elevates his local "characters" to be representatives of something quintessentially American.

WYETH (left)
Nick and Jamie, 1963
Many of Wyeth's works seem to be charged with an electric poignancy; this is particularly true of some interiors and landscapes that are portraits and yet unpeopled. Wyeth has discovered a way to invest objects and places with the presence of those no longer there; thus two sacks on a late autumn day evoke the artist's sons.

WYETH (left)
River cove, 1958
Tempera, for Wyeth, is almost a building material, and crucial to his aims: "I love the quality and the feel of it ... to me, it's like the dry mud of the Brandywine valley in certain times of the year, or like these tawny fields ... I really like tempera because it has a cocoon-like feeling of dry lostness – almost a lonely feeling."

WYETH (above)
The hunter, 1943
Apart from his holidays in Maine, on the Olsons' farm, Wyeth has spent his entire life in the small village of Chadds Ford, Pennsylvania. That is in part why his art is remote: these two regions form his world, he lives their landscapes, people and animals, while most artists, he has said, "just look at an object and there it sits".

awkwardly in the expanse of grass, is focused on the house on the crest of the slope. This house and the second house, seen directly behind Christina's head, and Christina's body are linked inexorably, pinioned on the three corners of a triangle, yet the sense of huge distance, seemingly unbridgeable, physically or psychologically, between the woman and the main house on which the grey sky sits so claustrophobically is overwhelming. Many, perhaps most people assume at once that the subject is an attractive young girl, an interpretation prompted by what could be a youthful abandon in the grass, and by the slightness of the body, the adolescent fragility of the arms. In fact Christina Olson was at this time a mature woman, somewhat gaunt, and so severely crippled that she proceeded by dragging herself on her arms. Several of Wyeth's initial rough drawings (not shown) record his determination to discover the exact articulation of the maimed body, which in the finished painting seems to express both the tragedy and the joy of life with such vivid poignancy that the painting becomes a universal symbol of the human condition – and is recognized as such: the picture has had a continuing fan mail from people who have identified with it.

Wyeth has described his sequence of portraits of Christina: "I go from *Christina Olson* (1947), which is a formal one, a classic pose in the doorway, all the way through *Christina's world*, which is a magical environment, that is, it's a portrait but with a much broader symbolism, to the complete closeness of focusing in *Miss Olson* (1952; not shown). *Miss Olson* was a shock to some people who had the illusion that the person in *Christina's world* was a young, beautiful girl. And that is one reason why I did it, in order to break the image. But I didn't want to ruin the illusion really, because it's not a question of that. One has to have both sides – one, the highly poetic; the other, the close scrutiny ...."

Wyeth has denied any fundamental influence on his development from other painters, though he has acknowledged generously inspiration from artists as diverse as Winslow Homer and Albrecht Dürer. His affinities with the impassioned detail of Dürer (particularly the watercolours) are obvious, and his technique of dry brush over watercolour is close to Dürer's, and not far short of him in brilliance and virtuosity. In his large paintings, too, his techniques are resolutely traditional; he uses tempera rather than oil, with extreme sensitivity and with a range of earth colours. His practice is minute, laborious and slow, and the paintings are prefaced in great detail by preparatory drawings.

Wyeth's work at its best demonstrates that the traditional subjects, media and techniques of Renaissance painting can still result in images that have a profound significance. His work is also quintessentially American, and in a sense, though so different in technique, he offers the rural counterpart to Edward Hopper's earlier characterization of American urban townscape. A comparable sense of vastness, and of isolation and loneliness, invests the work of both, but is expressed by Wyeth in the intensity of his realization of detail.

After 1945: Old Masters of the New

Picasso established a new type of career as a desirable norm for many artists – a career consisting of a sequence of discoveries, of new periods or styles, each style being worked until its possibilities were exhausted, at which point a new discovery, a fresh point of departure into a new seam, was necessary. In fact Picasso himself could work in entirely different styles at the same time (see p. 202). None could match his prodigal inventiveness, the speed with which he would see and grasp possibilities before anyone else, the ruthlessness with which he executed his *volte-faces*, his independence, his charisma, his legend. There were, however, other outstanding artists of the pre-War generation who were content to develop after World War II along their own lines. Their progress tends to be unjustly overlooked in the historians' compulsive charting of the new, but artists whom one tends to regard as pre-World War II figures (or even as pre-World War I figures) were producing superb work from the late 1940s even into the 1970s. This is true not least of Braque, who in his later works, before his death in 1963, achieved a series of masterpieces, notably one famous sequence, *Ateliers*. He worked always within

the Cubist idiom: still life provided his most constant theme as it had half a century before, but it yielded now compositions of superbly resolved balance and serenity, yet sensually rich in colour and texture.

Picasso occupied a place apart, even if, in the last 20 years before his death at the age of 91 in 1973, he was more a monument to be skirted respectfully by younger artists than an active influence. For the general public, for the media world-wide, he remained a focus of unflagging fascination. In a secular age, he was almost venerated. Through a series of acts, as copious as the rain of heaven – his pictures, sculptures, graphics – he created not least money by a process as mysterious and incomprehensible to most people as were once the miracles of the saints. Waiters snatched the table-cloths on which he had doodled during a meal; his signature was a blank cheque.

The work itself was a different matter. After *Guernica* and *The charnel-house* (see p. 203), his recharged energies exploded in some splendid affirmations of hope (at the same time he joined the Communist Party, though it cannot be said either that it had much influence on his work, or that his work had a discernible

PICASSO (above)
The painter and his model, 1963
This had been a favourite theme of Picasso's since the early days, one which he revived with new vigour in the early 1960s after his second marrage. His young wife, Jacqueline, was often the model. Her bland sexuality contrasts with his uneasy self-consciousness.

PICASSO (left)
Mounted rider, c. 1951
In the late 1940s Picasso began working within the small community of ceramic artists in Vallauris near Antibes. Other painters, notably Gauguin and Miró, had turned to ceramic art, but Picasso's reputation and his magical charisma stimulated new interest in this "minor" art form.

BRAQUE (above)
Atelier II, 1949
The spectator enters the artist's private world as if through veils of space wrought with signs of his presence – the palette and brushes, the head, the bird on a canvas. No suggestion of location detracts from the decorative surface patterns of the great *Atelier* series.

PICASSO (right)
Women of Algiers, 1955
Between December 1954 and February 1955, Picasso carried through 15 variant reworkings of Delacroix's painting of the same title (see p. 81). He retained the perfumed vermilions and smoky golds, also the voluptuous curves of the famous original in each.

MATISSE (above)
The snail, 1953
Crippled with arthritis, Matisse directed from his chair the execution of this huge work, a slow winding surge of glorious colour.

influence on the Communist Party). The best known of his later paintings are the series of variations in his own manner on masterpieces of the past – by Velazquez and Poussin, by Delacroix and Manet – reflecting once again the inescapable obsession of twentieth-century art with art; and his often moving variations on the theme of the aging artist and his young nude sitter. Much of this shows supreme virtuosity, but often not much more (the famous film made by Henri-Georges Clouzot in 1955 of Picasso painting with a light-bulb was revealing – in effect the recording of a performing juggler or conjuror). The quality in his work that so often confounded the critics, that irreverent wit, also expressed itself in sculpture – in sheet-metal cut-outs sometimes colossal in scale, in ceramics, in bronzes of figures and animals, sometimes painted. Of these last, some famous examples – the bull's head which is a bicycle saddle and handlebars, the ape whose head is a toy motorcar – delighted multitudes but encouraged a suspicion that Picasso was not perhaps wholly serious. It is too often forgotten that one of his great achievements was to add to the gaiety of nations, over and above enlarging the scope of

art with Braque way back about 1910.

The grand old man who in his late work proved a more exploratory and inspirational figure was Henri Matisse: during the 1920s and 1930s (see p. 184) he had pursued his own way, stubbornly independent of Picasso, almost deliberately unprovocative and aloof from the social or political mission of many other artists, intent on producing paintings serenely resolved and luminous with colour, to give pleasure. From 1948, in addition to a continuing output of exquisitely reductive yet vital linear work (ranging from book illustrations to the monumental simplicity of his wall and stained-glass decorations (1949-51) for his chapel at Vence near Antibes) he embarked on a series of famous compositions in cut-out paper (*gouaches découpées*). In some of them, he came far closer to extreme abstraction than he had before. He did not revert to sculpture; he spoke, however, of his cut-outs in three-dimensional terms. "Cutting into living colour reminds me of the sculptor's direct carving" – in this sense he had distilled a new mode for painting. It was in one way comparable to the Minimal art of the rising generation, yet was also an exhilaration of radiant colour

acting and interacting, a triumphant affirmation of the fullness of life. Matisse died in 1954, nearly 20 years before Picasso, but it was his last work rather than Picasso's that younger artists found stimulating.

Other masters of the school of Paris continued to develop within their own terms of reference – notably Léger, returning from America after the War, who died in 1955. The later work of European and American artists who made their impact before World War II has mostly been discussed when their names have first come up (Calder and Giacometti had perhaps greater impact after the War (see over), though we have glanced at their earlier work in context). They were generally impervious, though seldom oblivious, to the cut and thrust and the new arguments of the younger generation; to this Ben Nicholson and Oscar Kokoschka were no exception, but they have perhaps been too little considered. Kokoschka, who died in 1980, made little change to his masculine Expressionist style (see earlier p. 195); Nicholson (see previously p. 198) after World War II went on to a superb synthesis of severe abstraction with an evocation of English mist and light.

MATISSE (above)
The Tree of Life in the Chapel of the Rosary, Vence, 1949-53
Matisse himself thought the Chapel was his masterpiece. It exemplifies his mature style: here simple organic shapes flow across azure and turquoise; the walls are black and white.

NICHOLSON (right)
Poisonous yellow, 1949
The still life on a table was a recurrent theme in Nicholson's work: in this he was trying to achieve, as he said, such an effect "as if the paint had been wished on to the canvas".

LEGER (below)
The builders, 1950
Léger has used the frame of a modern building under construction as if it were a prefabricated Cubist form. His distinct late style has the sturdy, free directness of Naive art.

KOKOSCHKA (below)
Louis Krohnberg, 1950
Kokoschka continued in a long series of portraits to explore personality in corrosively Expressionist brushwork. His colours became noticeably brighter and happier after the War.

Post-War Sculpture 1

World War II caught several major sculptors in mid-career. In England Moore (see p. 200) and Barbara Hepworth (see p. 199) steadily continued to develop along lines established earlier, while the international reputations of both rose higher. Moore opened the way for other sculptors in Britain, and the important talents that emerged mainly in the 1960s owed much to him, although formally their work was mostly in sharp reaction to his (see p. 246). In France, Picasso's energies were unleashed in sculpture of great variety and invention (see preceding page), culminating, in size at least, in his colossal, sheet-metal monument of 1966 for the Civic Center in Chicago, 20 metres (65ft) high. In Switzerland Alberto Giacometti had shifted from "orthodox" Surrealism about 1935, but the remarkable originality of his new style was only revealed after the War (see over); and after 1945 the work of some other European sculptors of the same generation, whose reputations had hitherto been confined to their native countries, almost abruptly took on international significance. All had achieved in different ways an original synthesis of traditional values with a contemporary sensibility.

Marino Marini (1901-80) in Italy had discovered his enduring theme of *Horse and rider* even before the War. His inspiration came rather from the medieval equestrian statue at Bamberg (see vol. 2 p. 76) than the classical *Marcus Aurelius* (see vol. 2 p. 51) in Rome or the heroic Renaissance variations of Donatello and Verrocchio; close parallels are perhaps also to be found in the equestrian figurines of Tang pottery (see p. 37). The theme in his hands became the reverse of triumphant, seemingly the expression of anguished despair at a hostile fate. His elemental imagery, handled with almost primitive roughness, so that the figures seemed to have been recently excavated from centuries of oblivion, certainly touched responsive chords in a wide public, with the force of a new but valid and recognizable mythology. In the 1950s Marini drove his theme to the extremes of stylization, in the 1960s into an abstraction sometimes recalling Moore's recumbent figures (the two sculptors shared a mutual admiration). He was also a painter and printmaker, and not least a consistently powerful portraitist, succeeding in capturing remarkable likenesses of his sitters without diluting his personal style at all.

MARINI (left)
Horse and rider, 1946
There is no suggestion of the movement of riding; Marini's interest is the tension between horizontal and vertical. In the lively skew of faces and limbs, in the spontaneity of the childlike image and its modelling, there is an instant appeal.

MARINI (below)
The miracle, 1943
Marini was trained both as painter and as sculptor, and his textures reveal a painterly sensibility. He patinates his bronzes with acids, and adds dashes of colour to his plaster. His bust carries both Gothic and Expressionist echoes.

RICHIER (above)
Storm, 1949
Female companion to this
menacing personification was *Hurricane* – scabrous, stark, elemental spirits.

MANZU (left)
Detail of the Portals of Death in St Peter's, Rome: *The stoning of St Stephen; the death of St Gregory the Great; death in space; death on earth*, 1950-64 Manzù succeeds where other religious sculptors of today have failed: he invigorates Neoclassicism.

MANZU (right)
Great cardinal, 1955 Manzù made more than 50 *Cardinals*, varying in size from bust to larger than life: this is 2m (7ft) high. He insists that they are really still lifes, that he intends to capture "not the majesty of the Church, but the majesty of form".

Likewise, in France, Germaine Richier (1904-59) created a personal mythology with something of the same elemental, universal quality, though the general public found her work shocking. She used traditional forms – animals, birds, insects or the human figure – but their traditional anatomies are savaged or decomposing in places – in a sort of visceral symbolism grafted on to realistic detail. When she applied what seemed a morbid Expressionism to sacred themes such as Christ's crucifixion she provoked outrage. The new aspects of death and mutation revealed by the destruction of Hiroshima seemed never far from her thoughts. She was a pupil of Antoine Bourdelle, who was himself a pupil of Rodin, and her violence extended some of the idioms of Rodin's later work, but her imagery also recalls Giacometti and Dubuffet.

The aims of the Italian Giacomo Manzù (born 1908) have been very different, although he has aligned himself firmly with the great, unbroken European tradition from Donatello to Rodin, Degas and Maillol. His life-size bronze nudes (not shown), at first glance "cast from the life", and his chairs with bronze still lifes of vegetables on the seats evoke un-expected echoes of the work of Johns or some Pop artists. The naturalistic detail is in fact fused with artistry into the volume of the whole. In his long series of tented *Cardinals* in their copes, begun as early as 1936, he pushed towards simplification and monumentality. He also returned to the tradition stemming from Ghiberti's Baptistery doors (see vol. 2 p. 100): not without controversy, he was commissioned to make bronze doors for St Peter's in Rome and for Salzburg Cathedral.

In America, there was no immediate revelation in sculpture to parallel the explosion of Abstract Expressionism in paint – it is difficult indeed to imagine the equivalent of a Pollock "drip" painting in stone or metal. Alexander Calder, however, the most delightful and joyous sculptor of the twentieth century, had far from exhausted his invention. His mobiles had created dreamy arpeggios in the middle air already in the 1930s (see p. 181); after the War he continued to play variations with these, but developed them, and his standing mobiles, and his stabiles, to a monumental scale. His later colossal stabiles – *Man* (1967, not shown) soars 29 metres (95ft) high – are like a new breed of fossilized anthropomorphic dinosaurs, and have a strong architectural presence, relating to the ground more like an Eiffel Tower than a sculpture. His mobiles continued, and they also now demonstrated conclusively that the traditional base was not an inevitable component of sculpture – a vital fact in the work of David Smith.

David Smith (1906-65) had turned from painting to sculpture about 1930-33, much influenced by the metal sculpture of González and Picasso. Vigorously exploratory, before arriving at his most original and successful forms he experimented in many modes, from Surrealist fantasy to "drawing in space" with steel, from the use of found objects (usually elements of farm machinery) to Cubism. His last, most celebrated sequence, *Cubi*, was based on a grammar of cubiform elements in stainless steel, polished and then abraded, arranged at odd angles, and raised on a monumental scale against the sky with an extraordinary authority, a totemic expressiveness. Smith was the reverse of the Bohemian type: allied with the working man, the factory technician, he had a strong social conscience, and was aware both of the splendour and of the miseries of mechanized civilization.

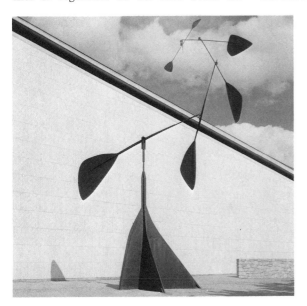

CALDER (left)
The spiral, 1958
Calder's undertakings since 1945 have included a series of large-scale commissions for public places. Beside his giant indoor mobile at John F. Kennedy Airport or his acoustical ceiling in Caracas his standing mobile outside the UNESCO building in Paris is quite modest, but it, too, is a feat of construction engineering.

CALDER (below)
Slender ribs, 1943
Calder wished to enable "nature and chance to replace the mechanical and calculable as the motive forces". For his friend Sartre his sculptures were at once "almost mathematical technical combinations, and symbols responsive to Nature".

SMITH (above)
11 books, 3 apples, 1959;
Zig II, 1961; *Cubi II*, 1963
The photograph was taken by the sculptor in 1965 in the field behind his studio. *Zig II* is painted; *Cubi II* is just behind a forerunner of the series, the polished steel *11 books, 3 apples*.

SMITH (right)
Head, 1959
Smith once said feelingly: "Steel is so beautiful because of all the movement associated with it, its strength, its functions. Yet it is also brutal, the rapist, the murderer, and death-dealing giants are often its offspring."

Giacometti: Man Pointing

GIACOMETTI
Man pointing, 1947

MICHEL DESJARDINS (above)
Alberto Giacometti, c. 1965
The artist is moulding clay

or plaster round a stick: the
model was cast in bronze,
often issued in a set of six.

GIACOMETTI (above)
Dog, 1951
"It's me. One day I saw
myself in the street just
like that. I was the dog."
Dog has accordingly been
read as a *Self-portrait
in a moment of depression.*
Subjects other than men
and women are very rare in
Giacometti's post-War art.

GIACOMETTI (right)
*Composition with seven
figures and one head (The
forest),* 1950
"The composition with
seven figures reminded me
of a forest corner seen for
many years (it was during
my childhood) where trees
. . . with their naked and
slender trunks, limbless
almost to their tops, had
always appeared to me like
personages immobilized in
the course of their wanderings and talking among
themselves." The figures
of the forest are all women.

About 1935 Alberto Giacometti (1901-66) had
become increasingly dissatisfied with his work,
and returned to direct study of the life model:
"I saw afresh the bodies that attracted me in
life and the abstract forms which I felt were
true to sculpture, but I wanted the one without
losing the other." He then worked almost
exclusively, throughout the War, on the
human figure, from life and then from memory, but he emerged into public attention only
in 1948, with an exhibition in New York,
introduced by the Existentialist philosopher
Jean-Paul Sartre. Painting, which he had
abandoned altogether in 1937, he resumed in
1946. In both painting and sculpture, he
pursued his quest, primarily in terms of the
human figure, until his death in 1966.

GIACOMETTI (above)
Caroline, 1962
Giacometti's paintings are

most commonly portraits
– of Caroline, his model, or
of his wife or his brother.

The process of his search for truth was
essentially reductive – at first almost catas-
trophically so: ". . . to my terror the sculptures
became smaller and smaller. Only when small
were they like (reality), and yet these dimensions revolted me, and tirelessly I began again,
only to end up, a few months later, at the same
point. A big figure seemed to me to be false and
a little one just as intolerable, and then they
became so minuscule that with a final stroke of
the knife they disappeared into dust. But the
heads and figures only seemed to me to have
any bit of truth when small." Finally about
1945 he was able to make figures to a larger
scale, finding "to my surprise that only when
tall and slender were they like", but the
reductive principle was never abandoned. His
vision was always conditioned by his knowledge that reality escapes clear definition: he
once said that he tended to see people as if
against the setting sun, their edges "whittled
away by the light refracted about them".
"Whatever I look at, everything gets beyond
me and astonishes me, and I do not know
exactly what I see. It is too complex . . . It is as
if reality is continually behind curtains that
one tears away – and then there is another,
always another . . . And so one goes on, know-
ing that the nearer one comes to the 'thing', the
more it recedes. The distance between me and
the model tends always to increase . . . It is a
quest without end." So, too, his figures seem to
exist not at the apex but within the cone of the
spectator's vision: the focus of one's eyes is
always on some elusive point beyond them.
Giacometti's world was that of the modern
physicist: it was composed not of solid, inert
matter but of entities apprehensible only as
centres of energy. Especially in his paintings
his sitters become a sort of vortex of energy,
re-creating their own spatial environment.

Possibly the relevance of Giacometti's art
will diminish, but in the 1950s and 1960s it was
quite startlingly real; the works of Giacometti
and of Francis Bacon (see over) were compelling evidence that the figurative tradition still
had profound importance. Sartre found the
essence of Giacometti's art to exist in absolute
freedom – the Existentialist *Angst.* He noted
more specifically: "What must be understood
is that these figures, who are wholly and all at
once what they are, do not permit one to study
them." It is perhaps the physical presence of
Giacometti's people, combined with the difficulty of grasping that presence, that is the most
compelling quality of his art. They are there,
but they are also "other"; they keep their
distance. The men may walk, may point: the
women, whether the size of a pin or giants
anchored on huge feet, are immobile with such
intensity that their rigidity can affect the way
people stand as they look at them. They reject
ownership: they are metaphors of human isolation, even more tellingly when grouped in
clusters or groves, often in entirely disparate
sizes. Though their ancestors in art are clearly
discernible (and Giacometti himself was fully
aware of them – Etruscan bronzes, Egyptian
sculpture, Oceanic art), they remain disturbing. They are Existentialism personified, having heroic loneliness (which some have compared to the dour and doomed integrity of
characters in Samuel Beckett's plays).

Bacon: Figures in a Landscape

The emergence – eruption almost – of Francis Bacon's work in the 1950s was a shock to international art. Critics at first found his paintings hard to accept; his expressionist images forced attention in a context of all-conquering abstract or near-abstract art, developed in the early post-War years by Pollock and the Abstract Expressionists in America, by Ben Nicholson in England, and by Nicolas de Staël or Hans Hartung in Europe. Picasso, working in the figurative tradition, was already regarded as an Old Master.

However, the pictures of Francis Bacon (born 1909) were disturbingly relevant; and their formidable immediacy made it necessary to reconsider the assumptions made about figurative painting. Its once basic function, to achieve "a good likeness", had been undermined by photography a century earlier – portraiture especially seemed to be surviving as a social rather than as an artistic phenomenon – but this was not a return to naturalism. Bacon, abandoning the abstract decorations of his pre-War years, exploited photography for his own artistic ends. It became a springboard for a figurative art that was fundamentally unphotographic. Bacon also works from the life, but the results are not what an old-fashioned sitter would accept as portraiture. Though Bacon himself might not agree that this was his intention, he transmutes these given images into fluid, mutating visions that convey horror, violence and suffering. In his early figurative work, such as *Figure in a landscape* of 1945, he used some more or less traditional devices of Surrealism, but by 1950 he was concentrating on the theme, seemingly inexhaustible, that he has explored ever since – studies of a single figure in spotlit isolation, or two figures locked in struggle (or perhaps sometimes in love).

The origins of his images are usually clearly discernible, but always they have suffered melting, dissolving, change. Often his imagination seizes on one particular image from which a sequence of variations develops. The first and most famous of these was the *Screaming Popes* series, based on one of the most vividly sane and seemingly definitive portraits in all European painting, Velazquez's *Pope Innocent X*. This Bacon has avoided seeing in the original, but knows only from reproductions. Subsequent series included one based on van Gogh on his way to work, and one developed round the life-mask of the poet-painter William Blake. Other pictures, including *Figures in a landscape*, 1956, are inspired by the rapid-sequence photographs of the human body in action made by Eadweard Muybridge (see p. 127). In Bacon's portraits a constant theme is the confined, clinical space in which the isolated sitter is trapped.

Superficially, Bacon's compositions have a traditional structure, a perspective recession into depth; but once having entered the picture's space, the viewer's eye is puzzled and baffled. In *Figures in a landscape*, 1956, the subject seems unfocused, ambiguous – here the vertical stripes of green at the back might be a fence, or a curtain; the central landscape sprouts grass of some kind, but reads more like a pit or an arena; the two naked figures are certainly human – or used to be, or are about to be, human. Are they wrestling? If so, in hate or love? Even their sex is unclear. The subject rejects exact definition, and yet mesmerizes.

Bacon's appeal to post-War sensibility lies in the fact that while his creatures are indisputably flesh and blood and compel our unwilling identification with them, they are also convincing embodiments of mental anguish. Bacon has invented a new grammar and imagery of human expression. Its frame of reference is contemporary awareness of the horrors of the twentieth century – concentration camps, gas chambers, the continuing techniques of torture throughout the world – as well as the private mental disturbances revealed by psychoanalysis or described in Kafkaesque literature of claustrophobia and alienation. Bacon's use of a glass box (not only holding his figures in focus but trapping them) even prophesied a haunting image of post-War reality – Press photographs of the Nazi war criminal Eichmann in an armoured-glass dock at his trial in Israel.

BACON (right)
Figures in a landscape, 1956
The naked human body is a main theme of Bacon's; a powerful sense of flesh as heir to pain and decay may stem from his view of man as "an accident, a completely futile being".

BACON (left)
Study after Velazquez, 1953
Among the sources for this early study in the series of *Screaming Popes* are not only Velazquez's painting but a photograph of Pope Pius XII borne in a litter above the crowds and the sketch of a howling face by Poussin for his *Massacre of the Innocents* (not shown).

VELAZQUEZ (right)
Pope Innocent X, 1650
The very opposites of the qualities Velazquez set himself to convey – spiritual authority and temporal might – inspire Bacon: his studies of agonized beings are seemingly gripped by a horrific, negative vision of life. Feeling for colour and texture, however, is something in common.

BACON (right)
Figure in a landscape,
1945
A photograph of a friend
dozing in the park becomes
an image of menace; hands
rest casually on the arm
of the chair, but the head
has melted away and at the
elbow is a machine-gun.

BACON (above)
Isabel Rawsthorne, 1966
Features grossly distorted
by dynamic brushwork, as if
rent by an obsessive scream,
are typical of Bacon's
expressive portraiture.

EISENSTEIN (below)
Still from the film *The
Battleship Potemkin*, 1925
The helpless individual, a
children's nurse caught in
a Revolutionary chaos, was
a potent image for Bacon.

Johns and Rauschenberg

Two young American painters emerged into the ferment of the New York artistic scene almost simultaneously in 1955 – Jasper Johns (born 1930) and Robert Rauschenberg (born 1925). When Abstract Expressionism seemed in the intensity of its subjectivity to have reached a point of no return – or at least to offer no future in its own terms – these two offered a way forward, and were to have a profound effect on the development of several currents in painting during the next two decades.

Rauschenberg had the more varied apprenticeship, in Kansas, briefly (1947) in Paris and then at Black Mountain College in North

Jasper Johns
In contrast to his friend Rauschenberg, Johns has a rather reserved, precise temperament; in the words of one interviewer, "He has a remoteness that, while very amiable, makes all questions sound vaguely coarse and irrelevant."

Carolina; there, too, came Johns. The presiding gurus of the college were Josef Albers and the philosopher-musician John Cage (born 1912). The austere detachment and geometric clarity of Albers' work (see p. 220) has affinities more with Johns' early practice than with Rauschenberg's, but Albers' approach to art, his persistent questioning of its philosophy and its aims, his intellectual seriousness, certainly influenced both of them. Cage's music reached out of the conventional framework of the art into (in one form) silence: the listener was to identify, even create, his own music in the silence beneath the surface of random sounds. "The thing to do is to keep the head alert but empty. Things come to pass, arising and disappearing. There can be no consideration of error. Things are always going wrong." Cage's principle of "unfocusing" the mind – which owes much to Japanese Zen Buddhism – was equally applicable to art.

The most obvious novelty of Johns' and Rauschenberg's work was their return to representation. Johns' early work was often literal, illusionistic. He tended to paint series as Albers was doing, and to represent objects that were both everyday, even banal, yet also

charged with universally recognizable symbolism. His most famous series was *American Flag*. The flag is often copied faithfully in detail, and its proportions determine exactly those of the canvas on which it is painted – if it were painted on both sides you might fly it as a flag. Yet it is worked in a positively tactile, sensitively textured, painterly medium of pigmented encaustic, so it is also very firmly a work of art. In a way this is an alternative position to Marcel Duchamp's. Duchamp's ready-mades were posited as works of art by the act of the artist simply designating them as such; Johns, as it were, took ready-mades and with uncompromising objectivity painted them back into art – or sculpted them, as in his notorious painted bronze facsimiles of beer-cans. He could also, however, introduce weird and disturbing extraneous elements: the most famous of his *Target* series has four half-seen plaster casts of impassive faces built into it – like the masked faces of a firing squad, or the blindfolded faces of victims. Here the heritage of Dada and Surrealism is obvious.

The impact of Johns' one-man show of 1958 was very great, partly because it offered avenues of development out of Abstract Expres-

JOHNS
(left) *Three flags*, 1958; (below) *Target with four faces*, 1955
"Using the designs of the American flag took care of a great deal for me because I didn't have to design it, so I went on to similar things like the target – things the mind already knows. That gave me room to work on other levels." Ambiguity and paradox are central to John's vision: things are not necessarily what they seem. Abstract qualities – texture, colour, drawing – are emphasized in a representational painting; a *Flag* is not only a flag or a reproduction of a flag but also neither – a third object in its own right.

JOHNS (left)
Painted bronze II, 1964
The object was back, if not quite figuration in the old sense. It is quite clear that these exact reproductions of beer-cans are not beer-cans: they are art, and they look like it. The step that Warhol then took, with his *Brillo* sculpture (see over), was to remove this quality.

JOHNS (below)
Untitled, 1972
The four sections of the work portray a progressive abstraction from right to left. The pattern of the "real" elements of wood and plaster is repeated in the representation of flagstones in the centre and in the cross-hatched abstraction on the left.

sionism without overturning the dogma that a painting was primarily a worked surface, subject and object in itself. Johns then, however, shifted his own attitudes: "The early things", he observed in 1965, "to me were very strongly objects. Then it occurs that, well, any painting is an object, but there was . . . I don't know how to describe the sense alterations I went through doing this, in thinking and in seeing. But I thought then, how to make an object which is not so easily defined as an object?" By 1974, he was stating his wish "to focus the attention in one way, but leave the situation as a kind of actual thing, so that the experience of it is variable". Thus he offers his work to the spectator not only to arouse a traditional aesthetic response but also as a platform for open-ended dialectical discussion.

In this he is sometimes very close to Rauschenberg. Rauschenberg moved through experiments with all white, all black and all red paintings in the early 1950s to what he called "combine-paintings", a development of collage and montage techniques, first seen in exhibition in 1955. Some were quite modest, but the notorious *Bed* (not shown) of that year incorporated a real quilt and pillow amidst Abstract Expressionist splashes and runs of paint on the canvas. Four years later, *Monogram*, since widely exhibited, presented a complete stuffed angora goat or ram girt with an automobile tyre standing on a horizontal canvas treated more conventionally with collage and paint. Other works have incorporated items such as radios and clocks. At this stage, Rauschenberg was not transforming objects for his imagery, but simply transferring them. "I am, I think, constantly involved in evoking other people's sensibilities. My work is about wanting to change your mind. Not for the art's sake, not for the sake of that individual piece, but for the sake of the mutual co-existence of the entire environment." In the 1960s, he reverted to a flat surface, and implanted much of his imagery in the form of silk-screen transfers – at one remove from the real objects – but the method of heterogeneous juxtaposition remains much the same. Latterly he has emphasized its casualness, its dissociation from the traditional conception of making and using pictures, by suspending his canvases slack and loose, even behind a slightly opaque covering. Like Johns, he presents art as an idea to be cogitated by the viewer; in both their work there is implicit criticism of the long-standing Western acceptance of art as a commodity to be owned or merely enjoyed.

The work of Johns and Rauschenberg proved a rich mine for subsequent movements. Pop was to take heart from Johns' use of the most contemporary, banal and ephemeral imagery, though adapting it for different ends. Both Johns and Rauschenberg continually stretched the constraints of painting; Rauschenberg has danced on stage (on roller-skates). Indeed Happenings may seem only an intensification, animation and expansion into real life of his "combine-paintings".

Robert Rauschenberg
"Everything goes crazy whenever he is here", said his printer. "You work his hours, his way, non-stop . . . It's incredibly exciting and incredibly exhausting."

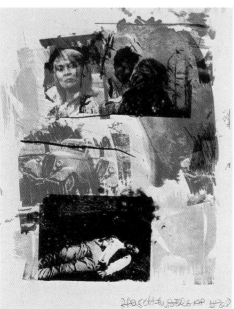

RAUSCHENBERG (above)
Monogram, 1959
"Painting relates to both art and life. Neither can be made. (I try to act in that gap between the two.)" Out of his materials he tries to conjure latent meanings, new references.

RAUSCHENBERG (left)
Story-line 1, 1968
This includes stills from the film *Bonnie and Clyde*, which established a cult following in the late 1960s. The images are set in an abstract mosaic – content is played against form.

RAUSCHENBERG (right)
Sleep for Yvonne Rainer, 1965
The artist believes that "there is nothing that everything is subservient to": therefore in his work no element is given more importance than any other.

American Pop Art

The "pop" in Pop art is for "popular", but also for a bright explosive quality, a visual counterpart to "snap-crackle-pop". Its application to a strong, controversial and highly publicized trend in the art of the 1960s originated in a painting of 1956 by a British artist, Richard Hamilton (see over), but though the British Pop movement preceded the American one in time, the American version originated independently; and it was in New York and also in California, sunlit home of Hollywood fantasy, that the style found its fullest and most spectacular destiny.

Pop art is often seen as part of a reaction against Abstract Expressionism, but from Abstract Expressionism Pop art inherited various elements, not least an immensely enlarged sense of the possibilities for art in general, and, specifically, for the effects of large-scale work and "all-over" painting. In contrast to Abstract Expressionism, however, it is, most obviously, a return to figuration; and the paintwork is often clean and crisp. The subject matter represented is the material of contemporary urban life, the new, the instantly banal, the consumable, the ephemeral, the highly sophisticated "folk art" of the second half of the twentieth century – comic strips, giant billboards, slickly styled automobiles, cigarette packets or film-star pin-ups. Pop art did not so much draw from these as reproduce them in different terms.

Pop artists exploited ground already opened up earlier in the twentieth century by Dada, by the Surrealists. Pop, however, even though it was sometimes called "neo-Dada", did not have the satirical or anarchic edge of the original Dada. Pop was affirmative rather than destructive, though the artists celebrated at a distance, with detachment, objects not previously found worthy of celebration, and objects that had already been processed – even reproductions of reproductions.

The immediate, most direct forebears of Pop were Johns and Rauschenberg (see preceding page), though they always held somewhat apart, and their painterly interests were not followed. Another in-between figure was Larry Rivers (born 1923), whose very sensitive and sensuous pleasure in paint traditional connoisseurs gratefully recognize. By the late 1950s he was applying it to a mixed and fragmented imagery, a free play of words and images. Rivers is an empiricist, often irre-

WARHOL (above)
Liz no. 2, 1962
The glamour of fame and the media obsesses Warhol; in a sense it is the main-spring of his work, though his view of it is typically ironic. It is all surface, but surface is the interest.

WARHOL (below)
Brillo, 1964
"I adore America", Warhol said, explaining his work. "My image is a statement of the harsh impersonal products and ... material-istic objects on which America is built today."

RIVERS (right)
French money, 1962
Johns and Rauschenberg and Larry Rivers bridge the gap between Pop and Abstract Expressionism, relating everyday objects and sensuous paint – even if Rivers is less dialectical. His canvases are not large, but cool, relaxed, elegant. He has perhaps influenced British Pop rather more than American; he denies, however, any "super visual strength and mystery in the products of Mass Culture ... I have a bad arm and am not interested in the art of holding up mirrors."

LICHTENSTEIN (left)
Masterpiece, 1962
Lichtenstein has described in detail how he set about making one of his "cartoon" paintings. Having selected a self-contained "frame" from a comic, he made a pencil drawing, introducing perhaps a few changes. He projected the drawing on to canvas, painted in the main lines, and made dots with a toothbrush through a per-forated screen. The result works on several levels, but is also entirely "straight".

INDIANA (right)
Yield brother, 1963
Indiana (the name is that of his native state) is an aggressive, bold nationalist committed to an American style of hard-edged, sign-like painting, which often looks like a giant badge – hammering its message. "I propose to be an American painter, not an internation-alist speaking some glib visual Esperanto – possibly I intend to be a Yankee."

verent and witty, rejecting dogma; he was nevertheless probably the first to treat the "vulgar" subject matter of Pop seriously.

Roy Lichtenstein (born 1923) has been one of the most consistent and pure practitioners of Pop ideas – a painter of types and media ideals. He is best known for his recycled extracts from comics, blown up, hugely enlarged: in these the stencil-like dots of cheap reproduction printing processes are faithfully reproduced, but the whole image is simplified into a unified design, a controlled composition. Later, he abstracted similar giant simplifications from reproductions of "fine art" – the brush-marks (see p. 254) of Abstract Expressionists, even the diagrammatic analysis by an "art-appreciator" of a Cézanne painting. One objective may be to force the spectator to question his own scale of values. Andy Warhol (born 1930) in some works questions specifically the traditional values of the hand-made and unique art-object and, even more forcefully, the concept of originality. He uses mechanical processes – especially silk-screens – facilitating repetition, and employs assistants like factory hands: all traces of personal involvement by the artist with the work are

avoided. His subject matter varies from the banal – a battalion of identical Coca-Cola bottles; sleep recorded in a film six hours long of a man asleep; a stack of Brillo boxes – to the ideal – a popular beauty or sex symbol, Marilyn Monroe, Liz Taylor, Jackie Kennedy, dehydrated in turn to banality – to the horrific – a deadpan juxtaposition of almost endless prints of the electric chair. So, too, in the glare of publicity the artist's own personality is simplified, enlarged and drained of reality until it becomes as impersonal as an image on the film screen. When, in 1968, Warhol was shot and severely wounded by an acolyte, it seemed almost another dimension of his work, though it proved him human after all.

Warhol makes no overt comment. Often he seems to register boredom by boring the spectator, but on an heroic scale with mesmeric intensity. Robert Indiana (Robert Clark, born 1928) in contrast was positively Romantic and Symbolist, though generally non-figurative, combining letters and slogans in very clear-cut designs (his colour and clarity owe something to Ellsworth Kelly). He has functioned as a social and political commentator, and imbued his work with a strong sense

of American history and literature. James Rosenquist (born 1933) worked for a time as a billboard painter, and in his enormous Pop paintings used the impersonal, generalized billboard techniques of representation – fragmented, the fragments juxtaposed in disarray. This can be read as a modern variation on the theme of Vanity of Vanities, and Rosenquist's formal inventiveness does seem to have a moral import. Tom Wesselmann (born 1931) produced a celebrated set of variations on the theme *The Giant American Nude*, simplified almost to silhouettes of sharp clear colour, their erotic content tantalizingly set at a great distance. Wesselmann has also been closely involved with an expansion of collage, "assemblage" art – incorporating real objects such as ringing telephones or televisions switched on.

Claes Oldenburg (born 1929) and Jim Dine (born 1935) can also be considered Pop artists, although their work crosses many boundaries. Oldenburg's giant soft sculptures of everyday objects and Dine's incorporation of similar real objects in his paintings are consistent with the idea of Pop. Both, however, are equally well known for their participation in the development of Happenings (see p. 242).

ROSENQUIST (above)
Flamingo capsule, 1970
Rosenquist's imagery, taken from advertising and colour magazines, then expanded to huge proportions, bombards the spectator with scale and glaring, aluminized colours as in a free fall or a car crash. The two ends reach out to enclose the viewer, so as to increase the effect.

WESSELMANN (below)
Great American nude no. 14, 1961
After an initial training in Abstract Expressionism, Wesselmann went figurative.
But he considered that "to paint a flower would be boring": he used collage – or three-dimensional bits. His nudes belong not to the life-class but to magazines.

DINE (above)
Things in their natural setting, 1973
Dine's work is openly autobiographical, concerning his life (his grandfather owned a hardware shop) and experiences as a painter.

OLDENBURG (right)
Giant fag-ends, 1967
The foam-filled cigarettes are truly gigantic; they are intended to get in the way, almost ludicrous in their very obvious irony. Like Warhol, Oldenburg annoys.

British Pop Art

British Pop art took shape in a group of young artists and critics (The Independent Group) at the Institute of Contemporary Art in London in the early 1950s. It was in part a revulsion against the grey austerity of post-War Britain (where rationing still persisted) and the anticlimax of an impoverished peace following an alleged victory. It celebrated the delights of Western, especially American, materialism, and came as a shock to the still-new orthodoxy of belief in abstraction, in underlying values, and equally to a more traditional pastoral romanticism that had revived in the 1940s. Pop artists proposed in contrast initially a blatant, even vulgar, emphasis on figuration, but the subject matter they figured, and the way they figured it, bore little relation to previous movements, whether Romantic or Realist, idealist or naturalistic. The imagery that excited them was extruded by mass-produced urban culture – the movies, advertising, science fiction, pop music, consumer goods and their packaging.

The first Pop art work exhibited was *Just what is it that makes today's homes so different, so appealing?* by Richard Hamilton (born 1922), a small, almost miniature, collage blown up to life scale at the entrance to the exhibition "This is Tomorrow" held in London in 1956. The exhibition was concerned with wider problems of the way art could and should affect urban man's total environment, and brought together artists, architects and critics of very different persuasions, including the severest of abstract Constructivists and the two leading figures of early English Pop art, Hamilton himself and Eduardo Paolozzi (born 1924). For "This is Tomorrow" Hamilton wrote: "Tomorrow can only extend the range of the present body of visual experience. What is needed is not a definition of meaningful imagery but the development of our perceptive potentialities to accept and utilize the continual enrichment of visual material." The qualities he then identified as most desirable were "transient, popular, low-cost, mass-produced, young, witty, sexy, gimmicky, glamorous and big-business". Hamilton is a spiritual heir of Dada, and specifically of Marcel Duchamp: he executed a meticulous copy of Duchamp's "*Large Glass*" (see p. 168).

Paolozzi has been equally original and even more inventive and exploratory. He is best known as a sculptor, but, like Hamilton, is also

HAMILTON (right)
Just what is it that makes today's homes so different, so appealing? 1956
Pop says the racket-like lollipop Charles Atlas is holding. Irony and parody were constituents of the movement from the start, but Hamilton makes myths even as he debunks them. The wit is celebratory; the joy in advertisement images and consumer goods is real; and Pop flourished until disillusion and credit squeeze bruised its roots.

PAOLOZZI (above)
Japanese war god, 1958
Paolozzi has always been fascinated by the world of science fiction. His robot is like a junk King Kong.

SMITH (below)
Giftwrap, 1963
"Everything", says Smith, "comes in boxes; you buy boxes when you're shopping, you do not buy visible goods; you don't buy cigarettes, only cartons. The box is your image of the product." The boxes here dominate the canvas, forced by them into high relief.

PAOLOZZI (left)
Conjectures to identity, 1963
The assorted images are unified by the medium into a coherent pattern; each print of the edition came in variant colours.

KITAJ (below)
Where the railroad leaves the sea, 1964
Bright, clear, slick, Pop in style, Kitaj's work has a wider range of image and allusion than typical Pop art, seeming to occupy an arcane dimension of the imagination. The literary element is subservient: "The picture always takes over, but you can't help being moved by the great cultural issues peripheral to the picture", he says.

important as a printmaker. In the early 1950s he was experimenting with a variety of assemblage, building up fragments of mechanical junk into enigmatic but brooding sculptures suggesting slot machines or rudimentary computers. He is sometimes excluded from the Pop category, as he always transmuted his found objects, consolidating his multi-source imagery in bronze. But, like Hamilton, he insists on the right to use whatever lies to hand for the purposes of art. "It is conceivable that in 1958 a higher order of imagination exists in S.F. pulp produced on the outskirts of L.A. than (in) the little art magazines of today."

This first, precocious wave of British Pop was in a sense highly romantic, celebrating consumer goods with the fervour of those seeking the Promised Land – which was virtually America. The work of younger artists following fast on the heels of Hamilton and Paolozzi took on a more abstract form. The characteristic early paintings of Richard Smith (born 1931) were giant interpretations of cigarette packets. Significantly, he has worked much in America, moving more recently into large, purely abstract compositions on elaborately shaped canvases. R.B. (Ronald) Kitaj

(born 1932), however, moved from his native America to Britain in 1957, to become a determining influence in British Pop, when Pop was becoming an international movement.

Kitaj combines a virtuoso, intellectual eclecticism with a most sensitive mastery of colour, texture and composition. According to a younger painter, Allen Jones, his widely admitted influence "wasn't one of imagery but of a dedicated professionalism and real toughness about painting". His imagery is, however, striking and often complex: fragments of incidents – from comic strips, famous murder stories, classical mythology, learned journals – are jumbled, shuffled and reshuffled in amongst the paint. Allen Jones (born 1937) and David Hockney (born 1937) have both reflected his inspiration, though both have moved on to their own individual styles, and Hockney has become a popular and international celebrity. The delicacy, certainty and wit of Hockney's early talent found its most congenial medium in graphics – almost parodies of child art; his most satisfactory works are perhaps his prints and drawings. His developed painting style, apparently as bland and inert as travel posters, celebrates a con-

tinuing love-affair with consumer society, especially with golden California. Perhaps because so blatantly decorative, his *Splash* series of swimming pools has disappointed some critics, but he has the power to invest familiar topics with electric strangeness, and in his portraits – especially the double ones – to indicate troubling psychological tensions. Jones, however, has become notorious for his unabashed use of kinky, erotic subject matter, inspired by the imagery of sex magazines, of fetish rubber and leather garments, painted in simplified flat planes of colour (often garishly acid); this tends to obscure his talent for formal invention. Patrick Caulfield (born 1936), who shows no such eroticism, is the nearest in England to Lichtenstein's adaptation of the visual clichés of cheap magazine reproduction; he makes no comment, but presents what are almost huge diagrams (heavily outlined as if for painting-in by numbers) of banal scenes, or of exotic scenes that he presents as banal.

Pop Art caught on with the general public throughout the Western world and the media as has no other modern movement in art, but it was in Britain and America that it found its true and most concentrated expression.

HOCKNEY (left)
The sprinkler, 1967
Glass and water, whether transparent or reflecting, are often prominent in the cool, spare vision of which Hockney is a main exponent: they assist in reducing the world to flat, sharp, air-brushed-looking colour.

HOCKNEY (below)
Christopher Isherwood and Don Bachardy, 1968
There is a tense balance between the cool, severe, toned-out interior with its stilled still life and the more emphatic modelling of the faces; the movement is frozen, almost repressed.

JONES (left)
Red latex suit, 1973
Jones always insists that "the shapes themselves suggest the subject, not the subject the shapes". Sometimes he seems ready to explore how far erotic shapes can be abstracted and still be erotic; more often his aim seems to be to titillate or scandalize.

CAULFIELD (below)
Town and country, 1979
The cool, impersonal, uncommitted style in which Caulfield works has more in common with American Pop than British; here he is perhaps suggesting the heterogeneous décor of a brashly ghastly snack-bar.

Environmental Art, Happenings and Performance

In a sense Environmental art is nothing new: it is the distant heir of tribal ritual, of medieval pageant, of Baroque church interiors, even of Wagner's opera; a more direct ancestor was Dada, especially Schwitters' *Merzbau* (see p. 167). But in the 1960s it was the expression particularly of an urge to free art from the frame and the wall, where it was set apart from life, and to involve art with life, until art should become indistinguishable from life. In order to achieve its purposes art could call on the resources of any and all techniques and media – three-dimensional sculpture and sound; time and motion; living people. "Happenings" or "Performance" art can be seen in one way simply as activated Environmental art, and in another way virtually as theatre – exhibitions could become very like showbiz. Central to it all was the desire to dissolve the barriers that separated the various disciplines of art.

A starting point was a now legendary lecture given at Black Mountain College in 1952 by John Cage, musician and intellectual progenitor of late twentieth-century avantgarde experiment in all media. The lecture, given from the top of a ladder, featured long silences, music both live and mechanical, poetry, dance.

From Black Mountain College came also Johns and Rauschenberg (see p. 236), whose work had anticipated aspects of Environmental art, and was soon extended into it: Cage and Rauschenberg were both involved in an elaborate showpiece of the movement in 1966, *Nine evenings of theatre and engineering*.

Two artists, classifiable basically as sculptors, early extended their practice to the scale of the Environmental or to the actuality of the Happening, injecting a disturbing, surreal element – Edward Kienholz (born 1927) and George Segal (born 1924). Both can in fact be seen as practitioners in modern dress of traditional genre themes. Kienholz, not an academically trained artist, has drawn on his experience of mental hospitals, drinking clubs, dance bands for constructions that have grown in size and detail since 1954, sometimes to become replicas of entire rooms. The tableau offered is generally sleazy in feeling, a comment, moral and satirical, on the condition of modern urban humanity. Segal has also created settings featuring real furniture, but peopled by plaster casts from living bodies. These date from 1961, and what was at first a

SEGAL (right)
The photo booth, 1966
Segal casts his friends in plaster; the casts give the impression that there is still someone inside. The works have an eerie quality, and are pervaded by an intense feeling of loneliness – the painter Rothko once aptly called them "walk-in Hoppers".

KAPROW (below)
Basic thermal units, 1973
A Happening, according to Kaprow, is "a convergence of events which are being performed in more than one unity of time and place . . . In contrast with a piece of theatre, a Happening can take place in a jam factory . . . or in a friend's kitchen . . . the Happening unfolds according to plan, but without repetition, without audience, without rehearsal. It is art but it seems nearer to life." The only materials needed in his *Basic thermal units* were thermometers and ice.

KIENHOLZ (right)
The birthday, 1964
Kienholz's brutal, seedy but also bizarre, surreal art reflects the dire side of life in California – Kienholz is a product of Los Angeles and the West Coast, not of New York. Grey, in dirty grey garb, a woman becomes a victim not so much of the pain of childbearing as of the squalor of her situation.

OLDENBURG (left)
Model for *Monument for Grand Army Plaza, New York*, 1969
This is one of the few Environmental projects by Oldenburg executed as yet. More than 7m (24ft) high, it was built by the Colossal Keepsake Company at Yale University, though in time opposition to it there has caused it to lead a rather nomadic existence. The lipstick is telescopic, and the monument moves around on its tank base. Oldenburg's work shocks: "I have tried to make it in every way so that anyone who comes into contact with it is . . . inconvenienced."

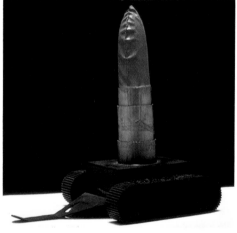

KLEIN (right)
Anthropometry: ANT *63*, 1961
Klein was fascinated by the culture of Japan: he visited the country and learnt judo – it was the ceremonial that specially interested him. Ritual is vital to the creation of the works in the *Anthropometry* series; here female nudes lay on the canvas as paint was sprayed round and about them; in others they covered themselves in blue paint and rolled and shifted on the canvas to the artist's directions.

neo-Dadaist joke has grown into a new, continuing mythology. He has experimented with Happenings, but prefers a static presence for his figures, caught, it seems, in an instant deep-freeze and drained to unearthly pallor – an essence of reality contrasted with the contrived art of their settings.

Allan Kaprow (born 1927) has been a central organizing figure in the development of Happenings. Starting in New York as an Abstract Expressionist, he studied with Cage, and in the mid-1950s developed increasingly complex assemblages. Set at first in the context of a gallery or museum, these grew into total environments; he moved his events to parking lots, gymnasia or stores, including spectators as his cast, using any techniques and materials that might be available, from sophisticated mechanisms to found junk. These events, however, while welcoming accidents of chance, always had a basic programme or "plot", unlike some developments, notably in Europe. Later, he experimented with simpler, more austerely Conceptual ideas (*Fluids*, of 1967, consisted of 20 monumental blocks of ice left to melt in city streets). Kaprow also established a sort of information centre, encouraging the pooling

and recording of Happenings.

Pop artists involved with Environmental or Happening experiments include Dine and Oldenburg (see p. 239). Dine staged an ambitious and well-publicized "psychodrama", *Car crash*, in 1960. Oldenburg in 1961 opened a store on East Twenty-first Street, New York, in which he sold, in manic parody of a commercial operation, various bits and pieces he had made, including painted plaster replicas of food. Oldenburg exploits the banal, with an inspired sense of the absurd on a Rabelaisian scale; he has suggested gigantic designs for urban monuments – a ballcock floating in the Thames by the Houses of Parliament, but bigger; lipsticks, ironing-boards, electric plugs as tall as the Empire State Building.

Environmental art and Happenings seem to have flourished particularly in America, but the trend has its practitioners both in Japan and in Europe. In France the short-lived Yves Klein (1928-62) was a brilliant forerunner. His reductive approach produced canvases of pure blue ("the most cosmic colour"), and an exhibition consisting of the white walls of an empty gallery, and he also painted by exposing canvases to the weather, or by using a blowlamp

as a brush. Very germane to the ideas behind Happenings were his ceremonial *Anthropometries* of 1958-61: one featured naked girls being dragged across canvas to the accompaniment of an orchestra sustaining a single note. A later variant on Happenings is "Body" art, in which the artist's body, in action, is used as both subject and object. Body art has been practised by the American Vito Acconci (born 1940) and in Europe by the Italian Gina Pane (born 1939). And yet the approach of Body artists has been as much Conceptual (see p. 246) as experiential.

The work of the German Joseph Beuys (born 1921), who achieved an international reputation in the 1970s, has a firm conceptual basis. His activities have often been Happenings, having weird, transcendental overtones, in which Beuys has the character of both high priest and research scientist. He sees himself primarily as a teacher, crossing disciplines, and acts out art as if it were life – it is for him. He has taken the interaction of art and life further than anyone – if not always to the immediate enlightenment of those who behold him, as other artists of revolutionary originality have previously found.

ACCONCI (left)
Rubbing piece, 1970
The work consisted of the artist, Acconci, sitting in a restaurant rubbing one arm (being photographed every five minutes) until a distinct weal appeared.

PANE (right)
Action psyche, 1974
"My corporeal experiments . . . have the aim", states Pane, "of demystifying the common image of the body experienced as a bastion of individuality." Body art is, more generally, an experiment with roles – relationships of audience, performance and performer.

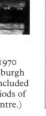

BEUYS (below)
Room installation, 1968
Beuys, having started his career as an artist in the early 1950s with sculpture, has worked with materials that are for him symbolic, mystic – especially felt and fat, by which his life was saved after an air crash in World War II. In spite of permanent injury he has involved himself in acts of extreme endurance. But most recently his art has become above all teaching: he teaches those who come about art (the marks made by him on the blackboards are sprayed with fixative).

WELFARE STATE (below)
Action, 1972
Welfare State was one of a number of British art-orientated theatre groups touring in the early 1970s.

"We will react . . . spontaneously and dramatically, and . . . fake unbelievable art as a necessary way of offsetting cultural and organic death", they cried.

BEUYS (above)
Scottish symphony, 1970
Enacted at the Edinburgh festival, this work included tapes, films and periods of silence. (Beuys is centre.)

Kinetic and Op Art

Kinetic means relating to motion – causing it or resulting from it. The aspect of kinetic art that startled popular and journalistic attention in the early 1960s was optical or retinal art, which was inevitably dubbed "Op" art, following so closely as it did on Pop. Kinetic art embraces works that themselves move, or (the kind known as Op art) that induce on the retina the illusion of movement, though physically static. Op art exploits or manipulates, even to the point of inducing physical dizziness, tendencies in the physiology and psychology of human sight that in everyday life are normally corrected or ignored. Kinetic and Op art is generally conceived, however, as essentially non-figurative: the natural or biomorphic references that persist in the work of Calder (see p.231), an obvious precursor, distance him from the recent kinetic movement, and the experiments of Maurits Escher (see p.175) with disturbed perspective, though they also exploit the fallibility of the human perceptual system, are concerned to extract surreal effects from what seems at first sight real.

The senior exponent, and pioneer of Op art effects even as early as the 1930s, is Victor Vasarély (born 1908), Hungarian in origin, but working in France since 1930. He has taken a radically sceptical view of traditional ideas about art and artists: in the light of modern scientific advances and modern techniques, he claims that the value of art should lie not in the rarity of an individual work, but in the rarity and originality of its meaning – which should be reproducible. He began as a graphic artist; much of his work is in (easily reproducible) black and white, though he is capable of brilliant colour. His best work is expressed in geometric, even mechanistic terms, but integrated into a balance and counterpoint that is organic and intuitive. He claims that his work contains "an architectural, abstract art form, a sort of universal folklore". His vision is of "a new city – geometrical, sunny and full of colours", resplendent with an art "kinetic, multi-dimensional and communal. Abstract, of course, and closer to the sciences".

Vasarély's work can sometimes dazzle the eye, but he does not aim to disturb the spectator's equilibrium. The effect of the work of the British Bridget Riley (born 1931) can be to produce such vertigo that the eye has to look away. Though carefully programmed, her patterns are intuitive and not strictly derived from

VASARELY (above)
Arny-C, 1969
The circle and the square, intercut and combined, are the prime constituents of Vasarély's repertoire. The eye automatically creates, in the contrast of dull and brilliant coloured tones, the illusion of instability, shift.

SEDGLEY (below)
Wind Tone Tower, 1979
Dominant in Sedgley's art is the idea of translating (with highly sophisticated technology) movement and sound into light. His Tower, constructed of sail-cloth and steel, plays patterns of light blown by the wind.

VASARELY (right)
Zebras, 1938
Vasarély's early works, though figurative, showed already his delight in an optical trickery. He was later a main inspiration to many in early 1960s Paris.

RILEY (below)
Cataract 3, 1967
Riley's canvases, despite their austere abstraction, carry allusions in both title and overall effect to natural phenomena, to sources of energy such as water, fire and wind.

scientific or mathematical calculations, and their geometrical structure is often disguised by the illusory effects (as Vasarély's structure never is). Riley refuses to distinguish between the physiological and psychological responses of the eye. Peter Sedgley (born 1930), a Briton living mainly in Germany, became known about 1965 for his experiments with one of the recurrent images of late twentieth-century painting, the "target" of concentric rings of colour. The effect was intensified by changing lights of red, yellow and blue, electrically programmed. Later he developed "video-rotors", stippled with brilliant fluorescent colour, rotating and still further animated by the play of ultraviolet and stroboscopic light upon them. His latest work has explored relationships between light and sound, with screens on which the noise and movement of spectators or passers-by are reflected in coloured light.

Ideas similar to those behind Sedgley's screens have dictated the work of the Venezuelan Jesus-Raphael Soto (born 1923), working in Paris, who started with transparent images layered in depth so that they seemed to move, but only as the spectator moved; later Soto produced very elegant linear designs across which suspended rods introduced changeable variations, and then he created total environments necessitating spectator participation, not only optical, but tactile and aural – neither paintings nor sculptures but experiments or games for each spectator. As early as 1960 the extension of kinetic art into the Environmental, virtually into Happenings, was a central aim of GRAV (Research Group for the Visual Arts) founded in Paris by artists including Vasarély's son Yvaral and the Argentinian Julio Le Parc (born 1928; not shown) under Vasarély's auspices.

Kinetic or mobile sculpture more closely linked with the inter-War experiments of Gabo or Moholy-Nagy (see pp. 180, 190) has been produced by the American George Rickey (born 1907; not shown), who has built austere, deeply cogitated abstracts in stainless steel, all wind-driven, and by the Greek Takis (Panayotis Vassilakis, born 1925), working in Paris, who used slender rods that vibrated gently in moving air, almost like bulrushes. Light is a dominant medium in recent kinetic art – Takis' *Signals*, appearing in 1954, were flashing lights at the end of long, wavering rods – but Takis, like other artists, also used noise, and then began extensive experiments with electromagnetic sculpture: he aims to induce spiritual contemplation, to suggest the presence of invisible energy ("If only I could capture the music of the beyond with an instrument similar to radar").

Some of the most spectacular and delightful creations of kinetic art have been those of the Swiss Jean Tinguely (born 1925), who constructs elaborate nonsense machines, manic sometimes to the point of self-destruction. In 1959 he invented a "*Métaméchanique*" (Meta-machine) that gallivanted about the floor recording its hiccoughing progress on a roll of paper built into itself. *Study no. 2 for the end of the world*, a complex construction in the Nevada desert near Las Vegas, worked itself into a frenzy in March 1962 and blew itself up. Tinguely's works verge on Happenings but also on the surreal, and often are definitely figurative in an eccentric way. Though much more abstract, the extremely spooky moving constructions of the Belgian Pol Bury (born 1922) again have surreal overtones; their elements shift very gently, articulating long periods of silence with a sigh or a click (their motors are always concealed, and noiseless).

SOTO (left)
Cardinal, 1965
Soto here exploits "the *moiré* effect": a diagonal line drawn across narrow parallel lines will appear to break where it intersects. Thus Soto's coloured rods, suspended before a thinly lined background, flicker.

TINGUELY (right)
Puss in boots, 1959
Tinguely's work has been likened to the fantasies of his fellow-Swiss Klee, but translated into three dimensions. Tinguely also has roots in Dada: this is obvious in the absurdity of his often self-destructive rubbish-dump machinery.

BURY (below)
3,069 white dots on an oval ground, 1967
Bury sets out to create a movement "anonymous, silent and supernatural". Here the shiver of these "feelers" is suddenly shot with a scarcely perceptible twitch at long intervals, to marvellous eerie effect.

TAKIS (above)
Signal: Insect animal of space, 1956
Railway signals inspired the series: to Takis they were "a necessary part of our century ... I used thin wires as bodies to hold the signals, accidentally they started moving."

Post-War Sculpture 2: Minimal and Conceptual

In the attempt to emancipate art from what appeared to some as the stultifying bonds of tradition, radical spirits have concentrated more and more on the idea of art or the idea behind art. In order to widen the scope of art, or at least to alter its references, or to purify it of conventional dross, artists have stripped art down to its essentials – Minimal art – or to its definition or basic idea – Conceptual art. Both approaches lead ultimately to a contradiction in terms – Minimal art tending perhaps towards a reduction to nothing, to the absurd, Conceptual moving from the visual to the purely mental, from the physical to the metaphysical. Some of the artists who identify themselves as Conceptual acknowledge the problem – thus Joseph Kosuth: "There is always something hopelessly real about materials, be they ordered or unordered."

Conceptual art reveals itself in as many ways as there are Conceptual artists. The first true conceptualist was no doubt Marcel Duchamp (see p. 168), who seemed finally to abandon both art and anti-art in favour of silence and chess, yet Duchamp's influence, from his emergence in 1912 until his death in 1968, has proved endlessly and most variously fruitful.

Modern self-acknowledged Conceptual artists include the Frenchman Daniel Buren (born 1938; not shown), the Briton Victor Burgin, the Japanese On Kawara (born 1933) and the Americans Don Burgy, Joseph Kosuth (born 1945) and Bruce Nauman (born 1941). To the layman their productions may seem generally incomprehensible or meaningless (and usually are unintelligible unless accompanied by explanatory texts); and even their positive contribution to visual or anti-visual metaphysics may seem an inadequate replacement for the sensory enrichment of life which they strive to eliminate. And yet, as with Duchamp, the feedback from their explorations will certainly nourish the mainstream of art, even if they prove not to be a decisive current within it.

The conceptual approach has in fact affected virtually all the non-figurative trends in art since Abstract Expressionism. The various types of art that emerged in the 1960s and 1970s – Minimal, Conceptual, Environmental, Performance, Process, Land, Earth, even "Real" – have often been used by the same artist, and they are best seen as different modes of working, rather than as different styles – as different indications of the artist's theoretical

CARO (above)
The month of May, 1963
From 1951 to 1953 Caro was assistant to Moore, enlarging his maquettes to actual size. This contact with the older sculptor's work was surely formative, although Caro's straight-edged and rambling style is partly in strong reaction. He painted his work so as to deny the physical nature of his metals, but recently has returned to "truth to materials". Caro's work has aspects in common with that of David Smith (see p. 231).

KOSUTH (above)
Chair I and III, 1965
Kosuth is concerned with "art language": he probes the nature of visual and verbal presentations of objects. Here the concept "chair" is arrived at by the bringing together of a wooden chair, a photograph of it and a photocopy of the dictionary definition of "chair". Kosuth finds philosophy and religion bankrupt, sterile, useless, no longer valid: only art can investigate "the state of things beyond physics".

KAWARA (right)
Today series: *April 5th, 1966*, 1966
Since 1966 Kawara has been producing the paintings in this series with obsessive, unveering regularity – each is accompanied by a newspaper clipping of that day. By his constant reckoning of himself against the outside world he seems to be seeking reassurance of his need to exist. A further development has been series of postcards, sent on consecutive days, stating his precise time of getting up.

NAUMAN (above)
Perfect door: perfect odor: perfect rodo, 1972
Nauman is an artist typical of that international trend or school of experimental "art workers" who function usually in "workshops" and work not in one medium or kind of art but freely, interacting, communicating and creating ideas almost in a kind of group therapy. Nauman, for instance, has practised Body art (see p. 243); he has also explored neon and fluorescent light in a controlled environment: his intention here is the "examination of physical or psychological response to simple or even oversimplified situations". The audience also participates.

NEVELSON (above)
Royal tide IV, 1960
Nevelson's sculptures are composed of found objects more or less altered, most of wood, arranged in boxes or shelves occupying a wall, taller than the spectator. The assembled sculpture is sprayed on completion in white, black or gold, which unifies the objects and reduces the shadows: the effect produced is of a multifaceted low relief in some homogeneous, even nondescript material. The works are often installed in the gallery in groups, sometimes forming rooms which seem like mysterious caves or tombs, stuffed full of trophies or tributes from a forgotten, mystic past.

approach. The Minimal was already emerging in the late 1950s in the work of colour-field and hard-edge painters (see p. 222) such as Reinhardt, Newman, Noland, Stella or even Olitski (although Olitski's output was dismissed by some as "visual Musak"). These artists, rather than painting pictures in the traditional sense, often seem to be illustrating or demonstrating ideas about making a painting. But the label "Minimal" was first applied to sculpture, and found even more (or, literally, less) expression in three dimensions, though it was only one trend in 1960s sculpture.

One very powerful and influential sculptor was the Englishman Anthony Caro (born 1924) who, while reducing his materials to a minimum – pieces of industrial cast metal – assembles them in positive shapes that may be completely abstract but which also strongly suggest analogies in nature. With Caro, sculpture demonstrates its new ability to get down from the plinth and extend across the floor. Caro's work, however, which is very open and involved with space, interpenetrated and interpenetrating, is atypical of the general trend in Minimal sculpture, which has been towards the smooth, closed and impersonal.

An older sculptor who came to prominence at about the same time was Louise Nevelson (born 1899), an American of Russian origins. She found her most characteristic mode of expression only in the 1950s and 1960s, in a constructive, assemblage method in which she produced huge walls built of wood filled with objects – geometric blocks, or bits and pieces of furniture. These, painted monochrome, can produce the effect of a mysterious Environmental shrine, almost a Byzantine iconostasis.

The Americans Tony Smith, Robert Morris and Carl Andre are more strictly Minimal innovators. Tony Smith (born 1912) has speculated with pure form often on a monumental scale – ranging from a two-metre (6½ft) plain cube of painted metal to vast geometric complexes the size of a large gallery. Robert Morris (born 1931) proceeds very strictly from theoretical considerations, and the visible results range from geometric metal shapes as basic as those of Tony Smith to exercises in felt, rope, wood or fibreglass, or even earth and grease. Working mostly in Europe, Carl Andre (born 1935), theorist, poet, likes to use as his material standard constructional elements such as 2×4 in timbers, or (most provocat-

ively) common building bricks. He began with pyramidal forms, and then spread his forms horizontal on the floor. Bricks or tiles can be arranged in symmetrical, repetitive sequences according to the extent and shape of floor space available. His avowed prime inspiration is Brancusi's *Endless column* (see p. 146).

Sol LeWitt (born 1928) and Donald Judd (born 1928) are two of the most rigorous American conceptualists still making art objects. LeWitt deploys grids, progressions, modules in strictly neutral materials, often in basic geometric forms arranged to a strict serial formula (he is fascinated by architectural modular systems and by serial music). "Conceptual artists", he has said, "are mystics rather than rationalists. They lead to conclusions that logic cannot reach." For Judd, the "extreme structivist", progressions with constant ratios between the successive quantities, expressed severely in enamelled metal, have provided a typical basic theme, fruitful in variation. The spectator is expected to react intellectually to his work. A more instinctual response is aroused by the no less controversial development, with some Conceptual element, of Earth and Land art.

SMITH (left)
Gracehoper, 1972
Smith was assistant to the American architect Frank Lloyd Wright for several years before he turned to sculpture – he had found that architects have to compromise their ideas to meet the needs of people; sculptors can more easily stay true to their original ideas. It was the extreme geometric simplicity of the forms used by Smith and other sculptors that earned the label "Minimal" art.

LEWITT (right)
Cube structure, 1972
The idea which LeWitt is exploring in his grids and modular structures is the conflict that is inevitable between "conceptual order and visual disorder". A number of identical cubes, when joined together, can no longer remain identical, because of the effect of perspective, of the play of light, of the spectator's always varying viewpoint.

ANDRE (above)
Proposal for The Hague Museum – *Lock* series, 1967
Andre exemplifies a main trend in recent sculpture – the installation. Formerly sculptors have often made works for specific outdoor locations, but not for one particular gallery. Running parallel is the trend to make the sculpture transformable, with components that are interchangeable, so that new combinations are always inherent in it. Andre has minimal interest in the form or aesthetic of his work; he wishes to materialize a concept.

MORRIS (above)
Untitled, 1966-67
Strips of black felt fall like pasta from a fork to a writhing mass. Morris, like Oldenburg before him, rejected the traditional hardness of sculpture; and he wanted the material he used to speak for itself. He has also worked in Earth, Happenings, Performance.

JUDD (above)
Untitled, 1974
Judd, like Caro, has used colour in order to disguise the intrinsic properties of his materials. He covers his aluminium in brilliant paint, creating unexpected sensuous qualities. Like LeWitt and other Minimal artists, Judd usually has his work made from blue-prints by professionals: this detaches him from the final outcome and confirms the premise of Conceptual art, that "the execution is a perfunctory affair" He is a learned and acute historian and critic, and calls on Alberti's Renaissance theories of harmonic proportions in statuary as precedents for his own art.

Land and Earth Art

One of the most intriguing elements in the almost infinitely variegated texture of art in the late twentieth century has been one that stresses landscape, the land, the earth itself. In some of its forms, this new development becomes as mystical or transcendental in its moods as the paintings of Washington Allston or the poems of Wordsworth: some purist critics have diagnosed in it an archaizing, "back-to-nature" ideology, a nostalgic leaning to woolly Romanticism. Land and Earth artists work in matter – rock, soil, turf, snow – without making an object or work of art in the traditional sense. Their product is essentially anonymous and often impermanent. Though in stark contrast to the geometric, structural concerns of artists such as Judd or LeWitt (see preceding page), their art is at one with Conceptual and Minimal theory in its rejection of traditional methods and forms, and it rejects even more emphatically the traditional outlook in which the work of art is a rare and precious commercial object, a mere decoration of life as jewellery is a decoration of the body. Most of its practitioners have nevertheless come to terms to some extent with the gallery system, as it is still their major source of livelihood.

The best-known and indeed most spectacular artist in Land (rather than Earth) art is Christo (Christo Javacheff, born 1935), who has moved through Sofia, Prague, Vienna, Paris, New York. In Paris he was associated with Yves Klein (see p. 242), and by the early 1960s was already executing fairly spectacular Environmental projects, such as blocking the Rue Visconti in Paris with a wall of oil-drums (*Iron curtains*). The works for which he became internationally notorious, his packaging projects, have been proceeding since 1968, when he wrapped up a monumental public building, the Kunsthalle in Berne, in plastic sheeting like some vast parcel. The effect close to is rather like that of a building shrouded for washing, but the realized concept, though lasting only a matter of a day or days, establishes the artist's control: he sets up a mystery, upsets the passer-by's expectations. Christo can lift what is in part uselessness and absurdity to epic scale, as when in 1976 he built across two counties in northern California his *Running fence*, a nylon fence 5.5 metres (18ft) high and nearly 40 kilometres (24 miles) long. Its lifespan was two weeks; the mechanics of setting it up, its impact on the landscape and

not least on its human neighbours, its environmental, social and scandalous effects, its sheer effrontery and economic nonsense – these were all important elements in the concept of the whole. Christo has wrapped skyscrapers, and in *Wrapped coast, Little Bay, Australia* (1969, see vol. 1 p. 204) packaged a million square feet of Australian seaboard.

For Christo, landscape or architecture is something that can be parcelled up or parcelled out. Land is used by two British artists in rather different ways. Hamish Fulton (born 1946) records landscapes by camera in what is almost "straight" photography, but his photographs, juxtaposed in a discernible composition, suggest spatial structures and circumstances in an almost abstract way, with landscape as the vehicle. Richard Long (born 1945) also depends on photographic documentation but he marks and alters the ground outdoors or moves indoors, into the gallery, earth or rocks, vegetation or driftwood. His work can be seen as a metaphor of human permanence and impermanence on earth.

The American Michael Heizer (born 1944), the son of a geologist, has been called "the boldest, most intransigent of the Earth work-

CHRISTO (right)
Project for Milan: *The Arco della Pace wrapped*, 1970
Christo has extended his work to encompass both the land untouched by man and the shapes of civilization. In the tradition of Dada, his aim is to provoke in the spectator questions about the object or area he has wrapped or shrouded.

CHRISTO (below)
Running fence, 1972-76
This work, which like the rest of Christo's projects was extensively documented, was designed to be viewed along a stretch of road in Sonoma and Marin counties. "I want to present", he said, "something that we never saw before ... not an image but a real thing like the pyramids in Egypt or the Great Wall of China."

LONG (right)
A line in Australia, 1977
Long's work in particular surely corresponds to an interest that has grown in the 1970s in prehistoric sites, from the mysterious ancient patterned tracks in the Nazca Valley, Peru, (man-made, but their forms can be seen only from an aircraft) to the "avenues" or lines of direction that seem to link in a colossal nexus mounds and henges near Salisbury, England. His arduous and lengthy journeys across the globe seem to have a ritualistic intensity: in lonely sites he makes some mark of his presence – for instance he creates a line by walking continually to and fro along it, or with stones, as here. In the gallery he exhibits variously marked maps, or arrangements of unworked found pieces of stone, in lines, circles, squares or spirals – very obvious forms invested with a mysterious significance, "a paradox of the perfectly explicable and the finally secret."

FULTON (left)
Untitled, 1969
Fulton and Long are both extremely reticent about themselves, their ideas and their work; thus the photographs which Fulton shows, rarely having any explanation, take on an aura of romantic mystery. His presentations are the product of a journey to a predetermined site and serve as a souvenir or witness to the artist's feeling about the event. Fulton is at the Minimal extreme of Land art.

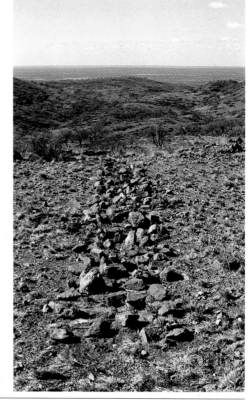

ers in his insistence on large-scale works, remote from the galleries and museums". His work, too, approaches the Minimal extreme – thus *Double negative* (1969, reworked 1970) is two cuts in a remote mesa, each nine metres (30ft) wide and 15 metres (50ft) deep. This should or can evoke Conceptual questionings, for example, which is the negative and which the positive shape? "I want to create without mass and volume", Heizer has said; nevertheless he produces exhibition works for galleries in the form of very austere geometrical paintings. There is a similar dichotomy in the work of Walter De Maria (born 1935); he has made earthworks, but also produced relatively traditional, though ultra-Minimal, objects in sculptural form. His most celebrated exhibit, in Munich in 1968, was a gallery containing 45 cubic metres (1,600cu.ft) of level dirt (not shown). The archetypal Earth artist, however, was Robert Smithson (1938-73), who plummeted to premature death from an aeroplane over Texas while surveying a potential site. Though Smithson, too, developed a form of art commensurable with gallery exhibition, in his most remarkable work he used the landscape as his raw material, choosing sites where he could set the theme of the inexhaustible fertility of nature against that of decay, fossilization and entropy.

Some Earth artists of the 1970s have turned more to man-made landscapes than to the desolate wilderness. In France Anne and Patrick Poirier (born 1942) have constructed immensely detailed models of archaeological sites, as if they were laying bare the skeleton of some embedded racial memory. The German Hans Haacke (born 1936), who has lived in New York since 1967, has advanced from installing miniature ecosystems in the gallery to surveys of the patterns of ownership in Manhattan. Haacke has consistently challenged both the enshrining of art in museums and the validity of boundaries between branches of art or between art and life, raising ecological and sociological issues without comment but insistently. The late twentieth-century art scene has not remained unchanged by the fact that man since 1945 has possessed instruments which can destroy all life whatsoever; and it continues to alter its scope as the effects of the computer, the silicon chip, the laser beam and microbiology alter us.

SMITHSON (right)
Spiral jetty, 1970
Projected by bulldozers into Salt Lake, Utah, in 1970, the work consists of black basalt, limestone, earth and the red algae that thrive in the otherwise desolate water. The spiral, 450m (1,500ft) long, 2,700 cubic metres (nearly 100,000cu.ft) in volume, 6,650 tons in weight, was a gigantic, unanswerable question mark. The simple shape and obvious symbol took on a new meaning as materialized on such a vast scale, though Smithson was concerned particularly with the theme of change; the jetty soon began to decay.

DE MARIA (right)
Vertical earth kilometre, 1977
De Maria was responsible for the first (unexecuted) Earth work, *Art yard* of 1961, in which spectators were to watch a large hole being dug. He also proposed in 1968 parallel lines 3.7m (12ft) apart and 800 metres (half a mile) long across the Nevada desert, where his fellow-earthworker Heizer (left) later moved a quarter of a million tons to create his *Double negative*. This project De Maria managed to execute, sinking in the ground (rather than erecting) his sculpture, a metal rod one kilometre long: only the base of it is visible.

HEIZER (above)
Double negative, 1969-70
"In the desert I can find that kind of unraped, peaceful, religious space that artists have always tried to put in their work", Heizer has commented.

THE POIRIERS (right)
Ancient Ostia, 1971-73
This scale model of ruins of the port of antic Rome was stimulated by a visit which the Poiriers made to Cambodia in 1970: there they saw venerated, ruined temples being lived in. It prompted interest in the past experienced through the present environment, on "the role of emotional radar in our relations with our ancestral wombs". The model is not a reconstruction but a facsimile.

HAACKE (above)
Rhine water installation, 1972
Haacke has extended the scope of Earth art into water and ice, or even into complete ecologies.

In this work a comment on the current pollution of the Rhine is implicit. As Haacke sees it, "An artist is not an isolated system ... there are no limits to his involvement."

Traditional Easel-Painting

The rapidly expanding scope of art since Pop has been a development less from one style to another, more from one kind of art to another – Environmental, Conceptual, Junk, Land, Earth – as art has climbed first off the wall or plinth and then out of the gallery. It has seemed at times that to paint on canvas at all, whether abstract or figurative, was reactionary or obsolete. Nevertheless ordinary picture-making – generally, if loosely, called the academic tradition – has continued in flood, both figurative and non-figurative, though figurative art seems to retain a more direct, empathetic appeal to the wider public. This is partly due to recognition of, or identification with, the subject matter, and many people look to art for comfort – as Matisse suggested they were by no means wrong to do. Visions of the rustic past, for example, offer a dream of security, of a Golden Age (even if it never was): in Britain, reproductions of Constable's *Haywain* (see p. 71) head the bestseller list. In figuration, not least, the erotic element is also an enduring attraction.

Quite apart from the sensory pleasures it offers, figuration also fulfils some specific social functions, and, both in totalitarian and in other states, some pronouncedly political ones. Photography is still far from killing the demand for portraiture in oil-paint or in stone or bronze, especially for formal and commemorative purposes. At its worst this kind of art degenerates into kitsch; but Kokoschka (see p. 229), still painting some portraits in the 1970s, or Sutherland, who turned to portraiture only in the late 1940s (see p. 199), remained uncompromisingly artists. As a result their work was not always acceptable to subject or patron: Sutherland's portrait of Sir Winston Churchill (not shown) was subsequently destroyed at Lady Churchill's order (Churchill had held that a portrait should be 75% sitter and only 25% artist).

The appeal of "primitive" or Naive painters, or those seeming to be so, has increased since the Douanier Rousseau's day (see p. 141). Like the glimpses of a pastoral, pre-industrial Eden offered by Constable, they, too, offer a vision of innocence. The most celebrated of genuinely Naive painters was Mary Anne Robertson (1860-1961), known as Grandma Moses, who, aged about 60, began first embroidery and then painting: her first one-woman show was in New York in 1940,

when she was 80. She did without traditional perspective, consistency of scale or of subject matter, but spelled out in minute detail across the picture surface a section of New York State, a countryside she peopled with animals, characters in all sorts of historical costume, and farm equipment, all drawn as if from stiff toys rather than nature, but conveying nevertheless a quick response to nature through a sure sense for brilliant colour and pattern.

Many other artists, though academically qualified, strive with more or less success to preserve a primitive vision – especially in France, where the Douanier Rousseau is a continuing inspiration. In Britain, the traditional visionary strain of Blake and Samuel Palmer was still strong in Stanley Spencer (see p. 199), but the painter to achieve widest recognition, his work welcomed on the walls of the middle-class parlours of England as Spencer's never quite was, was L.S. (Laurence Stephen) Lowry (1887-1976), who painted in greys, blacks and white the industrial townscapes of northern England, haunted with a mute poetry of desolation and an unexpectedly idyllic nostalgia. In France, Bernard Buffet (born 1928) propagated a spiky,

GRANDMA MOSES (left)
In harvest time, 1945
In her embroideries and her paintings the old lady evoked with great feeling a nostalgia for the customs and way of life which she had seen disappearing over the course of her many long years as a farmer's wife.

BUFFET (right)
Two Breton women, 1950
Buffet worked in France at the same time as Wols, Fautrier, Hartung (see p. 224), but unlike them used an anguished figuration to express the anger, sorrow and also bewilderment of the post-War generation.

GUTTUSO (below)
Occupation of the land, 1947
Guttuso is committed to an eloquent exposition of all social injustices. Picasso's *Guernica* (see p. 203) has much influenced his work.

LOWRY (above)
Industrial landscape, 1955
Lowry's snow-bright landscapes of a grim northern England harked back to the Depression years, 1922-35,

when he collected rents in Manchester, in daily, close contact with the poverty and deprivation rife there. He shows little sympathy, however; indeed he sought

the absurd: "I like the look of ill-fitting clothes, big bowlers and clumsy bodies", and his small, matchstick-thin people are impassive inhabitants of his vistas.

near-monochrome style, portraying a bleak world fit for Existentialist heroes, a style that was nevertheless also very seductive, then later more patently decorative, and from the beginning commercially hugely successful.

Established modern traditions have by no means been exhausted in Europe or in America. The austere painterly preoccupations of the "Euston Road" school in Britain, headed by Sir William Coldstream (born 1908; not shown) stem from the ideas of Cézanne. Some of the preoccupations of the School of Paris between the Wars live on in the emotionally charged realism of Balthus (see p. 185). The very different politically committed social realism of Renato Guttuso (born 1912) in Italy adapts and expands Cubist techniques. In Britain again Frank Auerbach (born 1931) has evolved his own powerful, highly personal development of Expressionism, figuration battling its way through turbulent paint. Sidney Nolan (born 1917), a remarkable colourist, has established Australian painting on the international map; his most famous sequence, variations on the Australian folk legend of the bushranger Ned Kelly, merged Expressionist techniques with Surrealist fantasy.

Landscape still answers many different styles and techniques. Nicolas de Staël (see p. 224) achieved a remarkable synthesis (now generally underrated) of abstract colour with the evocation of landscape. The Icelander Gudmunder Gudmundsson (born 1932), known as Erro, has replaced the traditional concept of landscape with other "scapes", in which with the clarity of Pop art he piles food upon food or 'plane upon 'plane. In America Milton Avery (1893-1965) and Richard Diebenkorn (born 1922) both adapted, in different ways, the discoveries of post-War abstraction to landscape themes with brilliant success.

All the revolutions in twentieth-century art seem not yet to have abolished or dislodged the traditional urge to realistic depiction. Since the pioneering Constructivism of the early Revolution the dominant style in the USSR has been a literal, sometimes melodramatic, realism: artists such as Arkady Plastov (1893-1972) have infused images of the everyday with heroic virtue. Then in the late 1960s and 1970s there was an international surge of interest in an extremely meticulous, photographic brand of realism – Superrealism.

NOLAN (left)
Kelly in landscape, 1969
The bandit Ned Kelly was famous for his iron mask; out of scale, it assists the sense of lunar mystery in this vision of the outback.

ERRO (below)
Plainscape, 1972
Erro's "scapes" bombard the senses of the viewer with a seemingly endless proliferation of objects, mute comment on the waste and consumerism of society.

AUERBACH (left)
E. O. W. nude, 1953-54
Auerbach has said the aim of his crusted paintwork is "to render a sensation . . . fully tangible". E. O. W. are his model's initials.

AVERY (below)
Morning sea, 1955
Avery's landscapes have an aura of joyous well-being and subtle thin colouring reminiscent of the artist he most admired, Matisse.

DIEBENKORN (left)
Ocean Park no. 108, 1978
Diebenkorn continues to move between abstract and figurative with assurance. His *Ocean Park* series, in progress since 1967, makes evocations of the dry, sun-drenched and shaded streets of California, the artist's adopted home. His feeling for space is superlative.

PLASTOV (right)
The tractor drivers' dinner, 1951
One of Plastov's favourite themes is the harmonious integration of old and new ways of life. The peasant farmer is mellowly depicted as being content and at one with both nature and the machine that has replaced the old ways of working.

Superrealism

The fascination of creating a facsimile that gives the illusion, as completely as possible, of being what it represents has been recurrent since the Renaissance. The object represented may range from a human being to a flower to a beer-can. At an instinctive level the pleasures of conjuring are involved, of *trompe-l'oeil*; on an intellectual level the artist questions ideas of illusion and reality, the reality of reality.

The immediate progenitor of the vigorous resurgence of this kind of realism in the 1970s – Superrealism – was clearly Pop art, although elements were inherited also from earlier post-War American movements – largeness of scale, all-over painting, and a coolness, a distancing, in the approach to subject matter. The overt comment (and also humour) often present in Pop is very rare in Superrealism; also completely absent is the kind of comment central to the form of realistic art that had been continuous and dominant in the communist states of the Western world since the 1920s – social-realist art which is essentially propaganda. The Superrealists often use similar everyday subject matter but never vitiate their art with heroics or sentimental rhetoric. (They seem also almost as suspicious of the interpretative

approach of the traditional figurative realism practised, for instance, by Andrew Wyeth (see p. 226) in a closely similar technique.)

Already in the 1950s several artists both in Europe and the USA were working towards an uncompromising attempt to transcribe reality in precise detail. Thus in Britain Lucian Freud (born 1922), though not using photographs, achieved and achieves a photographic verisimilitude: his studies of the nude seem naked rather than nude, and his portraits trace every furrow and wrinkle. The intensity of Freud's scrutiny produces Surrealistic overtones, although these are said not to be intended. The American Philip Pearlstein (born 1924) likewise painted realistic "nakeds" rather than nudes in the 1960s, and then concentrated on portraiture – portraiture not of celebrities but of ordinary people, and as dispassionate as a photograph. As he put it, "I'm not painting people ... I'm concerned with the human figure as a found object."

The Superrealists concentrated, however, not directly on real life, but on real life held at arm's length, pre-frozen by the camera. Probably for the first time the photograph became the prime, often the sole source of the art and

aesthetic of painting. For the Superrealist, a photograph can be virtually the equivalent of what Nature was for Constable. Working from photographs, sometimes from colour slides projected on to the canvas on which he paints, a Superrealist can achieve a remarkable, detached intensity: often a strange tension is created by the banality of what is represented, realized with such skill and often on a large scale on a gallery wall.

Superrealism seems quintessentially American, but became rapidly international, and even before its emergence several artists in Europe were working in closely allied idioms. One highly original example was the Italian Michelangelo Pistoletto (born 1933): his point of departure was life-size photographs, tracings of which were cut out, painted, and pasted to reflecting sheets of steel, so that the spectator, seeing both himself and the painted photographic image, had to adjust to two levels of perception. The Frenchman Jacques Monory (born 1934; not shown) often conjoins in one frame two or more images resembling film-stills, evoking in virtual monochrome the disillusioned memory of some unresolved action; he avoids the gloss, the surface lustre, of

FREUD (above)
John Minton, 1952
Lucian Freud, grandson of the famous psychologist, has been interested in the portrayal of human faces since childhood. Friends of his such as John Minton and Francis Bacon appear in inquisitorial close-up.

PISTOLETTO (right)
Marzi with the little girl, 1964
Although Pistoletto has since moved on to work in other media it was his mirror art of the 1960s that made his reputation. The cut-off silhouette of a woman and child, affixed to the reflecting steel, is the only object: everything else seen is a reflection.

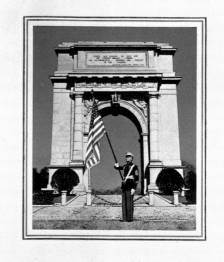

PEARLSTEIN (left)
Female nude reclining on an Empire sofa, 1973
Pearlstein, unlike other Superrealists, never uses the camera, but through his dispassionate recording of the human body adopts the

role of a camera himself. This effect is increased by his use of peculiarly photographic techniques such as cropping and odd angles. "Stilled-action choreography" is his own description of the nudes.

ESTES (left)
Grossinger's bakery, 1972
In reproduction, Estes' work often looks exactly like a photograph because his paintwork is invisible. He exploits photographs in much the same way as Roy Lichtenstein uses cartoon strips – changing, cutting, editing their composition. He has gone on to make the most elaborate silk-screen prints, superimposing bland reflection on reflection to make a curtain-glass maze.

MORLEY (above)
United States Marine at Valley Forge, 1968
In order to be objective about his subject matter, Morley often cuts up the photograph he is copying and then paints one piece at a time, the rest of the canvas remaining covered until the whole is complete. The "wedding photograph" white border, which he uses as a substitute for the traditional picture frame, emphasizes the flat image.

the American practitioners. In fact the first painter to work in a pure Superrealist style, Malcolm Morley (born 1931), was English, though he had been established in New York since 1964. He works from photographs, but the subject matter of the photographs is unimportant: "I accept the subject matter as a by-product of surface"; seen close to, his work becomes visibly "painterly".

Of the Americans, Richard Estes (born 1936), while concentrating on street scenes, store fronts, reflections in curtain-glass buildings, nevertheless regards photographs "as a sketch to be used" rather than as "a goal to be reached". There is something perhaps of the sense of American urban reality that Hopper had, but drained of Hopper's latent mystery. Ralph Goings (born 1928) has said: "The subject matter is what the painting is all about. I don't select it because it has dramatic compositional elements." On the other hand, "It's not the object I'm concerned with, it's the painting of the object." Several artists have developed the gigantic close-up of a face, most famously Chuck Close (born 1940): his heads, maybe two metres or more high, are painted from blown-up photographs of people chosen

at random: the human face is simply another phenomenon in a world full of phenomena. His medium is usually acrylic through an airbrush, avoiding any hint of the artist's personality in the handling of the paint.

Superrealist sculptors have obvious precursors in Pop and Environmental artists such as Segal or Kienholz (see p. 242). Their concern is to produce simulacra in the round, as literally and as impersonally as the painters: using painted fibreglass or other plastics, real hair or clothes, they produce presences from everyday life – tourists, shoppers in supermarkets – that are horrific precisely in their illusionistic common ordinariness. John De Andrea (born 1941) produces nudes that all but breathe. The best-known of the Superrealist sculptors, Duane Hanson (born 1925), is, however, not neutral in his attitudes, but in his commonplace people congealed in banal action suggests the spiritual void of a materialistic society: "I just want to express my feelings of dissatisfaction." These sculptures often achieve the macabre "otherness" of an older tradition of modelling, not generally categorized as fine art – waxworks, most famously Madame Tussaud's

GOINGS (left)
Twin Springs diner, 1976
There is often an empty, brittle quality present in Superrealist art which is due in part to the subject, in part to the labour of its technique. Goings has often spent a day painting only three square inches.

CLOSE (left)
Keith, 1970
Close's concern here is the discrepancies between a photograph and what it reproduces; he faithfully copies the areas which are out of focus and reveals, on a magnified scale, the limitations of the camera.

HANSON (right)
Couple with shopping-bags, 1976
Hanson has commented on his recent sculpture: "My most successful pieces are naturalistic or illusionistic, which results in an element of shock, surprise or psychological impact for the viewer. The subject matter that I like best deals with the familiar lower- and middle-class American types of today." His work reveals "the emptiness and loneliness of their existence".

DE ANDREA (above)
Seated woman, 1978
Unlike Hanson, with whom he is often bracketed, De Andrea deals not with the type but the particular; he is neutral in attitude, even though, despite their nudity, his subjects betray their background and personality,

by their stance, their hair, their make-up, etc. They are extremely lifelike, but aptly enough the effect is even more pronounced in a photographic reproduction. The woman is made of oil-painted polyvinyl, life-size; she is unerotic (if perhaps shocking), unselfconscious.

The Popularization of Art

During the last century the proliferation of images across the face of the world has intensified at an astonishing rate. Art history, the history of images, once the speciality of the German philosophic genius, is now a standard part of the academic curriculum in the universities of the world. The critic can become more famous than the artist whose work he comments on: in the nineteenth century John Ruskin had the stature of a prophet, and in the twentieth century Kenneth Clark, expounding culture and civilization on colour television, has achieved an enormous audience.

By art history and art criticism modern art is provided with an ancestry, with status and by implication with a future. The complaint has indeed been made that today art historians dictate their future to artists, and that modern artists have made art-history or painted theories rather than made or painted art. In 1975, in a brisk attack on modern art entitled *The Painted Word*, Tom Wolfe suggested that a great retrospective art show of AD 2000 would consist of enlarged reproductions of crucial texts from the critics, with small photographs of works of art alongside. Verbal commentary and explanation have become increasingly

necessary not only because modern art has become ever more private, more esoteric, but also because the conventions dictating the art of the past have become increasingly remote.

On the other hand the opportunities for people to see works of art in the original or in reproduction have increased enormously. The growth of museums and galleries, and of educational courses in art, together with the sponsorship, organization and cataloguing of major and minor retrospective exhibitions, have brought works of art before a huge new public. As a result of technical improvements in the processes of reproduction, works can also be more faithfully and cheaply copied and broadcast than ever before, in books, colour slides and films.

For drawings and prints, the standard of reproduction can now be so high that even the expert can mistake facsimile for original, but the very best reproductions of an oil-painting can still only offer at obvious second-hand, diluted, its original complexity, the texture and specific gravity of the paint. Both subtly and in obvious ways – by change of scale – reproductions distort the original. Outside the Bargello in Florence platoons of coarsened

WARHOL (below)
Thirty are better than one, 1963
What is probably the best-known portrait in the world becomes an image to rank beside contemporary icons

such as pin-ups of movie-stars. The context, the true meaning of the original, is swamped by its fame – its only real life today is its life as a reproduction; no-one can see it as it is.

(left) *Kenneth Clark* with Nôtre Dame, Paris, in the background, in part of *Civilization*, 1969
Lord Clark's television series *Civilization* was shown all over the world. Specifically intended "for the layman of no specialized knowledge", the series helped millions who had perhaps never visited an art gallery to appreciate their heritage.

LICHTENSTEIN (below)
Brush-strokes, 1967
The creation of prints is a natural extension of this artist's preoccupation in his painted work with the comic-strip image. He has made two prints and a few paintings showing enlarged details of brush-strokes – caricatures, he says, of the gestural marks made by Abstract Expressionists, in particular De Kooning.

MCKNIGHT-KAUFFER (left)
Winter sales, 1924
The artist developed his "Cubo-Vorticist" style in a series of posters made in the 1920s and 1930s for London Transport, then following a policy of using the services of modernist artists to brighten up its stations and fill trains.

MATISSE (right)
The swan, 1930-33
Matisse's earliest prints date from 1903, but he created what are perhaps the consummate examples of his reductive line in the illustrations he made in the early 1930s for an edition of Mallarmé. The prints are the product of many drawings, honed to absolute essentials, to one unwavering line that contains in its arabesque body, neck, head and beak. Picasso, too, turned his talents to illustration.

diminutive replicas of Michelangelo's *David* await sale, and what was the over-life-size embodiment of a proud city's independence becomes a decorative accent in a suburban sitting-room. This, the translation of masterpieces into other forms – a Morandi still life into a cheap mosaic, "*The Venus de Milo*" into a lamp-stand – is a version of the taste known as "kitsch", but is also evidence of the endlessly changing function of art. As its boundaries and definitions shift, what once was kitsch becomes museum art, as recently the decorative arts of the 1930s became Art Deco.

It is long since Duchamp thumbed his nose at art by adding a moustache and a pun to a postcard of the *Mona Lisa* (see p. 169). Andy Warhol in 1963 produced a barrage of *Mona Lisas* in his *Thirty are better than one*, reduplicating her in exactly the same deadpan presentation as his *Marilyns* or his *Soup-cans*. Lichenstein turns strip-cartoon imagery into monumental gallery paintings (and vice versa). The feedback into late twentieth-century art of the dazzling speed and ease with which art can be broadcast is incalculable: while some artists have delighted in it, especially since Pop, others have defied it, producing works that require the physical presence of the spectator – whether because of their scale, or because they are kinetic, or because the spectator's participation completes the work.

It follows, too, that it is impossible for the public to ignore modern art, whether they like it or not. If in no other way, and usually in very diluted and distorted form, the public of the capitalist world becomes conscious of the innovations and discoveries of modern artists through commercial advertising. Advertisers have adapted for their own purposes styles developed from all sources, from Picasso and Mondrian to Op art and even Land art. The particular form in which they began to exploit advanced visual imagery, in the late nineteenth century, was the poster. When artists of the stature of Bonnard or Toulouse-Lautrec (see p. 121), or Jules Cheret or Alphonse Mucha, began to demonstrate that the poster was a form in which highly original artistic work could be developed, it became almost immediately also a collectors' field – museum art. Though much poster art is ephemeral, of no artistic value, it has, in the hands of artists as various as the Russian Constructivists, Beardsley, the American Ernie McKnight-Kauffer (1891-1954), Munch, Picasso and Matisse, produced its own masterpieces.

Advances in graphic processes also assisted in the same period the revival of the illustrated book – the Symbolist *livre d'artiste* (see p. 122). Especially since 1945, the production of prints has increased enormously and has become for many artists a major source of livelihood. The traditional methods of printmaking are still extensively practised – engraving, etching – but lithography and silk-screen printing are particularly favoured media. Published in limited editions, original works by important artists do thus become available for people of moderate income to own. Meanwhile the borderlines between the traditional categories of art are further eroded, when cartoonists and illustrators start to put on sale their original artwork, and when commercial manufacturers issue limited editions of prints of their most successful advertisements. Whether or not a new artistic orthodoxy emerges from the constant flux of late twentieth-century art, it seems certain that technical innovation will continue to go hand in hand with creative innovation, even though the future of art lies still in the imagination of the individual artist.

ADAMI (right)
Arabian landscapes, 1969
Valerio Adami (born 1935) spent two years in London in the early 1960s, when he came into contact with British Pop. His style, close to Caulfield's in its bold, flat colours in black contour, is one that transfers particularly well to prints; Pop found its art form in silk-screen, as Expressionism in woodcut.

STEADMAN (below)
Illustration to Hunter S. Thompson's *Fear and Loathing in Las Vegas*, 1970
Ralph Steadman (born 1937) is one of many artists who have moved "up" from newspaper cartoons to book illustrations and prints. Images such as this are an accompaniment to the new journalism of writers such as Norman Mailer, Hunter S. Thompson, Tom Wolfe.

MIRO (left)
Marvellous puzzles, 1970s
Art has always been an investment, originally in materials and craft, then in the artist's prestige, too. An artist's own "handwriting", as opposed to the reproducible design, still has a value. An "authored" modern print has not much inherent rarity value, but it makes "real" works of art available to more people.

COLLETT, DICKINSON, PEARCE & PARTNERS (below)
(*Government warning: Smoking can seriously damage your health*), 1979
When a set of 12 of these slick, beguiling cigarette advertisements was printed in a limited edition of 250 in 1979 they were snapped up. They seem to exploit the Superrealist idiom, with visual puns perhaps after Salvador Dali.

List of Illustrations and Acknowledgments

Works of art illustrated are listed in the order in which they appear in the book. In general, the order runs from top to bottom and left to right on each page, though works by the same artist or of the same origin are grouped together.

The name of the artist (or, if the artist is not known, the place of origin) and the title or description of each work are followed by its medium, its dimensions (metric) and its present location and ownership. Photographic credits are given in brackets, unless the photograph has been supplied by the owner. Scala, the major supplier of photographs, is abbreviated as S.

Though every effort has been made to check the accuracy of these specifications, it has not always been possible to verify all of them.

2-3
RAUSCHENBERG: *Monogram*, 1959, oil and mixed media, height 122 cm, canvas 183 × 183 cm, Stockholm, National Museum. GERICAULT: *A kleptomaniac*, 1822-23, oil on canvas, 60 × 50 cm, Ghent, Musée des Beaux-Arts (S).

8-9 Eastern Art
ISFAHAN: View of the court of the Madraseh Chaharbagh, 1706-14 (Spectrum Colour Library). ANGKOR WAT: View of the temple in the centre, early 12th century (ZEFA).

10-11
(Map by Colin Salmon and Dinah Lone)

12-13 Indian Art 1
HARAPPA: *A buffalo*, c. 2500-2300 BC, steatite, 4 × 4 cm, Lahor, Museum (William Macquitty); *Ceremonial dancer*, 3rd millennium BC, limestone, height 9 cm, New Delhi, National Museum of India (Ravi Bedi). SARNATH: *Lion capital*, 240 BC, sandstone, height 213 cm, Sarnath, Museum (René Roland). BHARHUT: *Yakshi*, 2nd century BC, sandstone, height 2.1 m, *in situ* (India Office). DIDARGANJ: *Yakshi? or Royal devotee?* mid-1st century BC?, sandstone, height 163 cm, Patna, Museum (René Roland). SANCHI: The eastern gate of the Great Stupa, inner side, 1st century BC, sandstone, height about 10 m, *in situ* (Giraudon). KARLE: *The Buddha preaching, flanked by worshippers*, 1st/2nd century AD, sandstone, height of larger figures about 2.5 m, *in situ* (Ann and Bury Peerless). AMARAVATI: *The presents of King Bandhuma*, from the *Vessantra Jataka*, late 2nd century AD, marble, diameter about 90 cm, Madras, Government Museum and National Art Gallery (Giraudon). KATRA: *Seated Buddha*, mid-2nd century AD, sandstone, height 68 cm, Mathura, Archaeological Museum (René Roland). MATHURA: *Yakshi*, 2nd century AD, sandstone, height 140 cm, Calcutta, Indian Museum (S).

14-15 Indian Art 2
GANDHARA: *Standing Bodhisattva*, 2nd century AD, sandstone, height 109 cm, Paris, Musée Guimet (Giraudon). AJANTA: *Flying nymph*, late 5th century AD, fragment of a mural in Cave 17, tempera on plaster (Ann and Bury Peerless). PAHARPUR: *Shiva and dancing girls*, 8th century AD, terracotta, Durham, Gulbenkian Museum. SARNATH: *The first sermon*, 5th century AD, sandstone, height 160 cm, Sarnath, Museum (René Roland). NALANDA: *Seated Bodhisattva*, 8th or 9th century AD, stucco, Durham, Gulbenkian Museum. BENGAL: *The Ashtasahasrika Prajnaparamita: The Bodhisattva*

Samantabhadra with Tara, the incarnation of Buddhist wisdom, and the dwarf Acharya Vajrapani, c. 1120, colour on palm-leaf, 54 × 6 cm, London, Victoria and Albert Museum. SULTANGANJ: *Standing Buddha*, early 9th century?, bronze, height 226 cm, Birmingham, Museum and Art Gallery. TIBET: *The Heruka in union with his shakti Nairatmya*, 17th century?, gilt bronze, Germany, Private Collection (Claus and Liselotte Hansmann); *Thangka* (temple banner): *The goddess Tara, the incarnation of Buddhist wisdom*, late 17th century, paint on cotton, 62 × 41 cm, Durham, Gulbenkian Museum.

16-17 Indian Art 3
AJANTA: *Panchika and Hariti*, 6th century, from Cave 2, sandstone (Robert Harding Associates). BADAMI: *Vishnu sitting on Ananta*, 578, sandstone (Robert Harding Associates). MAMALLAPURAM: *The descent of the goddess Ganga*, mid-7th century, granite (A.F. Kersting). ELEPHANTA: *Shiva*, 8th century, sandstone, Cave of Maharastra (Giraudon). SIGIRIYA: *Apsaras*, c. 480, wall-painting from the rock fortress (Douglas Dickens). TANJORE: *Dancing girl*, c. 1000, wall-painting (Ravi Bedi). ELURA: *Shiva's dance in the elephant skin*, c. 580-642, stone relief (Robert Harding Associates). MADRAS: *Parvati*, 10th century, bronze, height 92 cm, Washington DC, Smithsonian Institution, Freer Gallery of Art. COCHIN: *Vishnu*, late 17th century, wall-painting, the Maharajah's Palace (Douglas Dickens). BELUR: *Heavenly nymph*, 12th/13th century, sandstone (William Macquitty).

18-19 The Kandarya Mahadeva Temple
ORISSA: *Shiva and Parvati*, 12th century, stone (Claus and Liselotte Hansmann). KONARAK: The Surya temple, detail: *A wheel, emblem of the chariot of the sun-god Surya*, 13th century, sandstone, *in situ* (A.F. Kersting). BHUVANESHVARA: The Rajarani temple, detail, c. 1000, sandstone (Michael Ridley). DEOGARH: *Vishnu lying on Ananta*, 6th century, sandstone (Robert Skelton). KHAJURAHO: The Kandarya Mahadeva temple, details of the Heavenly Bands, c. 1000, sandstone (*An Apsara* Ann and Bury Peerless; general view René Roland).

20-21 Indian Art 4
DELHI: Detail of the sculptured calligraphy on the Q'utb Minar, c. 1200, sandstone (Lawrence Clarke). WESTERN INDIA: *The Uttaradhyayana Sutra: Mahavira surrounded by dancers and musicians*, c. 1460, gouache on paper, height 11 cm, London, Victoria and Albert Museum. RAJASTHAN: *The marriage of Vasudeva and*

Devaki, 1525, gouache on paper, 17 × 23 cm, London, Victoria and Albert Museum. AKBAR'S ATELIER: *The Hamsanama* (Deeds of Mohammed's uncle, Hamsa): *Gardeners beating a giant trapped in a pit*, c. 1570, gouache on paper, 67 × 51 cm, London, Victoria and Albert Museum (Michael Holford); *The Akbarnama* (Deeds of Akbar): *Akbar's officers reconcile a rebel*, c. 1590, gouache on paper, 32 × 19 cm, London, Victoria and Albert Museum (Michael Holford). SCHOOL OF NIHAL CHAND: *Radha*, c. 1750, gouache on paper, 22 × 35 cm, Kishangarh, Collection of the Maharaj of Kishangarh (Studio Vista). SHAH JAHAN'S ATELIER: *Jade cup*, 1657, jade, 5 × 17 cm, London, Victoria and Albert Museum (Michael Holford). JEHANGIR'S ATELIER: *The zebra*, 1621, gouache on paper, 20 × 25 cm, London, Victoria and Albert Museum (Michael Holford). KANGRA: *Krishna and Radha in a grove*, c. 1780, gouache on paper, London, Victoria and Albert Museum (Michael Holford).

22-23 Islamic Art 1
IRAQ OR SYRIA: Chapter heading from a Koran, 9th/10th century, MS no. 1407, colours on paper, 33 × 23 cm, Dublin, Chester Beatty Library. BAGHDAD: Frontispiece from a Koran, early 16th century, MS no. 1544, colours on paper, 18 × 13 cm, Dublin, Chester Beatty Library. IRAN: Text from a Koran, 11th/12th century, MS no. 1436, colours on paper, 33.5 × 49 cm, Dublin, Chester Beatty Library. TURKEY: *Hilyah* (Description of the Prophet), 1691-92, from a Koran, colours on paper, 46 × 33.5 cm, Dublin, Chester Beatty Library; *Basmallah* (In the name of God the compassionate, the merciful), 1834, from a Koran, colours on paper, Dublin, Chester Beatty Library. NORTH AFRICA OR SPAIN: Text from a Koran, 11th century, MS no. 1424, gilt on vellum, 28 × 23 cm, Dublin, Chester Beatty Library. IRAN: Frontispiece from a Koran, early 16th century, MS no. 1544, colours on paper, 35.5 × 23 cm, Dublin, Chester Beatty Library; *Tailor at work*, early 17th century, ink on paper, 71 × 11 cm, Washington DC, Smithsonian Institution, Freer Gallery of Art. NISHAPUR, IRAN: Earthenware bowl, late 10th century, London, Bluett and Sons (Cooper-Bridgeman Library).

24-25 Islamic Art 2
IRAQ: A fragment of silk, 9th/10th century, London, Victoria and Albert Museum (Michael Holford). IRAN: Carpet, 16th century, silk, Washington DC, National Gallery of Art, Widener collection; Bronze cauldron, 12th/13th century, Baltimore, Walters Art Gallery; Standard, 16th century, gilt steel, Stockholm, Livrustkammaren; Tiles, late 14th century, glazed terracotta, Copenhagen, C.L. David Collection. SYRIA: Brass inlaid basin, 1240, inlaid with silver, Paris, Louvre (Documentation Photographique de la Réunion des Musées Nationaux); Bowl, 12th/13th century, earthenware, Copenhagen, C.L. David Collection. EGYPT: Inscribed marble slab, 9th/10th century, London, British Museum; Pair of doors inlaid with ivory, 13th/14th century, wood and ivory, New York, Metropolitan Museum of Art, Edward C. Moore Bequest. TURKEY: Mosque lamp, c. 1557, ceramic, London, Victoria and Albert Museum (Michael Holford).

26-27 Islamic Art 3: Representational Art
IRAN: Firdausi's *Shahnameh: Bahram Gur slays a dragon*, c. 1340, colours on paper, 40 × 30 cm, Cleveland, Museum of Art, Grace Rainey Rogers Fund. MIR SAYYID

ALI?: Firdausi's *Shahnameh: Bahram Gur slays onagers*, detail, c. 1525-30, colours on paper, New York, Metropolitan Museum of Art, Gift of Arthur A. Houghton Jnr. EGYPT: Panel, 11th-12th century, ivory, West Berlin, Museum für Islamische Kunst (Bildarchiv Preussischer Kulturbesitz). HERAT, IRAN: Hafiz's *Divan: Dancing Sufi dervishes*, c. 1490, colour on paper, New York, Metropolitan Museum of Art, Gift of Arthur A. Houghton Jnr. SULTAN MUHAMMAD?: Nizami's *Khamseh: The ascension of Mohammed*, early 16th century, folio 195r, colours on paper, London, British Library. AQA MIRAK?: Firdausi's *Shahnameh: King Khosroes I's war prizes are pledged for*, c. 1530, colours on paper, New York, Metropolitan Museum of Art, Gift of Arthur A. Houghton Jnr. TURKEY: Murad III's *Surnama: Sweepers performing before the sultan*, c. 1582, folio 341, colours on paper, 30 × 21 cm, Istanbul, Topkapi Palace Museum. MIRZA ALI?: Jami's *Haft Aurang: A father's discourse on love*, mid-16th century, colours on paper, 34 × 23 cm, Washington DC, Smithsonian Institution, Freer Gallery of Art.

28-29 South-East Asian Art 1
SUMATRA: Ancestor figure?, stone, on the island of Samosir in Lake Toba (Vautier-De Nanxe). NORTH VIETNAM: *The god of wine*, 1st century BC, bronze candelabrum, height 33 cm, from a tomb at Lach Truong, Hanoi, National Museum (Werner Forman Archive). KALIMANTAN: *Ikat* textile (Werner Forman Archive); *A hornbill*, wood, Liverpool, Merseyside County Museums. SULAWESI: Ancestor figures, Toraja (Claire Leimbach); The façade of a house, Toraja (Vautier-De Cool). IRIAN JAYA: Ancestor figure, stone and bone, height about 1 m, Leyden, Rijksmuseum voor Volkerkunde. BALI: *Kris* and scabbard, wood, gold and bronze, length about 50 cm, Bali, Collection R. Draptowi-Hardjo-Jogjakarta (Vautier-De Nanxe). JAVA: *Batik* textile (Werner Forman Archive).

30-31 South-East Asian Art 2
BOROBUDUR: *Pippalayana and Bhadra*, 8th/9th century, stone, *in situ* (Werner Forman Archive); One of the 72 *Buddhas*, 8th/9th century, stone, *in situ* (Vautier-De Nanxe); *The story of King Sibi*, detail: *Visitors arrive in their ship*, 8th/9th century, stone, *in situ* (Werner Forman Archive). CHANDI MENDUT: *The Bodhisattva Vajrapani*, 8th century, stone, *in situ* (Werner Forman Archive). PRAMBANAN: *Rama and Sita with Lakshmana*, early 10th century, stone, *in situ* (Werner Forman Archive). BELAHAN, EASTERN JAVA: *Vishnu seated on Garuda*, c. 1042, tufa, height 190 cm, Djakarta, National Museum. UPPER BURMA: *The Buddha in the bhumisparsamudra*, 17th century, bronze, Oxford, Ashmolean Museum. PAGAN, BURMA: Frescos decorating an arch in the temple of Muy-tha-kut, 11th or 12th century (Werner Forman Archive); Terracotta ornament, 12th century (Werner Forman Archive). BURMA: *Sutra* chest, 18th century, Oxford, Ashmolean Museum.

32-33 South-East Asian Art 3
CAMBODIA: *Vishnu*, late 7th century, sandstone, height 86 cm, Cleveland, Museum of Art, Gift of Hanna Fund. SULAWESI: *The Buddha*, detail, 3rd/5th century, bronze, height 75 cm, Leyden, Rijksmuseum voor Volkerkunde. ANGKOR WAT: *Apsara*, 12th century, stone, *in situ* (Mireille Vautier); Detail of the great frieze showing *The battle of the Pandavas and the Kauravas* on an outer gallery, early twelfth century, stone, *in situ* (Mireille Vautier). BANTEAY SREI:

Pediment, 10th century, stone, Paris, Musée Guimet. ANGKOR THOM: *Devata*, early 13th century, from the Bayon temple, stone, *in situ* (T.J. Mair); Details of reliefs from the outer terrace of the Bayon temple: *A military parade*, early 13th century, stone, *in situ* (William Macquitty). CHAIYA, THAILAND: *Bodhisattva*, mid-8th century, bronze, height about 50 cm, Durham, Gulbenkian Museum. CENTRAL THAILAND: *The Buddha calling the earth to witness*, 14th century, bronze, West Germany, Private Collection (Claus and Liselotte Hansmann). THAILAND: *The Buddha with two Bodhisattvas attended by spirits*, 18th century, paint on cloth, Munich, Museum für Volkerkunde.

34-35 Chinese Art 1
NORTHERN CHINA: Incense burner, *c.* 200 BC, inlaid bronze, height 18 cm, Washington DC, Smithsonian Institution, Freer Gallery of Art; Pictogram, and inscription, from bronze vessels, *c.* 1200 BC, rubbings, Durham, Gulbenkian Museum; Animal-shaped plaques, *c.* 1200 BC, jade and bronze, Durham, Gulbenkian Museum. ANYANG: Bronze vessel, *c.* 1200 BC, height 24 cm, Washington DC, Smithsonian Institution, Freer Gallery of Art. MANCHENG: Burial suit, *c.* 113 BC, jade plaques sewn with gold, length 188 cm (Michael Ridley). WUWEI, WESTERN CHINA: *"Flying Horse"*, 2nd century AD, bronze, length 45 cm, from tomb at Lei T'ai, Gansu (Robert Harding Associates). LONGQUAN: *One of the Emperor Taizong's chargers*, *c.* AD 649, sandstone, 165 × 191 cm, Xiangdu, Nan Yiian Museum (Richard and Sally Greenhill). XIANYANG: *Recumbent horse*, *c.* 177 BC, stone, height about 1 m, Xiangdu, Nan Yiian Museum (Richard and Sally Greenhill). MT LI: *A warrior*, *c.* 246-210 BC, terracotta, height 195 cm, *in situ* (Xinhua News Agency).

36-37 Chinese Art 2
YUNKANG: *The Buddha*, *c.* 460-70, stone (Michael Ridley). LONGMEN: *An empress visits Longmen*, *c.* 522, stone, height 198 cm, Kansas City, William Rockhill Nelson Gallery of Art. NORTHERN CHINA: *Maitreya*, 522, gilt bronze, New York, Metropolitan Museum of Art, Rogers Fund; *Bodhisattva*, 8th century, stone, Washington DC, Smithsonian Institution, Freer Gallery of Art. XIANGTANGSHAN: *Bodhisattva*, *c.* 550-77, stone, height 188 cm, Philadelphia, University of Pennsylvania, University Museum. WESTERN CHINA: Devotional stela, 554, stone, height 214 cm, Boston, Museum of Fine Arts. YICHOU: *Luohan*, late 10th century, glazed terracotta, London, British Museum. NORTHERN CHINA: Hanging scroll, 14th century, colour on silk, whole scroll 132 × 71 cm (Michael Ridley); *Guanyin*, Song dynasty, wood and plaster painted and gilded, height 225 cm, Kansas City, William Rockhill Nelson Gallery of Art.

38-39 Song Porcelain
HEBEI: Spitoon, *c.* 850, height 10.5 cm, China, Collection the People's Republic of China (Robert Harding Associates). HAIDIAN, PEKING: Vase and cover, late 14th century, height 66 cm, China, Collection the People's Republic of China (Giraudon). JINGDEZHEN: Stem cup, *c.* 1426-35, height 10 cm, and Plate, *c.* 1723-35, diameter 21 cm; Jar, *c.* 1506-21, diameter 15 cm; *Meiping* vase, *c.* 1662-1722, with enamels, height 14 cm, all porcelain, all Durham, Gulbenkian Museum. CHINA: Items of Song porcelain: A: Northern celadon bowl, 11th century, porcelain, diameter 21 cm; B: Jun bowl, probably 12th century, porcelain, diameter

13 cm; C: Ding bowl, 12th century, porcelain, diameter 23 cm; D: Cizhou vase, 12th century, stoneware, height 32.5 cm, all Durham, Gulbenkian Museum. SOUTHERN CHINA: *Bodhidharma*, 18th century, porcelain, London, British Museum (William MacQuitty).

40-41 Chinese Art 3
FAN KUAN: *Travelling among the mountains and streams*, early 11th century, ink and colour on silk, 155 × 74 cm, Taiwan, National Palace Museum. AFTER GU KAIZHI: *Admonitions of the instructress*, original *c.* 375, ink and colour on silk, height 25 cm, London, British Museum (Cooper-Bridgeman Library). MI FEI: *Spring mountains, clouds and pine-trees*, *c.* 1050-1100, ink and slight colour on paper, height 35 cm, Taiwan, National Palace Museum. MUQI: *A mother gibbon and her baby*, *c.* 1250?, part of a triptych, ink on silk, height 178 cm, Kyoto, Daitoku-ji (Tokyo, Kodansha Ltd). GUO XI: *Early spring*, 1072, ink and light colour on silk, 158 × 108 cm, Taiwan, National Palace Museum. WANG MENG: *Forest dwellings at Juqu*, *c.* 1370, ink and colour on paper, 69 × 43 cm, Taiwan, National Palace Museum. TANG YIN: *A poet and two courtesans*, *c.* 1500, ink and colour on paper, Taiwan, National Palace Museum. SHITAO: *The gleaming peak*, *c.* 1700, light colour on paper, 24.5 × 17 cm (Cologne, Rheinisches Bildarchiv).

42-43 Korean Art
KYONGJU: Royal crown, 4th/6th century, gold and jade, Seoul, National Museum (Mikihiro Taeda on loan from Hans Hinz). KOGURYO: *A nobleman and his wife*, mid-5th/6th century, mural, Anak, Tomb 3 (Werner Forman Archive). SILLA OR PAEKCHE?: *Maitreya*, early 7th century, gilt bronze, height 93.5 cm, Seoul, Toksu Palace Museum (Colorphoto Hans Hinz). KANG HUI-AN: *A sage resting on a rock*, 15th century, ink on paper, 23.5 × 16 cm, Seoul, National Museum (Charles E. Tuttle Co. Inc., Tokyo). KOREA: Wine pot, late 12th century, porcelain, Seoul, Toksu Palace Museum (Colorphoto Hans Hinz). AN KYON: *The dream of the peach-blossom garden*, 1447, colour on silk, 39 × 106 cm, Nara, Tenri Central Library. CHONG SON: *The mountain by the river*, 18th century, ink on paper, Kyongju, Museum (Werner Forman Archive). YI IN-MUN: *Young Immortal under a fir tree*, 18th/19th century, ink on paper, Pyongyang, Museum (Werner Forman Archive).

44-45 Japanese Art 1
JAPAN: Jomon figurine, 1st millennium BC, terracotta, height about 30 cm, Tokyo, National Museum (Vautier-De Cool); A *haniwa*: *A warrior*, 3rd/6th century AD, terracotta, height about 70 cm (Vautier-De Cool); *"The Kudara Kannon"*, 7th century, wood, height 205 cm, Nara, Horyu Daitoku-ji (Benrido Company Ltd, Kyoto). TOHAKU: *Pine-trees*, detail of screen, late 16th century, ink on paper, height 155 cm, Tokyo, National Museum (The Zauho Press). KENZAN: Ceremonial tea-bowl: *Evening glory*, late 17th or early 18th century, pottery, height 9.5 cm, Nara, Yamato Bunkakan Museum. NITEN: *Bird and branch*, late 16th or early 17th century, ink on paper, Philadelphia, Museum of Art, Fiske Kimball Fund. KOETSU AND SOTATSU: *Deer*, detail of a scroll, 17th century, gold, silver and ink on paper, height 33 cm, Shizuoka, Atami Museum. BUNCHO: *Heron wading among lotus flowers*, 18th/19th century, ink on paper, 83 × 26 cm, Durham, Gulbenkian Museum.

46-47 Japanese Art 2
SESSHU: *Autumn landscape*, late 15th

century, ink and colour on paper, height 46 cm, Tokyo, National Museum (The Zauho Press). BUNSEI: *The layman Vimalakirti*, 1457, ink on paper, 92 × 34 cm, Nara, Yamato Bunkakan Museum. MOTONOBU: *The small waterfall*, early 16th century, ink and colour washes on paper, 45 × 87 cm, Nara, Yamato Bunkakan Museum. EITOKU: *Plum trees by water*, 16th century, ink and colour washes on paper, height 172 cm, Kyoto, Juko-in (Kodansha Ltd, Tokyo); A Matsuura screen, early 17th century, colour on gold paper, 152 × 366 cm, Nara, Yamato Bunkakan Museum; Lacquer box, late 18th century, painted lacquer, Vienna, Kunsthistorisches Museum (Claus and Liselotte Hansmann). MORONOBU: *A riverboat party*, *c.* 1682, coloured woodcut, London, British Museum (Cooper-Bridgeman Library). JIHEI: *An insistent lover*, *c.* 1685, coloured woodcut, Chicago, Art Institute (Cooper-Bridgeman Library).

48-49 Japanese Art 3
TAKANOBU: *The courtier Taira-no-Shigemori*, late 12th century, colour on silk, 137 × 112 cm, Kyoto, Collection Jingo-Ji (The Zauho Press). MITSUNAGA: *Ban Danaigon: The flight of the court*, late 12th century, ink on paper, height 31 cm, Tokyo, National Museum (The Zauho Press). KORIN: *White plum-trees in spring*, *c.* 1705-10, colour on gold paper, 166 × 172 cm, Shizuoka, Atami Museum. UNKNOWN ARTIST: *The Tale of Genji: An interior with figures*, 12th century, colour on paper, height 22 cm, Nagoya, Tokugawa Museum (The Zauho Press). YAKUSHI-JI, NARA: *The Buddha and two Bodhisattvas*, *c.* 726, bronze, height of central figure 3.3 m, *in situ* (Zentrale Farbbild Agentur). HORYU-JI, JAPAN: *The death of the Buddha*, 711, clay, figures life-size, Nara, Horyuji Temple (Benrido Company Ltd). TOSHODAI-JI, JAPAN: *"The Kannon with 1,000 arms"*, after 759, gilt and dry-lacquer, height nearly 5.5 m; *The priest Ganjin*, before 763, dry-lacquer, height 80.7 cm, both Nara, *in situ*. JAPAN: *Fudo*, 13th century, wood, height about 2 m, London, British Museum; *The Bodhisattva Fugen*, 12th century, colour on silk, 160 × 73 cm, Tokyo, National Museum (The Zauho Press).

50-51 Japanese Art 4
KAIGETSUDO: *A courtesan*, *c.* 1714, coloured woodblock print, Chicago, Art Institute. UTAMARO: Folio from *The poem of the pillow*, 1788, woodblock colour print, London, art market (Angelo Hornak). HARUNOBU: *A lady dressing her hair*, 1768, woodblock colour print, West Germany, Private Collection (Claus and Liselotte Hansmann). KIYONAGA: *Cherry blossom*, *c.* 1787-88, woodblock colour print, London, British Museum (Cooper-Bridgeman Library). KORYUSAI: *At the gate*, *c.* 1771, woodblock colour print, Chicago, Art Institute (Cooper-Bridgeman Library). SHARAKU: *The Actor Otani Oniji as Edohei*, 1794, woodblock colour print, 38 × 23 cm, Chicago, Art Institute. HOKUSAI: Folio from *Little Flowers: Peonies and a sparrow*, 1828, woodblock colour print, West Germany, Private Collection (Claus and Liselotte Hansmann); Folio from *Thirty-six Views of Mount Fuji: Southerly wind and fine weather*, *c.* 1823-29, woodblock colour print, 25.5 × 38 cm, London, Victoria and Albert Museum (Cooper-Bridgeman Library). HIROSHIGE: Folio from *Fifty-three Stages of the Tokaido Highway: A shower at Shono*, *c.* 1833, woodblock colour print, 22 × 35 cm (Claus and Liselotte Hansmann). KUNIYOSHI: Folio from *The Heroes of Suikoden: Tameijiro dan Shogo grapples with his enemy under water*, 1828-

29, woodblock colour print, London, B.W. Robinson Collection (Cooper-Bridgeman Library).

52-53 The Age of Revolutions
PARIS: View of the grand staircase of the Opéra, 1861-74, by Charles Garnier (Giraudon). BARCELONA: The façade of Casa Batlló, began 1905, by Antoni Gaudi (ZEFA). CHICAGO: The Carson Pirie Scott store, 1899-1904, by Louis Sullivan (Angelo Hornak).

54-55
(Map by Colin Salmon and Dinah Lone)

56-57 David: The Oath of the Horatii
POUSSIN: *Extreme Unction*, 1644, oil on canvas, 117 × 178 cm, Edinburgh, Duke of Sutherland Collection, on loan to the National Gallery of Scotland. GREUZE: *Septimius Severus reproaches Caracalla for seeking his death*, 1769, oil on canvas, 124 × 160 cm, Paris, Louvre (Documentation Photographique de la Réunion des Musées Nationaux). MENGS: *Parnassus*, 1760-61, ceiling fresco, about 3 × 6 m, Rome, Villa Albani (The Mansell Collection). VIEN: *The cupid seller*, 1763, oil on canvas, 95 × 119 cm, Château de Fontainebleau (Giraudon). HAMILTON: *The oath of Brutus*, *c.* 1763, oil on canvas, 208 × 270 cm, London, Drury Lane, Theatre Royal (The Iveagh Bequest). DAVID: *The oath of the Horatii*, 1784, oil on canvas, Paris, Louvre (Documentation Photographique de la Réunion des Musées Nationaux); *The lictors bringing Brutus the bodies of his sons*, 1789, oil on canvas, 325 × 425 cm, Paris, Louvre (S).

58-59 Neoclassical Painting
DAVID: *The intervention of the Sabine women*, 1799, oil on canvas, 386 × 520 cm, Paris, Louvre (S); *The death of Marat*, 1795, oil on canvas, 165 × 126 cm, Brussels, Musées Royaux des Beaux-Arts (S); *Mme Récamier*, 1800, oil on canvas, 173 × 243 cm, Paris, Louvre (Documentation Photographique de la Réunion des Musées Nationaux); *Napoleon in his study*, 1812, oil on canvas, 202 × 124 cm, Washington, National Gallery of Art, Andrew W. Mellon collection. WEST: *The death of Wolfe*, 1771, oil on canvas, 151 × 213 cm, Ottawa, National Gallery of Canada. STUART: *George Washington*, 1795, oil on canvas, 122 × 94 cm, Washington, National Gallery of Art, Andrew W. Mellon collection. TRUMBULL: *The death of General Warren at the Battle of Bunker Hill*, 1786, oil on canvas, 61 × 86 cm, New Haven, Connecticut, Yale University Art Gallery. COPLEY: *A boy with a squirrel* (The artist's half-brother), *c.* 1765, oil on canvas, 77 × 63 cm, Boston, Museum of Fine Arts. GIRODET: *Atala's entombment*, 1808, oil on canvas, 205 × 284 cm, Paris, Louvre (S). GERARD: *Mme Récamier*, 1802, oil on canvas, 225 × 148 cm, Paris, Musée Carnavalet (Giraudon). PRUD'HON: *Justice and Divine Vengeance pursuing Crime*, 1808, oil on canvas, 243 × 292 cm, Paris, Louvre (Documentation Photographique de la Réunion des Musées Nationaux).

60-61 Neoclassical Sculpture
HOUDON: *Voltaire*, 1778, terracotta, height about 40 cm, Versailles, Musée Lambinet (Giraudon); *Denis Diderot*, 1791, terracotta, height 41 cm, Paris, Louvre (Documentation Photographique de la Réunion des Musées Nationaux); *George Washington*, 1788-92, marble, height of figure 188 cm, Richmond, Virginia, State Capitol (Photri). CANOVA: *Theseus and the Minotaur*, 1781-82, marble, height 147 cm, London, Victoria and Albert Museum; *Cupid and Psyche*, 1789-93, marble, height 155 cm, Paris, Louvre (Documentation

Photographique de la Réunion des Musées Nationaux); Sketch for *Cupid and Psyche*, 1787, terracotta, height 16 cm, Possagno, Museo Canova (Courtauld Institute of Art); *Paulina Borghese as Venus Victrix*, 1805-07, marble, height 160 cm, Rome, Villa Borghese (S); Monument to Archduchess Maria Christina, 1799-1805, marble, height of pyramid nearly 6 m, Vienna, Augustinerkirche (Vienna, Österreichische Nationalbibliothek). THORVALDSEN: *Hebe*, 1806, marble, height 150 cm, Copenhagen, Thorvaldsen Museum (S). SCHADOW: *Field-Marshal Blücher*, 1819, bronze, height of figure about 2.5 m, Rostock, Universitätsplatz (Courtauld Institute of Art). PIGALLE: *Voltaire*, 1770-76, marble, height 147 cm, Paris, Louvre (Documentation Photographique de la Réunion des Musées Nationaux).

62-63 Neoclassics and Romantics in England
FLAXMAN: Illustration to the *Iliad: Princes all Hail!*, 1795, engraving, 30 × 45 cm (The Fotomas Index); Illustration to Aeschylus' *The Furies*, 1795, engraving, 29 × 46 cm (The Fotomas Index); Monument to Sophia Hoare, 1821, marble, 78 × 132 cm, Streatham, Parish Church (Courtauld Institute of Art). BLAKE: *The good and evil angels struggling for the possession of a child*, 1795, monotype finished in pen and watercolour, 43 × 58 cm, London, Tate Gallery; *Newton*, 1795, monotype finished in pen and watercolour, 46 × 58 cm, London, Tate Gallery; *The circle of the lustful*, from Dante's *Inferno*, Canto V, c.1824, pen, pencil and watercolour on paper, 37 × 52 cm, Birmingham, Museum and Art Gallery; *Thenot under a fruit tree*, 1821, monotype, 3 × 7 cm, London, Tate Gallery. FUSELI: *The artist moved by the grandeur of ancient ruins*, 1778-79, red chalk and sepia wash on paper, 41 × 35 cm, Vienna, Kunsthistorisches Museum (S); *The nightmare*, 1781, oil on canvas, 101 × 127 cm, Detroit, Institute of Arts, Gift of Mr and Mrs Bert L. Smokler and Mr and Mrs Lawrence Fleischmann. PALMER: *Early morning*, 1825, sepia and gum on paper, 19 × 22 cm, Oxford, Ashmolean Museum.

64-65 Francisco de Goya
GOYA: *Los Caprichos*, frontispiece: *Self-portrait*, 1798, etching, 21 × 13 cm (The Fotomas Index); The dome of Nuestra Senora del Pilar, Saragossa: *The Virgin, Queen of martyrs*, detail, 1781, fresco (Ampliaciones y Reproduciones Mas); *The sunshade*, 1777, oil on canvas, 104 × 152 cm, Madrid, Prado (S); *The Duchess of Alba*, 1797, oil on canvas, 210 × 149 cm, New York, Hispanic Society (S); *Nude maja*, 1802-05, oil on canvas, 97 × 190 cm, Madrid, Prado (S); *Don Manuel de Godoy*, 1801, oil on canvas, 181 × 268 cm, Madrid, Academy of San Fernando (S); *Two majas on a balcony*, c.1800-14, oil on canvas, 195 × 125 cm, New York, Metropolitan Museum of Art, H.O. Havemeyer collection; *Charles IV and his family*, 1800, oil on canvas, 280 × 336 cm, Madrid, Prado (S); *May 3rd, 1808*, 1814, oil on canvas, 266 × 345 cm, Madrid, Prado (S).

66-67 Goya: The Colossus
GOYA: *The Disasters of War: This is how it is; This is worse*, c.1810-15, both etchings, 16 × 22 cm (The Fotomas Index); *The straw manikin*, 1791-92, oil on canvas, 267 × 160 cm, Madrid, Prado (S); *Los Caprichos*, plate 43: *The sleep of Reason*, 1799, etching, 21 × 13 cm (The Fotomas Index); *Self-portrait with Dr Arrieta*, 1820, oil on canvas, 117 × 79 cm, Minneapolis, Institute of Arts; *Saturn*,

1820, fresco transferred to canvas, 146 × 238 cm, Madrid, Prado (S); *The colossus*, 1808-12, oil on canvas, 116 × 105 cm, Madrid, Prado (S).

68-69 Romantic Landscape in Britain and America
LOUTHERBOURG: *Coalbrookdale by night*, 1801, oil on canvas, 68 × 106 cm, London, Science Museum. MARTIN: *Joshua commanding the sun to stand still*, 1816, oil on canvas, 149 × 231 cm, London, Freemasons' Hall, United Grand Lodge of England (Cooper-Bridgeman Library). CROME: *The Poringland oak*, c.1818, oil on canvas, 71 × 110 cm, London, Tate Gallery. COTMAN: *Greta Bridge*, 1805, watercolour on paper, 23 × 33 cm, London, British Museum. JOHN ROBERT COZENS: *Lake Nemi*, c.1778-79, watercolour on paper, 36 × 50 cm, London, Victoria and Albert Museum. GIRTIN: *Kirkstall Abbey*, c.1800, watercolour, pen and pencil on paper, 39 × 52 cm, London, Victoria and Albert Museum. ALLSTON: *Moonlit landscape*, 1819, oil on canvas, 61 × 89 cm, Boston, Museum of Fine Arts, Gift of William Sturgis Bigelow. COLE: *Sunny morning on the Hudson River*, c.1827, oil on panel, 47 × 64 cm, Boston, Museum of Fine Arts, Mr and Mrs Karolik collection. DURAND: *Kindred spirits*, 1849, oil on canvas, 111 × 91 cm, New York, Public Library. BINGHAM: *Fur traders descending the Missouri*, c.1844, oil on canvas, 73 × 93 cm, New York, Metropolitan Museum of Art, Morris K. Jessup Fund.

70-71 Constable: The White Horse
CONSTABLE: "*The White Horse*", 1819, oil on canvas, 131 × 188 cm, New York, Frick Collection (copyright); Oil-sketch for "*The White Horse*", c.1819, oil on canvas, 127 × 183 cm, Washington, National Gallery of Art, Widener collection; *Clouds, Sept. 5th*, 1822, oil on paper, 29 × 48 cm, London, Victoria and Albert Museum; *The haywain*, 1821, oil on canvas, 130 × 185 cm, London, National Gallery; *Stonehenge*, watercolour, 38 × 59 cm, London, Victoria and Albert Museum; Pencil sketch, 1814, from sketch-book no. 132, on paper, 8 × 11 cm, London, Victoria and Albert Museum.

72-73 Turner: Dawn after the Wreck
TURNER: *Dawn after the wreck*, c.1840, watercolour on paper, 34.5 × 36 cm, London, Courtauld Institute Galleries; *Tintern Abbey*, c.1795, watercolour over pencil with pen and ink, 33.5 × 26 cm, Oxford, Ashmolean Museum; *The slave ship*, 1840, oil on canvas, 91 × 122 cm, Boston, Museum of Fine Arts, Henry Lillie Pierce Fund; *Venice: S. Giorgio Maggiore*, 1819, watercolour on paper, 22 × 28 cm, London, British Museum (Cooper-Bridgeman Library); *Sun rising through vapour: fishermen cleaning and selling fish*, 1807, oil on canvas, 134 × 179 cm, London, National Gallery; *The Thames near Walton Bridge*, c.1807, oil on panel, 36 × 73 cm, London, Tate Gallery; *Snowstorm: Hannibal crossing the Alps*, 1812, oil on canvas, 144 × 236 cm, London, Tate Gallery.

74-75 German and Scandinavian Romanticism
JUEL: *Northern lights*, c.1790, oil on canvas, 31 × 39 cm, Copenhagen, Ny Carlsberg Glyptotek. KOCH: *Schmadribach waterfall*, 1808-11, oil on canvas, 123 × 93 cm, Leipzig, Museum of Fine Arts (S). DAHL: *Clouds*, 1825, oil on paper, 21 × 22 cm, West Berlin, Staatliche Museen (Bildarchiv Preussischer Kulturbesitz). FRIEDRICH: *Monk by the sea*, 1809, oil on canvas, 110 × 171 cm, West Berlin, Schloss Charlottenburg (Staatliche

Schlösser und Gärten). RUNGE: *Morning*, 1808-09, oil on canvas, 152 × 113 cm, Hamburg, Kunsthalle (S); *Morning*, from *The Phases of the Day*, 1803, engraving, 72 × 48 cm, Hamburg, Kunsthalle (S); *The artist's parents and children*, 1806, oil on canvas, 194 × 131 cm, Hamburg, Kunsthalle (S). CORNELIUS: *Faust and Mephisto on the Brocken*, c.1811, engraving, 40 × 34 cm, Frankfurt, Stadelisches Kunstinstitut (Bildarchiv Preussischer Kulturbesitz). PFORR: *The entry of Emperor Rudolf of Hapsburg into Basel in 1273*, 1808-10, oil on canvas, 90 × 119 cm, Frankfurt, Stadelisches Kunstinstitut (S). OVERBECK: *Italia and Germania*, 1811-28, oil on canvas, 95 × 105 cm, Dresden, Gemäldegalerie (S).

76-77 Friedrich: Man and Woman Gazing at the Moon
FRIEDRICH: *Abbey graveyard under snow*, 1810, oil on canvas, 121 × 170 cm, West Berlin, Schloss Charlottenburg (Bildarchiv Preussischer Kulturbesitz); *Moonrise over the sea*, 1822, oil on canvas, 55 × 71 cm, West Berlin, Staatliche Museen (S); The Tetschen altar: *The Cross on the mountains*, 1809, oil on canvas, 115 × 110 cm, Dresden, Gemäldegalerie (S); *A dolmen near Gützkow*, c.1837, pencil and sepia, 22 × 30 cm, Copenhagen, The Library of Her Majesty Margrethe II, Queen of Denmark (Hans Petersen); *Man and woman gazing at the moon*, c.1830-35, oil on canvas, 34 × 44 cm, West Berlin, Staatliche Museen (S); *The stages of life*, c.1835, oil on canvas, 72 × 94 cm, Leipzig, Museum der Bildende Künste (S). KERSTING: *Friedrich in his studio*, oil on canvas, 51 × 40 cm, West Berlin, Staatliche Museen (S).

78-79 French Romanticism
GROS: *The plague at Jaffa*, 1804, oil on canvas, 532 × 720 cm, Paris, Louvre (Documentation Photographique de la Réunion des Musées Nationaux). GERICAULT: *An officer of the Chasseurs*, 1812, oil on canvas, 349 × 266 cm, Paris, Louvre (Documentation Photographique de la Réunion des Musées Nationaux); *A wounded cuirassier leaving the field*, 1814, oil on canvas, 358 × 294 cm, Paris, Louvre (Documentation Photographique de la Réunion des Musées Nationaux); *The raft of the Medusa*, 1819, oil on canvas, 491 × 716 cm, Paris, Louvre (S); *A kleptomaniac*, 1822-23, oil on canvas, 60 × 50 cm, Ghent, Musée des Beaux-Arts (S). DELACROIX: *The barque of Dante*, 1822, oil on canvas, 189 × 246 cm, Paris, Louvre (Documentation Photographique de la Réunion des Musées Nationaux); *The departure of the volunteers*, 1833-36, stone relief, 12.7 × 6 m, Paris, Arc de Triomphe (Giraudon); *The awakening of Napoleon*, 1847, bronze, 215 × 195 cm, Fixin (Côte d'Or), Parc Noisot (René Roland). BARYE: *Jaguar devouring a crocodile*, 1850, bronze, length 32 cm, Copenhagen, Ny Carlsberg Glyptotek.

80-81 Delacroix: The Death of Sardanapalus
DELACROIX: *The death of Sardanapalus*, 1827, oil on canvas, 395 × 495 cm, Paris Louvre (S); *The massacre at Chios*, 1824, oil on canvas, 422 × 352 cm, Paris, Louvre (S); *Still life with a lobster*, 1827, oil on canvas, 80 × 106 cm, Paris, Louvre (Documentation Photographique de la Réunion des Musées Nationaux); *Women of Algiers*, 1834, oil on canvas, 180 × 220 cm, Paris, Louvre (S); *Baron Schwitter*, 1826-30, oil on canvas, 218 × 143 cm, London, National Gallery; *Liberty leading the people*, 1830, oil on canvas, 260 × 325 cm, Paris, Louvre (S).

82-83 Painting in Victorian Britain
FRITH: *Derby Day*, 1856-58, oil on canvas, 101 × 223 cm, London, Tate Gallery. WILKIE: *Chelsea pensioners reading the Gazette of the Battle of Waterloo*, 1822, oil on canvas, 91 × 152 cm, London, Victoria and Albert Museum. MILLAIS: *Christ in the house of his parents*, 1850, oil on canvas, 86 × 137 cm, London, Tate Gallery. HOLMAN HUNT: *The awakened conscience*, 1852-54, oil on canvas, 76 × 56 cm, London, Tate Gallery. LANDSEER: *The monarch of the glen*, 1850, oil on canvas, 162 × 167 cm, London, Dewar House (John Dewar and Sons Ltd). ROSSETTI: *The Annunciation*, 1850, oil on canvas, 71 × 41 cm, London, Tate Gallery. MADOX BROWN: *Work*, 1852-63, 134.5 × 196 cm, Manchester, City Art Gallery; *Pretty baa lambs*, 1851, oil on wood, 20 × 26 cm, Oxford, Ashmolean Museum. BURNE-JONES: *King Cophetua and the beggar maid*, 1884, oil on canvas, 292 × 135 cm, London, Tate Gallery. WATTS: *Hope*, oil on canvas, 141 × 110 cm, London, Tate Gallery.

84-85 Ingres: La Grande Odalisque
INGRES: "*La Grande Odalisque*" (The concubine), 1814, oil on canvas, 91 × 162 cm, Paris, Louvre (S); "*The Valpinçon Bather*", 1808, oil on canvas, 146 × 97 cm, Paris, Louvre (Documentation Photographique de la Réunion des Musées Nationaux); *The Turkish bath*, 1859-62, oil on canvas, diameter 108 cm, Paris, Louvre (S); *The apotheosis of Homer*, 1827, oil on canvas, 386 × 515 cm, Paris, Louvre (Documentation Photographique de la Réunion des Musées Nationaux); *Oedipus and the Sphinx*, 1808, reworked 1825, oil on canvas, 189 × 144 cm, Paris, Louvre (S); *Louis-François Bertin*, 1832, oil on canvas, 116 × 95 cm, Paris, Louvre (Documentation Photographique de la Réunion des Musées Nationaux); *Joseph Woodhead, his wife Harriet and her brother Henry Comber*, 1816, pencil on paper, 30 × 22 cm, Cambridge, Fitzwilliam Museum; *La Comtesse d'Haussonville*, 1845, oil on canvas, New York, Frick Collection (copyright).

86-87 Academic Art in Europe
COUTURE: *The Romans of the Decadence*, 1847, oil on canvas, 466 × 775 cm, Paris, Louvre (Documentation Photographique de la Réunion des Musées Nationaux). GEROME: *The gladiators*, c.1859, oil on canvas, 97 × 149 cm, Phoenix, Art Museum. MEISSONIER: *Napoleon III at the Battle of Solferino, June 24th, 1859*, 1863, oil on canvas, 44 × 76 cm, Paris, Louvre (Documentation Photographique de la Réunion des Musées Nationaux). INGRES: "*La Source*" (The spring), 1856, oil on canvas, 164 × 82 cm, Paris, Louvre (S). FLANDRIN: *Theseus recognized by his father*, 1838, oil on canvas, Paris, Ecole des Beaux-Arts (Giraudon). CHASSERIAU: *The toilet of Esther*, 1841, oil on canvas, 44 × 36 cm, Paris, Louvre (Documentation Photographique de la Réunion des Musées Nationaux). LEIGHTON: *The Garden of the Hesperides*, 1892, oil on canvas, diameter 169 cm, Liverpool, Walker Art Museum. CABANEL: *The birth of Venus*, 1863, oil on canvas, 130 × 225 cm, Paris, Louvre (Documentation Photographique de la Réunion des Musées Nationaux). REGNAULT: *Automedon with the horses of Achilles*, 1868, oil on canvas, 54 × 45 cm, Paris, Louvre (Documentation Photographique de la Réunion des Musées Nationaux). ALMA-TADEMA: *The Baths of Caracalla*, 1899, oil on canvas, 152 × 94 cm, Wynyard Park, Co. Durham, Lord Londonderry collection (Dennis Wompra).

88-89 French Realism

NADAR: *Charles Baudelaire*, c. 1863, photograph, Paris, Caisse Nationale des Monuments Historiques et des Sites. DAUMIER: *Ratapoil*, c. 1850, bronze, height 44 cm, Buffalo, Albright-Knox Art Gallery, Elizabeth H. Gates Fund; *Rue Transnonain, April 15th, 1834*, 1834, lithograph, 29 × 44 cm, Paris, Bibliothèque Nationale (Immédiate 2); *Nadar in a balloon*, 1862, lithograph, 27 × 22 cm, London, British Library; *The dream of the inventor of the needle gun*, 1866, lithograph, 23 × 20 cm, London, British Library; *The third-class carriage*, c. 1862, oil on canvas, 65 × 90 cm, New York, Metropolitan Museum, of Art, H.O. Havemeyer collection. GUYS: *Two ladies with muffs*, c. 1875-80, wash drawing, 18 × 14 cm, London, Courtauld Institute Galleries. MILLET: *The sower*, 1850, oil on canvas, 101 × 82 cm, Boston, Museum of Fine Arts, Shaw collection; *The angelus*, 1855-57, oil on canvas, 55 × 66 cm, Paris, Louvre (Documentation Photographique de la Réunion des Musées Nationaux). MERYON: *The morgue*, 1854, etching, 190 × 213 cm, London, Victoria and Albert Museum.

90-91 Courbet: The Artist's Studio

COURBET: *The artist's studio*, 1854-55, oil on canvas, 361 × 598 cm, Paris, Louvre (Documentation Photographique de la Réunion des Musées Nationaux); *Self-portrait with black dog*, 1844, oil on canvas, 46 × 55 cm, Paris, Louvre, Petit Palais (S); *The stone-breakers*, 1849, oil on canvas, 165 × 238 cm, formerly Dresden, Gemäldegalerie, destroyed (Courtauld Institute of Art); *The bathers*, 1853, oil on canvas, 227 × 193 cm, Montpellier, Musée Fabre (Claude O'Sughrue); *A burial at Ornans*, 1849-50, oil on canvas, 314 × 663 cm, Paris, Louvre (S); *Pierre-Joseph Proudhon and his family*, 1865, oil on canvas, 147 × 198 cm, Besançon, Musée des Beaux-Arts (S).

92-93 French Landscape

ROUSSEAU: *A group of oaks near Barbizon*, 1852, oil on canvas, 63 × 99 cm, Paris, Louvre (S). BONINGTON: *View of Normandy?*, c. 1824, oil on canvas, 38 × 53 cm, London, Tate Gallery. HUET: *Elms at St-Cloud*, 1823, oil on canvas, 36 × 27 cm, Paris, Louvre, Petit Palais (Photo Bulloz). MICHEL: *The storm*, c. 1820-30, oil on panel, 58 × 73 cm, Chicago, Art Institute. DAUBIGNY: *Snow scene: Valmondois*, 1875, oil on canvas, 89 × 153 cm, Perth, Art Gallery of Western Australia. MILLET: *Spring*, 1868-73, oil on canvas, 86 × 111 cm, Paris, Louvre (Documentation Photographique de la Réunion des Musées Nationaux). COURBET: *The Loue valley in stormy weather*, c. 1849, oil on canvas, 56 × 66 cm, Strasbourg, Musée des Beaux-Arts. DIAZ DE LA PENA: *Gypsies going to a fair*, 1844, oil on canvas, 99 × 80 cm, Boston, Museum of Fine Arts, Bequest of Mrs Samuel Dennis Warren. COROT: *The island of San Bartolommeo in Rome*, 1825, oil on canvas, 25 × 43 cm, Boston, Museum of Fine Arts, Harriet Otis Cruft Fund; *View of Avray*, c. 1835-40, oil on canvas, 53 × 78 cm, Metropolitan Museum of Art, Bequest of Catherine Lorillard Wolfe.

94-95 Edouard Manet

FANTIN-LATOUR: *Edouard Manet*, 1867, oil on canvas, 117 × 90 cm, Chicago, Art Institute. MANET: *The absinth drinker*, 1858, oil on canvas, 180 × 106 cm, Copenhagen, Ny Carlsberg Glyptotek; *Olympia*, 1863, oil on canvas, 150 × 190 cm, Paris, Louvre, Jeu de Paume (S); "*Le Déjeuner sur l'Herbe*" (The picnic), 1863, oil on canvas,

208 × 264 cm, Paris, Louvre, Jeu de Paume (S); Oil-sketch for *The execution of Maximilian*, 1867, oil on canvas, 252 × 305 cm, Copenhagen, Ny Carlsberg Glyptotek; *Emile Zola*, 1868, oil on canvas, 190 × 110 cm, Paris, Louvre, Jeu de Paume (S); *Chez Père Lathuile*, 1879, oil on canvas, 92 × 112 cm, Tournai, Musée des Beaux-Arts (René Roland); *Argenteuil*, 1874, oil on canvas, 92 × 112 cm, Tournai, Musée des Beaux-Arts (S); *Civil war*, 1871, lithograph, 39 × 50 cm, London, British Museum.

96-97 Whistler: Falling Rocket

WHISTLER: *Falling rocket: Nocturne in black and gold*, c. 1874, oil on panel, 60 × 47 cm, Detroit, Institute of Arts, Dexter M. Ferry Jnr Fund; *At the piano*, 1858-59, oil on canvas, 66 × 90 cm, Cincinnati, Art Museum, Louise Taft Semple Bequest; *Cremorne lights: Nocturne in blue and silver*, 1872, oil on canvas, 49 × 74 cm, London, Tate Gallery (Angelo Hornak); *Wapping-on-Thames*, 1861-64, oil on canvas, 71 × 101 cm, New York, Collection of Mr and Mrs John Hay Whitney; *The white girl: Symphony in white no. 1*, 1862, oil on canvas, 214 × 108 cm, Washington, National Gallery of Art, Harris Whittemore collection; *The artist's mother: Arrangement in grey and black no. I*, 1862, oil on canvas, 145 × 164 cm, Paris, Louvre (Documentation Photographique de la Réunion des Musées Nationaux); *Venetian palaces: Nocturne*, 1879-80, etching, 29 × 20 cm (Courtauld Institute of Art).

98-99 Impressionism 1

RENOIR: *At the inn of Mother Anthony*, 1866, oil on canvas, 195 × 130 cm, Stockholm, National Museum; *Monet working in his garden*, 1873, oil on canvas, 50 × 62 cm, Hartford, Connecticut, Wadsworth Atheneum. BOUDIN: *The jetty at Deauville*, 1865, oil on canvas, 235 × 325 cm, Paris, Louvre, Jeu de Paume (S). PISSARRO: *Red roofs*, 1877, oil on canvas, 53 × 64 cm, Paris, Louvre, Jeu de Paume (S). MONET: *Impression: Sunrise*, 1872, oil on canvas, 50 × 62 cm, Paris, Musée Marmottan (S). BAZILLE: *The artist's family*, 1867, oil on canvas, 152 × 230 cm, Paris, Louvre, Jeu de Paume (S). SISLEY: *Floods at Port-Marly*, 1876, oil on canvas, 60 × 81 cm, Paris, Louvre, Jeu de Paume (S). RENOIR: *Mme Charpentier and her children*, 1878, oil on canvas, 154 × 190 cm, New York, Metropolitan Museum of Art, Wolfe Fund. MORISOT: *The butterfly chase*, 1874, oil on canvas, 47 × 56 cm, Paris, Louvre, Jeu de Paume (S).

100-101 Claude Monet

NADAR: *Claude Monet*, 1899, photograph, Paris, Caisse Nationale des Monuments Historiques et des Sites. MONET: *The cart – snow-covered road at Honfleur*, 1865, oil on canvas, 65 × 92 cm, Paris, Louvre, Jeu de Paume (S); *Ladies in the garden*, 1867, oil on canvas, 254 × 206 cm, Paris, Louvre, Jeu de Paume (S); *La Grenouillère*, 1869, oil on canvas, 75 × 99 cm, New York, Metropolitan Museum of Art, H.O. Havemeyer collection; *Gare St Lazare*, 1877, oil on canvas, 75 × 100 cm, Paris, Louvre, Jeu de Paume (S); *Two haystacks*, 1891, oil on canvas, 64 × 99 cm, Chicago, Art Institute; *The cliff at Etretat*, 1883, oil on canvas, 64 × 81 cm, New York, Metropolitan Museum of Art, Bequest of William Church Osborne; *The lilypond*, after 1900, oil on canvas, 89 × 100 cm, Paris, Louvre, Jeu de Paume (S); *Two haystacks*, 1891, oil on canvas, 60 × 100 cm, Paris, Louvre, Jeu de Paume (Documentation Photographique de la Réunion des Musées Nationaux).

102-103 Impressionism 2

PISSARRO: *A view from the artist's window, Eragny*, 1888, oil on canvas, 55 × 81 cm, Oxford, Ashmolean Museum; *The Boulevard Montmartre at night*, 1897, oil on canvas, 55 × 65 cm, London, National Gallery; *The potato harvest*, 1886, etching, 28 × 22 cm, New York, Public Library. RENOIR: *Umbrellas*, c. 1881-84, oil on canvas, 180 × 116 cm, London, National Gallery; *The bathers*, c. 1884-87, oil on canvas, 115 × 170 cm, Philadelphia, Museum of Art, Mr and Mrs Carroll S. Tyson collection; *Ambroise Vollard*, 1908, oil on canvas, 81 × 64 cm, London, Courtauld Institute Galleries; *The washerwoman*, 1917, bronze, height 120 cm, New York, Museum of Modern Art, A. Conger Goodyear Fund. GAUGUIN: *Harvest in Brittany*, 1888, oil on canvas, 29 × 36 cm, Paris, Louvre, Jeu de Paume (S). MONET: *Rouen Cathedral: full sunlight*, 1894, oil on canvas, 107 × 73 cm, Paris, Louvre, Jeu de Paume (S).

104-105 Degas: The Little 14-Year-Old Dancer

DEGAS: *The Bellelli family*, 1858-59, oil on canvas, 199 × 252 cm, Paris, Louvre, Jeu de Paume (S); *The glass of absinth*, 1876, oil on canvas, 94 × 69 cm, Paris, Louvre, Jeu de Paume (S); *The little 14-year-old dancer*, 1880, bronze, muslin, satin and paint, height 98 cm, Paris, Louvre, Jeu de Paume (both views Documentation Photographique de la Réunion des Musées Nationaux); *A dancer on stage with a bouquet*, 1878, pastel on paper, 72 × 76 cm, Paris, Louvre, Jeu de Paume (S); *Woman drying her feet*, c. 1885, pastel on paper, 53 ×/51 cm, Paris, Louvre, Jeu de Paume (S).

106-107 Sculpture in the Later 19th Century

GIBSON: *The tinted Venus*, 1851-52, marble and paint, height 198 cm, Liverpool, Walker Art Gallery. POWERS: *The Greek slave*, 1843, marble, height 157 cm, Washington DC, Corcoran Gallery of Art, Gift of William Corcoran. STEVENS: Monument to the Duke of Wellington, detail: *Valour and Cowardice*, 1858-1912, marble and bronze, London, St Paul's Cathedral (Angelo Hornak). HILDEBRAND: The Hubertus fountain, detail: *The archer*, marble, Munich, Waisenhausstrasse (Courtauld Institute of Art). CARPEAUX: *The dance*, 1866-69, plaster, height 232 cm, Paris, Louvre (Documentation Photographique de la Réunion des Musées Nationaux). RODIN: *The Age of Bronze*, 1875-76, height 175 cm, Paris, Musée Rodin; *Honoré de Balzac*, 1892-98, bronze, height 275 cm, Paris, Musée Rodin; *The burghers of Calais*, 1884-86, bronze, height of figures about 2 m, Paris, Musée Rodin. ROSSO: *Conversation in a garden*, 1893, plaster, 33 × 67 cm, Milan, Collection Gianni Mattioli (Fabbri/Joseph P. Ziolo); "*Ecce Puer*", 1910, wax over plaster, height 43 cm, Piacenza, Galleria d'Arte Moderna (S). MAILLOL: *Young girl with drapery*, 1910, bronze, height 175 cm, Paris, Musée National d'Art Moderne (Caisse Historique des Monuments et des Sites).

108-109 Rodin: The Gates of Hell

RODIN: *Crouching woman*, 1882, bronze, height 83 cm, Paris, Musée Rodin; *The Danaïd*, 1885, marble, height 33 cm, Paris, Musée Rodin; *The thinker*, 1880, bronze, height 200 cm, Paris, Musée Rodin; *Nero*, c. 1900-05, pencil and gouache drawing, 31 × 25 cm, New York, Metropolitan Museum of Art; The Gates of Hell, 1880-1917, bronze, 550 × 370 cm, Paris, Musée Rodin (detail, *Ugolino*, also Musée Rodin).

110-111 Seurat: La Grande Jatte

SEURAT: *La Grande Jatte*, 1884-86, oil on canvas, 205 × 305 cm, Chicago, Art Institute; "*Une Baignade, Asnières*" (A bathing scene at Asnières), 1883-84, oil on canvas, 200 × 301 cm, London, National Gallery; *The yoked cart*, 1883, oil on canvas, 33 × 40 cm, New York, Solomon R. Guggenheim Museum (Robert E. Mates); *The "Bec du Hoc" at Grandchamp*, 1885, oil on canvas, 64 × 81 cm, London, Tate Gallery; *Seated boy with a straw hat*, 1883-84, Conté crayon on paper, 22 × 28 cm, New Haven, Connecticut, Yale University Art Gallery, Everett V. Meeks Fund; Study for *The circus*, 1890, oil on canvas, 55 × 46 cm, Paris, Louvre, Jeu de Paume (Documentation Photographique de la Réunion des Musées Nationaux). SIGNAC: *View of the marina at Marseilles*, 1905, oil on canvas, 86 × 114 cm, New York, Metropolitan Museum of Arts, Gift of Robert Lehman.

112-113 Post-Impressionism 1

GAUGUIN: *Vincent van Gogh*, 1888, oil on canvas, 73 × 91 cm, Amsterdam, Museum Vincent van Gogh. PISSARRO: *Paul Cézanne*, 1874, oil on canvas, 74 × 61 cm, Private Collection (Sotheby Parke Bernet). VAN GOGH: *Self-portrait*, 1888, 62 × 52 cm, Cambridge, Massachusetts, Harvard University, Courtesy of the Fogg Art Museum, Bequest of Maurice Wertheim; *Montmartre with windmills*, 1887, oil on canvas, 94 × 119 cm, Amsterdam, Stedelijk Museum; *The bridge at La Grande Jatte*, 1887, oil on canvas, 32 × 40.5 cm, Amsterdam, Museum Vincent van Gogh. CEZANNE: *The rape*, 1867, oil on canvas, 90 × 117 cm, Cambridge, Fitzwilliam Museum; *Achille Empéraire*, 1868-70, oil on canvas, 199 × 122 cm, Paris, Louvre, Jeu de Paume (Documentation Photographique de la Réunion des Musées Nationaux); "*La Maison du Pendu*" (The suicide's house), 1873, oil on canvas, 56 × 66 cm, Paris, Louvre, Jeu de Paume (S); *The little bridge at Maincy*, 1882-85, oil on canvas, 53 × 78 cm, Paris, Louvre, Jeu de Paume (S).

114-115 Vincent van Gogh

VAN GOGH: *Self-portrait*, 1890, oil on canvas, 63 × 53 cm, Paris, Louvre, Jeu de Paume (S); *The potato eaters*, 1885, oil on canvas, 82 × 114 cm, Amsterdam, Museum Vincent van Gogh; *The night café*, 1888, oil on canvas, 70 × 89 cm, New Haven, Connecticut, Yale University Art Gallery; *Sunflowers*, 1888, oil on canvas, 93 × 73 cm, London, National Gallery; *Sailing boats coming ashore*, 1888, ink on paper, 24 × 31 cm, Brussels, Musées Royaux des Beaux-Arts; *Field with a stormy sky*, 1890, oil on canvas, 50 × 101 cm, Amsterdam, Museum Vincent van Gogh; "*La Berceuse*" (Mme Roulin rocking a cradle), 1889, 92 × 73 cm, Otterlo, Museum Kröller-Müller; *Dr Paul Gachet*, 1890, oil on canvas, 68 × 57 cm, Paris, Louvre, Jeu de Paume (S); *Country road by night*, 1890, oil on canvas, 93 × 73 cm, Otterlo, Museum Kröller-Müller.

116-117 Paul Gauguin

GAUGUIN: *Bonjour, M. Gauguin*, 1889, oil on canvas, 92 × 54 cm, Prague, National Gallery; *Self-portrait*, 1888, oil on canvas, 71 × 89 cm, Amsterdam, Museum Vincent van Gogh; *Be in love and you will be happy*, 1889-90, painted wood, 96 × 72 cm, Boston, Museum of Fine Arts; *The vision after the sermon*, 1888, oil on canvas, 73 × 92 cm, Edinburgh, National Gallery of Scotland (Tom Scott); *The spirit of the dead watching*, 1892, oil on canvas, 73 × 92 cm, Buffalo, New York, Albright-Knox Art Gallery, A. Conger Goodyear collection; *Noa Noa*, c. 1893, woodcut, 14 × 8 cm, Paris, Bibliothèque Nationale (Immédiate 2); *Where do we come from? What are we? Where are we going?*, 1897, oil on canvas, 139 × 374 cm, Boston, Museum of Fine Arts; *Nevermore*, 1897, oil on canvas, 54 × 115 cm, London, Courtauld Institute Galleries.

118-119 Cézanne: Mont Ste-Victoire
CÉZANNE: The Philadelphia *Mont Ste-Victoire*, 1904-06, oil on canvas, 53 × 91 cm, Philadelphia, Museum of Art, George W. Atkins collection; *Mont Ste-Victoire with a great pine*, 1885-87, oil on canvas, 66 × 90 cm, London, Courtauld Institute Galleries; *Still life with onions*, c.1895-1900, oil on canvas, 63 × 78 cm, Paris, Louvre, Jeu de Paume (S); "*The Great Bathers*", 1898-1905, oil on canvas, 208 × 249 cm, Philadelphia, Museum of Art, William P. Wilstach collection (S); *Mont Ste-Victoire*, watercolour, 1906, on paper, 36 × 54 cm, London, Tate Gallery; *Self-portrait with a goatee*, c.1906, 63 × 50 cm, Boston, Museum of Fine Arts.

120-121 Post-Impressionism 2, and Art Nouveau
SÉRUSIER: "*The Talisman*": *landscape in the Bois d'Amour in Brittany*, 1888, oil on panel, 27 × 22 cm, Alençon, Collection F. Denis (Giraudon). VUILLARD: *Mother and sister of the artist*, c.1893, oil on canvas, 46.5 × 56.5 cm, New York, Museum of Modern Art; *The laden table*, c.1908, pastel and gouache and distemper, 47 × 54 cm, London, Tate Gallery. BONNARD: *Nude in the bath*, 1937, oil on canvas, 93 × 147 cm, Paris, Louvre, Petit Palais (René Roland); *La Revue Blanche*, 1894, lithograph poster, 77 × 60.5 cm, New Haven, Connecticut, Yale University Art Gallery. TOULOUSE-LAUTREC: *Self-portrait*, c.1890, black chalk, 25.5 × 16 cm, Rotterdam, Museum Boymans-van Beuningen; *The English girl at "Le Star", Le Havre*, 1899, sanguine and gesso on paper, 62 × 47 cm, Albi, Musée Toulouse-Lautrec (Cooper-Bridgeman Library); *Jane Avril at the Jardin de Paris*, 1893, lithograph poster, 130 × 95 cm, Albi, Musée Toulouse-Lautrec. BEARDSLEY: *Salomé*: "*J'ai baisé ta bouche, Iokanaan*", 1894, printed illustration to Oscar Wilde's *Salomé*, 26 × 13 cm, London. KLIMT: *Judith*, 1909, oil on canvas, 84 × 42 cm, Vienna, Österreichische Galerie (S).

122-123 Symbolism
MOREAU: *The unicorns*, c.1885, oil on canvas, 115 × 90 cm, Paris, Musée Gustave Moreau. PUVIS DE CHAVANNES: *Hope*, 1872, oil on canvas, 70 × 82 cm, Paris, Louvre. REDON: *Meadow flowers in a vase*, after 1895, pastel, 57 × 35 cm, Paris, Louvre, Jeu de Paume (Documentation Photographique de la Réunion des Musées Nationaux); *On the horizon, the angel of certainties*, 1882, lithograph, 27 × 20.5 cm, Chicago, Art Institute; *Orpheus*, after 1913, pastel, 70 × 31 cm, Cleveland, Museum of Art, Gift of J.H. Wade. ROSSETTI: *Astarte Syriaca*, 1877, oil on canvas, 185 × 109 cm, Manchester, City Art Gallery; BURNE-JONES: *The mill*, c.1870-82, oil on canvas, 90.5 × 195.5 cm, London, Victoria and Albert Museum. KHNOPFF: *Memories*, 1889, pastel on canvas, 127 × 200 cm, Brussels, Musées Royaux des Beaux-Arts; BÖCKLIN: *The island of the dead*, 1880, oil on panel, 74 × 122 cm, New York, Metropolitan Museum of Art.

124-125 American Art
JOHNSON: *The old stagecoach*, 1871, oil on canvas, 93 × 155 cm, Milwaukee, Art Center, Layton Art Collection. HOMER: *Inside the bar, Tynemouth*, 1883,

watercolour on paper, 39 × 72 cm, New York, Metropolitan Museum of Art; "*Breezing up*", 1876, oil on canvas, 61 × 97 cm, Washington, National Gallery of Art. EAKINS: *The Gross Clinic*, 1875, oil on canvas, 244 × 198 cm, Philadelphia, University, Jefferson College (Cooper-Bridgeman Library). HARNETT: *My gems*, 1888, oil on panel, 46 × 35.5 cm, Washington, National Gallery of Art, Gift of the Avalon Foundation. RYDER: *Moonlit cove*, c.1890-1900, oil on canvas, 35.5 × 43 cm, Washington DC, Phillips Collection. SARGENT: *The daughters of Edward D. Boit*, 1882, oil on canvas, 221 × 221 cm, Boston, Museum of Fine Arts; *Mme Gautreau*, 1884, oil on canvas, 209 × 110 cm, New York, Metropolitan Museum of Art, Arthur Hoppock Hearn Fund. CASSATT: *The bath*, 1892, oil on canvas, 100 × 66 cm, Chicago, Art Institute (S).

126-127 Art in the 20th Century
MONET: *Waterlilies*, 1900-09 (*Morning III*), oil on canvas, 197 × 425 cm, Paris, Louvre, Orangerie (whole and detail Joseph P. Ziolo/René Roland). CÉZANNE: *Ambroise Vollard*, 1899, oil on canvas, 100 × 81 cm, Paris, Louvre, Jeu de Paume (Joseph P. Ziolo/René Roland). UNKNOWN RUSSIAN: *A yellow cat*, early 20th century, woodcut (S.C.R. London). PICASSO: *Ambroise Vollard*, 1910, oil on canvas, 92 × 65 cm, Moscow, Museum of Modern Art (Joseph P. Ziolo/A.P.N. Paris). UNKNOWN AFRICAN: Ancestor figure, late 19th century, wood, height about 1 m (Werner Forman Archive). TOLTEC ARTIST: *Chacmool*, 12th century, stone, Chichen Itza, Temple of the Warriors (ZEFA/K. Rohrich). DEGAS: *Princess Metternich*, 1861, oil on canvas, 41 × 29 cm, London, National Gallery. MUYBRIDGE: *Two men wrestling*, 1887, photograph, Kingston-on-Thames, Museum and Art Gallery. DISDÉRI: *Prince and Princess Metternich*, c.1860, photograph, Melton Constable, Aaron Scharf Collection. *Paul Cézanne and Camille Pissarro*, 1872, photograph, Paris, Collection Roger Viollet. ARNATT: *I'm a real artist*, 1972, from "The New Art", London, Hayward Gallery, 1972 (courtesy of the artist).

128-129 Edvard Munch
MUNCH: *Self-portrait in Hell*, 1895, oil on canvas, 82 × 59.5 cm, Oslo, Munch Museet (S); *Madonna*, 1895, oil on canvas, 91 × 70.5 cm, Oslo, National Gallery (S); *Vampire*, 1895-1902, lithograph, 38.5 × 54.5 cm, Oslo, Munch Museet (S); *The kiss*, 1892, colour woodcut, 47 × 47.5 cm, Oslo, Munch Museet (S); *Puberty*, 1895, oil on canvas, 151 × 110 cm, Oslo, National Gallery (S); *The scream*, 1893, oil and pastel on cardboard, 91 × 73.5 cm, Oslo, National Gallery (S); *History*, 1910-11, oil on canvas, 455 × 1160 cm, Oslo, University Hall (S); *The scream*, 1895, lithograph, 35 × 25 cm, Oslo, Munch Museet (S); *Self-portrait between clock and bed*, 1940-42, oil on canvas, 149.5 × 120.5 cm, Oslo, Munch Museet (S).

130-131 Impressionists and Expressionists in Germany
TOOROP: *The three brides*, 1893, crayon on paper, 78 × 98 cm, Otterlo, Museum Kröller-Müller. LIEBERMANN: *The parrot man*, 1902, oil on canvas, 110 × 71 cm, Essen, Folkwang Museum. ENSOR: *The murder*, 1888, etching, 18 × 24 cm, Stuttgart, Staatsgalerie, Graphische Sammlung; *The entry of Christ into Brussels*, 1888, oil on canvas, 258 × 431 cm, Antwerp, Musée Royal des Beaux-Arts. UHDE: *At the summer resort*, 1892, oil on canvas, Munich, Neue Pinakothek (Blauel). CORINTH: *Morning*

sunlight, 1910, oil on canvas, 68.5 × 81 cm, Darmstadt, Hessisches Landesmuseum. BARLACH: *The solitary one*, 1911, oak, height 59 cm, Hamburg, Kunsthalle. KOLLWITZ: *Woman welcoming death*, 1934-35, lithograph, 31.5 × 31 cm, Washington, National Gallery of Art. LEHMBRUCK: *Kneeling woman*, 1911, cast stone, height 179.5 cm, Buffalo, New York, Albright-Knox Gallery, Charles Clifton Fund. MODERSOHN-BECKER: *Mother and child*, 1906, oil on canvas, 84 × 125 cm, Bremen, Ludwig-Roselius Sammlung (Angelo Hornak).

132-133 Nolde: The Last Supper
NOLDE: *The Last Supper*, 1909, oil on canvas, 83 × 106 cm, Seebüll, Nolde Foundation; *A Friesland farm under red clouds*, c.1930, watercolour on paper, 32.5 × 46.5 cm, London, Victoria and Albert Museum; *The prophet*, 1912, woodcut, 32 × 22 cm, Washington, National Gallery of Art, Rosenwald collection; *Early morning flight*, 1940, 70 × 86 cm, Seebüll, Nolde Foundation. ENSOR: *Intrigue*, 1890, oil on canvas, 90 × 150 cm, Antwerp, Musée des Beaux-Arts.

134-135 Expressionism 1: Die Brücke
KIRCHNER: *Artists of Die Brücke*, c.1926, oil on canvas, 167 × 125 cm, Cologne, Wallraf-Richartz Museum (S); *Street scene*, 1913-14, oil on canvas, 125 × 91 cm, Stuttgart, Staatsgalerie; *The artists' group of the bridge*, 1906, woodcut, Dresden, Staatliche Kunstsammlungen; *The couple*, 1923, oil on canvas, Paris, Musée National d'Art Moderne (S). SCHMIDT-ROTTLUFF: *The sun in a pine tree*, 1913, oil on canvas, 76.5 × 90 cm, Amsterdam, Collection Thyssen (S); *The head of Christ*, 1918, woodcut, 50 × 39.5 cm, New Haven, Connecticut, Yale University Art Gallery. HECKEL: *Two men at a table*, 1912, oil on canvas, 97 × 120 cm, Hamburg, Kunsthalle. PECHSTEIN: *The harbour*, 1922, oil on canvas, 80 × 100 cm, Amsterdam, Stedelijk Museum. MUELLER: *Nudes on a beach*, 1920, oil on canvas, Hamburg, Kunsthalle.

136-137 Expressionism 2: Der Blaue Reiter
KANDINSKY: *Composition no. 4 (Battle)*, 1911, oil on canvas, 159.5 × 250.5 cm, Düsseldorf, Kunstmuseum Nordrhein-Westfalen (Joseph P. Ziolo/M. Babey). MARC: *The fate of the animals*, 1913, oil on canvas, 195 × 263 cm, Basel, Kunstmuseum; *Deer in a forest II*, 1913-14, oil on canvas, 100.5 × 100.5 cm, Karlsruhe, Kunsthalle. MACKE: *Kairouan I*, 1914, watercolour, 20.5 × 24.5 cm, Munich, Neue Pinakothek; *People at the blue lake*, 1913, oil on canvas, 60 × 48.5 cm, Karlsruhe, Kunsthalle. KLEE: *An animal suckling its offspring*, 1906, drawing, Munich, Neue Pinakothek. MÜNTER: *A man at a table (Wassily Kandinsky)*, 1911, oil on cardboard, 51.5 × 68.5 cm, Munich, Lenbachhaus. JAWLENSKY: *Woman meditating*, 1912, oil on canvas, Lugano, Collection Thyssen (S). KUBIN: *The egg*, c.1900, etching, Vienna, Albertina.

138-139 Kandinsky: Study for Composition no. 7
KANDINSKY: Study for *Composition no. 7*, 1913, watercolour, 78 × 100 cm, Berne, Collection Felix Klee; *Improvisation no. 30 – Cannons*, 1913, oil on canvas, 110 × 110 cm, Chicago, Art Institute; *Composition no. 7, fragment no. 1*, 1913, oil on canvas, 87.5 × 100.5 cm, Milwaukee, Art Center, Gift of Mrs Harry Lynde Bradley; *The first abstract watercolour*, 1912, watercolour, 50 × 65 cm, Paris, Musée National d'Art Moderne; *Black*

lines, 1913, oil on canvas, 130 × 130.5 cm, New York, Solomon R. Guggenheim Museum; *Two poplars*, 1913, Chicago, Art Institute.

140-141 Le Douanier Rousseau: The Merry Jesters
ROUSSEAU: *The merry jesters*, c.1906, oil on canvas, 145.5 × 113 cm, Philadelphia, Museum of Art, Louise and Walter Arsenburg collection; *The toll station*, c.1890-91, oil on canvas, 41 × 33 cm, London, Courtauld Institute Galleries; *The ball players*, oil on canvas, 100 × 80 cm, New York, Solomon R. Guggenheim Museum. SÉRAPHINE: *The paradise tree*, 1929, oil on canvas, 195 × 129 cm, Paris, Musée National d'Art Moderne. VIVIN: *Notre Dame*, Paris, oil on canvas, 65 × 81 cm, Paris, Musée National d'Art Moderne. BAUCHANT: *Cleopatra's barge*, 1939, oil on canvas, 84 × 100 cm, New York, Museum of Modern Art, Abby Aldrich Rockefeller Fund.

142-143 Fauvism
DERAIN: *The harbour at Collioure*, 1905, oil on canvas, 72 × 91 cm, Paris, Musée National d'Art Moderne (Documentation Photographique de la Réunion des Musées Nationaux); *Effects of sunlight on water*, 1905, oil on canvas, 81 × 100 cm, St-Tropez, Musée de l'Annonciade (Documentation Photographique de la Réunion des Musées Nationaux). BRAQUE: *The little bay at La Ciotat*, 1907, oil on canvas, 38 × 46 cm, Paris, Musée National d'Art Moderne. MATISSE: *The gypsy*, 1906, oil on canvas, 55 × 46 cm, St-Tropez, Musée de l'Annonciade (S). DUFY: *Riders in the wood*, 1931, oil on canvas, 213 × 260 cm, Paris, Musée National d'Art Moderne (S). VLAMINCK: *Landscape with red hues*, 1906-07, oil on canvas, 65 × 81 cm, Paris, Musée National d'Art Moderne (Documentation Photographique de la Réunion des Musées Nationaux). MARQUET: *Hoardings at Trouville*, 1906, oil on canvas, 81 × 65 cm, Paris, Musée National d'Art Moderne (Giraudon). ROUAULT: *The face of Christ*, 1933, oil on canvas, 91 × 65 cm, Ghent, Musée des Beaux-Arts (S); *The prostitute*, 1906, gouache, watercolour and pastel, 71 × 54 cm, Paris, Musée National d'Art Moderne (Photo Bulloz).

144-145 Matisse: Le Luxe II
MATISSE: "*Luxe, Calme et Volupté*", 1904-05, oil on canvas, 86 × 116 cm, Paris, Mme Signac Collection (Cooper-Bridgeman Library); *The dance*, 1910, oil on canvas, 260 × 391 cm, Leningrad, Hermitage (Joseph P. Ziolo/Studio Adrion); "*La Joie de Vivre*", 1905-06, oil on canvas, 175 × 238 cm, Merion, Pennsylvania, Barnes Foundation; "*Le Luxe I*", 1907, oil on canvas, 210 × 138 cm, Paris, Musée National d'Art Moderne; "*Le Luxe II*", 1907-08, oil on canvas, 210 × 139 cm, Copenhagen, Statens Museum fur Kunst.

146-147 Brancusi: The Kiss
BRANCUSI: *Sleeping Muse*, 1910, bronze, length 27 cm, Paris, Musée National d'Art Moderne; *Sleeping Muse*, 1906, marble, height 27.5 cm, Bucharest, National Museum; *The table of silence*, 1937, stone, height of table 80 cm, diameter of stools 55 cm, Tirgu Jiu, Public Park (Susan Grigg Agency/AdamWoolfitt); *Bird in space*, 1919, bronze, height 137 cm, New York, Museum of Modern Art; *The kiss*, 1910, stone, height 50 cm, Paris, Musée National d'Art Moderne (Joseph P. Ziolo/René Roland).

148-149 Cubism 1
PICASSO: *Life*, 1903, oil on canvas,

197 × 127 cm, Cleveland, Museum of Art, Gift of Hanna Fund; "*Les Demoiselles d'Avignon*", 1907, oil on canvas, 244 × 233 cm, New York, Museum of Modern Art, acquired through the Lillie P. Bliss Bequest; *Daniel Henry Kahnweiler*, 1910, oil on canvas, 100 × 73 cm, Chicago, Art Institute, Mrs Charles B. Goodspeed collection; *Still life with chair-caning*, 1911-12, oil and pasted oil-cloth, length 33 cm, Paris, Estate of the Artist (Documentation Photographique de la Réunion des Musées Nationaux). BRAQUE: "*Grand Nu*" (Large nude), 1908, oil on canvas, 136 × 102 cm, Paris, Private Collection (Joseph P. Ziolo/André Held); *Houses at L'Estaque*, 1908, oil on canvas, 73 × 60 cm, Berne, Kunstmuseum; *Still life with fish*, c. 1909-10, oil on canvas, 61 × 75 cm, London, Tate Gallery; *The man with a pipe*, 1912, papier collé on paper, 62 × 48 cm, Basel, Öffentliche Kunstsammlung.

150-151 Cubism 2, and Orphism
GRIS: *The wash-stand*, 1912, oil with mirror and *papier collé*, 132 × 90 cm, Paris, Private Collection (Colorphoto Hans Hinz); *Homage to Picasso*, 1911-12, oil on canvas, 74 × 94 cm, Chicago, Art Institute, Gift of Leigh B. Block; *Landscape at Ceret*, 1913, oil on canvas, 180 × 65 cm, Stockholm, National Museum. LEGER: *Nudes in the forest*, 1909-10, oil on canvas, 122 × 173 cm, Otterlo, Museum Kröller-Müller; *Contrasting forms*, 1913, oil on canvas, 80.5 × 60 cm, Düsseldorf, Kunstsammlung Nordrhein-Westfalen. DELAUNAY: *A window*, 1912, oil on canvas, 111 × 89 cm, Paris, Musée National d'Art Moderne (S); *The Eiffel Tower*, 1910, oil on canvas, 202 × 138.5 cm, New York, Solomon R. Guggenheim Museum; *Circular forms: sun and moon*, 1912-13, oil on canvas, 100 × 68 cm, Zurich, Kunsthaus. KUPKA: *The disks of Newton: Study for a fugue in two colours*, 1911-12, oil on canvas, 49.5 × 67 cm, Paris, Musée National d'Art Moderne.

152-153 Futurism
BALLA: *The street lamp*, 1909, oil on canvas, 175 × 115 cm, New York, Museum of Modern Art, Hillman Periodicals Fund; *Dynamism of a dog on a leash*, 1912, oil on canvas, 90 × 110 cm, Buffalo, New York, Albright-Knox Art Gallery, Bequest of A. Conger Goodyear to George E. Goodyear. BOCCIONI: *The city rises*, 1910-11, oil on canvas, 200 × 300 cm, New York, Museum of Modern Art, Mrs Simon Guggenheim Fund; *Farewells*, 1911, oil on canvas, 70.5 × 96 cm, New York, Nelson A. Rockefeller Collection (S); *Unique forms of continuity in space*, 1913, bronze, height 109.5 cm, New York, Museum of Modern Art, Lillie P. Bliss Bequest; *Development of a bottle in space*, 1912-13, silvered bronze, height 38 cm, New York, Museum of Modern Art, Aristide Maillol Fund. CARRA: *The funeral of the anarchist Galli*, 1910-11, oil on canvas, 200 × 259 cm, New York, Museum of Modern Art, Lillie P. Bliss Bequest. SEVERINI: *Pam-Pam at the Monico*, 1910-12, oil on canvas, 113 × 162 cm, Paris, Musée National d'Art Moderne (S). RUSSOLO: *The revolt*, 1911-12, oil on canvas, 150 × 194.5 cm, The Hague, Gemeentemuseum.

154-155 British Art: The Vortex
STEER: *Children paddling, Walberswick*, 1894, oil on canvas, 64 × 92 cm, Cambridge, Fitzwilliam Museum. SICKERT: *Ennui*, c. 1913, oil on canvas, 76 × 56 cm, Oxford, Ashmolean Museum. AUGUSTUS JOHN: *David and Dorelia in Normandy*, c. 1907, oil on canvas, 37 × 45 cm, Cambridge, Fitzwilliam

Museum. GILMAN: *Mrs Mounter*, 1917, oil on canvas, 36 × 23 cm, Leeds, City Art Gallery. GWEN JOHN: *Girl with bare shoulders*, c. 1910, oil on canvas, 43.5 × 26 cm, New York, Museum of Modern Art, A. Conger Goodyear Fund. LEWIS: *Ezra Pound*, 1939, oil on canvas, 76 × 102 cm, London, Tate Gallery (Angelo Hornak). ROBERTS: *The diners*, 1919, oil on canvas, 152 × 83 cm, London, Tate Gallery (Angelo Hornak). BOMBERG: *In the hold*, 1913-14, oil on canvas, 196 × 231 cm, London, Tate Gallery (Angelo Hornak). GAUDIER-BRZESKA: *Red stone dancer*, 1913, sandstone, height 43 cm, London, Tate Gallery (Angelo Hornak). EPSTEIN: *The rock-drill*, 1913-14, bronze, height of torso 71 cm, London, Tate Gallery (Anthony d'Offay).

156-157 Russian Art 1: From Symbolism to Suprematism
VRUBEL: *Six-winged seraph*, 1904, oil on canvas (S.C.R. London). BENOIS: Backdrop for Stravinsky's *Petrouchka; The fair*, 1911, Hartford, Connecticut, Wadsworth Atheneum. BAKST: "*L'Après-midi d'un faune* (Vaslav Nijinsky)", 1912, 40 × 27 cm, Hartford, Connecticut, Wadsworth Atheneum. GONCHAROVA: *Monk with a cat*, 1910, oil on canvas, 100 × 92 cm, Edinburgh, National Gallery of Modern Art; *Cats*, 1911, oil on canvas, 85 × 85.5 cm, New York, Solomon R. Guggenheim Museum. LARIONOV: *Summer*, 1912, oil on panel, Paris, Collection Mme Larionov. MALEVICH: *Suprematist composition: white on white*, c. 1918, oil on canvas, 79 × 79 cm, New York, Museum of Modern Art; *Woman with buckets*, 1912, oil on canvas, 80 × 80 cm, New York, Museum of Modern Art; *Black trapezium and red square*, after 1915, oil on canvas, Amsterdam, Stedelijk Museum.

158-159 Russian Art 2: Constructivism
MAYAKOVSKY: Set design for *Misteria Bouffe*, 1919 (S.C.R. London); *Revolutionary poster*, 1920 (S.C.R. London). TATLIN: *Relief construction*, c. 1915, destroyed (S.C.R. London). UNKNOWN ARTISTS: "Agit" train, c. 1919 (S.C.R. London). RODCHENKO: *Composition*, 1918, gouache on paper, 33 × 16 cm, New York, Museum of Modern Art, Gift of the artist; *Hanging construction*, c. 1920, destroyed (Oxford, Museum of Modern Art). AFTER RODCHENKO: *Hanging construction*, original c. 1920, reconstruction by John Milner, painted plywood, width 110 cm, England, Collection John Milner (Oxford, Museum of Modern Art). LISSITZKY: *Proun 99*, 1924-25, oil on panel, 128.5 × 99 cm, New Haven, Connecticut, Yale University Art Gallery. GABO: *Head of a woman*, 1917-20, celluloid and metal, height 62 cm, New York, Museum of Modern Art.

160-161 Tatlin: Monument to the Third International
Vladimir Tatlin beside the maquette for his Monument to the Third International, photograph (Stockholm, Statens Konstmuseer); *Monument to the Third International*, c. 1920, drawing, Stockholm, Statens Konstmuseer; *Letatlin*, 1932, wood, cork, silk, ball-bearings, Stockholm, Statens Konstmuseer; *Bent-tube chair*, 1923, wood, leather (Arts Council of Great Britain). RODIN: *Monument to Labour*, 1893-99, drawing, Paris, Musée Rodin (Joseph P. Ziolo/René Roland).

162-163 Art Since 1915
BRASILIA: The Foreign Office, begun 1957, by Oscar Niemeyer (Spectrum Colour Library). BERLIN: The AEG Turbine Factory, 1909, by Peter Behrens

(Bildarchiv Foto Marburg).

164-165
(Map by Colin Salmon and Dinah Lone)

166-167 Dada
ARP: *Collage of squares arranged according to the laws of chance*, 1916-17, collage of coloured papers, 45.5 × 33.5 cm, New York, Museum of Modern Art, Gift of Philip Johnson; PICABIA: *I see again in memory my dear Udnie*, 1914, oil on canvas, 250 × 199 cm, New York, Museum of Modern Art, Hillman Periodicals Fund. MAN RAY: *The rope-dancer accompanies herself with her shadows*, 1916, oil on canvas, 132 × 186.5 cm, New York, Museum of Modern Art, Gift of G. David Thompson; *Crossroads*, 1934, photomontage, Paris, Man Ray Archive. PICABIA: "*M'Amenez-y*", 1919-20, oil on cardboard, 129 × 89 cm, New York, Museum of Modern Art, Helena Rubinstein Fund. SCHWITTERS: "*Arbeiterbild*" (Worker-picture), 1919, collage, 125.5 × 91 cm, Stockholm, Moderna Museet; *Ambleside*, 1945-48, mixed media, height about 3 m, Little Langdale, University of Newcastle upon Tyne. HAUSMANN: *The art critic*, 1920, drawing in ink, chalk and pencil, with collage, 32 × 25.5 cm, London, Tate Gallery. BAADER: *Collage A92-22*, c. 1920, collage, Paris, Musée National d'Art Moderne.

168-169 Marcel Duchamp
Marcel Duchamp, photograph by J.S. Lewinski (Camera Press). DUCHAMP: *A cemetery of uniforms and liveries – the bachelors*, 1914, pencil, ink and watercolour on paper, 66 × 100 cm, New Haven, Connecticut, Yale University Art Gallery, Gift of Katherine S. Dreier; *Nude descending a staircase no. 2*, 1912, oil on canvas, 148 × 90 cm, Philadelphia, Museum of Art, The Louise and Walter Arsenberg collection; AFTER DUCHAMP: *The bride stripped bare by her bachelors, even* ("*The Large Glass*"), original 1915-23, oil and other media on glass, reconstruction by Richard Hamilton, 277 × 176 cm, London, Tate Gallery; *Fountain*, original 1917, replica 1964, vitreous enamel, height 63 cm, Milan, Galleria Schwartz. DUCHAMP: "*The Large Glass*" (broken state), 1937, oil and other media on glass, 277 × 176 cm, Philadelphia, Museum of Art, Katherine S. Dreier Bequest; *L.H.O.O.Q.*, 1918, postcard retouched in pencil, 19 × 12 cm, Stuttgart, Staatsgalerie; "*Etant Donnés …*", 1946-66, assemblage, height of door 242 cm, Philadelphia, Museum of Art, Gift of the Cassandra Foundation. AFTER DUCHAMP: "Ready-made", original 1913, replica 1951, wooden stool and bicycle wheel, height 126 cm, New York, Sidney Janis Gallery.

170-171 Art in Italy: Metaphysical Painting
CHIRICO: *The enigma of the hour*, 1912, oil on canvas, 71 × 55 cm, Milan, Collection Gianni Mattioli (S); *The child's brain*, 1914, oil on canvas, 80 × 63 cm, Stockholm, Statens Konstmuseer; *The dream of the poet* (Guillaume Apollinaire), 1914, oil on canvas, 89 × 39.5 cm, New York, Solomon R. Guggenheim Museum, Peggy Guggenheim collection; *The nostalgia of the infinite*, 1913-14, oil on canvas, 135 × 65 cm, New York, Museum of Modern Art; *The mathematicians*, 1917, pencil on paper, 32 × 21.5 cm, New York, Museum of Modern Art, Gift of Mrs Stanley B. Resor. CARRA: *The engineer's mistress*, 1921, oil on canvas, 55 × 40 cm, Milan, Collection Gianni Mattioli (S). MORANDI: *Still life*, 1938, oil on canvas, 24 × 39 cm, New York, Museum of

Modern Art; *Still life with a pipe*, 1918, oil on canvas, Milan, Collection E. Jesi (S); *Still life*, 1937, oil on canvas, 27 × 40 cm, Hamburg, Kunsthalle; *Landscape with the River Saverna*, 1929, etching, 26 × 25 cm (Arts Council of Great Britain).

172-173 Max Ernst
Max Ernst, photograph (Agence Rapho). ERNST: *Katerina ondulata*, 1920, wallpaper overlaid with gouache and pencil, 30 × 25 cm, London, Sir Roland Penrose Collection (Eileen Tweedy Archive); "*Aquis Submersus*" (Plunged in the waters), 1919, oil on canvas, 54 × 43 cm, Frankfurt, Stadelsches Kunstinstitut; *The elephant Celebes*, 1921, oil on canvas, 130 × 110 cm, London, Tate Gallery; *Men shall know nothing of this*, 1923, oil on canvas, 81 × 65 cm, London, Tate Gallery (Angelo Hornak); *Hundred-headed Woman: Germinal, my sister*, 1929, printed illustration (Courtauld Institute of Art); *The great forest*, 1927, oil on canvas, 115 × 147 cm, Basel, Kunstmuseum (Colorphoto Hans Hinz); *Europe after the rain*, 1940-42, oil on canvas, 54 × 147.5 cm, Hartford, Connecticut, Wadsworth Atheneum, Ella Gallup Sumner and Mary Catlin Sumner collection; *Man intrigued by the flight of a non-Euclidian fly*, 1942, oil and varnish on canvas, 82 × 66 cm, Zurich, Private Collection.

174-175 Surrealism 1: Figurative
MAGRITTE: *The human condition*, 1933, oil on canvas, 100 × 81 cm, Choisel, Private Collection (P. Willi/Agence Top); *Time transfixed*, 1939, oil on canvas, 146 × 97 cm, Chicago, Art Institute; *Man in a bowler hat*, 1964, oil on canvas, 64 × 50 cm, New York, Private Collection. DALI: *The persistence of memory*, 1931, oil on canvas, 24 × 33 cm, New York, Museum of Modern Art; *The temptation of St Anthony*, 1947, oil on canvas, 89.5 × 119.5 cm, Brussels, Musées Royaux des Beaux-Arts; *The Venus de Milo of the drawers*, 1936, plaster, height 100 cm, Paris, Private Collection (Joseph P. Ziolo/Robert Descharnes). DELVAUX: *The village of the sirens*, 1942, oil on canvas, 105 × 127 cm, Chicago, Art Institute. DALI AND BUNUEL: Still from *Un Chien Andalou*, 1929, photograph, London, National Film Archive (Stills Library). ESCHER: *Still life and street*, 1937, woodcut, 49 × 49 cm, The Hague, Gemeentemuseum.

176-177 Surrealism 2: Abstract
MASSON: *Furious suns*, 1925, ink on paper, 42 × 32 cm, Paris, Galerie Louise Leiris; *The battle of the fishes*, 1927, sand, gesso, oil, ink and charcoal on canvas, 36.5 × 73 cm, New York, Museum of Modern Art. TANGUY: *The more we are*, 1929, oil on canvas, Paris, Collection Collinet (Giraudon); *The palace of windows*, 1942, oil on canvas, 163 × 132 cm, Paris, Musée National d'Art Moderne. MIRO: *Dog barking at the moon*, 1926, oil on canvas, 73 × 92 cm, Philadelphia, Museum of Art, E.A. Gallatin collection; *Painting*, 1933, oil on canvas, 130 × 161 cm, Hartford, Connecticut, Wadsworth Atheneum; *Aerial acrobatics*, 1934, Courtauld Institute; *The wall of the moon*, 1957, ceramic tiled wall, Paris, UNESCO Building (Michel Claude).

178-179 Cubist Developments
ARCHIPENKO: *Walking woman*, 1912, painted bronze, height 67 cm, Denver, Art Museum. DUCHAMP-VILLON: *The horse*, 1914, bronze, height 100 cm, New York, Museum of Modern Art, Van Gogh Purchase Fund. LIPCHITZ: *The bather*, 1915, bronze, height 80.5 cm, New York, Private Collection. PICASSO: *The glass of absinth*, 1914, painted bronze with silver

sugar strainer, height 22 cm, New York, Museum of Modern Art, Gift of Mrs Bertram Smith. ZADKINE: *The destroyed city*, 1953, bronze, height 6.4 m, Rotterdam, Schiedamse Dijk. BRAQUE: *Kanephoros*, 1922-23, oil on canvas, 180 × 72 cm, Paris, Musée National d'Art Moderne. OZENFANT: *The jug*, 1926, oil on canvas, 301 × 148 cm, Providence, Rhode Island, Rhode Island School of Design. LEGER: "*Le Grand Déjeuner*" (The feast), 1921, oil on canvas, 151 × 183.5 cm, New York, Museum of Modern Art, Mrs Simon Guggenheim Fund; *Still life with arm*, 1927, oil on canvas, 55 × 46 cm, Essen, Folkwang Museum.

180-181 Sculpture between the Wars
PEVSNER: *Torso*, 1924-26, plastic and copper, height 75.5 cm, New York, Museum of Modern Art; *Marcel Duchamp*, 1926, celluloid on copper (originally zinc), 94 × 65 cm, New Haven, Connecticut, Yale University Art Gallery. DUCHAMP: *Rotative plaques*, 1920, wood, metal and glass, 120 × 184 cm, New Haven, Connecticut, Yale University Art Gallery. GABO: *Sculpture*, 1954-57, bronze and stainless steel, height 25.5 m, Rotterdam, at Bijenkorf's store (Rotterdam, Museum Boymans-van Beuningen); *Kinetic sculpture (Standing wave)*, stone and metal, motorized, height 62 cm, London, Tate Gallery. CALDER: *Romulus and Remus*, 1928, metal wire, length 284.5 cm, New York, Solomon R. Guggenheim Museum. GIACOMETTI: *The cage*, 1932, wood, height 48.5 cm, Stockholm, National Museum. ARP: *Human concentration*, 1934, marble, height 78.5 cm, Paris, Musée National d'Art Moderne (S). GONZALEZ: *Maternity*, 1934, welded iron, height 128 cm, London, Tate Gallery.

182-183 Modigliani: Chaim Soutine
MODIGLIANI: *Reclining nude*, c. 1919, oil on canvas, 72 × 116.5 cm, New York, Museum of Modern Art, Mrs Simon Guggenheim Fund; *Study for a stone Head*, 1909-15, coloured chalks on paper, 34 × 22 cm, London, Victoria and Albert Museum; *Head of a young woman*, 1908, 56 × 55 cm, Marvaux, Private Collection (René Roland); *Head*, 1911-12, stone, height 63 cm, London, Tate Gallery (Angelo Hornak); *Chaim Soutine*, 1917, oil on canvas, 92 × 60 cm, Washington, National Gallery of Art, Chester Dale collection.

184-185 The School of Paris
MATISSE: *Odalisque in red trousers*, 1922, oil on canvas, 57 × 84 cm, Paris, Musée National d'Art Moderne (S). SOUTINE: *Oscar Miestschaninoff*, 1923, oil on canvas, 82 × 64 cm, Paris, Musée National d'Art Moderne; *The carcase of an ox*, 1925, oil on canvas, 140 × 82 cm, Buffalo, New York, Albright-Knox Art Gallery. UTRILLO: *Sacré Coeur, Paris*, 1937, gouache on canvas, Indianapolis, Museum of Art. PASCIN: *Nude with a green hat*, 1925, oil on canvas, 92 × 77 cm, Cincinnati, Ohio, Art Museum. CHAGALL: *The cock*, 1928, oil on canvas, Lugano, Collection Thyssen (S); *The Asher window*, Haddassah University Medical Centre, Jerusalem, 1960, stained glass, 3.5 × 2.5 m (Haddassah Medical Relief Association). BALTHUS: *The living-room*, 1941-43, oil on canvas, 114 × 147 cm, Minneapolis, Institute of Arts.

186-187 Art in Holland: De Stijl
VAN DOESBURG: *The cow*, 1916-17, oil on canvas, 37.5 × 63.5 cm, New York, Museum of Modern Art; *The card-players*, 1916-17, tempera on canvas, 147 × 169 cm, Meudon, Mme van Doesburg Collection (Joseph P. Ziolo/A.

Held); *Contra-composition V*, 1924, oil on canvas, 100 × 100 cm, Amsterdam, Stedelijk Museum; *The card-players*, 1917 (*Composition IX*), oil on canvas, 116 × 106 cm, The Hague, Gemeentemuseum. VAN DER LECK: *Composition*, 1918, oil on canvas, 101 × 100 cm, Amsterdam, Stedelijk Museum. MONDRIAN: *Composition*, 1917, oil on canvas, 108 × 108 cm, Otterlo, Museum Kröller-Müller. RIETVELD: Armchair, 1917, painted wood, height 87 cm, New York, Museum of Modern Art, Gift of Philip Johnson. VANTONGERLOO: *Construction of volume relations*, 1921, wood, height 41 cm, New York, Museum of Modern Art, Gift of Silvia Pizitz.

188-189 Mondrian: Composition in Yellow and Blue
MONDRIAN: *Composition in yellow and blue*, 1929, oil on canvas, 52 × 52 cm, Rotterdam, Museum Boymans-van Beuningen; *The red tree*, 1908, oil on canvas, 70 × 99 cm, The Hague, Gemeentemuseum; *Fox-trot A*, 1930, oil on canvas, height 110 cm, New Haven, Connecticut, Yale University Art Gallery; *Broadway Boogie-Woogie*, 1942-43, oil on canvas, 127 × 127 cm, New York, Museum of Modern Art; *The flowering apple-tree*, 1912, oil on canvas, 78 × 106 cm, The Hague, Gemeentemuseum.

190-191 Art in Germany: The Bauhaus
KANDINSKY: *On high*, 1920, oil on canvas, New York, Solomon R. Guggenheim Museum (S); *Rows of signs*, 1931, ink on paper, Basel, Kunstsammlung (S). KLEE: *Italian town*, 1928, watercolour on paper over cardboard, 35 × 27 cm, Berne, Felix Klee Foundation. FEININGER: Frontispiece for the Bauhaus *Manifesto*, 1919, woodcut on brown paper, 30.5 × 19.5 cm, Cambridge, Massachusetts, Harvard University, Busch-Reisinger Museum, Gift of Mr and Mrs Lyonel Feininger. MOHOLY-NAGY: *Light-space modulator*, 1922-30, steel, plastic and wood, height with base 151 cm, Cambridge, Massachusetts, Harvard University, Busch-Reisinger Museum, Gift of Mrs Sibyl Moholy-Nagy (Diana Wyllie Ltd); *Yellow cross*, c. 1923-28, oil on canvas, Rome, Galleria d'Arte Moderna (S). GROPIUS: The director's office at the Weimar Bauhaus, 1923 (Diana Wyllie Ltd). ITTEN: *Benign light*, 1920-21, oil on canvas, Lugano, Collection Thyssen (S). BREUER: Steel chair, 1925, tubular steel, height 71 cm, New York, Museum of Modern Art, Gift of H. Bayer (Architectural Association). SCHLEMMER: *Concentric group*, 1925, oil on canvas, 97 × 62 cm, Stuttgart, Staatsgalerie.

192-193 Paul Klee
Paul Klee, photograph, Berne, Felix Klee Collection. KLEE: *The country child*, 1923, oil on canvas, Grenoble, Musée des Beaux-Arts (S); *Motif of Hammamet*, 1914, watercolour on paper, 20 × 15 cm, Basel, Öffentliche Kunstsammlung; *The vocal fabric of the singer Rosa Silber*, 1922, gouache and gesso on canvas, 52 × 42 cm, New York, Museum of Modern Art; *Mask with small flag*, 1925, watercolour on paper, 65 × 49.5 cm, Munich, Neue Pinakothek; *Fire in the evening*, 1929, oil on cardboard, 34 × 33.5 cm, New York, Museum of Modern Art, Mr and Mrs Joachim Jean Abelbach Fund; "*Ad Parnassum*", 1932, oil on canvas, 100 × 126 cm, Berne, Kunstmuseum; *Death and fire*, 1940, oil and distemper, 46 × 44 cm, Berne, Kunstmuseum; *Under the angel's wing on a steep path*, 1931, pen and ink on paper, 56 × 43 cm, Berne,

Felix Klee Collection.

194-195 Expressionist Developments
GROSZ: *Eclipse of the sun*, 1926, oil on canvas, 210 × 184 cm, Huntington, New York, Heckschet Museum; *Dusk*, 1922, watercolour on paper, 52 × 40 cm, Lugano, Collection Thyssen (S). DIX: *The matchseller*, 1920, oil on canvas, 141 × 166 cm, Stuttgart, Staatsgalerie. HEARTFIELD: *War and corpses*, 1932, photomontage, printed in Arbeiter-Illustrierte-Zeitung, April 27, 1932 (Arts Council of Great Britain/John Webb). HOFER: *Three masqueraders*, 1922, oil on canvas, 129 × 103 cm, Cologne, Wallraf-Richartz Museum. SCHRIMPF: *Boy with a rabbit*, 1924, oil on canvas, 56 × 42 cm, Marburg, Marburger Universitätsmuseum für Kunst und Kulturgeschichte. SCHIELE: *The embrace*, 1917, oil on canvas, 110 × 170.5 cm, Vienna, Österreichisches Galerie. KOKOSCHKA: *Lovers with a cat*, 1917, oil on canvas, 93 × 130 cm, Zurich, Kunsthaus (S). PERMEKE: *The sower*, 1933, oil on canvas, 200 × 100 cm, Jabbeke, Provincial Museum Constant Permeke.

196-197 Beckmann: Departure
BECKMANN: *Self-portrait with a red scarf*, 1917, oil on canvas, 80 × 60 cm, Stuttgart, Staatsgalerie; *Quappi in pink*, 1932-34, oil on canvas, Lugano, Collection Thyssen (S); *Night*, 1918-19, oil on canvas, 134 × 154 cm, Düsseldorf, Kunstsammlung Nordrhein-Westfalen; *Self-portrait with Quappi Beckmann*, 1941, oil on canvas, 194 × 89 cm, Amsterdam, Stedelijk Museum; *Departure*, 1932-35, oil on canvas, centre panel 215 × 115 cm, side panels 215 × 98 cm, New York, Museum of Modern Art.

198-199 Art in Britain between the Wars
EPSTEIN: *Jacob Kramer*, 1921, bronze, height 63.5 cm, London, Tate Gallery (John Webb). NICHOLSON: *White relief*, 1935, painted wood, 101.5 × 165.5 cm, London, Tate Gallery. NASH: *Landscape from a dream*, oil on canvas, 67.5 × 101.5 cm, London, Tate Gallery; "*Totes Meer*" (Dead sea), 1940-41, oil on canvas, 101.5 × 152.5 cm, London, Tate Gallery (Angelo Hornak). SUTHERLAND: *Entrance to a lane*, 1939, oil on canvas, 61 × 51 cm, London, Tate Gallery; *Somerset Maugham*, 1949, oil on canvas, 137 × 63.5 cm, London, Tate Gallery. HEPWORTH: *Three forms*, 1935, marble, 20 × 53.5 × 60 cm, London, Tate Gallery. PASMORE: *The quiet river: the Thames at Chiswick*, 1943-44, oil on canvas, 76 × 101.5 cm, London, Tate Gallery (Angelo Hornak); *Snowstorm (Spiral motif in black and white)*, 1950-51, oil on canvas, 119.5 × 152.5 cm, Arts Council of Great Britain. SPENCER: *The resurrection of the soldiers*, 1928-29, mural, Burghclere, Sandham Memorial Chapel (Jeremy Whitaker/National Trust).

200-201 Henry Moore
Henry Moore, photograph (Henry Moore Foundation). MOORE: *Mother and child*, 1924, Hornton stone, height 57 cm, Manchester, City Art Gallery; *Composition*, 1932, marble, height 44 cm, London, Tate Gallery (Angelo Hornak); *Bird basket*, 1939, lignum vitae and string, height 42 cm, Much Hadham, Collection Mrs Irene Moore (Henry Moore Foundation); *Reclining figure*, 1929, Hornton stone, length 84 cm, Leeds, City Art Gallery; *The Tilbury shelter*, 1941, watercolour and gouache on paper, 42 × 38 cm, London, Tate Gallery (Angelo Hornak); *Reclining figure*, 1945-46, elmwood, length 190.5 cm, formerly Bloomfield Hills, Michigan, Cranbrook Academy of Art (Henry Moore

Foundation); *Helmet head no. 1*, 1950, lead, height 33 cm, London, Tate Gallery; *Two forms*, 1966, Soraya marble, length 152 cm, Zurich, Collection Dr and Mrs Staehein (Henry Moore Foundation); *Madonna*, 1943-46, Hornton stone, height 150 cm, Northampton, St Matthew's (Henry Moore Foundation).

202-203 Picasso between the Wars
Pablo Picasso, photograph (Popperfoto). PICASSO: *Three women at the fountain*, 1921, oil on canvas, 204 × 131 cm, New York, Museum of Modern Art; *Ambroise Vollard*, 1915, pencil drawing, 47.5 × 32.5 cm, New York, Metropolitan Museum, Elisha Whittelsey Fund; *The three dancers*, 1925, oil on canvas, 215 × 145 cm, London, Tate Gallery; *Guitar*, 1920, oil on canvas, Basel, Emmanuel Hoffman Foundation (Colorphoto Hans Hinz); *Seated bathers*, 1930, oil on canvas, 163 × 129.5 cm, New York, Museum of Modern Art, Mrs Simon Guggenheim Fund; *Nude in an armchair*, 1932, oil on canvas, 130 × 97 cm, London, Tate Gallery; *Woman's head*, 1931, metal assemblage, height 81 cm, Paris, Estate of the artist (John Hedgecoe); *Guernica*, 1937, oil on canvas, 351 × 782 cm, New York, on loan from the artist's estate to the Museum of Modern Art; *The charnel-house*, 1945-48, oil and charcoal on canvas, 200 × 250 cm, New York, Museum of Modern Art.

204-205 Early Modernist Art in America
HENRI: *The masquerade dress*, 1911 (Mrs Robert Henri), oil on canvas, 194 × 92 cm, New York, Metropolitan Museum of Art, Arthur Hoppock Hearn Fund. SLOAN: *McSorley's Bar*, 1912, oil on canvas, 66 × 81 cm, Detroit, Institute of Arts. LUKS: *Hester Street*, 1905, oil on canvas, 66 × 91 cm, New York, Brooklyn Museum, Dick S. Ramsay Fund. BELLOWS: *Stag at Sharkey's*, 1909, oil on canvas, 92 × 122.5 cm, Cleveland, Museum of Art, Hinman B. Hurlbut collection. STELLA: *Brooklyn Bridge*, 1917, oil on canvas, 216 × 190 cm, New Haven, Connecticut, Yale University Art Gallery; MARIN: *Maine islands*, 1922, watercolour on paper, 43 × 51 cm, Washington DC, Phillips Collection. DEMUTH: *I saw the figure 5 in gold*, 1928, oil on board, 91 × 76 cm, New York, Metropolitan Museum of Art, Alfred Stieglitz collection. HARTLEY: *A German officer*, 1914, oil on canvas, 173 × 105 cm, New York, Metropolitan Museum of Art, Alfred Stieglitz collection. SHAHN: *The prisoners Sacco and Vanzetti*, 1931-32, tempera on paper over board, 27 × 31 cm, New York, Museum of Modern Art, Gift of Abby Aldrich Rockefeller (S).

206-207 Hopper: Nighthawks
HOPPER: *The automat*, 1927, oil on canvas, 71 × 91 cm, Des Moines, Art Center, James D. Edmundsen Fund; *Approaching a city*, 1946, oil on canvas, 69 × 91 cm, Washington DC, Phillips Collection; *Night shadows*, 1921, etching, 18 × 21 cm (Courtauld Institute of Art); *Nighthawks*, 1942, oil on canvas, 84 × 152 cm, Chicago, Art Institute, Friends of American Art collection. BURCHFIELD: *The old farmhouse*, 1932, watercolour on paper, 38 × 53 cm, Cambridge, Massachusetts, Fogg Art Museum. BENTON: *City activities*, 1930-31, tempera on linen, 231 × 818 cm, New York, New School of Social Research (Snark International).

208-209 Mexican Muralism
POSADA: *The alcoholic*, c. 1912, etching (Courtauld Institute of Art). RIVERA: *A hymn to the earth*, 1926-27, fresco, total painted area 700 square metres, Chapingo,

Mexico, Chapel of the Agricultural College (Desmond Rochfort); *Mexico today, Mexico tomorrow*, 1936, fresco, area of south wall 65 square metres, Mexico City, National Palace, main staircase (Desmond Rochfort). OROZCO: *The people and their false leaders*, detail, 1937, fresco, Guadalajara, University of Guadalajara Assembly Hall (Desmond Rochfort); *Man of fire*, 1938-39, fresco, Guadalajara, Hospicio Cabanas (general view of cupola and detail Desmond Rochfort); *Machine horse of the conquest*, 1938-39, fresco, on the vault neighbouring the cupola, Guadalajara, Hospicio Cabanas (Desmond Rochfort); SIQUEIROS: *For the full safety and social security at work of all Mexicans*, 1952-54, pyroxiline and vinylite paint on celotex, total painted area 310 square metres, Mexico City, La Raza Hospital, vestibule to the auditorium (Desmond Rochfort); *The portrait of the bourgeoisie*, 1939, pyroxiline paint on a cement base, total painted area 100 square metres, Mexico City, Electrical Trades Union Building, stairwell (Desmond Rochfort). TAMAYO: *Sleeping musicians*, 1950, oil on canvas, 135 × 192 cm, Mexico City, Museu Nacional d'Arte Moderno (René Roland).

210-211 The Sources of Abstract Expressionism
DAVIS: *Lucky strike*, 1921, oil on canvas, 84 × 46 cm, New York, Museum of Modern Art, Gift of The American Tobacco Co. Inc.; *Ultra-Marine*, 1943, oil on canvas, 51 × 102 cm, Philadelphia, Pennsylvania Academy of the Fine Arts, Temple Purchase Fund. NAVAJO ARTIST: "Sand-painting", 1966, coloured sand, 175 × 175 cm, London, Horniman Museum. O'KEEFFE: *Light coming on the plains II*, 1917, watercolour on paper, 28.5 × 22 cm, Fort Worth, Texas, Amon Carter Museum. MATTA: *Stop the age of Hemorr*, 1948, Paris, Galerie du Dragon (P. Willi/Agence Top). HOFMANN: *Radiant space*, 1955, oil on canvas, 152.5 × 122 cm, New York, André Emmerich Gallery; *Untitled*, 1943, mixed media on paper, 61 × 84 cm, New York, André Emmerich Gallery. GORKY: *Water of the flowery mill*, 1944, oil on canvas, 107.5 × 123.5 cm, New York, Metropolitan Museum, George A. Hearn Fund; *The limit*, 1947, oil on paper, 128.5 × 159 cm, London, Mrs A.M. Phillips Collection (Michael Holford). TOBEY: *Forms follow man*, 1941, gouache on cardboard, 34.5 × 49 cm, Seattle, Washington, Art Museum, Eugene Fuller memorial collection.

212-213 Jackson Pollock
NAMUTH: *Jackson Pollock*, 1952, photograph (Hans Namuth); *Pollock painting*, 1950, photograph (Hans Namuth). POLLOCK: *Self-portrait*, c. 1933, oil on canvas, New York, Marlborough Gallery; *Going west*, 1934-35, oil on gesso over composition board, 39 × 52.5 cm, Washington DC, Smithsonian Institution (Cooper-Bridgeman Library); *Pasiphaë*, 1943, oil on canvas, 143 × 244 cm, New York, Marlborough Gallery; *No. 32*, 1950, 269 × 457.5 cm, Düsseldorf, Kunstsammlung Nordrhein-Westfalen; *Convergence*, 1952, oil and enamel on canvas, 237 × 396 cm, Buffalo, New York, Albright-Knox Art Gallery, Sherwin Greenberg collection.

214-215 Abstract Expressionism
STILL: *1957-D no. 1*, 1957, oil on canvas, 287 × 404 cm, Buffalo, New York, Albright-Knox Art Gallery. GUSTON: *Dial*, 1956, oil on canvas, 183 × 193 cm, New York, Whitney Museum of American Art, Gift of friends of the Whitney Museum; *Untitled*, 1958, oil on canvas, 165.5 × 188 cm, New York, David McKee

Gallery (Steven Sloman). KLINE: *Orange and black wall*, 1959, oil on canvas, 169 × 366 cm, Amsterdam, Collection Thyssen (S); *Mahoning*, 1956, oil on canvas, 203 × 254 cm, New York, Whitney Museum of American Art. MOTHERWELL: *The voyage*, 1949, oil and tempera on paper over composition board, 122 × 239 cm, New York, Museum of Modern Art, Gift of Mrs John D. Rockefeller III; *Elegy to the Spanish Republic no. 34*, 1953-54, oil on canvas, 203 × 254 cm, Buffalo, New York, Albright-Knox Art Gallery. GOTTLIEB: *Black and black*, 1959, acrylic on canvas, 202 × 183 cm, London, art market (Sotheby's). FRANCIS: *Summer no. 2*, 1958, oil on canvas, 183 × 244 cm, New York, André Emmerich Gallery.

216-217 De Kooning: Woman I
DE KOONING: *Woman I*, 1950-52, oil on canvas, 192 × 148 cm, New York, Museum of Modern Art; *Woman sitting*, 1943-44, oil and charcoal, 122 × 106.5 cm, New York, Xavier Fourcade Inc.; *Woman*, 1943, oil on canvas, 114 × 71 cm, USA, Collection of the artist (Visual Arts Library); *Excavation*, 1950, oil on canvas, 204 × 254.5 cm, Chicago, Art Institute; Study for *Woman*, 1949-52, oil and charcoal on canvas, 117 × 81 cm, Private Collection (Visual Arts Library); *Woman on the dune*, 1967, oil on paper, 137 × 122 cm, New York, Xavier Fourcade Inc.

218-219 Abstract Developments 1
ROTHKO: The Rothko room, Tate Gallery, London, 1958-59, all paintings oil on canvas, London, Tate Gallery (John Webb); *Central green*, 1949, oil on canvas, 171 × 137 cm, London, art market (Sotheby's); NEWMAN: *The third*, 1962, oil on canvas, 256.5 × 307.5 cm, New York, Estate of the artist (Visual Arts Library); *Concord*, 1949, oil on canvas, 227.5 × 136 cm, New York, Metropolitan Museum of Art, George A. Hearn Fund. BAZIOTES: *White bird*, 1957, oil on canvas, 152.5 × 122 cm, Buffalo, New York, Albright-Knox Art Gallery, Gift of Seymour A. Knox. LOUIS: *Floral*, 1959, acrylic on canvas, 256 × 362 cm, New York, Private Collection; *Gamma zeta*, 1960, acrylic on canvas, 258 × 377 cm, New York, André Emmerich Gallery. FRANKENTHALER: *Mountains and sea*, 1952, oil on canvas, 221 × 297 cm, Washington, Collection of the artist, on loan to the National Gallery of Art.

220-221 Albers: Homage to the Square
ALBERS: *Variation in red*, 1948, oil on canvas, 51 × 77 cm, London, art market (Sotheby's); Studies for *Homage to the Square: Rain forest*, 1965, oil on board, 74 × 74 cm, London, art market (Sotheby's); *R-NW IV*, 1966, oil on masonite, 122 × 122 cm, Basel, Galerie Beyeler; *Fugue*, 1925, oil on glass, 24.5 × 66 cm, Basel, Kunstmuseum (Colorphoto Hans Hinz); *Transformation of a scheme no. 24*, 1952, engraved vinylite, 43 × 57 cm, New Haven, Connecticut, Yale University Art Gallery; Study for *Homage to the Square – Confirming*, 1971, oil on masonite, 79.5 × 79.5 cm, London, art market (Sotheby's).

222-223 Abstract Developments 2
REINHARDT: *Untitled*, 1938, oil on canvas, 193 × 366 cm, New York, Private Collection (Visual Arts Library); *Black painting*, 1960-66, oil on canvas, 60 × 60 cm, New York, Pace Gallery. OLITSKI: *Green goes around*, 1967, acrylic on canvas, 153 × 227 cm, New York, Mr and Mrs Arnold Ginsberg Collection (André Emmerich Gallery). NOLAND: *Ember*, 1960, acrylic on canvas,

179 × 178 cm, New York, André Emmerich Gallery; *Apart*, 1965, acrylic on canvas, 178 × 178 cm, New York, André Emmerich Gallery. KELLY: *Four panels*, 1964, silk-screen, 92.5 × 157.5 cm, Los Angeles, Gemini Gallery. STELLA: *Port aux Basques*, 1969, silk-screen, 96.5 × 178 cm, Los Angeles, Gemini Gallery; *Black adder*, 1965, metallic powder in polymer emulsion on canvas, 195.5 × 352 cm, New York, Leo Castelli Gallery. HELD: *Greek garden*, detail, 1964-66, oil on canvas, 366 × 1607 cm, New York, André Emmerich Gallery.

224-225 Informal Abstraction in Europe
FAUTRIER: *Head of a hostage*, 1945, oil on canvas, 35 × 26 cm, London, art market (Christie's). HARTUNG: *T 1955-23*, 1955, oil on canvas, 162 × 122 cm, Collection of the artist. WOLS: *The blue phantom*, 1951, oil on canvas, 60 × 73 cm, Milan, Collection Riccardo Jucker (S). MATHIEU: *Painting*, 1952, oil on canvas, 51 × 64 cm, London, Gimpel Fils Gallery. DE STAEL: *Figure by the sea*, 1952, oil on canvas, 161.5 × 129.5 cm, Düsseldorf, Kunstsammlung Nordrhein-Westfalen. TAPIES: *Pale blue composition*, 1956, oil and sand, 97 × 161 cm, London, art market (Sotheby's). DUBUFFET: *The very rich earth*, 1956, oil on paper, 156 × 117 cm, France, Private Collection (Visual Arts Library); *Uncertain situations*, 1977, acrylic on canvas, 213 × 353 cm, New York, Pace Gallery. APPEL: *A bird with a fish*, 1956, oil on canvas, 130 × 145 cm, London, Gimpel Fils Gallery. BURRI: *Sacking with red*, 1954, acrylic and mixed media, 86.5 × 100 cm, London, Tate Gallery.

226-227 Wyeth: Christina's World
WYETH: *Christina's world*, 1948, tempera on panel, 82 × 121 cm, New York, Museum of Modern Art; *Christina Olson*, 1947, New York, Private Collection (Visual Arts Library); *Grape wine (Willard Snowden)*, 1966, tempera on panel, 66 × 74 cm, New York, Metropolitan Museum of Art, Gift of Amanda K. Berls; *Nick and Jamie*, 1963, Richmond, Virginia, Museum of Fine Arts (Visual Arts Library); *River cove*, 1958, USA, Private Collection (Visual Arts Library); *The hunter*, 1943, Toledo, Ohio, Museum of Art (Visual Arts Library).

228-229 After 1945: Old Masters of the New
BRAQUE: *Atelier II*, 1949, oil on canvas, 131 × 162.5 cm, Düsseldorf, Kunstsammlung Nordrhein-Westfalen. PICASSO: *Women of Algiers*, 1955, oil on canvas, 114 × 146 cm, New York, Victor Ganz Collection (S); *Mounted rider*, c. 1951, ceramic, London, Victoria and Albert Museum (Michael Holford); *The painter and his model*, 1963, oil on canvas, 195 × 160 cm, Paris, Private Collection (S). MATISSE: *The snail*, 1953, gouache and coloured paper on paper, 286.5 × 287 cm, London, Tate Gallery; *The Tree of Life*, 1949-51, stained glass, height of windows 515 cm, Vence, Chapel of the Rosary (Visual Arts Library). LEGER: *The builders*, 1950, oil on canvas, 302 × 216 cm, Biot, Musée Fernand Léger. NICHOLSON: *Poisonous yellow*, 1949, oil on canvas, 124 × 162 cm, Venice, Galleria d'Arte Moderna (S). KOKOSCHKA: *Louis Krohnberg*, 1950, oil on canvas, England, Private Collection (Cooper-Bridgeman Library).

230-231 Post-War Sculpture 1
MARINI: *Horse and rider*, 1946, bronze, height 52 cm, Rome, Galleria d'Arte Moderna (S); *The miracle*, 1943, painted plaster and collage, height 70 cm, Milan, Collection E. Jesi (S); MANZU: *The stoning*

of St Stephen; *the death of St Gregory the Great; death in space; death on earth*, detail from the Portals of Death, 1950-64, bronze, Rome, St Peter's (S); *Great cardinal*, 1955, bronze, height 2 m, Venice, Galleria d'Arte Moderna (S); RICHIER: *Storm*, 1949, bronze, height 200 cm, Paris, Musée National d'Art Moderne (S). CALDER: *The spiral*, 1958, painted steel, height 500 cm, Paris, UNESCO Building (S); *Slender ribs*, 1943, painted steel, height 358 cm, Humlebaek, Louisiana Museum (Visual Arts Library). SMITH: *11 books, 3 apples*, 1959; *Zig II*, 1961; *Cubi II*, 1963, Bolton Landing, New York, Estate of the artist (Visual Arts Library); *Head*, 1959, steel, height 56 cm, Bolton Landing, New York, Estate of the artist (Visual Arts Library).

232-233 Giacometti: Man Pointing
MICHEL DESJARDINS: *Alberto Giacometti*, c. 1965, photograph (Agence Top). GIACOMETTI: *Man pointing*, 1947, bronze, height 176 cm, London, Tate Gallery (Angelo Hornak); *Dog*, 1951, bronze, Lugano, Collection Thyssen (S); *Composition with seven figures and one head (The forest)*, 1950, painted bronze, height 58 cm, London, Thomas Gibson Fine Art; *Caroline*, 1962, oil on canvas, 100 × 81 cm, Basel, Kunstmuseum (Colorphoto Hans Hinz).

234-235 Bacon: Figures in a Landscape
VELAZQUEZ: *Pope Innocent X*, 1650, oil on canvas, 140 × 120 cm, Rome, Galleria Doria-Pamphili (S). BACON: *Study after Velazquez*, 1953, oil on canvas, 152 × 117.5 cm, New York, Museum of Modern Art, Gift of Mr and Mrs William A.M. Burden; *Figures in a Landscape*, 1956, oil on canvas, 152.5 × 119.5 cm, Birmingham, City Art Gallery; *Figures in a landscape*, 1945, oil on canvas, 145 × 128 cm, London, Tate Gallery; *Isabel Rawsthorne*, 1966, oil on canvas, 81 × 68.5 cm, London, Tate Gallery. EISENSTEIN: Still from the film *The Battleship Potemkin*, 1928, photograph, London, National Film Archive (Stills Library).

236-237 Johns and Rauschenberg
Jasper Johns, photograph by Judy Tomkins (Leo Castelli Gallery). JOHNS: *Painted bronze*, 1960, bronze, height including base 137 cm, New York, Collection of the artist; *Three flags*, 1958, oil on 3 canvases, 78 × 115 cm, New York, Leo Castelli Gallery; *Target with four faces*, 1955, oil and mixed media on canvas, 28.5 × 21 cm, New York, Museum of Modern Art; *Untitled*, 1972, oil, encaustic and collage, with objects, on canvas, 183 × 488 cm, Cologne, Collection Ludwig (Leo Castelli Gallery). RAUSCHENBERG: *Monogram*, 1959, oil and mixed media on canvas, height 122 cm, canvas 183 × 183 cm, Stockholm, National Museum; *Story-line 1*, 1968, silk-screen, 43 × 57 cm, New York, Museum of Modern Art; *Sleep for Yvonne Rainer*, 1965, mixed media on canvas, 213.5 × 152.5 cm, London, art market (Sotheby's); *Robert Rauschenberg*, photograph (Sunday Times).

238-239 American Pop Art
LICHTENSTEIN: *Masterpiece*, 1962, oil on canvas, 137 × 137 cm, New York, Private Collection (Leo Castelli Gallery). RIVERS: *French money*, 1962, oil on canvas, 46 × 81 cm, London, art market (Gimpel Fils Gallery). WARHOL: *Brillo*, 1964, painted wood, 43 × 43 × 35.5 cm, New York, Collection of the artist (Leo Castelli Gallery); *Liz no. 2*, 1962, silk-screen, 101.5 × 101.5 cm (Visual Arts Library). INDIANA: *Yield brother*, 1963, oil on

canvas, 152.5 × 127 cm, London, art market (Sotheby's). ROSENQUIST: *Flamingo capsule*, 1970, oil on canvas with aluminized myler, each panel 290 × 175 cm, New York, Collection of the artist (Leo Castelli Gallery). DINE: *Things in their natural setting*, 1973, oil on canvas and mixed media, 183 × 152.5 cm, London, art market (Christie's). OLDENBURG: *Giant fag-ends*, 1967, canvas, foam formica and wood, height 244 cm, New York, Whitney Museum of American Art (Visual Arts Library). WESSELMANN: *Great American nude no. 14*, 1961, oil on canvas and collage, 122.5 × 122.5 cm, London, art market (Sotheby's).

240-241 British Pop Art
PAOLOZZI: *Japanese war god*, 1958, bronze, height 153 cm, Buffalo, New York, Albright-Knox Art Gallery; *Conjectures to identity*, 1963, screenprint lithograph, 76 × 51.5 cm, London, Tate Gallery (Visual Arts Library). SMITH: *Giftwrap*, 1963, oil on canvas and plywood, 203 × 528 × 79 cm, London, Tate Gallery (Visual Arts Library). HAMILTON: *What is it that makes today's homes so different, so appealing?*, 1956, collage, 26 × 24.5 cm, Tübingen, Kunsthalle, Professor Dr Georg Zundel collection. KITAJ: *Where the railroad leaves the sea*, 1964, oil on canvas, 122 × 152.5 cm, London, Marlborough Fine Art. HOCKNEY: *The sprinkler*, 1967, acrylic on canvas, 122 × 122 cm, London, art market (Sotheby's); *Christopher Isherwood and Don Bachardy*, 1968, acrylic on canvas, 212 × 304 cm, USA, Private Collection (Visual Arts Library). JONES: *Red latex suit*, 1973, oil and latex on canvas, 122 × 122 cm, London, art market (Christie's). CAULFIELD: *Town and country*, 1979, acrylic on canvas, 231 × 165 cm, England, Private Collection (Visual Arts Library).

242-243 Environmental Art, Happenings and Performance
KAPROW: *Basic thermal units*, 1973, activity with thermometers and ice at Essen, Duisburg, Bochum and Remscheid, March 14-18 (Galerie Inge-Baecker). SEGAL: *The photo booth*, 1966, plaster, plastic, glass, metal, wood and electric lights, height 183 cm, Toronto, Collection Dr and Mrs Sidney Wax (Visual Arts Library). KIENHOLZ: *The birthday*, 1964, plastics and other media, figure life-size, Collection of the artist (Visual Arts Library). KLEIN: *Anthropometry: ANT 63*, 1961, acrylic on paper over canvas, 153 × 209 cm, Paris, Flinker Gallery (Visual Arts Library). OLDENBURG: Model for *Monument for Grand Army Plaza New York*, 1969 (Sunday Times). ACCONCI: *Rubbing piece*, 1970, activity at Max's Kansas City Restaurant, New York (John Gibson Commissions Inc./Betty Jackson). WELFARE STATE: *Action*, 1972, activity (Visual Arts Library). BEUYS: *Scottish symphony*, 1970, activity at the Edinburgh Festival, Edinburgh, 1970 (Visual Arts Library); *Room installation*, 1968, mixed media, 10 × 12 m, Darmstadt, Hessisches Landesmuseum, Karl Stöher collection (Visual Arts Library). PANE: *Action psyche*, 1974, activity at Paris, January 21, 1974 (Visual Arts Library).

244-245 Kinetic and Op Art
RILEY: *Cataract 3*, 1967, emulsion PVA on linen, 222 × 223 cm, British Council. VASARELY: *Zebras*, 1938, print, Paris, Collection of the artist; *Arny-C*, 1969, Paris, Collection of the artist. SEDGLEY: *Wind Tone Tower*, 1979, steel, sailcloth and electronics, height about 10 m, West Germany, Collection of the artist. SOTO: *Cardinal*, 1965, mixed media, 156 × 105.5 × 25.5 cm, London, Tate Gallery. TAKIS: *Signal: Insect animal of space*, 1956, metal, kinetic, height 205.5 × 35.5 × 37.5 cm, London, Tate Gallery. BURY: *3,069 white dots on an oval ground*, 1967, metal and cork, kinetic, 67 × 120 × 25.5 cm, London, Tate Gallery. TINGUELY: *Puss in boots*, 1959, painted wire and steel, motorized, 77 × 17 × 20 cm, New York, Museum of Modern Art, Philip Johnson Fund.

246-247 Post-War Sculpture 2: Minimal and Conceptual
KOSUTH: *Chair I and III*, 1965, photographs and chair, Aachen, Ludwig Collection (Visual Arts Library). NAUMAN: *Perfect door: Perfect odor: Perfect rodo*, 1972, neon tubing, New York, Leo Castelli Gallery. KAWARA: *Today*, series: *April 5, 1966*, 1966, liquitex on canvas, 20.5 × 25.5 cm, London, Lisson Gallery. NEVELSON: *Royal tide IV*, 1960, painted wood (Visual Arts Library). CARO: *The month of May*, 1963, painted steel, height 280 cm, length 358 cm, London, Kasmin Ltd. TONY SMITH: *Cigarette*, 1966, plywood, height 4.6 m, length 8 m, New York, Fischbach Gallery (Visual Arts Library). MORRIS: *Untitled*, 1966-67, thickness of felt 10 mm, New York, Leo Castelli Gallery. JUDD: *Untitled*, 1974, anodized aluminium, length 172 cm, New York, Leo Castelli Gallery. LEWITT: *Cube structure*, 1972, painted wood, 62 × 61 × 122 cm, London, Lisson Gallery. ANDRE: Proposal for the Hague Museum – *Lock* series 1967, felt pen on paper, 21 × 30 cm, Aachen, Ludwig Collection (Visual Arts Library).

248-249 Land and Earth Art
CHRISTO: *Running fence*, 1972-76, erected in California, Sonoma and Mann Counties, 1976 (Wolfgang Volz); Project for Milan: *The Arco della Pace wrapped*, 1970, drawing and collage, 50 × 70 cm, Milan, Collection Françoise Lambert. FULTON: *Untitled*, 1969, photomontage, New York, John Gibson Commissions Inc. LONG: *A line in Australia*, 1977, earth and stones (Lisson Gallery). HEIZER: *Double negative*, 1969-70, rhyolite and sandstone, 24,000 tons displaced on the Virginia river mesa, Nevada (Xavier Fourcade Inc./Gianfranco Gorgoni). SMITHSON: *Spiral jetty*, 1970, black basalt, limestone, salt crystal, red algae and earth, at Rozelle Point, Great Salt Lake, Utah (Visual Arts Library). THE POIRIERS: *Ancient Ostia*, 1971-73, soil and fixative, France, Collection of the artists (Visual Arts Library). DE MARIA: *Vertical earth kilometre*, 1977, at Kassel, West Germany (New York, Dia Art Foundation/Nic Tenwiggenhorn). HAACKE: *Rhine water installation*, 1972, fish, Rhine water, chemicals, plastic container and pump,

West Germany, Collection of the artist (Visual Arts Library).

250-251 Traditional Easel-Painting
GRANDMA MOSES: *In harvest time*, 1945, oil and tempera on cardboard, 45.5 × 71 cm, New York, Grandma Moses Properties Inc. LOWRY: *Industrial landscape*, 1955, oil on canvas, 114.5 × 152.5 cm, London, Tate Gallery (Visual Arts Library). GUTTUSO: *Occupation of the land*, 1947, Italy, Private Collection (Fabbri). BUFFET: *Two Breton women*, 1950, oil on canvas, France, Private Collection (Maurice Garnier). NOLAN: *Kelly in landscape*, 1969, oil on canvas, 122 × 152.5 cm, London, Marlborough Fine Art. AUERBACH: *E.O.W. nude*, 1953-54, oil on canvas, 51 × 77 cm, London, Tate Gallery (John Webb). DIEBENKORN: *Ocean Park no. 108*, 1978, oil on canvas, New York, Knoedler Gallery. ERRO: *Plainscape*, 1972, Paris, Private Collection (Visual Arts Library). AVERY: *Morning sea*, 1955, California, Private Collection (Visual Arts Library). PLASTOV: *The tractor drivers' dinner*, 1951, oil on canvas, Moscow, Tretyakov Gallery (Visual Arts Library).

252-253 Superrealism
FREUD: *John Minton*, 1952, oil on canvas, 40 × 25.5 cm, London, Royal College of Art (Visual Arts Library). PISTOLETTO: *Marzi with the little girl*, 1964, photographic transfer on steel, 200.5 × 119.5 cm (Visual Arts Library). PEARLSTEIN: *Female nude reclining on Empire Sofa*, 1973, oil on canvas, 122 × 152.5 cm, Private Collection (Visual Arts Library). ESTES: *Grossinger's bakery*, 1972, oil on canvas (Visual Arts Library). MORLEY: *United States Marine at Valley Forge*, 1968, oil on canvas, 150 × 125 cm, Paris, Collection Daniel Hechter (Visual Arts Library). GOINGS: *Twin Springs diner*, 1976, oil on canvas, 96.5 × 132 cm, New York, OK Harris Gallery (Eric Pollitzer). CLOSE: *Keith*, 1970, acrylic on canvas, 130 × 105 cm, Paris, Private Collection (Visual Arts Library). DE ANDREA: *Seated woman*, 1978, painted polyvinyl, life-size, New York, OK Harris Gallery. HANSON: *Couple with shopping bags*, 1976, painted vinyl, life-size, New York, OK Harris Gallery.

254-255 The Popularization of Art
MCKNIGHT-KAUFFER: *Winter sales*, 1924, poster, 76 × 51 cm, London, London Transport Ltd. (Sunday Times). MATISSE: *The swan*, 1930-33, pen and ink on paper, Baltimore, Museum of Art. Kenneth Clark, photograph, still from *Civilization* (BBC Picture Library). WARHOL: *Thirty are better than one*, 1963, silk-screen, New York, Leo Castelli Gallery. LICHENSTEIN: *Brush-strokes*, 1967, London, British Museum. STEADMAN: Illustration to Hunter S. Thompson's *Fear and Loathing in Las Vegas*, 1970, pen and paper (Visual Arts Library). ADAMI: *Arabian landscapes*, 1969, silk-screen (Visual Arts Library). MIRO: *Marvellous puzzles*, 1970s, lithograph, London, art market (Christie's). COLLETT, DICKINSON, PEARCE & PARTNERS: (*Government warning: Smoking can seriously damage your health*), 1979, photomontage, London, Gallagher Ltd.

Index

Page numbers in **bold** refer to the main entries; *italic* numbers refer to the illustrations.